Latinos in
American Football

Latinos in American Football

Pathbreakers on the Gridiron, 1927 to the Present

MARIO LONGORIA *and* JORGE IBER

McFarland & Company, Inc., Publishers
Jefferson, North Carolina

ALSO OF INTEREST

Mike Torrez: A Baseball Biography
by Jorge Iber (McFarland, 2016)

LIBRARY OF CONGRESS CATALOGUING-IN-PUBLICATION DATA

Names: Longoria, Mario, author. | Iber, Jorge, 1961– author.
Title: Latinos in American football : pathbreakers on the gridiron, 1927 to the present / Mario Longoria and Jorge Iber.
Description: Jefferson, North Carolina : McFarland & Company, Inc., Publishers, 2020. | Includes bibliographical references and index.
Identifiers: LCCN 2020002675 | ISBN 9781476668864 (paperback : acid free paper) ♾
ISBN 9781476636689 (ebook)
Subjects: LCSH: Hispanic American football players—Biography. | Hispanic American football players—History. | Football—United States—History. | National Football League—History.
Classification: LCC GV939.A1 L663 2020 | DDC 796.332092/368 [B]—dc23
LC record available at https://lccn.loc.gov/2020002675

BRITISH LIBRARY CATALOGUING DATA ARE AVAILABLE

ISBN (print) 978-1-4766-6886-4
ISBN (ebook) 978-1-4766-3668-9

© 2020 Mario Longoria and Jorge Iber. All rights reserved

No part of this book may be reproduced or transmitted in any form or by any means, electronic or mechanical, including photocopying or recording, or by any information storage and retrieval system, without permission in writing from the publisher.

On the cover: Southern Cal offensive tackle Anthony Munoz (center) blocks Texas Tech defender Andrew Thomas (46) at the Los Angeles Memorial Coliseum on September 9, 1978 (Mario Longoria collection)

Printed in the United States of America

*McFarland & Company, Inc., Publishers
Box 611, Jefferson, North Carolina 28640
www.mcfarlandpub.com*

Table of Contents

Introduction: Latinos/Hispanics in "American" Football — 1

1. Latinos Take to the Gridiron: The 1920s–1940 — 15
2. Slowly Moving the Ball Down the Field: 1941–1950 — 59
3. The McCarthy Era and the Age of Activism: 1951–1970 — 104
4. Increased Numbers and Diversity at All Levels, 1971–1990 — 166
5. Latinos on the Gridiron from Coast to Coast, 1991–2018 — 241

Conclusion: The Historical Significance of Latinos on the Gridiron and Their Future in the Game — 311

Chapter Notes — 319

Bibliography — 351

Index — 363

Introduction
Latinos/Hispanics in "American" Football

> Heroes, whether they be from sport or some other area of life, are essentially people who embody in some way the stated ideals rather than the realities of a society or culture.[1]

There are few things more "American" than having the family gather for annual Thanksgiving Day festivities in the later days of each November. Since the 1890s, competition on the gridiron (at the high school and collegiate levels) has been a mainstay of this celebration throughout the nation—even before Congress resolved officially to mark the day as the fourth Thursday of November in 1941. Since 1920, contests among the various clubs of the National Football League (NFL) have also been a part of Thanksgiving. While numerous franchises participated in the early years of these contests, starting in 1934, the host team for the tilt has been the Detroit Lions. The one-game offering expanded into a doubleheader (starting in 1966), and is always hosted (with the exceptions of 1975 and 1977) by, appropriately enough, "America's Team," the Dallas Cowboys. More recently, as if that is not sufficient, the NFL has added a third clash on this day, with rotating teams, starting in 2006. No doubt about it, football and consuming gigantic portions of turkey and pumpkin pie have long gone hand-in-hand in the United States.[2]

For our neighbors north of the border, the commemoration of Thanksgiving Day has been in place since 1879, though a permanent date was not affixed until 1957 (when Parliament declared that it was to be observed on the 2nd Monday of each October). Following the pattern of its United States counterpart, Canada's professional football association, the Canadian Football League (CFL), began playing at least one game (referred to as the

Thanksgiving Day Classic) for this holiday the very next year.[3] As of 2016, the second most frequent participant in these contests is the Montreal franchise (known originally and currently as the Alouettes, but also as the Concordes between 1982 and 1987), with a total of 31 appearances (exceeded only by the Hamilton Tiger-Cats with 32).[4]

Going into the October 10, 2011, Classic at Molson Stadium between the home-standing Alouettes and their bitter rivals the Toronto Argonauts, the two franchises were on totally different paths. Montreal was in the midst of a playoff push, sporting an 8–5 mark, while the Argos were the cellar-dwellers of the East Division with a putrid record of 3–10. As with most contests (no matter the sport) between the two largest Canadian cities, the roughly 24,000 Quebecois in attendance hoped to see their hometown squad crush the foes from Ontario. The fans were also there in hope that they would witness history, as the starting quarterback for the Alouettes was a mere 258 yards behind CFL legend Damon Allen, for the mark of most total passing yards in a professional football career.

The name of the athlete about to shatter this impressive record was Anthony Calvillo, a self-described poor Mexican American "kid from La Puente (California.)" The fans were not disappointed, as when Calvillo completed a 50-yard strike to wide-receiver Jamal Richardson on the final play of the third quarter he surpassed Allen's figure of 72,381 passing yards. In addition, Montreal triumphed over the Argos that October day, 29–19 and eventually made it to the first round of the playoffs, (where they lost to the Hamilton Tiger-Cats, 52–44); all the while riding the strong right arm of this Spanish-surnamed quarterback. All told Calvillo, who finished his career after the 2013 season, amassed an astonishing 79,816 yards through the air; all in the CFL. In addition to being the most prolific passer in the history of the professional game (both north and south of the border), Calvillo also chalked up eight Grey Cup (the CFL's championship game) appearances; winning three, three Most Outstanding Player trophies (MVP of the league), seven Terry Evanshen trophies (the Most Outstanding Player from a CFL East Division team), and a certain spot in the Canadian Football League Hall of Fame once he is eligible. After all of his success on the field, Calvillo continues to serve the franchise, first as receivers coach, and starting in 2016, as offensive coordinator. The full story of Calvillo's unlikely path from La Puente High School, to Utah State University, to the CFL, and finally to this all-time professional passing standard will be recounted later in this work, but for now suffice it to say that his history features many of the same elements (both positive and negative) that dot the stories of the majority of the athletes whose exploits are explored in this book.[5] The story of Hispanics and their participation in American-style football (at all levels of the sport) is, to the surprise of many, of long standing (about 100 years) but, unlike the story of other ethnic or racial groups, a more than cursory examination of that history has only recently commenced in both academic and popular literature.

While the genesis of the game that would become football first took root in the elite environs of institutions which now comprise the Ivy League (read that to mean that it was played almost exclusively by white athletes), the rough and tumble physical nature of the sport soon attracted individuals of varied racial, ethnic and religious backgrounds. The story of the participation of Native Americans, African Americans, Jews, Italian Americans and other groups is extensive and well documented.[6] A recent publication, *Bibliography of Books About American Football, 1891–2015*, compiled by Ralph Hickok, serves as a handy reference (mostly for popular literature) of the lacuna that exists in regard to the participation of the Spanish-surnamed in this field of athletic endeavor. For example, in a brief section entitled "Race and Ethnicity," there are but two books, both of which will be discussed below, that provide any sense of the contributions of Latinos to the professional and collegiate gridiron. Next, in another chapter entitled "Coaches," there is only one book, a biography of the University of Wisconsin's legendary coach Barry Alvarez (he is of Spanish descent) noted. Finally, in a segment headed "Players," which features hundreds of books, there are but three biographies/autobiographies of Latino players: Victor Cruz, Tom Flores, and Tony Romo.[7] As readers will note in this work, there have been several hundred Spanish-surnamed professional and collegiate football players over the past century. True, not all are meritorious of book treatments, but surely the life stories (and historical significance) of some, such as, for example, George Mira (of the University of Miami), Danny Villanueva (of New Mexico State University), and Joe Kapp (of the University of California, Berkeley) are worthy subject matter for such efforts—others of similar merit will be discussed later. Suffice it to say that the lack of attention to such *atletas* pales in comparison to the extensive treatment available on other groups of participants in the history of the game.

One of the most thorough, academic discussions of the significance of football to varied racial, ethnic and religious groups can be found in the works of Michael Oriard; specifically in *King Football: Sport and Spectacle in the Golden Age of Radio and Newsreels, Movies and Magazines, the Weekly & the Daily Press* which appeared in 2001.[8] The late 19th and early 20th century gridiron, Oriard rightly argues, served as a definite agent of "Americanization" (similar to arguments made for baseball) for young immigrants (or sons of immigrants) who hoped for greater acceptance by the broader society while maintaining a sense of their ethnic backgrounds:

> Sport meant one of two things within immigrant communities: the neighborhood and local sport clubs ... that both preserved ethnic identities and fostered assimilation into mainstream American culture, and the school and professional sports that meant distinctly American success and more thorough absorption into the mainstream. To

play football, whether at the high school or on a college or professional team, was to be thoroughly American.[9]

In addition to the more ambiguous notion of "greater acceptance" by the wider and more conventional social circles, Oriard also notes an even more basic reason for the attraction of strong-bodied youths to the football field: the possibility of gaining prestige in their local academic setting and community, as well as the possibility, for the truly talented, of attending institutions of higher learning; an aspiration often out of reach for many immigrant families of recent vintage.

> Polish and Italian youths were simply drawn to football in high school as a vehicle for achieving status. College coaches grabbed them not as aliens to be Americanized but as rugged and hungry football players. Seeing them succeed, their communities celebrated such achievements highly prized in their new country, and more and more youngsters saw an opportunity to make it in America by following this example. Through this more "natural" process football contributed to the new immigrants' acculturation over time far more powerfully than such concerted efforts as the Americanization movement during the First World War.[10]

Another important contributor to the literature of European ethnics and football is Gerald Gems. Among his many important studies are *For Pride, Profit and Patriarchy: Football and the Incorporation of American Cultural Values* in 2000, and *Sport and the Shaping of Italian American Identity*, which appeared in 2013.[11] The newer work provides an overview of various sports in which Italian Americans participated over the twentieth century, and Gems' conclusions are along the same lines as those articulated in Oriard's studies. An effective way to summarize the significance to these individuals is, as Gems states, that "Sport fitted not only economic but social and psychological needs as well. Italian athletes moved beyond their closed social circles and won greater self-esteem and they contributed to community pride."[12]

In regard to football, Gems provides a myriad of examples, but encapsulates the totality of his argument by focusing on the legendary Vince Lombardi, an individual who experienced unparalleled success on the collegiate gridiron (as one of the legendary "Seven Blocks of Granite" of Fordham University in the 1930s), and generated singular accomplishments as head coach of the Green Bay Packers. Still, Gems notes, Lombardi went beyond mere achievement on the gridiron, and utilized his notoriety to challenge assumptions about, and discrimination against, peoples of different backgrounds.

> Although Lombardi adhered to strict discipline, the work ethic, and a conservative ideology, he also worked diligently for racial progress. Having felt the sting of inferiority, he admonished his players and the Green Bay community regarding equality for all. When preseason exhibition games were played in the South he insisted that black players not be subjected to segregation practices. Lombardi ruled his team as a dominant Italian father presiding over his family. He required discipline and adher-

Introduction 5

ence to rules and regulations, with an occasional stroke of benevolence for wayward children.[13]

Even with all of these positives, this author argues, sport, and the notoriety it can provide, did not overcome all obstacles. "Assimilation, however, did not mean the inevitable, nonreversible linear progression.... Although Italians moved from exclusion to marginality and finally to incorporation ... that ... process has not been complete for all Italian-Americans."[14] It is significant to note that coaches who felt the sting of discrimination, such as Lombardi, often used their positions to improve the lives of not only their players, but of an entire community. Several individuals whose careers exemplify this theme will be discussed in this work.

In his earlier book Gems provides a sense of the significance of football to many different ethnic and racial groups throughout, but primarily accomplishes this task in a chapter entitled "The Huddle: Multicultural Football." Here is found a brief discussion of how the game moved beyond the hallowed halls of Ivy to become "the" game of the broader American (even recent immigrant) populace starting in the 1880s and 1890s. Initially, as elite leaders argued, the sport was merely for the educated and select few, as noted in a letter between Caspar Whitney and Walter Camp, wherein the two men argued that "What do we care for ... the men in the Fall River Mills [read that to mean Portuguese immigrants] or the silk mills at Patterson [Italian immigrants] ... the only Foot Ball in America is the Inter-College game."[15] Soon, however, as the games, and victory therein over arch-rivals became increasingly important, cracks appeared in this narrow line of thinking. As Gems noted, "victories required talent, regardless of lineage, and the spread of the game induced an inevitable leveling effect. As early in 1894, a proponent of the game extolled that it 'dissapated [sic] bigotry and intolerance.'"[16]

While we have discussed the general lack of coverage for Latinos in the literature of American football, it is by no means to imply that the cupboard is completely bare. In fact, starting in the early 1990s, there have been a limited quantity of substantive studies, both academic and popular, that have begun to shed light on this mostly overlooked story. Among the individuals who have performed groundbreaking spade work in order to peer into the historical and social significance of this topic are writers such as Jorge Prieto, Joel Huerta, Frederick Luis Aldama and Christopher Gonzalez, and the two authors of this work.

One important place to commence any discussion regarding the story of the significance of football in the lives of the Spanish-surnamed (in this case, Mexican Americans in particular), is with the autobiography of Dr. Jorge Prieto, a Mexican-born physician who learned to play football in California, and then excelled at the sport in his native country. He later came to the Chicago area (in 1949) and plied his profession mostly among the city's poorer environs. Prieto worked at various facilities starting in the 1950s through the 1980s; including Columbus Hospital, Cabrini Hospital, and Cook County Hospital, finally retiring in the late 1980s. In addition, he also owned and operated several clinics, mostly in African American and Hispanic neighborhoods. No doubt Dr. Prieto was a highly intelligent man, who overcame myriad obstacles. Part of what helped encourage him toward his noteworthy life and career was his love for, and desire to play, football. In this way, he embodied many of the "stated ideals" of the U.S., overcoming both medical and social obstacles, in his drive to improve the realities faced by Latinos in the Midwestern metropolis during the middle of the 20th century.[17]

Prieto's autobiography supports many of the points raised by both Oriard and Gems in their respective works concerning the motivations and hopes of Italians and other ethnics. Jorge first became enthralled with football as a youngster who watched "in wonder as my neighbors threw long, arching spirals.... The graceful flight of that oblong leather ball seemed a thing of beauty to me."[18] He eventually asked a friend who helped teach him the game the question that most football-loving youths in southern California ultimately ask: could he ever play for USC? "He laughed good-naturedly and told me that was impossible because the university did not accept Blacks or Mexicans.... When I asked about UCLA, or Stanford, I got the same discouraging answer."[19] This reply might have been sufficient to crush many a young athlete's dreams, but another player, this one a Catholic, encouraged Prieto to think about another alternative, one a bit further east: Notre Dame. It just so happened that the Irish were playing the Trojans in Los Angeles the very same week that the young Prieto was informed of this magical campus dedicated to both his faith and preferred sport. Upon arriving home, Jorge asked with great urgency for his mother to pray rosaries on behalf of the Indianans. Her supplications were answered and, no doubt, helped generate Notre Dame's triumph over the Trojans by a score of 27–0.

Given his love of football, Jorge's mother encouraged him to read about the sport, as well as classic works in both English and Spanish. There would always be books on the game, but Prieto also became enamored with the Spanish-language encyclopedic set known as *El Tesoro de la Juventud* (The Treasure of Youth).[20] It was the combination of interests that sustained Jorge through some difficult years during which he suffered severe medical issues. While convalescing, he also came across an athlete who would become a personal hero: Jose Martinez-Zorilla, who played halfback for Cornell University in the early 1930s and was named to the All-American team for 1932. Martinez-Zorilla would eventually return to his native Mexico and become a coach at the collegiate level. Through tremendous effort and sacrifice, Prieto persevered and actually played high school football on the same field as his hero, *El Parque Espana*, in 1939. He completed his career by playing and coaching at the collegiate level (even winning a national championship in 1945). He even spent time studying at Norte Dame prior to completing his medical training in his homeland.[21] All told, Jorge Prieto's experiences with football helped him gain confidence, overcome obstacles, and embrace a significant part of the culture of his adopted nation. In part, what he learned on the gridiron helped channel his drive to use his medical degree to benefit others. At the end of his memoir, Prieto summarizes his ties to football by saying:

> We did not realize at the time that we became champions because we had become better persons.... In a city, indeed in a whole nation plagued by *machismo*, decency was once again seen as our ancestors had seen it, as a primary virtue.... In 1945 we needed to see ... how vigorous and wholesome a disciplined life can make a man. We needed to be reminded ... of the truth of the old Mexican adage, "*Lo cortes no quita lo valiente*" ("Courtesy does not diminish courage").[22]

Several recent works have provided some sense of the significance and participation of the Spanish-surnamed in American football at the high school level. One of the most important is by Jorge Iber and examines the historic run in 1961 of the only team from the Rio Grande Valley of Texas (an area that is today over 90% Latino[23]) to win a state title in football: the Donna Redskins. In this work, which will be discussed more fully in a later chapter, Iber tracks this team's unlikely charge toward a championship by a unit comprised mostly of Mexican Americans. Further, he cites interviews with some of these athletes that articulate the notion that success not only impacted players, but the entire community in this deep-South Texas locale. One player, Oscar Avila, who intercepted a pass to seal his team's victory in the championship game against the Quanah Indians, noted that he and his Spanish-surnamed teammates already had much to be proud of even before going into this fairy-tale season. "We ... were always proud of who we were and were full of self-confidence. We were tough because of our fathers and the hard work we did and not because a coach told us we were." While that quotation presents a player's perspective, it is noteworthy to reference, almost four decades later, the impact that the 1961 title had on subsequent generations of Latinos in the town. In a 1999 interview with Cathy Harasta of the *Dallas Morning News* then principal of DHS, Fernando Castillo, detailed the formidable influence of that squad upon the youth of Donna. "I was born in 1963 and heard about that team all of my life. That was the big talk. To be like that team was everyone's dream."[24] The story of this team, in football-mad Texas, emphasizes a potent argument by Gems when he stated that, "athletic feats and successes destabilized norms, expectations, and stereotypes ... [still] they [minorities] remained ... marginalized with dual identities, and limited inclusion, particularly off the field."[25]

Another important essay that focuses on the role of the sport, both positive and negative, upon an individual and a *comunidad* is found in the work of Joel Huerta.[26] In his essay, "Friday Night Rights," Huerta documents notions embraced by state of Texas officials during the 1900s and 1910s in regard to the social and personal value of playing football. The game, educational bureaucrats believed, could serve as an outlet for civilizing "aggression and energy … [and would] teach the Texan boy how to cooperate, how to win honorably; it could give the rustic boy structure, polish and a public role without making him soft and sweet."[27] Having articulated this notion, Huerta then goes on to see how this idealized version of the goals of football played out in the life of a man who would become a Texas legend: Everardo Carlos (E.C.) Lerma.

The main obstacle Lerma faced was that many Texans, by the 1930s completely enthralled by the game, did not believe that Mexican Americans were capable of performing well on the field nor benefitting from the values taught by football. In 1932, E.C. made it onto the freshman squad of his local team, the Kingsville High School Brahmas. Making the squad was simple, gaining acceptance from his "teammates" proved far more problematic. "Nobody would talk to me…. When they did talk to me, it was an insult. So I just did what he {the coach} told me to do. To the players I was like a ghost, or the brunt of jokes." Even with such adversity, Lerma persevered and became an all-district performer who was offered a scholarship to play at Texas Christian University in 1934; a rare feat indeed for an athlete of Mexican descent at that time. Still, he persevered. "I cried many times, not because of the blows, but because of the discrimination. It was very hard to take, but I just loved playing sports…. To me there was nothing better. I was an athlete."[28]

Although the offer to attend a Southwest Conference power was tempting, Lerma decided to remain at home and instead attended his local institution of higher learning, Texas A&I (now Texas A&M University, Kingsville). He graduated with a teaching degree in 1938 and from there commenced a legendary career, beginning as head coach of the Benavides Eagles in nearby Duval County in 1940. The full story of Lerma's significance will be detailed in a subsequent chapter, but for now, suffice it to say that he well understood the important place he held as one of the first Mexican American head football coaches in the state of Texas. He drilled into the young men in his charge at BHS (and later, at other such institutions) the "radical" notion that success could be earned on the gridiron and the lessons learned thereon could translate into other areas of life. As Huerta summarizes his subject's life work, "It … [was] clear … that Mexican Americans, especially kids, were watching him. If he succeeded he might encourage them to claim their rightful place on the playing fields, classrooms, marching bands, and drill teams—the heart of South Texas youth culture."[29] As will be detailed, Lerma (and others like him) did this, and much, much more.

Given the significant role that coaches such as Lerma have played in the past in developing (both on the field and off) Latino student athletes, it is troubling to note that some areas of the state of Texas (as of the 2015 season), such as Dallas–Fort Worth–Arlington (the "Metroplex" in Texas-speak) which have many Spanish-surnamed majority high schools, still do not have very many head coaches of such backgrounds. While it is not absolutely necessary for an Hispanic player to play for a coach of their same (or similar) background, it is crucial to keep the importance of such matters in mind when hiring at certain schools. As one Metroplex field general, Michael Ramirez of Carrollton R.L. Turner High School, noted in a recent *Dallas News* article by Corbett Smith:

> "I'm trying to hire the best guys for the job, and I'd never, ever say that you have to be the same race to have great relationships with kids. When I was a player, I was drawn to a coach not just because he had a similar last name, or similar skin color, but to those coaches that cared about your and showed a desire to help you develop." Yet Ramirez said he "definitely felt more weight on his shoulders," wanting to be a role model for his predominantly Latino team by showing it is possible to become a head coach and a good steward to other Latinos who might want to coach in the area. "It's a responsibility that I feel I certainly have, trying to perform and be successful, in order that you might be able to earn some opportunities for those who come after you."[30]

Other work by Iber has brought the story of Spanish-speakers and football at the high school level in other parts of the country closer to the public's attention as well. In a co-authored book entitled *Latinos in U.S. Sport: A History of Isolation, Cultural Identity, and Acceptance* the authors examined various individuals and teams of note who have demonstrated the abilities of Latinos on the gridiron in the past. Additionally, the book also details how Spanish-surnamed athletes have become increasingly common in locales not usually associated with such populations: for example, in places such as West Liberty, Iowa and Springdale, Arkansas. Here, Iber and cohorts note, that as the Latino population, attracted by jobs in agriculture and food processing, increases in such locales, the number of athletes representing area schools is continuing to increase. While not all issues of bias have been eliminated in locales throughout the nation,[31] there is evidence that suggests that the goals of the late 19th century bureaucrats, such as using football as an entry into broader American society for ethnic minorities, is actually occurring in various milieus. An example of this comes from Iowa (playing for the West Liberty Comets), where these authors cited an ESPN story about a son of Mexican immigrants who used athletics as a way to build and strengthen his bond to a teammate (the two have been pals in school since second grade) of a non–Spanish-speaking background. The analysis of this relationship (one among many taking place on football fields, and off, throughout the country one would hope) is worthy of an extensive quote.

> What he [the Latino player] is used to is a town where, at least for kids, skin color had become almost a non-issue.... If anything, some Hispanic parents are growing increasingly frustrated that their teenage children are becoming *too Americanized* (emphasis mine). They're playing American sports, they're eating American food and they're speaking Spanish with an American accent. "I'll say something in Spanish with an accent and my mom will start yelling, 'Talk like you know how to talk...' But she doesn't understand. We just want to bridge both of our cultures together."[32]

In regard to the participation of Spanish-surnamed players at the collegiate and professional levels, the two books mentioned in Hickok's work are *Athletes Remembered: Mexicano/Latino Professional Football Players, 1929–1970* by Mario Longoria, and *Latinos in the End Zone: Conversations on the Brown Color Line in the NFL* by Frederick Luis Aldama and Christopher Gonzalez. Of these offerings, the Longoria piece is principally a straightforward recounting of the careers and statistics of these players, while Aldama and Gonzalez present an effort aimed at critical analysis of the NFL and the game of football as part of Latino life in the United States.

Longoria's exhaustive research and collaboration with the Pro Football Hall of Fame, the Canadian Football League Hall of Fame, and myriad NFL, CFL and collegiate teams, as well as private individuals, reveals that almost 100 Spanish-surnamed (though not all would self-identify as "Latino" or "Hispanic") played the professional game prior to the NFL-AFL (American Football League) merger in 1970. He also details *jugadores* who played in the defunct AAFC (All American Football Conference) as well as the CFL. The book features straightforward background info of each player, and is a basic introduction into this "lost history." This is critical spade work which will be expanded upon in this book, as well as moving on to the stories of gridiron warriors of the years since 1970.[33] Aldama and Gonzalez, on the other hand, are more analytical in their tome and examine how Latinos have been perceived ("construed") by coaches, media, and others tied to football. They summarize their exploration of this complex relationship by stating that:

> In so many respects, sports are used as a marker of humanity. Recall those minority players who were not allowed to play professional sports. Remember the stereotypes that even persist to this day that claim certain marginalized groups incapable of playing one type of sport or another. A way to mark someone as "other" or not equal is to keep him or her from playing professional sports. To dispel with those exclusionist policies, and stereotypes is a healthy thing for American sports.[34]

As is often necessary at the start of books dealing with the Spanish-surnamed population of the United States, there is a need to engage the matter concerning the "appropriate" pan-ethnic term to utilize for this populace: Latino or Hispanic. One of the authors of this current work has dealt extensively with this matter in a previous manuscript project on *atletas*, so the discussion here will be limited.[35] There are supporters and detractors on both sides of the fence for the two terms. Some writers argue that "Hispanic" was created by faceless bureaucrats at the Census Bureau and has implications of "colonialist" relationships. On the other hand, supporters believe that the word effectively captures the importance of the Spanish element in the history of Latin America.

Those who prefer to embrace the term "Latino" posit that it is "more authentic," "grassroots," and is a term that "we" ourselves have chosen. Finally, critics of "Latino" counter by postulating that the term has racial implications and connotes that there exists a direct link by all Spanish-surnamed persons to the original native populations of the Americas. Given the complexity and discord that surrounds this intellectual and political wrangling, we have decided to take the "middle road" suggested by Juan Gonzalez in his superb work, *Harvest of Empire: A History of Latinos in America*.

> I believe needless time has been spent by Latino intellectuals in this country debating whether the term "Hispanic" or "Latino" best describes us. Neither is totally accurate but both are acceptable, and I use them interchangeably in this book. Much as blacks in this country went from being comfortable with "colored," then Negro, then black, then African American, so will U.S. Latin Americans pass through our phases.[36]

In summary, we will use the two terms when referring to players and communities whose backgrounds tie them to the various nations of Latin America; whether individuals were born inside or outside of the United States. In addition to utilizing pan-ethnic idioms, we will also utilize terminology which specifies the particular group(s) being described; such as Mexican, Cuban, Mexican Americans, Cuban American, and so forth.

This book will be divided into five chronological chapters. These will contextualize the historical settings in which these players lived, and will also include subsections on some of the more prominent competitors at all levels. Chapter 1 will discuss a general overview of Latino life in the United States between the 1920s and 1940, and hash out how some of *atletas* managed to play football at the high school level; focusing on the sometimes herculean efforts required. We will also take note of how football spread into various regions with relatively high percentages of Hispanics, locales such as Texas, California, New Mexico, and parts of Florida, for example, providing for a few individuals of this background an opportunity to play the game in an organized/scholastic setting. Further, we will briefly itemize how American football spread into of Mexico and the Caribbean (primarily, Cuba). These locales would, eventually, begin to send a few more *jugadores* to the gridirons of the U.S.

Chapter 2 will focus on the years 1941–1950, with particular emphasis on the post-war years. Here, we will see how the return of thousands of *soldados*, after their military experiences in Europe and the Pacific, stimulated a civil rights movement that helped further open the doors of schools (and also playing fields) to an increased number of Hispanic children. A fair number of these young men played at the high school level, and some even went on to the collegiate and professional ranks. Chapter 3, which will cover 1951–1970, will build upon the main theme expounded previously and scrutinize the impact of the Chicano Movement upon football: particularly focusing on events in the states of Texas and California. This struggle opened doors to Latinos in athletics at the high school and collegiate echelons, and many noteworthy players, such as Tom Flores, Joe Kapp, and Danny Villanueva played during this era. Additionally, we will detail efforts to include Spanish-surnamed young women in the rituals surrounding football games; particularly in high schools.

Chapter 4 will continue to flesh out this topic over the years 1971–1990 but will also note the increased presence of other ethnic groups, such as Cuban Americans and Puerto Ricans. Finally, Chapter 5 will bring us to the present day were Latinos are more prevalent than ever on the gridiron at all levels. Still, there remain issues worth discussing: such as why players (and coaches) of the caliber of Jim Plunkett and Tom Flores, remain on the outside looking into the NFL's Hall of Fame. Additionally, it is necessary to examine how football, at the collegiate and NFL levels, interact and seek to attract the monies of Spanish-surnamed *fanaticos*. Will the NFL, for example, be able to attract recent immigrants, or is their devotion to soccer/*futbol* simply too intense for even "the Shield" to overcome? If the NFL does wish to make inroads, how will they achieve this goal; will the language of this pitch be in Spanish, English, or a combination of the two (Spanglish)?[37]

In summary, the goal of this work is to detail the participation and significance of the role which Hispanics/Latinos have played in the football fields of the United States (and elsewhere) over the past 90+ years. As is to be expected, we proffer copious amounts of statistics, play-by-play action, and a synopsis of glorious feats achieved so as to commemorate what these players accomplished. In addition, their personal stories of overcoming odds and achievement are contextualized into broader themes of American sport and general U.S. history. What role did such competitors play in helping to breakdown stereotypes of Spanish-speakers? How did success on gridirons across America challenge expectations and notions of the physical and intellectual capabilities (or lack thereof) of Spanish-surnamed persons in the minds and hearts of the general population? How did the civil-rights struggle of Latinos help to open doors to more students and thus made it possible for even larger numbers of such youths to play football? Why was this struggle significant beyond the gridiron? Finally, how have the demographic changes that have been taking place in the United States since the 1960s lead to major corporate entities, such as the NFL and collegiate football, to begin paying attention to the burgeoning presence (and economic power) of what is now the largest minority group in the nation? These are among the question we will address. Still, primarily, this is a book about the stories of athletes and their triumphs; and there are many, many to share. Thus, the ultimate goal is to make accessible the tales and triumphs of a mostly overlooked group of athletes who have contributed a great deal to the game of football.

1

Latinos Take to the Gridiron

The 1920s–1940

Before we can move on to detail the tribulations confronted, and successes achieved, by individual Latinos on the football field (at all levels of competition), it is necessary to scrutinize how this population first encountered the game of American football: both in the United States and in parts of Latin America. As noted in our introduction, scholars such as Michael Oriard and Gerald Gems (and others) have discussed how different ethnic groups were introduced to the sport, and how both the minority and the majority believed that there were benefits to be gained from participation. On the one hand, football would teach "appropriate American" values and "toughness" to recent arrivals and their offspring (the white/majority perspective). On the other side of the equation, involvement might serve as a vehicle with which to break down barriers to social acceptance, and could possibly (in a few cases) lead to entry into an institution of higher learning, thus helping to change the economic and societal trajectory of a family (the ethnic minority's standpoint).

While this may have been the assumed impact of football upon recent arrivals from various parts of Europe, similar expectations did not necessarily apply to Latinos and their ability (or lack thereof) to play this game. A few examples will suffice to make our point. First, was it possible for Spanish-surnamed to even comprehend the intricacies of the sport? Next, did they have the physical capabilities and stamina to play at a high level? After all, as Walter Camp and others (as noted in the introduction) believed, the game was the rightful purview of the scions of elite families who attended the most exclusive institutions of higher learning. The writings of Mark C. Anderson, Carlos Kevin Blanton, Miroslava Chavez-Garcia, Rodolfo Acuna, Elmer D. Mitchell, and two master's theses from the 1940s will be used to demonstrate what academics (and the general public) viewed as the aptitudes of such individuals in both the academic and physical realms.

Anderson, in a 1998 article, examined how Mexicans were presented in the American press during the early years of the 1910s. His findings led him to conclude that most English-language, major newspapers throughout the nation held similar, and quite negative, beliefs. Being that they were a mixture of Native American and Spanish genetic matter had produced in the Mexican a "'mongrelized' heritage both of which 'had been cast as inferior in their own right, but also as parts of a whole that amount to less than the sum of their parts.'"[1] Carlos Kevin Blanton, in a 2000 essay, focused on the early use of IQ testing during the 1910s and 1920s, and how this damaged educational opportunities for Mexican American children. In a particularly powerful source from that era, Blanton quotes Professor Lewis Terman (an early proponent of such measurements) arguing that the offspring of "'Spanish-Indian and Mexican families of the Southwest'" must be "'segregated in special classes and be given instruction which is concrete and practical.'" Overall, Terman's assessment was that such pupils "'cannot master abstractions, but they can be made efficient workers.'"[2] Another scholar who wrote about such matters is Miroslava Chavez-Garcia, who focused on such examinations in the Whittier School in California. This author also quotes Terman who, noted that "feeble-mindedness [low IQs] 'was very, very common among Spanish-Indian and Mexican families of the Southwest…. Their dullness seems to be racial, or at least inherent in the family stocks from which they come.'" In regard to the results from the institution noted specifically, Chavez-Garcia summarized that "Mexican and Mexican American youths continued to be identified explicitly by inherent racial attributes and implicitly by mental deficiencies."[3] In the area of academic and social proficiencies, it is also of value to quote from Rodolfo Acuna's textbook, *Occupied America* in regard to how Americans fathomed Spanish-speaking adults and children. Quoting from the National Flag Conference (sponsored by the Daughters of the American Revolution) in 1923, it was assumed that Mexicans had to be taught the "proper" way to live because they were "'dirty, shiftless, lazy, irresponsible, unambitious, thriftless, fatalistic, selfish, promiscuous, and prone to drinking, violence, and criminal behavior.'"[4] Taken together, the above listed traits do not seem to make for a stock of people who will benefit from participating in the intellectual rigors demanded by football.

Two final quotes, the first from a 1944 master's thesis, reveals how educators and law enforcement officials hoped to use football (and other team sports) as a mechanism to help reduce "gang activity" and juvenile delinquency among, in this case, Mexican American youths. The study, written by Lillian Emrick while at the University of Southern California, focused on how to deal with aspects of the "Mexican problem" in the border city of Nogales, Arizona. Emrick's work calls for the municipality to provide a greater amount of opportunity for high schoolers to participate in recreational activities, for through "team games it is possible to promote desirable moral and social qualities such as appreciation of the value of cooperation, self-subordination, obedience to authority, courage, wholesome interest and higher ideals...."[5]

A research project by one of Emrick's contemporaries, but focusing on a Los Angeles topic, generated a survey of the (mostly) Mexican American young men at Andrew Jackson Industrial Arts High School in 1942. Again, the principal concern lay in how to get such students to behave, work hard, avoid legal trouble, and keep them away from the influence of *pachucos* (gangs). Like the educators and police in Nogales, the southern California officials turned to football. The author of this thesis, Charles Dinnijes Withers, argued that the notion of prevention through sports was "beginning to have an effect ... by the fact that 60 percent to the boys' gangs played football as organized clubs." The participants so engaged tended to keep out of trouble while, "the delinquent boy is something of a lone wolf. Fewer played football as an organized club...."[6]

In addition to social and intellectual "issues," Spanish-speakers were also perceived as being inadequate in their physical faculties. In a landmark study from 1922, Professor Elmer Mitchell traced the athletic capabilities of 15 "races," organizing the groups in descending order. "Latins" by which Mitchell means French, Italians and Spaniards, were in the "second tier" of competitors. The noted scholar summarized his assessment of this "race" by arguing that:

> the emotions, being more on the surface, make the Latin more lighthearted ... and, at the same time, more quickly aroused to temper and more fickle in his ardor. [The Spaniard, in particular] tends to an indolent disposition.... He has less self-control than the Frenchman or the Italian ... [and he] is cruel, as is shown by the bull fights in Mexico and Spain.[7]

In the final, and lowest level of racial groups, Mitchell included the "South American" which incorporated the populations under examination in this work: primarily Mexicans/Mexican Americans and Cubans/Cuban Americans. Given the weight of his scholarship (at that time), and severity of his condemnation, it is essential to quote Mitchell at length:

> The South American has not the physique, environment, or disposition which makes for a champion athlete. In build he is of medium height and weight, and not rugged. The games he has borrowed from foreign countries are conducive to leisurely play.... [He] has inherited an undisciplined nature. The Indian in him chafes at discipline and sustained effort, while the Spanish half is proud to a fault.... [His] disposition makes team play difficult ... the steady grind and the competition involved in winning a place on the Varsity has no attraction for them.[8]

Thus, it was abundantly clear to many in the later part of the 19th and early 20th centuries that Spanish surnamed athletes could not possibly succeed in a game as modern, sophisticated and rugged as American football. They had neither the acumen nor prowess to survive the rigors of the gridiron. As the reader will note in the pages to follow, the actual historical record diverges starkly from the sentiments noted.

This chapter, then, will present information on the arrival of the game to areas of the U.S. with substantial pockets of Spanish-speakers, as well as on to Cuba and Mexico. Regarding individuals already living within the borders of the United States, as the game became popular in the late 19th and early 20th centuries, we will review how the sport moved into locations such as Texas, New Mexico, California and Florida. How did American football get to these locales? In regard to the game outside of the national boundaries, who played the sport initially in these *naciones* (nations) and how did it spread? Once this foundation is discussed, we will move on to detail the achievements of specific individuals.

While the game of football is now played everywhere in the U.S., as most followers of the sport are aware, its origins lay in the recherché setting of Ivy League universities. Under the tutelage of Walter Camp, Yale became the first major power in the sport.[9] In the later part of the 19th century, from the hallowed environs of New Haven, went forth multiple Camp disciples who helped spread the game to distant environs (indeed, even outside of the United States). Most devotees found fertile ground in which to sew their devotion, but one of the most successful was an individual named James Perkins Richardson who arrived to teach at Ball High School in Galveston, Texas. Here, he met up with a fellow Ivy Leaguer named John Sealy (from Princeton) who had already established a team named the Galveston Rugbys (comprised of young college graduates and local businessmen). Just as November 6, 1869, is memorialized as the "first" football game in the nation, Christmas Eve of 1892 marks the "first" recorded contest staged within the boundaries of the Lone Star State; it was the genesis of a passionate love affair which continues to the present. "Over the next decade, Sealy and his athletes played squads (both club and high school) in Dallas, Fort Worth, and San Antonio. By 1900, secondary schools ... were competing against each other in the increasingly popular sport."[10] As it spread, football gravitated eventually into locations where a substantial percentage of the population was (predominantly) of Mexican descent. Newspapers from cities such as El Paso, Laredo, and the region known as the Rio Grande Valley,[11] cited by contributors to Bynum's *King Football*, recorded the existence of scholastic squads as early as 1895, the early 1900s, and 1911.

One scholar who has written extensively about football in "the Valley" is Greg Selber. His work will be referenced extensively later, but at this point it is significant to address a meaningful feature about football in these heavily-Latino regions of Texas in the late 19th and early 20th centuries: the almost total lack of participation by Spanish-surnamed athletes on local teams. The reason for this was that very, very few of these young men made it to high school, and if they did, their families often needed assistance on the economic front; leaving no time to participate in athletic competition. Emrick noted this pattern as well in 1944 in her study on Nogales. While the high school in town was almost 90 percent Latino, "few pupils engage in athletics after school. There are never more than thirty boys participating in any season in football, basketball, or baseball.... It is true, too, that many have jobs after school and many children shop each day for their parents."[12]

Additionally, Selber recounts, in this region, "there was consistent racial strife ... and most accounts ... indicate that the Anglo kids did not exactly welcome their Latino Valley mates into the [football] fold."[13] Take this to mean that the more "dark skinned" (mostly of Mexican descent) were not welcomed, even if they did make it all the way to high school. For example, some teams did not get their first athletes of this background until well into the 1920s. A particular case noted elsewhere highlights the story of one of the first schools from the Valley to field a team (Edinburg High Bobcats) not fielding such an athlete until 1927 (Amador Rodriguez—now a local legend).[14] Not all players with Spanish surnames were ostracized, however. Those considered to be not of Mexican but rather "Spanish" background (read that to mean higher socioeconomic status) could play. One such player was the "'blue-eyed, blond-haired Spaniard' Rodolfo Samano," one of the earliest participants (1929) in the gridiron history of the Brownsville High School Eagles.[15]

A 2009 article by Joel Huerta entitled, "Friday Night Rights: South Texas High School Football and the Struggle for Equality," quoted a coach from McAllen who wondered aloud why there were not more Mexican Americans playing football in the Valley by the early 1930s. The field general in question, Chatter Allen, eventually comes to a significant, though only partial (not focusing on the economics, for example), realization which Huerta summarized by stating: "Was it something cultural? Was there something about football that the Mexican mind did not find conceptually interesting.... Finally, it clicked. In the stands and on the field, brown athletes faced racist, vocal crowds. What attraction did that hold?"[16]

Another legendary player (and later, coach) from southern Texas (though not from the Valley) was Everardo Carlos Lerma, originally from Bishop (born in 1915), but raised in Kingsville. He was the youngest of 11, and both parents had passed by his eight birthday. His brothers and sisters were determined that he would have a chance to complete his education. Like Dr. Jorge Prieto mentioned in the introduction, Lerma was fascinated by football and when he arrived at Kingsville High School in the late 1920s, he was determined to make the squad. As noted in Selber's research, Lerma, too, faced teammates who did not want to play alongside a "Mexican." Still, he persevered and earned all-district honors in 1934. Because of his performance, he was offered a scholarship to Texas Christian University, but instead chose to remain at home and attend Texas A&I (now Texas A&M University, Kingsville). Again he met with resistance, but ultimately earned a place as a starter for the Javelinas. He completed his education degree in 1938, and he and his new bride moved to the Duval County town of Benavides where Lerma first served as an assistant coach and high school teacher. After a down year in 1939, the administration of Benavides High dismissed their coach, and the young coach applied for the field general post at the institution. "E.C. recalled that he had a great deal of difficulty convincing the school board to give him a chance because 'people just couldn't believe that a Mexican American could do as good of a job as an Anglo. Well, I think I proved them wrong.'"[17]

A jaunt to the other end of Texas (El Paso) reveals similar issues. By the early 1930s, football had become an important way for the predominantly Mexican American high school, Bowie (Bears) to challenge notions of inferiority. One participant told researcher Victor M. Aguilar that the battle on the gridiron between Bowie and the mostly white Austin High was more than just about the numbers on a scoreboard. "Each side of town saw the game as a battle between the two cultures, one trying to prove their supremacy while the other was trying to prove they were equal." Another player, this one who donned the royal blue and white between 1932 and 1936, recalled that when his squad played a playoff game against Big Springs, that he and his teammates were "permitted to stay at the local hotel ... [but they were] put on the top floor so that we would be out of everybody's way. In the morning ... our ride to the stadium [was] this big old cattle truck."[18]

A recent work by Fred Morales provides further details concerning the prowess of the El Paso Bowie High School Bears on the gridiron. The school, which began in 1922 was established to serve the Segundo Barrio on the south side of the city. From its inception, the institution provided both a place (and teams) to fuel ethnic pride, while simultaneously also being a place where grievous stereotyping took place. For example, even before Bowie became a high school, athletic squads gave the mostly Mexican American student population a chance to shine. The soccer team in late January of 1924 claimed the city championship and finished its campaign both undefeated and unscored upon. Certainly a proud moment. Barely a week later, the administration instituted "tooth-brush drills" to be certain that all Bears were properly instructed in oral hygiene. Toward the end of 1925, the principal, Robert C. Jackson, lectured civic-minded El Pasoans at the Forum Club that in the area of the city in which the school resides, "there is no home life" among the Spanish-speaking inhabitants.[19]

In regard to football, the Bears claimed the city's junior high school title in late November of 1927, and then proceeded to triumph at a regional level by defeating a school from Alpine, 44–0. The 1928 squad was even more impressive, repeating as city champs and trouncing Austin Junior High, 73–0. The significance of such triumphs can be seen in the reaction to yet another victory, this time against Denning High on October 26th of 1929 when, after the game, a large group of boys were led ... from the stadium to downtown, then to the Segundo Barrio.... It was a large parade of supporters celebrating a decisive victory." The joy was cut short the following week, however, as the Bears lost to El Paso High, 12–0 in the city title tilt.

By the early 1930s, it was quite common for Bowie games to attract crowds of more than 3000 fans in a weekly basis. In 1933, for example, in a clash against their mostly–Anglo rivals from Austin High, the boys from the barrio won, 29–13, in front of a raucous gathering of approximately 5000. The season culminated with and 38–0 thrashing of Ysleta to win the district title. "It was the first district championship for the school in football and Porfirio Diaz was the quarterback Jose 'Crash' Chavez was the fullback and Gustavo Casarez was the halfback." One final note on this season, the administration from Austin did not surrender the Silver Cup, emblematic of city-wide gridiron supremacy until January of 1934. Not to be deterred, the Bear gridders instead "made a 'Pink Teacup' to represent a temporary emblem ... and it was taken through a ceremony held at the school."[20]

Under the leadership of Coach Guy Davidson, who would remain at Bowie between 1929 and 1949, the Bears continued to experience success in the later part of the 1930s. Even with wins on the field, disturbing discriminatory events marked the relationship between the mostly white teacher rank and the overwhelmingly Mexican American student body. For example, in November of 1937, a major squabble took place at the school as one teacher, Elvira McLaughlin (dean of girls), contacted the *El Paso Herald-Post* appealing for citizens to donate money to help feed hungry students. This petition proved a direct challenge to the sensibilities of many in the community, and they responded vigorously. Led by a 15-year-old student named Ruth Lopez, marchers went down to the newspaper's offices, and "stated [that] 'they were not hungry.'" The spat was finally resolved when the administration urged parents to increase participation in the P.T.A., and petitions for funds would be solicited "without publicity."[21]

The history of the game in neighboring New Mexico has been ably covered by Dan Ford in various manuscripts. In his first work, *The History of New Mexico High School Football: Volume I: The First 100 Years, 1892–1992*, the author noted an entry in the *Albuquerque Democrat* in late November of 1892 which stated that a new sport had arrived in the territory. "'This afternoon a game of foot-ball will be played at 3:00 on the first street grounds, between the High school and University boys. An interesting game is anticipated.'" In the same section, Ford cites information regarding the start of what is now the long-standing University of New Mexico vs. New Mexico State University rivalry the following year. By the early 1900s, seven high schools in the Land of Enchantment were fielding squads and playing a fairly regular schedule of games. Ford notes some of the earliest individuals of Latino background to make their mark on the gridiron in this locale were the Hernandez brothers, Louis and Walter, who played for Albuquerque High School (AHS) and the UNM Lobos, as well as coached for an extended period of time in the state. Louis was head coach at Menaul High for more than two decades, and his brother served as his assistant. One particularly noteworthy season for the institution under the Hernandezes' leadership was 1937, when the Panthers not only completed their campaign with a perfect 8–0 record, but outscored their opposition by a mark of 192–0. Finally, another significant marker involving Latino footballers in this era of New Mexico high school football occurred in 1934, when Clovis High School (on the border with the western part of Texas) played a predominantly Mexican American squad from El Paso Bowie in the first-ever night game in the state. The tilt, played in Carlsbad just before Thanksgiving, saw the Wildcats claim a 22–6 victory over the visiting Texans.[22]

Another researcher who has documented the role of Latinos in New Mexico football is Ricardo Dow Anaya in his dissertation entitled "An Historical Prospective of Influence Sport Had on Sport Legends of New Mexico, 1925–1975." Here, the author noted other early athletes on the state's gridirons. One individual of importance was Tony J. Valdez of Cimarron High School who not only played football, but also basketball, baseball and track at his alma mater. Then, he attended the University of New Mexico between 1935 and 1939 earning four varsity letters there as well. After graduation, he pursued a career as an educator at Albuquerque High School until the late 1970s.[23] A contemporary of Valdez was Albuquerque High School's Abbie Pais, a legendary performer on the football fields of New Mexico who graduated in 1932 and went on to coach at Belen High School until 1971. Pais' story encapsulates many of the issues concerning why so few Latinos played competitive football during the first few decades of the 20th century. In visiting with Dow Anaya, Pais recounted that, at age six, his father died and "my mother had to struggle to get me through high school. She could never have sent me to college. I played well at AHS ... [and my coach] recommended me highly to the University of New Mexico. I got the scholarship. It brought me many years of happiness and a college education."[24]

A final couple of players worth noting from this era in New Mexico are the Apodaca cousins, Lauro and Anastacio (known as "Hookey"), who played for the New Mexico Aggies (now New Mexico State University) in the late 1930s. The NMSU fan site bleedcrimson.net highlights some of the contributions of these two athletes to some very successful squads in 1935 and 1936. The Apodacas both played on the line for the Aggies and helped their side finish 1935 with a 6–1–1 mark, followed by a trip to the inaugural Sun Bowl in El Paso on January 1, 1936. Walter Hines' summary of the game noted that the 14–14 tie between the Aggies and the Cowboys of Hardin Simmons featured 10 fumbles, 5 interceptions and 29 punts. With the Las Cruces–based squad trailing 14–7 in the fourth quarter, the NMSU coaches "called a trick play that made use of the speedy Apodaca cousins. Pratt (the QB) pass to Hooky [sic] at the 35 who whirled and fired a long lateral pass to Lauro. Lauro, who had great speed, caught the ball and raced untouched into the Cowboy end zone…. The extra point [by Anastacio] was good, making it 14–14." This was just the start of a long line of Apodacas to play for the Aggies. As Mario Longoria noted from a local paper, in "those days of the 1930s and early 1940s, there were always some Apodacas on the New Mexico Aggies squads, but Lauro and his cousin 'Hookey' were competitors in a class by themselves."[25]

Moving further west, to California, reveals a very limited amount of research on the early participation of specific Spanish-surnamed individuals in the game of football. In a 1989 essay scholar Joel Franks documented the arrival of the sport in the state. Not surprisingly, the game's birth in the Golden State paralleled what occurred in other locales. Franks noted that by 1886, the University of California had played its first contest under "American rules" (as opposed to British Rugby, Gaelic and Australian regulations). Not to be outdone by their rivals, just six years later, the young men of Stanford fielded their first squad and "provided the sport with the needed impetus to attract a passionate following in California—a rivalry resembling that of Harvard and Yale." From that instant, "The Game" sought to match clashes from New England in both style (who attended) and substance (the reason/meaning of the game).

Anastacio F. (Hookey) Apodaca, 1935 (courtesy New Mexico State Athletics).

Franks noted that "society's upper echelons eagerly commanded the limelight at the annual event," and also "evoked sickly sentimental images of medieval knighthood." From a "modern" perspective, football "appealed to the era's call for machine-like teamwork and stout good fellowship."[26] Given how football was perceived, its exclusivity and appeal to elites, meant that, at least initially, there would be few Americans of Mexican background playing the sport. The writing of Arnoldo De Leon provides a sense, however, that "American" sports were making inroads with at least some individuals of this upbringing in locations such as California. "Some Mexicans no doubt found appeal in at least some of these newer contests ... [and] joined athletic teams or tried their hands at individual sports."[27]

Lauro Apodaca, 1935 (courtesy New Mexico State Athletics).

A 1996 dissertation by Deana Anderson Lamont entitled "Sport and Leisure in the Building of an Urban Community: The Case of Oakland, California, 1850–1906," while not providing any specific info on Latino players, does provide a timeframe of when high school football commenced, at least in the northern environs of the Golden State. Even before the first Berkeley and Stanford face off, Oakland High "also fielded a 'foot-ball' team. There had been significant interest in the sport, [but] the team always struggled because, it was reported, it had lacked a practice field." While the club may not have had the best facilities, it was part of an organization known as the California Foot Ball League (CFBL), the first iteration of which existed briefly and disbanded in 1886. The CFBL was supplanted by the Amateur League (but for only one year), which featured teams comprised of high schoolers, local clubs, and college-aged men. Under this organization, and then the reconstituted CFBL, Oakland High played against private and military schools as well as other public institutions.

By the last years of the 1880s, the league had begun to utilize intercollegiate rules to guide play. Just as with the collegiate version, the games were popular, but also tended to attract persons from further up the social ladder. "Significant crowds were expected at the League's games.... [But]

[o]nly those with invitations were 'admitted to the grounds' on game days and two policemen were hired."[28] In the southern part of the state, a 1942 article on the history of Los Angeles High noted that the institution fielded a football team as early as 1894 and often competed against colleges such as Occidental and Pomona. Further, one of the greatest distinctions of the school's gridiron program, was its success against another university for, "in 1908 and 1909 the Los Angeles High School defeated the University of Southern California."[29]

A more specific example for our purposes comes from the work of Jose Alamillo in a 2010 essay on transnational sport (between California and Mexico) in the early 1930s. In conjunction with the 1932 Olympic Games, the city of Los Angeles' Department of Playgrounds and Recreation worked with Mexican American groups to stage track and field events at the Evergreen Playground in May of that year. This lead to a collaborative effort between the city and the *comunidad* (community) to establish an organization known as the Mexican Athletic Association of Southern California (MAASC). The entity's offerings included football; though baseball, basketball, track and boxing were the most popular offerings. Further, the MAASC worked with a Mexican-based association, the *Confederacion Deportiva Mexicana* (Mexican Sports Confederation), or CDM. One of the most significant cooperative projects between these groups resulted in the playing of a gridiron contest between UNAM (*Universidad Nacional Autonoma de Mexico*) and Occidental College in September of 1935. The game featured segregated seating, and deriding of UNAM athletes as "Mexican jumping beans" and being like "chili con carne, they have a lot of pepper" in local newspapers. Alamillo's sources indicated that well over 6,000 Mexicans and Mexican American attended the contest, which Occidental won by three touchdowns.[30] We will provide a brief overview of how American football began in Mexico later in this chapter.

A final early 20th century note from California high school football is worth mentioning at this point. In a wonderful 2003 documentary entitled "Symbol of Heart," the producers tracked the longstanding rivalry between Roosevelt High School (located in Boyle Heights) and Garfield High School (located in East Los Angeles). The two schools, both of which opened in the 1920s, have played (with a pause between 1939 and 1948) continuously since 1926. At first, the Bulldogs from Garfield tended to contain the more Mexican American–laden roster, with the Rough Riders being comprised initially of Japanese Americans, Jews, and other ethnics (with some Mexican Americans as well). A 1936 survey of Roosevelt's student body noted that "Americans" were the largest segment of the populace (around 28 percent), followed by "Jews" at 26 percent, and then Mexican Americans, at roughly one quarter of all students. A student from that era indicated that the football team was representative of the total student populace.[31] After World War II, however, the demographics of the schools began to change, and by today, the "East

L.A. Classic" is overwhelmingly a Mexican American/Latino athletic spectacle. Indeed, the game usually attracts well north of 20,000 *fanaticos*, a figure that is difficult to achieve on Friday nights, even in football-crazy Texas. This game is a touchstone for civic and ethnic pride for thousands of Roosevelt and Garfield alumni all over southern California. More details on this civic and athletic event will be presented later.[32]

Moving east to the state of Florida, we encounter some research on football in the writings of Gary Mormino and George Pozzeta in their work on the Cuban-Italian community located in Ybor City and West Tampa: referred to in locale parlance as "Latins." These neighborhoods have produced many greats, among them legendary individuals such as Al Lopez in baseball and Ferdie Pacheco in boxing. In regard to football, the "Fight Doctor" recounts that at Tampa Jefferson and Hillsborough High Schools "our folk heroes were the fellows who wore ... [lettermen] sweaters." As early as 1920, players such as "Big Joe" Domingo terrorized opponents as "one of the best fullbacks that Hillsborough has ever produced, perhaps All-state." Between 1920 and the start of World War II, "Latins" comprised approximately 50 percent of the starting line-ups for Hillsborough High. Mormino and Pozzeta summarized playing high school football for the young men of these barrio as something that "'transported Latins away from the sheltered immigrant neighborhood and into rival arenas.'"[33]

Given the brief overviews of the tentative start of Latino participation in football within the borders of the United States noted above, we now briefly turn to the spread of the game in Latin America. As of the later years of the second decade of the 21st century, the sport has a burgeoning presence in most of Latin America; though interest is of fairly recent vintage in most locales. The most protracted historical narrative, comes from two specific nations: Mexico and Cuba.

In Mexico, as noted in a short film produced by UNAM, the initial development of the sport is credited to two forces: first, the arrival of U.S. Marines to Veracruz and to the tireless promotion by a war correspondent for Hearst Newspapers named Arthur Constantine. After the Marines played a game in the port city in 1896, they left balls and other materials with locals upon their departure. Among those who came into possession of these implements was the son of the state's governor, Raul Dehesa, who, due to time spent at American institutions, was familiar with the sport. Shortly thereafter, in the nearby city of Xalapa, Raul and friends became, most likely, the first *Mexicanos* to play this version of football. The game remained predominantly a curiosity among elites until the later part of the 1910s, however.[34]

The other historical actor credited with diffusing the game in Mexico was Arthur Constantine, who arrived to cover the nation's revolutionary turmoil, and married into a prominent Mexican family. His spouse, Amanda

Moran de Constantine, had a long and distinguished career as a professor at both Mexico City College (which would also develop into a prominent player in Mexican football) and UNAM. It was in part through the connection to UNAM that Constantine became acquainted with Mexican students who like Dehesa, after that university's reconstitution in 1910, where familiar with the game from having spent time in the United States. By the late 1920s, Constantine, in cooperation with students such as the Noriega brothers, Alejandro and Leopoldo, and American industrialists, got a team started. One highlight of this early era was UNAM playing against Mississippi College in 1929 with Emilio Portes Gil, President of Mexico between 1928 and 1930, in attendance. The American influence at UNAM, through Constantine and others, was prevalent until the 1940s, as eight of the first eleven head coaches were Americans, and, not surprisingly, there was a Yale connection here as well, as Reginald Root guided UNAM in 1933 and later went on to coach (with limited success) at his alma mater.[35]

Between 1933 and 1944, UNAM won a dozen consecutive *Liga Mayor* (the principal league for collegiate football in Mexico until the late 1960s) titles. During this time, additionally, there developed the most significant rivalry in the nation's collegiate football history between UNAM and the *Burros Blancos* of the *Instituto Politecnico Nacional*, or the IPN (National Technical Institute). The first showdown, referred to as the *Clasico-Poli-Universidad* (Poli-University Classic), between the two early titans of Mexican collegiate football took place in 1936, surprisingly, with IPN shutting out their rivals, 6–0. This tilt would continue in its in initial format until 1957. The rivalry featured legendary coaches and athletes of Mexican football, such as IPN's icon Salvador "Sapo" Mendiola and UNAM's great Roberto "Tapatio" Mendez (who would rename the UNAM team, Pumas, in 1942). The era before the 1940s also witnessed the development of what was known as *Segunda Fuerza* and *Tercera Fuerza* which were roughly equivalent to high school and youth football throughout many parts of the nation.[36] Given these developments, it is apparent that many Mexicans were familiar with the sport of American football prior to their arrival in the United States.

There is abundant similarity between the inceptions of American football in Cuba with that of the sport in Mexico. First, the game was "demonstrated" to Cubans by sailors from two American ships in January of 1899. A game between American sailors and Cuban "youths" (no affiliation given) took place in April of 1900. Then, as noted earlier in Gems' work, by 1902, the game began to filter into the island via connections established through interactions of the nation's elites during time spent at American universities. As a result, in October of that year, students at Havana University commenced practices and played intramural games: mostly between the various schools (Law, Medical, and Engineering). From these squads, came the first varsity in November 1904. The first exhibition game for the side took place on the 22nd of that month, a 22–5 victory against an artillery unit from Santa Clara.[37]

According to research conducted by Michael T. Wood, the first game played on Cuban soil between two Cuban teams was in January of 1905 and featured members of the Vedado Tennis Club (VTC) and the University of Havana. Wood also notes that the game remained the domain of more fashionable set of *alta sociedad* (high society) as, "Cuban colleges and athletic clubs, particularly in Havana, organized amateur leagues and played against each other.... The number of teams ... varied from year to year, depending on the condition of the clubs and political stability on the island."[38] In addition to playing against other *Cubanos*, the youths of VTC and Havana University soon began to test their mettle against Yankees: with very limited success. The first recorded tilt took place in late November of 1906, with the Caribes playing against a team of sailors from the naval ship USS Columbia: the *Americanos* emerged with a 15–0 triumph in a game played in Havana.

Another consequential encounter, and thoroughly studied for its social and historical significance, is a Christmas Day contest between the Caribes and the Louisiana State University Tigers in 1907, with the southerners trouncing the Cubans, 56–0. As Wood notes in a recent article, the substance of this match went well beyond what happened on the gridiron to provide a sense of, among other historical topics, "North American perceptions of race and ethnicity." In a nutshell, the Louisianans, and a group of American sailors who witnessed the game, perceived the match as a competition between inherently unequal "races." The Cubans, they believed, were simply cast as insignificant "others" who were going to be taught a football lesson (as the Yanks supposedly had taught the Cubans lessons in democracy, modern government, and economics during their occupation of the island). As further proof of this sense of American superiority, it is noteworthy to cite a cheer heard that day which included an ethnic slur ("Lick the Spicks, Kill the Spicks!"), as well as noting one of the stipulations placed on the game by LSU: "The dark-skinned natives could play anybody they wanted on their team, excepting Negroes and Americans." The American team, hailing from a southern state, brought its racial prejudices to this game.

The students of Havana University, on the other hand, sought to demonstrate their "worthiness" to play this "scientific" and "modern" sport. As one Havana paper argued, the student population at the institution was quite up-to-date on the pomp and circumstance that surrounded collegiate games back in the United States. "There will be plenty of college spirit shown, and the Havana University students are practicing their yells, their college songs, and various institutions of noise-making will convey enthusiasm to the players, while the colors of the colleges will be seen on all sides." The Cubans' preparation for the contest certainly approximated that of most colleges and universities in the United States.³⁹

Although the Cubans proved no match on the field, they did show "the greatest cordiality, friendship and enthusiasm" to the American teams. In total, over a fifty-year span, teams comprised of Cubans with university, athletic club, military, and police affiliations played 62 games against U.S.-based teams. The last game in this series, which took place on November 30, 1956, in Key West, Florida, saw Stetson University trounce the Caribes, 64–0. Overall, the islanders' mark against American-based competition was unimpressive, but the most notable victories were an 11–0 triumph over Tulane University by the Cuban Athletic Club (CAC) in 1910, and another triumph by CAC over the University of Mississippi, 13–0 in 1921.⁴⁰

In addition to these contests, there is documentation of Cubans playing in the NFL early in the league's history (Ignacio Molinet in 1927 with the Frankford Yellowjackets).⁴¹ Other evidence comes from the site profootball-daily.com, which shows a 1944 clipping entitled "Redskins Sign Cuban for Football Tryout," about Eneas Munoz. The same article also notes that another Cuban, Manuel Rivero, played for Columbia University and had a tryout with the Chicago Bears.⁴² Although failing to make it in the NFL, Rivero, however, became a successful multi-sport coach and administrator at a historically black institution between 1933 and 1977, Lincoln University, located in Oxford, Pennsylvania. His tenure and contributions were so significant, the institution's gymnasium was named in his honor in 1986.⁴³

Given the developments noted above, it is evident that a number of Mexicans and Cubans who emigrated had some familiarity with the sport of American football prior to their arrival in the United States. Thus, even with the economic hardships and the prejudice faced, there was not an insignificant pool of Spanish-surnamed talent ready and willing to put on helmet and pads to participate in the intellectually challenging and physically rigorous action on gridirons throughout the nation. It is to the specific stories of some of these individual athletes from the 1920s through 1940 to which we now turn. The athletes we will discuss are: Ignacio Saturnino Molinet, Jesse and Kelly Rodriguez, Waldo Don Carlos, Jim Schuber, Aldo Richins, Jose Martinez-Zorrilla, and further info on the previously mentioned Jorge Prieto.

Ignacio Saturnino Molinet

On July 5, 2000, Mario Longoria received a telephone call from Mr. Jason Aikens, Collections Coordinator, Pro Football Hall of Fame, Canton, Ohio, to advise he recently spoke with Ms. Heidi Caldwell from Mason,

New Hampshire. Ms. Caldwell identified herself as the granddaughter of Mr. Ignacio S. Molinet, who played collegiate football at Cornell University and with the 1927 Frankford Yellow Jackets team of the old National Football League (NFL). She contacted Mr. Jason Aiken to donate her grandfather's old NFL contract to the Pro Football Hall of Fame. In this matter, Mr. Aikens requested assistance in verifying his ethnic background and playing dates with the Frankford Yellow Jackets Team. The reason was that historical documentation in the book *Athletes Remembered: Mexicano/Latino Professional Football Players, 1929–1970*, listed a player named Jesse Rodriguez, punter/fullback with the 1929 Buffalo Bisons as the first Latino athlete in professional football. Mr. Aikens requested research on the matter to verify if indeed Molinet had preceded Rodriguez as the first athlete of this background in professional history of the sport.[44] Further, I researched the matter to verify Molinet's background and his contractual association with the NFL's Frankford Yellow Jackets. Thus it was confirmed that the Cuban-born Molinet was the first Latino athlete in the NFL.

The research into Ignacio's personal, collegiate and pro football career revealed he was one of the talented sons of Joaquin and Conchita Molinet from Chaparra, Oriente Province, Cuba. Both parents were Cuban citizens and after serious illnesses, both died in the same year, 1927. The family was well connected politically, as Ignacio's uncle, Ernestino Molinet, served as Cuba's Minister of the Secretary of the Interior under the Machado Government. According to Ignacio's daughter Teresa Van De Carr, the Molinet family wanted the best for their children and, like many Cuban elites, sent their sons to the United States for their education.[45] Older brother Joaquin was also an accomplished athlete, part of the Cornell Class of '21 and member of the institution's Sports Hall of Fame, being inducted in 1988. Still

Ignacio Saturnino Molinet, 1927 (courtesy Cornell University Athletics).

another family member Joaquin Ernesto Molinet, Cornell Class of 1949, won varsity letters in basketball in 1946, 1947 and soccer in 1947 and 1948.[46]

Ignacio began his American education at the Peddie School of Hightstown, New Jersey. Upon completion of his studies, he transitioned into Cornell University in Ithaca, New York. There, he was an outstanding basketball and football player for the Big Red, earning varsity letters in two sports (basketball '25, '27 and football '24, '26).[47] On the gridiron, "the big Cuban," as he was referred to in the *1925 Cornell University Yearbook—The Cornellian,* Ignacio starred in games against Columbia, Dartmouth, and Pennsylvania, and he cites his first varsity game against Columbia, played on November 1, 1924, by stating, "Molinet, the big Cuban sophomore, played his first game for the varsity, and was notably the star of the game." He was a hard-hitting, line plunging fullback who scored several touchdowns against Ivy League opponents. According to the university yearbook, "Molinet improved with each game,"[48] and was scouted by a professional club, the Frankford Athletic Association of the NFL.

To his collegiate peers and later pro teammates, Ignacio was also known as "Molly" and "Lou." This was a far cry from the phonetically pronounced (Ig-nah-see-o), and one can only speculate how troublesome it was for his Anglo-counterparts to correctly address him. Instead, it was linguistically easier for them to shorten or invent nicknames. Undaunted by the nicknames he received, "Molly" and "Lou," Ignacio pressed on with his academic and athletic pursuits. He ultimately received a degree in Mechanical Engineering the same year of his parent's deaths,[49] but it was his athletic achievements that eventually led him in the NFL.

After his collegiate career, he was contacted by the Frankford Athletic Association of Philadelphia to play professionally. The NFL draft was still nine years away so recruitment and negotiations were often conducted through referrals, correspondence, telegrams, and telephone. Savoring the opportunity to play for the Frankford Yellow Jackets, who were the 1926 defending NFL Champions, Molinet appreciated the offer and embraced the opportunity to discuss his prospects. He began the process in the summer of 1927 while he was in Cuba tending to his seriously ill parents.

The contract process with Frankford actually became an international business transaction. It began with a letter from Mr. Robert B. Haines, Treasurer of the Frankford Athletic Association, located at Frankford Avenue and Paul Street in Philadelphia, Pennsylvania, to Mr. Ignacio. S. Molinet in Chaparro, Oriente, Cuba. The opening letter information greets Mr. Molinet with contractual and financial information. The letter information specifies:

> Dear Sir: We are glad to have your letter of July 8th, and note that you are interested in playing pro-football. In order to save time, we are enclosing herewith a regular National Football League contract. Our Association offers you the salary of $100.00

per game for 13 Saturday games at home and $60.00 per game for 7 Sunday games away from home. This would net you $1720.00 for the season. In addition to this we will pay you $30.00 per week for living expenses during the two weeks training period. We will also allow you $50.00 toward your transportation from Cuba to Philadelphia. We do not, however, allow any return transportation. As we advised in our last letter your salary is guaranteed. That is you will receive full salary for all the games cancelled or games lost through personal injury. We believe that this feature is only offered by the Frankford Athletic Association.[50]

The letter noted the difference in the Saturday and Sunday games was necessary due to fact the team receives a minimum flat guarantee on Sunday as a traveling team. It also referred the enclosed contract information regarding pay is made out for $50.00 with the additional $50.00 added by the Exhibit A statement attached to the contract. The letter states, "This is necessary in order to keep our total salary limit within the League requirements. You will note the white copy of the contract, which goes to the League, does not contain the Exhibit A."[51] While the last paragraph of the letter states the following:

We have been fortunate in securing some of the most outstanding college players of last year's teams and at this time we have a number of applicants who desire to play on a Championship Club. May we ask that you give this matter your immediate consideration and advise us of your decision at once. We would appreciate if you would sign the pink and white copies, returning them to us and retaining the brown for yourself. You can understand that with a limited squad we must know definitely as early as possible who will make up our team. Very truly yours, Frankford Athletic Association. Robert B. Haines, Treasurer.[52]

The letter and NFL contract were mailed to Mr. Ignacio S. Molinet in Cuba with the anticipation of receiving a prompt reply. However, after an extended period there was no response, and Frankford followed up by sending a telegram. The correspondence was dated August 19, 1927, and asked the following, "Have you decided to play football, cable immediately, Frankford Athletic Association."[53]

Ignacio S. Molinet replied with a letter that addressed the questions posed in both the Frankford Athletic Association letter and the telegram. Mr. Molinet replied:

Gentlemen: This will acknowledge receipt of your cable of even date, to which I replied by wire immediately. Your letter of July 21st, enclosing contract for the 1927 football season has been in hand for some time, but I have been unable to answer before this, in view of the serious illness of my father which resulted in his death on Wednesday last. Your offer is attractive, but after having carefully gone over the terms of the contract, I find some points which are not quite clear to me, and would request that you answer the following questions—Do I understand that the player receives compensation for games scheduled, but in which, by complying with orders from the management, he does not participate?—Are the player's living expenses for his or the

1. Latinos Take to the Gridiron

club's account?—In the case of a controversy between player and the club, would the Exhibit "A" attached to the pink and brown copies, but not mentioned on the white copy, be accepted as valid by the league?[54]

The next paragraph in the letter asks another question concerning the approximate costs of travel to Philadelphia. He asks the question because he approximates the travel costs from Cuba to Philadelphia is $150.00 and requests Frankford reconsider the proposed allowance be increased to at least $100.00. The last paragraph in the letter addresses his questions:

> By your giving this letter your immediate attention, I should have your reply in my possession by September first, and I shall immediately give you my definite decision by cable, and in the case of accepting all the terms, forward you the signed contracts. Anxiously awaiting your reply, and feeling assured that we will be able to come to an early agreement, I remain, Yours, very truly. Ignacio S. Molinet.[55]

Eight days later on August 28, 1927, the Frankford Athletic Association wired a reply telegram to Ignacio S. Molinet. The telegram provided the following information:

> Salary guaranteed for twenty games as outlined—players pay living expenses from salary—we allow thirty dollars per week for two weeks training—exhibit a valid with league will allow you one hundred dollars toward the travelling expenses—team must report here September eleventh—Frankford Athletic Association.[56]

After Ignacio read the telegram, he drafted a letter reply to the attention of Mr. Robert S. Haines, Frankford Athletic Association. In the letter he acknowledges the receipt of the cable and acceptance of the contract terms. He writes:

> I am receipt of your cable of yesterday's date reading: Salary guaranteed for twenty games as outlined. Players pay living expenses from salary. We allow thirty dollars per week for two weeks training. Exhibit "A" valid with league. Will allow you one hundred dollars towards traveling expenses. Team must report here September eleventh.[57]

Mr. Molinet agreed to the terms with the following acknowledgment, "I herewith confirm my reply as follows—Cable received, terms accepted. Signed contracts mailed today. He also referred to the contract copies. "In accordance with my above cable, advice I attach hereto the pink and white copies of the contract duly signed, having retained the brown copy, as per your indication, my files." In the final paragraph of the letter, Molinet advised Mr. Haines about his travel plans to Philadelphia. He wrote:

> My present plans are to leave here Monday September 5, reaching Havana Tuesday, September 6th, leaving the following day by rail for Philadelphia, and if not delayed in Havana by the existing immigration restrictions should arrive in Philadelphia on September 9th. I think, however, unlikely that there be any delay but in case difficulties arise, I shall cable you from Havana. Yours very truly, Ignacio Molinet.[58]

Molinet also sent a cable to the Frankford Athletic Association to advise them of his acceptance of the contract terms and signed contracts mailed today. At this point in the negotiation process, Molinet technically began his professional football career with the Frankford Yellow Jackets of the old NFL becoming a historical first in the history of the league.

Ignacio wrote a separate letter on the same date to the American Consul in Havana, Cuba. In this correspondence, he sought advice from the American Consul regarding his immigration status. In doing so, Mr. Molinet explained the circumstances, reasons of his stay in Cuba, and requested the Consul's assistance with a re-entry permit to return to the United States. The letter to the Consul explains:

> The writer, a Cuban citizen, for the past twelve years has been traveling to the United States in the capacity of student, and is desirous of returning in the same capacity on or about September 7th. I do not hold the United States Bureau of Immigration permit to re-enter the states, for reason which I now wish to explain. Sometime before I planned to leave Ithaca, N.Y., I forwarded my application to re-enter the states, to the Department of Labor, accompanying the stipulated fee of $3.00, and hold receipt from this Dept. for my application. Sickness in my family made it necessary for me to leave for Cuba earlier than I had expected, consequently did not have sufficient time to terminate negotiations for obtaining necessary re-entry permit.[59]

Molinet specified in the letter that he possessed a communications from the Commissioner General of Immigration requesting certain information, which was forwarded from his address in Ithaca, N.Y. He further requested from the Consul what steps he should follow to return to the United States on or about September 7th without the permit.[60] It appears from this exchange of information, although not verified by any other documentation between the Frankford Athletic Association and the U.S. Consul that Ignacio S. Molinet was successful in securing the necessary paperwork to return to the United States.

Once the immigration and travel issues were resolved, Ignacio reported to training camp where he earned a backup fullback position as the season began. Interestingly, the Frankford Yellow Jackets played a pre-season baseball game in Atlantic City against an American Legion Post 211 baseball club, in which, Ignacio is listed as the left field fielder. The game was organized and played to celebrate the Legion's 3rd Annual Pageant.[61] *The Philadelphia Record* reports how and where the game took place:

> The baseball game formally opened the year 1927 for the Yellow Jackets, who play their first football game in Atlantic City today, an exhibition tussle with the Atlantic City Roses, and open their home stand next Saturday, with their first league grid tussle....[62]

Throughout the 1927 season, Ignacio saw action in nine games and garnered a total of 125 yards in total offense including a rushing touchdown against the Buffalo Bisons on October 16, 1927. The Frankford Yellow Jackets defeated Buffalo 23–0. Charley Rogers, halfback for the Yellow Jackets wrote in an article titled, "Jackets Again Buffalo the Bisons in Sunday Tilt—23–0," He describes Molinet's scoring play:

> Molinet crashed through the Buffalo line for the only other score of the game after Frankford opened up with a successful aerial attack which carried the leather down to the one-yard line. At the close of the game the Buffalo eleven crumbled. Had the contest lasted a few minutes longer no doubt the score would have been almost doubled.[63]

In another game played on October 1, 1927, Frankford defeated the New Britain Englanders 21–0. The entire Yellow Jackets team played in the game, as the coach substituted many players to keep a fresh team on the field at all times. According to the newspaper account, Ignacio Molinet substituted for Charlie Rogers at left halfback as the game concluded favorably for the Yellow Jackets.[64]

For the rest of the season, Ignacio carried the ball 17 times, caught two passes, and completed three passes to help the Yellow Jackets to a seventh-place finish in league standings. It was a great adventure for the Cubano athlete to be the NFL's first Latino player and he loved the competition. However, the experience was sadly interrupted by the death of his parents in Cuba that same year. Disheartened by the loss, Ignacio did not return to Cuba after his parents' passing, and upon conclusion of his single season in the NFL, he left pro football to establish his residency in the United States, became a U.S. citizen, married, raised a family and enjoyed a successful career in engineering.

A generation or so later, it is his grand-daughter Heidi Caldwell who contacted Jason Aiken at the Pro Football Hall of Fame in Canton, Ohio, to inquire about the process to donate her grandfather's original pro football contract. In the ensuing process it becomes evident to Ms. Caldwell that her grandfather was a pioneer in the history of professional football. More importantly for Heidi Caldwell, it also rekindled beloved memories and a renewed pride in her grandfather, while the rest of us celebrate the important discovery of a 1927 Frankford Yellow Jacket fullback, who pioneered the Latino experience in the NFL.

Jesse Rodriguez

The first Latino brothers in professional football were Jesse and Kelly Rodriguez who immigrated to the United States from Spain in 1912. Similar to Ignacio S. Molinet's immigration to the United States to receive an education and start a new life, it appears the entire Rodriguez family, parents and 10 children, came to the United States for similar reasons. They settled in

Clarksburg, West Virginia, to raise a family and begin a new life in their new country. In a 1982 letter to Mario Longoria, Jesse provided a brief personal description of his family and where they settled in the United States:

> I was born in Aviles, Asturias, Spain on August 7, 1901. My father owned a factory that manufactured lime and bricks. My parents had 10 children—5 boys and 5 girls. We lived in Aviles until I was 11 years old when our family came to the United States in 1912. We settled in the Clarksburg, West Virginia area. I went to Victory High School where I was the first student from that school chosen to the West Virginia High School All-State Football Team.[65]

Also noted was a mention that his wife Helen had written the letter for him due to health issues. Recently, Rodriguez had suffered a stroke which left him with various physical ailments, among which were a constant shaking of his hands. He also said he would like very much to talk but that his hearing was almost gone.[66] Therefore, we exchanged letters until 1983. Contained therein was invaluable information about Rodriguez's collegiate career, as well as recollections of the Buffalo Bison ball club and professional football in 1929.

This trailblazer's football story begins at Victory High School in Clarksburg, West Virginia, where he learned this new American game and became the first alumni of the high school selected to the West Virginia All-State Football Team. As a result of his skills and achievements on the gridiron, he was recruited by several West Virginia colleges and universities. His football success and assistance from family friend Senator Jennings Randolph actually made is possible for him to leave high school after his junior year and complete his secondary education at an academy affiliated with Salem College. He entered Salem College in the fall of 1925 to continue his education and begin his collegiate football career.

Early in his first season on campus, Rodriguez replaced the starting fullback and also played linebacker. Later, he became the team's regular kicker. The first two seasons at Salem were developmental years for Jesse, given how little time he had played the sport. In 1925, the Tigers were successful,

Jesse Rodriguez, 1929 (courtesy Salem University Athletics).

posting a record of five wins, two losses, and two ties. In the 1926 campaign, Rodriguez's skills improved and he began to impact the team's success. This trend was noted and recognized by the *Clarksburg Telegram* newspaper:

> October 9, 1926 ... Salem 20 ... Shephard 0 ... Jess Rodriguez, fullback, consistent player. October 23, 1926 ... Rodriguez displays best form and Bethany gets way back when he prepares to punt.... Salem upsets Bethany ... October 30, 1926, in Davis-Elkins game against Salem.... Rodriguez did well.[67]

One of Rodriguez's teammates, Art Goldchien, recalls that "Jesse was considered one of the finest football players in the state, both at Victory High School in Clarksburg and later at Salem College, where I came to know him when we played on that team. He was one of the finest punters I have ever seen, including today's pros that specialized in punting."[68] In fact, Rodriguez's trademark was in his powerful leg which could kick a football for great distance. Jesse remembered one occasion when he booted a 95-yard punt and he described what happened: "I was seven yards deep in the end zone ... in the game when Salem College was playing Marietta College of Ohio." Rodriguez took his usual three steps and booted the ball. It went to [the opponent's] 5-yard line. Salem won that particular contest, 12–0.[69] Sports reporter Bruce Harton attested to Rodriguez's punting ability in the local newspaper stating that, "When his educated toe sends the leather oval sailing into the air for a distance to his old, but praised record, he gives his head a determined shake and resolves to do better. A great change has come over this sterling athlete from Clarksburg."[70]

During the 1927 season, Rodriguez's playmaking and punting contributed greatly to the Tigers' success in West Virginia Intercollegiate Athletic Conference play. Against Broaddus College, Rodriguez helped his team win by scoring two touchdowns on remarkable runs. He towered above all other players as he knifed through the Broaddus line at will for large gains. Before the first quarter ended, Rodriguez dashed for 30 yards to place the ball in scoring territory and after two goal line plays, punched the leather over for the score. Against Wilmington College of Ohio, Rodriguez's placekick accounted for the difference as Salem scored a one-point victory, 7–6.

Rodriguez's most significant game of the 1927 season was against the rival West Virginia Wesleyan. The game featured both Jesse Rodriguez and his younger brother Kelly, who was a running back for the Bobcats. The newspaper headline read, "Here Today, Rodriguezes, Kelly and Jesse, Two Brothers Pitted One Against the Other, Score Both Touchdowns of Game."[71] The memorable game was played in Clarksburg. Wesleyan scored first, as Kelly Rodriguez scored the touchdown and Louis Kolopus kicked the extra point. Next, the Salem Tigers took possession and Jesse Rodriguez rushed for the touchdown after a series of running plays. Unfortunately, Jesse's extra point attempt was blocked and the play proved a turning point for the game. The remainder of the scrum generated a punting duel between the brothers. Late in the contest with the Bobcats controlling the football, Kelly crashed the Tigers defensive line and broke into the secondary. Jesse recalled that he was on the ground and saw his brother racing toward the goal line. Determined to make the play, he sped toward Kelly and caught him before he reached the goal line. The game ended with West Virginia Wesleyan on top, 7–6.[72]

In 1928, Jesse Rodriguez continued to be a dominant force for the Tigers. *The Clarksburg Exponent* described one particular game against Bethany College, "The toe of Jesse Rodriguez served the Salem team well. Time after time the Spanish youth got off kicks which caught the Bethany secondary defense napping and as a consequence the greater part of the game was played with Bethany up against the goal posts. He clearly out kicked Bethany's punter by 15 yards on every exchange."[73] Additionally, Rodriguez, who had been playing a great defense as linebacker scooped up a Bethany fumble and dashed 70 yards for a touchdown. He also kicked four of five extra points to seal the Salem victory, 34–0. In the Marietta College of Ohio game, Salem's first touchdown came as a result of brilliant passing quarterback Rodriguez as fired a 20-yard pass to teammate Batson, who side-stepped and dodged an additional 10 yards to score. In addition to being a fine carrier and passer, Rodriguez contributed considerably to the game with his splendid punting. His kicks invariably carried more distance than the Marietta defensive backs could cover. Final score: Salem 12 Marietta 0.

In the four years Rodriguez played with Salem College, the team posted a record of 20-9-2 in the West Virginia Intercollegiate Athletic Conference (WVIAC) play. Also in 1928, the WVIAC selected its first all-conference team; Rodriguez received Honorable Mention.[74] Shortly after graduation, Jim Durfee, a college referee who had worked Salem games, approached Rodriguez about playing professionally. Rodriguez responded affirmatively and received an invitation to play for the Buffalo (NY) Bison Football Club. Rodriguez wrote, "After I finished college, a referee by the name Durfee,[75] who worked many of our college games, came to me and asked if I would consider playing professional football. I told him I would. Later I received a letter from the Buffalo Bison office requesting me to come to Buffalo for an interview. I went and was hired. I was used as the regular fullback and kicker same as in college."[76] Rodriguez signed to play for the 1929 season.

That year the Buffalo roster consisted exclusively of first-year and inexperienced players. To attract more spectators, prior to the start of each home game, ownership asked Rodriguez to give exhibitions on barefoot kicking. Jesse recalled that Coach Al Jolley asked him to perform this task and he replied, "At first I refused, but, after being pressured by the other players, I finally agreed and continued to give an exhibition before each game as long as I remained with the team."⁷⁷ A 1929 *Buffalo Courier Express* article tells the story of Rodriguez's exploits in the Bisons' first game of the season against the Chicago Cardinals, "Jesse Rodriguez, halfback of the Buffalo team will give an exhibition of barefoot kicking, a department in which he excels. Fans in attendance will be really surprised by the distance that Rodriguez can send the pigskin."⁷⁸ Another newspaper article, this one from Rodriguez's hometown of Clarksburg recounts that, "a curious grin spread across Rodriguez's face when he reminisced about the time he used to give football kicking exhibitions with the Buffalo team, billed as the 'barefooted wonder' from West Virginia."⁷⁹ Because he took off his shoes and kicked the ball, "They thought nobody in West Virginia wore shoes. You get a better spiral. Your shoe does not interfere. With a shoe on, sometimes your toe sticks up too high to punt well, you have to touch the ball at impact just right."⁸⁰

That first campaign the Bisons posted a mark of 1–7–1. In the season opener Rodriguez stifled the Cardinals attack with his punts throughout the game. In one instance, Chicago pinned Buffalo on their own two-yard line. With their backs against their own goal, the Bisons sent Rodriguez in to punt them out of danger. In the third quarter, the Bisons again were backed up and Rodriguez booted a long spiral to Cardinals' Chief Elkins, who fumbled the ball when tackled by Walter "Tillie" Voss. The Bisons recovered the ball on the Cardinals' 23-yard line and settled for a field goal. Buffalo lost the game 9–3.⁸¹

In games against the Frankford Yellow Jackets, Rodriguez started at halfback, but once again it was his punting that most helped his squad. *The Buffalo Courier Express* attested that "Rodriguez punting and dogged resistance shown by the Bison battered line when backed up against their goalpost were the redeeming features from a local standpoint. With the Yellow Jackets threatening the local goal … the Bison forward wall stiffened and finally took the ball on downs. Rodriguez immediately punted them out of danger. Early in the second period, Chuck Weimer made one of the prettiest plays of the game when he sped down the field under a Rodriguez punt, smashed his way through two blockers, tackled the ball carrier and flopped him to the turf with a thickening thud."⁸²

Against the Chicago Bears, Rodriguez played tackle, substituting for player-coach Al Jolley. *Buffalo Courier* sportswriter Jack Laing wrote, "The Chicago Bears with Red Grange, Paddy Driscoll, and Joey Sternaman, made their first appearance at Bison Stadium. Bill Senn scored both Chicago touchdowns while Grange; 'The Galloping Ghost' played an important part in the scoring. The Bison with a bolstered and revamped backfield showed a better offensive punch but their fumbling ruined their chances to score."⁸³ They fumbled twice near the Chicago goal line and lost the game 16–0. In the next game that season the Bisons showed improvement and played the Providence Steamrollers to a tie. Rodriguez's returns to the fullback position as Buffalo came from behind to knot the score at 7–7.[84] The Bisons had indeed improved, tying the 1928 defending NFL Champions. On November 24, 1929, the last game of the season Buffalo defeated the Chicago Bears 19–7 at Wrigley Field in Chicago to post their only victory.[85]

Jesse Rodriguez finished 1929 with what he estimated to be an unheard-of average of 72-yards per punt. Unfortunately, the league did not keep such statistics at this time and newspaper accounts did not list punting yardage in their box scores. Therefore it was difficult to verify an accurate figure. However, disappointed with the Buffalo team, Rodriguez packed his bags and returned to West Virginia. He talked about his disappointment as a team member in a letter to this author, stating "That year, in my opinion, was a total disaster. There was another fullback on the team from Wisconsin, who sat on the bench and never played one minute of football.... He didn't pass up an opportunity to let me know he was being paid more than I was and I was doing all the work. The coach and players all gambled and somehow the coach managed to take the entire player's money. They would come to me to borrow money because I wouldn't gamble. The coach wasn't happy because I did not give him a chance to take my money too. I decided if I continued to lend them my money the day would surely come when I wouldn't be repaid. I didn't like the odds. I didn't like the whole set-up and left."[86] Thus Jesse concluded his single year in the NFL. Rodriguez died on October 12, 1983, in Clarksburg, West Virginia. A close friend and collegiate teammate Art Goldchien summed up what many people felt about Jesse Rodriguez, "Jesse passed away leaving a void, but one must remember there are those who gained from being associated with him, young and old."[87]

Kelly Rodriguez

The other half of the Rodriguez professional football duo was Jesse's younger brother Kelly. The two were outstanding football players who greatly respected and complimented each other over the years. Kelly's story begins with quotes from his letters providing insights into his era and the game both he and his brother played so well. "My brother Jess and I started out playing soccer football which helped our kicking game later. In my opinion Jess was the greatest punter in football. I saw him kick 85 yards in the air in a college game against Marietta College of Ohio. Jess played pro ball with the Buffalo Bison."[88] Kelly was several years younger but only one year behind Jesse academically.[89]

In another letter, Kelly expressed gratitude about his football career and reminisced about his playing days, though certainly not all was wonderful for him at West Virginia Wesleyan College. "As I recall I made Intercollegiate Conference First Team three years straight. We did not have Intercollegiate Conference my first year at Wesleyan. I was Honorable Mention on the All-Eastern Team that year, which was better. While playing for the Frankford Yellow Jackets, we purchased the Minneapolis Red Jackets at mid-season and finished their remaining schedule of games, plus our own. As I recall, Cliff Battles (who played with Kelly at Wesleyan), the Hall of Famer made second team Intercollegiate Conference. I do not understand how he made the Hall of Fame and I did not because I was a better football player than he was. If only my name had been Jones or Smith instead of Rodriguez, I'm sure I would have made it [to Canton]. There was great prejudice against Hispanics and we were treated like so much trash. Thank God that has changed now." No doubt Kelly Rodriguez and Cliff Battles were friends for many years but his commentary on prejudice is significant, and more a statement about the times they lived in and the treatment of Spanish-surnamed persons he experienced.[90]

The most well documented aspect of Kelly Rodriguez's life in the United States and football career comes from the *1935 Boston Redskins Press Guide*.

Kelly Rodriguez, 1930 (courtesy of the West Virginia Wesleyan College Archives).

From way over yonder in Aviles, Spain, came the infant Kelly Rodriguez, who bloomed into manhood in West Virginia and subsequently carved his niche in football's hall of fame. This fiery fellow, born August 9, 1907, is 5'10" tall, weighs 185 pounds and has black hair and brown eyes. Ever since he tackled the gridiron sport as a prep athlete, he has been listed as a halfback or fullback. Rodriguez graduated from West Virginia Wesleyan in 1930 and belongs to the Kappa Alpha Fraternity. His brother Jesse played professionally with the Buffalo Bison in 1929 and that season Kelly was earning honors galore as the most valuable performer on the Wesleyan team.[91]

Professionally, Kelly played with the Frankford Yellow Jackets and Minneapolis in 1930, and briefly in 1935 with the Boston Redskins.

From the very beginning of his athletic endeavors, Rodriguez reached for excellence and became an All-State selection at Victory High School. With his illustrious prep football career concluded, Rodriguez attended West Virginia Wesleyan College from 1926 to 1930. He became an immediate success, with overpowering talent that earned him the moniker the "Spanish Armada." An all-around player, Rodriguez played offense, defense, and did all the punting for the Bobcats. His fierce competitiveness became a trademark, and his gridiron exploits became legendary in the history of West Virginia collegiate football.[92] In 1926, Rodriguez's freshman season, the Bobcats won four and lost six in a very tough schedule. The victories came over Salem College 15–0; Bethany 19–7; Broaddus 13–0; and Davis & Elkins 9–7. In the 1927 season Wesleyan lost to West Virginia University 27–7, and except for the passing of Mickey McClung and the running of Forest Bachtel and Kelly Rodriguez, Wesleyan did not show much power.

Within a short period of time, Rodriguez took over the team's leadership and the signal calling on both offense and defense. The season's highlight of 1927 occurred on October 27 when the Wesleyan Bobcats played Salem College. The highly publicized game featured both Kelly and his brother Jesse. Kelly scored the initial touchdown on a pass interception and converted the extra point while Jesse rushed for Salem's touchdown. The difference in the game was Salem's failed extra point conversion that enabled Wesleyan to triumph 7–6.[93]

During the 1928 season, Rodriguez scored ten touchdowns to lead the team offensively. He began his great year against Xavier College of Cincinnati, Ohio. Author Kent Kessler wrote in his book about Rodriguez's exploits. "Xavier had lost only one game and expected to beat Wesleyan with ease; however, Rodriguez showed Cincinnati the best football player it saw all season. Rodriguez, a triple-threat man and almost spectacularly invincible on defense and offense ... shone like a star as he scored one touchdown and converted the point after, Wesleyan 19 Xavier 7."[94]

In another commentary, John J. Carroll, a friend of Rodriguez, wrote to him about the game, "your play in 1928 was the greatest he had ever witnessed ... if you were with Ohio State or other big school you would have been an All-American."[95] In the rest of the season, Wesleyan steamrolled their way to victory over Fairmont College, 43–0. In this contest, Rodriguez intercepted a pass and returned it 44 yards for a touchdown. Against New York University (NYU), Rodriguez scored Wesleyan's only touchdown in a game they lost, 26–7. At Concord State College, Wesleyan played well as Rodriguez scored two touchdowns in the first quarter to earn an 18–0 triumph. Against Georgetown, Wesleyan struggled against a productive passing game and lost, 34–7. In this game, Rodriguez returned a fumble for a score and added the extra point. The Waynesburg College Yellow Jackets came next and posed no threat to Wesleyan. The Bobcats trounced them 34–0. In the game, a beautifully executed lateral pass from Batchel to Paul Watson to Rodriguez was good for 70 yards and a touchdown. Rodriguez scored again in the third play of the second quarter to dominate the scoring. Against Navy, the *Clarksburg Telegram* reports, "A rampant Navy team ripped their way through Wesleyan for a 37–0 victory leaving the Wesleyan team dumbfounded and Rodriguez restricted solely to his kicking game for more yards than their rushing."[96]

Next on the schedule was Salem College. This game, like in the previous season, pitted Rodriguez against Rodriguez. However, this time around the game became a punting duel between the brothers, with Kelly's boots carrying a little further than his brother Jesse. Wesleyan got the better of the fight on a mud-soaked gridiron and triumphed, 12–0. In the game Kelly intercepted a pass and raced 40 yards on a broken field run for one of the two Wesleyan touchdowns.[97] In the season finale, Wesleyan took on the "Thundering Herd" from Marshall College. Kelly scored in the first quarter on a 26-yard touchdown and kicked the extra point successfully to led Marshall 7–0. However, momentum switched over to Marshall in the second half, and they went on to win, 13–7. It was nonetheless a great season for Kelly Rodriguez, who was selected to the All-West Virginia Intercollegiate Athletic Conference (WVIAC) First Team.

In his final collegiate season, Rodriguez and the 1929 Wesleyan Bobcats opened their schedule with a victory over Concord College. He picked up where he left off the previous year by scoring the first touchdown en route to a 39–0 shutout of the Mountain Lions. Throughout the season, Rodriguez and Cliff Battles led the Wesleyan offense. The 1929 squad experienced a losing season, finishing with four victories and five defeats. All of their triumphs, however, were shutouts. In addition to beating Concord, the Bobcats also beat Salem College 47–0, Bethany 32–0, and Marshall 28–0. Rodriguez tallied four touchdowns and three extra points.[98]

With his collegiate career concluded, Rodriguez did not have to wait long for a professional football offer. The Frankford Athletic Association of Philadelphia was interested in his skills and proposed an offer. On April 26, 1930, Rodriguez received a letter from Frankford Yellow Jackets' Manager Robert B. Haines to advise him they had received his signed contract. The correspondence stated:

> I was certainly glad to have your signed contract and feel sure that you have made no mistake in joining our club. The schedule meeting of the National Football League will be held sometime in July, after which time I shall notify you of the date to report for training. I would appreciate your advising me your summer address where I may reach you after you leave school.
> We intend to make an official announcement of the new members of our club after

the college season is over, and I would appreciate if you would send me a good picture of yourself as soon as possible. An action picture would be preferred. It is quite possible that if you do not have a photo you could secure one from a local newspaper. I am trusting you have an enjoyable summer, and that you will be graduated with honors.[99]

The agreement Kelly Rodriguez signed was the standard NFL Uniform Player's Contract. He received $75.00 for each regularly schedule game and an additional $50.00 for each Sunday game played away from home.

Rodriguez's initial year in pro football with the Frankford Yellow Jackets was frustrating and disappointing. Frankford went 4–13–1 and Rodriguez played a utility role in the Yellow Jackets backfield. In the first exhibition game against Clifton Heights, Rodriguez played quarterback and threw a touchdown pass to teammate Royce Goodbread for the third score of the game. Frankford won, 13–6, but the game performance was not a glimpse of the rest of the season. In their opener versus the Staten Island Stapletons, Rodriguez tossed a 19-yard touchdown pass to Cookie Tackwell for the only touchdown of the contest as the Yellow Jackets squeeze a 7–3 victory. The next ten consecutive games were losses, though Rodriguez's highlights for the season included a 50-yard kick-off return versus Staten Island, a 45-yard punt against the Chicago Bears, 62 yards rushing and a 56-yard punt in the Portsmouth game, and a 3-yard touchdown catch and 73-yard punt against the Green Bay Packers.[100] Overall, Rodriguez's 1930 season statistics included 30 rushing attempts for 87 yards, 12 passing attempts for 41 yards and 1 touchdown, 6 pass receptions for 115 yards and 1 touchdown, 1 kick-off return for 50 yards, 2 punt returns for 41 yards, and 14 punts for 576 yards, averaging 41.1 yards per punt.

Part of what marred Rodriguez's rookie NFL year was that the league continued to undergo severe growing pains. In addition to Rodriguez's participation and contribution to the 1930 Frankford Yellow Jackets' team, he recalled the situation with the Minneapolis franchise. "We (meaning Frankford) purchased the Minneapolis Red Jackets at mid-season and we finished their remaining games in addition to ours."[101] Although this arrangement was contrary to NFL rules, they were permitted to assist the Minneapolis team in hopes of improving league competition.[102] Rodriguez remained with the Yellow Jackets through 1931. That year Frankford played only eight games and did not finish the season.

Shortly thereafter, he retired from professional football and returned to West Virginia to plan his future. He wrote about his plans after football, "While playing pro football I was under great pressure from my father-in-law to quit and go into the family business with him. He owned the greatest fleet of trucks in West Virginia and was a contact hauler for the A& P Tea Company. They served 144 stores in West Virginia, Pennsylvania, and Maryland.

But I stayed with the Yellow Jackets until they dissolved their franchise before I retired."[103] In 1935, however, at the request of former collegiate teammate Cliff Battles, Rodriguez came out of retirement and signed to play for the Boston Redskins. That year, Rodriguez played sparingly and left the Redskins early in the season. He did not specify any particular reason(s) for leaving the Redskins. A year later (1936), he received another offer to play professional football, this time in the California Professional Football League on the West Coast. The letter read:

> We wish to take this opportunity to inform you that a corporation for a Professional Football League has been formed on the Pacific Coast.
> The League will be composed of six teams. You have been recommended to us for your ability to play high class football out here on the coast. We have a very fine proposition to make to you if you are at all interested in playing out here on the coast this fall. Besides a very fine salary for your services as a football player, we have a limited number of jobs for those who wish to make this their permanent home. If you are at all interested, we will be glad to hear from you immediately, Yours truly, L.F. Mansean, President.[104]

Although it appeared Rodriguez was impressed with the offer, he declined to play in California and resumed his work with the family business.

In 1974, both Kelly and his brother Jesse Rodriguez were honored and enshrined on the All-Time West Virginia Intercollegiate Athletic Conference Team for the years 1925–1965.[105] The Rodriguez brothers were greatly respected and admired for their excellence not only in the sport of football but in the game of life as well. They were indeed extraordinary people, who like Ignacio S. Molinet a couple years earlier, pioneered the Latino presence in professional football.

Waldo Don Carlos—The Champion

Waldo Emerson Don Carlos, a descendant of Spanish conquistadores, became a skillful football player and fierce gridiron competitor for the Drake University Bulldogs of the Missouri Valley Collegiate Conference, and he played professionally for Green Bay. Don Carlos played during the "Iron Man" era in the NFL and earned the distinction of being the first Latino athlete on a championship team—the 1931 Packers.

When the authors began research on Don Carlos, the belief was he was of Spanish origin. His last name "Don Carlos" implied a Spanish title or a first name, but the author was uncertain it was a last name. Research eventually confirmed this athlete's Spanish ancestry, as Don Carlos graciously responded to a series of questions pertaining to his background, his football career, and life after football. He wrote:

Our family came to this country about 1750, landing on the Carolina coast and over the years working our way to Greenfield, Iowa about 1878.... I am in the seventh generation of our family in the United States and probably have very little of the original Don Carlos blood. We understand that our Spanish ancestor was a son of Don Carlos who claimed the Spanish throne in the early 1700's, but whether or not that is true we don't know for sure. I was born in Greenfield, Iowa on October 16, 1909. We moved to Des Moines, Iowa about 1917. I graduated from Theodore Roosevelt High School in January 1927 and attended Drake University for the next six years, graduating from Law School in June 1933.

In 1926, I played center on the football team of our high school. We won the city championship and claimed the state title. I was All-City center and perhaps All-State, but I do not remember. At Drake ... freshmen did not play varsity ball at the time. I played center on the team during 1928, 1929, and 1930. As I recall it we won the Missouri Valley Championship each of those years.... In 1931, I played on the Green Bay Packers' Team and we won the National Football League (NFL) championship. I went back to law school at Drake University, attended summer school in 1932 and graduated with my class in 1933.[106]

Waldo Don Carlos, 1931 (courtesy Drake University Athletics).

The years that Don Carlos played for the Bulldogs were among the greatest in the history of Drake University football.[107]

After sitting out 1927, Don Carlos took the field with the varsity as Drake opened the 1928 season against Simpson College. The game was historic because it was the first night game played west of the Mississippi River. Huge floodlights illuminated the action as Drake defeated Simpson 40–6. Don Carlos played center on offense and backed up the line on defense, as well as disrupting Simpson's passing attack. Drake then beat Marquette and Grinnell before facing Notre Dame in South Bend. The Irish played splendidly and handed the Bulldogs their only loss of the season, by a score of 32–6. While outplayed, Drake was not outfought and Don Carlos stood out in general line play. For the next two seasons in which Drake played Notre Dame, Don Carlos turned in stellar performances against the Fighting Irish.

The 1929 campaign began with victories over Simpson College, Oklahoma A & M and Washington. Drake then tied Grinnell, and lost to Missouri,

Temple, and Notre Dame for a season record of 5-3-1. In their annual Notre Dame clash, the Bulldogs led 7-6 for the first three quarters. But in the fourth, the Irish scored two touchdowns to eliminate Drake's hopes for an upset. Don Carlos recalls the aspirations of the game. "The game was played at Soldier's Field in Chicago, Illinois. We led Notre Dame the first three quarters.... Finally, Notre Dame won by the score of 19-7. Our total squad consisted of 28 men and Notre Dame had a hundred or so dressed for the game."[108]

In his senior year of 1930, Drake continued to dominate the Missouri Valley Conference, winning the league title for the third consecutive year. In the school's publications, Don Carlos is remembered as having played superbly against the University of Oregon in a losing effort and solidly in the school's victory over Iowa State.[109] As in previous games against Notre Dame, Don Carlos left an impression due to his aggressive play versus the Irish. Drake's 1931 university yearbook, *The QUAX*, documented his performance by stating that "Don Carlos has been styled by the Notre Dame Football Review as the sparkplug of a fighting Drake line that held Notre Dame at bay. Tim Moynihan, Notre Dame's center who has met some of the best pivot men in the country says Don Carlos is the best center he played against all year."[110]

At season's end, Don Carlos was chosen to Knute Rockne's All Western Team and for the second consecutive year (1929-1930) was All Missouri Valley Conference selection.[111] His success at the Des Moines institution helped catapult Don Carlos into professional football. Since the NFL did not have collegiate draft until 1936, coaches or team representatives contacted individual players and enticed them to play professionally. Don Carlos received contract offers from both the Green Bay Packers and the Portsmouth Spartans. The Spartans later moved to Detroit, Michigan, where they became the Lions. Waldo chose Green Bay partly because of his having played against Notre Dame and Earl "Curly" Lambeau, the Packers' coach. Don Carlos recounted his early pro football experiences by stating that: "We started practice early in August. We didn't have a regular stadium to play or practice at the time. There was only one coach and we practiced only running plays. In our only scrimmage before our first game, over 3000 people came out to watch us play. The state of Wisconsin really supported the team."[112]

Don Carlos recalled that there were several notable players on the team, such as Cal Hubbard who played tackle and was the biggest man at 265 pounds. Bo Molenda of Michigan was the fullback. Vern Lewellen of Nebraska was a halfback and could punt a ball 70 yards. Mike Michalske of Penn State played left guard. Johnny "Blood" McNally was a great left end and Tom Nash of Georgia was the right end. "Our old center weighed 250 pounds with whom I alternated was Jug Earp. Red Dunn of Marquette was our quarterback and Roger Grove of Michigan was my roommate. We also had a halfback by the name Arnie Herber who could throw a pass seventy yards."[113] These vivid recollections of his teammates by Don Carlos are significant because several are now members of the Pro Football Hall of Fame in Canton. No doubt Don Carlos held his own among some of the best players in the history of the NFL.

Pro football provided a rewarding experience for Waldo E. Don Carlos. At first, he received two offers to play in the NFL and, interestingly, the two teams finished one and two in league standings in 1931. The Packers were the defending NFL Champions and began their 1931 season with a 26–0 victory over the Cleveland Indians. For the next eight games the Packers were invincible and raced from one victory to another. The Packers' closest challengers were the Spartans but through a scheduling quirk, the teams did not play that season.[114] The Green Bay winning streak ended as Ernie Nevers led the Chicago Cardinals to an upset victory, 23–13. Nevers threw two touchdown passes and kicked two extra points to hand the Packers their first defeat of the season. The following game, the Packers regained their momentum, beating New York 14–10.

Elsewhere, Ernie Nevers helped the Packers' cause by leading the Cardinals in a second consecutive upset, a 20–19 triumph over Portsmouth. This placed the Packers ahead of the Spartans in the win-loss record. Green Bay won their next two games but lost the season finale to the Chicago Bears 7–6. This gave them a 12–2 season record compared with Portsmouth's 11–3 mark. The 1931 campaign thus concluded with a schedule dispute. In *The Football Encyclopedia: The Complete Year-By-Year History of Professional Football from 1892 to the Present*, editor David Neft documents what happened at the end of the season.

> Portsmouth could tie for the title with a victory over the Packers in a game they said had been scheduled for December 13th at Portsmouth. To their surprise, Green Bay refused to play. The game they explained, was not on the official league schedule but had been only tentatively scheduled after the official schedule had been drawn. As such, either party had a right to cancel it. NFL President Joe Carr agreed with the Packers, giving Green Bay its third straight championship."[115]

Throughout the season, Don Carlos had alternated with Earp at the center position and was an important cog for this championship squad. The 1931 season was the only campaign for Don Carlos, however, as other opportunities beckoned. Throughout his football career he had not experienced a losing season, and even though Green Bay continued their winning tradition, the talented Don Carlos determined that it was better to study law at his undergraduate alma mater. Anxious to get started, he attended summer school in 1932 and graduated with a law degree in 1933.

Don Carlos went on to practice law in Greenfield, Iowa, for the next 50 years, interrupted only by World War II, when he served as a lieutenant in the U.S. Navy and was a communications officer aboard the battleship USS *Pennsylvania*. Recalling his tour of duty, he describes, "The Pennsylvania was to be the flagship for the planned invasion of Japan. However, while in Buckner Bay, Okinawa, the ship was hit by an aerial bomb that blew a hole in the hull about 60 feet by 40 feet, and our quarterdeck was flushed with water in about 30 minutes. There were about 1200 ships in the bay at the time and the repair ships were alongside very quickly and kept us afloat. I believe this was on August 9, 1945, and the war ended on August 12, 1945."[116]

With the war over and victory achieved, Don Carlos returned to family and friends in Iowa and continued his law career. He eventually served on the Board of Governors of the Iowa State Bar Association and as Adair County District Attorney. He was a member of the Iowa Trial Lawyers Association and Fellow of the Probate Organization for the United States. He retired from his practice on July 1, 1984.[117] His retirement was a welcome change as the Don Carlos family resided in the community of Sun City West, Arizona, where he passed on June 18, 1997, less than one year after he responded to this author's letter about his football career.

Non–U.S. Born Latinos

The early Latino athletes were a diverse group; all born in Latin American countries and immigrants who sought refuge and a new home in the United States. Their birthright for all intents and purposes defines their "Latino" designation, but it is the life they made in the U.S. that is important and meaningful. Initially we have examined the "accepted meaning" of the term because it is often misunderstood or misapplied. For example, the accepted dictionary definitions of "Latino" over the years are not the best resource to help clarify the complete significance. One reference states that this group includes all people who speak any one of the following Romance languages such as Latin, Spanish, Portuguese, French, Italian or Romanian; while another specifies "Latinos" as those who hail from any of the 20 independent Latin American countries. Although this information is the accepted norm of the definition, dictionary definitions do not consider or include items such as customs, linguistic competence, folklore, and traditions that predominate each of the respective cultures. This is important because they differ from one another in many identifiable ways. For example, James B. Schuber was born in Panama; therefore, his nationality is Panamanian. However, in appearance, language and as a cultural practitioner, he is different from the native Panamanians; but this does not change the fact he is "Latino" by definition. The same can also be said about Aldo Richins and many other Latinos who will appear throughout the remainder of this work. Therefore within the cultural paradigm we briefly note the stories of four athletes from Panama and Mexico, who through birthright, immigration, and citizenship came to the

United States to live and educate themselves. In the process they prospered, and very importantly, were inspired to learn the sport of American football which eventually led them to the professional ranks.

James Buchanan Schuber

James Schuber was born on June 23, 1904, in Ancon, Panama, Canal Zone. His early life and circumstances in Panama is relatively unknown but resulted in the immigration to the United States. What is known of Schuber is that he attended the United States Naval Academy starting in 1924, graduating in 1928. This is where his story begins. The 1928 Naval Academy annual entitled *The Lucky Bag* provides a profile of the Latino Naval Midshipman:

> Jim Schuber—a man of many fascinations whose sheer versatility of character remains unparalleled. His mind is a flash of intelligence, his body a dash of recklessness. Born in Panama and cradled in the exhilarants of every clime, he came to the Naval Academy with the nonchalant stride of an adventurer whose steel blue eyes snapped with the precision that was only equaled by muscles destined to figure in many a Navy victory.... This Spanish Don, like the owl, slept by day and roamed by night. His varied and mysterious nocturnal adventures, unwritten and unpublished, were wont to leave but a single trace, an empty bed and an open window.... Whether the sport is an Army-Navy game, a gang fight in the dark, an Argentine tango, or an ordinary pair of dice, Jim Schuber is yet to meet his superior....[118]

The profile is both romantic and colorful in its treatment of his personal characteristics, and also reveals his athletic participation in other sports while at Annapolis. Schuber alternated at quarterback and played defense throughout his collegiate career. He initially played on the B-squad one season and moved on to varsity football his junior year 1926—the year Navy was co-national champion.[119] The midshipmen went unbeaten that season. The only blemish was a 21–21 tie with their hated rival, Army. The other unbeaten was Stanford University, who shared the title with the Midshipmen. This co-championship was an extraordinary matter that involved a split decision amongst the various national rating systems. For example, the "Boand Rating System,"[120] and the "Houlgate Rating System"[121] selected Navy, while Stanford was selected by the "Dickinson System,"[122] the Helms Athletic Foundation,[123] and the third survey operated by Mr. Jeff Sagarin,[124] who was a noted American Sports Statistician, all of whom sanctioned by the NCAA. Nonetheless, the Panamanian-born Jim Schuber contributed to the 1926 National Collegiate Football Championship experience.

In Schuber's final year at the Naval Academy, *The Lucky Bag* described the 1927 football team as optimistic and hopeful of repeating. The annual cited two factors from the 1926 team that appeared promising; one was the coaching staff remained intact from the championship season. Another was the number of returning players, including Schuber.[125] The season began with a 35–6 victory over Davis-Elkins followed by a win over Drake University 27–0. In the Drake game, Schuber scored his only touchdown of the season in the third quarter. Navy then proceeded to win another five games but lost to Notre Dame, Michigan, and Army to finish their season with a mark of six wins and three losses.

Upon graduation, Ensign Jim B. Schuber received orders for duty aboard the battleship USS *Colorado BB-45* ported at San Pedro, California. However, his tour of duty in the Navy was limited to less than two years. After a cruise to Hawaii and a series of sea trials and readiness exercises, it appears he expressed a renewed interest in football that eventually led him to the NFL, in particular the Brooklyn Dodgers. Unfortunately, there is no documentation of interest or recruitment from Schuber or the Dodgers to describe the processes that delivers him to the club. What is known about Schuber and the NFL comes from pro football references such as David Neft et al., *The Football Encyclopedia* (1994) and Beau Riffenburgh, *The Official NFL Encyclopedia* (1986), which lists him on the Brooklyn Dodgers' roster for 1930 along with height, weight, position, and college. Thus Jim Schuber's single season tenure in the NFL was a matter of change and another winning experience as the Dodgers posted seven victories, lose four, and tie one in league play. Unfortunately, there are no professional statistics listed for Schuber as a member of the Brooklyn Dodgers' team.

After his brief stint in pro football, Schuber's career returned to a lifetime of military service. According to his obituary,[126] he returned to Panama, where he became a Canal Zone employee. In later years, he returned to military service, this time in the Spanish Civil War of 1933 as a pilot. Later, he enlisted in the United States Army Air Corps in World War II where he was wounded in action against Germany and medically discharged. After World War II, he joined the Merchant Marine and served another 21 years until 1966, which also included duty in Vietnam. Jim Schuber died on May 27, 1982, in Naples, Florida[127] after an illustrious life of being a dedicated patriot, collegiate football champion, and professional football athlete, who unknowingly became an integral part of the Latino history in professional football.

Aldo Osborn Richins

The Aldo Richins football story is another "Latino by birthright" tale that has its beginnings in Colonia Diaz, Meoqui Municipality, Chihuahua, Mexico. The Richins were a Mormon missionary family from Utah, who along with numerous other co-religionists, immigrated south of the border in the late 1880s. The reason for immigration into Mexico was to negotiate the settlement of a permanent Mormon colony in Mexico to provide refuge for Mormon families being persecuted by the United States Government.[128] Although the initial circumstances for the settlement were problematic, the differences were resolved by the Mexican government and that caused the colony to be named in honor of Mexican President Porfirio Diaz—thus the name "Colonia Diaz." Unfortunately, the complete settlement of the Mormon colonies were interrupted by the start of the Mexican Revolution in 1911 and resulted in the eventual destruction of Colonia Diaz by federal troops causing the Mormon families to return to the United States.[129]

Within this series of tumultuous life events, Aldo Osborn Richins was born on November 2, 1910, in Colonia Diaz. The Richins family was in Mexico only a few years, while the young Aldo spent less than a year in Mexico before his family's return to Salt lake City, Utah. Back in the United States, the young Aldo Richins developed into a superb athlete who garnered various football awards. He attended West High School in the Utah capital and received "Athlete of the Year" honors in 1929, and later was inducted into the West High School Athletic Hall of Fame. He also played collegiate football at the University of Utah and was a star athlete on the Redskins' 1932 and 1933 Rocky Mountain Athletic Conference title teams.[130] An example of Richins' collegiate athleticism is documented by the *Utah Daily Chronicle* dated May 24, 1934. The report cites, "Aldo Richins, stellar football, basketball and track performer was today awarded the '1934 Ute Trophy,' given annually to the most outstanding athlete of the school by the *Utah Chronicle*. The trophy, a handsome 17 inch cup surrounded by a victory statue, is considered the highest award an athlete can achieve."[131] According to the rest of the newspaper article, he amassed more points than other competing athletes for the award. The newspaper also cites Richins being named third All-America Team.[132]

In 1935, Richins signed with the Detroit Lions. He was recruited to play wingback on a very talented Lions team that finished second in league play. According to his obituary, Aldo Richins was hopeful for the opportunity to play for Detroit. Unfortunately, he was released from the team only after two games into the season. The Lions were deep and apparently Richins did not figure in their season plans. His early departure was a disappointment that deprived him of the association to Detroit's 1935 NFL Championship. He returned home to Utah to family and friends where he entered into private business and a brief career in law enforcement.[133] However, professional football would once again call upon Richins to give it another try. In 1946, Salt Lake City, Utah, was presented the opportunity to venture into professional football that recruited a reluctant Aldo Richins to be a player/coach for the Salt Lake Seagulls of the Pacific Coast Football League.

Local writer Mel "Buck" Bashore noted that, "Salt Lake City officials paid $5,000 to the Pacific Coast League for the right to take over the defunct San Jose Mustang's franchise, to recruit players and coaches. The temporary head coach Fred Tedesco, who was also Richins' teammate at the University of Utah, sought players with NFL experience."[134] The article describes the recruitment efforts, training camp successes and disappointments that led to the start of the 1946 season. The Seagulls managed two victories and five defeats in 1946. In 1947, their second and final year in the Pacific Coast League, the Seagulls' won a single game to conclude their participation in professional football. Writer Buck Bashore summed up the Seagulls' two years in the league, "Although Utah's only pro football team ended on an acrimonious note ... four decades later the players recall those years with wistful fondness.... Utah's memories of the Seagulls has mostly faded. Nonetheless, the Seagulls deserve to be remembered as filling a unique niche in Utah's sports history."[135] Aldo Osborn Richins died on April 19, 1995, in Midvale and is remembered as a stellar competitor and the first ever Mexican born athlete to play in the National Football League.

Jose Martinez-Zorrilla—All American

The Jose Martinez-Zorrilla story is a brief and significant account of another football player from Mexico, whose accomplishments in the sport also impacted the early experiences of Dr. Jorge Prieto who cites him in his book *The Quarterback Who Almost Wasn't* as an inspiration and role model:

> My first high school championship game was played in an old and almost venerated soccer stadium, "El Parque Espana." During my years of convalescence, I had seen Jose Martinez-Zorrilla play there. As an end at Cornell University he had been the only Mexican to be selected AP First Team All American in the United States.[136]

Prieto further stated that he watched Jose with great envy and sadness during the time he believed he would never again play football. He further recalled, in the spring of 1939, that he was excited to run onto the grass of the same stadium where Marinez-Zorrilla had played.[137] Jose C. Martinez-Zorrilla was born in Mexico in 1912 to a prominent Mexican family who owned one of oldest haciendas in the country. The origins of the Martinez-Zorrilla hacienda date back to the time of the Spanish conquistadors in 1548.[138]

By comparison, Martinez-Zorrilla was very similar to his Cuban counterpart Ignacio Saturnino Molinet, as his family also sent him to the United States for a college education. Molinet prepared at the Peddie School of Highstown, New Jersey, while Martinez-Zorrilla prepared at Ithaca High School, Ithaca, New York. Both attended Cornell University and received engineering degrees, both also had brothers who attended and played sports at the same university; however, the football difference between the two is Molinet's single season in the NFL with the Frankford Yellow Jackets in 1927. Martinez-Zorrilla, on the other hand, did not play professional football but ended his collegiate career with the distinction of being a first team All-American (1932) and selected to play in the East-West game (1933).

The Cornell University Sports Publicity Office profile on Martinez-Zorrilla provides the following information:

> Jose C. Martinez-Zorrilla was born in Guadalajara, Jalisco, Mexico. Civil Engineer. Prepped at Ithaca High School, New York.... Freshmen Football 1, Varsity Football 2, 3, 4 ... Football Club.... All East Selection First Team '31,'32 at Tight End.... All-American '32, 1st Team Associated Press.... All-American honorable mention 1931 ... played in the '32 East-West Game....[139]

Martinez-Zorrilla also competed as a fencer in the saber and epee events and captained the team as a senior. He also lettered in lacrosse in 1932 and outside the university reached the semifinals of the 1936 Berlin Olympic Games for Mexico in fencing. In addition, he also played on the Mexican national polo team in international competition.[140]

Older brother Cristobal Martinez-Zorrilla, Cornell Class '31, also played football for the Big Red over the years of 1929–1931. As the team captain, he also earned Associated Press All-American honorable mention honors as a senior. Years later, both Martinez-Zorrilla brothers were inducted into the Cornell University Sports Hall of Fame (in 1981 and 1984 respectively). Ignacio S. Molinet's brothers Joaquin Molinet (class of '21) and Ernesto Molinet (class of '49) also received athletic recognition.

Jose Martinez-Zorrilla's life after football, fencing, and polo continued with successful ventures in commercial aviation, ranching, cattle, agriculture, and public relations. He was married to Asuncion Gangioti Fernandez del Valle from Spain. The union produced two sons, Jose Jr. and Gonzalo.[141] He passed away, based on available sources, sometime after 1995.[142] His

Jose Martinez-Zorrilla, 1932 (courtesy Cornell University Athletics).

American football legacy and athleticism is remarkable and historically significant. He came to the United States as a Mexican immigrant to get a formal education. In the process, he readily adapted and successfully met the educational standards of Cornell University that also led him to learn and master the sport of American Football to the level of All-American recognition, an accomplishment only the best in the history of collegiate football have achieved.

Jorge Prieto

The Jorge Prieto football story is a slight departure from those of his Latino counterparts Jim Schuber and Aldo Richins because his information is autobiographical as well as culturally diverse in its presentation of life in both Mexico and the United States. Thus, his football story is unique and influenced by many circumstances and events that begin with the exile of the Prieto family from Mexico into the United States. Within this paradigm of change and adaptation, Jorge Prieto narrates in his autobiography, *The Quarterback Who Almost Wasn't*, his views, remembrances, and adjustments he and his family made to gain acceptance in a new and different country, as well as their return to Mexico. But equally important for him was the discovery of the game of American football, which greatly influenced Prieto's life and led him to dedicate his energies to learn the history, philosophy, and skills to play the sport. But more importantly, Jorge took his acquired knowledge and skills back to Mexico to affect change, understanding, and greater acceptance of the gridiron.

Unlike many of the other Latino athletes documented here, Jorge Prieto did not play American football at the professional level,

Jorge Prieto, 1940 (courtesy the Jorge Prieto Family).

but his determination as an exile/immigrant in the United States to learn and play the game was truly remarkable and inspirational. His story serves as a template of survival and determination for many immigrant athletes entering this country who are confronted and deal with the issues of race, language, and discrimination.[143] His autobiographical information documents that the young Prieto seemed only temporarily distracted by obstacles as he pushed forward to learn the game and then to transplant the game to his native homeland. His personal ambitions in American football were to become a passing quarterback, to lead a team to a national collegiate championship, and, interestingly, to attend the University of Notre Dame. Although these were lofty goals for the young Prieto, he believed that such aspirations were achievable.[144]

His football story begins in the Los Angeles neighborhood where his family moved into and settled. The process of getting acquainted quickly revealed differences and realizations. He writes in the autobiography about being different: "I knew my family was different because we were from Mexico and this was not our permanent home."[145] In this statement Prieto suggests they would eventually return to Mexico once the revolutionary violence subsided. Otherwise, for the time being, his interactions in the neighborhood included the acquaintance of many nationalities and ethnicities such as the Irish, German, Italian, French Canadian, Jewish families and a single African American family.[146] It was a diverse community but not without its prejudices that reflected early 1930s attitudes.

His interactions with neighborhood children began with an encounter that challenged Prieto's status and ethnicity. He was greeted with the following nativist commentary, "no greaser can come in here," meaning the alley he had to pass through leading to the football field was no place for Mexicans.[147] The two of the biggest and toughest boys in a neighborhood stood between him and the gridiron. According to Prieto, the initial confrontation yielded a fight and positive results but, "it took more than one fist fight to get on those teams."[148] Prieto did not back down and eventually gained admittance as his determination and talents ended the fights. But there were still a few other obstacles for him to endure. The next one was the local football coach who took an interest in Prieto's desire to play football but continued to racialize his status. He responded to a question about the possibility of him playing at USC, and was told that USC, UCLA, and Stanford did not accept Mexicans and Blacks into their schools and athletic programs, but added that the University of Notre Dame in South Bend did, because it was a Catholic university and would accept Mexicans because of their affiliation.[149] The response was discouraging but he was pleased to know that there was a university that would accept Mexicans. Also, during these years he was tagged with the nickname "Chili Beans."[150] This moniker came from the same coach who told him about USC, as he had difficulty in pronouncing "Jorge."[151]

Although these examples of racial bias were a part of Prieto's initial football learning experience, it did not deter him from pursuing his goals, instead prompting him to prove his courage as well as his ability to play.[152] During the years from 1929 to 1933, Prieto established himself in neighborhood football and learned as much as he could. But the time had arrived to start over again in his native country. Despite initial travel problems, he returned to Mexico armed with knowledge of the sport which he quickly shared with new school mates and coaches.

He recalled, "on that spring day of 1933, I was just fifteen years old and remember my parents and family viewed the return with some apprehension." Prieto described the family's uncertainty because "the return trip was a prolonged and frequently painful cultural shock."[153] He noted that they went from paved roads to dusty dirt roads and from joy to bewilderment. He also endured a bias against his linguistic abilities. Apparently, learning to speak and write English affected the Prietos' Spanish pronunciation, and that set them apart from others in their neighborhood. The realization resulted in a persistent and malicious ridicule that generated chastisement for having a "gringo accent." In the process, Prieto picked up a new nickname, "Pocho," which made the homecoming even less comfortable.[154] The football field, however, was a different matter. He recalled that in 1934 there were only a few high schools club and the National University with football teams in Mexico. The school he first attended only had soccer, but it was here that he began to promote and convince his classmates about American football and the courage required to tackle and block rather than simply to kick a round soccer ball.[155]

For the next two years, Prieto recruited and organized neighborhood football teams and helped to instruct officials. Then he was unexpectedly sidelined by rheumatic fever in 1935. However, during his illness and recuperation (which lasted until 1937), he zealously studied the intricacies of American football. "I read just about everything there was about the game.... This included the ... philosophy of Amos Alonzo Stagg, Knute Rockne, Frank Carideo, Coach Pop Warner of Stanford, and Fritz Crisler of Michigan."[156] Prieto also noticed the innovation of the lateral and the great passers of the game in the mid–1930s, including Sammy Baugh and Davey O'Brien of Texas, Sid Luckman of Columbia, and Frankie Albert of Stanford.[157] He also studied and thought about the passing game.[158]

After his recovery, he returned as a healthy young man to enroll in the Technological Institute, a large public junior high school in Mexico City which fielded American football teams.[159] He competed for the position of quarterback in 1938 and recalled that he could out-pass, out-kick, and out-run his competitors.[160] For the next five football seasons, Prieto played at three levels of football competition—junior high school, high school, and college. He attended the Instituto Technico (Technological Institute), Instituto Politecnico Nacional (National PolyTechnical Institute), and Universidad Politecnico (PolyTechnical University), and quarterbacked teams to city championships in 1938 and 1940. He was also a volunteer quarterback coach with the Universidad Politecnico in 1945, the team which won Mexico's national collegiate championship. In 1940, the Mexican press and football coaches named him the "All Mexico" Quarterback, an honor similar to the Heisman Trophy. That same year was also significant for the history of the game in Mexico because football was recognized as a sport by the government. The acknowledgment coincided with the conversion of two soccer stadiums to American football fields by adding goal posts and marking off the 100-yard gridiron.[161] All told, Jorge Prieto was a significant force in the development of American football in Mexico. He noted that:

> For me, two seasons of college ball satisfied all my dreams except that of leading a college team to a national championship. But the junior high school championship in 1938, the high school championship in 1940, and the great college victories in 1940 and 1941 had fulfilled my most important dreams of becoming a good quarterback.[162]

Notwithstanding, his goal of attending the University of Notre Dame was unexpectedly realized when he received a partial scholarship to the university's Medical School to help him complete his medical studies. Upon completing medical school, he returned to Mexico for his internship, married Luz Maria Davila, set about raising a family, and ultimately helped serve the health needs of immigrants and the poor. After a brief stay in Mexico, Dr. Prieto returned to the United States, where his medical career spanned from 1949 to 2001. He established health clinics in Chicago and Evanston, Illinois; co-founded the Illinois Migrant Council and the Evanston Latino Association; was the Director of Community Medicine at Cabrini Hospital; Chairman for family practice at Cook County Hospital; president of the Chicago Board of Health; and had a school named in his honor—the Dr. Jorge Prieto Math and Science Academy. He received four honorary degrees; particularly of note was one from the University of Notre Dame.[163] *Evanston RoundTable* reporter Janet G. Messenger graciously sums up the significance of his life: "Numerous honors came his way but, at heart, his family says, he was still an unpretentious man, a family, a doctor who believed in family medicine and a former athlete who loved his football."[164]

Dr. Jorge Prieto passed away in 2001, leaving a sacred legacy of family medicine, of serving immigrants and impoverished communities, and significantly, helping to foster the early development of American football in Mexico.

2

Slowly Moving the Ball Down the Field
1941–1950

As noted in the previous chapter, there were a few Spanish-surnamed athletes who took to the gridirons of the United States during the 1920s and 1930s. It is undeniable, however, that there remained substantive social, economic, and educational impediments which constrained greater participation in football by this populace in locales such as Texas, New Mexico, California, and to a lesser extent Florida. The coming of World War II, and the myriad changes it produced, set the stage for enhanced prospects, including a push for greater access to scholastic opportunities for barrio children of returning combatants. While not overcoming all obstacles, the 1940s saw increased expectations for the post-war era. As noted academician Zaragoza Vargas argued in his 2011 textbook, *Crucible of Struggle: A History of Mexican Americans from Colonial Times to the Present Era*, involvement in both the military and wartime industrial production

> contributed to the rapid rise of a Mexican American civil rights movement. It provided Mexican Americans with opportunities to realize the gap between the doctrine of democracy the United States advocated abroad and the racial practices maintained at home. The war heightened their assertiveness and desire to change their conditions. Increasingly dissatisfied with the barriers blocking their advancement, Mexican Americans began voicing their demands for equality more vigorously.[1]

Numerous researchers of Latino/a history have focused on how this era generated increased undertakings designed to challenge discriminatory practices, but little has been done to examine how such endeavors helped open the doors to a greater number of *atletas* to make their marks on gridirons, courts, and diamonds across the nation. Before moving on to discuss circumstances on the fields of competition, it is necessary to tap the research of Professor Vargas and others to scrutinize aspects of the day-to-day existence of the Spanish-surnamed populace (primarily Mexican Americans) in the years just before, and after, the end of World War II.

Vargas' synopsis of the period reveals heterogeneous social and economic outcomes for the Spanish-surnamed. Among the negative consequences cited was how mobilization throughout the West and Southwest "produced a volatile social climate on the home front as relocation, rationing, overcrowding, and ... the influx of newcomers into the nation's booming war production centers ... led to racial clashes." Many who pursued such occupations were previously tied to the migrant stream and thus not well-prepared to enter industrial work settings. Vargas notes that a proportion were poorly educated and "thus ... caught in a trap of inadequate education and job skills." In addition, those who did get jobs in war production were often confined to the lowest-paying and least skilled occupations. For example, in Texas, "less than five percent ... [of this population] held jobs in war-related industries because of labor market discrimination." Workers additionally confronted housing discrimination, with circumstances in the Los Angeles area documented as being particularly problematic. Further, local newspapers (in southern California and elsewhere) regularly and directly associated Mexican Americans with violence, sexual crimes, and drug usage and sales.[2]

Although some research indicates that treatment was, at times, more just within the military for the scores of Mexican Americans who enlisted during the war (an estimated 500,000), there are also myriad examples of abuse.[3] After the conflict, negative events continued as returning veterans were mistreated in movie theaters, restaurants, and other facilities in Texas and other states. In Kansas, for example, Spanish-surnamed veterans were forced to establish their own Veterans of Foreign Wars (VFW) posts due to discrimination by their former colleagues in arms.[4] The most egregious and infamous of such episodes was the abominable Felix Longoria affair in Three Rivers, Texas, where the family of a *soldado* killed in action in the Philippines was denied an opportunity to hold services in the community's one funeral home.[5] Vargas summarizes the importance of such deleterious developments by arguing that these trends made Mexican Americans more assertive in their pursuit of justice in various aspects of daily life.

> Because exposure to a larger world transformed the Mexican American World War II veterans' understanding of their future, they would lead the fight for citizenship in the postwar years. Many war veterans used their military service as a basis to argue for further rights as American citizens. Although workplace discrimination and restrictive housing covenants existed, many Mexican Americans were active in breaking down their quest for equality ... [and] helped lay the ground work for the postwar civil rights movement.[6]

There were also substantial positive changes, however. For example, in New Mexico, due in part to efforts by Democrat Senator Dennis

2. Slowly Moving the Ball Down the Field 61

Chavez, federal government training programs were made available to serve Spanish-speakers during the years of the Great Depression. This, in turn, "prepared them in numerous occupational fields previously closed to them." Once the war began, "thousands ... entered war work as riveters, airplane mechanics, electric welders, and machinists and in airplane construction in defense plants in Arizona and California."[7] Franklin Delano Roosevelt's signing of Executive Orders 8802 and 9346 established and strengthened the Fair Employment Practices Committee. The war years (and just after) witnessed the establishment of important organizations that precipitated and participated in challenges against discrimination. Some (not an exhaustive list) of the critical groups involved included: the Congress of Spanish-Speaking Peoples (which held its first convention in 1939), the Sleepy Lagoon Defense Committee (1942), the National Farm Labor Union (1947), and the American GI Forum (1948), which often joined in such endeavors with another important entity: the League of United Latin American Citizens (begun in 1929).

In addition to the establishment of associations designed to counteract prejudiced practices, there were also efforts in the courtroom that had significant impact on making the opportunity for a high school education more readily available. In Chapter 1, we discussed how many educators had negative perceptions of the intellectual and physical capabilities of Mexican American children. A recent publication by Estela Godinez Ballon, *The Mexican American Experience: Mexican Americans and Education: Saber es Poder*, provides myriad examples that typify such assumptions (before 1940). For example, she quotes *The Report of Illiteracy in Texas* from 1923, where it was argued that "There is but one choice in the matter of educating these unfortunate children and that is to put the 'dirty' ones into separate schools til they learn how to 'clean-up' and become eligible to better society." The author cites a 1937 piece which condemns all Mexican American pupils as substandard. "We segregate for the same reason that southerners segregate the Negro. They are an inferior race; that is all."[8] It was against such attitudes that reformers and their organizations struggled, particularly after the conclusion of World War II.

Of specific importance to our analysis of partaking in football (and athletic competitions in general) before 1950, are four court cases, two each from California and Texas. These were *Independent School District v. Salvatierra* of 1930 (San Antonio Court of Appeals), *Alvarez v. Lemon Grove School District* of 1931 (California Superior Court), *Mendez v. Westminster* of 1947 (U.S. Court of Appeals, 9th District) and *Delgado v. Bastrop Independent School District* of 1948 (U.S. District Court of Appeals, Western District). In *Salvatierra*, the court ruled that, while Mexican American pupils in this Lone Star State district could not be segregated due to race, they could "by their ability to learn English." In *Alvarez*, the courts determined that the district's attempt to segregate all Mexican American children (who were considered to be "white" by California state law), based on the need for some to have "special instruction," was not permissible. If students had a language barrier, they could be separated, but it was not legal to assume that all had to be removed from "regular" classrooms. *Alvarez* was a notable case because it was "the nation's first successful class action lawsuit against segregation, [but] like previous cases, its influence was strictly local, lacking a national, or even state, impact."[9]

The *Mendez* and *Delgado* cases were the first Mexican American–initiated federal court cases and further solidified the notion that Spanish-surnamed children should not be separated. In *Mendez*, the plaintiffs argued that separate facilities were inherently unequal and that such institutions were a violation of the 14th amendment to the Constitution. Further, the judge found that segregation produced "no evidence that … [it] helped students to develop English proficiency. Instead, evidence indicated that it retarded language and cultural assimilation. The *Mendez* case's greatest success was in ending de jure segregation in California." *Delgado* produced more mixed results. The judge in this Texas case determined that Mexican American children could not be segregated, but also ruled "that schools could segregate first-grade Mexican American students who were not English proficient within integrated schools."[10] In summary, by the first years after the conclusion of World War II, some progress had taken place, but there still remained much to do. As Godinez-Ballon noted:

> While each of these early desegregation cases provided some victories … unfortunately, segregation continued and increased. Many school districts did not comply with the court rulings by professing ignorance of the law and refusing to go against local custom and practice of segregation. School districts used the language proviso in many of the rulings as a form of second-generation segregation by segregating students by English language proficiency in a single school…. Nevertheless, these first cases demonstrate the desires and efforts of Mexican American parents and organizations to obtain equal opportunities for their children.[11]

Limited economic circumstances, however, continued to hinder the opportunities for many to complete a secondary education, as well as to participate in athletics.

Additionally, educators maintained their ambivalence about the physical capabilities of such youths, although here, too, a more realistic assessment evolved. A 1936 thesis by Genevieve King, for example, argued that "the Mexican Americans studied in San Antonio have little interest in exercise." Just a few years later, Albert Folsom Cobb presented a similar argument when he noted in his MA study that such pupils simply were "not as interested or eager to participate in physical education program[s], particularly in inter-school competition, as are Anglo American boys." Finally, yet another writer criticized such youths as being "fond of all sports, especially athletic contests. They excel in these but they mar the [games] ... by being poor losers."

While these results follow key elements of the argumentation laid out by Mitchell's work of the 1920s, there were some educators who noticed (grudgingly) a smattering of positive traits among the Spanish-surnamed regarding athletic ability. In a 1951 University of Texas thesis, Bruce Walsh Shaw argued that his results concerning physical traits revealed that his Mexican American test subjects actually outperformed white students. Further, "athletic ability did have a slightly positive impact on how Anglo children perceived their ... counterparts." An earlier (1942) study by Merrell E. Thompson and Claude C. Dove, the results of which were published in an academic journal, argued likewise. The researchers believed that since most of these youths came from poorer families, such "children seem to lead a more vigorous physical life than do the Anglos. This condition seems to produce ... physical development and thereby superiority in the events ... tested."[12]

The preceding materials have focused exclusively on individuals of Mexican background. Now we will briefly turn to Cubans. Before the massive migration of *Cubanos* seeking to escape Fidel Castro's revolution, there were pockets of concentration for this group in various American seacoast cities. In regard to their participation in athletics (besides those who were playing baseball for Major League and Negro Leagues teams), however, there is scant information. Some of the few items at hand deal with the Cuban/Spanish/Italian neighborhood of Ybor City in the Tampa area. As authors Gary Mormino and George Pozzetta noted, the experiences of individuals such as Ferdie Pacheco were in many ways dissimilar from those of Mexican Americans. As Mormino and Pozzetta argued, the schools in Hillsborough County did not practice direct discrimination against such students (known locally as "Latins") if they were light-skinned. Mulattoes and "black" Cubans were treated similarly to African Americans. By the early 1920s, however, many of the more "Spanish-looking" Latins were able to remain in school, graduate, participate in athletics, attend the University of Florida, and even join fraternities. "As early as 1932 ... Sigma Iota [was] populated exclusively by young men of Ybor City." In regard to sports, the historians cited above contended that participation "speeded acculturation, introducing Latins to the outside world, forcing individuals and groups to mingle with others in schools, gyms and on playing fields." The most important athlete to hail from this community in the years right after World War II was known as the "Tampa Torpedo," the great Rick Casares, who had a long and distinguished career in the NFL with the Chicago Bears, and briefly, with the expansion Miami Dolphins.[13] Given the dramatic increase in this population after 1959, the story of Cuban American athletes will be of greater significance in Chapter 3 and beyond.

In summary, shortly after the cessation of hostilities in 1945, a series of stimuli coalesced to provide greater opportunities for Spanish-speakers in the United States to compete in inter-scholastic athletics such as football. Certainly obstacles remained, but there were openings and the genesis of a more determined effort to make it possible for more and more Latinos/as to complete at least a high school education. The rest of this chapter will examine the presence of Latinos on the gridirons of states such as Texas, New Mexico, California, and Florida. The discussion will not only focus on what players accomplished on the field, but will contextualize their historical and social significance. At the end, as previously, we highlight the careers and achievements of several key, but representative, individuals at the collegiate and professional levels.

Before delving into particulars concerning Latino participation in football in Texas during this era, it is necessary to reemphasize how monumental an undertaking/achievement it was for some of these athletes to compete on the gridiron. Greg Selber's research into the sport in the Rio Grande Valley region noted that during the middle of the decade in question, this densely Mexican American sector featured almost an all-white district squad. Particularly, in the 1943–1944 academic year, "on the ... 14-AA team that year, halfback Ramiro Guerra of Edinburg was the only Hispanic to be named, and McHigh [McAllen High School] at that stage had an all-Anglo team. It wouldn't be until the 1950s that the ethnic makeup of the Valley squads started to change."[14] Joel Huerta supports this contention in his dissertation on high school football in southern Texas. One of his interviewees recalled that, even if you made the team, "'Who in the hell was going to play a Mexican when they had an Anglo? It was an absurd idea.'"[15] Therefore, if in one of the three regions (the others being El Paso and Laredo) most jam-packed with Spanish-surnamed population, only one such player made it on an all-star team, and the largest high school in the region featured an all-white squad, Mexican Americans were indeed a rarity on the gridiron. Still, as the following sections will show, just because they were an oddity did not mean that there were not some great athletes and, by 1950, even a coach or two.

In Chapter 1 we discussed the beginning of the athletic career of Everardo Carlos (E.C.) Lerma and brought his story up to the point when he was hired as the head coach of the Benavides High School (BHS) Eagles for the start of the 1940 season. In the late 1990s, as Coach Lerma reminisced about his career, he indicated on more than one occasion that "I proved them wrong" regarding questions about his abilities as a leader because of his background. The success for the Eagles began in his third season on the sidelines, with BHS claiming a district crown. This was followed in 1943 with a perfect season and a regional title. At this time, schools the size of BHS did not compete for state titles; therefore, this was the highest prize they could achieve.

2. Slowly Moving the Ball Down the Field

The Eagles repeated the honor in 1949. More accolades came in 1947, 1950, and 1952 (district), and 1948 and 1951 (bi-district). Even by Texas standards, this was an impressive run of gridiron glory. All of this was accomplished with Mexican Americans comprising the majority of the team's roster. Lerma also enjoyed similar success with BHS's basketball and track teams. He left Duval County in 1955, taking a job with Rio Grande City High School (RCG). From the year he departed, the Eagles did not make the state playoffs again in football until 1984. The school immortalized Lerma by naming its football field in his honor in October of 1991.[16]

Although Lerma brought much success on the fields of athletic competition, an assessment of this pioneer's historical influence reaches well beyond noting scoreboard tallies and win-loss records compiled during the 1940s. Lerma the player and coach, one researcher has noted, "presented a dilemma for Texans who believed in the athletic and intellectual inferiority of Mexican Americans. Clearly, here was an individual who did not fit the perception of the typical 'greaser.' If a Spanish-surnamed individual could help the local team win, perhaps he could be treated as an equal, at least on the football field."[17] But that is not all to this story, as Joel Huerta argues in his dissertation. Of even greater significance was what Lerma's success on the sidelines meant to his charges. Here was a man who was college educated, successful in his field, and directing one of the most important elements of Benavides' present and future. Perhaps there was, indeed, room for individuals of this background as professional and community leaders. As Huerta argues, Lerma's importance arose when it became "Clear to Lerma that Mexicanos, especially kids, were watching him. If he succeeded he might encourage them to claim their rightful place on playing fields, classrooms, marching bands and drill teams—the mainstream of South Texas everyday culture." This was certainly a crucial message to pass along to the youth of Duval County. He made his players tough on the field and elsewhere. Lerma most assuredly prepared these young men to tackle bigger issues later on in life.

> Lerma's strict, paternalistic coaching style ... dovetailed with South Texas ranch country ethic ... [ultimately] the 1940s and 50s saw increased racial contact and a slow and steady dismantling of segregation in sports, schools, and the broader society—often in that order. Lerma and his ... [teams] were trigger points, bell-weather of the changes afoot in this football-obsessed province of Mexican America.[18]

The Mexican American population of Benavides had the good fortune of working with a coach such as Lerma much earlier than did most families of a similar background in Texas. Ironically, another early coach in southern Texas was Joe Martinez, head coach at Rio Grande City between 1948 and 1952. His mark with the Rattlers was nowhere near as successful as Lerma's, however (10–37–2). In research discussed in the following chapter, a perusal of the *Texas Sports Guide of High Schools and Colleges* demonstrates that for the years prior to the late 1960s Mexican American head football coaches were few and far between (and they continue to be). One extraordinary exception who bears mention is the legendary Nemo Herrera, although he did not coach football.[19]

A few other notable athletes who made their mark on the gridiron during this era warrant mention. Gonzalo Garcia was a two-way lineman for Brownsville High in the 1940s and became a Little All-American for the Southwest Texas State (now Texas State University) Bobcats in 1949. He had offers to join teams in the NFL but instead enlisted in the military and later returned to the Valley as a coach at his alma mater. Rene Manuel Hinojosa played football, basketball and track at Mercedes High School during the 1940s and subsequently coached Sharyland High School to three straight post-season appearances in the 1950s. Efraim Vela played football for the legendary Chuck Moser at McAllen High School and is acknowledged as one of the first Mexican Americans to play football (and basketball) at the institution. He also earned All-Valley honors in 1948. He moved on to coaching at RGC, following E.C. Lerma starting in 1966. The story of R.C. "Frito" Flores is particularly unique. Because of a lack of players at Edinburg High School during the war, he joined the varsity as an 8th-grader, playing on both lines. Flores has the distinction of being the only player in the region to earn five letters in football at a single institution. He later played two years at the University of Colorado, went into the Air Force, and returned to get his degree at Pan American College (now University of Texas–Rio Grande Valley). Joe R. Sanchez, Jr., was born in Del Rio, but was a Rattler at RGC in the 1940s before playing his collegiate football at Sul Ross State Teachers College (now Sul Ross University) in Alpine, Texas. He was an All-Lone Star Conference performer, earned Little All-America honorable mention in 1948, and signed with the Los Angeles Rams. His professional career was cut short due to injury, and Sanchez returned to the Valley to serve as a coach and administrator in the RGC school district for almost four decades.[20]

On the other side of the Lone Star State, the young men who played football for El Paso Bowie continued to make their mark as well. By the year before the start of American participation in World War II hostilities, the institution had grown to over 1,200 students. One highlight from the 1940 schedule occurred on October 3, when the Bears competed against the Mexico City Y.M.C.A. in El Paso. The divisions between Mexican Americans and Mexicanos were apparent on this day, as "both teams were involved in quite a bit of name calling and the team from Mexico City was ridiculing the Bowie players." Most likely, the term "pochos," a derogatory label used to make fun of American-born/raised Mexicans by natives of the "old country," was hurled at the locals. Fred Morales' recounting of the game does not present a positive portrayal of either squad and their fans. The game ended in a 13–13 tie, as Bowie was unable to line up and kick an extra point due to a melee.

> In the final minute of play Bowie scored a tying touchdown, 3,000 of the 7,000 spectators swarmed the field, and officials tried in vain to keep crowds off.... Then a flurry of fist fights broke out among players and spectators massed tightly around the two teams. Game officials and the police broke up the disturbance.... Following the game, spectators "ganged" the Mexico City players downtown at a scheduled dinner at the Hotel Paso del Norte. Another riot occurred there and the police and MPs from Ft. Bliss broke up the fight. Then players of both teams shook hands at the joint banquet and the hatchet was buried. Despite the incidents, the school would later go to Mexico City to play the same team next fall.[21]

The visit by the football team to Mexico City scheduled for the following year was put off until 1946, however. The reason for the delay was euphemistically noted as being due to the "unsettled transportation and other difficulties at the time."[22]

In 1941, the Bears were involved in another significant tilt against the San Antonio Lanier Voks, one of the earliest (as far as we have been able to determine) high school gridiron games in Texas featuring almost exclusively Mexican American-laden squads. This contest took place on September 26, and the El Paso paper took note of the import. "The game is a natural, in that players from both teams are largely of Spanish-American extraction; but Bowie, with its best club in several years, must be rated a heavy favorite."[23] Although the hometown scribes predicted a Bears victory, the teams battled to a scoreless tie. In its next edition, the *Times* praised the athleticism and work ethic of both sides, though author Grenville Mott could not help but sneak in what can only be construed as a snide remark. "The teams were much alike, with both fast and both tricky, both displaying good blocking and murderous tackling." Additionally, Mott noted that the game ended in "hysteria," though he did not provide further details about what caused the agitations.[24] Unfortunately, this year did feature one actual melee involving Bowie; that came on November 7 against El Paso High. As Morales stated, "600 people slung fists, bottles and cushions," and several youths were arrested. After the game, the "crowd attempted to break down the restroom to free the ... youths ... [who] were then rushed to a squad car through the school and taken to the city jail." The Tigers defeated the Bears in this contest, 21–0.[25] In 1942 the Bears claimed a district title, defeating Ysleta, 12–0, on November 13, before bowing out of the state playoffs by losing to San Angelo on December 5, 20–6.[26]

By war's end, Bowie had grown to 1,599 students, almost exclusively of Mexican descent. In the last years of the decade, the institution's students and alumni were presented regularly with both positive and negative experiences of education and athletics for Spanish-surnamed students in Texas. On positive side of the ledger, the Bears traveled to Mexico City in 1946 and played before an estimated crowd of 25,000, defeating a team called the Spitfires, 26–0. The school honored the many youths who gave their lives during the conflict, dedicating an impressive on-campus memorial in 1948. Finally, and most significantly in regard to sports, the Bears won the state title in baseball under the leadership of Nemo Herrera. Among the negative experiences were occurrences such as students being suspended for speaking Spanish on campus, a heated debate as to whether to classify students as "Mexicans" or "Americans," and finally, during the Bears' drive to the state title on the diamond, players and coaches

> had to sleep in cots beneath the stands of Memorial Stadium at the University of Texas and they were not allowed to stay in local hotels. Racial segregation was still in force, and they were despised by the local population after their victory. After the game, both teams did not shake hands, and the team was awarded the trophy with no formal presentation. When they boarded their bus back home, a few rocks were hurled at them and the local police did nothing. They reached a restaurant in Ft. Stockton that day, and they had to ferry food to the bus, because they would not be served inside.[27]

Even success on the fields of athletic competition and of battle in World War II were not sufficient to overcome the negative perceptions of many Texans.

In summary, for high school football in the Lone Star State before 1950, the number of Mexican American competitors was undoubtedly limited. This does not mean, however, that the players and the few coaches did not have a significant impact on the lives of their co-ethnics. In a 1987 undergraduate paper by Victor M. Aguilar entitled "Mexican American in Sports: A Survey of Ex-Bowie High School Football Players, 1932–1954," the author captured important aspects of what playing football meant to athletes, their classmates, and parents. One player, Jesus "Jessie" Bullos, recalled that during one playoff game in Lamar, some locals held up a sign that read: "It takes 1000 Mexicans to defeat one Texan." "Bullos and his teammates used this insult for motivation because 'we all realized that most of us were Texans anyway so we just went out and beat their butts.'" Of particular importance, many argued, was playing, and defeating, their mostly white city rivals at Austin High School. The white players thought as did the folks in Lamar, that Mexican Americans would be easy to defeat on the gridiron. As Aguilar argued at the conclusion of his essay, most of his interviewees

> agreed that this was a major weakness in the Anglo thinking because when they competed against these Mexicans, the Anglos expected the stereo-type lazy, good for nothing Mexican that Anglo society had grown to look down upon. With this style of thinking, the Mexican American athlete had an important advantage because they knew what they were up against and what they could do and had to do, to beat

the Anglo at his own game and prove himself and his race as equals.... [One player noted that] "with pride like ours, we felt important enough that we could change the world, and many of us did just that by doing our part by serving in the wars, civil and military service, political life, education, joining together to support the cause ... and becoming responsible citizens of the city and of our country."[28]

Dan Ford's work once again serves as a key source to highlight players and field generals in New Mexico. The years covered in this chapter saw an increased number of coaches and players, as well as the retirement of one of the legendary figures noted in Chapter 1. Coach Louis Hernandez, who began his tenure in the 1920s, continued his success at Menaul High School, winning a state crown in 1937. Ford compares him to other early prodigies of the state's football history and argues that "not only did they coach on the gridiron but also usually their duties included all other sports.... Those dedicated coaches of the development era ... are little remembered even by the most avid fan but their contributions to the sport are felt by all athletes who feel the hereditary pride when they don school colors."[29] Hernandez retired in 1945 and turned over the program to another New Mexico icon, Dave Tomlinson, who coached at Menaul for 30 years and highlighted his career by leading the Panthers to a title in 1959 as well as an undefeated, and unscored upon, campaign in 1975.[30]

On the plains, another individual with a Spanish-surnamed background made his mark at Carlsbad. Sam Etcheverry, born in 1930, was the offspring of a Basque sheep rancher who had immigrated to New Mexico. He was a member of the 1945 and 1946 state title-winning Cavemen, and after graduating in 1948 went on to star as a quarterback with the University of Denver Pioneers between 1949 and 1951, participating in the 1952 Pineapple Bowl against the University of Hawaii (a 28–27 loss). At the end of his collegiate career, he held almost all passing records for the school (the Pioneers dropped the sport in 1961). Etcheverry went on to have an illustrious career with the Alouettes of the CFL, playing in two Grey Cup finals (1955 and 1956) and coaching and winning the trophy for Montreal in 1970. He was the team's field general from 1969 through 1972. In the year he became head coach, he was inducted into the CFL Hall of Fame, and he ranks as the 26th-best player in league history. Sam Etcheverry passed away in Quebec in 2009.[31]

Another significant individual in the story of New Mexico football is Guillermo Rudolfo "Rudy" Camunez, who spent many years as the head coach of the Las Cruces High School (LCHS) Bulldawgs (this is how the school has spelled the team's name since 1980). The family was prominent in the community with Rudy's father, Jose, serving as a town trustee in the mid-1910s and later as fire chief. The family's domicile was built in 1920 and is still part of a walking tour of the city. Camunez, who was born in 1922, was a part of a state title basketball team (as manager) at the local high school in 1940 and graduated in 1941. This was only the first state championship tie between Camunez and LCHS.

Camunez eventually returned to his alma mater and was in the right place at the right time to begin his coaching career. In the years after World War II, there was much pressure on state officials to erect a bureaucratic scaffolding, to establish a football playoff system and crown a "real" champion.[32] The Bulldawgs were always in "the conversation" concerning state gridiron supremacy, but there was also a lack of clarity concerning which side ultimately was supreme. As Ford notes, "Anybody that could finish the season without a loss within state play, no matter how few games they played, could claim the title." In order to further bolster LCHS's chances, administrators hired a Texan named Aulton "Bull" Durham to lead their student athletes starting in 1944. Durham had some successes (for example, he led the basketball team to a state title in 1944), but abruptly resigned just at the end of school in the spring of 1948. Locals were outraged and there were walkouts and demands for an explanation concerning the move. It turned out that Durham had violated more than a few state and school regulations, such as scheduling camps and games on his own as well as utilizing ineligible players. As a result, the state athletic association banned LCHS from competing against other New Mexico schools in all sports for the academic year of 1948–1949. The institution then turned to a "local boy made good" and hired Rudy Camunez as head coach; he would continue at this post until 1961.

Sam Etcheverry, 1961 (Canadian Football Hall of Fame).

In his first year at the helm, his charges finished 0–3, playing two games against El Paso Cathedral and a town team from White Sands. The dismissal of Coach Durham was perceived as a positive step by the state organization, which lifted the ban just in time for basketball season (November). After this rough start, Camunez brought much glory to LCHS, leading his alma mater to the state title game in 1955, losing to Roswell, 19–14. A review of the New Mexico Activities Association (NMAA) listing of football champions (and their coaches) reveals that Rudy Camunez was the first Spanish-surnamed coach to lead a squad to a state title game (in the "modern" era—since the start of NMAA). Later, Camunez captured the first recognized state title for LCHS in 1959, defeating Artesia, 31–7. Even more significant than his leadership in football and other sports, Camunez, a 1979 inductee into the NMAA Hall of Fame, worked to integrate both African Americans and Latinos into the high school athletic teams in this border town beginning in 1949; the local school board acquiesced to this request in 1951. In honor of his civil rights activities, as well as his importance as a coach, teacher, and administrator, the city of Las Cruces designated the Wall of Honor at the local sports complex in his name in October of 2016.[33]

In addition to the athletes and coaches Ford noted, we return briefly to research by Ricardo Dow Anaya in his 1997 University of New Mexico dissertation. Two legendary athletes and coaches filled very much of a "Lerma-esque" role in the communities of Las Vegas and Artesia. The story of Gilbert S. "Gillie" Lopez is instructive in the significance of a coach and administrator at a local school. Lopez was born in Wagon Mound in 1922, the descendant of a family that had lived in the northern section of New Mexico since at least the 1700s. Gillie was an excellent all-round athlete, played basketball, ran track, and played football (during the three-year stretch his high school existed prior to World War II). It was a tall order for the small player and school. "We had to play the bigger schools. It was kind of hard because we had to play Roy, Raton, Las Vegas Robertson, and we were just a tiny little school in Wagon Mound." Although the institution dropped football during World War II, Lopez learned the game and eventually played the sport at New Mexico Highlands University, where he earned a Master's in Education after the war. He was hired as the first coach at West Las Vegas High School shortly thereafter.

Like Coach Lerma, Lopez wore many coaching hats during his career; finding the most success on the hardwood. Indeed, the school's current gym is named in his honor. Much of what Lopez learned in the classroom and the military, he put to work with his charges. "As a coach I never had a losing season … the records show I have never had a losing team in any of the three sports I coached…. Material wise, I'd say my athletes were dedicated. The boys … knew how to win. I think my kids enjoyed athletics and competition." Coach Lopez's success actually helped to reopen the school after it was closed in 1950. "Students not only dropped out of school, they left the community. When the high school was reopened, our student enrollment came back and our students … completed their education." Gillie Lopez was also involved in state politics and was an ardent Democrat. He retired in 1981 and passed away in 2005. As Dow Anaya summarizes, here was an individual who took what he earned on the gridiron and the court and turned the passion for competition and improvement to the benefit of all. Lopez "maintained a strong advocacy for the traditions, culture and heritage of his family ... [and] will be long remembered for his intensity on the field of play and ... in standing up for his people and his community."[34]

The experiences of another legendary New Mexico athlete and coach, Jimmy Juarez from Artesia (in the southern part of the state), share some similarities with those of Lopez, though his experiences with racism appear to have been much harsher than what Lopez endured in the northern reaches of the territory. Juarez's family had a much shorter connection to New Mexico than Lopez. His mother was born in Italy, and his father hailed from Juarez, Mexico. Jimmy was born in 1933, graduated from his hometown high school, attended the University of New Mexico, and worked in the public schools of Albuquerque. He recalled that his hometown "was not a good place for some of the Hispanic people there. Artesia was a very prejudiced community." Among the practices Juarez confronted was being allowed to swim in city pools only on Fridays, the day when the facility would be cleaned. It was his success on the football field, however, that mitigated some of the discriminatory practices used against him. "If I went by myself, I could swim because I was from an athletic family and I was also beginning to be known as an athlete."

Like his co-ethnics in El Paso, Jimmy Juarez realized that he could challenge discrimination by success on the football field and baseball diamond. Such events "motivated Juarez, his brothers, and their Hispanic friends to organize teams to go across town and challenge teams.... He believed those to be the years that really developed his competitive nature." During his time at Artesia High School, he lettered in various sports, including three years on the gridiron. He even played in the state all-star game as a senior. He summarized his athletic career with the Bulldogs by stating that "I accepted the challenge of being one of the few Hispanic kids ... that was playing a lot, so I took that as setting an example that someone else could follow.... I took that upon myself." As a result, he promised himself that, given the chance, "I would never treat any kid differently, no matter if he was white, black, brown or whatever. Individuals would solely be judged on their merit." He put this ideology into practice starting in 1956 and remained a coach, administrator, and official for almost four decades. Among the highlights of his coaching career was taking West Mesa High to the state title game in 1971, where the Mustangs came up short, 24–21, against Mayfield. At the end of his career, Juarez summarized his ties to football (and sports in general) in the following way:

> Athletics allowed me to do a lot of things ... go to college, have a professional goal which later turned into a personal one and to succeed. Coming from Artesia, there was only one thing that was possibly going to happen to me. If I stayed there, I was going to scratch for whatever jobs were available to a Hispanic person there.... Ath-

2. Slowly Moving the Ball Down the Field

letics teaches you that kind of things. You develop a common bond with one another and a dedication to friendship. I have friends that I have competed against throughout my life. We see each other every now and then and we still have that bond, that special bond that only an athlete, coach or teacher knows.[35]

The story of Latinos playing football in the state of California is not as methodically documented as in Texas and New Mexico. Therefore, the section on this state focuses primarily on the experiences of a few individuals who made it to the collegiate and professional ranks. The majority of this research was conducted by Mario Longoria.[36] We will discuss the experiences of the following: John Sanchez, Gonzalo Morales, and "Mean" Gene Brito. In addition, we will briefly note what was happening with the Roosevelt vs. Garfield rivalry in Los Angeles. Finally, other Californians will be discussed at greater length at the end of the chapter, when we provide more extensive, individual coverage of particularly outstanding/significant players.

John Sanchez was born in October 1920, the offspring of a Mexican mother and a Spanish father. By the time he graduated high school Sanchez, a lineman, had blossomed into a 6'2" frame and weighed over 200 pounds. Given this bulk, he was surprisingly nimble, as his Los Angeles City College newspaper noted how he would race "down the field with the agility of an ambitious hepcat and being as immobile as the rock of Gibraltar." In 1940, Sanchez was part of a team that finished 6–3–1. He subsequently transferred to the University of San Francisco and played defensive end for the Dons in 1941 and 1942. By this time, he had grown an extra two inches in height and added almost 40 pounds to his frame. After the 1942 season, the *Associated Press* selected Sanchez for the annual All-Pacific Coast Football Team. He was also honored by his academic institution with the Martin O'Brien Trophy, awarded to the best all-around player on the squad. Shortly thereafter, Sanchez enlisted, was sent to Marine Corps officer school at the University of the Redlands, and completed his training at Parris Island. Ultimately, he was commissioned and served with the Second Marine Division at Okinawa.

After the war, Sanchez returned to the Dons and captained the 1946 squad. He also played semi-pro football with the San Francisco Clippers of the Pacific Coast Football League. This stellar athlete graduated with a degree in romance languages in 1947 and decided to try his hand at professional football. He had been selected by the NFL Giants (in the ninth round of the 1944 draft) while with the Marines, but signed with the Chicago Rockets of the All-American Football Conference (AAFC) instead. This was a poor franchise (1–13 in 1947) and Sanchez decided to move on, contracting with the Lions (another team destined to finish last in its division that year, with a 3–9 mark). He asked Detroit to waive him and became a member of the Washington Redskins. This was still not a high-caliber team (4–8, in next-to-last place in the Eastern Division), but here Sanchez made his mark. His most significant play that year was an interception against the Boston Yankees in the last game of the season, a 40–13 triumph. In this year and his second season with the Redskins, Sanchez played on the line and often opened holes for his fellow Mexican American, Eddie Saenz (who will be discussed later). After a few games with Washington in 1949, Sanchez signed with the team that had originally drafted him, the New York Giants. He was part of a 1950 team that played the Cleveland Browns for the AAFC Championship game, a tilt which Paul Brown's squad ultimately won, 8–3. As Sanchez recalled, "The game was closely contested on frozen ground. Conerly was quarterbacking and it was Kelly Note who dropped the pass in the end zone. Had he caught it, we would have won the game and the championship." After this season, Sanchez retired from professional football and spent the rest of his working life in construction contracting. He was inducted into the Dons' Hall of Fame in 1975 and passed away in 1992.[37]

Gonzalo Morales was another excellent athlete from the Golden State who parlayed his athletic abilities into a collegiate scholarship, as well as brief time in the NFL (with the Pittsburgh Steelers) in the late 1940s. "Ganzie," as his teammates called him, was the son of two Spaniards who had immigrated to the San Francisco area. He was born in 1922 and played his high school football at Mission High. In his senior season, he earned the distinction of being named his squad's MVP as well as to the All-City Team. This, in turn, led to a scholarship offer from the St. Mary's Gaels in 1941, where he played quarterback and in the backfield. He participated in the East-West Shrine Game in the post-season of 1942 and was part of the All-Northern California Football Second Team named by the *San Francisco Examiner*. Morales interrupted his collegiate athletic career and served in the Coast Guard; he was discharged in 1945. After the 1946 season, he was part of a Gaels team that played in the Oil Bowl in Houston against Georgia Tech on New Year's Day. He provided some of the few highlights for St. Mary's, returning a Yellowjackets kickoff 62 yards. The Californians lost the contest, 41–19.

The Philadelphia Eagles had selected Morales in the fifth round of the 1945 draft, but he never donned their colors. Instead, he continued his schooling, and the Eagles eventually traded him to their cross-state rivals. His totals in two years for the Steelers were not impressive, though he did average over 21 yards per kickoff return. The 1947 team, which finished 8–5, is considered to be the best Pittsburgh squad before the Chuck Noll era. After the 1948 season, Morales decided to retire, though Art Rooney personally reached out and asked him to reconsider his decision. Morales stood firm and returned to San Francisco with his wife, Helen. He eventually became a member of the San Francisco police department, retiring after an almost three-decade career. Gonzalo Morales passed away in 2002.[38]

"Mean" Gene Brito was born in Huntington Park in 1925 and grew up in

East Los Angeles. He played high school football at Lincoln High and starred in basketball, baseball, and track. Upon graduation, he entered the U.S. Army as a paratrooper, serving in the Philippines. He achieved the rank of staff sergeant and received an honorable discharge after the conclusion of hostilities. He returned to the gridiron, playing both lines as well as serving as a viable pass receiving option (with 15 receptions and one touchdown in his senior season of 1950) over his four years with the Loyola (now Loyola Marymount) University Lions. He was named a member of that season's UPI All-Coast Independent College Team and was a 1951 draft choice of the Washington Redskins. He had hoped to become a teacher but decided to give professional football a try. We will provide further details on his professional career, in both the NFL and CFL, in Chapter 3.

It is imperative, however, to note here that Brito did more than just play football. He would always return to his hometown during the off-season in order to work with what were described as "incorrigible and disadvantaged children." As Brito noted to a colleague at Lincoln High concerning his desire to work with such youths:

The fact that I'm a football player makes it also easier but the problem with these kids is that they need love, kindness and attention. I've sacked many a quarterback and have made many a tackle, but to me the greatest thing I've ever done in life is to see these kids come back after a few years as good citizens of the community.

Gonzalo Morales, 1947 (courtesy St. Mary's College of California College Archives).

Tragically, Brito passed away in 1965 at the young age of 39, but his work with children, as well as his success on the field, earned him an honored place in Redskins lore. In 1976, the Touchdown Club of Washington, D.C., established the "Gene Brito Achievement Award," which was presented until 1987 to persons who demonstrated the traits of faith, perseverance, and fortitude. Among the recipients were Rocky Bleier of the Steelers and Darryl Stingley of the Patriots.[39]

A quick mention of the Garfield High School and Roosevelt High School rivalry in Los Angeles is warranted at this point. The competition between the two institutions was discontinued between 1939 and 1948. Three key developments that impacted opportunities for Latinos (mostly Mexican Americans) to play football took place during the rivalry's dormancy, however. First, as noted in Chapter 1, there existed organizations such as the Mexican Athletic Association of Southern California, which had fielded teams during the 1930s and allowed some of these youths to play football (and other sports). Next, as noted in the video on the Garfield-Roosevelt story, the Roughriders' campus, while housing a not insignificant number of Mexican American students, was still mostly Jewish and Japanese in population up until the late 1940s, and "the game was not as significant then" as it would become. As the population of families of Mexican heritage increased, there was a concerted effort to increase the number of Spanish-surnamed youths who remained in school. The noted historian of East Los Angeles, George J. Sanchez, has argued in his seminal work, *Becoming Mexican American: Ethnicity, Culture and Identity in Chicano Los Angeles, 1900–1945*, that organizations such as the Mexican American Movement (MAM) worked tirelessly from the late 1930s to provide role models, leadership training, and other efforts to keep kids in school. Sanchez summarizes the efforts of MAM by citing the organization's three reasons for Mexican American students to remain in school:

> First, educated Mexicans were less likely to be targets of discrimination and prejudice. A college degree, therefore, held out the possibility of acceptance by the larger society despite one's race. Second, MAM members saw education as key to understanding the world and, thereby, transcending the limited confines of the barrio. Finally, they understood education to be a way of advancing socioeconomic mobility. Social mobility, they argued, promoted not only personal advancement but progress for Mexican American people as a group.[40]

Although not overcoming (by a longshot) all of the obstacles, both social and economic, the increasing number of Mexican Americans in both schools had mechanisms in place to help improve educational outcomes. As more of these young men managed to stay in school, their presence on the gridiron increased. The years beyond 1950 would see the rivalry between the Bulldogs and the Roughriders achieve great social significance among the denizens of Boyle Heights and East Los Angeles.

The most significant Latino footballer from the state of Florida during this decade was the late Rick Casares, who passed away in 2013. Born in Tampa on July 4, 1931, Casares was the offspring of Spanish and Italian parents. As a youth, he played baseball, basketball, and football, ran track, and boxed. He was so prolific in the ring that he earned a New Jersey Golden Gloves championship in 1946 before returning to his hometown to attend Jefferson High School. In 1947, the Dragons, which was the "Latin" institution and which had not been very successful, defeated Hillsborough High

(6–0) on a touchdown pass from Casares to Johnny Alonso. That same year, Jefferson claimed the city title, and did so again in 1949. In 1948 he was selected as a national high school All-American. As a final example of his high school athletic prowess, Rick Casares won the state title in the javelin throw at Miami in 1950; that was the first time he had ever picked up this projectile. This talent attracted many collegiate coaches' attention. Ultimately, Casares decided to stay close to home and joined many of his fellow *Tampenos* at the University of Florida. Details of his collegiate and professional careers will be discussed in Chapter 3.[41]

The story of Latino history in the United States had, for years, been focused mostly (and with good reason) on the story of Mexican Americans in states such as Texas and California. Over the past two decades or so, however, a profusion of research has shed light upon the experiences of communities in other parts of the nation. For example, Juan Garcia's *Mexicans in the Midwest, 1900–1932* and Zaragoza Vargas' *Proletarians of the North: Mexican Industrial Workers in Detroit and the Midwest, 1917–1933* both examine the genesis and daily existence in "non-traditional" locales. Further, one of the authors of this work, Jorge Iber, has written extensively about the significance of sport in the lives of such *comunidades* in his biography of major leaguer Mike Torrez, whose family hailed from Topeka, Kansas.[42] Another recent article, this by Julie M. Weise and entitled "Mexican Nationalisms, Southern Racisms: Mexicans and Mexican Americans in the U.S. South," introduced many readers to the history of this population in places such as New Orleans and Baton Rouge. Not surprisingly, the families of the individuals discussed below came to locales such as Illinois, Kansas, Iowa, and Louisiana in search of better job opportunities and life possibilities. What was unusual was that through familial determination and athletic skills, the following four players managed to make a mark for themselves on the high school and collegiate (and later, professional) gridirons during a time when only a very few Latinos of working class backgrounds completed a high school education: Peter Perez, Ray Romero, Lupe Joe Arenas, and Vincent Gonzalez.

Peter Perez was born in Aurora, Illinois, in 1924, the offspring of a couple who had immigrated to the Midwest from the state of Zacatecas in Mexico. Through much sacrifice, the Perez clan managed to send their son to the Marmion Military Academy, where Peter, on the recommendation of his coach, Hank Fallon, showed enough talent on the field to merit a scholarship offer from the University of Illinois. He played but one season for the Fighting Illini, 1943. Perez started at offensive tackle for a 3–7 squad in Ray Eliot's second season. After the conclusion of the campaign, Perez sought to volunteer for the military, but a perforated eardrum kept him from the service. Instead, he fulfilled his patriotic duty with the merchant marine in Europe. He returned to Illinois after the war and, with Eliot's recommendation to the Bears, signed with Chicago, starting three games for the Bears. He was eventually released and played (and coached) for three more seasons of professional ball with the Akron Bears and the Bethlehem Bulldogs. By 1949, Perez retired and became a police officer in Aurora. Pete and his wife, Maria, had six children. Of their five sons, two played collegiate football: Pedro for Eastern Illinois, and Paul for the University of Wisconsin. Although he had a successful career and loving family, Perez always regretted not finishing his academic requirements at Champaign. "If I had to change or do anything different, I would return to the University of Illinois and finish my college education." Given the circumstances then extant for most Mexican Americans, Pete Perez accomplished much more than most and helped pave the way for future Latinos on the football field.[43]

Ray Romero's story is similar, though the Wichita, Kansas, native was much more open about some of the difficulties he endured while growing up in this region of the United States during the 1930s and 1940s. Romero, the offspring of parents from Guadalajara and Chihuahua, was born in 1927 and became a legendary performer for the Kansas State University (KSU) Wildcats. Before making it to the fields (and mats) of Manhattan, however, he endured much discrimination. As he noted to Mario Longoria:

Peter Perez, 1945 (courtesy University of Illinois Division of Intercollegiate Athletics).

I remember many incidents that happened to me as a boy in Wichita, Kansas. But the most outstanding was when I was forced to leave a movie theater because I had taken a seat on the first floor with an Anglo friend from school. The Mexicans were to sit only in the far balcony that was roped off. A Mexican ... in the early years of my life was considered stupid, dirty and immoral. My parents were decent, hard-working people who raised four children. They taught us to be proud of our heritage and to be the very best at what we did.

For Ray Romero, what he did best was compete in sports. He not only played football, but he also wrestled at KSU, lettering in both sports between 1947 and 1949. The highlight of his career came in his last season, though he played in only three games due to a shoulder injury. His efforts on the Wildcats' line were so impressive that he was named Honorable Mention to the All-Big-7 Conference Team. While he healed, he was not selected in the 1950 NFL draft, though he did sign as a free agent with the Philadelphia Eagles for 1951. He played that season, but was then drafted to fight in Korea.

Romero made his mark on the football fields of the military, earning a place on two *Army Times* all-star teams. Upon his discharge in 1953, he sought to return to the Eagles, but was cut. His final attempt to play in the NFL came with the Chicago Bears, but an injury ended that effort. Additionally, younger brother Eli, who played collegiately at Wichita State University (WSU), was also cut by the Bears at the end of the 1953 pre-season. After the end of his professional career, Ray Romero enrolled at his hometown institution and earned a Master's degree in education. He went on to an almost 40-year career in the field. As with others noted in this chapter, Ray Romero's life work impacted more than just athletics. In 1993, the Hispanic Leadership Conference in our nation's capital selected him as one of eight national honorees for success in various fields of endeavor. Romero's reaction to his honor was to recall being kicked out of the movie theater many years before. "Later, I realized that moment was a positive one. It motivated me to show I was just as good as anyone. I can remember when I was put down for being Mexican.... I guess you live long enough, things change."[44]

The career path of Guadalupe (Lupe) Joe Arenas was different from that of others noted here, for he did not play high school football, though he did go on to star at the University of Omaha (now University of Nebraska–Omaha) and, later, the San Francisco 49ers (his professional career will be discussed in Chapter 3). Arenas, the son of Mexican immigrants, was born in Cedar Rapids, Iowa, in 1925. Shortly after graduating from high school in Lincoln, Nebraska, however, he enlisted in the Marines and served in the Pacific. Arenas was one of the heroic fighters who landed on Iwo Jima in February of 1945. During this campaign, he was wounded and was decorated for his courage. Upon completion of his service, he returned to Nebraska and enrolled in college. Although he did not play in high school, Lupe Arenas became a weapon in the Mavericks' backfield. His best season was 1950, when Omaha finished 6–3. Arenas rushed for almost 500 yards, threw for 15 touchdowns, and passed for more than 800 yards. He also scored 46 points. These statistics helped him earn a spot on the Little All-American Team at the conclusion of that season. The 49ers then selected Arenas in the 8th round of the 1951 NFL draft.[45]

Vincent Gonzalez was born in New Orleans in 1933, the son of Mexican and Italian parents. His parents moved to Brooklyn, and the young "Vicente" grew up with his grandmother in the Crescent City. He attended Holy Cross High School and helped the Tigers to three consecutive city gridiron championships. In 1951, he was named New Orleans' Outstanding High School Athlete and accepted an athletic scholarship to Louisiana State University (LSU). He had an impressive career with those Tigers, as well as a brief tenure in the CFL (cut short because of injury) and a stellar high school coaching career in his adopted community of Baton Rouge. More details on Gonzalez will appear in subsequent chapters.

Having laid a substantial groundwork on the role of Latinos on the gridiron in the 1940s, we now turn to four individuals whose careers earned them even greater acclaim: Joe Aguirre, Eddie Saenz, Steve Van Buren, and Tom Fears.

Joe Aguirre

The story of Joseph (Joe) Aguirre is a history of a Latino athlete whose mastery of American football included a memorable collegiate career at St. Mary's College of California and a very productive professional career with teams in three professional leagues (NFL, AAFC, CFL). His personal background reveals a Basque ancestry from northern Spain though he was born in the United States.[46] The family's information is scarce, but we do know he was born on October 17, 1918, in Rock Springs, Wyoming, where he spent his childhood. He played high school football in Ogden, Utah, and was described as a tall and talented individual.[47] His football skills were apparently good enough to draw the attention of St. Mary's College of California, which offered him the opportunity to play collegiately under coach "Slip" Madigan.

In 1938, Aguirre's sophomore year, the St. Mary's Gaels won six of nine games. Their wins included a victory over the Texas Tech Raiders in the Cotton Bowl, 20–13. Aguirre continued to develop his skills during the 1939 season. The most impressive victory for the Gaels that year was a 40–7 triumph over Loyola University.[48] By his senior year, Aguirre had developed into an exceptional receiver and proficient place-kicker. In the eight games he played that season, Aguirre's best performances came against Loyola and Fordham. Against the Rams, his 30-yard field goal gave the Gaels a 9–6 win. At season's end, his efforts brought him recognition as an All-American Honorable Mention selection.[49]

In 1941, Joe Aguirre made history as the first Latino athlete chosen in the NFL collegiate draft when the Washington Redskins selected him as their 9th-round choice.[50] From the beginning, Aguirre showed promise as Bill Dismar, sports columnist for the *Washington Star*, noted on September 11, 1941, a week before Aguirre's first professional game:

> Big Joe Aguirre of St. Mary's College of California and equally husky Sam Goldman of Howard College of Alabama stood head and shoulders above the rest figuratively

as well as literally. Each weighs in the low 220's, stand[s] 6 feet 3½ and are strong and rugged.

Aguirre and the other Redskins rookies melded well with the team's veterans, and the Redskins led the NFL's Eastern Division in 1941 with an impressive 5–1 record. Aguirre's greatest moment up to that point of the season occurred when he kicked a 36-yard field goal to beat the Brooklyn Dodgers, 3–0. The *New York Times* described it as follows:

> Although the mercury hovered around 90 degrees, the rivals waged a grueling duel on the sun-baked turf. Both failed to capitalize on several opportunities as the outcome remained in doubt down to the final moment.... Regaining the ball at the Brooklyn 49 following a quick kick by Parker, the Redskins, with Filchock leading the way, moved 20 yards quickly. The attack stalled and Aguirre stepped back to the 36 to boot the ball squarely between the uprights.[51]

But then came December 7, 1941, and the U.S. entry into World War II. Aguirre left the Redskins to serve in the Merchant Marines from December 1942 to November 1943.[52]

Upon his return to professional football and the Redskins, Aguirre resumed his career with a championship team that had won the NFL East-West

Joe Aguirre (19) fighting off a defender, 1941 (Pro Football Hall of Fame).

playoff in 1942 and for the third time in four years were playing the Chicago Bears for the NFL Championship. One year plus away from the game had not lessened Aguirre's skills. In the title tilt, he caught a 25-yard touchdown pass from Sammy Baugh and kicked the extra point. His kicking and pass-receiving abilities were important cogs of the Redskins' success. In 1944, Aguirre became the first Latino professional football player named All-Pro; during this season he caught 34 passes for 410 yards and scored four touchdowns.[53]

The 1945 campaign was a very successful one for Aguirre and the Washington club. Quarterback Sammy Baugh set an NFL standard

Joe Aguirre, 1941 (courtesy St. Mary's College of California College Archives).

with an incredible 70.3 percent completion rate, helping generate an 8–2 mark. Aguirre proved his importance to the Redskins as a kicker when, in a game against the Chicago Cardinals, he booted a 19-yard field goal with 25 seconds left to secure the victory, 24–21.[54] The *New York Times* featured Aguirre's name in the headlines and described the winning field goal as follows:

> An early 21–0 lead wiped out, Washington's Redskins had to call on Joe Aguirre's unerring toe today to beat the underdog Chicago Cardinals, 24–21. Aguirre booted the ball between the uprights from 19 yards out in the last twenty-five seconds to break a 21–21 deadlock.[55]

The Redskins captured the Eastern Division championship and played the Cleveland Rams (who moved to Los Angeles the following year) for the NFL Championship. Unfortunately for Washington, the season ended in disappointment after an otherwise very successful year.[56]

The heartbreaking game was played on December 16, and freezing weather played havoc upon the players' performances. The day of the game, the weather was bitterly cold, minus 7 degrees Fahrenheit with strong gusting winds; the field had been covered with bales of straw and tarps to prevent freezing. There was also a disagreement between the Redskins' coach, Dud DeGroot, and Cleveland's Adam Walsh over the use of cleated shoes. Although both agreed to wear cleats, the Redskins brought along sneakers in case the field was frozen solid. The sneakers were never used even though their utilization could have made a difference in the game.[57]

Early in the first quarter, the Rams blocked a punt and forced the Redskins back to their own goal line. Sammy Baugh dropped back in punt formation deep in his end zone, but instead of kicking, he executed a fake and passed toward receiver Wayne Millner. The ball did not reach Millner. Instead, the spheroid slipped from Baugh's hands, hit the goalpost and rebounded into the end zone for a Rams safety.[58] In the second quarter, halfback Frank Filchock threw a 38-yard touchdown pass to Steve Bagarus for the Redskins. Aguirre converted the extra point to put the Redskins in the lead, 7–2. In the same quarter, the Rams added a touchdown and a conversion to make it 9–7 at the half. In the third quarter, both teams scored again, making the score 15–14, Cleveland. But then came the heartbreaker.[59]

With time running out, Washington moved into position for a field goal attempt from 31 yards with 6:16 left to play. Baugh took the snap and held the football on the frozen ground while Aguirre kicked. The kick was long enough, but a sudden gust of wind blew it off course. Al Costello of the *Washington Post* described the events in these words: "As the ball sailed high everybody held their breath as referee Ronald Gibbs hesitated momentarily before waving the 'No Good' signal. The leather was only a few feet to the right of the goalposts." The Washington Redskins lost, and the defeat ended an era of Redskins success; it would be another 25 years or so before Washington had a championship team again—a team that would compare with that of the first half of the 1940s. Although remembered for this miss, Joe Aguirre led the NFL that year in the number of converted field goals (7) for the entire season, but did not repeat as an NFL All-Pro. After the 1945 NFL season, Joe Aguirre entertained an offer from a rival league—the All-America Football Conference (AAFC)—and concluded his time in the nation's capital.

The All-America Football Conference (AAFC) of 1946–949 is, according to historian Beau Riffenburgh credited with having a substantial influence on professional football; it reached more people, and made more inroads against the strength of the National Football League (NFL), than any other previous league.[60] The AAFC produced the Baltimore Colts, Cleveland Browns, and San Francisco 49ers. The league also produced a host of players who went on to star in the NFL. Its first permanent franchise in California was the San Francisco 49ers. Its teams were also the first to travel by air, and some franchises had a better average attendance than the NFL.[61]

In terms of racial diversity on its rosters, African American athletes were numerous. This ran counter to the NFL, which had excluded them since 1933.[62] The AAFC afforded the likes of Marion Motley and Bill Wills of the

Cleveland Browns, Len Ford of the Los Angeles Dons, Buddy Young of the New York Yankees, and Joe Perry of the San Francisco 49ers the opportunity to play.[63] Among the Latinos who played in this league were John C. Sanchez (Mexican American) with the Chicago Rockets and Dan Garza (Mexican American) with the New York Yankees.[64]

Joe Aguirre signed with the Los Angeles Dons and played through the 1949 season. During his first season (1946) with the Dons, he set a point after touchdown record for a single game (with eight conversions) when the Dons crushed the Buffalo Bisons, 62–14. The *New York Times* reported:

> The Los Angeles Dons set an All-American Conference scoring record in defeating the Buffalo Bisons, 62–14, today before a crowd of 27,000 fans at Memorial Coliseum.... In scoring 62 points, the Dons displaced Cleveland as the league's high scoring team. The previous record was Cleveland 51, Chicago Rockets 14 in a game played Nov. 17.... Joe Aguirre kicked all but one extra point and that was missed from the 25-yard line after the Dons were guilty of holding on the first kick.[65]

In an earlier game against the Bisons, Aguirre had a pass reception for 67 yards and a touchdown in the final minutes of play, to help tie that contest. The game took place in Buffalo on September 29, 1946. Once again, the *New York Times* provided a game summary:

> The Bison beaten in their previous four games, led by 21–14 four minutes before the gun, but Charley O'Rourke threw a 48-yard pass to Joe Aguirre, who made the catch on the Bison 28 and scored. The played covered 67 yards. Aguirre's third conversion tied. Another O'Rourke—Aguirre pitch barely missed in the end zone 35 seconds before the finish.... The game was brilliantly contested, despite intermittent rain that made the field treacherous.[66]

Against the mighty Cleveland Browns, Aguirre booted an 11-yard field goal in the last 20 seconds to provide the Dons a 17–16 victory over the league-leaders. Once again, the *New York Times* noted the game's outcome:

> Big Joe Aguirre booted a field goal in the last twenty seconds today and gave the Los Angeles Dons a 17–16 victory over the loop-leading Cleveland Browns of the All-America Conference. The largest crowd of the Dons' season here, 24,800, saw the local team come from behind to hand the favored Browns their second loss of the campaign in a hard battle that started and ended with a bang.[67]

For his outstanding play in 1946, Joe Aguirre was named to the AAFC All-Pro Second Team and finished as the fifth-highest scorer in the league with 31 extra points.[68] His four-year tenure with the Dons yielded 63 pass receptions for 1,040 yards, 16 touchdowns, five field goals, and 33 extra points after touchdown for a total of 144 points. The best finish in the league for the Dons was a third place in the Western Division in 1947.[69] After the 1949 season, the AAFC merged with the National Football League (NFL). However, big Joe Aguirre accepted an offer to play in his third professional league, from the Winnipeg Blue Bombers of the CFL for 1950.

Aguirre's initial season north of the border was successful as he led the Blue Bombers and the CFL Western Conference with 57 points to capture the Dave Drysborough Memorial Trophy for Scoring.[70] He was also selected to the CFL Western All-Star Team as the Blue Bombers posted a 10–4 record and played the Argonauts in the Grey Cup. The squad from Manitoba lost to Toronto, 13–0. After the 1951 season, Joe Aguirre joined the Edmonton Eskimos for a single season and earned himself a place in their record book. On September 1, 1952, facing the Calgary Stampeders, Aguirre caught eight passes for 204 yards, to rank him fifth in Edmonton's All-Time pass reception statistics for a single game.[71] For his final three professional seasons (1953–1955), Aguirre played for the Saskatchewan Roughriders. A *1953 Saskatchewan Roughrider Game Program* introduced Joe Aguirre to the fans in Regina:

> Joe the Toe is no stranger to Saskatchewan fans, having played previously with Winnipeg and Edmonton, while with the former team he was 1950 Conference scoring champion. Last season, his third in Canada, he broke his ankle early in the season but played with Edmonton as a line coach. A graduate of St. Mary's of California, with pro experience at Washington and Los Angeles, Aguirre is 35 years old, weighs 215 pounds and is six feet, two inches tall.[72]

In 1954, Aguirre scored 85 points to lead the CFL Western Conference in scoring one last time.[73] The history-making Latino football star played a combined 14 years in three professional leagues.

For Joseph Leonard "Joe" Aguirre, it was a long journey from the football gridiron of St. Mary's College to his retirement in Saskatchewan, Canada. In each of the leagues he played in, he was a star, but no one could tell by his quiet demeanor. Although an excellent football player for many years and in varied locales, Aguirre has not been duly acknowledged for his talent and accomplishments. But someday soon, Big Joe Aguirre, the Latino football hero, will receive the recognition he most assuredly deserves.

Edwin "Eddie" Matthew Saenz

One of the most prominent Latino running backs in college and the NFL during the 1940s and 1950s was California-born Edwin "Eddie" Matthew Saenz. He was one of five brothers and one sister and grew up in an exceptionally athletic environment. His father, Cy Saenz, was a boxing promoter and owned the Culver City Boxing Arena, which was built on family property inherited from Cy's father, Jesus.[74] According to Edwin's son, Edward D. Saenz, with whom Mario Longoria spoke with and exchanged correspondence over the years regarding his father's background and football career, he initially emphasized that the highlight of his father's life was his family and provided some very interesting family history. He writes:

Edwin Mathew Saenz was born on September 21, 1922, and raised in Culver City and Venice, California. His grandfather, Jesus Saenz, migrated from Mexico in the 1880s. He became the first postmaster of Palms, California and owned extensive property in West Los Angeles and Long Beach. His paternal grandmother was descended from a Spanish soldier named Manuel Valenzuela, who disembarked from a Spanish ship at Santa Barbara, California in 1780 to claim a royal land grant. His mother Rose, from the Peralta family, was also from the early Southern California settlers, from the days of the Dons.[75]

The Saenz family was very prominent in Southern California and like their father Cy, the Saenz brothers were all boxers at one time or another, but they did not limit themselves to the ring. The oldest, Gabriel, went to California Polytechnic University and excelled as the college's starting quarterback. Manuel, a wiry lightweight, showed his reach, quick reaction, and wallop as one of the all-time volleyball greats of Southern California. Daniel, in turn, was the boxer who saw the most action in the ring and the only one to fight professionally. Ernie, like Gabriel, was a star quarterback at both Santa Monica City College and Santa Barbara State University.[76]

And then there was Eddie. He took to football with the vengeance and heart of a boxer. Eddie knew about being game and how to fight. He began his collegiate football career at Loyola University of Los Angeles, where he played from 1940 to 1942. These early seasons were developmental ones for the elusive Saenz. They were competitive and successful, as the *New York Times* reported their victory and Saenz's mishap at the beginning of a particular game:

> A fighting Loyola football team came from behind with five minutes left to play today to upset a heavily favored University of San Francisco Tigers 7 to 2 at Kezar Stadium before 12,000 fans. Victory came after the Tigers three times had missed field goals by inches. With the Loyola attack apparently halted on their opponents' 31, fullback Vince Pacewic fired a pass to End Carl Sweeters on the 10 and [he] stumbled across the goal line. Halfback John McCaffery converted.... Loyola halfback Eddie Saenz slipped in his own end zone in the opening minutes of the game to provide San Francisco the initial two-point advantage.[77]

The war was on, and shortly after the season ended, Eddie Saenz entered a U.S. Naval Reserve Program and was assigned to the V-12 program at University of Southern California (USC) in 1943. Saenz's football skills developed further, and he was an even more potent threat than when he played at Loyola.

As a student at USC, Eddie Saenz led the Trojans through battle after battle as their leading ground gainer. In 1943, he was instrumental in helping USC win the Pacific Coast Conference Championship with spectacular performances against UCLA, St. Mary's College, the University of San Francisco, and the University of California. Against UCLA, Saenz romped 86 yards for a score and returned a UCLA punt 40 yards for another. In the St. Mary's contest, he returned an interception 39 yards to set up a Trojans score. And against the Dons he sped 43 yards for a touchdown. Saenz sparked an offensive drive with runs that led the Trojans to a score versus the Golden Bears.[78] He also shined against the Washington Huskies in a game that ended 29–0 in favor of the men of Troy. In 1944, USC earned a trip to the Rose Bowl, and Saenz's participation earned him the distinction of being the first Mexican American to play in the classic. Prior to the start of the next collegiate season, Eddie Saenz's gridiron success was nationally recognized by the *Official National Collegiate Athletic Association Football Guide and Official Rules*, as he appeared on the publication's cover, illustrating an exciting moment from the Rose Bowl.[79]

Saenz's meteoric career was interrupted by the war as he enlisted in the Navy shortly after his heroics in Pasadena. He was sent to Illinois to train at the Great Lakes Naval Training Center, where his reputation as a player preceded him. Shortly after arriving, he began training, both for naval service and as center for the football team. During that period, many military installations fielded teams that played competitive collegiate schedules. Saenz's teammates at Great Lakes included Paul E. Brown and Ara Parseghian. Brown later became owner and coach of the Cleveland Browns of the National Football League—for those who wondered where the team got its name—and would later also own and coach the Cincinnati Bengals. Parseghian became the legendary football coach of the Northwestern Wildcats and the Fighting Irish of the University of Notre Dame.

When the 1944 season opened against Fort Sheridan, Saenz was nursing an ankle injury.[80] Though used sparingly, he drew first blood on the season, scampering around left end for an 11-yard touchdown run as the Bluejackets demolished their opponents, 62–0.[81] As his injuries healed, he saw more action. Against Western Michigan, he scored another touchdown, this one on a short dive into the end zone that apparently delighted fans who had heard of this young Mexican American's California successes. The game was a prelude to the anticipated tussle against the University of Wisconsin. The *Great Lakes Bulletin* reported that the Bluejackets looked forward to playing the Badgers and that this game marked the second meeting of the teams during the war. Wisconsin had upset Great Lakes two years previous at Soldier Field in Chicago, 13–7.[82] Saenz had an exceptional game against the Badgers in Madison as the *New York Times* reported, "Great Lakes roared back from its defeat by Ohio State last week to smother Wisconsin's young Badgers, 40–12 … Saenz scored three times.[83]

Chicago Tribune reporter Irving Vaughan saw this performance a little differently. He wrote, "In the last few minutes of the opening period, the sailors from the Great Lakes, particularly Jim Mello and Eddie Saenz, moved the ball from their own 20 yard line to the Badgers' one yard line. In the first play of the second quarter, Saenz was stopped, but he tried again, and this time slipped through Wisconsin's right guard for the score." As it turned out, Saenz was just getting started. In the third quarter, he scored on two runs, one from the 40-yard line. The other was described by the *Tribune* as follows: "The sailors recovered a Badger fumble on their own 23-yard line. Four rushing plays later, the ball was spotted on the Wisconsin 25-yard line. Saenz took a lateral from quarterback Jim Youel and charged the remaining 21 yards for the touchdown."[84] In spite of his late-season start, his rushing in the Wisconsin game advanced Saenz to the high end of the team's stats. He was second in scoring and rushing. His 135 yards against Wisconsin increased his season rushing yardage to 288 yards on 36 carries, and his three touchdowns moved him to 30 points, second only to Jim Mello. Saenz started at halfback the rest of the season in games against Third Air Force, Marquette, Fort Warren, and Notre Dame. He scored against Marquette on a 9-yard run as Great Lakes finished the season with an impressive 9–2–1 record. Saenz finished third on the team in scoring with 36 points and second in rushing with 465 yards. He accumulated 569 total yards and was named one of the three most valuable players on the now-legendary Great Lakes Team.[85]

A month after finishing the season, in January of 1945, Saenz received his orders and shipped out to the West Coast.[86] While on duty, he received news of his selection as the 13th-round draft choice of the Washington Redskins. The annual NFL collegiate draft was held on April 6, 1945.[87] Given the circumstances, it would be some time before he could play in the NFL. More than a year later, the speedy Culver City native signed with the Redskins. The *Los Angeles Times* reported:

Edwin "Eddie" Saenz, 1946 (Pro Football Hall of Fame).

> Eddie Saenz, star halfback at Loyola, Southern California and the Great Lakes Naval Training Station in the last several years, was signed yesterday by George Preston Marshall to play pro football for

the Washington Redskins during the next three years.... "He is the fastest man, I've ever signed to the Redskins, said Marshall in Washington yesterday"[88]

In 1946, Seaman Saenz joined the Redskins, and he played six seasons in Washington. In the days when few Latinos lived or worked in the nation's capital, Saenz is remembered for his quickness and his ability to evade the defensive protection schemes of so many NFL teams. He was frequently on the receiving end of Sammy Baugh passes. In 1947, Saenz claimed the title as the NFL's most dangerous kickoff and punt return specialist. He returned 29 kickoffs for 797 yards and two scores. His longest jaunt was 94 yards, a feat he accomplished twice during that campaign. The first return was against the Philadelphia Eagles, who featured another Latino running back named Steve Van Buren. This is historically significant for the Latino American pro football experience because Steve Van Buren was Honduran-born and Eddie Saenz was of Mexican ancestry. The *New York Times* recounted the high-scoring game as follows:

> The Eagles and Redskins smashed all NFL scoring records today with the Eagles finishing on the long end of a 45–42 count before a crowd of 35,400 at Municipal Stadium. In piling up a total of 87 points and topping the previous high of 70 by Green Bay and the Chicago Cardinals in 1942.... But Steve Van Buren personally conducted the Eagles back into the lead on a 95-yard kick-off return before the half ended.... Each team scored twice in the third, the Skins counting on the opening kick-off as Eddie Saenz raced 94 yards with the ball.[89]

Later, in a game versus the New York Giants, noted *New York Times* sportswriter Joseph Sheehan described Saenz's second kickoff return for a touchdown:

> Paced by the incomparable Sammy Baugh and the mercurial Eddie Saenz, the Washington Redskins sent the New York Giants down to their second straight NFL defeat 28–20.... After a New York threat fizzled, Baugh hit Saenz with a long pass and the fleet Californian galloped the last 40 yards of a 74-yard pass untouched, to make it 21–7 in the third period. In the final quarter, Saenz took the next kick-off on his 6-yard line, burst into the clear on the 20 and went all the way, four blockers convoying him past Ken Strong and into the end zone.[90]

Saenz's career in the pros also featured difficulties. Injuries cut his career short at the end of the 1951 season. And although he never publicly complained about it, he was also at the receiving end of a lot of anti–Mexicano discrimination. His son, Edward D. Saenz, in 1985 mentioned that these incidents bothered his father, who did not care for the nickname "Tortilla," which was listed in the team's 1947 and 1951 media guides. Edward recalled that his father did not like the moniker, but it was beyond his control. In 1948, the *Los Angeles Times* discussed Eddie Saenz's contract holdout but did not specify the reason(s) for his actions. The newspaper story finished on a positive note, stating, "Washington's stock zoomed sharply upward on the pro pigskin market yesterday when Eddie Saenz, the holdout halfback, signed his 1948 Redskin ticket."[91] The story described Saenz' background with verbiage that can only be considered derogatory:

> The speedy Spaniard from Culver City was adamant to the bitter end, and wasn't even listed on the Redskins roster, but when the team came to town Sunday, Senor Saenz couldn't stand it any longer. Smiling somewhat sheepishly, but glad to be back with the gang, dark-eyed Eddie was on hand yesterday when Coach Turk Edwards called the first workout at the Occidental College Training camp.[92]

In six productive seasons (1946–1951) with the Redskins, Saenz caught 84 passes for 1,327 yards, rushed 190 times for 619 yards, returned punts for 643 yards, and returned 93 kickoffs for 2,191 yards.

After finishing his gridiron career, Eddie Saenz—not one to seek the mundane or the ordinary—returned to California and became a noted stuntman in the motion picture industry. Westerns were at their peak, and Saenz was a fights and falls specialist, working as a double for Tyrone Power, Steve Cochran, Anthony Quinn, Charles Bronson, and others.[93] Edwin "Eddie" Mathew Saenz died on April 28, 1971, survived by his wife Helen, eight sons, and one daughter. But his football exploits against numerous college opponents, against a host of NFL teams, and against numerous celluloid bad guys are all remembered. Eddie Saenz was a great talent with an illustrious career that to date has not been properly honored and recognized.[94]

Steve Van Buren

Mario Longoria's first inquiry into the personal history and football career of Latino Steve Van Buren resulted in a four-page letter from Mr. Jim Gallagher, Director of Public Relation for the Philadelphia Eagles. Mr. Gallagher provided personal information as well as brief collegiate and pro football information on Van Buren. The information revealed personal insights that normally are not included in profiles. Nonetheless, the information provided access into Van Buren the person, football player, and Hall of Famer. This starting point provided the impetus to further research into a man who was born in Honduras, migrated to the United States, and after his youth in Louisiana, achieved the ultimate honor in professional football. Gallagher's information, it appears, was based on an interview he did with Van Buren. He wrote:

> Born in Tela, Spanish Honduras, [Steve Van Buren] was the son of a fruit inspector for one of the large American Fruit Companies. His remembrance of his parents and his early life in Honduras is extremely vague—practically non-existence. His earliest recol-

lections are of New Orleans and his life with his grandparents. While he is loath to talk about his boyhood days, casual conversations with him lead one to believe his boyhood surroundings smack strongly of the Tobacco Road atmosphere. Apparently his grandparents' interest in the boy ceased after they made sure he did all the chores and odd jobs about the house. Aside from this, they apparently exercised little or no supervision over the boy's habits or the manner in which he spent the little time he had.[95]

Mr. Gallagher's letter also includes Steve Van Buren's birthday, December 28, 1920, and indicates that the family moved first to La Ceiba when he was around two, and finally to New Orleans by age seven. He also indicates that Steve Van Buren remembers little about his past and suggests this was probably due to unpleasant memories or his conviction not to recall the past. We also discovered that Steve's mother was of Spanish ancestry and that he attended Warren Easton High School in New Orleans, where he played football and in his senior year earned an athletic scholarship to LSU.[96] Mr. Gallagher documents an incident involving Steve and his grandmother that provides a rather graphic picture of life with his grandparents:

> There was a time when his grandmother stopped him just as he was leaving the house to play with some of the neighborhood boys, and insisted that he clean up the backyard, which, according to Steve, was always littered with rubbish. To even the score with his grandmother for interfering with his plans for the afternoon, Steve stole the old Lady's spectacles, and buried them in the same back yard. For two months the old grandmother was unable to read the newspaper or do her knitting and sewing, and lived in a word of semi-darkness. At the end of that time young Steve made a bargain with her. In return for permission to go fishing, he revealed the hiding place of the spectacles.[97]

At this point, the young Steve Van Buren was about to attend high school, but not because of his grandparents' influence. Gallagher states, "This effort at early education was apparently the insistence by local authorities and not from any interest in the matter by Van Buren's grandparents."[98]

Van Buren's transition from grade school to high school was interrupted by the presence of an unnamed uncle who came to live with the family. Mr. Gallagher refers to him as a frustrated character and unsuccessful prizefighter who saw the young Van Buren as the one family member who might win big in that sport. Steve recounted his uncle's misguided preparations to train him as a pugilist:

> From Steve's description, it was understood why his uncle never attained any prominence in the ring. He taught him nothing but flailing way at another boy. Steve recalls the boy used to beat him until he ran out of breath, while Steve, whose wind was a little better, would beat the other boy until both were exhausted.[99]

Thereafter, Steve Van Buren entered high school and received his introduction to competitive athletics. He played baseball and football, but preferred the gridiron because he felt it taught him valuable lessons:

Steve Van Buren, 1944 (Pro Football Hall of Fame).

He became the star of the eleven and learned another lesson. If he wanted a good dinner, which seems to have been something of a rarity at home, he would go on strike, and refuse to report for practice. The high school coach would go into the huddle with him, find out what was troubling him, buy him a good chicken dinner, and Steve would be out for practice the following day.[100]

The arrangement served Van Buren well as he entered Louisiana State University, although by that time he had learned to demand more than just chicken dinners for his football prowess.[101]

2. Slowly Moving the Ball Down the Field 93

Van Buren's childhood was far from normal and was tragic in many ways. He was born in Honduras, which grants him a Latino birthright. He lived there only a short period of time, but there is no available documented recollection of his parents during the seven years he lived in Honduras. All the more mysterious are the parents, grandparents, and uncle who are part of his family but have no names listed. The omissions are intriguing and lead one to wonder about the actual circumstances of his early life.

Curious to know more about his early life in Honduras and New Orleans we interviewed Steve Van Buren in May of 1996. His contact information was provided by the Eagles organization. He was living in Ben Salem, Pennsylvania. He responded to questions and provided brief information during the telephone conversation:

> Both [of my] parents were from the United States, and my father worked for the United Fruit Company. I was born in Tela, Honduras, and we later moved to La Ceiba when I was very young. My brother Ebert Van Buren was also born in La Ceiba, and I have not seen him in many years. The last time I saw Ebert was the time I was sick. Ebert lived somewhere in Louisiana but I did not know for sure.... I attended Warren Easton High School in New Orleans, played on the football team, and received a football scholarship to LSU to play the end position.[102]

The rest of the interview was lively and friendly. He talked about initially being used as a blocking back at LSU in a single-wing offense and additionally playing linebacker and on special teams. He got his brother a scholarship to LSU and also helped him get selected in the NFL draft by the Philadelphia Eagles. Van Buren recalled he had established the NFL record for most rushing touchdowns in a single season—18—and talked about the 1949 championship game against the Los Angeles Rams. "We played in the mud, and this was my best game because I rushed for 196 yards. The Rams had Van Brocklin and others who are now in the Hall of Fame, but we beat them."[103]

Also, he informed me, "Yo hablo un poco Espanol." He demonstrated this ability during an interview he did with Telemundo in November 1993,[104] in conjunction with the National celebration of Hispanic Heritage Month. We were pleased that he brought up the fact that he was aware of the language of his birthplace. Our discussion was insightful and generated information similar to Gallagher's work. Van Buren again did not provide specifics about his family, the reasons are personal and should be left at that.[105]

At LSU, Steve Van Buren's first two football seasons (1941–1942) were primarily in a supporting role on offense. The LSU Tigers were a successful team, recording 11 victories and seven losses over the two seasons. They were nowhere near to competing in post-season games, however. Tigers head coach Ernie Moore admitted that he should have moved Van Buren from blocking back to the tailback position sooner to better utilize his speed and elusiveness.

In 1943, Steve Van Buren's senior year, he became their star tailback and began the season by scoring four touchdowns in a 34–27 win over Georgia, including the game-winning score with less than two minutes to play. For the remainder of the season, Van Buren and the Tigers ran roughshod with wins over Rice University, Louisiana, Army, Texas Christian University, and Texas A&M. Van Buren rushed for 847 yards and scored 98 points to lead LSU to six wins against three losses, and an invitation to play in the Orange Bowl. His rushing yardage ranked second nationally, and he led the SEC in scoring as well.[106]

In the 1944 Orange Bowl, LSU faced the Texas A&M Aggies for the second time in the season—losing during the season, but winning the bowl game, 19–14. Steve Van Buren was the star of the contest.[107] The *New York Times* account highlighted Van Buren's plays that resulted in two first quarter scores and the apparent winning score in the third period.

> The second period rocked with a few offensive fireworks as the Aggies threw back several LSU drives, but the colorful throng was brought to its feet three plays after the start of the second half when Van Buren again tore apart the Aggie defense. Smashing off his right tackle, the pile-driving star burst into the secondary to cover 63 yards for the Tigers' final touchdown.[108]

The Aggies scored in the first and third quarters. The first score was a pass play from Hallmark to quarterback Red Burditt. Their second tally was a 3-yard run by end Marion Settegast. Statistically, the Aggies completed 14 of 32 passes for 199 yards, but compared to Van Buren's 172 rushing yards it was not enough to afford A&M the victory.[109]

The next football chapter for Steve Van Buren was the NFL draft of collegiate players. It was anticipated that he would be a first-round selection, and on April 19, 1944, Philadelphia selected him as their number one draft choice.[110] For the next eight years (1944–1951), he outran, eluded, and ran over NFL defensive players to lead the Eagles to three divisional titles (1947–1949) and two NFL championships (1948–1949), and in the process, established league rushing and scoring titles that earned him a well-deserved induction into the Pro Football Hall of Fame in 1965.

The following are highlights of his career. In 1944, the Eagles finished in second place with a 7-1-2 record. Van Buren quickly adjusted to the "T" formation and began to perfect its operation. In wins against the Brooklyn Tigers, 21–7, and the New York Giants, 38–17, Van Buren scored four of his seven touchdowns in his rookie season. The *New York Times* described Van Buren's efforts:

> With the Eagles running from the T at all times, the one person who hurt the Tigers most was the Louisiana State rookie, Steve Van Buren, whose weak-side reverses were good for repeated gains. Van Buren scored two Philadelphia touchdowns, the second

on a 71-yard dash through the better-than-average Brooklyn line, late in the opening period.[111]

In the November game versus the New York Giants, Van Buren led the charge once again:

> The main offender in this respect was the light-footed Steve Van Buren, former Louisiana State University star, who scored two of the five touchdowns the Eagles made, and who covered 129 yards the nineteen times he was called upon to carry the ball.[112]

In the 1945 season, the Eagles finished 7–3 and Van Buren led the NFL in rushing for the first time with 832 yards and scored 110 points. The contests against the Pittsburgh Steelers and the Boston Yanks were banner performances for Van Buren. The *New York Times* reported:

> Steve Van Buren, the National Football League's leading ground gainer, scored two touchdowns today to lead the injury-riddled Philadelphia Eagles to a 30–6 victory over the Pittsburgh Steelers.[113]

Opposing the Boston Yanks in the season finale, Van Buren firmly established his place in the NFL record book. According to the *New York Times*:

> Steve Van Buren tallied tree touchdowns, placed-kicked two extra points and gained an even 100 yards as the Eagles walloped the Boston Yanks, 35–7, in the season finale, before 27,905 fans at Shibe Park today ... and yet there was consolation to the achievement of Van Buren who, in addition to clinching the individual ground-gaining championship of the league, 832 yards, wound up the campaign with a total of 110 points which gave him first place in that department over Green Bay's Don Hutson.... Van Buren established an all-time record for most touchdowns in a single season.[114]

In the 1946 season, the Eagles finished in second place for the third straight year with a 6–5 record.[115] Van Buren's statistics were less impressive than in the two previous campaigns, with only 529 total rushing yards and five touchdowns. However, the next year the Eagles made great strides and reached the NFL championship game, only to fall short. The Chicago Cardinals, who beat Philadelphia during the regular season, produced another victory, this time by the score of 28–21. Still, Van Buren led the league with 1,008 rushing yards to break the single-season record of 1,004 set by Beattie Feathers with the Chicago Bears in 1934.[116]

Also historically significant for the Latino pro football experience was the season opener at Shibe Park when the Philadelphia Eagles faced the Washington Redskins on September 28, 1947. First, the 12 touchdowns scored in the game set an NFL record, surpassing the previous high of 11 touchdowns established by the Green Bay Packers and the Chicago Cardinals in 1942.[117] Playing for the Washington Redskins was Mexican American halfback Eddie Saenz, from Culver City. Saenz played his collegiate football at USC and signed with the Redskins in 1945. Although both Van Buren and Saenz were unaware of the Latino birthright and ethnic backgrounds that bound them, the two halfbacks ran back kickoff returns for touchdowns in the contest. The first was a spectacular 95-yard return by Van Buren just before the half ended. On the opening kickoff of the third quarter, Eddie Saenz responded to Van Buren's run and raced, in the same spectacular manner, 94 yards for the score.[118] At the conclusion of the 1947 NFL season, Washington's Saenz ended up as the league's kickoff return leader with 797 yards and two touchdowns, while his Latino counterpart Van Buren led the NFL in rushing yardage.[119]

The following year, the Philadelphia Eagles claimed their first NFL Championship, defeating the Chicago Cardinals, 7–0, in a blinding snowstorm at Shibe Park. The Eagles amassed an overall season record of 10 wins, 2 losses, and 1 tie. The *New York Times* described the setting and outcome of the championship game:

> A driving snow storm providing a 4-inch fall that completely covered the gridiron eliminated any pretense of a true football test.... However do not say that in the presence of any faithful Philadelphia followers. Wet, cold, and uncomfortable though they might have been, they were happy because, on this snow-bound afternoon in the City of Brotherly love, a 16-year-old dream came true. The Eagles won their first.... World Championship by defeating the defending champion Cardinals 7–0.[120]

Statistically, Van Buren was held scoreless in the championship game until the start of the fourth quarter, when the sloshing and slipping in the snow for Van Buren was no longer a problem. The *New York Times* narrated the game's lone scoring drive:

> On a quarterback sneak, Thompson went for the first down but was stopped short. It was then that Van Buren, former Louisiana State star, turned the trick. Taking the handoff from Thompson, Van Buren crashed outside his right tackle and reached the end zone. Right then and there the Cardinals were beaten. The game's lone touchdown was fashioned in 0.53 of the fourth quarter. The remaining 14 minutes and 7 seconds saw the Eagles maintaining possession most of the time.[121]

The 1949 season was a year of change for the Eagles organization. The owner, Alexis Thompson, sold the team for $250,000 to a syndicate headed by businessman James P. Clark. During the transition, the Eagles drafted future Hall of Famer Chuck Bednarik to strengthen their offensive line. The Eagles won their third consecutive division title and repeated as NFL champs. Along the way, Van Buren collected his fourth NFL rushing title.[122] In the championship game, played in the Los Angeles Coliseum, the Eagles played in the mud rather than the snow and proceeded to blank the Los Angeles Rams, 14–0. The game's notable players included Eagles quarterback Tommy Thompson, ends Pete Pihos and Leo Sklahany, and halfback Clyde Scott, but the real star of the championship game, although he did not score, is cited in a *New York Times* article:

2. Slowly Moving the Ball Down the Field 97

> ...Van Buren, the Bull of the Bayous of Louisiana State, carried the ball thirty-one times and plagued the Rams with an accumulation of 196 yards gained. Twice Van Buren uncorked crushing gains that set up scoring opportunities.[123]

The Los Angeles Rams, on the other hand, credited Van Buren's rushing efforts and stated that they played both the Eagles and the weather with little success.[124] The Rams managed to accumulate only 119 yards of total offense as the game ended on a missed 45-yard field goal by Bob Waterfield.[125] Interestingly, Rams receiver Tom Fears, who is also a Latino, led the NFL in pass receptions in 1949, but was limited to only two receptions in the championship game for 15 yards.[126]

In Van Buren's final years (1950–1951), the constant pounding and crushing tackles took their toll. According to the *Victoria Advocate*, this punishment was a factor in decreased productivity. "Back, leg and neck injuries began to take a toll on Van Buren. In 1950, he broke a toe in the 1950 off-season and suffered a series of bone spurs that caused him to miss the pre-season games and season-opener."[127] Although the injuries continued, Van Buren led the NFL in carries but did not repeat as the rushing leader. In 1951, he played alongside his brother Ebert Van Buren, whom the Eagles selected in the draft, but his football playing days were numbered. He concluded his pro football career during the training camp period prior to the start of the 1952 campaign.

With his playing days over, Van Buren returned to football in a coaching capacity. He served as a head coach, a backfield coach, vice-president and director of player personnel for several minor league football organizations. Theses included the Atlantic Coast Football League (ACFL), the Continental Football League (CFL), and the North American Football League (NAFL). His leadership in the associations mentioned produced two championships, in 1962 and 1963. His coaching career ended in 1970.[128]

In 1965 Van Buren was inducted in the Pro Football Hall of Fame, another well-deserved honor in addition to being part of the AP All-Time Southeastern Conference Team (1950), the Louisiana State University Athletic Hall of Fame (1944), and the Louisiana Sports Hall of Fame (1961). The recognition and honors bestowed on Van Buren were numerous and meaningful. It appears he was also a man of few words, and according to his Pro Football Hall of Fame profile, his enshrinement speech consisted of only four sentences. Hall of Famer Clarke Hinkle introduced Steve Van Buren at the ceremony in Canton, Ohio. He thanked Mr. Hinkle and said:

> Thank you, Clarke Hinkle, I am glad to have broken your record. Since you people can't hear too good and I am not too good a speaker, I won't say much, but it's a great honor to be here. The two days I've spent in Canton will certainly bring me back every year from now on. Thank you very much.[129]

American football history remembers Steve Van Buren's career vividly. His childhood was far from normal, as best it can be assessed from available records, but his athletic career, although sketchy at first, transformed into a great one. The Steve Van Buren interview we conducted, although now many years ago, portrayed him differently from what was read and heard about him over the years. He was a common man, simple and easy-going. He was also direct in his responses. His mannerisms reminded us of men in the Latino culture that partially explains his privacy and short responses to questions, and possibly explains his short enshrinement speech and other matters pertaining to his early life. Nonetheless, he was a great professional football player who also happened to be a big part of the Latino professional football experience. Mr. Steve van Buren died on August 23, 2012, in Lancaster, Pennsylvania, at the age of 91.

Tom Jesse (Valdes) Fears

The Thomas Jesse Fears football story is unique and diverse because it involves many influences and experiences common to Latinos in the United States. It is a special history unknown to most football aficionados, including Latinos, and it must be recorded and given its proper acclaim. Mario Longoria did not know that Tom Fears was Latino until after he researched and published his first football book, *Athletes Remembered: Mexicano/Latino Professional Football Players, 1929–1970*. The book was published in 1997, and Longoria was on a book tour in Southern California, visiting area university campuses to present the Latino collegiate and professional football story. The book tour was arranged by his mentor, Dr. Rodolfo Acuna, noted Chicano historian and tenured professor at California State University—Northridge.

Shortly after presenting at his alma mater and the University of Southern California, he visited with a group of professors, students, and community people at California State University–Los Angeles, in March 1998. The attendees were cordial and very interested in the book. They asked many questions regarding the reasons for writing the manuscript and why such players had been ignored in the standard histories of the sport. One encounter involved a conversation with an elderly Latino gentleman in Spanish. He congratulated Longoria on the book and shared some information that opened his eyes and further stimulated his research. The informant stated that there was one very important football player not included in the work: Tom Fears. He stated, "He ... [had] an Anglo last name but [was] a great collegiate and professional football player." Longoria thanked him for the information, shortly thereafter discovered Tom Fears' significance, and understood why the elderly gentleman wanted Fears included. The Tom Fears discovery was an important revelation because the Latino gentleman also brought out the idea of an oral history in the Mexican American community of Los Angeles that recalls their sports heroes while the standard media and sports institutions overlook or present incomplete information about athletes from diverse communities.

Research uncovered that Thomas Jesse (Valdes) Fears was born in Mexico, grew up in a Japanese American neighborhood in Los Angeles, played collegiately at Santa Clara and UCLA, served in the U.S. Army Air Force during World War II, played professionally with the Los Angeles Rams, coached 16 years in the NFL and World Football League, and is now enshrined in Canton. The story begins with initial research information obtained from a telephone conversation with his widow, Louella Fears, on January 19, 2000, just two weeks after his passing (January 4, 2000) in Palm Desert, California. She stated that their marriage lasted 48 years and that she appreciated the telephone call. Louella answered questions regarding her husband's mother, Carmen Valdes. We thanked her and advised that a follow-up letter would arrive shortly. Unfortunately, there was never a reply.[130] Nonetheless, it is clear that Fears' story begins south of the Rio Grande.

Thomas Jesse Fears was born in Guadalajara, Jalisco, Mexico, on December 3, 1922. According to newspaper and other materials, the Fears' family lived in Mexico approximately six years before migrating to the United States. The sources do not specify any details concerning the family's years in Mexico. In 1975, *Los Angeles Times* sportswriter Earl Gustkey wrote an article about Coach Fears and mentioned that he "is the son of an American mining engineer—Charles William Fears; a Mexican Mother—Carmen Valdes; and an older brother—Charles William Fears, Jr."[131] The young Fears boys lived in a remote Mexican mining town (unnamed), and by 1930 their domicile was a one-story, two-bedroom structure in Los Angeles situated in a Japanese-American neighborhood.[132] Gustkey also mentioned that Fears' boyhood was spent emulating his older brother, Charles Fears, Jr., a football star at UCLA and played in the 1943 Rose Bowl. Gustkey added that Charles was also the university's heavyweight boxing champion.[133] Tom was two years younger than Charles, and it is safe to surmise that he anxiously awaited his time to embark on an equally stellar athletic career.

During his grammar and high school years, Tom Fears worked in numerous capacities to earn a little money. According to sources, he washed cafeteria trays to pay for his lunch. At Easter time, he unloaded Easter Lily boxes from trucks at the wholesale market and made 25 cents an hour. At the Los Angeles Coliseum, the youngster worked as an usher, earning 50 cents a day.[134] In between these jobs, however, he found time to play football and continue his academic pursuits at Los Angeles' Manual Arts High School. The future Hall of Famer recalled how his schoolboy Japanese American friends helped him develop his football skills:

The Japanese kids I knew were good, tough athletes. My best friend when I was in high school was a guy named Jerry Tageri. He got shipped out with his family to some camp after Pearl Harbor. I never saw him again. It was disgraceful the way the Japanese-Americans were treated during the war."[135]

In high school, Tom Fears filled out to a strapping 6'2", 200-pound player who became a star, achieving All-Southern California recognition. Not surprisingly, he was heavily recruited by most of the major football universities on the West Coast. As a devout and practicing Catholic, "he narrowed his choices to St. Mary's College of California and Santa Clara University, finally choosing the latter."[136] Fears attended and played football at Santa Clara for one or two seasons in either 1941 or 1942. Records indicate that Santa Clara did not play football in 1943–1944, which happened to correspond to Fears being drafted into the U.S. Army Air Corps.[137]

Tom Fears trained to become a pilot. Contemporary newspaper accounts and other sources reported that his father was taken prisoner by the Japanese and that this, in part, influenced his decision to join the military. The elder Fears was a civilian working in the Philippines when war broke out. The Japanese captured and sent him to Camp Holmes near Baguio, Philippines, where they held more than 500 Americans. His father's capture was first reported to the International Committee of the Red Cross on December 28, 1943. He was imprisoned for 20 months and ultimately returned home after cessation of hostilities.[138] It was with such concerns that Tom Fears entered the military. However, due to his football talent, the Army Air Corps authorities did not issue him combat orders. Instead he was assigned flight instructor duties at Colorado Springs Flight School and captained the 2nd Army Air Corps Super Bombers football team.[139]

In the spring of 1945, while Fears was still in the Army, the Cleveland Rams drafted him as a defensive back in the 11th round.[140] However, Fears thought seriously about his opportunity to become a professional football player. Earl Gustkey quoted Fears saying about the decision, "At first they offered me a $5,000 salary. But after they [the Rams] moved to Los Angeles, they were afraid of making UCLA upset. I'd made a commitment to play for UCLA after the war."[141] When World War II ended, Tom Jesse Fears kept his commitment to UCLA and in 1946 and 1947 produced a great deal for the Bruins. Under the leadership of Bert La Brucherie, the 1946 UCLA squad finished 10–1, captured the Pacific Coast Conference Championship, and played the University of Illinois in the Rose Bowl.[142] The Bruins were no match for the Fighting Illini and lost, 45–14. The 1947 squad was not as successful. The Bruins posted a 5–4 record and finished fourth in the Pacific Coast Conference.[143] Post-season accolades for Tom Fears included his selection to the 1946–1947 All-Coast and the 1947 All-Pacific Coast Conference Team(s),[144] as well as being named to the 1947 *New York Sun* All-America Team.[145]

2. Slowly Moving the Ball Down the Field   101

The next football stop for the talented young man was nearby, as the Rams had just moved to southern California. Fears was the first Mexican-born and second Latino player to be drafted into the NFL. Other firsts included: first Mexican-born player on NFL Champion team and first Mexican-born/ Latino Pro Football Hall of Famer. In his nine NFL seasons, Tom Fears caught 400 passes for 5,397 yards and 38 touchdowns. He led the league in receptions each of his first three NFL seasons with marks of 51, 77, and 84. In 1950, Rams quarterback Bob Waterfield and Fears spearheaded a playoff victory over the Chicago Bears, 24–14, with the end hauling in three touchdown receptions.[146] The following season, the Rams captured their third straight conference title and proceeded to defeat the defending champion Cleveland Browns at the Coliseum, 24–17. The margin of victory came in the form of a fourth quarter, 73-pass from Van Brocklin to Fears.[147] An *Associated Press* article in the *San Antonio Express* described the action:

> Los Angeles' spectacular Rams sweeping high on a tie-breaking 73-yard touchdown pass in the final quarter, captured the national League championship Sunday from the Cleveland Browns in a battle that belted the visitors out of a six-year rule in profes-

Tom Jesse (Valdes) Fears hauling in a pass, 1948 (Pro Football Hall of Fame).

sional football. The score was 24–17. Tommy Fears of the Rams, racing at mad speed down the field, gathered in a tremendous pass thrown by Norman Van Brocklin, Rams quarterback, and tore on to complete the day's longest play that sent the Rams off the field with a triumph and their first championship since the club moved here from Cleveland in 1946.... That one long throw ended the Browns' complete domination of the old National Football League and marked the first time they have been defeated in a title game in a string stretching back to 1946, when they became the rulers of the now-defunct All American Football Conference.[148]

Starting in 1952, the Los Angeles Rams underwent coaching and other changes. Head coach Joe Stydahar was replaced by Hampton Pool in 1953, and he was followed by Sid Gillman in 1955.[149] The Rams had winning records through 1955, when they again won the conference title but lost to the Browns for the championship, 38–14.[150] An excerpt from the *Rams 1956 Press Book*— Tom Fears' last active season—described the previous campaign:

> Fears had a great year in 1955. His 44 receptions tied him for fourth among all NFL pass catchers and resulted in his best season since 1952. Holder of two NFL receiving records, Fears has been a standout for the Rams since joining the club in 1948. He established NFL marks of most passes caught in one game—19 vs. Green bay in 1950 and most for one season—84 in 1950. With the retirement of team mate Don Paul, Fears now ranks as the oldest Ram on the team.[151]

The Los Angeles Rams had a losing record (4–8–0) in 1956, and Fears played in only two games, spending most of the time recovering from injuries. No doubt, the physical punishment of the years of gridiron battles was now apparent. Although Fears physically intimidated many defensive players over the years, he remembered a few of his opponents who helped to wear down his body, including Hardy Brown of the San Francisco 49ers, Don Shula of the Cleveland Browns, and the Philadelphia Eagles' Chuck Bednarik.[152]

Tom Fears had a brilliant career as a receiver, but he was not yet finished with the sport. He considered coaching, and this seemed a natural follow-up. He commented in a newspaper interview that coaching was a matter of luck and circumstance.[153] After retirement, Fears became an assistant coach for Vince Lombardi in 1959.[154] An excerpt from his biography in the *New Orleans Press Book* summed up the start of his coaching career:

> Fears started his coaching career in 1959 at Green Bay under Vince Lombardi, but he switched to Los Angeles Rams in 1960 and 1961. Then he was back at Green Bay in 1962 and remained there through the 1965 season, when he joined the staff of the Atlanta Falcons as chief offensive coach in 1966.[155]

Fears' tenure with the Falcons was limited to one season. He had clashed with Los Angeles Rams head coach George Allen over a matter of insider information that involved an accusation that Allen had attempted to get information from a former player. He was dismissed at season's end by Atlanta and once again, luck and circumstances intervened. In 1967, Tom Fears be-

2. Slowly Moving the Ball Down the Field

came a head coach for the first time when he was hired by the expansion New Orleans Saints.[156] Interestingly, Fears had applied in 1966 for the head coach position with the St. Louis Cardinals but was not selected. With this hiring, Fears became the first Latino head coach in the history of the NFL. Life with the expansion Saints was very challenging, however. Fears coached four years at New Orleans, finishing with a record of 14–40–2. On November 3, 1970, the Saints' front office decided on a coaching change and hired J.D. Roberts.[157] Tom Fears reappeared in 1971 as an offensive coordinator for the Philadelphia Eagles but was terminated at the end of the 1972 season.

These events concluded Fears' NFL coaching career, but there was more to come from the development of a rival professional football league in 1974. Once again, luck and circumstance sought out and found Tom Fears. In 1973, he was absent from football a single year but received attention from the Los Angeles franchise of the newly-formed World Football League (WFL). On January 14, 1974, Fears was named the head coach of the Southern California Sun team that competed in only two seasons (1974–1975) before the league folded in October 1975.[158] Fears guided the Sun to a 20–12 record and a playoff appearance in 1974.[159] Thereafter, he briefly coached at San Bernardino Junior College (1976) and Chapman College Club Football (1980), served as player personnel director of the USFL's Los Angeles Express in 1982, and coached the Milan franchise of the International League of American Football (ILAF) in 1990. In 1976, he was inducted into the College Football Hall of Fame and into the All-Sports Council of Southern California as a tribute to his collegiate football playing days. His coaching legacy, although not much discussed, is evident in the impact he had on a few great receivers along the way. At Green Bay, it was rookie tight end Boyd Dowler, who was the Rookie of the Year in 1959 and Ron Kramer, who became an All-Pro tight end in 1962 and 1963. With the Los Angeles Rams Fears coached ends Del Shofner and Red Phillips, who similarly achieved All-Pro status and credited Fears' tutelage for their success.[160] The crowning achievement for Tom Jesse (Valdes) Fears was his selection to the Pro Football Hall of Fame in 1970. His 46-year association with the sport is remarkable, as well as his record number of per game and season catches. His performances in the big games, including the NFL championship, his pass route techniques, his toughness and competitiveness all contributed to earn him a place in Canton. The remarkable Latino Tom Fears passed away on January 4, 2000, at the age of 77 years old, surrounded by family and friends in Palm Desert, California.

3

The McCarthy Era and the Age of Activism
1951–1970

The decade between 1941 and 1950 witnessed substantial Latino/a participation in the American military effort (both on the home front and overseas) and then an increased stirring of activity to challenge discriminatory practices in various aspects of daily life. Key to the history of Spanish-surnamed athletes' participation on the gridiron (and in other sports) were efforts undertaken to broaden educational and economic prospects. While there were successes, much remained to be done. Although the population of Mexican Americans (by far the largest component of this category) increased substantially in the American Southwest, topping 3.4 million (from 2.3 million a decade earlier) by 1960, their overall economic outlook did not advance in any substantive way.[1] Once again, we turn to the research of Zaragoza Vargas to provide summaries of demographic changes and other circumstances impacting this populace. For example, in regard to employment and financial wherewithal, Vargas indicates that by 1960:

> Sixty percent of this population expansion occurred in California ... [as] Mexican Americans from across the Southwest [came] in search of work and a better life. Texas had the highest density.... [But] Most remained concentrated in the agricultural counties of South Texas, one of America's poorest regions. Here, Mexican Americans lived meager lives in rural slums marked by high infant deaths, a tuberculosis rate seven times that of Anglos, a third-grade level of education, and segregation in public places.... Annual incomes ... averaged less than $3,000. For the small middle classes who took advantage of federal programs such as the GI Bill and the Federal Housing Authority loans ... the postwar years did bring prosperity and change, but discrimination limited social mobility.[2]

In the area of schooling, likewise, there remained many obstructions to attaining even a high school education, and this trend solidified societal impediments that kept many Mexican Americans in the lowest rungs of the economy.

3. The McCarthy Era and the Age of Activism   105

Segregation of school-age Mexican Americans was imposed by Anglo teachers and counselors, who tracked these students into vocational training classes because they shared the prevailing views of Mexican Americans' inherent intellectual inferiority. Those few ... who did gain knowledge and skills did not get jobs, because the employment market blocked people with dark skins and limited English-language skills.... By 1960 three-fourths of those in the Southwest were relegated to manual labor.[3]

To counteract this trend, one of the key sectors of resistance through the mid–1960s targeted often deplorable situations extant in classrooms throughout the Southwest, and particularly in Texas. During the height of the McCarthy era, many of the World War II and Korean War veterans who fought against such practices were branded as Communist agitators; therefore, to preserve their standing in the broader community, they had to tread lightly; quite often following a more conservative bent in their pursuit of modifications. Such efforts led to court cases such as *Mendez v. Westminster* and *Delgado v. Bastrop Independent School District* in the later years of the 1940s. It was hoped that having Spanish-surnamed pupils categorized as "white" would improve their educational level, expand overall opportunities and, ultimately, generate better occupational results. By and large, this did not turn out to be so. We will now present brief examples to demonstrate the status of such students and how they were still disadvantaged in the public scholastic institutions of Texas (in particular) well into the mid–1960s.

Vargas' work notes that one of the brightest lights in this era for Mexican Americans, Congressman Henry B. Gonzalez of San Antonio (while in the Texas Senate), battled constantly and vigorously against attempts by "colleagues" to roll back the Supreme Court's decision of *Brown v. Board of Education*. Although managing to mitigate against some of the more extreme aspects of the Southern Manifesto (the effort to defeat desegregation), the state of Texas had only integrated 75 school districts by 1957. "Nor had segregation in privately owned places of public accommodation and public facilities been eliminated. Signs in restaurant windows and posted at swimming pools remained ... stating: 'No dogs or Mexicans Allowed.'" Even with efforts in the legislature and in courtrooms, in Texas, "the gap between the status of Mexican Americans and that of the dominant group continued to widen ... [they] still suffered economic, educational, and social deprivation."[4]

An even more detailed analysis of efforts to improve academic outcome of Spanish-surnamed pupils in 1950s Texas can be gleaned from the works of Guadalupe San Miguel, Jr., and Thomas H. Kreneck. These scholars have written about endeavors such as the Little Schools of the 400 (to promote English language instruction).[5] San Miguel, a historian of education, takes a more negative view than does Kreneck, who has authored an excellent biography of Felix Tijerina, the man who pushed for the establishment of the Little

Schools of the 400. The courses were designed to provide Mexican American youths with a "head start" on the English language and introduce them to key words so as to prepare them to "succeed" once enrolled in pre-school. Although well-intentioned, results of this undertaking were mixed, and educators keenly concerned with the status of Mexican American children, such as H.T. Manuel and George Sanchez, believed benefits were marginal at best. As Manuel argued, "three months (of English language instruction) can add something to a child's experience, but they cannot make up for six years of privation." Sanchez concurred and stated that "it stretches credulity ... when it is alleged that a few weeks of vocabulary building ... can substitute for the ... years that a Spanish-language child otherwise would have to spend in the first grade!"[6] San Miguel's research goes on to examine aspects of the fight for better schools in Texas in the late 1960s (and beyond). In summary, as far as Spanish-surnamed students in the state were concerned, by the mid–1960s: "80 percent fall two grades behind their Anglo class mates, most were leaving school in their junior high school years and 89 percent were not completing high school."[7] Given a track record such as this, it is no wonder Mexican American athletes were so scarce on the gridiron.

In summary, before the mid–1960s, the primary goal was to get Mexican American students recognized as being "white," thus procuring for them the same treatment as all other students in that category. In some locations, in El Centro, California for example, Mexican Americans would make common cause with African Americans in the effort to desegregate schools. By the latter part of the decade, however, a new and more uncompromising (some would say, revolutionary) tactic would come to the forefront.[8] We now turn briefly to some of the other areas in which this group moved to challenge unfair treatment by coalescing under a new (though not centrally organized) banner: that of the increased militancy of the Chicano Movement.[9] All of these endeavors would ultimately have an impact on what went on, and surrounding, gridirons throughout the nation.

Again, the work of Professor Vargas can serve as a brief guide to the overall history of the Chicano Movement. We certainly do not intend to provide in-depth coverage of this period here, however, it is imperative that we proffer an overall sense of the movement and how it impacted the social significance of what gridiron athletes accomplished (and off-the-field issues as well) between the years 1951 and 1970. An effective place to start ties in with what we've previously discussed regarding the court cases of the late 1940s: how were Mexican Americans to be perceived? Where they "white," or were they "others?" How would this impact the way the wider society viewed this population?

Vargas spends much time discussing the consternation and division caused in the Mexican American community in regard to the repatriation efforts of the early 1950s, such as Operation Wetback and Operation Terror in 1954. The country was in the middle of an economic downturn in this year, and there was a determination to "round up" undocumented Mexicanos. Vargas notes that one of the conundrums of this effort was that "the U.S. government made few attempts to distinguish between American citizens of Mexican descent and ... Mexican aliens." In total, over one million people were removed beyond the Rio Grande. This left many adults penniless in Mexico and often separated parents from their American-born offspring. Beyond the human toll, there was a political premium paid as well: the division between more "conservative" groups, such as LULAC and the AGIF, which "endorsed the roundups," and more "progressive" elements, such as the Community Service Organization (CSO), which "protested loudly."[10] As the Chicano Movement developed, such philosophical divisions would become even more pronounced.

The dread caused by the deportations of, in some cases, persons of Mexican descent born in the United States helped to push for other types of action to break down barriers. For example, in Texas, there had been long-standing policies to exclude Mexican Americans from juries, making it difficult to get fair trials in many locales. In the same year as the actions noted above, a major case took place that helped to challenge discriminatory practices in the state's legal system, as the U.S. Supreme Court handed down the decision, *Hernandez v. the State of Texas*. Here, the tribunal determined that the plaintiff "was denied his rights to equal protection and due process ... because the county in which he lived did not allow Mexican Americans to serve on juries." The court, in keeping with the primary civil rights thrust by this group prior to the mid–1960s, "accepted arguments that ... Anglos treated Mexicans as nonwhites despite the fact that they were actually white."[11]

One final area that we will consider deals with the political ties between Mexican Americans and the Democratic Party. There were a few voices in Congress for this group by the late 1950s: the previously mentioned Henry B. Gonzalez from San Antonio, Edward Roybal from Los Angeles, and Senator Dennis Chavez of New Mexico. There were smatterings of representatives in the Texas and other legislatures, as well as Raymond Telles, who won the mayoralty of El Paso in 1957.[12] In addition, other new groups sprang up in the 1940s and 1950s: the Political Association of Spanish-Speaking Organizations (PASSO) in Texas and the Community Service Organization (CSO) and, later, the Mexican American Political Association (MAPA) in California.[13] Vargas summarizes the overall ties between the community and the Party as follows:

> Many Mexican Americans looked to the liberal wing of the party ... for support. Having come of age during the New Deal, these activists believed that change could come under the watchful eye of a strong and active federal government. Mexican American political influence in national elections derived not so much because of their numer-

ical strength but from their diffusion in Texas, New Mexico, and California, where electoral votes were considered vital.[14]

A further show of solidarity commenced for the 1960 presidential election cycle with the development of "Viva Kennedy" clubs.[15]

Unfortunately, Vargas acknowledges, this support did not translate into dramatic improvement, and by the early to mid–1960s, change was in the offing. "Just as it did with African Americans, … [Democratic Party] defaulted on … promises to Mexican Americans for social reform because it remained firmly beholden to its Southern wing."[16] One flashpoint occurred in the "Spinach Capital" of the Lone Star State, the town of Crystal City. In this locale, comprised of a population that was 80 percent Mexican American, the group had no political power. In 1963, through the work of PASSO, the Teamsters, and others, the community elected five "of their own" as city officials. Although they were voted out in 1965, "the Crystal City revolt was of symbolic importance; it was the starting point of what became known as the Chicano movement."[17] As we will detail an aspect of this revolt, led by Jose Angel Gutierrez and others associated with the *La Raza Unida Party* (The United Race Party, or LRUP), also played out on the gridirons of southern Texas.[18]

Elsewhere, during the mid– to late 1960s, other exertions and leaders came to the forefront. For example, Cesar Chavez and Dolores Huerta were significant in the struggle to organize farm workers and directed the first strike by their union, the United Farmworkers of America, in 1965 in Delano, California. In New Mexico, under the guidance of Reies Lopez Tijerina, the effort centered on the attempt to gain compensation for the descendants of Spanish land grant holders, many of whom had lost their lands through nefarious and legally disreputable means. In Denver, Colorado, under the aegis of Rodolfo "Corky" Gonzalez, the Crusade for Justice sought to confront, among other matters, problems of Mexican Americans living in urban cores.

As a challenge to poor treatment in schools, including a lack of a meaningful curriculum, and empowered by Chicano nationalism and its associated rhetoric, high school students in locales as varied as Los Angeles, Crystal City, and Kansas City (among others) staged "blow outs" to oppose the extant state of affairs. Likewise, at many universities, college students joined in the protest and established entities such as the *Movimiento Estudiantil Chicano de Aztlan* (Chicano Student Movement for Aztlan), or MEChA. Lastly, to push back against the overrepresentation of Spanish-speakers both serving and dying in Vietnam, a coalition underneath the banner of the National Chicano Moratorium Committee (NCMC) staged a huge rally against the military action and the draft in Los Angeles on August 29, 1970.[19] In summary, as Vargas states, the last years covered in this chapter were a period when, "wherever Mexican Americans lived a process of self-discovery was underway as a sweeping transformation took place. The Chicano movement

3. The McCarthy Era and the Age of Activism

linked education reform to wider social reform through an emerging brand of student activism and leadership."[20] Although not involved in football (both as coaches and athletes) in representative numbers, Mexican Americans, inspired by the social turbulence, continued to build on the endeavors of E.C. Lerma, R.C. "Frito" Flores, and others in earlier decades. This pattern was reflected at all levels of the sport, from high school all the way to the NFL.

As discussed earlier, the overwhelming majority of the materials covered focus on football players of Mexican background. However, during the period included in this chapter, the arrival of Cubans, fleeing the tyranny of the Castro Revolution of 1959, swelled that population in the United States, primarily in southern Florida. There is little research on this group and its participation in football either in Miami and other locales of the Sunshine State. We will present, however, some more information on George Mira, who starred for the University of Miami, as well as in the NFL, CFL, and World Football League (WFL) during the 1960s and 1970s. Mira is of Cuban/Spanish descent and is referred to in Florida parlance as a "Conch," that is, someone who hails from Key West. Finally, we interviewed one of the first Cuban Americans to merit substantial national attention for his play on the gridiron, the great Carlos Alvarez, also known as the "Cuban Comet," who played wide receiver for the Florida Gators in the late 1960s and early 1970s. In addition, Alvarez's story sheds light on the impact of the social upheaval of this era on the life of a Latino athlete. In many ways, Alvarez's story parallels the more famous counter-cultural accounts in works by other football players, such as Dave Meggyesy of the St. Louis Cardinals. Finally, in the individual stories section, we will present a discussion of the collegiate and NFL career of the "Tampa Torpedo," the legendary Rick Casares of the University of Florida and the Chicago Bears.[21]

In summary, the years between 1951 and 1970 produced dramatic changes in the ways that Latinos (and particularly, Mexican Americans) challenged discriminatory practices, especially after the mid–1960s. Of particular note, there were substantial efforts to counter the circumstances that prevented large numbers of Spanish-surnamed students from completing high school educations. In addition, there was a concerted attempt to instill (re-instill?) a sense of ethnic pride and cohesion. These trends bled onto the gridirons of Texas, New Mexico, California, and Florida. The discussion to follow will shed light not only on the accomplishments on the fields and sidelines, many of which were of great significance in challenging stereotypes, but will contextualize them into the broader historical framework of this highly transformative and combustible era.

In Chapter 2, we focused on the career of E.C. Lerma, both as an athlete and coach, and noted the tremendous impact he had upon the Mexican American youths of the region surrounding Duval County (Benavides), and later, in Starr County (Rio Grande City). Before moving on to the exploits of players, it is important to note that, following in the footsteps of Lerma and a few others, the 1950s through the 1960s saw some coaches of Mexican American descent taking the helm of programs in areas of the state with the largest concentration of this group. Not surprisingly, Lerma was the "dean" of this cadre, as he continued on at Rio Grande City until the end of the 1965 season. After his successful run in Benavides, Lerma took over a moribund program with the Rattlers, a team that had notched only five victories combined from 1952 to 1954. By the start of his third year with the Rattlers, Lerma had turned things around and even posted one of the best two-year marks in team history: 14 wins and 5 defeats over the 1957 and 1958 campaigns. As he wrapped up his coaching tenure (before moving on to become an administrator in various districts throughout the state), Lerma left the sidelines with an overall record of 154 wins, 98 losses, and 13 outright or shared championships. One of the players E.C. Lerma coached was his son, John, who would go on to make his own mark as a field general both in Texas and New Mexico.[22]

Given the level of obsession that exists for the sport in the state, it is important to understand the significance of having a person of this ethnicity leading what was and remains one of the "flagship" institutions of Texas communities. A 1998 work by Ty Cashion, *Pigskin Pulpit: A Social History of Texas High School Football Coaches*, examines the important role that these men played in towns and cities throughout the Lone Star State. While he does an excellent job of discussing the importance of both white and African American field generals, he fails to account for the experiences and significance of Spanish-surnamed colleagues.[23] By using another one of the "bibles" of the sport, the *Texas Sports Guide of High Schools and Colleges*, it was possible to track down the names and locations of 11 individuals who led programs between 1955 and 1965. Not surprisingly, all "worked in the Rio Grande Valley, in the El Paso area, or in San Antonio. Apparently, it was still too early in the game for school districts to be willing to take a chance on hiring such individuals in areas where Spanish-speakers did not predominate."

In other research for this work, Jorge Iber interviewed a series of then-current (in 2000) Mexican American coaches. While there were certainly more leaders of this background by the turn of the century, many of the field generals interviewed asserted that it was still difficult to get a job outside of the "traditional" areas of Mexican American concentration. One interviewee in particular, Joe Carillo, then at San Elizario High School (in El Paso County) insisted that there were areas of Texas where "no Hispanic coach would be hired." Another participant, from the other extreme of the state (Roque Hernandez of Calhoun County High School in southeastern Texas) supported this assessment by arguing that there is "an unspoken situation regarding the hiring of Mexican American head coaches," and that "outside

3. The McCarthy Era and the Age of Activism

of the Valley there is resistance to hire a Hispanic coach."[24] A more recent example (which will be fleshed out more fully in a subsequent chapter) of such sentiments comes from the Dallas-Ft. Worth-Arlington area (known as the "Metroplex"), in which similar circumstances were detailed, but in 2015.[25]

In Chapter 2, we mentioned Greg Selber's point that the Rio Grande Valley, although always overwhelmingly Mexican American in population, had, through the early post–World War II years, not many Spanish-surnamed athletes. This began to change by the early 1950s, however. With the added manpower, many teams from the Valley made deep runs into state playoff competition, though only one, the 1961 Donna Redskins, managed (and are still the only) to claim a gridiron title. Selber refers to the years between 1950 and the 1960s as the region's "Golden Era." While it is not possible to discuss all of the meritorious individuals and teams from this segment of Valley football history, we will discuss a few who made important marks and mention others in passing. For a more complete account, we refer readers to Selber's exhaustively researched works.

One of the first coaches to make a mark in this region was the previously mentioned Rene Manuel Hinojosa, who had been a noted athlete at Mercedes High School in Hidalgo County in the early 1940s. After a stint in the U.S. Navy, he served as head coach at Sharyland High School in Mission and led the Rattlers on the first of three consecutive trips to the state playoffs between 1956 and 1958. One highlight was the final campaign, in which the squad finished 10-1-1 and made it to the third round of the state playoffs before bowing out of contention. Hinojosa left Sharyland in 1958 and became an assistant principal at McAllen High. He subsequently served in other administrative capacities for the district. Coach Hinojosa passed away in 2008.[26]

Like Hinojosa, many other athletes from the area had stellar careers on the field and then returned to coach and serve as teachers and administrators in local schools. One of the earliest was Carlos Esquivel, from Edinburg High School, who achieved more on the field and sidelines than just about anyone else from the Valley. In 1953, he rushed for over 1,100 yards and scored 21 touchdowns for the Bobcats. This squad made it all the way to the state semi-finals, upsetting a team from San Antonio along the way, before losing on penetrations to Port Neches. Esquivel's performance earned him an almost unheard-of (for a Mexican American) All-State designation in December of that year. This success attracted the attention of Coach Paul "Bear" Bryant, who recruited Esquivel to Texas A&M. The highlight of Esquivel's Aggie career, in addition to surviving the "Junction Boys" training camp, was scoring a game-winning touchdown against LSU in 1956. One of his teammates was Heisman Trophy winner John David Crow. This Aggie legend noted that his teammate was "the first Hispanic I'd ever been around. I was just an ol' Louisiana boy, but you know, I didn't even realize he was Hispanic until months into the season. He was one of us. He was tough and played through all the injuries…. I don't mean to be too corny about it, but we would have fought for each other like brothers." After graduating in 1958, Esquivel became an educator and eventually moved into coaching at his alma mater, starting in 1970 through 1974.[27]

While Carlos Esquivel managed to play at the highest collegiate level, a Division I program under the tutelage of a legendary coach, other Valley athletes achieved great success, but at lower levels of competition. Nevertheless, their achievements were valuable and assertive challenges concerning the athletic and intellectual limitations of Mexican Americans shared by so many Texans in the early 1960s. Here, we turn to the story of two players, B.R. "Poppy" Rodriguez of Pharr, playing for the Pharr-San Juan-Alamo (PSJA) High School Bears, and Luz Pedraza of the Donna Redskins. Rodriguez was a tough, though minuscule (160-pound) running back who led the Valley in rushing in 1962 in over 350 carries. In addition, as of the late 2000s, his 1,730 yards on the ground that season remained a regional record. Rodriguez reminded Selber that in that era, the game was not as wide-open as it has become. "This was an era of running the ball; heck, we only had three plays, run left, run right, and run up the middle." In Rodriguez's senior season, the Bears made it all the way to the state title game, losing to Dumas, 14–3. This was the second consecutive state championship game to feature a Valley, and predominantly Mexican American, team. In 1963, PSJA would go back one more time to the finals, only to lose again, 7–0, to Corsicana (Rodriguez had already graduated).

When lining up against playoff teams in 1962, the Bears faced obstacles that were a rarity in the Valley. For example, they faced a team comprised mostly of African Americans in an early round and, as Rodriguez recalled, that "was the first time any of us had seen blacks, and we said 'uh oh, here it is. We were all scared before the game.'" The Bears won, 26–0. Next, they played a team from Orange (eastern Texas) whose offensive line outweighed PSJA by an average of 50 pounds. They won again. Finally, they made it to Ft. Worth to play against the Demons from the panhandle region. Here, the disparity was even greater, for "the Dumas offensive line also outweighed the University of Texas line that year, by the way." How did the Spanish-surnamed kids from the Valley manage to compete? Rodriguez postulated that tennis (and other sports like track) helped to whip these athletes into shape. "We felt that we could stay with teams and beat them by having fresh legs in the fourth quarter." While such a run of success should have attracted scholarship offers from large programs, Rodriguez was not considered much of a prospect. It was not unusual then (and remains so to this day) for major programs to overlook potential stars from the Valley. Rodriguez, however, begged to differ from that assessment. Particularly for the Mexican Americans athletes who were

3. The McCarthy Era and the Age of Activism

beginning to play in greater numbers, success on the gridiron was a badge of honor. "Some people try to tell me that that Valley never did much. But I say ... we did quite a lot, especially in the 1960s. We were always overachievers.... Every time someone told us we couldn't do something, it just made us work harder to prove them wrong."

Even the nearby Texas A&I Javelinas did not seek out his services. Instead, Rodriguez had to traverse a substantial part of Texas' vast geography in order to continue his playing career, winding up at Sul Ross State, more than 500 miles from home. Fortunately, he was not alone, as he joined Luz Pedraza and Alfredo Avila (also from Donna, and who would make Little All-American in 1965 and 1966 as a defensive back) with the Lobos in Alpine. "We became roommates and we really stuck together, that helped all of us having familiar faces from the same place." These three players from the Valley helped turn around what had been a moribund Lobos program and led to two of the greatest moments in Sul Ross football history: first, tying the Javelinas in 1964 and helping to deny A&I the Lone Star Conference title, and then winning the conference in 1965 with a perfect 10–0 mark. That year, Sul Ross made it to the NAIA playoffs, but lost to Linfield College of Oregon. Rodriguez eventually moved into education and coached a new school, McAllen Memorial, for its first four seasons, through 1984. He then became the Athletic Director for the McAllen Independent School District. Even with all of the success on the field and in administration, Rodriguez still looks back on his time as a player and notes the significant impact this had on his life. It is worthwhile quoting his discussion with Selber at length:

> "We were all, or most of us, from poor families, who were just waiting for the opportunity to achieve," said Rodriguez, who likes to brag more about academic success than his football accolades. "We were just taking advantage of finally getting a chance. There were a lot of first- and second-generation immigrants, whose parents had sacrificed so that their kids could have a better life, and we weren't about to let them down." He says that today Hispanics by and large have ridden the rails of education to better lives and it started back in the days of the Bears, Redskins.... When one had to be persistent to overcome what area youths were up against.... "That's the way it goes, folks work hard when they're hungry; later on, maybe their kids get complacent, some do, some don't. But for our generation that came of age in the '60s, we fought against the odds to make it, and education was the key."[28]

The story of one of Poppy Rodriguez's teammates, Luz Pedraza, is even more remarkable, for he was part of the legendary 1961 Donna Redskins, the only team from the Valley to reach the summit of Texas football glory. The success he achieved at Sul Ross (he was named Little All American in 1965), while socially significant, paled in comparison to what he achieved as the quarterback for his hometown high school. Even with the passage of more than half a century, "the team" remains one of the most powerful symbols of

Mexican American pride and success in the Valley. As one interviewee noted, "I was born in 1963 and heard about that team all of my life. That was the big talk. To be like that team was everyone's dream." That version of the Redskins allowed area youths to dream big dreams because "the success of these players permitted the Valley's Mexican American youths to envisage goals that previous generations could not."[29]

Given the importance of that season, it is essential to provide a brief overview of Donna's drive to the title. At the start of the year, pigskin prognosticators foresaw a good season for the District 32AA Redskins. They would, most likely, compete for a local crown, but not do much beyond that. The season did not get off to a promising start, as the team lost its first two games, the first to Lerma's Rattlers, 20–0, and the second to the Mercedes Tigers, 12–8. Part of the reason for many Valley teams' shortcomings can be attributed to the fact that many players had to work and could not train during the off-season. Luz Pedraza faced just such a circumstance. His family routinely travelled to Alabama and Illinois to work the fields. After the first two defeats, however, the team's strenuous conditioning drills (Pedraza noted in an interview that "We sprinted on changes of quarters. We sprinted to the huddle. We ran everywhere.") began to pay off with the arrival of district play, as the Redskins rattled off eight consecutive victories. Then they played four road playoff games and defeated Refugio, Devine, Sweeny, and Brady. The Sweeny game was particularly significant because, prior to kickoff, one of the Bulldogs coaches approached Redskins field general Earl Scott and asked: "Can these pepper bellies play? I mean, you never hear about any of them in the Southwest Conference." The final score in this matchup was 32–14. Guess they could play after all.

The championship tilt featured Donna versus the Quanah Indians, a team that tallied 483 points while surrendering only 56 over the 1961 season. As usual, the Redskins were decided underdogs. Things looked grim after a Pedraza interception led to a Quanah touchdown, making the score 21–12 early in the fourth quarter. A touchdown by Donna and a two-point conversion narrowed the lead to 21–20 with less than six minutes to go. After stopping the Indians, the Valley squad took over on a short field, starting on the Quanah 42-yard line. From there, the passing of Pedraza and running of Fred Edwards led to a final touchdown and made the tally 28–21. The Indians tried to rally, but their final threat was squashed with an interception by Oscar Avila, one of five brothers on the team. In a 2002 interview, Avila recalled how significant this victory was for Mexican Americans in the Valley by recounting an exchange with a local in the late 1990s. During a visit to his hometown, Avila was approached by an older gentleman who inquired as to whether he was a member of the 1961 team. When Avila answered in the affirmative, the gentleman turned to his wife and said, "Mira, viejita, este es uno de los Avilas

3. The McCarthy Era and the Age of Activism

que jugo en el equipo del '61 cuando les ensellamos a los gringos que nosotros tambien sabiamos jugar football." ("My dear, this is one of the Avila boys who played for the '61 team when we showed the gringos that we too knew how to play football.")

After completing his collegiate career, Pederaza played for another team that is legendary in Texas: the San Antonio Toros of the Texas Football League and the Continental Football League. The highlight of this professional (though minor league) career came in 1967, when Pedraza lead the Toros to a perfect season, including a victory in the title game, 27–7, against the Tulsa Thunderbirds that December. Pedraza was named All-League, finishing with over 2,300 yards passing and 22 touchdowns. He played professionally, off and on, until 1974, and he completed a second degree as well. After his success as a player, Pedraza went on to a stellar career as a coach and athletics administrator.[30]

Three other Valley greats from this era merit more extensive coverage: Lupe "Chipper" Zamora of Harlingen High School, Robert Cortez of San Benito High School, and Robert Vela of Edinburg High School. Zamora is, according to Selber, "a living legend" in the region. A quick perusal of his resume certainly seems to affirm this designation. Chipper Zamora's playing and professional careers feature several important pioneering roles: the first Latino quarterback in the history of the Cardinals (1957); the first such Athletic Director in Weslaco (in 1977); a member of Texas Education Desegregation Assistance Center (1970); coaching the Mercedes Tigers to their first district title since 1958 (in 1973); and later serving as Harlingen Athletic Director from 1992 to 2007. For Selber's book on the sport in the Valley, Zamora shared key recollections about how Mexican Americans were treated, how they were perceived as athletes, and how sports brought about certain change:

> I think that Harlingen was among the last schools to integrate at that position.... We just figured that's the way it is. I do remember wondering what happened to the Mexican American kids who had been successful at the lower levels. I grew up in Harlingen, and when we went to the movies, we had to sit upstairs, while the Anglos sat downstairs.... In sports I saw that there was more equality, ... I know we had discrimination in the Valley in the old days. But at the same time, my older brother was the first Mexican American to be named King Cardinal.... Some of us just kept working hard, through the obstacles.

Zamora, who earned his undergraduate degree at Pan American and a Master's at Sam Houston State, began his coaching career at Edinburg under Carlos Esquivel. Later, he coached at Mercedes, Weslaco, Brownsville, and Harlingen. Of all his success as a player, coach, and AD, Zamora noted that he was most proud of his 1973 Tigers team. Not only did they win, but "those kids who won the district title in '73, they are doctors, lawyers, and most of them have made it, and that makes me really proud."[31]

Another Valley product who followed on Carlos Esquivel's heels was Robert Cortez, who played for the San Benito Greyhounds. Initially, he was on the radar of Darrell Royal, who came to the region in 1961 to scout Jim Helms. Royal kept in touch with Helms' teammate, but Robert Cortez ultimately decided to attend A&M in part because "I just knew there was nothing going there in College Station, so I figured it would keep me out of trouble." He had a highly successful career with the Aggies, lettering from 1965 through 1967, being named team captain in 1967, and graduating in 1968. One of the highlights of his playing career came in helping A&M defeat Alabama in the 1968 Cotton Bowl. Before achieving success on the field, however, Cortez had to help some of his fellow students understand that a Mexican American in the late 1960s was not going to put up with any guff, even in College Station. In short, as Selber noted, Cortez "brooked no racial prejudice." In part, it was the difficult conditions in his hometown that shaped this player's attitude on the field. During practices, he would often be chided for being too aggressive. "They kept saying, 'Damn it, Cortez, take it easy, take it easy!' But I came from a family of 13 kids, most of them had to quit school to work, and I grew up competitive and hard-nosed, that's just the way it was for us back then.'" The San Benito product recalled that shortly after his arrival on campus:

> One night I was sitting in my dorm room, and some guy came in, and he looked at me and said, "Hey, how's it going, taco-maker?" I jumped up and socked that guy right in the mouth. I didn't want to hear any of that shit. After that, the teasing tailed off dramatically.... "That's one tough Mexican, don't mess with him." I got into several fights right off the bat until I let them know I wasn't going to stand for being called a taco-bender or a greasy Mexican.

One of the ultimate compliments paid to Cortez came from Coach Gene Stallings who, after several freshmen quit his team in 1965, was heard to say, "Hell, let them all quit, we'll just go out there on the field with Cortez and nobody else." After graduation, Robert Cortez played semi-professionally with the West Texas Rufnecks and then became a coach, working at Odessa Permian High School and finally returning to the Valley at San Benito in 1979. One interesting stop for this Greyhound led to his working as an assistant at Mexico's Monterrey Tech in 1974. Coach Cortez worked in Valley schools until 2004.[32]

Robert Vela graduated from Edinburg in 1964, having benefited from the tutelage of Fred Akers (the soon-to-be University of Texas head coach) during his junior and senior seasons. He was also influenced by the career of Carlos Esquivel, whom Vela got to see on a weekly basis during the 1950s as one of the "sideline rats" who would carry the helmets and pads of Bobcats players after games. Vela was also like many other Mexican Americans from the Valley in that "he was a migrant worker, riding with his folks to Hereford in the Panhandle every summer. They usually made it to Michigan too, to

3. The McCarthy Era and the Age of Activism

pick strawberries, pickles and cherries." After finishing his high school career, he enlisted in the Air Force, serving at Carswell AFB near Ft. Worth. There, he was encouraged by a fellow airman to begin taking classes at nearby Texas Christian University in 1965. Vela eventually earned more than 30 credits at TCU and then returned to Pan American to complete his undergrad degree. He also earned a Master's in Education from A&I.

Esquivel got Vela his first coaching job at Edinburg. After working for his boyhood idol, Vela eventually served as head coach for the Edcouch-Elsa Yellowjackets (also known as *La Maquina Amarilla*—"The Yellow Machine" in Valley parlance). Between 1989 and 1997, E-E made a habit of playoff appearances. The highlight was the 1989 season, when the Yellowjackets won their district for the first time in over two decades and made it into the state quarterfinals, tying Gregory-Portland, 13–13, but losing on penetrations, which are encroachments beyond the opponent's 20-yard line, a mechanism used to break ties before the advent of overtime.

Ten years later, now coaching his beloved Bobcats, Vela again moved his squad deep into the playoffs, losing to Aldine Eisenhower (from the Houston area) in the state semifinals. All told, his teams made the state playoffs in 14 seasons. After an uncharacteristically poor season of 3–7 in 2006, Vela noticed he was much more fatigued than usual. Unfortunately, it was the start of stomach cancer. Coach Vela passed away in August of 2007.[33] As a tribute to this local legend, his hometown board named a new high school in his honor. The Robert Vela High School SaberCats took to the field for the first time in 2012 and won a bi-district title in 2014. This is a fitting tribute to one of the most important Mexican American coaches in Valley history.[34]

Since we reside in Texas and do not want to be chastised by colleagues, it is only fair to balance out mentions of two Aggies greats with a couple of quick notations of Mexican Americans who played for the other large state institutions: Bobby Cavazos (from Kingsville) at Texas Tech University and Rene Ramirez (from Hebbronville), who played for the University of Texas Longhorns during the 1950s. Please note, however, that while both of these players can be said to be from "South" Texas, Kingsville (in Kleberg County) and Hebbronville (in Jim Hogg County), their hometowns, are too far north to be considered from "the Valley."

Bobby Cavazos was born on the famous King Ranch in 1931, the fourth of five children born to Lauro Cavazos, Sr. (the first Mexican American foreman in the Ranch's history) and Thomasa Quintanilla Cavazos. All five children earned degrees and made substantial contributions in various fields. Bobby's older brothers, Lauro and Dick, were true pioneers: Lauro as the first Latino president of Texas Tech as well as a member of a Presidential cabinet (as Secretary of Education under Ronald Reagan and George Bush), and Dick was the first Latino four-star general. Bobby made his mark on the football field, starring for the local team, the Brahmas. He starred on the basketball court as well and ultimately moved on to Tarleton Junior College (now Tarleton State University). There, he led the Plowboys in scoring and finished third in the Southwest Junior College Conference in scoring in 1949.

While he played against older athletes, the 19-year-old Cavazos excelled and earned a scholarship to Texas Tech University the following year. The local press took note of his background, as Spanish-surnamed individuals were quite rare at the Lubbock institution at this time. His goal was to win and to help Tech move into the Southwest Conference (they played in the Border Conference, which existed until the end of the 1961–1962 academic year, through 1956). Cavazos certainly did help in this regard. A local reporter even noted that Tech did not concern itself with the backgrounds of athletes (as long as they were not African American, of course), stating, "we don't care where the boys come from as long as they're the right kind of boys and can play winning football." The highlight of Cavazos' career came in 1953, when he lead the Red Raiders in scoring (80 points) and rushing yards (757). In that campaign, the team finished 11–1 and defeated Auburn at the Gator Bowl on January 1, 1954, 35–13. Cavazos was named the game's MVP, rushing for 141 yards and scoring three touchdowns. That season was quite helpful in bolstering Texas Tech's justification for admission into the Southwestern Conference in May of 1956.

In addition to Lubbock papers recording his exploits, Kingsville scribes took note of Cavazos' exploits. As Jorge Iber noted in an article on Bobby Cavazos in 2002, this material was of great significance to broader aspects of Mexican American history.

Bobby Cavazos, 1954 (courtesy Texas Tech Athletics).

The articles contained the story of a Spanish-surnamed individual who stood proud, successful, and victorious in an endeavor most Texans respected and glorified. Contrast this with the daily life of most of the region's Mexican Americans—segregation, racism, substandard schooling for their children, and dominance by Democratic political machines. Unintentionally, the articles on Bobby Cavazos' athletic brilliance provided a form of resistance against Anglo perceptions and dominance.[35]

Cavazos signed with the Chicago Cardinals, but a knee injury ended his career. He returned to the King Ranch and eventually published two fictional historical novels based loosely on his family's experiences at the facility. Cavazos died in November 2013 at the age of 82.[36]

The University of Texas, the state's flagship institution and football program, has had a few outstanding Latinos grace its gridiron over the years though, given the issues discussed throughout this work, their numbers have been limited. Among the earliest were Francis Dominques of Kerrville (a letterman in 1920–1921) and Richard Ochoa of Laredo, who played halfback and was the MVP of the 1953 Cotton Bowl. The next player in this line was Rene Ramirez of Hebbronville, where he was not only a standout athlete, but also the valedictorian of his 1956 class. When he arrived at Austin, the school had just made a coaching change, hiring Darrell Royal for the 1957 season. In Royal's first year, the Longhorns went 6–3–1 and earned a trip to the Sugar Bowl. The "Galloping Gaucho" led that team in all-purpose yards. In 1958, he highlighted another successful year (7–3) by scoring three touchdowns against the hated Aggies in a 27–0 Texas victory. Finally, in 1959, Ramirez was named first team All-Southwest Conference and was instrumental in leading a squad that finished 9–1 and played in the Cotton Bowl against Syracuse University. He earned a degree in Mechanical Engineering and has been in the insurance business in the Valley for many years. At Ramirez's induction into the UT Hall of Honor, David McWilliams of the Longhorn Association noted that "now you find more Mexican Americans playing ... not only at UT, but in the state of Texas and across the nation." It is, in part, because players such as Rene Ramirez that today's athletes have increased opportunities to play the sport.[37]

So far, our discussion has centered around athletes on the field or coaches on the sideline, but there were other elements to the football scene in southern Texas during these years that merit attention. For example, the halftime shows and homecoming events were influenced by the Chicano Movement. The Movement also helped spur a truly unique combination of that most Texan of sports with a Spanish-language radio program for fans, as well as the development of *corridos* (Mexican-style ballads dealing with heroic deeds) emanating from station KGBT (in McAllen) starting in 1970.

A 2005 book by Jose Angel Gutierrez—one of the leaders of the Crystal City Revolt and the La Raza Unida Party—documented how the Chicano Movement impacted happenings surrounding football games in this region of Texas by the late 1960s. *We Won't Back Down!: Severita Lara's Rise from Student Leader to Mayor* recounts the story of how the town's white minority controlled who could be cheerleaders, members of the homecoming court, and even the music played during halftime at Crystal City High School contests. The policy for selecting members of the court was deceptively simple and exclusive: only alumni association members were permitted to vote. Since the majority of the past graduates were white, even though the town was overwhelmingly Mexican American, the winners always came from the minority populace. A similar arrangement existed for the selection of members of the cheer squad. Severita and some of her classmates did not agree with this arrangement, and by 1969 they were prepared to challenge the policy. "Eighty five percent of the population was Mexican American, yet in all of our activities like … cheerleaders … there's always three Anglos and one Mexicana…. We started questioning. Why should it be like that?"

Likewise, students agitated for academic classes and arts that were more relevant to their lives. In Crystal, for example, there were changes in the marching band's halftime repertoire. Given the support for the Javelinas, Friday nights at the local stadium would now present not just football games, but also "ceremonies [that] made extensive use of Spanish, Mexican/Chicano music, and symbols such as raised clenched fists and Azltan eagle formations." Certainly, it was not the ultimate aim of the Chicano Movement to change the music played during halftime of gridiron contests; however, it is crucial to note how significant a transformation this was. As noted in a recent work on this topic, "the momentum and vitality of the Chicano Movement enabled Spanish-surnamed students … to challenge a great many discriminatory practices both in the classroom and in athletics."[38]

Not only had the fans of schools in the Valley fallen in love with football, as have most Texans, they, since the early 1970s, have also participated in a unique version of another aspect of the sport's culture: the call-in/scoreboard show. The distinctive version that emanated from McAllen for almost four decades was called "Football Scoreboard" and was hosted by Hugo De La Cruz, also known as "Mr. Nifu/Nifa."[39] Much of what is normally expected in such a program is part of the fare. Fans of teams call in, crow about victories, and complain after defeats. There is also a plethora of good-natured ribbing between aficionados of traditional rivals. However, there is an element that is truly inimitable about this show, and it stems directly from local history: corridos for each team. The most famous of these is the one tied to the *maquina amarilla*, the Yellowjackets of Edcouch-Elsa. Joel Huerta notes that these ballads form an integral part of the experience of high school football culture in the Valley. "Typically football is a kind of all–American sport, … but at the same time, the Valley's a pretty old place, it's been around a long time and there's a lot of exchange with mainstream America." It is no surprise that the show started at the height of the Movement. It became, and continues to be, an irreplaceable element of sports in this region. "The expressive culture that grew around borderlands football in the 1970s and 1980s in many ways resembles the vibrant fan culture found in European and Latin American rugby and soccer."[40]

3. The McCarthy Era and the Age of Activism

A few other notable athletes who made their mark during this era warrant mention. Celestino Avila, M.D., earned All-State honorable mention for Donna in 1960, the first team coached by Earl Scott. He is a member of the clan that helped put the Redskins over the top in 1961. Avila also played collegiately at Southwest Texas State (now Texas State University) and earned second-team Little All-American in 1963 and 1964. He also coached briefly before moving on to Monterrey Tech to earn his medical degree.

Ernesto Vela was an All-District player for the RGC Rattlers in 1953 and has the distinction of being the first player from the institution to earn a collegiate athletic scholarship, to Sam Houston State. He lettered three years for the Bearkats and helped them win the Lone Star Conference title in 1956. After graduation, he returned to the Valley and became an administrator in local schools.

Gus Zavaletta has the peculiarity of having won football titles in two countries. He coached at Brownsville's St. Joseph Academy for many years and guided the Bloodhounds to state titles in 1962 and 1980. He also guided the Monterrey Tech Borregos to state football titles in Mexico. One other element of note in Zavaletta's career was his encouragement of competition in football between Brownsville teams and nearby Mexican high schools.

Several other Valley natives were involved with championship teams: but these were at the national level. Alfredo Lugo (Donna) and Leonel Garza (Los Fresnos) both initially attended Trinity University in San Antonio, transferred to Livingston State College (now the University of West Alabama), and were part of a squad that won the NAIA championship in 1971. Their coach on that Tigers team was Mickey Andrews, who became a long-time assistant to Bobby Bowden at Florida State University. One final individual who claimed this distinction was Juan Jose Capello, M.D., who played multiple sports at Edcouch-Elsa. Capello was part of an A&I team that won the school's first national title (of eight) under Gil Steinke in 1959. This Javelina side had a total of ten players from the Valley on its roster.[41]

So far, we have discussed how victories and success impacted players, coaches and communities in southern Texas. While it is always pleasant to recount triumphs, there can also be great value in overcoming great odds, such as breaking a long losing streak. The example of the 1968–1972 Asherton Trojans (from Dimmit County) can also shed light on the importance of football to a group of Spanish-surnamed athletes. While the 1961 Donna Redskins reached the mountain top, the Trojans from this era were at rock bottom. Going into the 1972 season, the gridders had lost 40 consecutive contests, and their basketball team would go on a 62-game winless streak by the end of the decade. When legendary football essayist Carlton Stowers wrote about them in the early 1980s, a new coach had arrived and was hoping to end the Trojans' losing ways. The challenges these youths faced have been noted throughout this work, so there is no need to recount specifics. Things did not turn around, though, and the school ultimately closed in 1999. While not achieving the heights of Earl Scott at Donna or E.C. Lerma at Benavides and Rio Grande City, the new field general hoped to channel the same goals and aspirations for his Mexican American charges. There is value in the struggle, even if ultimate success was not achieved. "I'd like to think that despite the fact that we haven't had much success lately there is something that the kids get out of being part of the team. Playing football helps them grow up and accept responsibility. Clearly, here [was] a team and community that looked beyond the final score in measuring the value of competition for their youths."[42]

On the other side of the Lone Star State at Bowie High School in El Paso, the gridiron years between 1950 and 1970 featured tragedy, success, renewed sorrow, and finally a dry spell. These years were also significant in that the Mexican American population in the city began to flex its political muscle, starting with the election of Raymond Telles in 1957. The 1950s began with a new coach at the Bears' helm: Buryl Baty, who had graduated from Texas A&M in 1948 after serving his country in World War II. Although Coach Baty had been drafted by the Detroit Lions, he decided to pursue a career on the sidelines of Texas instead of pro ball. He spent the 1949 season at Lufkin and guided the Panthers to a mark of 8–2. In June of 1950, the young coach accepted the position of field general of the Bears.

The four years Baty coached Bowie provide a revealing overview of how Mexican American football players were perceived and treated during the 1950s. As noted in his wonderful tribute to his late father, R. Gaines Baty's book, *Champion of the Barrio: The Legacy of Coach Buryl Baty*, the school in the *Segundo Barrio*, while having some success, was not considered a plum job by any stretch of the imagination. The 1949 squad finished a miserable 2–7. Baty believed that there was potential for the team as the area had many fine athletes. In addition, the new coach laid down the law for his charges as far as expectations and comportment in the classroom and community. "You will be good citizens, respectful and respectable.... If I hear of anyone drinking, he is automatically off the team." In addition, he also began the practice, which shocked many parents in the barrio, of visiting his players' homes and emphasizing the need for education. One symbolic act that took place at his first team meeting occurred when Baty and his assistant, Jerry Simmang, handed out new jerseys and equipment. This was unheard-of by most of the Bears players. "Until this season the meager equipment room had contained only used, worn-out gear, and a depleted supply of that. The previous season ... [one player] had been forced to wait until someone quit before he could suit up for a junior varsity game."[43]

We are not going to cover the various seasons game by game, but will provide a few athletic and historical highlights of Baty's time at Bowie. The

1950 team began the turnaround of the school's gridiron fortune, although the players were exposed to some of the harsh realities of race in the America of that era. One of the first games they played was against a team from Douglas, Arizona. Game film showed that the squad had "several 'Negroes,'" but when the team visited El Paso, these players were nowhere to be seen. The Bowie players inquired and "they soon learned that these Bulldog team members had been left behind … due to a rule prohibiting their playing in Texas." A more direct example of such treatment occurred in Austin, when Bowie traveled again to play Stephen F. Austin High. Nemo Herrera had warned Baty of what to expect, given the baseball team's experience in the previous year's playoffs. Not surprisingly, this other group of "boys from the barrio" were turned away at various locales. A similar event took place in Plainview later that season. Baty took such actions very seriously. "At first, I felt sorry for the boys, then mad that anyone would treat my kids that way.... I must say that I never realized how demeaning it feels to be discriminated against. Now I know." The Sunday after the Plainview game, the first tragedy to strike the Bowie football program occurred when five fans were killed on the Carlsbad Highway, returning from the contest. An even more tragic event happened three years later. Even with the discrimination faced and misfortune suffered, Bowie earned a co-championship of their district in 1950. Even more pleasing was the fact that the Bears beat El Paso High and tied the mostly "white school" in town, Austin.

In 1951 and 1952 Baty had lost many of his better players to graduation, and these turned out to be a rebuilding years. The 1952 season featured another incident concerning the treatment of his players; this time in Snyder. Not only did Bowie lose, 27–0, to the Tigers, but their bus was pelted with rocks and the crowd chanted, "We're kicking your tamale butts!" and "Go home you greasy Meskins!" This was not the last time the Bears had to deal with the team and fans of Snyder. The 1953 season held greater promise and was highlighted by a victory over Austin High as well as an outright title. Bowie played, and lost to, Odessa High in the first round of the playoffs. Baty was named District Coach of the Year, and seven members of the squad earned first-team All-District.

The 1954 season featured a return trip to Snyder and more run-ins with their "progressive" populace. Again, the team made reservations at local eateries, only to be told there would be no service. By this point, Baty had had enough and threatened not to play the game on Friday night. Later, at the stadium, the visitors' locker room suddenly developed "plumbing problems," making it necessary to change on the bus. Finally, some of the players were flagged for personal fouls for speaking Spanish while on the field. Bowie lost, 19–0. Later that year, on October 8, Baty, Simmang, and a third coach, Fred Rosas (who survived the 1950 crash), were returning to El Paso after a scouting trip to Pecos. At approximately midnight, their car was struck head-on by a truck being driven on the wrong side of the road. Just like that, the life and career of a man who cared deeply for the athletic and academic futures of his charges from the barrio was gone. In 1998, the Bears' stadium was named in honor of Baty, Simmang, and Rosas.[44]

Nemo Herrera stepped in to complete the 1954 season, and he was replaced by Lou Robustelli. Fred Rosas became one of his assistant coaches. The shock and the damage, however, were done, and Bowie entered a period of decline on the gridiron. Still, there were some highlights. In 1956, Memo Gonzalez, just a sophomore, led the district in rushing. There was also a winning season in 1958, with the Bears finishing 6–4. The captain of that squad was Nolan Richardson, who would go on to great renown as a collegiate basketball coach. The school's enrollment continued to increase during these years and reached 2000 in 1960. The freshman team that year showed promise, finishing 6–0–1. Later in the decade, the varsity finished 6–4 , and the 8th-grade team won the city title. The two highlights for the 1960s came in 1965, when Bowie won their district (the first since the Baty years) but lost in the first round of the playoffs, and in 1969, when they again won their district and a playoff game, before falling in the bi-district before a crowd of almost 18,000, the largest gathering ever for a football game in El Paso up to that time.

On the social side of the equation, there were still issues both in the barrio and in the school. For example, as Morales notes, the area "had lots of juvenile delinquency and many Bowie students belonged to gangs." This issue was brought to the forefront on October 17 of 1961, when a student was stabbed at the school's game versus El Paso Cathedral High. Also, punishment for speaking Spanish in the school continued into the 1960s, with guilty parties having to write a 200-word essay, in English, as castigation for this serious infraction. The "English Only Law," which had been in place in El Paso schools since 1918, was finally terminated in 1968.[45]

Now we turn again to Dan Ford for an overview of key events on the gridirons of New Mexico. One significant trend that becomes apparent between 1951 and 1970 is that Spanish-surnamed coaches became more and more commonplace, with many quite successful. For example, as noted in Chapter 2, Rudy Camunez led Las Cruces High School to the state title in 1959. That season the Bulldawgs capped off a perfect campaign by defeating Artesia. In addition to running roughshod over all of their New Mexico opponents, the team also trampled some Texas competition, defeating both Bowie, 42–6, and El Paso High, 20–12, early that season. The competition between this institution and its Texas neighbors has continued to the present, with as many as three El Paso institutions competing against the Bulldawgs in one season.[46]

Other Latino field generals who participated in New Mexico's title games during these years were Jose Martinez at McCurdy High School, with a title in 1962 and championship game losses in 1957 and 1963; Evasalio Padilla led Belen against New Mexico Military Institute in 1963 in a battle of unbeatens, but lost, 3–0; Dennis Trujillo, Jr., guided Chama to the final against Carrizozo in 1960, losing 34–0; Finally, Melvin Romero was the head coach for Capitan in their 1965 loss to Roy, 30–7. All of the above coaches achieved the ultimate or penultimate goal: playing for, or winning, a state title. There are two coaches during this era, however, who merit a bit more attention: Ernie Abreu of St. Michael's (Santa Fe) and the legendary Sal Gonzalez, who, after a renowned playing career at Anthony Gadsden High, moved into the coaching ranks in the early 1960s.

The Abreu family has been in New Mexico since well before statehood and even the start of American dominion of the territory. Ernest Beaubien Abreu was born in August of 1933, a direct descendent of Santiago Abreu II, Governor of New Mexico. The family moved to Las Vegas in 1942 after his father found work with the railroad. By the time that he reached high school, Ernie was part of the initial freshman class at troubled West Las Vegas High School (WLVHS). The principal concern at WLVHS was based on class and ethnicity. The city was actually two communities, the Anglo (and wealthier) one concentrated on the east side, and poorer, mostly Spanish-surnamed on the west. "The affluent Anglos ... and had no strong reason to keep the school system alive in that area.... The conflict between those two parts of the small college town continued for several decades." Ernie Abreu played for WLVHS and was a fullback on a team that finished 11–1. The school closed in 1951 and did not field a football team again until 1954. Abreu, like many of his fellow Spanish-speakers, completed his high school education at a Catholic institution in town, Immaculate Conception.

After graduation, Abreu married his high school sweetheart, Mary Louise Wildenstein (they were married for 64 years) and began working at the local gas station. His former football coach, Gillie Lopez, helped him get a scholarship to New Mexico Highlands, and he graduated with a degree in education in three years; he also played football, basketball, and baseball for the Cowboys. In 1954, he was hired at the reopened WLVHS and began an almost four-decade career in the field. While there, he coached the Dons' football team. In 1961, St. Michael's in the state capital recruited Ernie Abreu to head their program, which he did until 1965. From there, he went on to serve as an administrator and superintendent at various districts. Coach Abreu passed away in March 2016.[47]

Ernie and Mary Louise's first-born, James "Jim" Abreu, also enjoyed much athletic success in his home state. Jim was born in 1951 and competed for WLVHS in football, basketball, and baseball. In 1968, all three of these

Dons squads made it to either the state semi-finals or finals. In 1969, the Dons gridders finally made it to the state championship game, under Coach Frank Herrera, only to lose to Lovington, 46–14. The younger Abreu played multiple sports for New Mexico Highlands as well, though his focus was baseball. He went on to a career in coaching and education, just like his father, though he earned a doctorate and eventually served as Dean of the College of Education at his undergraduate alma mater.[48]

After New Mexico consolidated its playoff format so as to establish a clear path for determining state champions in various divisions, one of the first schools to dominate on the gridiron was Gadsden High School from the community of Anthony. One of the principal reason for the Panthers' supremacy was the play of Sal Gonzalez. Dan Ford's work well documents the achievements of this great running back. In 1953 (the first of the school's three consecutive state titles), Gonzalez carried the ball on almost every play, running out of a single-wing formation, and earned his first of three All-State designations. The following year was more of the same as Sal scored a then-record 178 points in the season. Finally, in 1955, he scored another 158 as the Panthers defeated St. Michael's, 19–0 to complete the title trifecta. All told, the teams went 30–0 (their winning streak was actually 34 games, as they won their final three in 1952 and the first contest of the season in 1956 before losing to Deming, 13–7) between 1953 and 1955 as Gonzalez tallied a remarkable 608 points and almost 9,000 yards of offense. Coach Warren Woodson recruited the Gadsden legend for the University of Arizona, and he followed his mentor to finish out his career at New Mexico State. After earning a degree in Physical Education, Gonzalez coached at Laguna-Acuma between 1961 and 1965 (19-15-2 record), then at Los Lunas from 1966–1972 (28-31-8), before moving on to resuscitate the Cowboys' program in 1974.[49]

Several other high schoolers of note in New Mexico during this era included Bobby Santiago of Albuquerque High, who scored five touchdowns against New Mexico Military Institute in 1959, and then starred for the hometown university Lobos, winning All-Skyline Conference honors. He later coached at Rio Grande High. Cruz Flores of WLVHS broke Gonzalez's scoring record by tallying an incredible 208 points in 1961. Among his most impressive performances was a game against El Rito, which the Dons won, 61–6, and with Flores scoring 40 points. A similar effort took place against Santa Rosa in a 73–6 victory. Unfortunately, Cruz Flores' legacy was stained by a poor playoff game against Gallup Cathedral in his senior year which featured two fumbles and only one point scored in a 12–7 loss. Finally, one of Jim Abreu's teammates at WLVHS, Mike Lopez, was instrumental in getting the Dons to the 1969 title game as he scored 188 points that season.[50]

Several natives of the Land of Enchantment also distinguished themselves at the collegiate and professional levels during this era. The stories of two—Danny Villanueva and Al Gonzalez—not only demonstrate success and perseverance on the playing field, but also provide insight into the value of playing football as a mechanism to challenge assumptions about Spanish-speakers, both as athletes and in professional settings.

Daniel Villanueva was born in Tucumcari in November of 1937. His father was an itinerant Methodist preacher, and the family moved several times, including stops in Phoenix and Calexico, California. One of his brothers, Primo, went on to football stardom at UCLA, and his story will be detailed shortly. Daniel played quarterback, at Calexico High, but a shoulder injury forced him to make a fateful decision: he could either quit playing or acquire a new gridiron talent. He chose to learn to placekick and punt. He feared his mother's wrath if he quit football. He once noted that after a loss, "the house was dark. She'd lock me out and she'd let me think about it … and then she'd let me in." After his time with the Bulldogs in California, Danny Villanueva attended Reedley Junior College. His brief career there ended with another injury. He subsequently moved back to the state of his birth and latched on with the Aggies in Las Cruces, where he perfected his craft for kicking field goals and punting. He graduated in 1959 with a degree in English. While at NMSU, he also edited the school paper and played in the 1959 Sun Bowl, a 28–8 victory against North Texas State.

After completing his collegiate career, he was not drafted by any NFL squad, and he began to ply his trade in the classroom. Fortunately, an announcer recalled his exploits at the high school level and recommended Villanueva to the Rams. Satisfied with his capabilities, the L.A. franchise signed him to a 1960 contract for the princely sum of $5,500. He played with the Rams between 1960 and 1964. In 1965, he was traded to the Cowboys, and the new organization almost tripled his salary to $15,000. "I'd thought I'd died and gone to heaven." Villanueva thrived on the field for this new squad, notching 107 points as a kicker in 1966, and he converted a total of 56 consecutive extra points. He also played in one of the greatest games in NFL history, the 1967 "Ice Bowl" for the league title versus the Green Bay Packers.

After completing this season, Daniel Villanueva hung up his cleats and moved into broadcasting with KMEX in Los Angeles. Working as a reporter, he re-learned the Spanish he had forgotten. Ultimately, he moved from working in the field to owning the station, and then others. This enterprise was the precursor to what became Univision. In many ways, Villanueva's determination to have his stations serve the Spanish-speaking community came from his personal experiences. He not only wanted to provide a news outlet and a source for customers for Spanish-surnamed-owned business, he also wanted to connect with the community and bring to light its concerns and aspirations. "We don't have an *L.A. Times*. We don't have a KCET. We have to be a little bit more than a TV station to our viewers," he noted in 1985.

As recounted in Villanueva's obituary in the *New York Times*, there were incidents on the playing field that helped shape this entrepreneur's conscience in regard to racial matters. For example, he was chided in the Los Angeles media as "El Kickador" while with the Rams. His "place" as an "other" was made abundantly clear to Daniel Villanueva in the NFL. "'We had a black bus and we had a white bus in those days: we were segregated.' He recalled a teammate once announcing, 'All black guys get on that bus, white guys get on this bus, and Danny, you take a cab.'" Such experiences impacted Villanueva's role as a reporter and owner. "We were a transitional generation that thought that by distancing ourselves from our culture, our language and our ... roots, we were going to magically be accepted by the general community. It didn't work." Daniel Villanueva passed away in June 2015. He was 77.[51]

Al Gonzalez was born in Cedar Vale in November 1945. The family lived in an area described as full of "poverty" and "challenging because of the lack of opportunity for its inhabitants." Fortunately, the family moved to nearby Albuquerque during Al's childhood, and he began to thrive in the urban environment. He quickly became passionate about football and notes that "Had it not been for athletics.... I might have taken a different road and wound up in a lifestyle or situation less than positive." After a stellar career as a lineman and kicker at Albuquerque Rio Grande, he received offers from various schools, but settled on attending New Mexico State. The seasons that Gonzalez played were some of the glory years of the Aggies program; they did not lose a home game between 1964 and 1967. Going into his senior season, Gonzalez and teammate Tony Fields were the school's preseason All-American candidates. As a result of his line play and kicking, including connecting for 12 extra points in a 90–0 victory over Northern Arizona, Gonzalez earned Honorable Mention and was selected (though he did not play) to the East-West Shrine Game.

After Al Gonzalez finished his eligibility, the Oakland Raiders approached him about coming to training camp, but they gave him what he considered a "low ball" offer. Instead, as other Latinos have done, he went north of the border and played with the CFL's Saskatchewan Roughriders until a knee injury ended his playing career. He then returned to Las Cruces and finished his degree. In 1973, football once again beckoned, and Gonzalez became the line coach for the Aggies, serving in that capacity for four years. From there, he filled various administrative posts and eventually became the Athletic Director for NMSU. Even though he had starred for his alma mater, there was blowback against hiring a Spanish-surnamed individual to fill this important post. "Some of the letters said, 'You shouldn't be athletic director,' ... [or] 'you should go back to picking lettuce in the field,' just to quote a few of the remarks." Ultimately, with the administration's backing, the insults subsided and Gonzalez had a fairly successful run in many sports, though not

3. The McCarthy Era and the Age of Activism 129

in football. One highlight came in 1992, when the team went 6–5, their first winning season since 1978, when they also finished 6–5.

While the 1992 season turned out to be a positive, times were difficult for Gonzalez at the helm of a poor (financially) athletic unit. In August of that year, a story appeared in *Sports Illustrated* that documented how difficult it was for NMSU to compete. When the New Mexico Lobos, no football power either during this era, printed shirts emblazoned with "We May Not Win Very Many Games, But We Always Beat New Mexico State," you realize that your program has reached a nadir. Not only was Las Cruces out of the way, the facilities were poor, and in 1989 the recruiting budget totaled a mere $19,500. By 1997, a five-year extension for Gonzalez was one of the reasons why the Board of Regents fired the school's president. Although he has faced difficult times, Al Gonzalez is a prime example of the importance of success on the football field and how it can impact an individual and a community: "The road from the barrio ... was a rocky one. Simply stated, Gonzalez endured and succeeded by utilizing a strong work ethic, sound judgement, and the belief that virtue is its own reward."[52]

As we previously provided substantial coverage of educational issues (primarily in Texas) as impediments that kept the Spanish-surnamed off the gridiron, it is necessary at this point to provide a brief glimpse into similar matters in California. For that, we turn to a wonderful work by Mario T. Garcia entitled *Blowout: Sal Castro and the Chicano Struggle for Educational Justice*.[53] We will simply point out some of the connections Sal Castro recounts in this testimonial and how they relate to football. The pattern is not dissimilar to that of events/personages covered in Texas. For example, Castro recalls that during his high school years, he did not participate in varsity athletics, "not because I didn't want to, but because I had to work after school all four years." After finishing his primary education, Castro moved on to L.A. State, graduating in 1961 and moving into a teaching certification program. "My hope ... was to teach in the East L.A. public schools, where the greatest need existed and where few Mexican American teachers were to be found." The expectations of such pupils were, to say the least, limited. The circumstances, as summarized by Castro, did not lend themselves to many students participating in extracurricular activities such as football. "Our educational system was terrible.... Few Chicanos attended college. By 1964, the Fair Employment Practices Committee reported that less than 1 percent of Mexican American college-age students in California went to college."[54]

Sal Castro began his post-accreditation teaching career at Belmont High (in downtown L.A.) in 1963. He noticed various issues right away: Mexican American students were funneled into vocational tracks, did not partake in school governance, and did not go on to college. What they did do at Belmont was to participate, for as long as many could, given often trying financial circumstances, in playing football. Castro was determined to help out with the Sentinels' program. "I actually volunteered some of my time to help with the football team. I gravitated toward sports because that's where the Chicanos were." Clearly, the interest in the sport was there, but most of these students did not make it to graduation, and certainly not to the next level of competition. The result of all of these problems was that Belmont had at least a 50 percent drop-out rate, and other campuses, such as Garfield, were even higher, with attrition totaling approximately 60 percent.[55]

Eventually, Castro moved on to Lincoln High (which also had a 50 percent dropout rate), on the northern edge of East Los Angeles. The institution was 90 percent Spanish-surnamed. This was not the only school with such a population. As noted, one of the participants in the "Symbol of Heart" rivalry movie, Roosevelt High, had a student body that was 83 percent of this background. Early on, Castro was given the opportunity to, once again, tie in with the institution's sports program, this time by serving as athletic director. His recollection of his time at this post (1965–1968) is worth noting:

> The only problem with the sports program was that even though we had many good Chicano athletes, the mostly white coaches never tried to get them college athletic scholarships. They had the mind-set that college coaches weren't interested in Mexican players. As a result, many excellent athletes from Lincoln and other Eastside schools never got the chance to play ball in football, basketball, baseball, or track.[56]

Castro recalled that one of the Lincoln athletes who did merit a scholarship in football turned down an offer to play for San Jose State because it was too far from home. Rather, this young man preferred to join the Marines, where he would initially attend boot camp in North Carolina. "'Camp Lejeune! That's 3,000 miles away. You want to go 3,000 miles to be a Marine, but you won't go 385 miles to go to college?'"[57]

By the early 1970s, there was a direct connection between the sport and Castro's activities. He would set up visits for bright youths to institutions such as UCLA and USC. In order to fund scholarships, he approached the owner of the Los Angeles Dodgers, Peter O'Malley. The civic-minded entrepreneur agreed to provide half-price tickets to games which Castro could then re-sell at full price, with profits going to fund tuition payments. O'Malley even went so far as to allow the organization (Association of Mexican American Educators) to have musical entertainment (the band *Tierra* and Mariachi *Los Camperos*) before a game to attract customers. The result was the first Chicano Scholarship Night (there would be only two). The master of ceremonies that evening was the legendary California Golden Bear (and NFL and CFL veteran) Joe Kapp (whom we will detail at length in the individual stories section of the chapter)—also known as the "The Toughest Chicano," according to *Sports Illustrated*. Kapp is now enshrined in both the Canadian and Col-

3. The McCarthy Era and the Age of Activism 131

lege Football Halls of Fame. Given Kapp's experiences with discrimination as a youth and later in life, there is no surprise that he was willing to assist in such a cause. The efforts ultimately provided funds for about 20 students.[58] In sum, the discussion of these obstacles is presented here to provide a sense of the many impediments Latino athletes faced in California. Of course, as with the other states examined, there are far too many individuals to permit in-depth examination of all aspects of their careers. Therefore, we will focus on the following four, whom we consider to be among the most important: Primo Villanueva (of UCLA), Tom Flores (College of the Pacific), Hank Olguin (California), and Jim Plunkett (Stanford). We will also, once again, provide some information on the rivalry between Garfield and Roosevelt High Schools in Los Angeles.

Having noted the career and significance of Daniel Villanueva's athletic and professional work, we now detail the career of his brother, Primo, who starred for the UCLA Bruins in the 1950s. Primo was born in December of 1931, the oldest of 12 siblings. He, too attended Calexico High and was named to the All-Imperial Valley First-Half Century Team. His exploits earned him a full scholarship with the Bruins, arriving on campus in 1951. The success he achieved on the field did not come easily, as he was injured in his first spring practice and was ready to quit. Fortunately, as with Daniel, his mother intervened and reminded him of how fortunate he was to be playing football and to have a scholarship.

> I was ready to go back to Calexico and the vegetable fields.... I was having a terrible time with my classes; we had a little boy and it was hard to make ends meet. In fact, I was mowing lawns and doing anything I could on Sundays to make some money. Finally, Mother convinced me that I had to take full advantage of the opportunity for a college education that none of the other eleven kids had; that's why I'm still here.

The Bruin faithful were certainly glad he stayed.

By the time he reached his senior year of 1954, Villanueva had become a star. In that season, he scored the winning touchdown in the game against the Washington Huskies; scored twice in a 72–0 rout of Stanford; and threw a touchdown pass against the hated USC Trojans in the season's final contest, a 34–0 trouncing of the cross-town rivals. UCLA went undefeated and finished first in the Pacific Coast Conference, but was ineligible to go to the Rose Bowl because they had played in the "granddaddy" the previous season (a 28–20 loss to Michigan State). They did get a bigger prize, however, a national championship. Villanueva was one of the principal cogs in the offensive machinery. He carried the ball 101 times for 380 yards, threw for another 371 yards and scored six touchdowns. He was named to the All-Conference team and was invited to participate in the Hula Bowl All-Star Game.

While his statistics were impressive, apparently, they were not remarkable enough, and Primo Villanueva went undrafted. One scout for the Rams argued that, though Villanueva had faced good competition, he was "too small, no speed, and is no specialist." As a result, as other Latinos did at this time, he went north of the border and signed with British Columbia of the CFL. He spent his entire career with the Lions, playing all over the field: he rushed, passed, received, punted, returned punts, and played in the secondary. He was traded to the Montreal Alouettes for the 1959 season, but decided to remain in Vancouver. At this juncture, his Mexicano background proved of great value; as Primo Villanueva opened a restaurant that gave Canadians a chance to sample his ethnic group's cuisine. In 2009, he was inducted into the BC Restaurant Hall of Fame in the "Pioneer" category.[59]

In Tom Flores' autobiography, *Fire in the Iceman*, this legendary player and coach points out to his readers that "I was literally raised in fields." For athletes of other backgrounds, that might mean they were raised in the shadow of a gridiron, perfecting their craft under the tutelage of a father or other family member who coached or played the game. This was not so for Flores who, instead, worked in "lettuce fields, fruit orchards, berry patches. My family traveled from crop to crop in California's ... central valley. We picked whatever needed to be picked. We were like thousands of Mexican American families then and now." Even following the crops, Flores got a decent education and enjoyed his childhood. His father hailed from Durango, and his mother, though born in the United States, had roots in Jalisco. After settling in Sanger, the family sharecropped and eventually operated a corner grocery store. While all of this was happening, Tom discovered sports, and he proved quite adroit in this endeavor. To Flores' benefit, his father bought him a baseball glove and told him about a local celebrity of similar background: Mike Garcia, the great pitcher of the Cleveland Indians.

Flores played football at Sanger Union High School and was a backup quarterback (he also punted and played defensive back) until his senior season. Like many of his co-ethnics in Texas, he also worked all the way through high school, primarily as an iceman (hence, the nickname), while continuing to help in the store and working the fields. Although his goal was to attend Stanford (because they threw the ball more than most collegiate teams at that time), his lack of "college prep" courses prevented him from attending the Palo Alto institution. A good Mexican American student not funneled into college prep classes in the mid–1950s; wonder how that happened? Instead, he played at Fresno City College, where he was also a member of the baseball and basketball teams. Flores "was happy with [his] decision ... because it gave me time to become acclimated to college academics" while still playing sports. He wanted to transfer to San Jose State, but a scholarship that paid for all expenses to Pacific sealed the deal, and Flores became a Boxer.

In his junior year, Tom Flores had an excellent season, finishing fourth

3. The McCarthy Era and the Age of Activism

in the nation in completion percentage. Before the start of the campaign, however, he had broken his collarbone, and that limited his accuracy and velocity. Still, he played in the East-West Shrine Game and hoped to hear from an NFL team. Of course, that call never came. "When I was ignored for 30 rounds in the NFL draft—30 rounds, he'll still have a hard time believing it— Moose Meyers suggested that I go to Canada." This proved a wise decision, as he was given a chance with the Calgary Stampeders in 1958. The shoulder did not heal, and he wound up back in Sanger, where he finished his degree while tutoring and tossing pizzas at Lugo's Pizzeria. In 1959, after surgery, Flores got a tryout with the Redskins, though that did not work out either. By early 1960, he was offered a job at Roosevelt High School in Fresno, but was "too stubborn to let his dream [to play professionally] die." It was shortly thereafter that Lamar Hunt and "The Foolish Club" established the American Football League. In March of that year, Flores got an invitation to try out for one of the renegade franchises: the Oakland Raiders. We will continue the story of Tom Flores' career and significance at the end of this chapter in the extended, individual stories section.[60]

While we will discuss the career and significance of "The Toughest Chicano," Joe Kapp later, here we turn briefly to one of his teammates on the 1958 California Golden Bears squad that won the Pacific Coast title and played in the 1959 Rose Bowl against the Iowa Hawkeyes, Hank Olguin. This running back was born in Albuquerque but was raised in San Jose, California. He played various sports at Lincoln High, and although successful in athletics, he was also active in the band and theater, and he took college prep courses. "I did have to take some math and language classes at San Jose City College, that brought me up to speed. Once those were behind me, I got into Cal easily." Football, however, was his ticket to college, and that was apparent from the first moment he touched the ball at the high school level and ran 99 yards for a score.

The 1958 Golden Bears team was unique in that it had little in the way of size and included four Latinos: in addition to Kapp and Olguin, there were Bob Gonzalez and Mike Prado. The team did not start off well, losing its first two contests, to Pacific, 24–20, and Michigan State, 32–12, before reeling off victories in seven of its last eight games. Among those triumphs was a 16–15 victory over Stanford in "The Big Game." The success on the field was a thrill, but also limiting as Olguin and Kapp did not flaunt the fact that they were of Mexican backgrounds. It was "not exactly fashionable or cool to be Mexican in the '50s." Still, they did embrace their ethnic background and shared it when possible. That season, in the game against USC, Kapp and Olguin tackled a Trojans running back named Tony Ortega. As Olguin notes, "I playfully hurled Spanish profanities at him. 'Orale, cabron' or 'pendejo' elicited a knowing grin from Tony as he picked himself off of the turf."

As the Cal players entered the Rose Bowl for the contest, Olguin, already demonstrating character traits that would serve him well in years to come in his various jobs in communication and marketing (with specific efforts to change the way that Latinos are presented and perceived of in mass broadcasting), thought, "Of the tens of thousands in this grand arena and the millions watching on television, I wonder how many realize ... that Kapp and I are Mexicans?" Although he recognized how lucky he was to have played football, Olguin hung up his cleats after the Rose Bowl (and a brief flirtation with the Dallas Texans during which he was injured) and moved into media. "I became more aware of all the negative stereotypes of Latinos and wanted to do something about this." Among his undertakings was participating in a group called "Nosotros" with Ricardo Montalban, Joe Kapp, and others. In an article by Olguin, he notes that Kapp was quite active in *la causa* (the cause), giving speeches in support of Cesar Chavez and other elements of the Chicano Movement. There were times when he was joined by other famous Mexicanos, such as Anthony Quinn.

Part of Olguin's determination to "come out" as a Latino (and an advocate for the group) was his insistence that his surname be pronounced correctly. It was often pronounced "ALL-GWINN," whereas it should be "OHL-GEEN." When asked about his background, this firebrand has been known to retort: "I'm as Mexican American as apple pie!" One final aspect of Olguin's work is to seek greater recognition for fellow Spanish-surnamed competitors from this era. When asked by Frederick Luis Aldama about why people like Kapp, Flores, and Jim Plunkett are not in the Pro Football Hall of Fame, he noted, "I'd say we're being shortchanged. The committee making these decisions is made up of media professionals ... [and many] carry some of the misperceptions of Hispanics that I've been working to change. So I can see how some may be as ignorant ... about what we are and what we have to contribute" to the sport.[61] We will discuss this further when we review the some of the professional accomplishments of Flores and Kapp at the end of this chapter.

The career of Jim Plunkett in the NFL will be considered directly in Chapter 4, but here we present a bit of information regarding his upbringing and high school career. Once again, the offerings of Professor Aldama and his co-author, Christopher Gonzalez, are highly instructive. Jim Plunkett was born in San Jose in December of 1947. As is widely known, his parents were both blind, and as a young man the future Raider suffered from Osgood-Schlatter disease (which caused problems with his soft tissue and pain in his knees). In order to help his parents make ends meet, he picked fruit over the summers and worked in a gas station. Still, he played sports constantly with the ethnically mixed group of kids in his east-side barrio. "We all played sports ... and most of us were Hispanic. When I went to play football in high school ... there was quite a mixture of ethnicities and races.

Many of the team members were also Hispanic." He started at Overfelt, but finished at James Lick High School under the tutelage of Al Cementina. In this regard, Plunkett was fortunate, for the team threw the ball quite a bit (by the standards of the time). Further, the young Latino also credited his coach with keeping him focused on the goal of moving on to college. "Al ... was very clear-sighted about my academic and athletic abilities.... I had good enough grades and I was the perfect quarterback for ... a small team with a lot of Hispanics.... I am very proud of those tough, hard-nosed, scrappy Mexicans." After his career with the Comets, Plunkett went to Stanford to play for John Ralston with the Indians. Almost as soon as he arrived on campus, doctors discovered a tumor on Plunkett's thyroid. While it was benign, it cost Plunkett a great deal of strength, and he redshirted. He feared that he would lose his scholarship and educational benefits, but Rod Rusk, one of the men who recruited Plunkett, told him, "we want you to come to Stanford anyway, whether you play football for us or not." The fans of Palo Alto were certainly grateful that this Latino managed to play for their squad.

Aldama and Gonzalez, in an interview with Plunkett, asked him to recall what it was like to be a Latino on campus at this time (late 1960s). "I had no money. My parents didn't have some of the basics that other kids had, like a car. I felt a little embarrassed and out of place.... I was not doing well in football. This increased my sense of not fitting in and not doing well in my classes. I thought about leaving." Once Plunkett healed, he made it a daily chore to throw 500 to 1,000 passes in order to regain his strength and mechanics, and he settled into his role. Over his three years at the helm, he started 32 games, completed 55 percent of his passes, threw for more than 7,800 yards, and had a modern quarterback rating of 129.5. In his final year, Plunkett led Stanford to an impressive 9–3 season, including victories over Arkansas, USC, UCLA and, most importantly, Ohio State in the Rose Bowl on January 1, 1971. His reward was becoming the first Latino to lay claim to the Heisman Trophy as well as the Walter Camp Player of the Year Award for 1970. He was also the first pick of the 1971 NFL Draft by the Boston Patriots. That part of the story which does not turn out as positively, will continue in the next chapter.[62]

The movie "Symbol of Heart" brings into focus how the years of the Chicano Movement helped reconfigure how the Roosevelt and Garfield rivalry was presented to the broader society. While the game was always of great significance to the people in these communities, many whites in southern California had always derisively referred to the contest as the "Taco Bowl" or "Chili Bowl." By the early 1970s, the more empowered denizens of their neighborhoods worked to change the name to the East Los Angeles Classic (used for the first time in 1972) and thus took "away the negative moniker and [became a way of] demonstrating pride in their shared heritage, schools and athletic prowess." Much of the pageantry surrounding the contest ties in directly with some of the developments seen in South Texas during these years. As one local reporter noted just prior to the 2008 contest:

> It has been said that this is the oldest and largest high school football rivalries [sic] west of the Mississippi and definitely in the state of California. Annual attendance reaches 20,000 spectators at East Los Angeles College. Visitors to the game often note that the evening takes on a life of its own. The evening is more than a football game. It is often seen as a family reunion spanning several generations. It is not unusual for spectators from both schools to attend to meet with old friends and family members.... There is competition between the drum majors for the bands for their skill in tossing the baton. There is the battle of the marching bands, the drill teams, the dance teams, the cheerleaders, the leadership councils, and of course the mascots.[63]

The arrival of thousands of Cubans to the shores of southern Florida in the early 1960s brought more Latinos familiar with the game of football to a region obsessed with the sport. But these were by no means the first to arrive. For example, as we have noted earlier, the cigar industry brought many to the Ybor City (Tampa) area in the 1870s and 1880s. Earlier still, there were arrivals who reached Key West in the years just after the Civil War, as a result of the failed Ten Years War of 1868. In addition to seeking asylum, like their brethren further north, these Cubans also came to work in the cigar industry. "By 1876, more than 2,000 cigar-makers were producing 62 million cigars a year. That made Key West rich." By the mid–1880s, about one in three Conchs were of Cuban background. In 1876, the mayor of the community was Cuban-born. The area was even represented in Tallahassee by a member of this ethnic group. Finally, even the great patriot of the 1895 Revolution, Jose Marti, visited the community in order to raise funds for his party's activities. As recently as the 1950s, in *Cayo Hueso* (as the city was referred to in Spanish) it was possible to hear bolita numbers (the Cuban numbers racket) over local radios. It is from this older Cuban/Spanish lineage that George Mira, a University of Miami legend, sprang.[64]

While Key West has older ties to Cuban migration, what became ground zero during the 1960s, Miami, also goes further back in time than many may realize, as by the early 1930s, there were an estimated 1,000 Cubans in the city. As Jose Cobas and Jorge Duany noted in their study on Cuban Americans:

> Miami ... became an important Cuban migration center in the 1930s with the overthrow of Gerardo Machado (1924–1933). During the 1940s and 1950s thousands of Cubans migrated to the United States, especially New York City, searching for better economic opportunities. In 1958 about 40,000 Cubans lived in the United States; most of them were either political refugees or skilled workers in the tobacco industry.[65]

It is from this newer community that the second "Cuban Comet," Carlos Alvarez, not Minnie Minoso, sprang in the late 1960s to set records at Florida Field (as "The Swamp" was known until the late 1980s) with the Gators.

3. The McCarthy Era and the Age of Activism

While the University of Miami has had more than its share of great quarterbacks over the years—Jim Kelly, Vinnie Testaverde, and Bernie Kosar come to mind right off of the bat—one of the first great men under center for "the U" was George Ignacio Mira, the son of a former professional boxer, Jimmy Mira, Sr., who plied his trade in the Tampa area. While at Key West High (home of the "Fighting Conchs"), this descendant of Cubans and Spaniards lead his squads to a 21–8–1 mark in his three varsity years, graduating in 1959. He was also a member of the baseball (he was offered $13,000 to sign with the Orioles, after winning 31 of 33 starts) and basketball teams. In a September 23, 1963, *Sports Illustrated* article by John Underwood, the writer noted that Mira's desire to win sometimes got a bit out of hand, as in the case of an incident on his school's hardwood where "an opponent on a Miami team was giving him lots of hands. When both teams and the referees turned after one basket, Mira … stopped and decked the man with one punch, then trotted casually down-court and set up on defense."

Mira's career with the Hurricanes was outstanding, and most discussion of his feats included references to his ethnic background. He led Miami from 1961 to 1963, completing passes for over 5,000 yards and generating a QB rating of 104.2. Over these seasons, the team went to two bowl games (finishing 7–4 in both campaigns), the Liberty (a 15–14 loss to Syracuse) and Gotham (a 36–34 loss to Nebraska); however, they slumped to 3–7 in Mira's senior season. In his final collegiate post-season game, Mira completed 24 of 34 passes for 321 yards and was named MVP. He was drafted by the 49ers in 1964 and spent five seasons with the club, though he started only five games, backing up John Brodie. He was sent to the Eagles in 1969 and backed up Bob Griese with the 1971 Dolphins squad that lost to the Dallas Cowboys in Super Bowl VI, 24–3.

After his time in the "big" Cuban city, Mira moved on to Montreal, where he played for the Alouettes the following season, throwing for over 1,300 yards and 11 touchdowns on a poor 4–10 squad. He jumped to the WFL, guiding the Birmingham Americans to the lone championship of the association, 22–21, over the Florida Blazers in December 1974. Just as in his final bowl game with the Hurricanes, Mira was the title game's MVP. After the contest, it was clear that Mira had lost none of his bravado. "Hell, we're champions just like anybody else and I think we deserve a chance to play the NFL's best." Of course, it was not to be. Mira returned to his home state with the Jacksonville Express team that finished 6–5 as the league folded in October of 1975. He threw for over 1,600 yards and 12 touchdowns that season. He tried one final comeback in 1977 with the Toronto Argonauts, but played in only six games as a player-coach. After retiring, George Mira returned to his hometown and, eventually, Miami, as a restaurateur, most recently running the Native Conch in Coral Gables. The Mira name continues to sparkle in Hurricanes lore, as his son, George Mira, Jr., became an All-American defender at their alma mater. Most recently, the third generation, Jr.'s son Nick, was playing baseball for the state university in Miami, Florida International.[66]

The final player we will discuss before moving on to more extensive, individual stories is Carlos Alvarez, of the University of Florida. Alvarez's family left Cuba in May of 1960 and arrived in Key West shortly thereafter. The clan managed to get out a few possessions, but shortly after reaching Florida, Carlos's father informed all concerned that there was no going back. They were now "Americans" and had to make their way in this "new" land. For young Carlos, part of this process included learning about a game he knew nothing about: American football.

Like most other Cuban immigrants of that era, the Alvarezes worked diligently to gain a toehold in their new homeland. They did have the usual negative run-ins with some of the less enlightened. Carlos Alvarez recalled that, hoping to help out with family finances, he and his brother Arturo would deliver papers in the early morning hours in their North Miami neighborhood. "You little spic! Get the hell of my porch and go back to Cuba with your spic brother!" a nice lady remarked one morning. There was also an incident where another student called Carlos a slur at school and his brother came to his rescue. No doubt about it, not all Miamians were thrilled to have the waves of Cubans coming on to their shores in the early 1960s, particularly away from the friendlier confines of the poor, but ethnically wealthy, sector of Little Havana.

One of the ways in which Carlos Alvarez began to see another side of American life—he called it his "Dream"—was through learning to play on the gridiron. It was through the help of Rudy Freitos and a football coach named Mitch that he was introduced to the sport at the Boys Club of North Miami. "We only got 15 players, even if you don't know how to play, we could use you." Alvarez started in part to have something to do, but also was "the overwhelming desire to be American, like everyone else." Although fear of failure permeated his mind, play he did. He eventually became the quarterback of a poor team, but he was on his way; eventually, he was both a football and track star for the North Miami High Pioneers. While at NMHS, he also became involved in politics, seeking to right every wrong he perceived in the school, things such as the local police ticketing students for parking off campus. This element of Alvarez's character would return to the fore a few years later.

Going into the last few games of his senior season, Carlos Alvarez led Dade County in rushing and had attracted attention from substantive programs such as Vanderbilt and Georgia Tech. By this time, brothers Arturo and Cesar were at Florida, and when Lindy Infante promised Carlos a chance to play receiver (let's face it, not too many 160-lb. running backs can make it in the SEC—even back then), that sealed the deal, and Alvarez became a

Gator. It did not take long for the Cubano to make his presence known as he caught a 78-yard pass from John Reaves on the season's first play from scrimmage (versus Houston) in 1969. He went on to claim numerous records and honors, including: first-team All-SEC and first-team All-American in 1969, and the marks for catches in a season (88) and in a single game (15), and career receiving yards. Even more significantly, he was also a first team Academic All-American in 1969 and second team in 1970 and 1971. Knee injuries slowed him down in the last years at UF, but he was still named to the school's "Team of the Century" in 1999.

He graduated with a degree in Political Science in 1972, and though he was drafted by the Cowboys, he decided to attend Duke Law School. He earned his degree in 1975 and became a professor at Southern Methodist University until 1980. He has been a practicing attorney in Tallahassee (keeping an eye on the Seminoles, one must assume) since that time, focusing on environmental law and, more recently, alternative dispute resolution. A final point to bring up about Carlos Alvarez ties in directly with some of the social upheaval that took place during this era. While he loved the United States and the opportunities provided to his family, Alvarez also learned to stand up for what he believed; after all, his father had been a lawyer in Cuba, and his two brothers also earned legal degrees at UF. When he thought about what happened at Kent State, the Mai Lai Massacre, and the death of Martin Luther King, he decided to become politically active, not something that was particularly welcome by most football coaches in this era. Additionally, Carlos Alvarez questioned why Florida did not have African Americans on their various athletic teams. All of these circumstances led him to engage with more "progressive" voices on campus, and this was not always appreciated.

Two key moments, one more serious than the other, took place during his career: first, he participated in protest events on campus and spoke at banquets throughout the state after he won a major award from the Department of Health, Education and Welfare. A second, more comical event occurred at the Playboy Club in Chicago, where Alvarez was invited as part of the All-American team. When photographers took the squad's picture, there is Carlos Alvarez smiling and flashing a peace sign. Freedom to be an American meant that he could play football, earn respect for his ethnic group, and also speak out against the injustices he saw in the nation. Not a bad start for a future lawyer. Dave Meggyesy, the quintessential personification of the "rebellious" football player of this era, would have been proud.[67]

We now turn to four individuals whose careers have earned them even greater acclaim. The players we will discuss in greater detail are: Gene Brito, Tom Flores, Danny Villanueva, and Rick Casares. In addition, we present a short passage on the 1962 Brackenridge Eagles and their drive to the Texas State football title. This was the first fully integrated team (African Americans, whites and Latinos) to claim the ultimate prize in this football-mad state.

Genaro Herman "Mean Gene" Brito

The first Latino player ever to achieve multiple and consecutive All-Pro selection both in the National Football League (four times) and the Canadian Football League (once) was California-born Genaro Herman Brito. He was an outstanding defensive end who specialized in bone-jarring tackles and fumble recoveries. He was indeed a great athlete who helped sustain the fortunes of the Washington Redskins during the 1950s. He was also a very popular persona who even attracted the attention of a U.S. President. Genaro G. Brito was born on October 23, 1925, in Huntington Park, California. His parents were Genaro Brito and Trecia Cheavez. His mother's name was misspelled, which was not an common occurrence with Spanish surnames in locales such as Texas, New Mexico, and California.[68] Her name in another vital statistic certificate was corrected to read "Theresa Chavez." The certificate also indicates the "color or race" for both parents is "Spanish," and their birthplaces are noted as being in New Mexico. Additionally, the middle "G" in Genaro Brito was later changed to "Herman."[69] The misspellings by public agencies regarding proper identification were a problematic start to Gene's life, but this did not prevent him from achieving renown as a professional football player.

The young Genaro Brito grew up in East Los Angeles and attended Lincoln High School, located in the predominately Mexican and Mexican American part of the metropolis. World War II was in its early phases as the young Brito began his athletic career and excelled in football, basketball, baseball, and track. For most young men during the wartime, graduation from high school meant military service, and for Brito it was no different. He joined the U.S. Army and served and trained as a paratrooper, attaining the rank of staff sergeant. According to personal records, Brito made a combat jump over Negros Island in Philippines during the Pacific campaign.[70] He was honorably discharged after the end of hostilities and returned to Los Angeles, enrolling at Loyola University. While at Loyola, Brito was a good student who embarked upon a great football career. His last two years were the most eventful of his collegiate career.

The *1951 Loyola University Yearbook* documented that the previous season featured great enthusiasm and success for the Lions. The yearbook stated:

> An unprecedented winning streak, national recognition, and captivation of the public fancy were all achieved by last year's Loyola Lions varsity.... The 1950 Lions rolled off seven straight victories over Pepperdine, St. Mary's, San Jose State, College of the

Pacific, Nevada, Hardin-Simmons, and Fresno State before falling to Giant-killer Santa Clara, then rebounding to overwhelm the University of San Francisco Dons.[71]

Genaro Brito starred both on offense and defense and rated as the team's finest end. He never missed a game during his four-year tenure at Loyola, and his 1950 offensive statistics included 15 receptions for 199 yards and a single touchdown. At the end of the final season, "Mean" Gene Brito, as he was nicknamed by both teammates and opponents, was named to the UPI All-Coast Independent College Football Team.[72] In the spring of 1951, the Washington Redskins expressed an interest in the highly regarded Mexican American and selected him in the 17th round of the annual NFL draft. Brito was initially envisioned as an offensive end but shifted to defense in 1953. The transition to the other side of the ball was beneficial for both player and team.

Now a professional, Brito began to establish himself as a star. The 1951 season for Washington was dismal, and it marked the final year of play for Latino running back Eddie Saenz. Veteran quarterback Sammy Baugh was in the twilight of his career, and backup Billy Kilmer was still a journeyman. Nevertheless, Gene Brito hauled in 24 passes for 313 yards. The following season, the Redskins made a coaching change as Earl "Curley" Lambeau took over but the Redskins' offense continued to struggle. After a 2–2 start, Washington lost six games in a row until Sammy Baugh, who had broken a hand earlier in the season, returned to the starting lineup to lead them to two victories. Despite the problems behind center, Brito accumulated 21 pass receptions for 270 yards and two scores.[73] This would be his final year on the offensive side of the line of scrimmage. In 1953, the Redskins improved somewhat and finished third in their conference with a record of 6–5–1. The key to the Redskins' success, according to Beau Riffenburgh's *The Official NFL Encyclopedia*, "was a strong defense built around end Gene Brito, tackle Dick Modzelewski, linebacker Chuck Drazenovich, and defensive back Don Doll."[74]

The 1954 pre-season began with a feud involving Lambeau, Brito, and quarterback Eddie LeBaron. The players were at odds with management and left the Redskins to play in the CFL.[75] Brito played with the Calgary Stampeders and was utilized on both offense and defense. While he caught five passes for 60 yards with the Stampeders, it was his defensive skills that gained him notoriety. His defensive play was recognized and rewarded with selection to the CFL Western Conference All-Star Team at the defensive end position.[76] This award was the first of five consecutive All-Pro designations.

Brito and LeBaron rejoined the Redskins in 1955. All-American halfback Vic Janowicz had also signed with Washington, and the three rejuvenated the team. Grateful to be back in the NFL, Brito reversed the old saying that offense was the best defense and proved that great defense can sometimes sustain a pedestrian offense. The Redskins finished second in the Eastern

Conference with a mark of 8–4, and Brito was named an All-Pro. In the Pro Bowl, he garnered the game's Most Valuable Player Award.[77] The Touchdown Club of Washington, D.C., also selected him as the Pro Football Player of the Year, to cap a sensational year.[78]

The 1956 season was darkened with tragedy as Vic Janowicz was killed when he was thrown from a car and struck a tree during training camp. The accident greatly demoralized the team, and the after-effects lingered throughout the season. Washington could only muster a .500 mark. The only light that shone amidst the tragedy was Gene Brito's defensive play that earned him a second All-Pro selection at defensive end.[79] The 1957 campaign was no better. The Redskins lost another player during training camp, when defensive back Roy Barni was shot to death in a barroom brawl. Washington's defense was the one positive as they held the Chicago Bears, Pittsburgh Steelers, and Philadelphia Eagles to a combined total of 13 points. The offense continued to sputter, and the team finished 4–7–1. For the third consecutive year, Brito was selected an All-Pro. He repeated this achievement in 1958, once again garnering League-wide honors as well as being voted Outstanding Lineman in the Pro Bowl.[80]

As the 1950s wound down, Genaro Brito was considering a life outside of football. Prior to the Pro Bowl, he announced his retirement. Modestly he proclaimed, "My greatest thrill as a pro came when I made the Redskins squad in 1951."[81] He never missed a start with Washington and played 84 straight regular season games. Brito was also never penalized until the 1958 season, when he received a penalty for jumping off-sides. When Brito announced his retirement in the nation's capital, Vice President Richard M. Nixon commented about his decision, stating, "Brito symbolized the kind of spirit which, win or lose, has made the Redskins a great team to watch."[82] Brito ended his playing career in January 1959. He returned to Los Angeles and planned to devote his time to teaching and coaching at his alma mater, Lincoln High School. However, no sooner was Brito back in town than the Los Angeles Rams announced they had obtained the four-time NFL All-Pro defensive end from Washington in exchange for linebacker Larry Morris.

When Brito was notified of the trade, he recalled not considering the possibility of donning Rams colors, but welcomed the opportunity to return to his hometown club. Brito prepared for another NFL campaign, but in the second game of the season, versus the San Francisco 49ers, he suffered a fractured ankle and was out for the year.[83] In 1960, Brito returned for what turned out to be his final season as a professional. At training camp, he was in top form and eager to play. "He's quick as a cat," praised Rams coach Bob Waterfield. "He's not favoring that ankle at all … to watch Brito work out is a football education in itself. He spins, fakes, dips, and relies on 8 years of NFL experience to slip past an offensive lineman and smother the ball carriers on passes."[84] Brito started every game that 1960 season as the Rams finished in sixth.

The next football season would have been his tenth, and as in the past, he looked forward to playing again. However, at summer camp in Redlands, California, he was stricken with a paralyzing disease described as peripheral neuritis, an inflammation of the nerves of the lower body that ended his career.[85] As fate would have it, the well-respected All-Pro Defensive end was forced to leave the game he loved so much.

Brito was quoted in a *Los Angeles Times* article about his disease, saying, "I wish I could play this year, but I've had 10 years in this league and that's more than most. It's all been great!" Los Angeles Rams General Manager Elroy "Crazy Legs" Hirsch hailed Brito as a "wonderful person and player who will be missed by the game of football.[86] Thereafter, Brito waged a four-year battle with the paralysis and died on June 8, 1965. His passing was greatly mourned and remembered by many friends/teammates, opponents, coaches, and politicians. Daniel F. Reeves, team president, expressed his sorrow, noting, "The example of the courage he set for us will live long after his football feats are forgotten."[87] Rams star Les Richter added, "It is a very sad thing. The sports world has lost a true champion."[88] Rams coach Harlan Svare lamented Brito's passing, noting, "He was an inspiration to me as a man and a player."[89] Also, former Vice President Richard Nixon recalled the memorable Brito:

> His example of courage, determination, and spirit in the face of overwhelming odds, both on and off the football field and in his great battle for life, will be a lasting memorial to one of America's truly great athletes.[90]

Years later, Brito was nominated for election to the Pro Football Hall of Fame, but his candidacy gained little traction. He is, however, admired and remembered for his feats on the gridiron. The late, great Gene Brito continued to be a source of inspiration to all who knew and heard of him even after his passing. Not only was he one of pro football's best defensive linemen, he was also known for being a caring and extraordinary man. In between gridiron campaigns, Brito gave back to the community he was from, and in the off-season he taught at his alma mater, Lincoln High School. According to a close friend, Bob Addie, "Brito specialized in teaching incorrigible and disadvantaged children. They needed love, kindness, and attention, and this was the best thing he has done in life is to see these kids come back after a few years as good citizens of the Lincoln community. He had a soft heart for children and continued to work with the youth of Los Angeles until the very end."[91] Years later, the Gene Brito legacy was recognized in 1976, 1982, and again in 1987. The first tribute was by The Touchdown Club of Washington D.C. They honored Gene Brito by establishing "The Gene Brito Achievement Award" that was presented annually to individuals who demonstrated the virtues of faith, perseverance, and fortitude. The recipients of this award included physically-challenged individuals who overcame their disabilities to succeed in sports. Past award winners included Edward M. Kennedy Jr., amputee; Darryl Stingley, paraplegic; Jimmy Huega, multiple sclerosis; and Rocky Bleier, wounded Vietnam veteran. The award was presented to 11 individuals before being discontinued. A permanent plaque for the award, Brito's jersey and helmet are on display in the trophy room of the Touchdown Club of Washington, D.C.[92]

A second award received after Gene Brito's passing was induction into the Washington Hall of Stars in September 1982. He was recognized for his performance, popularity, and contribution to the sports history of the District of Columbia. As part of the induction ceremony, Brito was posthumously presented a gold and ruby ring; his portrait hangs in the StarPlex Clubhouse at RFK Stadium; and his name and plaque are on display in the mezzanine railing around the Stadium.[93] A final, and interesting, tribute for Brito was induction into the National Italian American Sports Hall of Fame in 1987. The honor was based on his gridiron prowess, his life-long association with this community, and his ancestry on the part of one of his grandparents.[94] Genaro Herman "Mean Gene" Brito was indeed memorable, extraordinary, and a lasting monument not only to the sport he loved so much but also to the family and people he touched and inspired.

Thomas Raymond "Tom" Flores

Thomas Raymond Flores is the son of Mexican American farmworkers who, throughout his lifetime, has transcended many obstacles and barriers to become a four-time champion in professional football. This accomplishment is a story of a Mexican American/Latino who dedicated himself to work hard to overcome the strife and uncertainty in his life, and did so with an extraordinary sense of determination and conviction that made him successful. His remarkable story began inauspiciously in the lettuce fields, fruit orchards, and berry patches outside of Fresno, California. At eight years of age, the young Flores first worked as a lettuce and fruit picker. In an interview with *Los Angeles Times* editorial writer Frank del Olmo in 1979, Flores said, "You name it and I picked it."[95] At 15, he transitioned from a farmworker into a job as an iceman, lifting 300-lb. blocks at an ice house in nearby Sanger.[96] He credited this task with building his arm strength and earning him "The Ice Man" moniker due to his implacable demeanor under heavy pressure.[97]

Flores was born in Fresno, California, on March 21, 1937, to Tom Cervantes Flores and Nellie Flores. Both parents were farmworkers, and toiling in the fields was a necessity and a family affair. When the time arrived for the children to attend school, they did so because education was also a family requirement.[98] In addition to Tom, there was older brother Bob. Both attended Sanger Union High School and shared a passion for music. Tom played the trombone, while Bob played a "pretty good saxophone" in the high school jazz band.[99] Tom also played and starred in football, basketball, and baseball.

Tom Flores attended Fresno City College, where he quarterbacked the 1954 and 1955 teams. He was the team captain in 1955, and his play that year earned him Honorable Mention Junior College All-American status.[100] After two years at Fresno City College, Flores initially planned to transfer to San Jose State University, but a scholarship offer from College of the Pacific changed his mind, and he headed to Stockton instead of San Jose. At Pacific, Flores split the duties under center with another Mexican American, Jim Reynosa. Flores' best collegiate game was against San Jose State, as he connected on 12 of 14 passes for 3 touchdowns and 200-plus yards; playing only one half.[101] He played two seasons (1956–1957) for the Tigers. He also injured his shoulder, which resulted in painful and disappointing performances. He concluded his tenure at Pacific on a positive note, however, being recognized as a Scholastic All-American, earning the 1958 Amos Alonzo Stagg Award, Honorable Mention All-American, and playing in the 1957 East-West All-Star game.

With his collegiate career concluded, Flores waited to hear from the NFL. However, the only contact was a telegram from the Cleveland Browns indicating that they would draft him, though they never did. Angered by his exclusion, Flores looked north to play pro football and tried out with the Stampeders. His was in Calgary for two months and then was released due to his shoulder injury.[102] Not one to give up easily, Flores returned to Pacific and worked on finishing his Master's Degree. In 1959, he tried out for the Washington Redskins, but was once again hampered by the shoulder problem and was not signed. Flores eventually found a medical answer to his problem in a new surgical procedure that permanently corrected the recurring shoulder issue in 1960.[103]

Finally, a professional opportunity presented itself when he signed in 1960 with the Oakland Raiders of the newly formed American Football League (AFL). Flores beat out a dozen quarterbacks for the starting job with the Raiders. As a rookie, he led the league with a 54 percent pass completion rate and also suffered the fewest interceptions (12). In 1961, Flores finished second in the AFL in passing behind the great George Blanda of the title-winning Houston Oilers. In 1962, Flores was sidelined with a severe case of tuberculosis, then returned in 1963 and led the Raiders to a 10–4 record.

In the last game of that season, he had his greatest statistical performance as a player against the Houston Oilers. It came in a classic AFL shootout where he outgunned Blanda. On a rainy December 22, 1963, at Frank Youell Field in Oakland, one of the most memorable games in AFL history took place, and footballs were flying everywhere. Tom Flores completed 17 of 29 passes for 407 yards and six touchdowns, four of which went to Art Powell. Not to be outdone, Blanda completed 20 of 32 passes for five scores. The game came down to a late 39-yard field goal by Mike Mercer to seal the 52–49 Raiders triumph. *Oakland Tribune* sportswriter Scotty Stirling summarized the events as follows:

> It's all over for the Raiders but you have to figure that is the best runner-up team the American Football League has ever seen. There was no help forthcoming from Denver in San Diego (Chargers 58, Broncos 20), so the Raiders magnificent 10–4 season record simply means they lost out in the divisional race by one game, while the Eastern Division champions, Boston and Buffalo, will meet in a playoff to decide which of the two 7–6 clubs will play San Diego for all the marbles.... But the Davis Damoes put it on for the home folks in yesterday's finale. They hooked up with the Houston Oilers in a ding-dong passing battle that left league records scattered all over the slippery Youell Field turf. The final score was 52–49, with a 39-yard field goal by Mike Mercer swinging it Oakland's way in the final five minutes but not before Oakland's Tom Flores and Houston's George Blanda threw touchdown passes with record abandon for most of the afternoon.... The only guy capable of stealing thunder from the unerring quarterbacks and ends was Raider fullback Clem Daniels, who gained three yards on the final play of the game to set a new single season AFL record for rushing yardage.[104]

Even with these fantastic numbers, Flores was left out of the AFL All-Star game. He noted in his autobiography that: "I finished the season with 11 touchdown passes in the last two weeks and I was third in the AFL in passing. I thought that was a good comeback for me and the Raiders. I felt I should have gone to the AFL All-Star game that year."[105]

Cotton Davidson, who won some games for the Raiders and finished eighth in the league in passing statistics, was selected as the West's quarterback. Although Davidson did admit that Flores deserved to go instead of him, he could not turn down the opportunity to play in the game.[106]

The 1964–1966 seasons were mediocre ones for the Oakland Raiders, who managed a 21–17–4 mark over that span. Davidson played the 1964 season and generated a third-place finish in the Western Division. Flores returned as the starter for the next two years and led the Raiders to eight victories each year.[107] However, Flores' playing tenure with the Raiders ended at the conclusion of 1966. He was traded to the Buffalo Bills where he spent two seasons 1967–1968, followed by two with the Kansas City Chiefs in 1969–1970. He finished his career as a Super Bowl winner, though he was the backup for Len Dawson. Flores described the time he spent with the Bills and the Chiefs:

> Buffalo was disappointing because I was physically hurt both years. The Bills were a good team ... honest fans but I never fulfilled my abilities there.... Kansas City was big as we became world champions ... it was dream come true.[108]

3. The McCarthy Era and the Age of Activism

In 1971, Flores returned to the Bills as quarterback coach, replacing John Rauch, who resigned prior to the season; he remained a single season. Given the opportunity to return to California in 1972, Flores signed on as an assistant for John Madden with the Raiders. During the next seven seasons, Oakland claimed five Western Division Championships and defeated the Minnesota Vikings 32–14 in Super Bowl XI. At this point, Flores now possessed two Super Bowl Rings; one as a player and one as an assistant coach.[109]

On February 9, 1979, Tom Flores was named the head coach of the Oakland Raiders, replacing John Madden, who resigned due to health issues.[110] Flores was the second Mexican American/Latino named to be a head coach in the NFL, following Tom Fears. In 1980, Flores guided the Raiders to victory in Super Bowl XV, a 27–10 triumph over the Philadelphia Eagles. This championship was particularly significant because Mexican American Jim Plunkett also played in the championship game. Plunkett, who had been released by the San Francisco 49ers and written off by other NFL teams, signed with the Raiders. He was a backup with little playing time and had requested a trade. Coach Flores kept him on the roster, and when an injury ended Dan Pastorini's season, Plunkett stepped in and led the Oakland offense.[111] *Los Angeles Times* sportswriter Bob Oates summed up the Raiders' victory and Flores' approach to the game:

> In the opinion of some of those analyzing the game, this pressure and the way the competing teams responded to it—was one of three reasons Oakland won. Here's what some of the most knowledgeable scouts and coaches in pro football are saying about the AFC's eight wins in the last nine games against NFC teams.... The first two cites [sic] quarterback Jim Plunkett outplayed Ron Jaworski, while the Raiders' decisive emotional performance disrupted the Eagles' execution. The third reason being, Tom Flores was the calming agent who kept the Oakland playboys on course. A former Raiders quarterback with a good mind and strong leadership qualities, Flores had his team well-prepared for Philadelphia's tactics and strategies. But his low-key nature even contributed more. Flores indeed is the lowest-keyed coach to reach this game since Minnesota's Bud Grant and the lowest to win it. He makes Dallas' Tom Landry look like a jumping jack.[112]

In the Premier issue of *PRO! The Magazine of the National Football League*, August 1981, Tom Flores and Jim Plunkett were featured on the cover with the caption, "Jim Plunkett and Tom Flores: Hispanic Pride, Poise, And an NFL Title." The issue featured an article written by Dwight Chapin entitled, "Dos De La Misma Clase," translated as "Two of a Kind," in which he described about the sometimes rocky road Flores followed before winning the title:

> When Flores was hired to become head coach, writer Steve Cassady asked him the difference between his regime and Madden's, "It will be a lot duller," Flores said.... But the Madden fire obviously wasn't there, on the surface, and when the Raiders sagged, it was suggested Flores might go. "I read what was being said," Flores says. "I

heard rumors, and I'd be lying if I said they didn't bother me. But I've been released and cut and traded as a player. I know the possibility exists as a coach, too. The only barometer is wins and losses."[113]

Interestingly, the Chapin article is congratulatory but limited in important respects. Although the writer does address the familial, social, and athletic background of Plunkett and Flores, the historical value of the Latino firsts is minimized/downplayed.

As so often happens following a title, the 1981 season was not a good one for Oakland. The age of the offensive line was an issue, as well as a lack of depth at several positions. Plunkett and backup quarterback Marc Wilson both took beatings. The Raiders were also in the process of moving to Los Angeles.[114] Things improved in 1982 as the Raiders boasted a record of 8–1 for the strike-shortened season. Flores achieved another milestone in his career that year, being named the 1982 UPI AFC Coach of the Year.

In 1983, Flores led the newly minted Los Angeles Raiders to victory in Super Bowl XVIII. The Raiders beat Pittsburgh, 38–10, in the divisional round, then Seattle, 30–14, for the AFC crown. They played the Washington Redskins in the title tilt. Coach Flores wrote in his autobiography that defense was the key to the Raiders' success and credited his defensive coordinator:

> This was all the design of defensive coach Charlie Sumner, who recalled that we used a similar approach against another tricky offensive line to get us into Super Bowl XI.... He remembered that in the AFC championship game against the Pittsburgh Steelers, the Raiders deployed an inside linebacker eyeball-to-eyeball with the offensive guard ... who became [so] confused that he didn't pull on running plays when he supposed to.[115]

The Raiders' attacking defense stymied John Riggins' rushes and Joe Theismann's passing game. The offensive line opened up huge holes and allowed Marcus Allen to set a new NFL Super Bowl Rushing record of 191 yards, with two touchdowns. Jim Plunkett contributed a 12-yard touchdown pass to Cliff Branch. The final score was 38–9.[116] In the locker room after the game, Raiders owner Al Davis complimented the team and coach about their victory:

> I think today this organization, this team, this coaching staff, dominated so decisively that two things must be said. Not only, in my opinion, are you the greatest Raider Team of all time to have ever played any professional sport. Tom Flores isn't just a great coach in our league, but with all due respect, he's one of the greatest coaches of all time.[117]

In his final four seasons, Flores and the team were stymied by injuries, poor performances, and other factors. However, the 1984 season began with a symbolic victory in the career of Tom Flores. On September 16, 1984, the date that commemorates Mexico's Independence, Flores won his 50th game. The *NFL GameDay Program* of September 24, 1984, reported:

3. The McCarthy Era and the Age of Activism 149

Lost in the excitement of the Raiders' latest comeback win over the Kansas City Chiefs in Arrowhead Stadium was a personal milestone for brilliant head coach Tom Flores. The pressure-packed 22–20 victory over the Chiefs was the fiftieth league game victory for Flores since he became head coach of the Silver and Black on February 9, 1979.[118]

From 1984–1987, the Raiders compiled a 36–27 mark. They lost the wild-card game to Seattle, 13–7, in 1984. They managed to win their division in 1985, but lost to the New England Patriots, 27–20, in the AFC title game. In 1986, *The Football Encyclopedia: The Complete, Year-by-Year History of Professional Football from 1892 to the Present* documented some factors for the Raiders' subsequent decline:

> The Raiders team begins to show their age. The offensive line was blitzed for 64 sacks.... By mid-season Flores benches Marc Wilson in favor of the ancient Jim Plunkett, who played well until he was injured. Running back Marcus Allen had a terrible year ... fumbling at inopportune times.... Even the defense, long a source of pride, showed some slippage....[119]

In 1987, Los Angeles acquired running back Bo Jackson in mid-season to complement Marcus Allen, but a seven-game losing streak and continuing injuries led to a season record of 5–10. At this juncture in his coaching career, Tom Flores decided to retire amidst a barrage of unsubstantiated speculation from the press. On January 20, 1988, the Raiders announced the parting of the ways.[120]

Although Tom Flores looked forward to retirement, there were feelings of uncertainty. After all, his career spanned 27 years, and other things besides football would have to occupy his mind. Flores' success attracted the attention of Seattle Seahawks owner Ken Behring, who offered him the position of president and general manager starting in 1989.[121] With little hesitation, Flores accepted, thereby extending his career for another six years. The first three seasons, he served in the dual capacity with oversight regarding management and player negotiations. In his autobiography, *Fire in the Iceman*, Flores mentioned the successful resolution of Steve Largent's contract as one of his key accomplishments in that regard.[122] In Flores' third year, Chuck Knox left the Pacific Northwest to accept the head coaching position with the Los Angeles Rams. Behring pressured Flores into relinquishing his front-office responsibilities to coach the Seahawks.[123]

The final three years (1992–1994) of Flores' tenure, however, were part of a difficult rebuilding project. In 1992, the Seahawks finished with the worst record in the league and lost their two top quarterbacks, but did produce the NFL's Defensive Player of the Year, Cortez Kennedy.[124] In 1993, there was cause for optimism as rookie signal-caller Rick Mire completed 486 passes for 2,833 yards while running back Chris Warren produced a second consecutive 1,000-yard rushing season. Unfortunately, the Seahawks' defense stumbled badly, dropping all the way down to 23rd in the NFL.[125] Overall, these

Tom Flores (right) with Art Shell of the Raiders (courtesy Corky Trewin/Seattle Seahawks).

three seasons generated a 14–34 mark. At the time of his release, the franchise argued that Flores had done his best in a difficult situation. "If there had been any justice, things would have gone better for Flores—and the Seahawks under him. His tenure was marked by class and honesty, both on and off the field, but simply not enough victories to offset some of the inconsistencies." Tom Flores' pro football career thus ended without fanfare or excitement, but this conclusion does not and should not detract from his numerous accomplishments, both on and off the field.

After his years in football, Tom Flores was still a prominent figure and became a point of reference for racial issues in the NFL. For example, in 1988, freelance writer Richard Keeton interviewed him for the article, "A Minority of None—Why are there no black coaches in the National Football League?" Keeton asked Flores his views on the matter. Initially the Mexican American was reluctant to respond because the race issue in professional sports was quite controversial. He did acknowledge the volatility, stating, "I do not want to comment on why there are no black head coaches, because anything I say might not sound right to somebody."[126] Flores instead offered general comments on the tension that comes with being a head coach in the NFL. "The tension is indescribable and the pressure to win has caused a head-spinning turnover rate ... [Flores] recalls that after his first four years as a head coach, only five of his counter-parts in the NFL had greater longevity."[127] The remainder of the Keeton articles includes commentary from notable NFL coaches and spokesmen, and sociologist Dr. Harry Edwards. The article also identifies the prospects of several assistant black coaches in the NFL being considered candidates for head coaching positions.[128]

Flores was also cited as a point of reference concerning the lack of African American quarterbacks in the NFL. This leads to another important element in Flores' career: his ties with Marlin Briscoe. Briscoe entered the NFL in 1968 after being the first black quarterback to start for an AFL team (Denver Broncos). At the time of Briscoe's historical starting role, Flores was an injured backup quarterback with the Buffalo Bills. Although Briscoe was successful with various AFL and NFL teams, he did have personal issues that Coach Tom Flores recognized and offered to help him with. In the book, *The First Black Quarterback: Marlin Briscoe's Journey to Break the Color Barrier and Start in the NFL*, Briscoe and his co-author, Bob Schaller, devoted Chapter 18 to expressing his thanks for Flores' intervention and help during the low time in his life:

> Tom Flores and I crossed paths again. He allowed me to visit him at the Raiders' complex in El Segundo, California. He would loan me money, trying to help me out. One day in 1986, I saw him—as I often did—after practice. Again he gave me some money. "Marlin what's going on with this?" Tom asked me.... He scratched his chin and then looked me in the eye. "Marlin, are you on drugs?" I was ashamed, but I could see in his eyes that he cared deeply for me.[129]

Briscoe noted that Flores put him up at the Raiders' training camp and facilitated his rehabilitation. He wrote that Flores was a person he could trust and recognized him as a friend; that, in the end, was a factor in regaining his self-determination, eventually beating the odds and regaining his self-respect.[130]

Since leaving the sidelines and front office, Tom Flores and Jim Plunkett have served as radio announcers for the Raiders, reporting and analyzing at home games for the black and silver faithful. They are honored and respected by peers and fans. A major tribute to Coach Flores' career was his induction into the Latin American International Sports Hall of Fame in Laredo, Texas, in January of 2006.[131] Flores was recognized for his sterling character, athleticism, being a role model for youth, and coaching two Super Bowl victories. One important question that remains unanswered for Flores is whether he will receive the ultimate recognition and induction into the Pro Football Hall of Fame. Are four Super Bowl rings not worthy of consideration?

Daniel Dario "Danny" Villanueva

The Danny Villanueva football story is, like those of other Mexican Americans of the era, an itinerant journey in the Southwest that is fraught with unexpected change and diverse experiences. Daniel Dario Villanueva was born on November 5, 1937, in what was described as a two-room earthen hut in Tucumcari, New Mexico. The small town was initially a railroad camp named Douglas in 1901 and became a permanent settlement named Tucumcari in 1908. Interestingly, the community's name is derived from a mixture of the Comanche word for "ambush" and an Apache legend pertaining to an Apache chief, his daughter, and two braves, whose undying love for the chief's daughter was their demise.[132] Thus we have a rustic and historical setting for one of the homes of the Villanueva family.

Danny Villanueva was one of 12 children born to the Rev. Primitivo and Pilar Villanueva. His father was an itinerant Methodist minister, and Danny and the other children grew up wherever the Reverend Villanueva took a pulpit, which included Phoenix, Arizona, and Calexico, California.[133] The Villanuevas were blessed in many ways. Their eldest son, Primo was a star tailback for the 1954 UCLA Bruins National Collegiate Football Championship Team, while the younger son, Danny, would become an NFL pro football kicker/punter and later the wealthy owner and President of the Spanish International Communications Corporation (later renamed Univision).[134]

Danny Villanueva began his football career as a quarterback at Calexico High School in California and continued his gridiron development at Reedley Junior College in California in 1957. Regrettably, it was a short-lived experience due to arm and shoulder injuries that caused his return to New Mexico to pursue an education and to play football at New Mexico State University. At New Mexico State, Villanueva ended his quarterbacking ambitions and instead learned to kick a football, earning a scholarship. For the next two seasons (1958–1959) Villanueva doubled as the punter and place-kicker for the Aggies. In his senior year, Villanueva kicked seven of eight field goals, the longest from 47 yards,[135] to help his team earn a bid to the 1959 Sun Bowl in El Paso, where the Aggies beat North Texas, 28–8.[136]

Upon his graduation from New Mexico State University with a Bachelor's degree in English, Villanueva anticipated some interest by the NFL during the 1959 draft; this never materialized. He became a teacher rather than a football player, but that soon changed unexpectedly as a matter of luck or providence when the Los Angeles Rams expressed a need for a kicker. Chuck Benedict, a radio broadcaster at the Rams' training camp, remembered Villanueva from his high school playing days and suggested that the team's coaches consider him for a tryout.[137]

When the Rams contacted Villanueva, he wasted no time and flew to the team's training camp in Van Nuys. Once there, the Rams drove him to Grant High School in Van Nuys, where he reported to coach Bob Waterfield. The field general evaluated Villanueva's kicking and accuracy. The *Los Angeles Times* reported Villanueva's performance and reactions:

3. The McCarthy Era and the Age of Activism

I thought he was the greatest thing I'd ever heard of and so I kicked and kicked. I don't recall the exact number anymore, but it was 30-something in a row and I never missed, and he said, "I've seen enough," so they offered me a contract.[138]

Villanueva received a $5,500 contract, a bargain for the Rams because he was both punter and place-kicker. The Rams' rookie free-agent enjoyed a good 1960 season but was initially reminded of his ethnic heritage when the time came for the players to board the buses that took them to the games. In a 2008 interview with ESPN, Danny Villanueva also remembers his nickname, "El Kickador," bestowed on him by the news media, as well as the bullfighting music that was played whenever he took the field. However, the point of his ethnicity was then made abundantly clear. Villanueva stated, "We had a black bus and we had a white bus in those days, we were segregated." He recalled a teammate announcing "all black guys get on that bus, white guys get on that bus, and Danny you take a cab." He understood that he was "neither fish nor fowl."[139]

The 1960 season ended with the Rams posting a 4–7–1 mark. Villanueva hit on 28 of 28 extra points and 12 of 17 field goals for a total of 64 points.[140] His biggest moment of the season came versus Green Bay, where he kicked a short field goal in the final 22 seconds of the game beat the Packers, 33–31.[141] In 1961, Villanueva and the Rams endured another tough season, finishing 4–10. Villanueva was, again, productive, connecting on all 32 extra points and 13 of 27 field goal attempts for 71 points.[142] In 1962, he set a Rams' record by averaging 45.5 yards per punt and scored 56 points. Los Angeles lost four of their five first games and continued to slide in the standings, so coach Bob Waterfield resigned after the eighth game of the season. Ownership problems added to the team's disorganization and problems on the field.[143]

The 1963 campaign was a productive year for Villanueva. He finished third among NFL punters with a 45.4 average and once again led the Rams in scoring with 52 points.[144] His best punting day that season was against the Chicago Bears on October 12, when he averaged 51 yards on five punts, the fifth-highest in Rams history. His place-kicking skills were among the few highlights of another unsuccessful Rams season when they finished 5–9.[145] In 1964, his final year with Los Angeles, Villanueva was solely a punter, as the Rams signed Bruce Gossett as their place-kicker. The reason for this move was not that Villanueva's place-kicking abilities had lessened, but to have him focus on punting. The decision was a good one, as his punts averaged 44.1 yards. Once again, the team struggled and finished a mediocre 5–7–2.[146]

At the end of the 1964 season, Villanueva was surprised to learn that he had been traded to the Dallas Cowboys for tight end Tommy McDonald. Although there was some bitterness, he maintained a positive outlook on the transaction, as evidenced in his comment to the *Los Angeles Times*' Al Wolf:

Last May, Los Angeles Rams kicking specialist (since 1960) Danny Villanueva purchased a new home for his family in Sepulveda. Two days later, he was traded to the Dallas Cowboys. If the 27-year old athlete harbors any bitterness or heartbreak, he keeps such emotions well hidden. "I have nothing but gratitude toward the Ram management," Danny said Friday at the Cowboys training camp in Thousand Oaks. "Everything I have—a job in the National Football League, two television programs, a newspaper column, and a partnership in two real estate developments.... I owe to the Rams for signing me as a free agent out of New Mexico State in 1960."[147]

Wolf also noted, "Villanueva may have nothing but kind words for his five years with the Rams, but he also has this to say about the *Los Angeles Times* Charity game between the two clubs, 'I'd like nothing better than to start my Dallas career by kicking a winning field goal against the Rams.'"[148]

For the next two seasons, Villanueva led the Cowboys in scoring with 85 and 107 points respectively. Unlike the Rams, the Cowboys were successful, making it all the way to the NFL championship game, only to lose to Green Bay. Villanueva had a stellar season. His 107 points were second-best in the NFL, and his 56 consecutive extra point conversions in a single season established an NFL record[149] Ray Wersching of the San Francisco 49ers tied the record in 1984.[150] A key moment that year was Villanueva's successful kick against the Washington Redskins on November 13, a 20-yard field goal with 15 seconds remaining in the game to defeat the Cowboys' hated rivals, 31–30. Sportswriter Carlton Stowers described the drive leading up to this kick:

Danny Villanueva, 1960 (courtesy Dallas Cowboys/James D. Smith).

> It was a game which had all the earmarks of defeat for the Cowboys, then still smoldering the stigma of not being able to win the big one. The fading minutes of the clock were fast escaping when Washington punter Pat Richter, protecting a 30–28 lead, punted the ball inside the Cowboys five-yard line. On the sidelines, Danny Villanueva had no reason to be nervous. This one he knew would not come down to him. There was simply not enough time. However, Cowboys quarterback Don Meredith had not given up. He threw

a long pass to Pete Gent and then one to Pettis Norman. Dan Reeves caught one coming out of the backfield and the miracle was beginning to take form.

It became a real possibility when Meredith, rolling out to his right, was knocked out of bounds and tackled by an over-zealous Redskins defender after he was clearly off the field of play. As the official stepped off the 15-yard penalty, 11 seconds showed on the clock. It had come down to Villanueva. Villanueva remembers, "It was just over 30 yards. But it looked a lot further. The holder, Dan Reeves, bobbled the snap and I had to wait. There was no timing on the kick; I just tried to nurse it over the goal posts. I've never in my life been so relieved to see an official raise his arms."[151]

As a souvenir of the winning field goal, the fan who caught the football was Pete Richert, former Los Angeles Dodgers and Washington Senators pitcher, who was seated in the end zone with his son. In a thoughtful gesture, Richert returned the game ball to Villanueva afterward. Surprised to retrieve the ball, the elated Villanueva noticed Richert's son had hopes of keeping the ball, so he got another ball from the equipment manager and traded pigskins with him.

But Villanueva's excitement was quickly suppressed when he returned to Dallas to learn that his two-year old son, Jimmy, had been saved from drowning by a conscientious neighbor, Robert Somerall. The near-tragedy occurred about the same time that Villanueva kicked the ball through the uprights for the win. Villanueva described his sentiments regarding his son's near-death experience. "When I got home and heard about it, the first thing I did was find the guy. I gave him a blank check and told him to make it out for whatever amount he wanted. He handed it back to me and said he would gladly settle for a couple of tickets to the playoff game."[152]

The Cowboys' victory propelled them into the playoffs for the first time in the history of the Dallas franchise. After Villanueva's dramatic kick in the Washington game, the Cowboys won four of their remaining five games to play the Green Bay Packers in the NFL Championship game. Unfortunately, they lost, 34–27. Villanueva contributed two field goals and three extra points. The Cowboys posted a season record of 10–3–1.[153]

The year 1967 was Villanueva's final as a pro, and it was business as usual. His kicking was effective and helped Dallas return to the playoffs. They battled the Browns for the Eastern Conference Championship and beat Cleveland, 52–14. Villanueva was perfect in his placements, converting seven of seven extra points and his only field goal attempt.[154] This set up the Cowboys' opportunity to get revenge against the Packers in the title tilt. This became the legendary "Ice Bowl" that sportswriter Mike Shropshire aptly described:

> An epic that contained so many elements of triumph and despair, of suffering and salvation, the term "frozen tundra" maintained a standard definition in the geological texts. It meant "a level or undulating treeless plain characteristic of arctic or subarctic regions that consist of black mucky soil with permanently frozen subsoil that supports a dense growth of often conspicuously flowering dwarf herbs."[155]

The teams played a closely contested game that turned on the last play. The Cowboys led the Packers, 17–14, in the fourth quarter on a 50-yard pass from Dan Reeves to Lance Rentzel, as Villanueva converted the point after. After a Villanueva punt, the Packers, led by Bart Starr, charged down the "frozen tundra" to the Dallas goal line. The field clock showed 13 seconds left when the home team utilized their last timeout. The final play of the game was a successful quarterback sneak that resulted in the winning touchdown and the Packers' third consecutive NFL Championship.[156] Although he was a part of a legendary game, the time had arrived, after eight successful seasons, for Danny Villanueva to announce his retirement.

The once self-described portly football player embarked on a new career as a Spanish-language sportscaster with radio/television station KMEX in Los Angeles. This choice soon produced great results and helped springboard Villanueva into a respected leadership position within the Spanish-language communications industry. He became a self-made millionaire and a very successful executive, including president and owner of the Spanish International (SIN) Communications Corporation. However, despite his remarkable pro football experience and business success, Danny Villanueva never lost sight of his identity, family, and his origins. His father and mother were always strong influences in his life until the very end. They initially wanted him to be a missionary and pressed upon him the notion that he had to serve people because that was the proper thing to do. He never forgot that goal, and despite all the successes, his charity work, as well as the disappointments, he remained true to that notion. In a newspaper interview in 1985, Villanueva expressed his thankfulness for family and success, and reflected on his life and parents' wishes. He stated, "I remember a phrase my father used to use: He said, 'Well done, my good and faithful servant.' Was all he said ... and one day I want him to tell me, 'Well done.'"[157]

No doubt that Daniel Dario "Danny" Villanueva received not only his parents' "well done," but "a well done" from the many people he knew and helped throughout his life and career. He passed on June 18, 2015, in Ventura, California, leaving a legacy of Latino community service and, significantly, a pro football first as one of the early Latino stars in the history of the sport. At the time of his passing, the Villanueva survivors include his wife, Myrna Schmidt; two sons, Daniel L. and Jim; four brothers, Samuel, Paul, Ben and Primo; four sisters, Mary Beth, Lily Hernandez, Noemi Prince, and Ester Aguilar; five grandchildren; and eight great-grandchildren.[158]

Ricardo Jose "Rick" Casares

The premier Spanish-surnamed running back in professional football history is Tampa, Florida-born Ricardo Jose "Rick" Casares.[159] The son of a

Spanish father and Italian mother, Casares played a tough and fierce brand of football at all levels of competition and is greatly remembered and respected by his coaches, teammates, fans, and opponents. Importantly and historically significant is the fact that Rick Casares is the first and only Spanish-surnamed athlete to hold a rushing yardage title in the National Football League.

His life's journey began during the Great Depression on July 4, 1931, in Tampa, Florida. According to Tampa sportswriter Paul Guzzo, the Casares family resided in Tampa during hard times and violence resulting from the ills of the Depression and other social and political events. When the young Casares was a seven-year-old, his father was gunned down in a gangland slaying, and his death forced the family to move to Paterson, New Jersey.[160] When asked about his father's death, Casares simply stated that he had no desire to provide details but added, "Tampa was a tough town then; real tough."[161]

In Paterson, New Jersey, Casares' family settled in only to learn that Paterson was not much different from the tough and violent conditions in Tampa. Casares knew that life in his new neighborhood was also a challenge. He and his friends regularly met in parking lots throughout the city to fight with other groups of neighbor kids. However, the fights were solely to determine which was the toughest area, and according to writer Paul Guzzo, "the large and athletic Casares never lost a fight for his neighborhood."[162]

When Casares turned 15, the street fighting moved into the boxing ring. Physical development and skill took place, and Casares scored victories in the New Jersey Diamond Gloves Tournament 160-pound weight division, New Jersey's version of the Golden Gloves. His performance in the tournament was so impressive that he caught the attention of a well-known boxing trainer and promoter who offered his mother a monetary consideration. The offer was made to his mother because the young Casares was still a minor. However, his mother adamantly said no because she did not want her son fighting for a living. The decision frustrated the rebellious youth, who wanted to box professionally. His mother, in turn, thought it best for her son to return to his late father's family in Tampa. Her decision proved to be the best remedy and resulted in a more peaceful and positive atmosphere for her son.[163]

Back in Tampa, Casares received support and positive influences, and was introduced to high school athletics. He attended Jefferson High School, where the teenage Rick Casares became the school's star athlete. He excelled in basketball, baseball, track, and not surprisingly, football.[164] There was no stopping him as he led Jefferson High School to the city championship in both 1948 and 1949; in the process, he was selected the Outstanding Player of the 1949 All-American Game played in Memphis, Tennessee.[165]

Recognized as a triple-threat athlete, Casares' reputation stretched statewide and collegiate coaches closely watched this future star with anticipation. When the time came, Casares chose the University of Florida in Gainesville and played for the Gators from 1951 to 1953. He was a powerful runner, considered by many experts of the time as the best fullback in the South.[166]

In the *1951 Florida Gators' Media Guide*, Rick Casares was listed under the category of "Non-Lettermen" as a quarterback and halfback.[167] At the end of the season, his contributions included 422 rushing yards, 25 points, 8 receptions for 120 yards, 1 touchdown pass, and 33 punts for 1,202 yards, an average of 39.1 yards per punt.[168] The Gators' record was 5–5.[169] It was an impressive year that moved Casares from the non-lettermen category into the starting lineup.

Casares quickly established himself in 1952 and averaged 28 carries per game, rushing for 635 yards, scoring seven touchdowns, converting 21 of 28 extra points, and averaging 41.2 yards on 24 punts. He led the Gators' offense as the team finished 8–3 and earned an invitation to play the University of Tulsa in the Gator Bowl.[170] The game was a close contest, and a penalty determined the winner. Casares rushed for 86 yards, scored a touchdown, and kicked two extra points, with the second making the difference. Casares missed on his second attempt, but a Tulsa penalty allowed him another try. With game in the balance, he split the uprights. The *New York Times* reported: "Rick Casares got a second chance to kick a conversion because of a Tulsa penalty today and that gave Florida a 14–13 victory over Tulsa in the eighth Gator Bowl football game before a crowd of 30,015."[171]

The 1953 season for Casares was a short one due to his military duty. After two games, the Gators' co-captain received a draft notice advising of his induction into U.S. Army. Complying with the notice, he reported for training and duty, but his football skills do not go unnoticed. During his brief stay in the Army, he performed for the Fort Jackson football team and garnered All-Army and All-Service accolades. He also played in the Chicago Collegiate All-Star Game and was selected by the Chicago Bears in the second round of the 1954 draft.[172] Casares recalled his reaction in Paul Guzzo's article:

> I was stationed at Fort Jackson in South Carolina when I got the call from the Bears telling me I was drafted.... Honestly, I never dreamt of playing professional football so when I got the call I was shocked. But then a short time later I got another call on base; it was from Canada. A team in the Canadian Football league offered me $20,000 to play as compared to the $8,000 the Bears offered me.[173]

Prior to his discharge in 1955, Casares reflected on the offers he received. He travelled to Toronto to evaluate his CFL possibilities. He liked the money in Canada but also talked with George Halas, who arranged a meeting in Chicago. Casares initially leaned toward Toronto but changed his mind after Halas offered him $10,000. While this was still less than Toronto offered, he realized that Chicago was a better choice to care for his mother. Also, he could not pass on the opportunity to play for the "Monsters of the Midway."[174] Upon

3. The McCarthy Era and the Age of Activism 159

separation from the Army, he reported to the Bears' training camp, donned the black and orange uniform, and became one of the NFL's most formidable running backs.

His rookie season was impressive, as Casares crashed his way through opposing defenses. Although he saw limited action in the first three games, the pattern changed by week four. On a running play, he raced 81 yards for a touchdown, the Bears' longest run from scrimmage that year. The run occurred on a play that was supposed to feature a handoff to halfback Bobby Watkins. Quarterback Ed Brown called for a halfback toss to Watkins, who advised Brown he was not feeling well. To give Watkins a rest, Casares suggested that he, instead of Watkins, be moved to halfback. Watkins agreed to trade places. This confused quarterback Brown as Casares took the pitch-out and began his outstanding run. What better way to start a pro football career?[175] Casares recollected:

> I'll never forget that as long as I live.... I can see it as if it were yesterday, all my cuts, one guy hitting me across the head. Practically everyone got a shot at me. Five yards from the end zone, somebody took a dive at me, so I went diving in and wound up lying on my back. I was so filled with exultation that I raised my legs up on my neck. I was so happy, well, I stood on my head.[176]

The Casares end zone celebration announced that he had arrived in the NFL, and there was more to come.

The 1956 season was historic as the hard-running Casares rushed for 1,126 yards on 234 carries to lead all NFL ground gainers. He set the rushing mark against the Detroit Lions, a game marked by fisticuffs and mayhem. From the opening kickoff, fights broke out and continued throughout the game. Casares exchanged fisticuffs with Lions players and left with an injured wrist with 6:30 left to play in the contest. The *New York Times'* Louis Effrat described the scene:

> Football and fisticuffs plus a considerable amount of no-holds barred grappling were on display at Wrigley Field today as the Chicago Bears walloped the Detroit Lions 38 to 21. Ignoring for the moment the outcome of the numerous extra-curricular activities, the principal prize—the Western Conference Championship of the National Football League—went to the Bears as a direct result of their convincing triumph.[177]

Richard M. Cohen book's *The Scrapbook History of Pro Football*, provided details of the game and the fighting:

> It was a rough, tough ball game in which several players were ejected for fighting and a free-for-all developed in the fourth quarter with players, fans, and police engaging in the melee. As best could be determined, the big battle featured Bear quarterback George Blanda and Lion tackle Gil Mains that held up play several minutes.[178]

Despite sitting out a portion of the contest, Casares was very productive, rushing for 190 yards, including a 68-yard touchdown jaunt. His rushing yardage not only gave him the annual NFL rushing title but also bettered the old Bears rushing record of 1,004 set in 1944 by Hall of Famer Beattie Feathers.[179]

Chicago won the Western title and prepared for the title game versus the New York Giants. Although the Bears were favored to win, the 20-degree weather severely hampered Chicago's offense. At the Polo Grounds in New York City on December 15, 1956, the New York Giants and Chicago Bears clashed. The Giants scored quickly and led by the score of 34–7 at halftime. The Bears scored their only touchdown on Casares' second quarter, 9-yard run. Although the Bears were favored, the New York defense, led by defensive end Andy Robustelli, limited Casares to a mere 43 yards on 14 attempts.[180] Although lacking the NFL championship to cap a great season, the Bears fullback was named to the NFL All-Pro Team in 1956, and he played in the first of five consecutive Pro Bowls (1965–1960). The Chicago Bears had winning seasons in 1958, 1959, 1961, and 1962. Time and time again, Casares pounded defenders for yardage. He led the Bears in rushing from 1956 to 1960 and in scoring in 1956 and 1959.[181]

The 1961 NFL collegiate draft was significant for Chicago as they selected their number one choice, tight end Mike Ditka, from the University of Pittsburgh. In two seasons, Ditka, quarterback Bill Wade, Casares (in a limited role), and other veterans helped form the core of the 1963 championship team. Ditka recalled Casares as follows:

> He was one of the most inspirational players I ever played with…. It was exciting to get into the huddle with him and look into his eyes because you knew he was all business…. He was a man's man. He did everything by example, nothing by word…. He was a tough guy that didn't wear it outside…. Although he was a very nice man, a quiet spoken guy, but no one ever messed with Rick Casares. He had a reputation.[182]

The 1963 season was one of great success for the Bears. Their defense made some adjustments and became one of the strongest in the NFL. According to Irv Goodman, sportswriter for *SPORT: The Magazine For the Sports-Minded*, the Bears' 1960s defense resembled the old "Monsters of the Midway" defense of years past. He wrote:

> In professional football, the club with the extra something—call it spirit, pride of heritage, old fashioned determination or whatever you will—is the Chicago Bears…. Now it appears that George Halas has another edition of the Monsters of the Midway, a loaded club that should be good for quite a few years.[183]

Goodman's article was lengthy and compares the players of the present and yesteryear, examining the attitudes, similarities, and differences. He described Casares as committed, very strong and hardworking, with good speed and great power.[184] Offensively, Casares, Joe Marconi, and Willie Galimore ran exceptionally well, while Ditka caught 59 passes. Casares was having a excellent year until he broke his ankle on November 17 against the Green Bay Packers and was out for the remainder of the season. This Bears team lost just one game that season and advanced to the NFL championship game.[185] Unlike the results of their previous championship tilt versus the New York Giants in 1956, this time the outcome favored the Bears. The sides played in 8-degree weather at Wrigley Field on December 29, 1963. The Chicago defense was the key as it rose to the occasion and intercepted five Y.A. Tittle passes. The victory was sweet revenge for the Bears as they defeated New York, 14–10, to capture their first NFL Championship since 1946.

In 1964, Rick Casares played his tenth and last season with the Chicago Bears. Nagging injuries kept him from performing at 100 percent, and the tough warrior gave way to other Bears runners such as Joe Marconi, Jon Arnett, and Ron Hall. He left Chicago as the team's all-time career rushing leader, a mark that has since been surpassed by the immortal Walter Payton. At season's end, the Bears traded Casares to the Washington Redskins. However, injuries continued to bother the former Gator. In his first game for the Redskins, Casares sustained a season-ending rib injury that resulted in his being released.[186]

Simultaneously, the American Football League (AFL) was expanding into Miami, and the Dolphins would begin play in 1966. On June 19 the team signed the Florida legend as a free agent. Dolphins coach George Wilson commented about the signing:

> When I was the head coach of the West, one year in the Pro Bowl, he played for me and turned in an outstanding performance. Last year (1965), I was an assistant at Washington and we were counting on him to be the number one fullback before he was injured, and I felt that with his experience and all-around ability, he could be of tremendous help to our offense.[187]

In Miami's AFL debut against Oakland, the aging Latino fullback caught a touchdown pass, but the Dolphins lost to the Raiders, 23–14.[188] For Miami, it was a typical expansion season, but for Ricardo Jose "Rick" Casares, it was his last glory on the field, bringing to a close a 12-year professional career.

From the very beginning, Casares seized the opportunity to play football and had all the necessary talent and instincts to be great. Nothing in the game escaped his scrutiny, and only injuries curtailed his performance. In retirement, the reclusive Casares wondered in 1977 about playing again. He was quoted in a Tampa Bay newspaper article titled, "Flashback of a Fullback":

> If there is one thing Casares envies about modern players, it is that they are playing and he is not. In his 11th year out of football, he's still wondering when retirement will start coming easier. "If anything," he says, "it's getting worse. I've just about realized that I'm not going to make a comeback, but I'd make a deal with the devil tomorrow if I could trade ten years of my life for one season with my full capabilities. Some players say football's just a game, but it was everything to me."[189]

Throughout his life and football career, Casares was well-respected by all who knew him. To him, actions spoke louder than words, and he is remembered not only for the records set, but also by the vigorous and determined way he set them. He passed away on September 13, 2013, in Tampa, Florida, survived by his wife Polly Casares, a daughter, grandson, sister and extended family. As a U.S. Army veteran, Mr. Casares was buried in the Sarasota National Cemetery. He will be both missed and genuinely remembered as a gentleman, athlete, and as of this writing, the greatest Latino running back of all time. His legacy lives in the tributes received: inducted into the University of Florida's Athletic Hall of Fame, the Bears' Ring of Honor, the Chicago Sports Hall of Fame, the Tampa Sports Hall of Fame, and the Italian American Sports Hall of Fame. However, one important honor remains that is lacking in the Casares resume: induction into Canton.

1962 Brackenridge Eagles—Texas Schoolboy Class AAAA State Football Champions

Like other late 50s' and early 60s' South Texas towns with large Mexican American populations, San Antonio exemplified the exclusionary treatment of Mexicans, Mexican-Americans, and Blacks. School segregation was the law, movie theatres maintained "colored balconies," and, separate water fountains also displayed signs that read, "Whites only," "Mexicans," and "Coloreds." All these restrictions were in place to separate peoples for reasons that were not in the best interest of humanity. Within this environment of exclusion, there appeared in 1962 a high school football team comprised primarily of Mexican American, Black, and a few Anglo athletes from the East and Westside neighborhoods of San Antonio. These courageous young men utilized the football field to challenge and overcome established racial stigmas and barriers and to win the 1962 Texas Schoolboy Class AAAA State Football Championship.

The championship journey began in 1958 with the hiring of head coach Weldon Forren, who despite the discouraging assessment of the team by the School District Athletic Director, accepted the position with a determination to make Brackenridge a football power.[190] In the seasons leading up to the championship run, the Brackenridge Eagles matured as a team and transitioned from winning just two games in 1959 to six wins in 1960 and seven in 1961 (including a District 16 AAAA crown). Needless to say, expectations for 1962 were high. The campaign began inauspiciously, however. The Eagles won the first two games, beating Uvalde, 42–0, and Stephen F. Austin of Austin, 31–14. They lost three of the next four. The only commentary by Coach Forren regarding the three losses was a reference to being careless on

3. The McCarthy Era and the Age of Activism 163

defense.¹⁹¹ The Eagles addressed their errant ways and completed a 5–0 run to win another district title.¹⁹²

The next hurdle in the journey was the Bi-District game against the cross-town Highland Owls. The game took place on November 30, 1962. The Eagles won, 21–3. The game's notable players included quarterback Victor Castillo and running backs Warren McVea and Robert Wade.¹⁹³ For the following week's quarter-final tilt, Brackenridge prepared for the Southernmost Brownsville Eagles, who were no pushover and equaled Brackenridge's speed on offense. The Eagles anticipated a close contest but it turned out to be no contest as they beat Brownsville, 38–13. Once again, Warren McVea led the offense with four touchdowns while quarterback Victor Castillo completed 9 of 18 passes for 189 yards. Other stars included Douglas Coffee, Isidro Villalobos, Louis Perez, William Hines, Robert Wade, Johnny Pesina, and Alfred Valdez. The victory moved Brackenridge into the semi-finals against one of

The Brackenridge High School Eagles, San Antonio, Texas, 1962. Texas School Boy State Football Champions (Allee Wallace photographer/The San Antonio Light Collections/The UT Institute of Texan Cultures at San Antonio. No.5131/ Zuma Press).

the state's powerhouse teams, the Spring Branch Bears.[194] On the Thursday before the game, the *San Antonio Express and News* provided pre-game analysis and reported that, "As one of the last two undefeated class AAAA schools in the state, the Spring Branch Bears find themselves just two games away from a possible perfect season and a state championship." The newspaper did not mention the Eagles and seemed to have conceded the contest to the Bears. The game was played on December 15 at Rice Stadium in Houston.[195]

For this contest, Brackenridge made sweeping changes to their defensive scheme so as to offset Spring Branch's strong offensive line. Spring Branch countered with changes to guard against Brackenridge's offensive speed. The favored Bears led 15–12 at intermission. The score could have been worse if not for excellent defensive plays by the Eagles' Edward Coleman and Robert Wade. For the rest of game, however, quarterback Victor Castillo was energized and put on a passing exhibition that left Spring Branch dumbfounded as he tossed five touchdowns passes to lead the Eagles to a 30–23 victory. Castillo passed for 368 yards. Game notables, in addition to other players already mentioned were: Pete Bautista, Johnny Pesina, and Floyd Boone.[196] Defensively several other players were credited for their outstanding play: Douglas Coffee, Alfred Valdez, Isidro Villalobos, Louis Perez, and Eddie Villarreal.[197]

The unheralded and underdog Eagles would play the other undefeated team, the Borger Bulldogs, for the AAAA Football Championship. The championship game was a dream come true for the Brackenridge players and coaches. Prior to the contest, Brackenridge Coach Forren commented on the players' game outlook, "Our boys seem to be in top physical and mental condition … and we hope our open field offense will be too much for the Bulldogs' close-in type of ball." The Brackenridge scouting reports, on the other hand, showed Borger as a team which operated from the straight "I" formation and liked to run tackle to tackle power plays behind a strong line.[198] The San Antonio newspaper further reported, "These boys aren't worried about playing Borger, or anybody else. This is just another ball game.[199]

At 2 p.m. on Saturday, December 22, the Brackenridge Eagles confidently marched out onto the field to play their foes at the new Abilene Public School Stadium. Borger drew first blood by forcing a safety just 70 seconds in the game and followed with a touchdown to make the score 8–0. Undaunted, the Eagles rebounded with Castillo's aerial heroics. The game was close, but Castillo's 14 completions of 26 passes for 256 yards and his three two-point conversions were the key to success. His principal receivers were Pete Bautista and Warren McVea. When the final whistle sounded, the scoreboard read Eagles 30, Bulldogs 26. The deserving and emotional Eagles were the 1962 state champs![200] Afterwards, there were great celebrations in all of San Antonio, but particularly in the respective Eastside and Westside neighborhoods.

Unfortunately, during this era, whenever non-whites were victorious in

3. The McCarthy Era and the Age of Activism 165

contests of this nature, there was almost always controversy. The week before Brackenridge played Borger, there was a dispute regarding the exchange and use of game films. Borger contended there would be no exchange, based on some obscure district regulation that prohibited such transactions. Soon thereafter, Coach Forren learned that Borger already possessed Brackenridge game films, and he quickly arranged to secure Borger film and scouting reports from other coaches.[201] Another controversy was the selection of the All-State Team. The Texas Sportswriters Association released their choices for the Class AAAA State Team on December 27, 1962. Regrettably, there was not a single Brackenridge Eagles football player selected as part of the first, second or honorable mention teams.[202] Suspiciously, the scribes explained that their reason for the release was a deadline of December 8 for their selections. The question was asked, why they did not release the All-State team selections at that time, but instead waited until after the championship game? It was pretty evident that their selections were racially motivated and a great injustice to all Texas players and to the history of sport in this state.

In 2011, some 50 years later, noted Mexican American sportswriter David Flores revisited a few of the Brackenridge football champions to reminisce about their glory days. He documented their remembrances:

> "It was special," said Claudis Minor, a 16-year-old senior offensive lineman that season.... "It will never happen again." Robert Wade commented, "It means a lot to get together with these guys.... It's good to reminisce about our games, practices and trips...." Fellow teammate Eddie Villarreal, a senior tight end/linebacker, agreed. Quarterback Victor Castillo said, "It's a unique situation as far as the cohesiveness that we have.... We accomplished something out of the ordinary and then there's the makeup of the team. We were very close." Starting safety on the team David Hardin, whose father was Anglo and mother was Hispanic, acknowledged the Eagles' roster was composed of Hispanics and African Americans.... He also kiddingly remarked that coach Forren referred to him as the Great White Hope on the team.... George "Mickey" Cook, a sophomore lineman on the varsity in 1962, said he believed the Eagles were underestimated in the playoffs because of their race and ethnicity.[203]

As a student (referring to the author Longoria) at another 1962 San Antonio public school that was also predominately Mexican American, I recall to this day how proud I felt to be a Mexican American; and more importantly, to see these young men succeed when they/we are always expected to fail. Their success instilled a great sense of pride in their communities, San Antonio, and more importantly, upon countless numbers of Mexican Americans and African Americans, young and old, throughout all of Texas.

4

Increased Numbers and Diversity at All Levels, 1971–1990[1]

The 1970 Census presented Americans with a new pan-ethnic term: "Hispanic." The purpose of this exonym was to capture (more effectively?) the totality of the burgeoning population of Spanish-speakers/surnamed individuals, be they descended of Mexican, Cuban, Puerto Rican, or other stock (or born in those countries) stemming from the Spanish Empire. As noted in Chapter 3, the 1960s generated substantial changes in many facets of Latino/a life in the United States. As a result of the marches, strikes, demonstrations, "blowouts" and other political actions, there were, eventually, improvements in the economic and social results for many. Of course, not all in the population benefited to the same extent. Again, we turn to Zaragoza Vargas for a brief synopsis (focused on Mexican Americans) of this overarching trend. By 1980, the start of the so-called "Decade of the Hispanic," it was clear that "Many Mexican Americans attained success, as the well-educated among them broke down barriers of discrimination and entered better paying professional jobs. However, many more ... were profoundly affected by ... the restructuring of the United States economy and ... the savage unemployment precipitated by deindustrialization."[2]

In addition to the Mexican American community flexing its muscle in substantive ways, the 1960s also began the process for bringing more and more diverse individuals of "Hispanic" background into the nation, initially through the Immigration and Nationality Act of 1965 (also known as the Hart-Celler Act) with its principal purpose being that of "family reunification." As historian Neil Foley articulates in his work, *Mexicans in the Making of America*, once within the national borders, these immigrants "could sponsor other family members to immigrate. Few realized that the family reunification provision of the law would set off a chain migration that resulted in the exponential increase of immigrants from Asia and Latin America. In less than

4. Increased Numbers and Diversity at All Levels, 1971–1990 167

two decades, almost two out of every three immigrants came from Asia and Latin America, a large percentage of them from a single country—Mexico."[3]

The results of the Chicano Movement and the immigration (both legal and illegal) fueled by the Hart-Celler Act increased both the variety and numbers of persons from Latin American backgrounds in the United States. There were both positive and negative results from these overarching trends. Not surprisingly, both major political parties sought to develop (or, in the case of the Democrats, strengthen) ties to this burgeoning population, and there were repercussions in other aspects of American/Latino social life as well.

Foley noted a few important (and generally positive) developments in this regard in business and in the marketplace. For example, Richard Nixon pushed for set-asides for federal contracts for minority- (and women-) owned companies and for providing millions of dollars for federal funds to school districts to back endeavors for children with limited English proficiency, through the 1968 Bilingual Education Act. This was done not only in hope of helping establish a firm commercial and educational foundation, but also with the anticipation of having some of these folks align themselves with the Republican Party. By 1980, it was common for large corporations, such as McDonald's, Coca-Cola, and even Coors, which had had a troubled relationship with Spanish-speakers, to demarcate millions specifically to target the proliferating segment. As a result of such developments, new organizations, the National Council for La Raza (NCLR) for example, commenced operations, not in "traditional" locales of residency (such as Texas and California), but rather in the heart of the nation's capital. Further, the leadership of this newly minted entity sought to serve as "an advocate for all Latino subgroups and produced a magazine, *Agenda* dedicated to 'Hispanic' issues." Rather than continue with a nationalistic (and often more radical) philosophical push and nomenclature (as in the 1960s), the NCLR instead sought to "cultivate ties to politicians and private-sector funding sources."[4]

The mushrooming Latino/a presence was also noticeable in the political arena with the creation of the National Association of Latino Elected and Appointed Officials (NALEO) in 1978 (it had a different name when it started in 1976, tied to the Democratic Party, the traditional political affiliation for Mexican Americans). The numbers of such officials (at all levels of government) more than doubled between 1974 and 1984, then grew another 40 percent by 1994, reaching a total of approximately 4,400. Among the most notable politicos of this era were Henry Cisneros (elected mayor of San Antonio in 1981, the first Mexican American since 1842), Federico Pena (elected mayor of Denver in 1983, the first Hispanic mayor in the city's history), and Gloria Molina (elected to the California State Assembly in 1982, the first Latina to achieve such office). Over 80 percent of these civil servants hailed from Texas, California, and New Mexico.[5]

To further build upon this development, Foley noted, by 1980 Los Angeles County's Spanish-surnamed population had swelled to 27.6 percent of all inhabitants. Elsewhere, "the Hispanic population increased dramatically in other cities outside of the border states: St. Paul, Newark, New Orleans, Kansas City, and Miami—the destination of many Central Americans as well as Cubans and Puerto Ricans. But two-thirds of all legal immigrants ... settled in just six states: California, New York, Texas, Florida, New Jersey, and Illinois." Over the period covered by this chapter, the nation's overall Spanish-speaking populace almost doubled, growing from less than five percent in 1970 to nine percent two decades later.[6] Given statistics such as these, it is no wonder that in this chapter (and in Chapter 5) we will see Latino football players hailing from an even larger variety of states.

Two final, but critical "positive points" need to be presented at this juncture. First, starting in 1982, with the introduction of the Simpson-Mazzolli Bill, the two major parties and the Reagan Administration began a long and contentious debate concerning: (1) amnesty for those who had entered the borders of the U.S. without permission; (2) employer sanctions (for hiring such persons); and, (3) increased border enforcement. By the time that the final version of the bill, known as the Immigration Control and Reform Act (IRCA) became law with Reagan's signature in 1986, a total of three million "unauthorized immigrants" received exoneration. Now these individuals could be out in the open and more fully participate in the national economy and society.[7] At about the same time as Senator Simpson and Representative Mazzolli introduced their legislative proposal, the Supreme Court ruled on the case of *Plyer v. Doe*. Here, the justices determined that a Texas law (from 1975) which disallowed children not "legally admitted" into the United States enrollment in public schools, was unconstitutional. By a 5–4 decision, the magistrates determined that denying such individuals (or charging their parents so that the children could attend public schools) was not appropriate policy. From that time on, it has not been permitted for school board authorities to question children's legal status when parents or caretakers attempt to enroll them in local academic institutions.[8] These two items, in combination with the trends noted above, helped make it possible for more Latino/a students to remain in school, and for a growing number to play football.

While much in the previous few paragraphs highlights somewhat positive patterns, it is important, at least briefly, to balance out this information with analysis by Zaragoza Vargas, which presents not as rosy a picture for Latinos/as. Vargas' work discusses a plethora of concerns, including: environmental pollution in poor neighborhoods, a resurgence of racism by whites who believed that progress by minorities had come at their expense, "the end of the New Deal social contract," Supreme Court decisions (such as *Regents of the University of California v. Bakke*) damaging to Affirmative Action policies,

4. Increased Numbers and Diversity at All Levels, 1971–1990   169

the process of deindustrialization, and greater class stratification (both within and outside of) the Latino community.⁹ He recaps these trends between 1970 and 1990 this way:

> Spanish-speaking communities steadily lost their working-class industrial base and faced growing economic inequality ... [where] low-wage service jobs replaced high-wage manufacturing jobs.... [Also] the mechanism of affirmative action ... [helped] college-educated Mexican American increase in the 1970s, 1980s, and 1990s, and entered corporate, educational, governmental, and professional positions of authority.... However, colleges and universities became the primary site for the struggle over affirmative action.¹⁰

In summary, the years between 1971 and 1990 generated significant changes in the lives of Latinos/as, as well as the nation as a whole. As this populace grew dramatically, it moved in more substantive numbers into "newer" areas. A recent work edited by Mark Overmeyer-Velazquez, *Latino America: A State-by-State Encyclopedia* provides some interesting observations regarding these changes.¹¹ Obviously, we do not have the space to describe all of these shifts, but a few, wherein we can see Latinos playing football (detailed in Chapter 5), will suffice at this point. The states we will discuss are Arkansas and Iowa, though arguments similar to those below can be made for other states.

The scholars who documented aspects of the Latino presence in the Natural State, Steve Striffler and Julie M. Weise, noted that the presence of such persons in Arkansas is of long standing (though on a limited scale). "For most of the twentieth century, the fate of Arkansas' Latinos and its cotton were intertwined." During the 1930s, the Lee Wilson Plantation (in Mississippi County) "was the most active in pursuing Mexican laborers." During World War II, thousands more came to work in agriculture (both native-born and braceros). The circumstances were not always pleasant, with many workers arrested and harassed without reason. Conditions were such that in 1949 the Mexican consul from Memphis, Ruben Gaxiola, visited the state in order to investigate complaints. The imagery of Spanish-speakers as migrant workers continued to prevail in the state through the early 1980s. At that point, Tyson Foods and other processors of fowl began to hire such persons in substantial numbers (as whites and African Americans left to pursue other occupations). "Latinos, many of whom moved from California, quickly obtained poultry jobs that, although difficult and dangerous, provided benefits, the potential for overtime, and relative job security, especially when compared to seasonal agriculture." The dramatic transformation of communities such as Rogers (roughly 25 percent Latino) and DeQueen (roughly 40 percent Latino) by 2000 attest to this important trend. As the sons of these now more economically secure *familias* moved into high school, many took to the gridiron.¹²

The pattern in the Hawkeye State more closely resembles that of Arkansas, with (primarily) Mexicans reaching the area to work in railroads, agriculture, construction, steel mills, beet sugar production, and tanneries by the early 1900s. The author of this essay, Jerry Garcia, notes that the first *Dieciséis de Septiembre* celebration in the state took place in 1906, with Mexican *honorificas* (mutual aid societies) extant by the 1920s. Seasonal agricultural work attracted many more Spanish-speakers (primarily from Texas) to Iowa during the 1940s and 1950s. Garcia describes political and labor activities by Latino/a activists in the state during the 1960s and 1970s; for example, the League of United Latin American Citizens (LULAC) filed a grievance with the Department of Defense in 1976 against International Harvester for discriminatory practices against such applicants.

By the early 1980s, as elsewhere, many Spanish-surnamed workers began to move into, you guessed it, food processing and packaging, working for companies such as ConAgra, Cargill, and Hormel. These occupational patterns, as well a high fecundity, helped generate a 169 percent increase in the numbers of this populace between 1990 and 2000.[13] Again, there is information that documents the impact of the Latino presence on the gridiron by the early years of the 2000s. While there may not be specific examples available of Latinos on the field during the 1971–1990 period, it is important to keep the demographic changes noted here in mind for Chapter 5; after all, as these populations grew, their children began to attend local schools and many eventually wound up playing football in locales that one would not necessarily correlate with Latinos. As we have done previously after providing the broader contextualization, we will begin our examination of events, both on the field and off, in Texas, New Mexico, California, and Florida.

One of the names that has recurred here is E.C. Lerma, who was not only a celebrity because of his accomplishments on the gridiron (and coaching other sports as well), but also because of what he meant to Mexican American youths in places such as Benavides and Rio Grande City. After wrapping up his coaching career, Lerma worked as a coordinator of physical education, director of migrant educational efforts, and adult learning. Additionally, he also served as a principal in various Texas cities, including a district in Dallas. One of his final posts was serving as superintendent of Benavides schools during the middle of the 1970s. He retired in 1980 and had the honor of having the field where he coached his Eagles to such success named after him in October of 1991. Coach E.C. Lerma passed away in April of 1998 at the age of 83.[14]

As part of Lerma's career, he also coached his son, John, who was a quarterback for the Rattlers at Rio Grande City. An all-around excellent athlete, the youth played in the Texas All-Star Game in 1964 and eventually attended Baylor University. Although his career statistics with the Bears were not extraordinary, rushing for around 50 yards in 1967 and 1968 and serving mostly as a receiver and punt returner, Lerma got his degree and decided to take up

4. Increased Numbers and Diversity at All Levels, 1971–1990   171

the family "business." As he was about to earn his diploma, his father had some sage advice: "There's a lot of hard work and you have to put up with a lot of crap. It isn't nearly as easy as some people think it is. If you are not in it for the love of the game and the kids, forget it, you'll never survive." As with most coaches, even the scion of a local legend, John Lerma cut his teeth at a middle school and subsequently as an assistant at McAllen High. He obviously did an effective job, as in 1972, when he was 24, Port Isabel came calling and offered him his first head coaching post. Over the years, the Tarpons have become a regional power, but that lay in the future in the early 1970s. "They had never won a district title ... [but] we went .500 the first year, then in '73, we were 8–1–1." Although he set up his charges for success, Lerma began a pattern that would continue throughout his career, "posting winning records but again usually firing out for greener pastures before too long." By 1976, when the Tarpons finally broke through to the playoffs, John Lerma was two jobs removed. The culture he established at Port Isabel, however, became celebrated, as the Tarpons would, after that initial trip to the postseason, total 29 playoff trips in subsequent decades, the most influential power in the Valley's gridiron history.[15]

By the time that Port Isabel began its dominance, Lerma had moved on to Robstown, and later, Corpus Christi Miller, where he reenergized the Bucs' program, going 8–3–1 in 1976. After the 1978 season, it was time to move again, this time, back to the Valley with Donna. Although not claiming another state title, between 1979 and 1983 his Redskins won approximately 70 percent of their games, with the highlight of his tenure in 1982, when Donna made it to the second round of the playoffs, losing 10–0 to New Braunfels Canyon. Another move took place in 1984, as he served as head coach at McAllen Memorial until 1989. Other stops included his father's alma mater (Kingsville High) between 1989 and 1991, and McAllen High as an assistant to Alex Leal in 1992. Hanna High School named him head coach in 1993, and in 1994 Lerma guided the Eagles to the first district title in school history. Finally, he had another opportunity to coach where E.C. had been field general: Rio Grande City. Unfortunately, this was not a successful stop, as Lerma could only muster a 6–24 mark between 1995 and 1997. In 1998, he served as an assistant at La Joya High School, and helped lead the Coyotes to their first-ever district title and a 10–0 mark. Even more importantly, "being at La Joya meant I could be close to my dad, who was dying of cancer at the time." John Lerma contemplated retirement from the sidelines after his stint with La Joya, but instead wound up as an assistant at Harlingen South until 2004.

Coach Lerma's two final stops on the coaching carousel were in New Mexico, where he was an assistant at Rio Rancho, then head coach at Belen from 2008 to 2015. As the coach of the Belen Eagles, Lerma outshined even his renowned father, posting a mark of 71–23, guiding his charges to six district titles, and making the state finals for 4A in 2009 and 5A in 2014, losing the title game on both occasions. Coach Lerma's contract was not renewed for the 2015–2016 academic year following his only losing campaign in the Land of Enchantment: 3–7. All told, the two Lermas guided their squads, comprised mostly of athletes of Mexican American backgrounds, to 370 victories.[16]

Another celebrated name in the Valley is that of Alex Leal, who finished his head coaching career as the winningest area coach in history: 224–105–6.[17] Again, Selber does an excellent job of detailing this legend's career, and it dovetails nicely with some of the social/historical changes discussed throughout that work. Leal was born in Lyford and graduated from the local high school in 1958. He attended both Texas Southmost College and Pan American, completing his teaching degree in 1964. His high school English teacher, Ruth Patterson, encouraged the young Leal to attend college. Like many of his peers in the late 1950s, the young Mexican American was contemplating a military career. Patterson ran interference and helped Leal procure a scholarship to Southmost. "I felt obliged to do my best.... I ended up making the dean's list the first semester down there, and then it became a matter of, how fast could I get out and go to work."

Having developed an affinity for coaching due to his time with the Bulldogs, Leal served as a volunteer (while teaching at L.C. Smith Elementary) with Raymondville under Carl Spoonemore, eventually coaching the junior high team. "I was the lowest man on the totem pole but I worked my way up.... I have always believed that through patience and hard work, that's possible." The job with the Bearkats turned into an assistant's position (with an actual salary), and eventually Leal took over the reigns of the program in 1973. By 1975, Raymondville began a decade-long period of success, including three consecutive district crowns through 1977. While he led his charges to accomplishments on the gridiron, by the late 1970s, feeling a bit underpaid, Leal jumped to Port Isabel, garnering three consecutive 10+ win seasons. By the early 1980s, he jumped at the chance to move to McAllen High, which was 5A (not 3A as were the Tarpons). He remained there until 1992, compiling a 52–29–1 mark. One more jump landed Leal at Harlingen South, where he steered the Hawks to regular playoff contention until retiring in 2000. Although Leal had (supposedly) left the sidelines for good, to go back to being a teacher, the institution where he began his career came calling again in 2006, and he took charge of the Bearkats one final time, until 2010, culminating his career with a bi-district title.[18]

Another field general worth mentioning here is Joe Solis, a Valley legend whose vocation, unfortunately, ended with controversy in 2012. Solis began his career in 1972, after playing at Lyford and attending Pan American. The motivation to get into coaching (and a college education) came early to Solis, courtesy of his father, who owned a bit of land and sharecropped. "He believed in hard labor, but I started to think, 'Do I really want to spend my life working in this hot sun?' I guess my dad wanted us to get our schooling in, and down the road, I traded the cotton field for the football field." Although determined, Solis, like many of his fellow Mexican Americans, endured ill treatment, particularly for speaking Spanish. "Kids don't believe me when I tell them how it was. They say, 'No way, sir.' In my family, Spanish was the first language, so it was tough for us at school. Now things are the other way around."

Solis' first job was at Los Fresnos, though he was only there for one year. In 1973, he followed Chipper Zamora to Weslaco as defensive coordinator, moving two years later to Edcouch-Elsa under Boxer Hernandez. By the early 1980s, Solis worked for John Lerma at Donna, and finally, at Raymondville under his cousin, Ray Solis. The chance to take over his alma mater finally came in 1988. Playing in a difficult district, the Bulldogs finally broke through in 1991 and went three-deep into the playoffs, the school's most successful season to date. Joe Solis eventually moved on to *La Maquina Amarilla* (Edcouch-Elsa) in 1997. While he loved his alma mater, the chance to move up in classification was too tantalizing. "You usually want to coach for a higher classification unless you have a particular tie to a place, but I left.... I joined the team in time for that quarterfinal trip, the coach was Chris Cavazos, and it was just a magic year."

Subsequent trips to the playoffs took place in 1998, 1999, and 2000. Having proven his mettle, Solis was given the keys to the machine in 2002 (he would also serve as Athletic Director for the district) and would steer the team to great success over the next decade with a mark of 99–24. In October of 2012, accusations were made that Solis had exceeded the number of hours that his charges could be on the practice field (eight hours per week), along with involvement of school personnel in the team's 7-on-7 workouts. In December of that year, the school board terminated the coach's contract.[19]

While there are many other coaches who can be discussed here (turn to the Selber book for more such stories), it is important to single out one final individual field general: Gus Zavaletta, from St. Joseph Academy and Brownsville High School. As noted earlier, Zavaletta guided the Bloodhounds to the TCIL (Texas Catholic Interscholastic League) state title in 1962, and repeated that feat in 1980 (the TCIL was renamed Texas Christian Interscholastic League in 1976). In between his stints at St. Joseph, Zavaletta guided national championship American football teams at Monterrey Tech in 1971 and 1972. His teams would often cross the border for international competitions with high schools in Texas. He also coached at Brownsville High in the late 1960s and finally at Brownsville Porter in 1992. Both of his sons, Bart and Gus Jr., played the sport at the University of Houston and became head coaches as well. "First and foremost, my father was a mentor. He wanted you to develop as a human being and as a Christian.... Just winning wasn't the most important thing.... He was a role model and a spiritual guide to lots of boys, and that's pretty uncommon now."[20]

There were many great football players from the Valley and southern Texas during this era, and Selber notes them in his work. A particularly interesting story to support one of our arguments in this book involves two players from Uvalde, who played for the Coyotes in the very early 1970s. Ruben Alcorta (tight end) and Lynn Leonard (quarterback) were the best of friends during that turbulent era, and remain so. As Charlie Robinson noted in 1973 piece for *Texas Coach*, the relationship between these two individuals demonstrated some of the benefits of bringing together athletes of different backgrounds on a football team. The tale began in Crystal City in the early 1960s, as Robinson noted, a "racial-torn town," and culminated in Uvalde, which was not much better regarding such relations.

In 1969–1970, Alcorta's mother was dying, and his father wanted to move his son to San Antonio while his wife received treatment. Into this dire situation stepped Leonard's parents who, seeing the close ties between the youths, took in Alcorta while the boys played the 1970 season for Crystal City. The turbulence at the local school led the Leonard family to transfer the boys to another district, and Ruben and Lynn joined the Uvalde Coyotes' junior varsity in 1971. That squad went undefeated, and the transplants then helped lead their new school to the state title in 1972. As Robinson stated about the pair, "So in this area of South Texas where so much is blown out of proportion about the racial strife, the same segment ... has said very little about a Mexican and a gringo who teamed up to bring harmony ... [and] that loved each other to the point of becoming brothers for life, [and] produced a state championship." While Robinson's article certainly simplifies and overlooks important historical issues, it is an interesting story about the power of sport. By the way, Alcorta and Leonard spent their collegiate careers at Angelo State in San Angelo, Texas, playing for the Rams between 1973 and 1976.[21]

Another remarkable athlete from this era who reached the pinnacle of the sport in Texas, earning admission to the state's Sports Hall of Fame was Nati Valdez, a receiver for the Mission Eagles, one of the most successful pass catchers in the state during the 1980s. In three years, he caught more than 250 passes for over 3,700 yards. His best season was in 1987, where he caught 104 throws for over 1,600 yards and 15 scores. As a senior, he caught 14 passes in one game against McAllen Memorial. These figures attracted the attention of LaVell Edwards and other coaches at pass-happy BYU. The Super Prep All-American signed with the Cougars and netted 38 receptions and six scores for the Provo-based institution, until a broken collarbone ended his career in 1991. Valdez was inducted into the Rio Grande Valley Sports Hall of Fame in 2015.[22]

4. Increased Numbers and Diversity at All Levels, 1971–1990 175

Another local who made a significant contribution to the Latino presence on the gridiron was quarterback Sammy Garza, who hailed from Corpus Christi but played his career at Harlingen High with the Cardinals. He guided his teams to a 30–10 mark during his career, but never had a chance to participate in the playoffs due to the format in use at that time. His statistics earned him a scholarship to play at the University of Texas at El Paso, where he competed between 1983 and 1986. Among his career highlights were 36 completions in one contest, 35 passing touchdowns (currently fourth all-time for the Miners), a school-record six touchdowns in one game (against Northern Michigan in his senior year), the fourth-highest single-game yardage (458 in the game where he threw for his record number of scores), and over 6,100 total passing yards. After he completed his tenure on the border, the Seattle Seahawks made him an eight-round draft choice in 1987. Garza was cut in training camp but caught on with the Cardinals as a replacement player. Like many other Latino players, Garza headed to the CFL and latched on with the Winnipeg Blue Bombers, helping to guide his team to the Grey Cup in 1993, a 33–23 loss versus Edmonton. Sammy Garza also played in the World League with the Frankfurt Galaxy in 1991, before returning to the Bombers from 1992 to 1994. His final professional stop was with the Ottawa Rough Riders in 1995–1996 before the team folded. In 2000, Garza's alma mater brought him in as quarterback coach, and he was dismissed after the 2003 campaign. He caught on with the Dallas Cowboys as a college scout in 2005, a position he held through 2017.[23]

While many stars brought recognition to Valley/southern Texas football during this period, there is no doubt that the most significant career on and off the gridiron was that of Juan Castillo, who played his football at Port Isabel and later at A&M Kingsville. The story of this Tarpons great has numerous twists and turns, yet shares many key aspects with other athletes discussed in this work. Castillo's parents immigrated to the United States from Mexico at the ages of 13 and 14. His father was a shrimper and early on accustomed his son to being diligent and waking up well before the crack of dawn. In a 2015 article for the Baltimore Ravens' website, Juan Castillo recollected that those early-morning sessions at the fish house were mandatory. As far as his dad was concerned, "you don't really ask, you just do."

The early-morning tasks with his father ended abruptly in 1970 as a tragic accident on a shrimp boat killed the elder Castillo. Overnight, 11-year-old Juan became "the man" of the house. His mother worked two jobs, as a maid and busing tables at a local restaurant. Although he had to help his mom take care of two sisters, Juan always found time to play football. He eventually played for the Tarpons as both a linebacker and a tight end. The tragedy that befell his clan helped mold the player he became. "He wasn't the fastest, strongest, or most talented, but he developed a work ethic that pushed him to become the first person in his family ever to graduate from high school." Although he made his mark on the gridiron, no U.S.–based institution of higher education offered him a scholarship to play the game he loved. Enter Monterrey Tech in his ancestral homeland. Castillo, though not well versed in using the Spanish language, accepted the opportunity.

The experience south of the Rio Grande lasted but one year, as the school suspended its football program. Back in Texas, Castillo reached out to his high school coach, who contacted the staff at A&M–Kingsville. Castillo walked on with the Javelinas in 1978 and earned his scholarship shortly thereafter. Graduating with a degree in Kinesiology, Castillo served as defensive coordinator with the Kingsville High Brahmas for four seasons before accepting a post with his alma mater as offensive line coach.

After Castillo spent one season on the offensive side of the ball, the secondary coach post came open at Kingsville. Given his background, he applied, but he did not get the position. Shocked, he inquired as to why he was not hired. "He found out it was because of one thing: a difference in the technique of backpedaling." Once again, the lessons ingrained after his father's passing came into play. Instead of complaining about his misfortune, Castillo drove to Tallahassee and learned to coach the technique from Mickey Andrews at Florida State. "If you don't know something, learn it." Another call, this time to Tony Wise with the Dallas Cowboys, led to a visit to their training camp. Likewise, Castillo also made contacts with Mike Berry at the University of Colorado and Marv Levy of the Buffalo Bills.

The connection that helped usher Castillo into the NFL coaching ranks came through the legendary coach of the Bills, as Levy helped him plug into the league's minority internship program. This lead to introductions to Tom Bresnahan and, eventually, Ray Rhodes, who hired Castillo as quality control coach for the Eagles' offensive coordinator, Jon Gruden. That legendary workaholic sounded much like the young coach's father when he stated that "Juan, when I did your job, I was always here at 4 in the morning." Juan Castillo would go one better, usually showing up

Juan Castillo, 1995 (courtesy Phil Hoffmann).

4. Increased Numbers and Diversity at All Levels, 1971–1990   177

around 3:30. By the time that he reached his fourth season with the Eagles, he was named offensive line coach. After Rhodes' termination, the new field general, Andy Reid, decided to keep Castillo; the job in Philadelphia would last more than one decade. Finally, after being switched to defensive coordinator, Castillo was fired after the 2012 season, but he quickly moved on to guide the offensive line with the Ravens (under John Harbaugh), and earned a Super Bowl ring in 2013 when Baltimore defeated the 49ers. After three seasons in Charm City, Castillo moved on to the same post with the Buffalo Bills. An effective summary of his career and significance can be gleaned from his statement in 2002: "There's a lot of people back in Texas just like me. I want to help pave the way. I want to do a good job for my boss but also for the people of my heritage so that the next time there's an opening, a Hispanic will get a good look."[24]

Another great player from southern Texas was Rene Amaya, who played his high school football at San Diego (Duval County) in the late 1960s and played for the Texas Longhorns in the early 1970s. Amaya was a 1973 letterman and played in the 1974 Cotton Bowl. An interesting issue is visible in the local newspaper's account of this player's upcoming campaign with the Longhorns. While noting that two locals, Amaya and James Johnston, were going to play for the Austin institution, the story focused on the Anglo player for 15 paragraphs, while Amaya merited but one. It seems that, in 1972, even playing for the state's flagship institution did not generate much appreciation for a home-grown Mexican American athlete.[25]

One final athlete from southern Texas with NFL ties during this era merits a mention: the great Gabe Rivera, who played high school football at San Antonio Jefferson and earned the moniker "Senor Sack" at Texas Tech University. Rivera was a first-team All-American on the defensive side of the ball in 1982 and earned honorable mention in 1980 as a sophomore. Over his career in Lubbock, he tallied 321 tackles, including 34 for lost yardage. He collected 14 sacks, but was an absolute terror and was the 21st player selected in the 1983 NFL draft. The Pittsburgh Steelers thought they had nabbed a critical cog to help birth a new version of the Steel Curtain, even passing over local hero Dan Marino to acquire Rivera. As a Steelers publication noted, he "started slowly, but as his NFL career progressed game by game, Rivera began making an impact stopping the run and pressuring opposing quarterbacks." Unfortunately, the former Red Raider's career would last but six games, and generated only two sacks.

On October 20, 1983, a legally intoxicated Gabe Rivera was speeding in his new 280ZX and was involved in a two-car accident. The crash lead to a crushed spine, punctured lung, and bruised heart. He was permanently paralyzed from the waist down. Suddenly, the promise of a football career at the highest level was gone. Most of the aficionados in western Pennsylvania remember Rivera not as "Senor Sack," but as the "Steeler that never was." Although he did not have the time to prove himself at the professional level, Rivera remains a fabled personage in Lubbock, San Antonio, and his hometown of Crystal City. In 1993, he was inducted into the Texas Tech Hall of Honor, followed by induction into the Texas Sports Hall of Fame in 2007. Two other important honors have followed: selection to the College Football Hall of Fame in 2012 and, most significantly to a Red Raider, Rivera was added to the Ring of Honor at his alma mater in 2014.[26] Gabe Rivera passed away on July 16, 2018.

Gabe Rivera (right) talking with "Mean" Joe Greene, 1983 (courtesy Texas Tech Athletics).

An effective way to summarize the significance of football to Latinos/Mexican Americans in this region of Texas comes from a 2012 dissertation by Victor Anthony Castillo of the University of Texas, San Antonio. In a work entitled "Pathfinders: A Life History of 10 Academically Successful Latinos from San Antonio," Castillo examined key traits shared by these men. Not surprisingly, half of them played on the gridiron, and only two did not participate in any type of athletic competition for their high school. One of these individuals, a man identified as "Hector," who went on to complete a PhD in Economics, argued that "Participating in sports [he played football] not only taught me discipline, it helped me build and maintain important friendships throughout my life…." Castillo summarized his research into how important activities such as football can be to Latinos who hailed from what are often socially disadvantaged backgrounds:

> The narrative that speaks on extracurricular participation suggests that this involvement establishes an identity that is affiliated with the campus culture, promotes a life-long social network that cultivates a reciprocal amount of support, while instilling discipline and resiliency that can be used as a sculpt for other aspects of life…. Sports and extracurricular activities as a sub-category of cultural capital are identified as salient aspects of the educational attainment of academically successful Latinos, and

a resource that allowed several of the men to overcome obstacles of: a hostile environment, time management, identity, deviance, inner-ethnic conflict, and the lack of confidence.[27]

On the other side of the Lone Star State, we once again reference the work of Fred Morales concerning his alma mater, Bowie High. The work's chronology concludes in May of 1973, and it does reveal some successes by the Bears during the late 1960s and early 1970s. In 1969, for example, under new head coach Don Reiderer, Bowie's varsity claimed its first district title since the Baty days of the early 1950s (1953, to be exact). The championship game was played in the Sun Bowl and attracted more than 17,000 fans. The following week, the Bears lost to El Paso Coronado, 29–16, for the bi-district title. Another important moment this year involved Manuel "Mel" Ramos garnering All-State honors in football. The Bears' success continued in 1970, as they again claimed the district title before losing to Coronado, 17–8, before more than 25,000 fans at UTEP's home stadium. That season, Bowie finished 10–1. Morales makes no mention of the 1971 season, but does note another championship, this time by the junior varsity, in 1972 with a perfect 6–0 mark.[28]

Unlike the 1961 Donna Redskins, who claimed the only state title by a team from the Rio Grande Valley, no team from El Paso has ever reached the pinnacle of Texas high school football, though some have made deep runs, including several during the era covered in this chapter. The 1973 version of the Coronado Thunderbirds surprised many fans in their community and around the state by going three-deep into the playoffs after compiling a mediocre 6–5–2 mark. The team lost its first four contests, then defeated Parkland and tied Hereford (advanced on penetrations) to become the first El Paso team to win a regional final. The 1975 version of the Thunderbirds is considered one of the best squads in the city's history. They went 10–1–2 and defeated Ysleta and Amarillo Caprock in the first two playoff rounds. Coronado tied Odessa Permian (of Mojo fame) in the quarterfinals, but lost on penetrations. The Panthers finished runners-up that year for the state title. A final playoff season of note for Coronado came in 1979 when they again reached the third round, this time losing to Lewisville, 15–7. That team finished 11–2. The only other team from El Paso to advance into the third round during this period was the 1990 Andress Golden Eagles (a 5A school), who defeated another legendary Texas program, Midland Lee, in the regionals that year, only to lose to Arlington Lamar, 49–7, in the quarter-finals.[29]

A final Latino football player of note from this era was Cuban American Kiki De Ayala, who made his mark at Houston Memorial High, the University of Texas, and with the Houston Gamblers and Cincinnati Bengals at the professional level. Like many individuals of his ethnic background, De Ayala was born in Miami, but after that his story took an interesting turn.

His father, Ralph, was one of the hearty souls who signed up to attempt to overthrow the Castro regime in the Bay of Pigs invasion in April of 1961. Kiki was born in October of that year. For a further six months, the family did not know what had happened to Ralph, who was thought to be one of the Cuban patriots captured in that ill-fated incursion. Fortunately, he had managed to hide in the Swiss embassy in Havana, and he eventually made it back to the United States. The family ultimately moved to Houston, and Ralph Sr., was employed by a Texas-based gas company.

After relocation to the Lone Star State, Kiki De Ayala became a star athlete in baseball and tennis, as well as on the gridiron at Memorial High School. He attracted the attention of the Longhorns and went to Austin as a highly touted linebacker. He did not disappoint, earned All-Southwest Conference designation, and was named Southwest Conference Defensive Lineman of the Year in his senior season, 1982. His statistics for the Longhorns were impressive. He still holds the record for most sacks and the single-season mark, 40.5 and 22.5. "I kind of found a niche for what I did. Sometimes, the light goes on, and you figure out how to defeat the pass blocker. I did a lot of film studying and understood his tendencies." His coach at Texas, Fred Akers, gave him high praise for his accomplishments on the field. "De Ayala is a consistently fine, fine football player. I can't imagine a defensive end anywhere being better than Kiki. He's smart, experienced, and he's a competitor." Given his success at the elite collegiate stage, he would have an opportunity to pursue the sport at the next level.

De Ayala was drafted by both the USFL and the NFL. Fortuitously, the opportunity to play in Houston permitted him to stay close to family as well as earn more than he could with the traditionally penny-pinching Bengals. De Ayala led the Gamblers' defense as a rookie and was named first-team All-USFL in 1984. The team finished 13–5 that year and made it to the quarter-final round of the playoffs. In 1985, he had four interceptions and five sacks. He started all 36 games he played for the Gamblers. Shortly after the 1985 season, the Houston franchise ceased operation, and De Ayala moved on to the Bengals. His time in the NFL was not as successful, and he recorded only one sack. What also transpired were two shoulder surgeries and six knee operations. After the 1987 season, Kiki De Ayala decided to follow a new path. "During the off-season, I started working for a commercial real estate company. When I retired, it was a smooth transition right into commercial real estate." In the subsequent years, De Ayala started his own firm, and since 2000 has been involved in this field with interests in Laredo, Houston, and San Antonio.[30]

We again turn to Dan Ford for information on events and key players in the Land of Enchantment. The era between 1971 and 1990 witnessed a wide array of significant moments concerning Latino participation in high school football in this state, including the rise of other Spanish-surnamed coaches into the elite ranks of New Mexico field generals, great stars who led their teams to much success, tragedies on the field, and even a national first: a Latina suiting up to play (ever so briefly, as you will see) on the offensive line for her squad.

Among the field generals of this background to have great success during this era, were Army Salinas, Eddie Castaneda, and Ernest Renteria (this last coached six-man ball). Salinas, a native of Woodrow, Texas, a suburb of Lubbock, became head coach at Hagerman High School in Chavez County in 1970, the first year the school fielded a team. He lead his baby Bobcats, a team comprised mostly of athletes with little or no football experience, to a 5-1 record as an independent team. Indeed, this squad was comprised mostly of youths not unlike Salinas, who played in the first football game he ever witnessed at Cooper High School. After his career with the Pirates, Salinas, who not surprisingly attracted no interest from larger colleges, made his way to Portales and tried out with the Eastern New Mexico Greyhounds. He went on to play as a tackle and graduated in 1968. He subsequently taught at a junior high for two years before hearing of the opportunity with Hagerman.

If the record in 1970 with a side full of gridiron newbies was impressive, then 1971 was even more extraordinary. That season, the Bobcats finished with a perfect mark in-district and played for the New Mexico Class A title versus Carrizozo. During the regular season, Hagerman's lone defeat came at the hands of a team from Dell City, Texas, 27–6. All contests with in-state opponents featured dominating performances, particularly on the defensive side of the ball, including four shutouts and victories against JVs from larger communities, such as Roswell and Tularosa. The Bobcats defeated the Navajo Mission Eagles, 31–26, in the playoff semi-finals before bowing to the Grizzlies, 20–7, in the title contest. For his outstanding efforts, Salinas was named Coach of the Year by the Associated Press and United Press International. Coach Salinas remained at Hagerman for one more season, before moving to a larger school in 1973. His mark with the Bobcats was 20–4–1. Not bad for a school just getting into gridiron competition.

Army Salinas led Portales until 1979, with his best campaign coming in 1978, when the Rams made it to the playoffs before losing to Bloomfield, 7–0, and finishing 7–3–1. Salinas ultimately returned to western Texas to take charge of the Lubbock High Westerners, a post he kept until 1983. His final stop in the coaching carousel would be with another small community, Seminole, Texas, in Gaines County. Success was plentiful with the Indians, making the playoffs in 1997, 1998, and a final hurrah in 1999 with a district title. Salinas also served as athletic director for Seminole between 1992 and 2004, when he wrapped up a 36-year career on the sidelines and in education.[31]

Another successful coach from this era was Eddie Castaneda, who lead the Socorro Warriors for almost two decades, starting in the early 1970s. Unfortunately, his tenure ended abruptly in 1989 due to the use of ineligible players. The two most significant seasons for Castaneda's squad came in 1976 and 1977, when they reached the state title game, losing in the bicentennial year, 46–7, to Artesia and then triumphing against (Albuquerque) Academy, 12–7, the following season. One of the key aspects of the championship season was that the Warriors had been fairly successful at the 3A level until 1974, but achieved their runs to the final contest of the season at the higher 5A classification. In 1978, however, Socorro slipped to 1–8, and the rest of Castaneda's tenure was not as successful, with no more playoff appearances. The last straw occurred in a 1989 game against Moriarty, a 17–8 Warriors win, that was subsequently turned into a 2–0 victory for the Fighting Pintos due to the utilization of barred athletes.[32]

A final coach of note from this era is probably the most successful of all mentioned here: Ernest Renteria, who made his mark with the Mountainair Bears. According to Dan Ford, Coach Renteria began his coaching career at Lordsburg and moved on to Mountainair in 1988. Before his arrival, the school's gridiron teams were 4–37 in their last years of 11-man ball. New Mexico adopted the downsized version of the game so popular in neighboring Texas in 1987. The Bears dropped down to six-man, and the turnaround was instantaneous and overwhelmingly dominant. Starting in Renteria's first year, his teams became a fixture in the state playoffs and in the winner's circle, garnering consecutive state titles through 1992. They lost in the semis in 1993 to eventual champion Lake Arthur. Over his first five years, Renteria's mark stood at 46–4. For the remainder of his tenure (ending in 2004), his Bears made the playoffs every year, but did not reclaim the top prize again, and reached the title tilt one final time, in 1997, a 63–42 loss to Roy. Starting in 2005, the coaching legend moved to Estancia, where he served that community as an assistant in football, co-athletic director, and head of girls basketball and track. His thin-clads won the state title in track in 2014.[33]

The state of New Mexico also generated a substantial number of excellent athletes who made their marks on the gridiron over this two-decade period. Willie Gallegos of Carrizozo helped get his squad to the finals versus Salinas' Hagerman Bobcats by scoring 164 points in 1971. This was the third consecutive championship for the Grizzlies. The following year, Sam Merlino of St. Michael's (Santa Fe) rushed for over 1,800 yards and scored 162 points to lead the Horsemen to a 28–6 victory over the Lovington Wildcats in the AAA title match. In 1974, Ernie Luevano of Tularosa scored 150 points and followed that impressive output in his senior year with 196, leading the Wildcats to a 10–1 mark and the first round of the playoffs, where they lost to the St. Pius Spartans, 29–25. Even more impressive was the number of points tallied by Reuben Nieblas of Animas, 508, over his three-year career which culminated in 1989 with a victory over the Santa Rosa Lions, 51–6, for the team's sixth consecutive AAA title (five outright and one shared). Although the Panthers won it all again in 1990, they did lose to Lordsburg, 9–8, and saw their 69-game winning streak snapped by the Mavericks. Finally, another celebrated athlete was quarterback Danny Vigil of the (Roswell) Goddard Rockets. In 1989, he led his squad to a 12–3 mark and a state title in AAAA versus Lovington, 6–0. Goddard returned to the playoffs in Vigil's senior year of 1991 and again won the title, defeating the Artesia Bulldogs, 28–14.[34]

Along with these successes, there were also two tragedies on the football fields of New Mexico during this era. Larry Sanchez of Albuquerque Valley High was killed during practice in 1974, and five years later, Martin Candelaria of Estancia died from an in-game head injury. Spurred by his memory, his teammates rallied around the Candelaria family and proceeded to claim the 1979 AAA title, defeating the Hatch Bears, 33–7.[35]

While these players were noteworthy in their communities and the state, many aficionados of New Mexico high school football would argue that the greatest gridder from these years was the incomparable Chano Talavera of Lordsburg High. His coach with the Mavericks, Louis Baisa, recalled that in one 1977 game the diminutive (5'3" and 125 pounds) running back scored nine touchdowns against Clifton, Arizona. The final score was 80–0. As the Hobbs paper noted, Chano "served notice early what was going to happen when he grabbed the opening kickoff and ran 90 yards to paydirt." In total, he rushed for 264 yards on only 13 carries. He notched 188 points that season. Not surprisingly, he was first-team All-State. Even with this tremendous output, the Mavericks, though making the playoffs in AAA each of Talavera's campaigns, made it through only to the second round on each occasion. Frustratingly, his last game was a 21–0 defeat against the Clayton Yellowjackets. Finally, it is worth noting that Talavera did not excel only on the gridiron. He was also quite successful in the Junior Olympics and in the AAU, finishing fourth in the 200 meters and being part of a second-place 4 × 100 relay team in 1977.[36]

A final story from the Land of Enchantment is truly unique and well worth some discussion. The tiny western community of Quemado in Catron County had not fielded a football team prior to 1974. In order to stimulate some interest in the sport, Dick Moore instituted an intermural version of the game which featured students of both sexes. One of the young women who became interested in playing varsity was Sally Gutierrez. In 1975 she was allowed by Coach Moore to practice on the offensive line. Soon, the New Mexico Athletic Association (NMAA) caught wind of this and warned the field general and his boss, Principal Owen Robinson, against inserting Gutierrez into a game. While the administrator took this to mean all games, Moore believed it applied only in contests versus other New Mexico teams. Thus, he inserted Sally Gutierrez into a contest versus a team from Sanders, Arizona, on September 19, 1975. She participated in but one snap. Once this information reached the NMAA, the oversight body suspended Quemado from playing the rest of its season. Of course, the matter eventually wound up in court. If she did not play football, were there any other athletic pursuits open to her? The answer to that was "no." Thus, she continued to play sparingly in parts of subsequent games in 1975, though Quemado was suspended for the 1976 season. As Dan Ford noted, "the questions raised by this issue were eventually answered … [and] It directly created girls' volleyball … in New Mexico."[37]

In 1987, reporter Barbara Armijo of the *Albuquerque Journal* caught up with Gutierrez, now living in Spokane, Washington, to reminisce about her playing days. This was due, in part, to another young lady, Cassey Pendergrass, attempting to play at Anthony Gadsden High. "Granted, we had a pretty small school and a pretty small team. I sure tried hard to be a good player. The whole thing was, I had my heart set on it. There wasn't anybody who could get in my way. I hope that Cassey is like that." While many in New Mexico were not supportive of her efforts, Gutierrez fondly recalls Coach Moore's efforts, as well as letters of encouragement that came to her institution. "I even got letters from women in Europe telling me to keep it up."[38]

The years between 1971 and 1990 witnessed a dramatic increase in the number of notable players from the state of California. Among the topics discussed in this section will be Joe Kapp, Jim Plunkett, Tom Flores, Anthony Calvillo, Mervyn Fernandez, Max Montoya, and, of course, the legendary Anthony Munoz. Additionally, we mentioned the rise of a plethora of "kickadores" (to follow up on the name given to Daniel Villanueva on the Rams) who would ply their trade both at schools in the Golden State and in the NFL.

Before we focus on some of these athletes, however, it is important to comment upon some of the changes that took place regarding the Garfield-Roosevelt rivalry, the East LA Classic, in Los Angeles. While these two teams never claimed the state title in football, their rivalry is indicative of the demographic changes that have taken place in the sport in this part of California; for example, both schools are now overwhelmingly Latino, and the 2017 teams certainly reflect this. Additionally, as noted in Chapter 3, it was in 1972 that the game's name changed from a the derisive "Taco Bowl" to the East LA Classic. Indeed, one local touted the tilt, played at Weingart Stadium (on the campus of East Los Angeles College), as "the Super Bowl of East L.A." The pride in the game, the athletes, and the community blossomed further during the years covered here. The rivalry is so intense and socially significant that it has now spawned a second film, "The Classic," directed by Billy McMillin.[39]

With the new name for the contest established, the denizens of Boyle Heights and East Los Angeles turned the bout into a community affair tied directly to a sense of pride in Mexican American/Latino cultural traditions. In a 2017 article leading up to the 87th renewal of the rivalry between the Roughriders and the Bulldogs, reporter Julia Wick documented quotations in local papers from the 1970s and 1980s concerning goings-on around the city and within families, many of which classified themselves as "houses divided" by loyalties to the rival institutions. One Rider aficionado noted in 1976, "in bars, guys will be making bets on the game." One teacher, Al Padilla, who coached at both schools recalled in 1985 that "The most fuddy-duddy teachers, who have not come out to any of the games, come out for Garfield-Roosevelt." In 1986, Julian Nava (Roosevelt, Class of 1945), a former U.S. ambassador to Mexico, stated, "Anyone who went to school in East L.A. identifies with either Garfield or Roosevelt." During these years, crowds swelled to Texas-size attendance, with 22,000 fans counted in 1969, 23,500 in 1974. Eventually, by the 1990s, there was discussion of moving the contest to the Los Angeles Coliseum. Indeed, the 2004 game took place in the home of the Trojans and attracted 33,000 fans. Although an impressive figure, the attendance was overwhelmed by the scope of the stadium, making for unattractive visuals. The game has since been returned to the confines of Weingart Stadium.

The allure of the contest starts at an early age. For decades, two Pop Warner teams, the Wolfpack and the Bobcats, "have trained youth from Boyle Heights and East Los Angeles to be leading players for their competing high school football programs. The two teams serve as a feeder, with their 6- to 13-year-old players dreaming of playing in … the Classic." The coach of the Riders, Javier Cid, saw this as a way to build community, as well as developing talent for future battles; "Pop Warner serves as 'our feeder program,' just as the professional teams have their minor league."[40]

In their discussion with Joe Kapp, Frederick Luis Aldama and Christopher Gonzales delved into the significance of sport to an individual, dubbed the "Toughest Chicano" in a 1970 *Sports Illustrated* article. In addition to his love for various sports, Kapp noted that he drew inspiration from the careers of men such as tennis player Pancho Gonzalez and golfer Chi Chi Rodriguez. "There weren't many Latinos playing football that I knew of when I was going to school." In the very next line, however, Kapp noted the importance of Sam Etcheverry (see Chapter 3) on his career. Still, "whether or not there were other Latino players didn't matter. I was ready, and nothing was going to hold me back." This attitude, and his skills on the gridiron, eventually helped pave the way for a tumultuous career in the CFL and the NFL.

Part of the significance of Kapp's playing days goes well beyond the field, given his contract disputes with Minnesota and Boston. Before the start of the 1969 season, the Vikings and Kapp did not agree on a contract, so the quarterback played out his option. Even though he had just led his team to Super Bowl IV, there appeared to be little interest in his services (sound familiar?).

Ultimately, the Patriots signed Kapp to a four-year deal. The association was not a prosperous one, as that version of the team finished a miserable 2-12, gaining them the first pick in the upcoming NFL draft. The team selected another Latino, Jim Plunkett, with the first pick of 1971. Kapp never played another down in the NFL because, he asserted, Pete Rozelle, Don Shula, and others denigrated him before other teams, ruining demand for his services. Joe Kapp did, however, triumph in the courts. "I won a summary judgement in 1976. [The] 9th Circuit Court of Appeals said ... this man's trade has been restrained. So what was the result of that? It was a legal point that the NFL had to give something away: the option clause."[41]

After his playing career ended, Kapp moved into roles in numerous movies and television shows and coached his alma mater (he was the coach for the California Golden Bears for the infamous "The Play" during the 1982 installment of "The Game" versus Stanford). Kapp earned Pac-10 Coach of the Year honors his first season. This was the highlight of his time as a field general at Berkeley, however, as the Bears never surpassed the .500 mark for the rest of his tenure (which ended after the 1986 season). Kapp finished with a 20-34-1 record. He eventually returned to Canada in the capacity of general manager for the British Columbia Lions in 1990. That tenure lasted less than one season, though it did feature the signing of Doug Flutie to his first CFL contract.

We previously discussed the high school and collegiate careers of both Jim Plunkett and Tom Flores. During the era covered in this chapter, these two Mexican Americans, through very circuitous routes, became pioneers in the NFL by helping the Oakland/Los Angeles Raiders claim two Super Bowl titles. After Plunkett's selection by the Patriots in 1971, the former Heisman Trophy winner got off to a good start in New England. Plunkett helped the Patriots improve to 6-8 and was named AFC Rookie of the Year. Unfortunately, the success did not last, and campaigns of 3-11, 5-9, 7-7, and 3-11 followed. In 1975, the Patriots selected Steve Grogan of Kansas State in the fifth round of the draft, and by the middle of his rookie season, the former Wildcat had taken over behind center for the "underachieving" Plunkett. He finished his time in New England with a 23-38 record, and had more interceptions than touchdowns (87 versus 62). This led to a trade back to the Golden State and the San Francisco 49ers for a bevy of choices: two first-round selections in 1976 and one first- and one second-round pick in 1977.[42]

The 49ers had not been the same since the retirement of John Brodie, and it was hoped that Plunkett could provide some stability and a return to better days. Things got off to a wonderful start, with the team winning six of their first seven games. Here was a "local boy makes good" story if there ever was one, as Plunkett tossed ten scores over the first half of 1976. Then injuries took their toll, particularly on the offensive line. The returning hero threw

4. Increased Numbers and Diversity at All Levels, 1971–1990   187

but three more scores over the final seven contests. Indeed, he was replaced behind center by rookie Scott Bull in game 13. The 49ers won, mostly because of their ground game, then lost the season finale to the Chargers. A year that had started out with such promise ended as an 8–6 clunker. Things got even worse in 1977. San Francisco started 0–5 on the way to a 5–9 finish, and Plunkett completed barely half his throws. He had nine touchdown passes and 14 interceptions over the season. In modern terms, his QBR was a very poor 62.1, and he was released.[43]

Now that he had faced NFL rejection on both coasts, Plunkett was at a loss. "There was quite a bit of self-doubt. It was probably the lowest point of my career.... Surgery after surgery, being beaten up quite a bit, almost always playing from behind.... It makes it tough on a quarterback." Into this dismal scenario rode a champion on a silver and black horse with a final opportunity: Al Davis, a specialist in rehabilitating NFL careers. The start to this fairy tale took a while, however. Plunkett, while happy to still be on a roster, mostly sat, first behind Ken Stabler (in 1978 and 1979, the year that Tom Flores took over for John Madden), and then, at the start of 1980, backing up Dan Pastorini (whom the Raiders acquired from the Oilers in exchange for Stabler). Circumstances would change dramatically after the fifth game of that season, however.

The other actor involved in this drama was Coach Tom Flores. In Chapter 3, we discussed his high school, collegiate, and part of his professional careers. After spending most of his time with the Raiders and two seasons with the Buffalo Bills, Flores signed in 1969 to back up Len Dawson with the Kansas City Chiefs. It is quite a coincidence that this Mexican American was on the other sideline during Super Bowl IV against a team guided by Joe Kapp. As he noted in his autobiography, "I am happy that I was part of the whole thing when the AFL went out with a bang.... Although I did not get into the game, I am grateful that [Hank] Stram gave me the chance to be part of that historical event."[44]

That was the last moment of Flores' playing career, as he was relegated to the taxi squad for 1970. In June 1971, he asked the club for his release. It was granted. "But the phone never rang. Suddenly, I was a former player." He commenced employment with a plastics manufacturing company, and a local television thought about using him for weekend sports. Then, just as abruptly as he was out of the game as a player, the Bills contacted him about serving as an assistant coach. While he was employed (for a princely $20,000), the season was a nightmare as Buffalo went 1–13. Flores recalls, "we were able to move the ball pretty good. But the defense was horrible.... After the season they ran me out of Buffalo again." The lone victory that year was, coincidently, against the Plunkett-led Patriots, 27–20, in week 11. Shortly after he was fired, the Raiders contacted Flores about a scouting post, and he visited lovely places such as Yankton State University, where the wind-chill hit -60. Just when Flores was close to calling it quits for good regarding the NFL, John Madden offered him a chance to coach receivers for the Raiders.[45]

The opportunity proved advantageous as Flores got to coach the likes of Fred Biletnikoff and Cliff Branch. He was even on the sidelines for the "Immaculate Reception" by Franco Harris in the playoffs. While remaining in the league, he felt that his career was not progressing. "To be an assistant coach in most places is to work in anonymity. To be an assistant with the Raiders is to be invisible." During his time under Madden, a few head jobs came open, but Flores was not seriously considered. The Rams' general manager, Don Klosterman, a long-time friend, advised him to "find somebody to toot my horn. He said I needed more exposure." It seemed that his chance would never come. Then, abruptly, Madden resigned in January of 1979. In early February, Flores was named head coach of the Raiders. He went 9–7 in his first season. By the end of that campaign, Stabler had had cross words with Davis and was traded to the Oilers. In the background was Plunkett, who would now be the backup to Dan Pastorini.[46]

The Plunkett that Tom Flores encountered with the Raiders in 1978 was but a shadow of the player he had been at Stanford. "You could see his passing motion was altered and his confidence was gone." When the Raiders traded for Pastorini, he wanted out of Oakland. "He was 32 years old with a 31-year-old starting in front of him and a first round draft pick sitting in the wings." Further, the two quarterbacks did not see eye-to-eye on much. The former Oiler was "high profile," and Plunkett "was quiet, conservative and didn't like Pastorini much." This is how things stood when the 2–2 Raiders played one of their archrivals, the Kansas City Chiefs on October 5 at Alameda County Coliseum. The game would go to the visitors, 31–17. After throwing seven passes and completing five for 43 yards, Pastorini was injured and left the game (to the derisive cheers of local fans). Enter Plunkett, who would go 20-of-52 for 238 yards (with five interceptions) in a desperate attempt to claw back from a 31–3 deficit. Not exactly an auspicious start to what would become a legendary run for these two Mexican Americans.[47]

The rest of the season could not have gone more providentially. The Raiders commenced a six-game winning streak that was broken by the Philadelphia Eagles in week 12, 10–7. Oakland won three of their final four games and clinched a wild-card slot in the final week of the campaign. Plunkett threw for almost 2,300 yards and 18 scores and guided the team to a 9–2 mark. The Raiders defeated the Stabler-led Oilers, 27–7, the Browns, 14–12, and the Chargers, 34–27. The final two victories came on the road. Oakland was now headed to Super Bowl XV to take on the Eagles once again. Unlike the regular season meeting, the Raiders, lead by Plunkett's 261 yards passing and three scores with no interceptions, crushed Philadelphia, 27–10. Shortly

4. Increased Numbers and Diversity at All Levels, 1971–1990   189

thereafter, in the premier issue of *Pro: The Magazine of the National Football League*, Dwight Chapin recounted the astounding turnabout in Plunkett's life. "Brilliantly, almost astoundingly.... The Incredible Shrinking Quarterback looked like a new-born giant as he accepted the game's most valuable player award."[48]

Of course, more honors followed, and among these were several for both player and coach directly connected to their ethnic background. Flores, for example, noted that "You are talking about a group of people here who seldom have had this type of national heroes—world champions." At about this time, he was asked to give a speech in Sonora and had to practice his Spanish. The coach and quarterback also did a lot of community work, primarily for Latino groups in the Bay area. Among these was a dinner in San Jose that Jim Plunkett used to begin a fund to sponsor scholarships for Latino youths. Flores summarized the chaos and joy of the victory by noting that he and Plunkett "were a couple of merry Mexicans, all right, even if neither of us could speak Spanish very well." The scenario would be repeated in 1983, when the Raiders (now based in Los Angeles) defeated the Redskins, 38–9. Plunkett had a good game, 172 yards passing and one score, but the star for the silver and black was Marcus Allen. Still, in the span of three years, two Latinos had guided an NFL team to Super Bowl victories. Even with these accomplishments, particularly Flores,' neither of these men is in the NFL Hall of Fame.[49]

Interviewed in 2016, Anthony Calvillo led off the conversation simply by mentioning a score, "58–56." Calvillo knew instantly that he was dealing with a person with ties to the state of Utah (although I [Jorge Iber] am a Ute and Anthony is a Utah State Aggie), as that was the score by which his alma mater defeated the BYU Cougars in 1993. The teams tallied 49 points in a wild final quarter and combined for more than 1,300 yards of offense. At the center of this titanic clash was this Californian who threw for 472 yards and five touchdowns, with a rating of 152.89.[50] This was just one of many highlights of Calvillo's career in Logan, and there would be plenty more in the CFL (as we will detail further in Chapter 5). This section however, will deal with his life and football career before he went on to collegiate and professional glory. This story is chronicled in the documentary about Calvillo entitled *The Kid from La Puente*.

The story of Anthony Calvillo encapsulates many of the themes that we have discussed in detailing the careers of other athletes, particularly, the necessity to overcome substantial odds against success. Three recent articles, a first-person account by Calvillo from 2017, one by Les Carpenter for Yahoo Sports in 2013, and a story by Bill Plaschke from 2011, recount what this all-time great endured while growing up. One of the first obstacles was an abusive father. "For months everything would be fine at the house. Then suddenly, he would start to drink more and it was chaos." Eventually, older brother David had enough and stood up to his violent parent at age 12. Anthony was a year younger and found his solace on the fields of athletic competition. "Playing sports was my life. It allowed me to think about other things." For David, things did not go as well, as he joined a gang and eventually went to prison for eight years for attempted murder. Still, he protected and encouraged his siblings. "Anthony and Mario [the youngest brother] had to pass through our park to get to their fields, and I made sure they never stopped. I told them, 'This is not going to be your life, keep going, keep going.'" The advice helped, as there were few role models available, on or off the field. "Where I come from … very few people ever go to university. In my family, we didn't go anywhere…. In my eyes, [La Puente] was the entire universe." Mother Christina did her best to make sure that the kids had a roof over their heads and food on the table, but that entailed having to be away from home for most of the day. This left Anthony in David's care most of the time.

Anthony was an excellent competitor at La Puente High School, playing both football and basketball. One of the earliest mentions of his athletic prowess came in the *Los Angeles Times* in 1989, when a report noted how Calvillo was helping the Warriors to one of their best seasons in two decades. After football season, he donned basketball shorts and continued to shine. In one game in February of 1990, he scored 57 of his team's 75 points to carry the Warriors to a victory over Bosco Tech by two points. When he graduated, his grades were not the best, and the only offer to play football was from Mt. San Antonio College in Riverside County. He played there during 1990 and 1991. By his second year, he was getting recognition among coaches in the Mission Conference. John Featherstone of El Camino College noted, as his team was about the play the Mounties, that, "Mt. SAC has one of the best offenses in the state and one of the best quarterbacks."

Anthony Calvillo would ultimately be inducted into the school's Hall of Fame in 2015. Although he put up gaudy numbers at Mt. San Antonio, there was little interest at the next level given Calvillo's relatively small size (6'2" 180 lbs.). At that moment, the young man's patience and perseverance paid off as another "overlooked" quarterback, Jim Zorn of Seattle Seahawks fame, had just been hired to serve as offensive coordinator at Utah State by Charlie Weatherbie. The young man from La Puente's two years at Logan were prolific and generated many great moments in Aggies history, including the school's first bowl victory in 1993 as well as the classic victory over the BYU Cougars. The details of this part of the story, as well as Calvillo's CFL career, will be covered in Chapter 5.[51]

Mervyn Fernandez was another great Latino athlete from the San Jose area. He played his high school football for the Andrew P. Hill High Falcons, where he was given the nickname "Swervin" by his quarterback. He became a Don at De Anza College in Cupertino, before finishing his collegiate career at San Jose State University. He was a letter winner in 1981, and the highlight of his season was catching nine passes for 152 yards in the California Raisin Bowl against the Toledo Rockets in a 27–25 SJSU defeat. Unfortunately, that was the climax of Fernandez's time as a Spartan, as he soon faced problems both in the classroom and off the field prior to returning for the 1982 season. In an article published in the *Spartan Daily* and dated February 1, 1982, reporter Michael Liedtke noted that Fernandez had been kicked off of the team by Coach Jack Elway due to both academic and legal issues. In regard to his academics, "it became apparent that he was not going to make it late last semester. We had trouble tracking down his progress in class. It didn't seem that he was going to class.... Mervyn was another case of a young man who had different priorities."[52]

Although he did not remain for long on the San Jose campus, this receiver's size and speed attracted the attention of the Raiders, who made him a 10th-round selection in 1983. Before he could play in the NFL, however, Fernandez made the trek up to Canada and played for the British Columbia Lions between 1982 and 1986. He had a spectacular career north of the border, and his statistics mark him as one of the top 50 players in CFL history (number 42). In his rookie year, he caught passes for over 1,000 yards, and he improved upon that figure each of his first four years in the league. His best season came in 1985 as he helped lead the Lions to the Grey Cup (though he did not play in the title game due to injury). That year, he caught 95 passes for 1,727 yards and 15 scores. During his last season in Vancouver, he suffered a broken finger which limited his totals to 48 catches and 865 yards. Overall, his CFL figures totaled 399 catches, 6,680 yards, and 57 touchdown receptions. In March of 1987, Fernandez made the jump to the NFL and inked a $7 million dollar deal with the Raiders. Here was another weapon for Tom Flores to exploit in the Los Angeles arsenal. "He's got size and also has speed. Watching films from his days in the CFL, he rarely gets caught from behind."

Almost from the start of his NFL career, Fernandez seemed to bring along some of his penchant for controversy from his days at SJSU. In August of 1987, for example, he was quoted as saying that the Raiders defensive backs were not "you know, a shut-me-down-totally type of guy." Over his first couple of years in the new league, he did not make much of a splash, catching only 45 passes for about 1,000 yards. Although he did have good seasons from 1988 to 1990, with 155 receptions for over 2,600 yards, by the start of 1991 Fernandez felt that he was merely a cog in the Los Angeles offense, and not the star he once was in Canada. "I knew they drafted Tim [Brown] and brought Willie [Gault] in. I just go out and play. If my talents were not good enough, then they'd let me go or do something else." As of 1991, Fernandez still kept Brown, a 2015 Hall of Fame inductee, out of the starting lineup, however.

After the 1991 campaign, once again Fernandez got into legal trouble, for an alleged indecent exposure incident. The 1992 season was not very productive, as Fernandez caught only nine passes and started one game (although he played in 15 contests). With the rise of Brown, other receivers, and the arrival of Raghib Ismail in 1993, Fernandez's time with the Raiders was over. "I wasn't in the picture, so I asked them what plans they had for me. They gave me permission to shop around, and [San Francisco] was the place we thought of because it was close to home." While convenient, this meant that Fernandez was now behind Jerry Rice, John Taylor, and Odessa Turner, quite an imposing troika! The writing was soon on the wall, as he played sparingly in an exhibition game for the 49ers versus the Steelers. "Just playing five minutes in the fourth quarter wasn't what I came here for. There comes a time in a man's life when he's got to look at himself and say, 'Is it really worth it?'" With that, Fernandez's career was done. Although he did not have as significant a mark in the NFL as in the CFL, all told, he caught passes for over 10,000 yards over an 11-year career.[53]

Anthony Calvillo was not the only Latino on the Mt. San Antonio Scots to make his mark on professional football. About one decade before the La Puente quarterback stepped on to the confines of Covina District Field, Max Montoya, another La Puente product, was beginning a career that would lead to his status among the all-time greats of the Cincinnati Bengals, lining up next to another Bengals legend, Hall of Famer Anthony Munoz, to form one of the best offensive lines of the 1980s, if not in NFL history. Mark Powell's 2017 book, *Legends of the Jungle: Introducing the Initial Candidates for a Possible Cincinnati Bengals Hall of Fame*, provides extensive coverage of his career with the team.[54]

Unlike his fellow Warrior, Montoya did not have much of an opportunity to prove himself on the field during his high school years. In his senior campaign, doctors detected a heart murmur, and that negated his opportunity to participate in either football or basketball. Not surprisingly, he had no offers from colleges when he graduated from La Puente. Enter an opportunity with the Scots. While not starting as a freshman, Montoya did play well enough as a sophomore to attract the attention of Terry Donahue, then coaching the UCLA Bruins, who offered him a scholarship for 1976. As was common in that era, UCLA redshirted Montoya, and he finally hit the field in 1977. The impact on the Bruins' running game was quite noticeable, as the team totaled over 2,900 yards on almost 600 carries in 1978. In his senior year, Montoya helped lead the Blue and Gold to an 8–3–1 mark and a birth in the Fiesta Bowl versus Arkansas (a 10–10 tie). In this game, again, the running game predominated, as the Bruins ran the ball on 55 of 59 total offensive plays, for 255 yards (out of 316 yards of total offense). Given his prominence on the offensive line of the 12th-ranked team in the nation, Max Montoya should have been a shoe-in for 1st Team All-Pac-10 Conference or All American honors.

That was not to be, as his competition for that slot on these squads was none other than Anthony Munoz of the hated cross-town Trojans. Still, "Montoya was ... considered a potential NFL prospect prior to the 1979 NFL Draft." The Bengals selected this Mexican American with the 168th choice in the seventh round. The team certainly got excellent value for a player taken so late in the process.

After a 4–12 campaign in Montoya's rookie year, the Bengals installed Forrest Gregg as coach, and plucked Munoz with the third overall pick in 1980. The combination that would come to be recognized as "The Mexican Connection" helped usher in an era of offensive excellence for Cincinnati. Powell notes that during this decade, the squad set season records for points scored, touchdowns, rushing touchdowns, and total net yards. Additionally, the Bengals made their two trips to the Super Bowl, following the 1981 and 1989 campaigns, only to lose both contests to the San Francisco 49ers. One other aspect of Montoya's time with the Bengals harkens back to the "Tough Chicano" designation of Joe Kapp. During the infamous "Freezer Bowl" (for the AFC Championship) in January of 1982 (against the San Diego Chargers, with the temperature hovering at around -40 degrees), Montoya, along with other linemen, went sleeveless. During his time with the Bengals, he made three Pro Bowl appearances (1986, 1988 and 1989), and was second-team All-Pro in his final year with Cincinnati. He had also put down roots in the community, not only raising his family in the area, but also becoming involved in the restaurant business and civic endeavors.

The Bengals, facing the establishment of the league's Plan B free agency, had to make a difficult choice after the 1989 season. "In short, they didn't have the salary resources to keep the entire team together as they entered a new decade." Montoya merited an approximately $475,000 offer, as far as the Brown family was concerned. "I think they were taking a calculated risk, knowing that I had a lot of ties in Cincinnati and ... was very comfortable with the situation." Enter Al Davis with a offer of more than $650,000 per season. Sam Wyche, the new Bengals coach, was appreciative of Montoya's decision. At that time, this was the most money ever offered to an offensive lineman. He played for the Raiders until 1994 and earned one final trip to the Pro Bowl in 1993. Overall, he played in 223 NFL games, starting 195. Although his final years were in silver and black, Powell (and many in Ohio) still see Montoya strictly as a Bengal. "The divorce between himself and the Bengals aside, there's no question Montoya is one of the greatest, if not the best, offensive guard in team history." Montoya remains a fixture in the Cincinnati area, as he owns several restaurants, and he and his wife Patty also raise horses in nearby Hebron, Kentucky. A final connection to his hometown high school took place recently, as Montoya returned in October of 2015 to present the Warriors with a Wilson Golden Football as part of the NFL's program to reconnect former Super Bowl participants with their alma maters. He was also inducted into the Mt. San Antonio Athletic Hall of Fame in 1992.[55]

Mark Powell quotes the NFL Alumni Association stating that the other half of the "Mexican Connection" for Cincinnati, Anthony Munoz, merited the following description as he was inducted into the Hall of Fame in 1998: "The NFL has three levels of offensive linemen. The bottom rung is for players aspiring to make the Pro Bowl. The next step is for those how have earned all-star status. Then there's Anthony Munoz. He's alone at the top."[56] That is indeed high praise and, as statistics bear out, well-deserved. Anthony Munoz, like many of the other athletes noted in this work, had to overcome many obstacles, personal, financial, and physical, to arrive at this lofty plateau.

Munoz was born in Ontario, California, in 1958, the middle child of five siblings. His father abandoned the clan, and his mother Esther raised the offspring on her own. Finances were always tight, but Munoz recalls these years as a time when "we were provided for, but we didn't have any extras." He channeled his energies into sports and academics. His first love was baseball, and that may have been in part due to his imposing size, which prevented him from playing Pop Warner football. As noted on his webpage in the Hall of Fame, "His size helped him become a power-pitcher and power-hitter and a much-in-demand player in the playgrounds near his home." Eventually, he grew to a point where football became the logical choice for his athletic pursuits, although the diamond held a continued attraction. Indeed, as part of his decision to attend USC, Munoz requested the opportunity to play baseball (and skip spring football) while with the Trojans. He became part of USC's 1978 national championship team in that sport.

On the football field, he was an imposing sight and lettered between 1977 and 1979. As a starter in his sophomore year, he was described as "an offensive tackle with 'the agility of a running back.'" Not a bad set of skills when wrapped up in a 6'6", 280-lb. frame. His career in garnet and gold was limited due to several knee injuries, though he proved his mettle by earning Second Team All-American and First Team All-Pac-10 honors in 1978. There were certainly doubters, and when the Bengals made him the third selection of the first round in 1980, many in the NFL felt that the team had made a huge mistake; after all, he did fail 14 physicals prior to the draft. One person who disagreed was his college coach, John Robinson, who boldly proclaimed, "Munoz is one of the best offensive tackles in America right now. He's one of the greatest football players I've ever been associated with in any position."

This selection provided instantaneous benefits to the Bengals, as Munoz started immediately and was named to the All-Rookie team. His excellence was a constant for many years, as he was an All-Pro each season between 1981 and 1991. During these years he protected both Ken Anderson, and later, left-handed thrower Boomer Esiason. His dominance was also felt in the

4. Increased Numbers and Diversity at All Levels, 1971–1990   195

ground game, as Bengals backs rushed for over 1,000 yards six times while he anchored the line. Additionally, he showed off his agility and good hands from time to time, catching four touchdown passes on tackle eligible plays over his career. He was the NFL Offensive Lineman of the Year in 1987 and 1988 and won the same recognition from the NFL Alumni Association in 1989–1991. The ultimate on-field recognition came in 1994, when he was named part of the league's 75th Anniversary All-Time Team. Anthony Munoz, hampered by shoulder and knee issues, played his final contest on December 27, 1992. At a special ceremony during halftime, he was honored for his efforts with the Bengals. One banner on display that day stated presciently, "Munoz: Next Stop Canton."

While he accomplished much as a player, he has done just as much, if not more, via his charitable work. Recognizing how much his family struggled, Anthony, his wife DeDe, and their children, Michael and Michelle, have been more than generous with their time, talents, and treasure to help the less fortunate in the Cincinnati area. A major element in their efforts is the Anthony Munoz Foundation, which commenced operation in 2002. Among its endeavors are various scholarship funds, youth seminars, and athletic, religious, and Hispanic-themed camps. One final note, both Michael and Michelle also competed at the highest levels of athletics, with the younger Munoz playing the offensive line for the Tennessee Volunteers, and Michelle starting her basketball career at the same school before finishing at Ohio State.[57]

Anthony Munoz, 1980s (Pro Football Hall of Fame).

We have covered a lot of athletes in the preceding pages, and they have played almost all positions on the gridiron, but we have not discussed many kickers. Daniel Villanueva was the first full-time Latino kicker in the NFL, though Joe Aguirre also plied this trade on a part-time basis for the Redskins, the Dons (AAFC), and the Bombers and the Saskatchewan

Roughriders in the CFL between 1941 and 1953.[58] Some of Villanueva's teammates attached the moniker "kickador" to their Rams teammate. The notion soon became widespread in football that Latinos only played this particular position. Of course, this impression was totally incorrect. During this era, however, many individuals made their mark on the high school, college, and professional fields of California. We will provide some brief details on Efren Herrera, Frank Corral, and the Zendejas family.

Herrera, who was born in Guadalajara in 1951, moved to southern California with his family when he was 15 and attended La Puente High School. There he played soccer and baseball, wrestled, and ran track in addition to playing football. At first, he was not familiar with the game, but a coach who saw him kicking a basketball approached him about the possibility of learning the sport. He did well enough to merit a scholarship to UCLA to play football and soccer. This squad made it to the national finals in 1972 and 1973, losing both times to the St. Louis University Billikins. He had a stellar career as a kicker for the Bruins and set some marks that still stand, such as most extra points in a game (9 in 1973 versus Utah), and some that were surpassed, such as most field goals in a game, four, and most extra points in a season with 60 in 1973 (surpassed in 1998 by Chris Sailer). Herrera played for the Lions, Cowboys, Seahawks, Bills, and Raiders in the NFL, and one season for the Oklahoma Outlaws of the USFL. Over his NFL years, he connected on 116 of 171 field goals, added 256 extra points, and even caught two passes for 29 yards with Seattle. After his year with the Outlaws, he was replaced by Luis Zendejas. Herrera was very philosophical about his situation. "If I can't play, I'm not going to be sour. I'm happy to have had chances to play football. I've been All-Pro, all-league, gone to a Super Bowl.... I've welcomed the challenge." He also recognized his importance to the burgeoning Latino/Hispanic population as far as promoting the game. "I felt that Hispanics didn't have enough role models in the NFL."[59]

Efren Herrera, 1974 (courtesy Dallas Cowboys/James D. Smith).

4. Increased Numbers and Diversity at All Levels, 1971–1990   197

Following on the heels of Herrera was another Mexican-born specialist, Frank Corral, out of North Vista High School and Riverside City College. He played for Bruins in 1977 and in 1978 was drafted by George Allen and the Los Angeles Rams. He served a dual purpose with the franchise, as both punter and kicker, the last player in the NFL to perform both functions. He led the NFL in scoring in his rookie year, and recorded an 80-yard punt. The highlight of his career came in 1979, when his 9–7 squad made it all the way to the Super Bowl against the mighty Steelers. He played for the Rams until 1982, when he was replaced by John Misko and Mike Landsford. He was very upset regarding his treatment by the Rams' management. He felt that serving double duty for the team increased his value as well as the franchise's appreciation for his contributions. But it did not turn out that way. "Now that I was down in the hole, they just let me go." He played the rest of his career in the USFL with the Chicago Blitz, the Arizona Wranglers, and the Houston Gamblers. As recently as early 2016, Corral worked for the city of Riverside.[60]

In a 1984 *People* article, the publication noted the presence of what would become one of the most noted professional football families of this era, the Zendejas of the Chino, California area. Two Mexican brothers, Genaro (who arrived in the U.S. in 1964) and Joaquin Sr. (who came to this country in 1970) raised a number of sons who proved to be excellent kickers. Tony Zendejas, the oldest son of Genaro, was born in Michoacan, but excelled in soccer and football at Chino High. He attended Mt. San Antonio (noticing a pattern here?) and eventually got a scholarship to Nevada. He played with the Los Angeles Express between 1983 and 1985, and in 1984 he connected on a dozen consecutive field goals and was perfect on 36 extra point tries. After the USFL's demise, he latched on with the Houston Oilers and kicked for them between 1985 and 1990. He then played for the Rams between 1991 and 1994, and finished his career by playing in four games in 1995. Overall, his mark in the NFL was 186 field goals made out of 252 attempts (78.3 percent) and 874 total points. After his retirement, he got into the restaurant business in southern California. In 2008, he was accused of rape, but was found not guilty in 2009.

Tony's cousins, Luis and Max, made substantial marks in the NCAA and the NFL. In 1983 these two siblings participated in a highly unusual kicking competition in the Arizona–Arizona State rivalry game. Luis was kicking for the Sun Devils, and Max plied his trade for the Wildcats. In that contest, Luis established two NCAA records and tied another, but it was Max, with a 45-yarder as time expired, to who won the game for the Red and Blue. Luis might have been on the losing side in this game, but he earned All-American status that season. He finished with 28 field goals out of 37 attempts (75.7 percent) and notched 112 points for ASU. Overall, he finished his career with only one extra point missed out of 138 attempts, 81 of 108 field goals made, and 380 points. The number of field goals was then a record and still ranks in the top 10. By the way, the individual with the most field goals at the time of this writing is another Latino, Zane Gonzalez, who played for ASU between 2013 and 2016 and connected on 96 attempts.

Luis played for one decade in professional football: first with the Arizona Outlaws of the USFL (1985), then in the NFL (1987–1989), four years in the Arena League (1992–1995), and finally one season with the Birmingham Barracudas during the CFL's star-crossed attempt to move into the U.S. Max played his four years with the Wildcats, connected on 77 of 104 field goal attempts (74.0 percent), earned Second Team All-American honors in 1983 and 1985, earned Second Team All Pac-10 honors the same years, and was Honorable Mention All Pac-10 in 1984. He had a brief career in the NFL with the Cowboys, Redskins, and Packers.[61]

A final individual with a California connection is the Cuban American, Luis Sharpe, who was born in Havana and played his high school football at Southwestern High School (closed in 2012) in an inner-city section of Detroit with a relatively high Latino concentration. After being part of the Prep All-America Football Squad for 1977, Sharpe earned a scholarship to UCLA and anchored the line as an offensive tackle between 1978 and 1981. He was the team's "rookie of the year" as a freshman and capped his career with Team Offensive MVP, All Pac-10 and All-American designations in 1981. In 2009, a "greatest of" team for the Bruins listed Sharpe as a backup on the offensive line (along with Max Montoya) behind such luminaries as Jonathon Ogden and Randy Cross. This success led to Luis' selection as a first-round pick by St. Louis Cardinals in 1982. He eventually became a three-time Pro Bowl player in 1987, 1988, and 1989. Altogether, he started and played in 189 NFL contests.

As his career wound down, he was injured against the Philadelphia Eagles in 1994 and became involved in drugs, particularly crack cocaine. In a recent interview with a Phoenix TV station, Sharpe pointed to this injury as an important moment in his path to addiction, though a

Luis Sharpe, 1982 (courtesy Arizona Cardinals Football Club).

4. Increased Numbers and Diversity at All Levels, 1971–1990   199

source from the Cardinals indicated that he was aware of Sharpe's usage as early as 1992. In short order, a man described by many as "Personable. Articulate…. He was fluent in two languages. He seemed the total package," began a downward spiral that culminated in a failed marriage, being shot twice, and serving more time incarcerated than he spent in the NFL. By 1995 he was involved in various drug offenses, including convictions in 2000 and 2004. After his first release, he became a preacher at a Salvation Army center in Phoenix, only to fall into the felonious routine yet again. While he was incarcerated the second time, his daughter Leah was murdered in a drug-related incident. Her death helped spark a reconciliation between Sharpe and his remaining offspring. His daughter Rebekah lives in the Detroit area, another daughter Sarah was attending the University of Arizona (as of 2011), and twins, Luis and Hannah, were attending Phoenix Mountain Pointe High. Luis Jr., eventually moved on to play defensive back with the Leathernecks of Western Illinois. According to the 2017 Phoenix station interview, Sharpe had been clean and sober since his most recent release in 2013. An excellent summary of his life and struggles is documented in the movie "Mountain Highs and Valley Lows."[62]

In Chapter 3, we noted the career of Carlos Alvarez, the "Cuban Comet" with the Florida Gators between 1969 and 1972. In 2017, he was inducted into the Miami Chamber of Commerce Sports Hall of Champions. The ceremony honored Alvarez for his tremendous athletic career at Gainesville, as well as his great success as an environmental lawyer for four decades in Tallahassee. As part of his visit with the *Miami Herald* to mark this august occasion, Alvarez brought up some interesting points that tie in with some themes articulated in this work. For example, he noted how significant it was to the Cuban American community to have him play in a game at the Orange Bowl against the Hurricanes. "Miami would normally draw 30,000 people, and there were 75,000 in the stands that day." Clearly, even at this relatively early period in this community's development, football, and success by a fellow Cubano, was significant indeed. Alvarez was also partially responsible for attracting yet another Cuban-born athlete to campus, Ralph Ortega (discussed below). Even with these two great examples, Cuban Americans have not been well represented at the highest levels of collegiate or professional football.[63]

A 2008 review by the *Herald* of Miami-Dade's "best" of all times (broken down by schools) revealed but a scant listing of Cubanos/Latinos. Ralph Ortega is on the list (Coral Gables High, 1971), as are Silvio Cardozo (Hialeah High, 1969), Jose Rios (North Miami High, 1970), and more recently Orlando Iglesias (Coral Park High, 1997, who played at the University of Houston and will be discussed in Chapter 5). Two other Latinos from this era that we highlight here are Colombian-born Fuad Reveiz and fellow kicker, Cuban-American Carlos Huerta. An earlier list, from 2007, included only Ortega and Iglesias.[64]

When Ralph Ortega signed with the Atlanta Falcons after his selection in the second round of the 1975 NFL draft, a Florida paper referred to him as a player who "will become the first Cuban born to play" at this level.[65] Obviously, that is not a correct statement. What can be said, however, is that Ortega had an illustrious, though fairly brief, amount of time in professional football, as well as boasting one of the finest careers ever for a member of the Florida Gators.

Ortega was born in Havana, his father a lawyer in Cuba, but his family fled to Miami, as did many of his countrymen shortly after the revolution. Ralph eventually attended Coral Gables High and benefited from the tutelage of south Florida head football coaching legend Nick Kotys, as well as being a shot-putter. By the late 1960s, the Cavaliers were a well-oiled machine that was one of the dominant powers in the state. Ortega played on one of those legendary squads, the undefeated 1969 version which the National Sports News Service proclaimed as mythical national champions. Four players from that historic side—Ortega, Neil Colzie, Glenn Cameron, and Gary Dunn—eventually played in the NFL.[66]

Ortega decided upon Florida in part because of Carlos Alvarez, but also because he wanted to play against his father's and brother's alma mater, Auburn. Indeed, it was his father who encouraged him to attend Florida. "Florida is offering you ... a lot more than Auburn can offer. You can play at home, before a home crowd and if you plan to live here, it is better for your future if you play here."[67] Ralph Ortega quickly made his mark and moved to the first team as a sophomore. His coach, Doug Dickey, noted going into the 1972 campaign that he expected the Cubano to "be one of our top linebackers for a long time. He plays the game in a bad humor."[68]

The Coral Gables product soon made a difference, and the Gators' defense improved dramatically from 1971. After a 3–3 tie against LSU, one Miami paper noted that it "marked the third time this season the Gator defense prevented their opposition from scoring a touchdown, an accomplishment which would not have been possible without linebacker Ralph Ortega."[69] He continued to make a difference as a junior and senior, earning 1st Team All-SEC status both years, and was a First Team All-American in 1974. In total, he tallied 357 tackles, five interceptions, and 12 forced fumbles. These statistics helped him earn the ranking of the 40th "greatest Gator" by the *Gainesville Sun*, as well as enshrinement as an SEC Legend in 2007. Ortega graduated with a degree in management in 1976.[70]

As a member of the Falcons between 1975 and 1978, Ortega was part of the legendary "Grits Blitz" defense that surrendered an NFL record-low 129 points in 1977. His recollection of that team includes needling a fellow Miami legend, Manny Fernandez (whom we will discuss later in this chapter), who helped anchor the "No Name Defense" of the Dolphins' perfect

4. Increased Numbers and Diversity at All Levels, 1971–1990 201

season. "I use to get into great arguments with Manny.... He'd talk about the 1972 Dolphins.... And I would always tease him that if the '77 Falcons defense with that offense, that would have been the dream team."[71] After four years with Atlanta, Ortega made the move back to Miami and completed his career after the 1980 season. Over his NFL career, he played in 81 games, started 24, forced seven fumbles, and had five interceptions. He has been involved in the financial sector in his hometown in the years since his retirement.[72] The next generation of the Ortega clan also played football, as his son Buck played quarterback at Gulliver Prep (coached by his dad) and helped the Raiders win the state Class 2A title in 2000. He played quarterback and tight end for the University of Miami, was an undrafted free agent with the Redskins in 2006, and finished his career with the Saints in 2009.[73]

Cuban American Carlos Huerta made his mark with another traditional south Florida powerhouse, the Columbus High Explorers. Not recruited by the University of Miami, he walked on and kicked for the Hurricanes between 1988 and 1991. In his senior year, he was part of a national championship team and was a consensus All-American. While with "the U," he kicked 73 field goals and tallied 397 career points. He played in the CFL with the Las Vegas Posse (at the same time as Anthony Calvillo) and scored 154 points for that ill-fated organization. He won the league's Jackie Parker Trophy (Rookie of the Year) for his efforts in 1994. When the Posse ceased operations, he moved on to another American-based CFL team in Baltimore. He had an even better season in 1995, scoring 228 points and helping the Stallions win the Grey Cup. His success "north of the border" garnered two brief stints in the NFL, with the Bears and Rams in 1996. Finally, he tried the Arena League, with the Florida Bobcats and the San Jose Sabercats.[74]

Fuad Reveiz was born in Bogota, Colombia, and his family moved to Miami in 1974. He played at Miami Sunset High, a school known for its success in tennis, volleyball, and soccer, but certainly not a football power. Like most players who suited up for the Knights, he was not necessarily on the radar of most major college football powers. Reveiz acknowledged that his hope was to be a running back, à la Larry Csonka, but he never developed into that type of body. During his sophomore year in 1978, however, he kicked a 60-yarder, then a record for the state of Florida, and that did garner some notice. This mark has since been surpassed by Graham Gano of Tate High School with a 65-yarder in 2004.

After finishing high school, Reveiz considered attending a California junior college when he was surprised by an offer from Coach Johnny Majors and the Tennessee Volunteers. According to the 1981 UT press guide, Reveiz had been brought to the school's attention by a South Florida contact. Going into the season, Majors and special teams coach George Cafego had trepidations as "after spring practice ... the more I looked at it, the more I was concerned that our place kicking wasn't stabilized." The opportunity presented itself, and shortly after the family returned to Florida from the West Coast, Majors offered the scholarship to Rocky Top. The Volunteers were very fortunate to bring the transplanted Miamian on to their squad, as Reveiz connected on 71 of 95 field goal attempts during his career. In 1982, he hit on 27 of 31 attempts and did not miss an extra point. He fell off a bit as a junior, but rebounded to make 20 of 23 kicks in his senior season. He earned All-SEC designation that year, and Gannett News named him to its All-American team. He scored a total of 314 points for Tennessee.

This success led his hometown Dolphins to make him a 7th-round pick in 1985. Again, he did not disappoint. By early October of the 1985 campaign, he had already kicked more field goals than his predecessor, and he wound up hitting 22 of 27 (and 50 of 52 extra points) that year. Over the next four seasons, he would not do as well, going only 31 for 45. After a partial season with the Chargers in 1990, Fuad Reveiz moved on to the Minnesota Vikings in mid-season and kicked through 1995. He set the single-season mark for that franchise, hitting 11 of 12 field goals after his move from San Diego. His most successful stretch came right at the end of his career, between October 1994 and September 1995, as he connected on 31 consecutive attempts (then an NFL record). He was forced to retire before the start of the 1996 season due to a painful foot. Since leaving the game, Reveiz has been involved in home construction and real estate development. He and his wife, Gail, have three children, and his two sons, Nick and Shane, played linebacker for the Volunteers between 2007 and 2010 and 2009 and 2011 respectively.[75]

We now present information concerning two noted Latino athletes who made their mark outside of the states noted above. While both had excellent collegiate careers, only one made his mark at the professional level. These individuals are Tony Casillas, who played for the University of Oklahoma Sooners, and Andre Herrera, who played for the Southern Illinois University Salukis.

Tony Casillas was born in 1963 in Tulsa, and he attended East Central High School, where he was an all-state performer on the defensive line for the Cardinals. He earned a scholarship to play for the Sooners, in part because of his play at the 1981 State All-Star Game at Owen Field. Barry Switzer, the legendary OU coach, was present and, to say the least, was impressed with Casillas' performance. "I had no idea this guy was that good. He'll be a great player for us. Which he was."

Casillas' time in Norman did not get off to a great start, however, as he suffered an ankle injury, contracted mononucleosis, and lost his entire first year. The following season, 1982, he played sparingly and accounted for only ten tackles. In 1983, switched to nose-guard, he began to blossom and was named second team All-Big 8. By that time, Switzer was comparing this Mexican American to one of the all-time Sooners greats, the immortal Lee Roy Selmon. Not bad for a young man who, for many years, did not really know or appreciate his ethnic background. He was the second Latino inducted into the College Football Hall of Fame (in 2008), alongside Joe Kapp. Jim Plunkett was the first individual so honored.

When Casillas was growing up in what he described as "a white neighborhood in Tulsa," he was taught by his family (his father is of Mexican descent, and his mother is Irish and Native American) to pronounce his name "Ca-sill-as" not "Ca-see-yas." This confused Tony, as he wondered why some of his relatives used the Spanish version of the surname. "I asked my mom and my dad and my family, but never really got an answer. They simply didn't want to expose us to anything negative. When I went to college is when I changed it back.... Even though we had a different background ... we were kind of sheltered." Although he came to appreciate his background, he struggled with his father's native language. "To this day, Spanish is a struggle for me."[76]

Casillas also did not do well at the start of his academic career at OU, and he grew frustrated with both situations. His GPA dropped to 2.3 before he became more acclimated to the academic rigors of university life and athletics. He recalled, "when I messed up in school ... it really bothered me because I knew if I had just taken the time and motivated myself to studying and doing the little things right that I wouldn't be in that situation." By the time he started his junior season in 1984, his grades had improved to above a 3.0. He would excel on the field as well and lived up to the Selmonian standards predicted by Switzer.[77] His performance earned him several major awards: first-team All-American as a junior and senior, UPI Lineman of the Year, the Lombardi Award, and Big Eight Conference Defensive Player of the Year, all in 1985. As frosting on the cake, Casillas was a major cog in the Sooners' National Championship that year. All of this helped make him the second selection in the first round of the 1986 draft by the Atlanta Falcons.

Tony Casillas played with the Falcons between 1986 and 1990, and he performed well when healthy. In 1986 and 1988, he recorded 111 tackles and started all 16 games. In the strike-shortened 1987 campaign, he started all of the games in which "the regulars" played and tallied another 72 tackles. His finest season came in 1989, though he experienced some issues off of the field starting the previous year. Shortly after the start of camp in 1988, Casillas left the facility for counseling due to stress-related symptoms. By the start of the next season, he was a changed man. "I just don't let little things bother me.... I don't try to put too much emphasis on myself to be perfect every play."[78] Although he felt better about his emotional status, Casillas and the Falcons soon became embroiled in a dispute over pay. He sat out most of the 1990 training camp and played in only nine games. Further, he missed a team flight back from a game in Los Angeles and was suspended for two weeks without pay. By July 1991, Casillas was openly discussing retirement. The Falcons traded him to the Cowboys instead. In his time in Atlanta, he accounted for 478 tackles, eight sacks and eight forced fumbles. As he left town, Casillas noted his appreciation for the new opportunity. "I was in a situation ... where I felt shafted and now I'm with an upcoming program.... I achieved my goal. I got out of Atlanta."

Over the next three seasons (he was signed through 1993) with the Cowboys, Casillas combined with Russell Maryland to form a fearsome front that was instrumental in claiming two Super Bowl victories. After leaving Dallas, Casillas signed with the Chiefs, but never played a down in the regular season. The issue, as far as he indicated, was medical, though the Kansas City organization thought otherwise. He stated that he had high blood pressure and might have to retire. The Chiefs thought he wanted to return to Dallas, which was now under the direction of Barry Switzer.[79] He subsequently signed with the Jets and played two years in the Meadowlands for teams that were the exact opposite of the situation in Texas, going 6–10 and 3–13. By this point in his career, his playing time had decreased, in part because of back surgery, and he recorded only 43 tackles over this two years in green and white.[80] A final opportunity to play in the NFL took place in 1996 and 1997, as he finished his career with Dallas. In his last season, he started 14 games (in place of Leon Lett) and tied his career high with three sacks. He retired in February of 1998. Many honors have followed since he left the field. He was enshrined in the College Football Hall of Fame in 2005 and was also inducted into the Oklahoma Sports Hall of Fame in 2008.[81]

Tony Casillas took a well-worn path to collegiate and professional football glory, but the story of Cuban American Andre Herrera was altogether different. His family lived in the Bronx after leaving the island. Given their economic circumstances, he did not have the opportunity to play high school football. Every morning, to attend

Tony Casillas, 1986 (courtesy Dallas Cowboys/ James D. Smith).

4. Increased Numbers and Diversity at All Levels, 1971–1990 205

DeWitt Clinton High School, he would take a four-bus, one-and-one-half-hour ride. While he saw many of his friends wearing Converse sneakers to play basketball, he had to work to get his. Instead of hitting the court or the gridiron, he "carried messages around downtown Manhattan, cleaned out stockrooms, and raked sanitation lots." This appeared to be his lot until, one year after graduation, he started to play football with a sandlot team known as the Pelham Spartans, and then at Westchester Community College in New York, before he came to the attention of the talent-starved Salukis. He did not contribute much to the 2–9 (1974) and 1–9–1 (1975) squads, totaling 758 yards on 160 carries. In 1976, new coach Rey Dempsey gave the Cubano a chance to be the featured back, and respond he did. In 11 games, he carried the ball 287 times for 1,588 yards, a 5.5 average. In one game, against the Northern Illinois Huskies, he ran wild, totaling 214 yards in the first quarter alone and ending up with 319 (including jaunts of 85, 53, and 45 yards) and five touchdowns. This unlikely Latino star came out of nowhere to finish second in the NCAA in total yards on the ground, just behind Tony Dorsett. Herrera was selected by the Kansas City Chiefs in the sixth round of the 1977 draft.

It would be wonderful to say that Andre Herrera went on to a long and successful career in the NFL, but that would be incorrect. He got barely a chance with the Chiefs, "partly, I did not get a lot of playing time. And then, when I was in there, they wanted to see me do something spectacular. I guess I wasn't spectacular enough." He was soon waived and went to the Toronto Argonauts in the CFL for a brief time. He then signed with Oakland, that football haven of misfits and individuals looking for another opportunity, but things did not work out there either. "It's been depressing, somewhat. You look back and you questioned what happened to you. And why it's happened. You wonder if maybe it's not time to give up, get a job and accept your responsibility elsewhere." Apparently, that is what happened, as Herrera never played a down in a regular season game in either league. His alma mater inducted him into its Hall of Fame in 1994, but that is the last information we found on him.[82]

At the start of this chapter, we quoted Christopher Gonzalez's statement about the need to get into the pipeline to have a chance to make it through. Given the increased numbers of Latinos playing football at various levels by 1990, it is apparent that progress had taken place. In our final chapter, we will look at a further expansion of these numbers, though obvious problems remain. In the late 2010s, Latinos still account for but a small percentage of the athletes playing the sport; particularly as we get beyond the high school level. Why is this? Alongside tales of on-field exploits, we will seek to address such issues. Now, as we have done in the previous chapters, we turn to individuals whose life stories and careers merit a bit more extensive discussion: Joe Kapp, Jim Plunkett, Ted Hendricks, Manny Fernandez, and Pete Rodriguez.

Joseph Robert (Garcia) "Joe" Kapp

The Joseph Robert Kapp football story, unlike the other Latino/Spanish-surname football stories, is the account of a Mexican American athlete who clearly confronted and overcame a variety of negative images/labels by reporters, players, and fans throughout his personal and professional career. Importantly, his identity remained intact although constantly challenged by the social climate of the times and people who intended to stigmatize his identity and actions. Joe Kapp, in turn, countered with a determination and fierce style of leadership that enabled him to endure and achieve a large measure of success in professional football.

Where does the story begin? Joseph Robert (Garcia) Kapp was born on March 19, 1938, in Santa Fe, New Mexico. He was the oldest son of five children in the Kapp family. His mother, Florence Garcia Kapp, was of Mexican ancestry; his father, Robert Douglas Kapp, was German.[83] Joe had a younger brother, Larry Kapp, a Sergeant in the U.S. Army and a wounded Vietnam veteran, and three sisters, Jonnie, Linda, and Suzie.[84] In 1940, the Kapp family migrated to several towns. They first moved to the San Fernando Valley, then to Salinas, a hundred miles south of San Francisco, where the young Joe Kapp experienced his first threat because of being Mexican ancestry. He recounted the incident in a 1970 *Sports Illustrated* article:

> We lived in a housing project with other pickers, Okies, Arkies, blacks, whites and browns. In the fifth grade, a bigger kid called me a "dirty Mexican," and at first I didn't challenge him. But when I got home I brooded on what he had said. My sense of justice was outraged. My mother is Mexican American, but my father is German; therefore at worst, I could only be half of what that kid called me. So I went back and found him and really whaled him.[85]

The confrontation for Kapp was the first of many similar incidents that occurred in later life. One important aspect of this incident was that Kapp learned not to back down from such confrontations. After the Salinas stay, the Kapp family finally made their way to Newhall in southern California, where the children attended local schools. Kapp attended Hart High School, where he was a star in both basketball and football. The young Kapp was a great competitor and captained both teams. His leadership earned All-California Interscholastic Federation (CIF) honors in basketball, and he was selected the Most Valuable Athlete at Hart High School his senior year.[86]

As a result, the University of California Berkeley Golden Bears offered Kapp a basketball scholarship, which he accepted, but it was football that distinguished his athletic career. During his first three years at Berkeley, his performances in both sports in Pacific Coast Conference competition were outstanding. He played on the Golden Bears basketball team that defeated West Virginia and Jerry West to win the 1959 NCAA Championship.[87]

4. Increased Numbers and Diversity at All Levels, 1971–1990 207

The football team, however, was not as successful. They had not won a conference title in years, and in the two previous seasons had won a total of three games. Bothered by his team's lethargy, Kapp worked diligently to motivate his teammates at every practice. His dedication paid off as he led his team to one of the most dramatic one-season turnarounds in college football history. The Golden Bears finished with a 7–3 record. They won the Pacific Coast Conference title and a date to play the University of Iowa Hawkeyes in the 1958 Rose Bowl.

Unfortunately, the powerful Iowa team wreaked havoc upon Kapp and the Golden Bears. Ron Fimrite reported Kapp's game experiences in a *Sports Illustrated* story, "'I remember it was a beautiful day,' says Kapp, 'because I spent most of it lying on my back looking up at the sky.'" Fimrite also quoted Iowa's halfback, Willie Fleming, about his encounter with Joe Kapp:

> In the game, I'm in the end zone after scoring and I see this mad man running straight at me and it's Kapp alright. He grabs me by the jersey and says, "we're gonna kick your ass," and I tell him, "hey, there's five minutes left and we're way ahead," but he said that with such conviction, he had me believing we were in trouble.[88]

For his leadership and inspiration, Kapp was selected by the Football Writers and *Time* magazine to their All-America Team. He was also named the team's Most Valuable Player and awarded the Andy Smith Trophy, given annually to the varsity player with the most playing time during the season. Kapp was also named to the All-Pacific Coast Conference Team.[89] According to a *CAL Athletic News* publication story, Kapp finished his collegiate career with impressive statistics:

> Kapp finished his Cal career as one of the most versatile athletes in the school's history. Wound up completing 154 of 303 passes for 2,023 career yards, while rushing for 965 yards, accounting for 16 touchdowns through the air or on the ground. When he graduated, he ranked second on Cal's all-time total offense and passing list.[90]

Awaiting the opportunity to play football at the professional level, Kapp anticipated numerous NFL offers, but the 1959 collegiate draft was a disappointment. The Washington Redskins selected him in the 17th round but never contacted him.[91] Instead, he opted to play in the Canadian Football League (CFL) and signed a three-year contract with the struggling Calgary Stampeders. No sooner did Joe Kapp arrive in Calgary than things began to happen. Kapp recalled in a *Sports Illustrated* article:

> The ink was hardly dry on the contract before I got into a battle that produced these scars on my face. It was a hot, humid night during the training season, and most of the Stampeders were sitting around drinking beer. We'd had the annual rookie show earlier and nobody felt like going to bed, and around one a.m., I walked into a room where the guys were talking. Without warning, a big linebacker [Doug Brown] broke a quart bottle across my jaw and raked it across my throat. We started to tangle, but

Joe Kapp (22), 1959 (Canadian Football Hall of Fame).

there was so much blood spurting out the room that the other guys jumped in and broke it up. At the hospital, they gave me 100 stitches, and the doctors said the broken glass had missed the jugular by about half an inch.[92]

The reason for the attack was never fully explained, but order was restored and differences set aside. The issue of race is a consideration for the attack. Kapp noted that the same linebacker killed a priest in Vancouver for no apparent reason and was institutionalized in a mental hospital, suffering from paranoid schizophrenia.[93]

The 1959 season opened auspiciously as the Stampeders beat Saskatchewan, 28–8, and Kapp passed for two touchdowns. They also beat Winnipeg and posted a 29–17 victory over British Columbia to take over first place in the conference with a 5–1 record.[94] The rookie Mexican American played brilliantly in his first pro season, rushing for 606 yards and completing 196 passes for 2,990 yards with an outstanding 59.7 percent completion rate and 21 touchdown passes.[95] It was a great start for both Kapp and Calgary, but the excitement would soon fade.

Calgary's 1960 season opener with Saskatchewan ended in a tie, 15–15, as Kapp was impressive with his passing efficiency. The Stampeders went 6–8–2 in regular season play but exceeded expectations. A head coaching change early in the season did not hamper their will to win, and Kapp led them into the playoffs. Against British Columbia, Kapp engineered a 22–10 victory over the Lions that finally returned Calgary to the playoffs after three years.[96] Unfortunately, their momentum ground to halt as the Edmonton Eskimos defeat Calgary, 30–7, and advanced to the Grey Cup.⁹⁷

At the start of the 1961 season, in what appeared to be a salary dispute, Kapp informed Calgary management that he wanted to play out his option and go to another team. This action caused tensions for the team leadership, and they opted to replace Joe Kapp with Washington Redskins punter/quarterback Herman Sidney Eagle Day. Throughout the exhibition season and the early part of the schedule, Kapp played a backup role until the granting of his trade request to the British Columbia Lions. In the meantime, the *Calgary Press* and fans criticized Kapp's reluctance to reconsider staying in Calgary. Kapp's decision for a trade was solidified after a series of negotiations between the two teams. The decision favored Kapp's request, and Canadian sportswriter Denny Boyd called it "the greatest trade in Canadian football history." In the deal, the British Columbia Lions gave up three players and the rights to a fourth player for Calgary quarterback Joe Kapp.

The *Touchdown—The All-Canadian Sports Magazine* writer Gorde Hunter described the controversial trade:

> Joe Kapp, the most controversial and one of the most colorful players in Western Conference football, has gone from the foothills but the memory lingers on. The rabid ones hereabouts had themselves a field day when it was announced the "Big Mex" had been peddled to the Vancouver Lions for Messrs. Ed O'Bradovich, Bruce Claridge, Jim Walden and Bill Crawford. There was no fence-sitting on the subject— they were either pro–Joe or violently anti-Joe.⁹⁸

The Hunter article presented a citizen's negative assessment of Kapp's tenure with the Stampeders that is racially intensified by the label "big Mex," which appears to connote the sale of a slave rather than a football player. Nonetheless, citizen commentary documented in the article centers on his play-calling and his refusal of all Calgary contract offers.⁹⁹ Although Jim Finks, Calgary General Manager, did not want Kapp to leave, he added, "I think we got the best of the deal. Otherwise we wouldn't have made it." Interestingly, Jim Finks would also figure in Joe Kapp's later move from British Columbia to the Minnesota Vikings of the NFL.¹⁰⁰

For the British Columbia Lions, the trade appeared to be a gamble due to Kapp's knee injury, and this caused some concern. However, off-season surgery restored mobility to his knee, and Kapp was ready to play. In the 1962 campaign, Kapp set a CFL season record of 3,279 passing yards with 28 touchdowns, while the season highlight was his performance versus the Edmonton Eskimos on September 29.¹⁰¹ Kapp passed for 433 yards and six touchdowns to set a Lions record for most touchdowns in a single game. It was a great performance by Kapp, which he would supersede in the NFL.

The 1963 Lions' season produced 12 victories against 4 losses and a trip to play in the Grey Cup. The *1987 B.C. Lions Fact Book* recaps the season:

With a great season from a veteran roster, headlined by Kapp and Fleming, the Lions' 12–4 record gave them first place (for the first time) and a two-one series victory of Saskatchewan put them in the Grey Cup.... With star player Fleming out with an injury and sent to the sidelines, the Hamilton Tiger-Cats took home the Grey Cup prize with a 21–10 victory over the Lions.[102]

Disappointed by the Grey Cup loss to the Hamilton Tiger-Cats, Kapp and the Lions regrouped in 1964. Interestingly, after the 1963 season, and as a result of Kapp's leadership and injuries during the campaign, he was given the nickname "El Cid." He explained who El Cid was and the symbolism for the moniker. "In the motion picture, El Cid is a feared and respected Spanish General who was killed in battle, but the enemy was not aware of his death. To gain an advantage over their enemies, El Cid is then strapped into the saddle to lead the Spanish into battle to scare and gain an advantage over the enemy." The implications of Kapp's description serve as metaphors for Kapp's leadership, his numerous injuries that did not keep him from playing, and the impression of fear that enabled him to overcome his critics.[103]

The team now possessed a new and inspirational identity provided by their Grey Cup experience, and they were determined to repeat. In the process, the Lions dug up an old club slogan, "Lions roar in '54," and updated the slogan to "Lions roar in '64" as their motivation to win.[104] They finished with an 11–2–3 record to meet the Hamilton Tiger-Cats once again in the Grey Cup. This time the Lions roared to victory, beating Hamilton, 34–24. Although the Tiger-Cats outpassed the Lions, Kapp kept the supposedly tough Hamilton defense off-balance most of the afternoon. Author Jack Sullivan writes that Kapp picked holes in Hamilton's deep pass defense and crossed them up by sending the 183-pound Fleming into the middle of the line rather than running him out wide.[105]

To the victor belong the spoils, and Kapp was selected to the CFL All-Pro team in both 1963 and 1964. He garnered the Jeff Nicklin Memorial Trophy for being the Western Conference Most Valuable Player, and was runner-up for the Schenley Award as the Most Outstanding Player in the CFL.

In 1966, Kapp played out his option with the British Columbia Lions and requested waivers that would permit him to play in the NFL. As expected, Lions management refused to waive him and continued to negotiate a deal to keep him with the Lions. Not surprisingly, Kapp had initiated his own talks with representatives from the AFL's Houston Oilers. This sent shock waves throughout professional football. Kapp's negotiations proposed a two-year, $100,000 per season contract with the Oilers that stipulated an early escape from the CFL, in time for the 1967 campaign, which would qualify him for a $10,000 bonus.

In Canada, the B.C. Lions realized they did not want a reluctant player on their team, so they sold their rights to Kapp to the Minnesota Vikings for

4. Increased Numbers and Diversity at All Levels, 1971–1990   211

$50,000. Once again, it was former Calgary General Manager Jim Finks, now with Vikings, who handled the negotiations. Finks first negotiated with the Washington Redskins, who had drafted Kapp back in 1959, to release him from their reserve list. Finks signed Kapp for two years plus an option season at $100,000 per year. Kapp's long-lasting desire to play in the NFL was now realized.

His initial season (1967) with the Minnesota Vikings was anti-climatic as the team faltered winning only three games. They beat Green Bay, 10–7, the New York Giants, 27–24, and the Pittsburgh Steelers, 41–27.[106] In the "Viking Team Season Records," stats reveal that they also had the fewest pass completions, the lowest pass completion percentage, the most penalty yards, and the fewest points scored.[107] It seemed as though the Vikings were in a deep sleep and needed mega-amounts of motivation. In his second season with Minnesota, as he had done previously at California, Calgary, and Vancouver, Kapp took on a bigger leadership role and provided the inspiration that helped turned the Vikings from a last-place team into a winner, as they claimed the Central Division title in 1968. The Vikings posted an 8–6 mark to advance to the playoffs, where they fell short to Baltimore, 24–14, and the Dallas Cowboys, 17–13.[108]

In the 1969 campaign, Kapp led Minnesota to a 12–2 record, the NFL Championship, and the Vikings' first appearance in the Super Bowl. Along the way, Kapp recorded one of the most remarkable performances in pro football history. On September 28, 1969, facing the defending NFL Champion Baltimore Colts, Kapp passed for 449 yards and seven touchdowns to become just the fifth man in NFL history to throw seven scoring passes in a game, joining pro football greats Sid Luckman, Adrian Burke, George Blanda, and Y.A. Tittle. The *New York Times* described the effort:

> Joe Kapp shredded the Baltimore defense for a league record-tying seven touchdown passes today as the Minnesota Vikings smashed the defending National Football League champion Colts, 52–14. Kapp, whose play elicited boos the last two seasons, joins the elite group of Sid Luckman, Y.A. Tittle, George Blanda and Adrian Burke for throwing the most scoring passes in a single game.... A sellout crowd of 47,644 saw Kapp hit 12 different receivers for a Viking record of 449 yards. His scoring strikes of 18, 83, 21, 13, 41, 1, and 15 yards went to six different men with Gene Washington taking in the 83 and 41 yard bombs....[109]

The 1969 regular season began with a loss to the New York Giants, followed by 12 consecutive victories and a loss to the Atlanta Falcons. In the playoffs, they beat Los Angeles and Cleveland to meet the Kansas City Chiefs in the Super Bowl.[110]

On January 11, 1970, the Minnesota Vikings and the Kansas City Chiefs met at Tulane Stadium in New Orleans to determine the Super Bowl IV Champion. However, the Vikings' Cinderella story ended unsuccessfully. The

Chiefs scored first on three field goals by Jan Stenerud and a 5-yard run by Mike Garrett. The Chiefs led at halftime, 16–0. In the third period, the Vikings marched 69 yards in ten plays, including 47 yards passing by Joe Kapp to set up Dave Osborne's 4-yard touchdown run. Late in the third quarter, the Chiefs scored once again when Otis Taylor evaded tacklers to score the final touchdown in the game. The Chiefs won, 23–7.[111] The Vikings, although they had looked forward to the contest with anticipation, did not perform well. Turnovers and mistakes rendered Minnesota's game plan ineffective. Toward the end of the contest, Kapp ran a bootleg into the Chiefs' Buck Buchanan and Aaron Brown; Brown clinched the tackle and pounded Kapp onto the turf shoulder to shoulder. This was the end of the game and the dream for Kapp.[112] He left the game with a separated shoulder, torn ligaments, and a pronounced sense of disappointment.

Lamenting the loss to Kansas City, Kapp praised their overall team effort and said, "Now my attitude is simply that we Vikings will have to go out there and do it all over again—the hard way."[113] However, there were contract matters yet to be resolved to allow Kapp to continue his career in the NFL.

Interestingly, several months after Super Bowl IV, *Sports Illustrated* ran a series of articles on Joe Kapp's tenure with the Vikings, beginning with the July 20, 1970, issue. Kapp was featured on the cover of *Sports Illustrated* with the caption, "The Toughest Chicano—Viking Quarterback Joe Kapp." The term "Chicano" on the cover was basically another reference to his ethnic background, while the term itself linguistically is a derivation of the word "Mexicano" that dates back to the 16th century. The word "Chicano" is a civil rights' Mexican American identity that gained notoriety during the 60s and 70s.[114]

After the Super Bowl and before the start of the 1970 season, Kapp became involved in contract negotiations that threatened his future with the Vikings, and he looked eastward to Boston. The Vikings offered Kapp $100,000 a year, but he wanted more money to stay in Minnesota. However, Minnesota was not willing to offer more. He was given an ultimatum to take the offer or leave it. Stunned and disappointed by the Vikings' refusal to negotiate, he responded, "I don't answer to ultimatums; I'm not some kind of slave."[115]

In the meantime, Boston Patriots head coach Clive Rush telephoned Kapp about the possibility of playing in Boston. Two days later, Kapp flew to Boston and signed a three-year, no cut, $200,000 temporary contract and became the Patriots' second-string quarterback. At the time, Kapp's three-year deal represented the biggest contract in football. However, rather than signing a standard NFL contract, Kapp signed a "Memorandum of Agreement" that covered the general terms that are normally included in the standard player's contract. This was an exception to standard procedure, but it allowed the NFL to expedite the signing, based on the expectations that he would eventually sign a standard player's contract.[116]

Kapp did not want to sign a standard player's contract because it was too rigid and did not provide any player rights. Instead, he was looking for the flexibility to negotiate a contract that never materialized. He believed that in signing the contract with the Pats, he gave up his rights and became the property of the team and the NFL. He also believed the team could fire him at any time, without a release, and thus prevent him from playing with another team. For the 1970 season, he was allowed to play, but his future was in jeopardy.

The 1970 Boston Patriots' season got underway with Mike Taliaferro at quarterback. The Patriots won the first game beating the Miami Dolphins, 27–14. But they soon faltered, losing the next nine games. Kapp entered the Patriots' huddle in the fourth game with little fanfare, little success, but high expectations. The Boston fans, according to the *Boston Globe*, referred to Joe Kapp as the "Mexican Messiah" and were willing to give him a few days, but they expected him to lead them to the green pasture called the Super Bowl.[117]

In Larry Fox's book, *The New England Patriots: Triumph & Tragedy*, the author also has a nickname for Kapp. He writes:

> Kapp's arrival did little to soothe their starting quarterback Mike Taliaferro's generally testy disposition, but "Super Mex" hardly proved the savior of Patriot football. He began playing in the fourth game and participated in only a single season victory the rest of the way. The unsettled coaching situation was also partly responsible, but he completed less than 45 percent of his passes for a mere 3 touchdowns, had 17 interceptions and was sacked 27 times. Kapp's greatest contribution was an unceasing effort to bring the team together, so they resembled, at least in this way, the Vikings he left behind and the old Patriots as well.[118]

It is obvious from the constant use of racial monikers for Kapp that his Mexican ancestry was singled out whenever something went wrong. Wherever Kapp went, his ethnic background was always identified, and used to question his performance or potential.

The Patriots of 1970 struggled to a record of 2–12. It was a season of disorganized football that everyone wanted to forget, but in the aftermath, it worsened over the matter of Kapp's "Memorandum of Agreement." It is clear that Joe Kapp did not want to sign a standard player's contract, which according to Kapp was too rigid and binding.[119] It seems he hoped to negotiate these conditions, but was unable to. Unfortunately, the business of pro football would take its toll, and eventually it cost him his career.

Moving into 1971, Kapp continued to oppose Pete Rozelle's mandate and was ordered out of training camp indefinitely. He wanted to negotiate and emphasized the legality of his "Memorandum of Agreement" with the Patriots, but this was not allowed. At the time, Rozelle's position on the matter became known as the "Rozelle Rule," in which the key factor is that the team(s) signing a free agent had to compensate the club from which he came. If teams did not agree on the compensation, Rozelle would make the determination himself (this rule is no longer applicable).[120] Thus, Rozelle personally saw to it that Kapp did not have any options whatsoever. Unsettled by the whole affair, Kapp continued to complain that the NFL had conspired against him, and he now sought a legal remedy.

Out of football and out of a job, Kapp and his attorneys prepared for legal action and filed an antitrust suit against the National Football League, contending that he was being deprived of his right to earn a living. The suit asked for $12 million in damages, and the trial began in the Superior Court of San Francisco. When the case finally went to trial in December 1974, Kapp appeared to win a major victory when U.S. District Court Judge William T. Sweigert issued a summary judgment which found the NFL Standard Contract and their reserve system "patently unreasonable and illegal." The court held that the player draft and the so-called Rozelle Rule, requiring compensation from a club signing a free agent to a team losing him, were "unreasonable restraints under the antitrust laws."[121]

However, the question of whether or not Kapp had been financially damaged by the action was left to the jury to decide. Two years later in the same San Francisco courtroom, a jury of two men and four women deliberated for almost six hours and ruled that $200,000 a year, which Kapp was being paid, was not exactly slave wages (although he thought he was being treated like one). He could very well have signed and played and still sued, as the judge had pointed out. In other words, Kapp was not entitled to any damages. The news agencies covering the trial reported the jury's verdict. One *Associated Press* headline dated April 3, 1976, read, "Mexican Joe thrown for million-dollar loss," once again referring to Kapp's Mexican ancestry. The article reports:

> Former quarterback Joe Kapp was dealt a staggering defeat Friday by a United States District Court which ruled in favor of the National Football League in his antitrust suit. Kapp, now 38, said he was forced out of football five years ago and sought a multi-million dollar settlement from the NFL. A six-member jury took six hours to decide Kapp had not suffered damages and should receive nothing.[122]

Subsequent appeals to the Supreme Court did not result in any positive changes. The court process took eight years. In the meantime, Kapp supported his family with monies from real estate ventures and acting in, and producing TV and feature films. Most notably, he co-starred in the Burt Reynolds film, *The Longest Yard*.

Kapp had pioneered "free agency" in the NFL long before its time, but it cost him his career. Years later in a television interview, Kapp recalled those difficult times: "I learned a lot about the business and the power of the NFL, but as you look back you see the growth of it too; we fought some issues—the draft, the Rozelle rule—in the court of law and won."[123]

Kapp won his legal battles except the one for damages, but even more costly to pro football, it lost one of its most charismatic and colorful players. According to an old gridiron saying, "Old quarterbacks never die; they just drop back and pass away." Kapp departed slightly from the saying as he stepped back onto the football field, not as a quarterback, but this time as a head football coach of his alma mater, the University of California at Berkeley.

However, as in his previous ventures, there would be controversy surrounding his opportunity to coach collegiate football. At California, the football program was struggling to produce winning seasons. The team, coached by Roger Theder, posted a 2–9 record for the 1981 season, the worst in 19 years. The last time the California Golden Bears had a Pacific Coast Conference championship and played for the "Roses" was in 1958—Kapp's senior year at Berkeley.[124] On December 5, 1981, University of California Athletic Director Dave Maggard announced the hiring of Kapp for the head coach position. The announcement brought reactions that differed from his previous hirings; this time, *Oakland Tribune* sportswriter Ralph Wiley gave Kapp a vote of confidence when he wrote: "Joe Kapp can make a great fist. His chin is square. He could stare down an eclipse. He makes even old men want to charge. He'll look good on the sidelines and if there is a way to light emotion under the California Bears, whom he will serve as head coach, Joe will find it."[125]

Kapp, the prodigal son, returned amidst some criticism from the coaching community about his lack of coaching experience and other related issues, but he overcame the criticism and pushed forward. Challenged by it all, Kapp donned his old letterman's jacket from past years and walked onto the field to begin the task of motivating his players into becoming believers and winners. Short of a miracle, the 1982 season was historic not only for the California Bears, as they went 7–4, but also for Coach Kapp. He was honored by his peers and named the Pac-10 Coach of the Year to silence his critics temporarily.

In another display of determination to win in Pac-10 play, California snatched a victory from their rival, Stanford University. The California Bears led early in the fourth quarter when future NFL star John Elway rallied Stanford to a 20–19 lead. With four seconds remaining, the Stanford fans and band members began to celebrate their apparent victory by prematurely invading the playing field. On the sidelines, Coach Kapp recalled, "We tried to talk about the fact the game wasn't over and that they—the fans—were partying a little too early." On the kickoff return that has now become legendary, the California Bears utilized five laterals and provoked a key block by a Stanford band member to score the winning touchdown and snatch the victory from Stanford. It was one of the most bizarre and thrilling plays in the history of collegiate football, and Kapp credited his players for their determination to win. The climax of the 1982 season was a thriller, and only a Kapp-coached team could accomplish such a rare and unusual feat to win a football game. Final score: Cal 25, Stanford 20.[126]

The following year (1983), Kapp and the Bears posted a 5–5–1 record, but the record did not reflect the quality of football played throughout the season. The Bears tied Arizona when the Wildcats were one of the best teams in the country, and they nearly defeated UCLA, which went on to win both the Pac-10 Championship and the Rose Bowl.

The following season for coach Kapp would begin with a trip to Canada to receive a well-deserved honor. Just prior to the start of the 1984 season, Kapp was notified by CFL officials of his selection for induction into the Canadian Football League Hall of Fame. Finally, Kapp was honored by his Canadian counterparts for the skills and leadership he displayed in the league for eight difficult and hard-fought years.[127] With his induction into the CFL Hall of Fame, he was the first ever Mexican American athlete to receive such an honor.

Back in California for the 1984 campaign, Kapp and the Bears began with enthusiasm but fell short of success. The California Bears finished 2–9. Their offense managed to score just 104 points, while the defense allowed 219 points. Turnovers, missed field goals, and the inability to stop the run and defend against the pass were costly mistakes for the Bears.[128] Unfortunately, the next two seasons (1985–1986) did not show any improvement as the Bears were anything but golden and went 6–16.[129] The competitive fire that burned brightly in 1982 was now almost extinguished, and at the end of the 1986 season, Kapp stepped aside for another coach, leaving behind a Cal football program that had learned to win and would do so in the future.

Joe Kapp's football story would have a few more stops before he returned to family and friends on a full-time basis. In June 1990, his former team, the British Columbia Lions, whom he led to the Grey Cup Championship in 1964, hired him as their General Manager. It was some time since Kapp was in Canada, and the "tough Chicano," as he referred to himself, returned for a brief sojourn in the business of pro football. The highlight of his short tenure with the Lions' management was the successful contract negotiations with and signing of NFL veterans Doug Flutie and Mark Gastineau. Flamboyant as ever, Kapp's marketing of these two players in the CFL and the B.C. Lions was a tremendous financial success for the team.[130] A couple of years later (1992), Joe Kapp was hired as the head coach of the Arena Football League's (AFL) Los Angeles Wings. Unfortunately, the franchise never materialized there instead and moved north to become the Sacramento Attack. The Kapp-coached team managed a 4–6 mark and made it to the playoffs, only to be eliminated. At season's end, Kapp retired again while the franchise moved to Miami, Florida.[131]

Shortly thereafter, Kapp finally cleaned out the old football locker and took his last walk from the dressing room, the stadium, and the office. He looked back nostalgically, remembering his glory days, the challenges, the disappointments, the battles he fought and survived. He loved football and he would miss it. But he loved his family more and laments: "There is too much good life and I am an optimist who looks for the good things.... Of course you look back with some regret, but you learn from the past and try to make new and better decisions from the battles you fought."[132]

In the years that followed his retirement, Kapp settled in to become a successful business owner and motivational speaker. Although football still coursed through his veins, he kept his distance from the sport until he received a surprising letter from a sports organization in Laredo, Texas. The letter informed him of his selection for induction into the Latin-American Sports Hall of Fame. On February 2, 2001, at the Laredo Civic Center Ballroom, Joe Kapp was inducted into their hall for his talent, skill, and achievement in the sport of football, and his influence as a role model for others. In essence, Kapp was recognized and honored by the Mexican/Latino American community of Texas.[133] A true champion and crusader, Joseph Robert Kapp was diagnosed with Alzheimer's disease in 2015. But he will long be remembered and respected as a man, athlete, and Latino who never lost sight of his identity and values.

James William "Jim" Plunkett

Jim Plunkett's life and football journey is a two-part story. The first part of the story is about the character-building phase of the Plunkett children, evidenced in the caring bonds that sustained and unified the family during difficult and impoverished times. The second part of the story focuses on the Plunketts' only son—Jim, who not only worked to support the family, but was an exceptional high school student/athlete who dedicated himself to family and his goals. One of his aspirations was an education, and he earned a scholarship to Stanford University for his success on the field and in the classroom. As a Stanford student/athlete, he was not only successful academically but also achieved college football's highest honor—the Heisman Trophy. Later, as a professional football player, he came back from a disappointing start in the sport to capture two Super Bowl rings.

The Plunkett story begins in quite humble circumstances in California, shortly after the Plunkett family left New Mexico. Jim Plunkett was born on December 5, 1947, in San Jose. He was the only son of William Gutierrez and Carmen Blea Plunkett. He had two older sisters—Genevieve and Mary Ann—all of whom comprised a very caring family. In his autobiography, *The Jim Plunkett Story: The Saga of the Man Who Came Back,* in the first chapter entitled "The Mind's Eye," Plunkett describes his warm family origins and background:

> My mother has never seen her three children. She has hugged us, scolded us, raised us and loved us, but she wouldn't know us by sight. My mother is totally blind. Typhoid fever seized her vision when she was 19. She lived in a world of darkness

ever since. My father's world was blurred, like a man who spent his life swimming under water. He was legally blind, though with the aid of thick glasses he could see well enough to work and get around on his own. His eyesight became progressively worse over the years, but his body deteriorated faster, and he died of a heart attack in 1969. He was 56.

They were born in New Mexico, my mother in Santa Fe and my father in Albuquerque, where they met at a school for the blind. My mother's given name is Carmen Blea. She is Mexican with a trace of Indian blood. Dad's full name was William Gutierrez Plunkett, though everyone knew him as Willie. He was Mexican with a few German and Irish branches hanging on his side of the family tree. Plunkett is an Irish name.[134]

In the remainder of the chapter, Plunkett provides descriptions and remembrances of early family life. He describes how his parents left New Mexico for California during World War II. He also notes his father's employment in the Richmond Shipyards in San Francisco and other jobs, including running a news stand in downtown San Jose. The family's search for low-cost housing caused their move from Santa Clara. He worked as a newspaper boy, grocery clerk, and gas station attendant to help support the unit.[135] Importantly, his parents did not consider themselves handicapped because his mother, though blind, possessed four sets of eyes (his father, himself, and two sisters) to guide her along. He writes, "My parents would go for walks, hand in hand. Dad would tell mom what kind of day it was. He would describe the flowers, the trees; and she would respond, 'how pretty they are.' My father delighted in coloring the day for my mother."[136] This quotation sums up the love and the caring environment in the Plunkett household. His family's closeness and background provided him the necessary strength to overcome the crisis that plagued him throughout his young life, and later in his professional football career.

The young Jim Plunkett attended Overfeldt High School for a year and a half before transferring to James Lick High School. In each school he was viewed as a promising and natural athlete, but he would disagree and play down his extraordinary athleticism. An example of his athleticism was brought to light on the practice field of James Lick High School in 1964. Sportswriter Dwight Chapin, who wrote an article about both Tom Flores and Jim Plunkett after their 1981 Super Bowl victory, begins the article titled "Dos de la Misma Clase" with a quote from Jim Plunkett's high school football coach:

> The Year is 1964. The place is the practice field of the James Lick High School Football team, and it's so late in the afternoon everybody should be inside washing up for dinner. But coach Al Cementina isn't ready to have his kids quit just yet, "It's getting almost too dark to see," Cementina says, when one of his players comes up to him and says, "guess what, coach? Jim Plunkett just threw the ball from the twenty yard line all the way down the field and hit the other goal post. That's ninety yards!"[137]

Jim Plunkett showed great athletic promise. According to author Dave Newhouse, "He was a standout pitcher and a .300 hitter in baseball; He was

4. Increased Numbers and Diversity at All Levels, 1971–1990 219

the first wrestler from the school to win four consecutive Mount Hamilton Athletic League individual titles. He was even more celebrated in football, leading his school, the James Lick Comets, to a 17–1 record and two league championships."[138] He was the biggest player on the high school team at 6'3" and 220 pounds.[139] In high school, he was one of the most heavily recruited players in the state. In his junior year, he received offers from California, Santa Clara, and Navy. In his senior year, other offers came from Notre Dame and Stanford. When deciding, the young Plunkett always considered the distance between his college and family. He settled on Stanford for athletic and academic reasons, but equally importantly, because it was close to his parents.[140]

In August 1966, just before attending Stanford, Plunkett noticed a growth/tumor on his neck and shoulder. The discovery alarmed him and, with much trepidation, he had it biopsied. The diagnosis was malignant and required immediate surgery. In his autobiography, Plunkett writes about his concern and the decision to have the operation. In doing so, he remained concerned about the outcome and his future at Stanford. After the surgery, he learned that the tumor was benign.[141] He enrolled at Stanford in September 1966, less than three weeks after his operation. Although he was anxious to play football, his recovery would require time, and he was disappointed when he was assigned to the freshman team. The following year, he was once again disappointed when advised by head coach John Ralston of his status as fourth-stringer. His coaches offered him the opportunity to play as a defensive end. Surprised by this suggestion, Plunkett's response was that he would prove himself under center.[142]

In his second year (1967) at Stanford, Plunkett suited out for the first three games but was then red-shirted. At this point, he was healthy and was the backup quarterback. The Stanford Indians posted a 5–5 record as he watched from the sidelines. The 1968 season saw Stanford improve to a 6–3–1 with Plunkett as the starting quarterback. He completed 142 passes for 2,156 yards, 14 touchdowns, and a third-place finish in the Pac-8 standings.[143] In the process, Plunkett broke school and conference records for yards gained passing in one season. He also ranked tenth nationally in total offense and eighth in passing yardage, and he received Stanford's De Swarte-Eller Memorial Award, presented to the team's Outstanding Sophomore Football Player.[144] In 1969, Plunkett and Stanford continued to improve in both wins and overall statistics. Plunkett commented, "The 1969 team was the best I played on in college."[145] They posted a 7–2–1 mark. Plunkett completed 197 passes for 2,673 yards and 20 touchdowns, but fell short of playing in the Rose Bowl as USC won the league title.

In his senior year, 1970,[146] Plunkett was spectacular. The Indians captured the Pac-8 crown with a 6–1 conference record, along with Plunkett's establishment of several collegiate career passing records—530 completions out of 962 passes thrown for a total of 7,544 yards and 53 touchdowns.[147] He was hailed as the top collegiate player in the nation and claimed the Heisman Trophy. *Los Angeles Times* reporter Frank del Olmo, in an article for *NUESTRO* Magazine, quoted what Plunkett told one interviewer about winning the Heisman Trophy: "The Mexican American can take pride in this award I have won. I hope it will help the Mexican American community."[148] This was indeed a great achievement by this young man, and equally important for him to recognize his background and community. Additionally, the nationally 12th-ranked 8-3 Stanford Indians would play the 2nd-ranked, 10-0 Ohio State Buckeyes in the 1971 Rose Bowl. The Californians were decided underdogs to their opponents from the Midwest.

Stanford's first offensive snap of the game was a successful misdirection play that netted 41 yards and fooled the Buckeyes' defense. Stanford scored shortly thereafter on a rushing play; next they kicked a field goal to take a 10-0 lead, but Ohio State led, 14-10, at the half. During the second half, both teams tightened up defensively as Ohio State eventually led, 17-13. Then came what author Herb Michelson called the pivotal play of the game:

> Ohio State hammered on the ground to the Stanford 20. It was fourth and one. They lined up for the next play, and Coach Ralston could see that Brockington was cheating towards the line.... But before they could get the play off, the third quarter ended. Ralston called the right defense in case they lined up again that way. That's exactly what they did, and we [Stanford] stopped them. Linebacker Kadziel hit Brockington a yard behind the line of scrimmage.... It was a great singular effort by Kadziel, and the turning point of the game.[149]

The Buckeyes did not recover enough from that misdirection play that enabled Stanford to score two additional touchdowns. Jim Plunkett completed 20 of 30 passes for 265 yards and was named Player of the Game.[150] His collegiate career ended on a glorious note, and a few months later he was the first player selected in the 1971 National Football League Draft of college players.[151]

According to *Los Angeles Times* editorial writer Frank del Olmo's analysis, Plunkett's number one draft selection meant he was a "can't miss" prospect for the struggling New England Patriots. The selection meant Plunkett was their primary hope to turn the team into winners. Unfortunately, there were circumstances throughout his tenure with the Patriots that prevented Plunkett from displaying his full talents. The start of his career with the New England Patriots was a marked improvement from the previous seasons. Ironically, he initially replaced the incumbent, Joe Kapp.[152] The first game of the 1971 season was against the Oakland Raiders, and Plunkett played well in his debut. He threw a pair of second-half touchdowns to upset the Raiders. A Boston newspaper described his debut:

> Plunkett, who only threw four times in the first two periods, took charge after the intermission and flashed the form which earned him All-America honors at Stanford

4. Increased Numbers and Diversity at All Levels, 1971–1990

in rallying the Patriots.... Plunkett directed the Patriots on a 70-yard scoring drive ... and then caught the Raiders by surprise with a pass to tight end Tom Beers on a 20-yard touchdown maneuver.[153]

For the rest of the season, Plunkett and the Patriots played well on occasion with victories against the New York Jets, Houston Oilers, Buffalo Bills, Miami Dolphins, and Baltimore Colts for a record of 6–8. This was the team's best record in five years. However, Plunkett's rookie year produced 19 touchdowns and he was honored as the NFL's Rookie of the Year.[154] The next four years in New England presented Plunkett with a series of nagging injuries that can be attributed to numerous causes, beginning with a coaching change and ineffective play-calling. John Mazur was replaced by Chuck Fairbanks and the implementation of the quarterback run option behind an exceptionally weak offensive line limited Plunkett's drop-back passing. Likewise, the lack of line protection hampered the passing game.[155] In his final year with the Patriots (1975), Plunkett injured his shoulder in a pre-season game against the San Diego Chargers. The injury prevented his playing until the sixth game of the season against the 49ers, when he suffered another injury. This time, backup quarterback Steve Grogan replaced Plunkett to finish out the 1975 season, in which the Patriots managed only three wins. As the season ended, Plunkett rethought his options and decided to leave New England; he looked into the possibility of a trade to San Francisco.[156]

Quarterback Jim Plinkett during Stanford's 27–17 win over Ohio State at the Rose Bowl on January 1, 1970, in Pasadena, California (Stanford Athletics).

In 1976, the Patriots granted Plunkett his wish, and he went west for draft picks and a backup quarterback.[157] It was an enormous deal that revealed Plunkett was not a wash-out but a still highly regarded football player. Unfortunately the 49ers were in a similar rebuilding phase. The *Los Angeles Times'* Frank del Olmo evaluated the 49ers' situation: "Sadly, the 49ers are a football team only on paper. With a weak blocking line, poor receivers and a porous defense, they consistently finish in the lower end of the NFL standings."[158]

Plunkett's first year with the 49ers began on the fast track and then faltered. After seven games, the 49ers held a 6–1 record, but they won only two more games for a final record of 8–6. It was a good start, but Plunkett was apprehensive about his future in San Francisco. At the time, the team ownership had just changed, and there was a new head coach and general manger. As a result of the changes, the team, including Plunkett, transitioned as best they could to compete in 1977. Unfortunately, the 49ers were less than successful and struggled to finish with a 5–9 record. The team's breakdown was attributed to many front office distractions and player personnel issues that included Plunkett's poor passing performance and high interception rate.[159]

In August 1978, a few weeks before the start of the season, Jim Plunkett was placed on waivers and released.[160] Without a team, he contemplated the significance of this turn of events and explored possible options. It was not long until, during first week of the 1978 season, he heard from his attorney, Wayne Hooper, who advised him that Al Davis of the Oakland Raiders had invited him to a tryout. Although skeptical at first, Plunkett agreed to attend the session in which Davis, John Madden, and Tom Flores put him through the drills. The Raiders signed him to a $125,000 contract, but he did not take a single snap that season.[161] The following year (1979), he played in a few games, threw a few passes, and accepted his backup role, though still hoping for playing time. In 1980, Plunkett expressed his concern and demanded to play or be traded. In response to Plunkett's demands, Coach Tom Flores reiterated the important role of a backup quarterback and asked him to be patient and wait his turn.

In 1980, Jim Plunkett got his wish to play but it came at another player's misfortune. Prior to the season, the Raiders' quarterback situation underwent significant changes. Starting quarterback Ken Stabler was traded to the Houston Oilers for quarterback Dan Pastorini. The transaction was in football terms, "a straight up" trade of one starting quarterback for another.[162] In other words, Plunkett's backup status did not change. He was still a backup as the season began. The Raiders won the season opener against the Kansas City Chiefs, 27–14, but lost two of the next three games. In the fifth game, Dan Pastorini was injured and lost for the year. Plunkett was the next man up. In recalling the events of Pastorini's injury, Plunkett wrote in his autobiography he did not want to become the starting quarterback in this manner, but there was no time to think about it; he had a job to do.[163] For the remainder of the season, the Raiders lost only to the Eagles and the Cowboys, finishing with an 11–5 record, tied for first place in the AFC West, and became the first wild card team to make it to the Super Bowl.

Jim Plunkett's day had finally arrived, January 25, 1981, at the Louisiana Superdome. After years of disappointment and injuries at New England and San Francisco, Plunkett had made it to the title tilt. The game got underway as the Eagles received the opening kickoff. From the beginning, the Raiders controlled the game. Eagles quarterback Ron Jaworski's first pass was intercepted by Rod Martin. A few plays later, Plunkett started to run with the

4. Increased Numbers and Diversity at All Levels, 1971–1990 223

ball but spotted Cliff Branch, who hauled in a Plunkett pass for the initial score. Later in the first quarter, Oakland lined up on the 20-yard line. Plunkett looked to pass once again but had to scramble. In the process, he saw Kenny King behind Herman Edwards. Plunkett launched a pass that cleared the defender's reach, and King broke the play for an 80-yard touchdown. In the second quarter, Eagles kicker Tony Franklin converted on a field goal. Oakland 14, Philadelphia 3. Just before halftime, Franklin attempted another field goal that was blocked by another Latino on the Raiders, Ted Hendricks. The score stood at Oakland 14, Philadelphia 3, at the half.

The Raiders received the kickoff to start the third quarter, and once again, Plunkett connected with Cliff Branch for a touchdown. On the Eagles' first possession, they moved the ball into Raiders territory, but Rod Martin intercepted another Jaworski pass. The turnover lead to a Chris Bahr field goal. In the fourth quarter, Philadelphia finally scored a touchdown. However, the final tally of the game was another field goal by Chris Bahr that sealed the Raiders' victory: Oakland 27, Philadelphia 10.[164] Jim Plunkett and the Oakland Raiders were now atop the world of professional football, and Jim Plunkett was the game's Most Valuable Player. From an historical perspective, Super Bowl XV was significant because of the roles played by Jim Plunkett and Tom Flores.[165] In addition to the Vince Lombardi Trophy, Plunkett collected the 1980 NFL Comeback Player of the Year Award.

From 1981 through 1986, the Raiders underwent changes due to injuries and the introduction of new personnel. In 1981, Plunkett and the Raiders experienced their first losing season (7–9) since 1964. Plunkett sustained a hand injury and was replaced by Marc Wilson, who finished out the season. The following year, the NFL players staged a 57-day strike that ended on November 22. After that, the games resumed with Marc Wilson at quarterback, and he managed an 8–1 record for the Silver and Black.[166]

In 1983, Plunkett was back as the starting quarterback. The Raiders won their first four but struggled while losing the next two. The Raiders then replaced Plunkett with Wilson for two games. After Wilson suffered an injury, Plunkett returned. It was like 1980 all over again as the Raiders rode Plunkett's play to a seven-game win streak and into the playoffs.[167] The win streak continued into the playoffs, and Plunkett and the Raiders became, once again, Super Bowl champions, trouncing the Washington Redskins 38–9.[168]

Jim Plunkett's final seasons (1984–1986) with the Raiders were injury-ridden, and he saw limited playing time. In 1984, he played a few games but injuries prevented his participation in the AFC playoff loss to the Seattle Seahawks, 13–7. The following year, Plunkett remained the backup to Marc Wilson, who struggled. When Wilson's performances were less than productive, and Plunkett was healthy, the Raiders continued to win and captured the Western Division title. Unfortunately, a recurring injury to Plunkett kept him out of the line-up for the AFC Conference Championship game against New England that resulted in the Patriots' 27–20 win.[169]

In Plunkett's final year, the quarterback situation only worsened in terms of injuries and performances. The Raiders won only eight games and did not qualify for the playoffs. Overall, Plunkett's career with the Raiders was a grand success compared to his two previous teams. After his on-the-field days, Plunkett remained connected to the Raiders organization by co-hosting their weekly television program for many years. He ultimately left the program to pursue other business ventures, football interests, and very importantly, his family. He is married to Gerry Plunkett. They have two children, son Jim William Plunkett, Jr. (deceased) and daughter Meghan Plunkett. We close his story with a quote from his autobiography that sums up his life's journey:

> People have asked me what my story means. I imagine it is about a young Mexican kid who learned from his parents that blindness and poverty aren't necessarily deterrents to happiness.... I also learned that not all tumors are malignant ... that I could have become a defensive end ... that I had a good college career. That I was lost for a while ... and that through an injury to someone else came an opportunity ... that I could have stepped in and failed ... but I came through ... and accomplished a goal I had set for myself many years ago.[170]

Theodore Paul "Ted" Hendricks

Chicago Tribune sportswriter Robert Markus referred to Theodore Paul "Ted" Hendricks as one of the few foreign-born players in the National Football league (NFL). He noted that Hendricks' mother was living in Guatemala when his father met her during World War II, and although they were residing in Miami, Florida, the family decided to return to Guatemala to be with Ted Hendricks' grandmother.[171] He was born on November 1, 1947, in Guatemala City, Guatemala. His mother was a native Guatemalan, Angela Bonatti, of Austrian-Italian descent, and his father Maurice "Sonny" Hendricks, was a native of McAllen, Texas. They had met in Central America while working for Pan Am Airlines.[172] They married and raised a family that included three children: Ted, his sister Sandy, and brother Mark. Ted recalls that his father worked many years for Pan Am, and every year they vacationed in Guatemala City, where he achieved fluency in Spanish. One article that addressed his background stated that Hendricks spoke fluent Spanish and read books on the Mayan culture that fortified his cultural identity.[173]

Ted Hendricks is one of two Latino birthright NFL football players from Guatemala. The other player was John Hendy, also born in Guatemala City in 1962, who played with the San Diego Chargers in 1985. However, Hendricks was unlike many other Latino pro football players because he readily embraced his Guatemalan culture and language, whereas other Latinos in the NFL were seldom associated with their respective Latino birthright for various social and political reasons. Ted Hendricks was the exception. He spoke Spanish, and throughout his professional football career did not lose sight of his Guatemalan ancestry. For example, a 1983 *Sports Illustrated* article by Paul Zimmerman described the many aspects of Hendricks' personal and athletic characteristics. One pertained to his roots and the penchant to travel. Zimmerman quoted Hendricks' commentary about visiting Guatemala when he stated, "My roots are in the banyan trees.... My cousin owns a rum factory in Quezaltenango ... where each city has its different costume ... the beauty there.... I get excited just thinking about it."[174]

Growing up in Miami, Hendricks matured into an extraordinary athlete and student. At 15 he was already a standout in football, track, and basketball at Hialeah High School, a working-class suburb of Miami. *The Sporting News* reported that by the age of 17, and a senior, Hendricks was an All-City, All-Southern, All-American offensive end, and additionally was named the state's outstanding lineman in the annual All-Star prep game.[175] Academically, Hendricks was just as astute; he was an A-B student at Hialeah and identified mathematics as his main interest. He was a promising scholar-athlete who chose to attend the University of Miami in Florida although there were offers from Princeton and other top schools. He chose Miami because it was close to home. It became the starting point for his rise to football stardom, not only with the Hurricanes, but in the NFL as well. His career spanned three NFL teams: the Baltimore Colts, Green Bay Packers, and Oakland/Los Angeles Raiders.

His first two years in Coral Gables, Hendricks participated in 247 tackles and recovered eight fumbles. Newspaper accounts and football records documented his unique ability to strip the ball away from quarterbacks, running backs, and receivers, as well as to block kicks. One particular feat occurred during the 1967 season when he blocked a quick kick against the University of Pittsburgh by grabbing the ball before it hit the ground and returned it to the Panthers' 16-yard line to set up a Miami touchdown.[176] Against Virginia Tech, he knocked the ball out of the quarterback's hand, chased the ball 20 yards, and recovered it. This also led to a touchdown. At Northwestern, Hendricks made a mid-air interception; at Tulane, he stole the ball twice; at LSU, he harassed the quarterback to the point of almost eliminating their passing game.[177]

His height, weight, and quickness gave him a particular advantage. Hendricks stands 6'8" tall and weighed 220 pounds with an expansive wing span. Originally he was an offensive end, and in his freshman year he set a single-game reception record. Head coach Ray Graves thought that Ted Hendricks was a player who could have competed for All-American recognition at four positions.[178]

Hendricks' career at Miami was very successful. Between 1966 and 1968, the Hurricanes went 20–11–1 in an independent schedule. Hendricks' performance during his collegiate tenure resulted in many awards, two bowl games, and an immortal nickname. He was an All-American three times; was the first University of Miami sophomore to achieve this distinction; won the Lineman of the Year Award from United Press International (UPI); and won the Washington Touchdown Club's Knute Rockne Memorial Award in 1968.[179] Hendricks and the Hurricanes played in two bowl games; the Liberty and Blue Bonnet Bowls in 1966 and 1967. Christened "The Mad Stork" by sportswriter Luther Evans of the *Miami Herald* because of his physical attributes, this thin and lanky defender was a force on the field.

When his collegiate career ended, there was substantial interest by NFL franchises. Pro scouts expressed some concern that his weight did not match up to the NFL's prototype for defensive ends, however. According to reports, several clubs thought he was too frail to be a defensive end and too tall to be a linebacker. The Baltimore Colts thought differently and drafted him in the second round of the 1969 NFL draft. He was the 33rd player chosen overall, and the 12th defensive player selected.[180]

Hendricks began his rookie season with the Colts as a defensive end. He played sparingly and mostly on special teams. However, the team struggled early in the season, losing to the Los Angeles Rams, and allowed 52 points in the loss to the Minnesota Vikings. This prompted head coach Don Shula to reassign defensive personnel. One of those changes was moving Hendricks from the defensive end position to right linebacker. This and other defensive changes enabled the Colts to improve as they posted a record of 8–5–1, good enough for a second-place finish in their division.[181]

In his second pro season (1970), Hendricks helped the Colts improve further, and the team made the playoffs. He adapted and learned the ways of a pro linebacker by stripping the ball, recovering fumbles, pass rushing, and blocking kicks. At the end of the regular season, the Colts were 11–2–1. They initially beat the Cincinnati Bengals 17–0 in the first playoff round and then claimed the AFC Championship by disposing of the Oakland Raiders, 27–17. The next step was to play the Dallas Cowboys in Super Bowl V in the Orange Bowl.[182] The Colts emerged victorious with the margin of victory being Jim O'Brien's 32-yard field goal with five seconds left to play. For Hendricks, this was the first of four Super Bowl championships in his career.

The next three seasons (1971–1973) with the Colts were not as productive. In 1971, Baltimore went 10–4. They beat the Cleveland Browns in the divisional round, but lost to the Miami Dolphins in the AFC Championship game. Hendricks was named to the All-Pro team and played in his first of eight Pro Bowls.[183] The 1972 season was fraught with disorganization and player personnel changes that resulted in a losing season (5–9). Amidst the turmoil, Hendricks was recognized for his field performance as his teammates voted him the club's outstanding player.[184] The 1973 season was a continuation of the previous year. At the start, the Colts' personnel issues worsened, which prompted Hendricks to request a trade to the Miami Dolphins. The *Boston Globe* reported:

> Ted Hendricks wanted to be a Dolphin but was not getting cooperation from the Colts' general manager Joe Thomas. "After the season I asked him if I could be traded to Miami…. Miami was my home and I owned a house there. I emphasized my request had nothing to do with the turmoil in Baltimore … and wanted to minimize the player outrage over the firings of coaches and the benching of quarterback Johnny Unitas."[185]

The Colts' new general manager, Joe Thomas, was at the heart of the personnel changes and was the main reason for low morale. Amidst the disharmony, there was also individual recognition. Hendricks was chosen to participate in his third consecutive Pro Bowl.[186] The turmoil continued, however. Another reason for Hendricks' trade request was that his business investments in South Florida required his attention. He wanted to stay in Florida, but his options were limited.

Still another distraction was the formation of another professional football organization: the World Football League (WFL). The new entity targeted NFL players with promises of large salaries. In Hendricks' case, the Southern California Sun identified him as their top prospect.[187] What happened? Hendricks signed a contract with the Jacksonville Sharks prematurely, and that disrupted his trade request. When approached by Joe Thomas, Hendricks assured him he would play for the Colts. This caused a breakdown in communications between the parties and precipitated his trade to the Green Bay Packers. In the exchange for Hendricks, the Packers traded their 1973 Rookie of the Year—Tom Macleod—and an eighth-round pick.[188] The only remaining obstacle in the Hendricks transaction was the Jacksonville Sharks contract which eventually disappeared when the WFL disbanded. Amidst all the changes, Hendricks played a single season with the Packers.[189] They went 6–8. Again, he was selected to the All-Pro Team.[190] At season's end, Hendricks and the Packers underwent another series of protracted negotiations that eventually produced another trade.

Al Davis, the managing general partner of the Raiders, successfully negotiated with the Packers to obtain Hendricks. The Raiders sent two first-round draft choices to Green Bay for the rights to Hendricks, and signed him as a limited free agent.[191] There was concern by some of the Raiders' coaches about the Hendricks acquisition, however. One reporter suggested that head coach John Madden disagreed with Al Davis' choice for unspecified reasons.[192] Nonetheless, Ted Hendricks eventually became a starter. In 1976, he played the weak-side linebacker and contributed to the Raiders' defense, which ranked sixth overall in the NFL. The Raiders posted a 13–1 record and another trip to the playoffs. In the AFC playoffs, the Raiders won a close game versus the New England Patriots, 24–21, and then beat Pittsburgh, 24–7, for the AFC Championship. In Super Bowl XI, the Raiders took control of the game to defeat the Minnesota Vikings, 32–14.[193] The Super Bowl victory was the first of three titles for the Raiders in seven seasons and Hendricks earned second team All-Pro recognition.

The following three seasons (1977–1979) were a preamble to the Raiders' next run to a Super Bowl appearance. The 1977 season produced a mark of 11–3. The Raiders made it to the playoffs, where they beat the Baltimore Colts, 37–31, but lost to the Denver Broncos, 20–17, in the AFC Championship game. The next two seasons, the Raiders posted identical win-loss records of 9–7. Head coach John Madden resigned on January 19, 1979, and Tom Flores was named as his replacement on February 8.[194] The coaching change was a positive move as the Raiders regained their winning tradition and claimed another opportunity to play in the Super Bowl. During the 1980 season, Hendricks had an excellent year that included nine quarterback sacks, three interceptions, three blocked kicks, and a safety to help the Raiders get into the playoffs.[195]

Though the start for that season was questionable, that quickly changed for the better as the Raiders, quarterbacked by Jim Plunkett, finished with an 11–5 record, making the playoffs as a wildcard. The underdog Oakland team made it to Super Bowl XV, matched against NFC Conference Champions, the Philadelphia Eagles.[196] The Raiders dominated the Eagles from the very start of the contest, as summarized in their publication, *Decades of Destiny 1960–1984—The Historic First 25 Years*:

> After missing the playoffs the previous two years, the Raiders entered the 1980 season as a consensus choice to finish last in the American Football Conference

Ted Hendricks, c. 1980 (Pro Football Hall of Fame).

Western Division.... On their first possession, the Eagles attempted their first pass ... [which] was picked off by Raiders' Rod Martin ... Cliff Branch grabbed a 2-yard toss from Plunkett.... Plunkett hit running back Kenny King ... to complete an 80-yard scoring play.... A subsequent 28-yard field goal attempt by the Eagles' Franklin with 54 seconds remaining in the first half was blocked by Raiders linebacker Ted Hendricks.... Another Plunkett to Branch pass, this time for 29-yards accounted for a touchdown.... Chris Bahr kicked field goals from 46 and 25 yards ... Raiders quarterback Plunkett was the game's Most Valuable Player.[197]

It was a convincing and meaningful win for the Raiders, who became the first wildcard team to win the Super Bowl Championship. For Hendricks, it was also a comeback. He was named to the First-team All-Pro and All-AFC Conference teams, and was selected to play in the Pro Bowl.[198]

Following the unexpected title run, the Raiders had their first losing season (1981) since 1964. But they returned to dominance shortly thereafter.[199] In 1982, the regular season began with two Raiders victories, but the season was temporarily halted by an NFL players' strike that began on September 12, 1982. The strike lasted two months and ended on November 22, 1982.[200] For the remainder of season, the Raiders posted eight victories and a single loss. They qualified for the playoffs and began with a victory over the Cleveland Browns, 27–10. However, they barely lost to the New York Jets, 17–14, in the second round.

The 1983 season, which turned out to be Hendricks' final year in pro football, proved to be a winner for the Raiders organization. The team underwent a name change, a location change, and another Super Bowl title. Prior to the season, the Raiders' petition to move the Oakland Raiders to Los Angeles, was finally heard and acted upon. On July 22, 1983, the California State Supreme Court upheld the Raiders' bid to move to Los Angeles.[201] The Oakland Raiders became the Los Angeles Raiders, and in their first season in Los Angeles went 12–4 in regular season play. They were primed for the playoffs and were very successful against the Pittsburgh Steelers, Seattle Seahawks, and ultimately the Washington Redskins.

Ted Hendricks' last football game was the Raiders' win in Super Bowl XVIII. He retired after 15 seasons and 216 consecutive games. In his second year of eligibility, Hendricks' strong and devastating style of play earned him nomination and election into the Pro Football Hall of Fame. His career statistics and honors were numerous and helped to establish the basis for his recognition. From his linebacker position, he specialized in blocking—25 punts, field goals, and extra points. He intercepted 26 passes and returned them for 332 yards and one touchdown. He recovered 16 opponents' fumbles; tied an NFL record by recording four safeties; played in eight Pro Bowls; played and won four Super Bowl Championships; was named to seven All-American Football Conference (AFC) teams and one All-National Football Conference

(NFC) team. On August 4, 1990, Ted Hendricks was enshrined.[202] He was the third Latino birthright in the history of professional football to receive that honor and distinction, the other two being Steve Van Buren (Honduras) and Tom J. Fears (Mexico).

Manuel Jose "Manny" Fernandez

Throughout the history of the NFL, there has never been a team so devastating on both offense and defense as the 1972 Miami Dolphins. They are the only NFL team to go undefeated the entire season. Among the key players who contributed to that success was Manuel Jose "Manny" Fernandez. By both collegiate and pro football standards, Fernandez was an exception. He was not big for a defensive lineman, not very fast, had poor vision, and his second collegiate football coach, Mike Giddings, was convinced he did not have the necessary skills to play professional football. Within a few years, Fernandez proved him wrong and became one of the most important/successful free agents in Miami Dolphins history.[203]

The Fernandez family story begins in Spain. In a recent interview with Jorge Iber, Fernandez discussed his family's origins in Spain and Hawaii, where they worked the fields and ran small businesses. Both maternal and parental sides of the clan eventually migrated to California, where fate brought them together at the start of World War II:

> My mother's [Dolores] parents were from Spain and Hawaii. My maternal grandparents moved to Hawaii around 1902. This side of the family then settled in the Mountain View, California area [what is now Silicon Valley]. The main occupation back then for the clan was farming…. After a brief period, there was another move to Monterey. Here my grandfather opened a small grocery store as well as a shoe repair shop. Dolores worked in the fields and sardine canneries when she was young.
>
> My father Manuel was born in Hawaii. But his family also came from Spain and worked in the dairy business on the Islands. Dad's family then moved to California when he was seven. When World War II broke out, he joined the U.S. Army and served in Europe, including being in the Battle of the Bulge.[204]

Manny's parents met at a USO dance at Fort Ord Army Base and stayed in touch during the years of the conflict. They were married right after the war, and he recalled that his Mom always worked when he was growing up. Her last place of employment was at a light fixture manufacturing company. There was not much emphasis placed on his ethnic background during his youth. His neighborhood was mixed: Italians, Mexicans, Asians, and Portuguese. "Race was not an issue." The family eventually made one further move to San Lorenzo.[205]

It was in this community, located south of Oakland, that Manuel Jose

4. Increased Numbers and Diversity at All Levels, 1971–1990 231

Fernandez was born on July 3, 1946. He was the first of three sons in the family. He attended San Lorenzo High School, where he starred as a football player, wrestler, and weightlifter. He was very interested and successful in sports; he was a state runner-up wrestler in his weight class, set a school record of 305 pounds in the bench press, and started out as halfback, then moved to offensive lineman on the gridiron. His football efforts and success gained All-League and All-Northern California accolades.[206] Fernandez received numerous scholarship offers to play at the collegiate level. He particularly liked Salt Lake City and the University of Utah. However, he lacked some foreign language credits and attended Chabot Junior College for a year to satisfy the requirements.[207] Upon successful completion, he entered the University of Utah in 1965.

From the start of his academic career, Fernandez chose to major in education and wanted to coach. He looked forward to playing football for the Utes, but encountered a few obstacles. In 1965, his freshman year, the University of Utah Utes, coached by Ray Nagel, finished 3–7 in Western Athletic Conference (WAC). They beat Montana, Wyoming, and Colorado State for their only victories and underwent a coaching change after the season.[208] The new field general was Mike Giddings, and the team improved to 5–5 in 1966. In 1967, they slipped back to a 3–8 mark.[209]

Fernandez felt that Giddings' leadership was not an improvement or inspiration for the team or for him personally. He remembered his coach telling him, to "overcome his background, suck it up, and play hurt to be successful."[210] Overall, Fernandez's experiences under Giddings were less than favorable. They did not get along, and when his college career ended, the 1968 NFL collegiate draft took place and his name was not called. Manny Fernandez recalled coach Giddings telling the interested Miami Dolphins that this now-former Ute couldn't make the pro grade.[211] Although Fernandez captained the Utah team, he lamented, "I wasn't hard to overlook.... At Utah, not only was I not all-conference, I barely was all-team."[212]

The negativity created by Giddings changed for the better as the Miami Dolphins took a chance, in part looking for a Spanish-surnamed player as a possible way to appeal to the city's Latino/Cuban population. Aside from the linguistic consideration, the Dolphins' scouts saw promise in Fernandez's football abilities and signed him as a free agent. Only later did the Dolphins learn that Fernandez could not speak enough Spanish to impact the Latino market. He admitted that he could not speak a word of Spanish and never learned.[213] Fernandez referred to this issue as an interesting reminder because his parents spoke Spanish, particularly when his grandmother was in the house.[214] However, the language deficiency was soon forgotten as the fans' attention focused on the head-knocking, body-slamming type of football Fernandez played for the next nine seasons with the Dolphins.

As a rookie, Fernandez played defensive end, and he switched over to defensive tackle in 1969. At tackle, Fernandez became a part of Miami's legendary "No Name" defense. It soon became evident that the quickness and strength he had developed in high school and college enabled him to out-maneuver bigger men. As a result of his continuing and fearsome style of play, he was voted the Defensive Lineman of the Year by the South Florida media for six straight years (1968–1973).[215] During the early years of the franchise, the Dolphins were not successful, but that all changed in 1970. That squad went 10–4 to begin a run for the championship. Under new coach Don Shula, Manny Fernandez remembered, "things changed radically … and the team made the playoffs in their first year under Shula."[216] That season the Dolphins made the post-season and met the Oakland Raiders in the playoffs, losing by a touchdown.[217] In 1971, the Dolphins signed former University of Miami All–American Latino quarterback George Mira as a free agent, posted their first-ever shutout over Buffalo and recorded eight straight wins, including a win in the longest game ever played in pro football history against the Kansas City Chiefs, 27–24.[218] Manny Fernandez contributed to the team's defense by recording eight quarterback sacks. He earned selection to the All AFC Team. In the seasons that followed, Fernandez made All-Pro, All-AFC and the team's Defensive Lineman of the Year award, and earned the prestigious Johnny Unitas Award presented by the South Shore Quarterback Club of Massachusetts given annually to an outstanding player who had come to professional football with little, if any, college fanfare.[219]

The pinnacle of Fernandez's career took place during the Super Bowl–winning years of 1972 and 1973. In those seasons, he made 107 and 113 tackles respectively. His finest game was Super Bowl VII, in which he manhandled the Washington Redskins with 17 tackles. Fernandez and the Miami Dolphins beat the Redskins, 14–7, to complete the first, and still only, perfect season in NFL history.[220] In Super Bowl VII, Fernandez disrupted Washington's offensive schemes throughout the game. Although Redskins coach George Allen did not single out a single Dolphins defensive player as the key to the defense, he did admit that Fernandez led the Miami charge.[221] Teammate Nick Buoniconti also commented on Fernandez's play:

> It was the game of his life—in fact, it was the most dominant game played by a defensive lineman in the history of the game, and he would never be given much credit for it. They should have given out two game balls and made Manny Fernandez the co-MVP with Jake Scott. Larry Csonka also said he thought Fernandez should have been the MVP.[222]

However, Manny Fernandez had a different recollection, "The play I remember most vividly from the Redskins game," recounts Fernandez, "was getting hold of Larry Brown, and then [my teammate] Nick Buoniconti, hav-

4. Increased Numbers and Diversity at All Levels, 1971–1990 233

ing a clear shot at Brown, hit me instead. Hardest lick I ever had. I was dazed for three plays afterwards."²²³ Fernandez did not leave the game and recalled that teammates had to tell him what to do for a while. While he had an outstanding game, teammate Jake Scott, who had two interceptions, took home the Most Valuable Player Award.²²⁴

In 1973, the Dolphins did not lose their championship form and determination. In season play, they lost only to the Oakland Raiders, 12–7, in September; and the Baltimore Colts, 16–3, in December. The Dolphins beat the Cincinnati Bengals, 34–16, in the first round of the playoffs and then the Oakland Raiders, 27–10, for the American Conference Championship. Once again, Miami was in the Super Bowl, and their opponents would be the Minnesota Vikings. According to Beau Riffenburgh's documentation of Super Bowl history found in *The Official NFL Encyclopedia*, the Dolphins had the game won from the very beginning: "The Miami Dolphins defeated the Minnesota Vikings 24–7 in Super Bowl VIII, a game in which the Dolphins took control on the first series of offensive plays."²²⁵ Offensively, fullback Larry Csonka, receiver Jim Kiick, and kicker Garo Yepremian accomplished all the Miami scoring. The "No Name Defense," anchored by Manny Fernandez, played exceptionally and held the Vikings to only 72 rushing yards, 166 passing yards, and a single touchdown. The Dolphins won their second consecutive Super Bowl and also set a record by making their third consecutive appearance in the game.²²⁶

The formation of the World Football League (WFL) in 1974 proved disruptive for the Dolphins. The new and ambitious league snatched Larry Csonka, Jim Kiick, and Paul Warfield from the Dolphins to place them in a tenuous but controllable situation. Additionally, the Portland Storm made Fernandez the 12th pick in their pro draft and, according to a *New York Times* newspaper story, Fernandez had a date to negotiate with the club.²²⁷ These actions shocked the Dolphins organization, and coach Don Shula took immediate action to sign the remaining 14 unsigned Miami players.²²⁸ Fernandez stayed on with the Dolphins and profited by signing a five-year contract worth $500,000. The Dolphins missed the offensive talents of Csonka and company but managed to continue their winning ways. They posted an overall mark of 21–7 over 1974–1975.²²⁹

In the 1975 season, Fernandez sustained an ankle injury and missed four games. The gridiron battles were taking their toll, and the ankle was added to a growing list of injured body parts. For Fernandez, his left knee had already undergone numerous surgeries and had more stitching tracks than a railroad station switching area. His shoulder was questionable, and it became evident that the healing powers of youth were quickly abandoning the once-quick and guile Fernandez.²³⁰ At the 1976 training camp, injuries continued to plague Fernandez, and he was placed on injured reserve. During this inactive period, he underwent knee and shoulder surgery with little success, and he was forced to conclude his career at the end of that season.

The Manuel Jose Fernandez football saga is one of personal belief and extraordinary determination to succeed; in spite of the racially biased attitudes and opinions expressed to him by coaches and others, from the outset of his college career and throughout his college and professional careers, he pushed on and overcame to succeed at the highest level of the sport. In 1981, the former Dolphin began to claim post-career honors; the first was from the *New York Times* sportswriters, who selected him to the All-Time Super Bowl Team. He was selected as one of the defensive tackles, along with Bob Lilly of the Dallas Cowboys. According to Dave Anderson, the selection to the All-Time Super Bowl Team was no easy task. He writes:

> Unfortunately, there is not enough evidence available to choose the all-time Super Bowl team.... But the games, for better or worse, are burned into memory. Some of the selections were easy, others difficult. When in doubt, those who had made big plays were given higher priority, if for no other reason than Super Bowl games are decided by big plays.[231]

In 2001, Fernandez was named *to Pro Football Weekly's* All-Time Super Bowl Team; *USA Today* named him to their version of this squad in 2007; Fernandez is also part of the Dolphins' All-Time Team; in 2014, he was inducted into the Miami Dolphins Honor Roll at Sun Life Stadium—all fitting tributes to one of the NFL's best defensive linemen. After football, Manuel Jose "Manny" Fernandez pursued a successful career in the mortgage/title and real estate business. In retirement, the Fernandez family enjoys life at their home in rural Georgia.[232]

Peter Paul "Pete" Rodriguez

The Pete Rodriguez story begins with a respectful note from his obituary that asks us to remember and celebrate the life of a man who accomplished much in his life, who took great pride in his family, who also possessed an unshakable faith, and whose strength and courage to build a remarkable career from some very humble beginnings.[233] Pete Rodriguez was the son of a Mexican immigrant. He was born in Chicago, Illinois, on July 25, 1940, and he was raised in an impoverished environment, but nurtured by a loving family whose influence shaped his character and inspired him to succeed in education and other endeavors. Early on, he learned about sports and dedicated himself to a football career that spanned over 40 years as a player and coach at four colleges/universities and nine professional teams.

His father, Francisco Rodriguez, was a migrant who left his country for many reasons, but primarily in search of work and a decent place to live. He

4. Increased Numbers and Diversity at All Levels, 1971–1990 235

entered the United States at an unknown port of entry and settled in Chicago. There he found work as a section hand/laborer for the Gulf, Mobile & Ohio Railroad Company, and the prospect of decent housing. At the time, the railroad offered its workers the free use of boxcars located in their yard to convert into housing. Without wasting time, Francisco took possession of one of the boxcars and converted it into what his son, Pete, later described and compared to a modern-day mobile home. The boxcar did not have any electricity or plumbing. The only toilet was an outhouse.[234] In later years, Rodriguez recalled the acquisition of a potbellied stove where they burned wood and coal for heat. An extra room was added eventually, as well as a cold-water sink, and if the family wanted a hot bath, they heated the water on the stove. Also, kerosene lamps lit up the home until electricity was finally connected, a hot-water tank was installed, and an inside bathroom was added.[235] While certainly humble, it was home for the Rodriguez family. Pete commented about this part of his life by saying: "We grew up that way and fast, but we never went hungry and everyone turned out well. It was a tough environment, but I'm sure people have grown up tougher. And my dad and mom always took great care of us."[236] His parents continued to live in the boxcar until they passed on shortly after seeing their son graduate from Western State Colorado University in 1973.[237]

As a youth, Peter Rodriguez attended Kelly High School in South Chicago and, against his mother's wishes, forged her signature on a consent form to allow him to play football. The secret was soon discovered and forgiven, allowing him to participate in other sports as well. However, football was his calling. Upon graduation he earned a football scholarship to Western State Colorado University in Gunnison. There he applied himself both academically and athletically, obtaining a degree in history and earning All-Conference honors at the linebacker position.[238] In 1963, his senior year, the Mountaineers, coached by O. Kay Dalton, finished 8–1 to capture the Rocky Mountain Conference Championship (RMAC).[239]

Following his collegiate football playing days, Rodriguez began his coaching career in 1964–1965 at Stratton High School in Colorado, where he served as assistant coach for all sports. After two years, he became the head football coach at Harrison High School (1966–1967) in Colorado Springs.[240] The high school coaching experience was beneficial, and his next coaching position elevated him into the college ranks as a graduate assistant coach in the University of Arizona Wildcats program. While at Tucson, Rodriguez toiled for two coaches; in 1968, he worked for and established a relationship with head coach Darrell Mudra, who coached the team to an 8–3 record and received an invitation to the Sun Bowl in El Paso, Texas. In 1969, Arizona released Mudra and replaced him with Bob Weber. However, Weber's tenure with the Wildcats was not a success. He was eventually replaced after a few years. However, the two years at Arizona also provided Rodriguez the opportunity to earn a Master's in Education, along with the necessary coaching experience to apply for the defensive co-coordinator position at Western Illinois University. He was hired in 1970 and was reunited with his former University of Arizona head coach Darrell Mudra. Rodriguez served in this capacity through the 1973 season.[241]

For the next five years, Rodriguez coached at three universities. The first was Florida State, where he coached two seasons (1974–1975). The Seminoles were winless and hired Mudra, who, in turn, brought along two of his staff from Western Illinois. They were Rodriguez and Cal Jones to assist him in improving the Seminoles' situation.[242] In 1975, the Florida State Seminoles improved only slightly to finish 3–8. Next, Coach Rodriguez moved to Iowa State University of the Big Eight Conference between 1976–1978. He was part of Earle Bruce's staff for three winning seasons, including two bowl game appearances. In 1977, the Cyclones played in the Peach Bowl but fell short, losing to North Carolina State, 24–14. In 1978, they finish third in the conference and played Texas A&M in the Hall of Fame Classic Bowl, but once again, the Cyclones could not muster enough offense and lost, 28–12.[243] With Florida State and Iowa State in his rearview mirror, Rodriguez pushed on and signed on with Western Illinois to become their head coach starting in 1979.

He went to Western Illinois to help transition the school into the NCAA Division I FCS level.[244] Unfortunately, Coach Rodriguez improved the program only slightly, but he did infuse them with a better outlook for the future. In the next four years, the Western Illinois Leathernecks played improved football. Their best season was 1981, when they transitioned to the NCAA Division I FCS level; they posted a 5–6 record and earned a second-place finish in the Mid-Continent Conference.[245] After the 1982 season, Rodriguez stepped aside to explore other coaching possibilities at the professional level. At this point, Rodriguez's resume included stints as defensive coordinator and head coach. The timing was also favorable for Rodriguez because a new pro football league sprang up in 1983 to challenge the NFL's supremacy. David S. Neft of *The Football Encyclopedia* wrote of the league:

> The USFL broke ground by playing from March to July, hoping to cash in on the American's insatiable appetite for football.... The USFL, like any other new league with big-time aspirations were manned mostly by anonymous rookies, NFL veterans, with a few big stars mixed-in.... The Philadelphia Stars played the Michigan Panthers in the very first title game ... the Panthers captured the first USFL title 24–22 before 50,906 fans in Denver.[246]

Rodriguez got his opportunity to break into the new league, signing on as the defensive line coach for the Michigan Panthers. The team was coached by Jim Stanley and struggled early in the season but rebounded to post a 12–6 record. In the playoffs, the Panthers overcame the Chicago Blitz and the

Oakland Invaders to advance to the USFL's first league championship game, where Michigan played the Eastern Conference champions, the Philadelphia Stars. Rodriguez was a key element in leading the Michigan Panthers to the USFL title as they defeated the Stars, 24–22.[247] That season, the Panthers registered 76 quarterback sacks.[248] In his second year (1984) with Michigan, the team completed their regular season with a 10–8 record but lost in the playoffs. It was a successful season for Michigan, but the league itself was beginning to unravel.[249] Prior to the start of 1985, the Panthers withdrew from the league, and the players and coaches were transferred to the Oakland Invaders franchise.[250] As a result, Rodriguez left the Panthers to join the coaching staff of the Denver Gold in 1985.[251] The Gold was a successful team and finished second in the Western Division, but did not make the playoffs. Shortly thereafter, Rodriguez's status was once again affected by the league's problems as Denver released him to the Jacksonville Bulls for 1986; that season did not take place. The USFL eventually folded.[252]

In 1986, Rodriguez interrupted his football journey to attend college and add another graduate degree to his resume. He attended Northern Iowa University, in Cedar Falls, to earn an MA in Political Science. Education had always been a big part of his life, and he always emphasized its importance.

Next on the agenda was his return to coaching, and he looked for an opportunity in Canada. Rodriguez found an interested team in the Ottawa Rough Riders. He was hired as defensive coordinator in 1987, but his tenure with the team was fraught with financial concerns and distractions. Although the Rough Riders and Rodriguez played and completed their schedule of games, posting a 3–15 record, the Canadian experience was very difficult, as *Sports Illustrated* writer Rick Reilly described in his story, "Staying Away In Flocks." The CFL generally, and several teams such as the Ottawa Rough Riders, were on the brink of bankruptcy. The fans were indifferent as the owners and teams struggled.[253] After the 1987 season, Coach Rodriguez concluded his stay with Ottawa and sought to find employment back stateside in the NFL.

Shortly thereafter, Rodriguez was offered a coaching position in the NFL. His ticket into the NFL was provide by Mike Shanahan, who contacted him with an offer, and in the process, changed his coaching career path from defense to special teams, to begin his 19-year career in the NFL.[254] Rodriguez commented on the conditions for the coaching position in a *Florida Times-Union* newspaper article:

> "Mike Shanahan had just taken over as coach of the Raiders, but Al Davis, the Managing General Partner of the Los Angeles Raiders only let Shanahan hire three of his own coaches," Rodriguez said. "I had always been a defensive coach, but that wasn't one of the openings. Special teams was the only choice."[255]

From the very beginning, Shanahan was limited in his offer to Rodriguez because of the arrangement he had with the team owner Al Davis. The special teams coaching job was the only position available, which prompted Shanahan to offer the possibility of switching him to defense for 1989. Rodriguez agreed to the offer with the understanding he would possibly move to defense.[256] However, this did not happen. Rodriguez was not switched to defense the following 1989 season. Instead, Shanahan was fired four games into the 1989 season, indirectly cementing Rodriguez into a special teams post for the rest of his time in the NFL.[257]

His two years with the Raiders were his introduction to special teams coaching, in which the focus of his responsibilities was the development of punters, kickers, long snappers, kickoff/punting blocking and coverage assignments, as well as kickoff and punt returns. His transition and efforts in this capacity produced the following results. Tim Brown led the NFL in kickoff returns and played in the Pro Bowl, while the Raiders' special teams ranked in the league's top three in both kickoff return and punt coverage.[258] For the next 15 years, Coach Rodriguez served in the same special teams capacity with the Phoenix Cardinals (1990–1993), Washington Redskins (1994–1997), Seattle Seahawks (1998–2003), and Jacksonville Jaguars (2005–2006). He concluded his football coaching career with the 2009 New York Sentinels of the United Football League (UFL).

In his stint with Cardinals, Rodriguez continued his special teams development. The Cardinals' coverage and return units during his four-year tenure (1990–1993) were rated at or near the top of the league's charts. Punter Rich Camarillo[259] made three consecutive trips to the Pro Bowl, while return specialist Johnny Bailey led the NFL in punt returns and played in the Pro Bowl.[260] At Washington, Rodriguez coached special teams' with the Redskins (1994–1997). On February 9, 1998, he was named as the Seattle Seahawks' assistant head coach/special teams by Coach Dennis Erickson.[261] The assistant head coach responsibilities were significant to Rodriguez but short-lived once Erickson was let go by the Seahawks. The following season, Rodriguez's title changed to Special Teams coordinator.[262] Nonetheless, Rodriguez began his 11th NFL season on a negative note that originated in the relationship with head coach Mike Holmgren. It seems Rodriguez's style of independent coaching caused friction with Holmgren. According to a *Florida Times-Union* newspaper article:

> Rodriguez's admitted independence, though, has caused friction ... and reportedly contributed to him leaving Seahawks coach Mike Holmgren last winter. Holmgren dismissed Rodriguez after the season in which Rodriguez produced the NFL's No. 1 ranked punt team, sent kickoff coverage specialist Alex Bannister to the Pro Bowl, and had rookie kicker Josh Brown miss just two of his 24 field-goal tries from inside 48-yards.[263]

4. Increased Numbers and Diversity at All Levels, 1971–1990   239

In reply to Holmgren's dismissal, Rodriguez said, "Some people like me, and some people don't."[264] However, during his six years (1998–2003) with the Seahawks, he left his mark on the special teams unit. In addition to the successes of Alex Bannister and Josh Brown, Seattle also led the NFL in lowest opponent punt return average (4.8) and set season records for fewest opponents punt returns—17, in 2002; fewest yards allowed in punt returns—140, in 2003; and lowest average allowed in punt returns.[265] He left Seattle with a sense of accomplishment but also a reminder that his ethnic background was still a factor in his career development.

In 2004, the Jacksonville Jaguars needed help with their special teams because in recent years, they ranked at or near the bottom of the league in every major statistical category in this area.[266] The time had arrived for a coaching change, and Jaguars Coach Jack Del Rio considered Rodriguez's availability as a means to solve their special teams issues. According to the *2006 Jacksonville Jaguars Media Guide*, Rodriguez was hired on February 9, 2004, as coordinator. He began to overhaul their special teams by developing numerous young players acquired from the draft. The process would take a couple of seasons but started to pay dividends with the arrival of rookie kicker Josh Scobee. In 2004 and 2005, Scobee connected on 47 of 61 field goals, earned AFC Special Teams Player of the Week honors three times in two seasons, and successfully kicked two 53-yard field goals, including a game-winner against the Indianapolis Colts. He also ranked second in the NFL with 20 touchbacks on 78 kickoffs in 2005.[267]

Likewise, Jaguars punter Chris Hanson joined Scobee with improved performances. He set the NFL record in 2005 with a team-record 33 of 82 punts inside the 20, finishing the season with a 42.9 average. Rookie kickoff returner Derrick Wimbush returned a 91-yard kickoff for a touchdown and set a club record with 955 kickoffs return yards on 39 returns.[268] Thus the Jaguars' special teams greatly improved under Rodriguez's tutelage. His style of coaching was the key to success. He was calm, mild-mannered in his approach, and motivated his players

Pete Rodriguez, 1988 (courtesy Corky Trewin/Seattle Seahawks).

to adopt and maintain a strenuous work ethic in all aspects of their responsibilities. Kicker Josh Scobee said, "Overcoming that rough beginning was a lot easier with Rodriguez in my corner." Chris Hanson recalled his recovery from an injury by stating, "Pete does a great job of instilling an everyday work ethic" that helped him regain his confidence.[269]

Unfortunately, a three-game Jaguars losing streak at the end of the 2007 season caused a firing of five coaching assistants, including Rodriguez. Among the reasons given was the Jaguars' inability to win consistently and get into the playoffs.[270] After three seasons, Rodriguez was dismissed and considered retirement. He had coached a total of 19 years. For his dedication and success with special teams, Rodriguez was honored in 1992 as the NFL's Special Teams Coach of the Year, and a few years later was named the "Special Teams Coach of the Decade of the 90's" by the *Dallas Morning News*. Additionally, he was selected on September 21, 2017, to ESPN's list of the "Best NFL Coordinators of the Past 25 Years." He was ranked the #3 Coordinator of the coaches selected by the sportswriters.[271]

Three years after leaving the NFL, Rodriguez came out of retirement to coach for the New York Sentinels of the newly formed United Football League (UFL). The league was comprised of four teams, played a six-game schedule, and then held a championship contest. Regrettably, the Sentinels were winless in season play and the UFL ceased operations after only that year. The UFL championship game was played on November 27, 2009, between the California Redwoods and the Las Vegas Locomotives.[272] For Rodriguez, there was no recognition or accolades in his final pro football season. It seems he just wanted one more opportunity to stand on the sidelines to coach his players or maybe just to walk one last time from the locker room, and look back at the years, good and not-so-good times, with a sense of acknowledgment to conclude what was a remarkable professional football coaching career.

Peter Paul "Pete" Rodriguez passed away on November 30, 2014, from complications after routine surgery. His passing was a great loss to family, friends, colleagues, and many fans. Nonetheless, he was a pioneer like other Mexican American/Latino/Spanish surname pro football players/coaches.[273] He struggled and worked hard to succeed and, importantly, he confronted and overcame the racial barriers familiar to all Latinos in the sport. His football legacy is inspirational while his personal legacy is simply that he was able to help people along the way as best he could without any fanfare or recognition; and very importantly, he appreciated everything and everybody in his life.[274]

5

Latinos on the Gridiron from Coast to Coast, 1991–2018

The idea for the title for this chapter comes from an anomalous source: it is not by a noted academician, writer (sports or otherwise), or politician. Neither is it the musing of a Spanish-speaker who resides in states traditionally associated with the group: Texas, New Mexico, California, or Florida. Rather, these are the prescient words of young Manny Gamon, the son of Mexican immigrants and a player for the 2006 West Liberty Comets football team. ESPN interviewed Manny Gamon for an essay authored by Wayne Drehs regarding the increased presence of Spanish-surnamed athletes on football teams in "new" pockets of concentration. The title of the story, "Cultures Are Teammates at Iowa High School," is particularly noteworthy and bolsters key assertions presented in this book.[1] Participation in football (and other athletic endeavors), while certainly not surmounting all social and economic divides, has certainly contributed to significant changes in many rural communities. Just as Jacques Barzun noted in the 1950s that "Whoever wants to know the heart and mind of America had better learn baseball … and do it by watching first some high school or small-town teams," we argue that whoever wishes to gain a sense of the demographic changes taking place in locations such as Lexington, Nebraska, Ulysses and Garden City, Kansas, and Springdale, Arkansas, can turn to an examination of these towns' high school football rosters.[2]

It is again necessary to contextualize/generalize the circumstances for Latinos/as in the United States during the period covered in this chapter. This is particularly significant for the years 1991–2018, given the group's dramatic growth and expanded geographic footprint. While the overwhelming majority of the Spanish-surnamed in the United States have ties to Mexico (either by ancestry or nativity), there has been a dramatic transformation of the overall populace. For some of this information we turn to a recent work by Rogelio Saenz and Maria Cristina Morales entitled *Latinos in the United States: Diversity and Change*.[3] These authors, one a demographer and the other a sociologist, have compiled and analyzed an enormous amount of information concerning myriad aspects of Latino life. One key statistic presented is the total number of persons obtaining legal permanent residence in the U.S. by periods. For the years covered in this chapter (Saenz's and Morales' information for this table covers through 2012), there were approximately 4.9 million such individuals from Mexico. Other countries providing substantial numbers were Cuba, roughly 532,000; El Salvador, around 577,000; and Guatemala, about 314,000. Overall, the number of Latinos meeting the criteria was 10.3 million. Out of this expanding pot, we can expect to see future generations of gridiron participants and coaches.[4]

These inhabitants tend to be younger, more fertile, and have a lower mortality rate than do our white countrymen. By the end of the first decade of the 21st century, Spanish-surnamed people accounted for more than one-half (55 percent) of the population growth in the United States. As Saenz and Morales summarized, "Latinos represent the engine of the US population."[5] Of further significance to a possible future increased presence on the gridiron is the percentage disparity of Latinos/as compared with whites in the high school age group (15–19) in both Texas and California (45 percent to 35 percent). It is estimated that by 2020, nonwhites will account for the majority of the nation's child population, "with Latinos becoming the largest group some time between 2050 and 2060." Spanish-surnamed students are already the most significant component of student bodies in K–12 in New Mexico, California, Texas, Arizona, and Nevada.[6]

Two other key issues to note are Saenz's and Morales' discussion of "new" destinations for the Spanish-surnamed and the number of such persons getting at least a high school diploma. Some of the states with the greatest increase between 2000 and 2010 were: Kansas, 67.9 percent (now 10.5 percent of the state's total inhabitants); Iowa, 57.5 percent (5.0 percent); Nebraska, 63.4 percent (9.2 percent); Oklahoma, 50.8 percent (8.9 percent); Arkansas, 40.9 percent (6.4 percent); Georgia, 27.9 percent (8.8 percent) and South Carolina, 22.9 percent (5.1 percent). In these (and other) states, the majority of Latino/a inflow is due to the arrival of foreign-born persons. Of additional significance is the fact that the under 15-year-old segment comprises approximately one-third of the Spanish-surnamed in many of the "new" destinations.[7] What this all means is that there is now an increased probability of seeing Spanish surnames on future rosters of high school football teams in such locales. This trend should become more pronounced the further we move into the 21st century.

While this population continues to grow, there is one other issue of significance: the high school graduation rate. Latinos/as continue to have the lowest percentage of this achievement in the nation. Compared with the national majority (based on 2010 figures), Spanish-speakers trail whites by almost 30 percentage points in this category (90.6 percent for males and 91.6 percent for females for whites, 61.8 percent for males and 64.5 percent for females for Latinos/as). Of course, there are specific national groups that do better in this regard. For example, Cubans have an overall mark of 77.8 percent (91.2 percent for native-born), Puerto Ricans come in at 74.8 percent and Colombians head the list with a mark of 86.6 percent (91.1 percent for native-born). The statistic that drags down the overall numbers is the figure for persons of Mexican ancestry, which is 56.5 percent (78.3 percent for native born, and 40.6 percent for foreign-born).[8] Overall, it is imperative to increase these figures, particularly for Mexican Americans, to better economic outcomes. The number of athletes participating in football (and other sports) should increase as financial circumstances improve.

Given that substantial numbers of the families living in "new" states are foreign-born, many may need to have children assist in making financial ends meet. This trend will mitigate the number of athletes who can play football (or other sports) for a time. What is in place, however, are demographic and social trends that, over time, will produce an improvement in education and economic levels. Thus, over the course of the 21st century, seeing a gridiron athlete with the surname of "Rodriguez" will become much more common throughout the nation. A 2006 census report by William Kandel and John Cromartie provides an overview of how this overall trend may come about:

> How Hispanics are viewed in new rural destinations depends on one's point of view. Hispanic population growth has helped to stem decades of population decline in some States, revitalizing many rural communities with new demographic and economic vigor.... In addition to increasing the local tax base and spending money on local goods, services and housing, recent immigrant workers may fill labor market demands that otherwise might force employers to relocate … or even abandon certain industries. Finally, new immigrants clearly provide social and cultural diversity that introduces native residents to new cultures, languages and cuisines.... Long-term prospects for Hispanic social and economic mobility … depend critically on the degree to which the educational attainments of Hispanic children match that of their peers.... As their experience in the United States increases, they will become socially and economically integrated through various mechanisms, including the acquisition of English language skills … marriage, and amnesty programs.[9]

We think it is only appropriate to add participation in football (and other sports) to this list of mechanisms that will help to make the Spanish-surnamed "socially and economically integrated" into the broader society, be they traditional or "new" areas of concentration.

The information Saenz and Morales provide, though of great value, does not put "meat and bones" on the historical trends that have impacted the U.S.'s Spanish-surnamed people over the past three decades (as we historians are wont to do). Once again, we turn to the work of Zaragoza Vargas to flesh out other relevant evidence. Further, as proof of the increased interest in this topic, we also draw upon one other important work: *Our America: A Hispanic History of the United States*, by Felipe Fernandez-Armesto.[10]

The final chapter of Vargas' work is entitled "Mexican Americans at the End of the Twentieth Century," and examines many key issues that have a bearing on the participation of Latinos/as in high school and collegiate athletics. For example, he spends a substantial amount of this essay focusing on anti-immigrant/Latino/a trends manifested in ways such as the push for Propositions 187 and 209 in California, the impact of NAFTA upon working Spanish-speakers in the U.S., court decisions such as *Regents of the University of California v. Bakke* (which challenged set-aside programs), the signing into law by President Bill Clinton of the Illegal Immigration Reform and Individual Responsibility Act of 1996, and the rise of protests (such as armed groups, like the Minutemen, on the border) against continued Latino/a migration, particularly from Mexico. All of these developments, plus continued de-industrialization and de-unionization, have made it more difficult for the Spanish-surnamed, particularly in "new" destinations, to begin the process of acclimating themselves, socially and economically, into their adopted homeland. On a few occasions, as we will also note in our conclusion, some anti-immigrant inclinations have spilled out onto the gridiron.[11]

Fernandez-Armesto's work provides much information concerning trends that have taken place within the Hispanic population since the 1960s. He documents developments in the three largest (traditional) communities: those being persons of Mexican, Puerto Rican, and Cuban descent. He also discusses the dramatic increase in diversity within this populace. An interesting point by this scholar is his mention of the various Latin American nations which joined in filing amicus briefs in court proceedings against "fastidious state immigration laws" in hope of helping the overall standing of Latinos in the U.S. While it is not surprising to see Mexico on this list, nations such as Nicaragua, Peru, and even Paraguay also joined. This clearly indicates a level of pan–Hispanism concerning how most Spanish-speaking nations view such matters in the U.S., whether their citizens are directly involved or not. Further, Fernandez-Armesto provides even more evidence of the expanding footprint of the group, citing statistics from places such as Hartford (with a population of around 110,000, which includes almost 50,000 Latinos) and three counties in Washington state, including Yakima, which are either Latino majority, or close to that figure (Yakima County is 45 percent Spanish-surnamed).[12]

A final issue discussed by this scholar ties in with the quote by Kandel and Cromartie noted above. What impact is diffusion throughout the nation having on the Spanish-surnamed? Are they assimilating? Fernandez-Armesto argues that this is happening, to an extent:

5. *Latinos on the Gridiron from Coast to Coast, 1991–2018*

> Diffusion probably increases pressure on Hispanics to assimilate—that is, forgo their own culture in order to be more like their non–Hispanic neighbors.... In the long term there is little chance that Hispanics will reunite enduringly around common political interests, because those interests are limited.... Latinos have behaved more like members of the "American" middle class than middle-class "Americans" themselves have: Latinos exhibit the most vigorous workforce participation; the lowest public welfare usage; the strongest family structures.[13]

Again, a lot of these trends indicate that there may be more and more Hispanics whose families embrace varied aspects of American life, including having their children partake in athletic competition on behalf of local schools; for some, that means participation on the gridiron. Now, as we have done in the previous chapters, we will discuss significant individual Latinos and their roles on the field and sidelines in the states of Texas, New Mexico, California, and Florida. As support for the contextualization provided above, we will also include a few stories of relevance from other states, including some which have experienced tremendous growth in this population since the turn of the 21st century.

Once again, we present some of the materials collected and analyzed by Greg Selber in his fine study of high school football in the Rio Grande Valley of southern Texas. Given the expansion of the region, and the fact that the area is approximately 90 percent Latino, this is a metropolitan statistical area (MSA) that currently houses many such football players and will have even more in the future. A report from August of 2016 estimated that the McAllen-Edinburg-Mission MSA was now the fifth-largest in the state. Robert Coronado, a senior economist for the Dallas Federal Reserve Bank, noted, "if you look at the population growth from 1990 to 2015 ... McAllen is responsible for almost half of the growth in population along the Texas-Mexico border." The MSA now has a population of approximately 843,000. Further, this region has a median age of 28.4 years, well below the figure for the state, which is 33.9, and the nation, 37.4.[14] This growing and youthful population will feed the area high schools, and these student/athletes will benefit from some of the current crop of coaches who are carrying on the traditions of E.C. and John Lerma, Alex Leal, Gus Zavaletta, and others.

One prominent clan that has been coaching in the Valley for decades is the Vela family. Pete Vela graduated from Edinburg High in 1965 and went on to Pan American. "Back then, we were just lucky to get to go to college." He earned two degrees, in education and management and administration (the second from A&I), with the goal of becoming a coach and athletic director. His mentor was Joe Green, who hired Vela for his first job at Lyford in 1969. He worked for Green for seven years. At that time, Vela also joined the reserves and was out in California when Green called to inform him that he had accepted a job at Tuloso-Midway High School in Corpus Christi. Green hired his protégé over the phone. Vela recalled that he was indeed a pathbreaker with the Warriors. "I was the first Mexican American coach in school history, but I never felt discriminated against up there."

He went on to a distinguished career as an assistant, working with the great Chipper Zamora and others. By the late 1970s, he was working as defensive coordinator for Bob Loomis at Mercedes, where he remained through 1984. "The pressure to beat Donna was tough ... and in 1984 when he lost to Donna again, that was it. You just had to beat the rivals or else. So that's when I became a head coach for the first time." Vela was very successful with the Tigers, going 9–1 his first year and going undefeated in 1988. Between 1988 and 1994, Mercedes and Edcouch-Elsa traded district titles, though Pete Vela had moved on to McAllen Memorial by 1991. The most difficult defeat he suffered while leading the Tigers came in 1989, when the Yellowjackets, under the guidance of his brother, Robert, defeated Mercedes, 14–9, for the district title, then went three-deep in the state playoffs. McAllen Memorial was a difficult place to establish a winning tradition, and Vela's overall record there was only 14–25. He was fired after a 1–9 season in 1994. "The Lord blessed me, because two months later I got the AD job at Weslaco." He remained with the Panthers until 2004, retiring after 35 years in the education and coaching profession.

In 2007, Pete Vela had the pleasure of speaking on behalf of Robert at his induction into the Rio Grande Valley Sports Hall of Fame. This is a wonderful memory for Pete, as Robert died not long thereafter. Pete's turn for enshrinement occurred in 2012, when he was recognized for his successful record as well as serving as a father figure to many hundreds of young men. In 2011, he was honored by inclusion into the Texas Athletic Directors Association Hall of Honor, along with other Valley greats, such as Richard Flores, Joe Rodriguez, Chipper Zamora, and Poppy Rodriguez. Selber summarized the careers of these two brothers by noting that "together they carved out a place in Valley football history as the siblings who eventually transferred their daily slugfests out of the house and onto the field." The Velas took many residents of the region along for the ride, one that instilled pride and a drive for success in untold number of youths.[15]

Another legendary clan on the gridiron of the Valley are the Villarreal family. Tony Villarreal, Jr., helped Brownsville High in 1951 reach the state semi-final. His son, Tony Villarreal III, did not know much about his dad's exploits, even as he took the field as a freshman at BHS in 1972. He was not very good, and many on campus reminded him (constantly) of the tradition he had to uphold. He graduated from Brownsville Hanna in 1976 and played baseball at Texas Southmost College, leading his squad to the 1977 Junior College World Series. After two years at TSC, he transferred to SMU and continued playing on the diamond for the Mustangs. He graduated with a degree in physical education and a minor in history in 1980.

Although he spent much time on the ball field, the gridiron retained its pull on Villarreal III. He served his apprenticeship at McAllen High under another area legend, Charlie Williams. "I had little success in football in my two years in high school. I didn't know I was going to be a football coach but I knew I had to go through that to be with the winners, and Charlie was probably the best coach in the Valley at the time." By 1982, he was running the Bulldogs' successful junior varsity program, and the following year moved on to be an assistant at Alice. He served there for three years, then went to Pharr–San Juan and eventually moved on to juggernaut Port Isabel, where he followed Chris Cavazos in 1990. He recalled that the admonition for the new head coach from his superintendent was simple: "Okay, you better win."

He did, but there were bumps along the way. While the Tarpons made it to the third round of the playoffs in 1993, they got crushed by Cuero High School (north of Corpus Christi), 63–8. "To this day, that was the worst beating I've ever gotten." In the finest tradition of many of the athletes and coaches noted in this work, Villarreal III prepared for a potential rematch against the Gobblers. He game-planned to no end and even subscribed to the Cuero paper in order to keep track of what was going on with the team. The opportunity for redemption came in 1994 as the Gobblers, ranked No. 1 in Texas, came into another contest with Port Isabel with a 12–0 mark. The hard work and perseverance of the coaching staff and athletes paid off, and the game ended in a 20–20 tie, with the Tarpons advancing on penetrations. Villarreal's squad lost to the eventual state champion Sealy Tigers. The victory, however, meant more to the region and to Latino athletes than met the eye. While many in Texas overlook the Valley (and El Paso, Brownsville, Laredo, and so forth) Villarreal noted, "I've always been one to think that Valley athletes can play at the next level. Ever since I was a young coach I always told the kids they could do anything.... But you have to get past the No. 1 team in the state.... I think us winning that game laid the ground work for all of the teams that have had deep playoff success."

Villarreal remained at PIHS until 1997, then moved on to Pharr-San Juan for one year, to his alma mater for the years between 1998 and 2004, and finally to Weslaco from 2004 through 2017. In 27 seasons, he took teams to the playoffs 20 times and claimed ten district titles. His overall record finished at 200–107–4. Unfortunately, there were some political issues in early 2017, and Villarreal, after filing a grievance against the school system, was reassigned to an administrative position away from the field. He finished his career with the Panthers with a mark of 88–50, making the playoffs in ten of his final 12 seasons.

One of his proudest achievements came off the field, however. Tony's son, Anthony, played for his dad for four years and later earned a dentistry degree from Texas A&M. The younger Villarreal noted, as his grandfather was being inducted into the Rio Grande Valley Hall of Fame, something that many of these coaches and players have passed along to their charges over the years: Latinos can accomplish whatever they set their minds to. As Villarreal IV stated, "it always comes back to the work ethic my dad [or coach] instilled.... Playing football for him was a full-time job with the amount of studying you had to do. Making it on a Tony-coached team made dental school seem survivable for me." No doubt words along the same line have been repeated often in the Valley as a result of the work of men such as Coach Tony Villarreal III.[16]

The chronicles noted in the previous paragraphs do provide a sense of the improvement in relations that have taken place over the past few decades in the Valley. Unlike the rosy picture painted above, there are examples of older, nastier circumstances still present on the gridirons of Texas. The story of Abel Gonzalez, who played at Rio Grande City and Texas A&M, Kingsville, and now is a head coach in his hometown, highlights both the good and the bad that continues to take place in the sport. First, the positive. Gonzalez was a great quarterback for the Rattlers and led them to the playoffs in his senior year of 1998. While that team barely got into the post-season with a 5–5 mark, they did major damage and made it the third round. Now the negative. While playing against MacArthur High School (San Antonio), a game the Rattlers lost, 24–14, Gonzalez heard vile comments directed at him and teammates. "I was in the middle of a dog-pile and a guy called me a 'spic.' It's something that stayed in my mind that was actually said. I never would have thought of saying anything to a black guy or a white guy."

In a 2007 story in the *Brownsville Herald*, Brian Sandalow reported having heard similar stories from numerous athletes. Slurs such as "dirty Mexicans," "wetbacks" and "you don't belong here. Get back across the border," were heard. Gonzalez, when taking his La Grulla Gators out of the Valley, reminds his kids that such comments sometimes cascade upon teams from this region. "Every time we play teams that are up North and have white guys and black guys ... we're going to get those comments.... I guess they just think we all just crossed the border."

When Greg Selber tells the story of Abel Gonzalez, he uses the word "agency" often. The comments and doubts are out there, but a player like Gonzalez did not let such matters stop him from playing, and now coaching, successfully in the sport he loves. In his senior season, besides playing quarterback, Abel Gonzalez also punted, kicked field goals, and played safety on the defensive side of the ball. He made All-District and honorable mention All-State. "Surely such a talented football star would have an easy time making the transition to college ... [but] once again, being from a tiny town in a small, isolated region would come back to haunt him."

The notion of an RGC Rattler moving on to play collegiately was so out of the norm in the late 1990s that Gonzalez and his family had not collected film of Abel in action. By the time he graduated, "all of the scholarships had passed." Fortunately, the Javelinas, who had become quite adroit at gobbling up RGV talent, were there to offer a chance. Boston College eventually came around to look, but by that time Gonzalez had decided to take the "sure thing" and go to Kingsville. Between 1998 and 2002, Gonzalez established himself, guiding the Javelinas to the playoffs in 2001 and 2002. In his senior year, the team defeated Nebraska-Kearney, 58–40, in the first round, then UC Davis, 27–20, before bowing out in the national semifinals, 21–12, against Valdosta State. This playoff run included Gonzalez being named National Player of the Week in the game against the California school. He was named as one of two quarterbacks on the all-decade team for the 2000s at TAMUK.

Abel Gonzalez signed with the Rio Grande Valley Dorados of Arena Football League 2 in 2004. As a hometown hero at the controls of a professional team, Gonzalez enjoyed his time in the AFL2 ranks. The Dorados finished that season with a 6–10 record. At this time, Gonzalez decided to begin his coaching career. He served as offensive coordinator at Pharr-San Juan-Alamo for two years, then went back to his alma mater until 2010. With the establishment of Grulla High, he got his chance to take over a program. He has been at Grulla for the past seven years, was named All-Valley Coach of the Year in 2012, and guided the Gators to their first district title in 2016. Given his success, and his modeling of good traits and determination for Valley youths, Selber summarizes Gonzalez's career by stating:

> [Here is a] boy who overcame the odds to make it in college and beyond. A humble example of the best that sports has to offer, having used it as a vehicle to battle poverty, disadvantage, and all of the crippling stigmas ... that go along with them. The rest of the country might not know about his story, but they would do well to hear it and understand it. Sometimes a guy works best when he's up against the wall.[17]

Another player of note from this era was "the face of Valley football," Mishak Rivas, who thrived under the tutelage, and slot-T offense, of Coach Villarreal at Weslaco. The most impressive season for this young legend took place in 2007, his senior year, in which he rushed for more than 3,000 yards and he scored around 100 touchdowns. The Panthers came into the year with high hopes, but standing in their way was La Maquina, which had won 37 consecutive regular season games. In a mythic clash of Valley titans, Rivas ran for 223 yards and four scores against the Yellowjackets, leading the Panthers to a 41–40 victory. Even more impressive, he rushed for 431 yards in one game against San Benito. In a rare feat for a Valley player, he was named Texas Preps Football All-Texas Player of the Year.

The scores and yardage helped lead Weslaco into the state playoffs, eventually falling to San Antonio Mission, 59–45, in the Region VI semifinals.

Rivas did not disappoint in the losing effort, generating 215 yards on the ground and nabbing passes for another 130 yards. Even these incredible numbers failed to generate much interest. Rivas received offers only from Fresno State and Texas State. He decided to stay close to home and signed with the Bobcats in San Marcos. His two seasons there did not produce anywhere near the same results. He was moved to wide receiver and caught 66 passes for 900 yards in his two seasons. He decided to come back to south Texas and play with the Javelinas. Unfortunately, he was declared ineligible for the 2010 season. A 2011 article in *Dave Cambell's Texas Football* noted that he had yet to play a down for TAMUK.[18]

At the other end of the Lone Star State, no team from this area has ever captured a state title in 11-man football. Charles Hill, on the website of local TV station KVIA, as recently as July of 2017 provided an excellent summary of some of the successes that area teams have had since the early 1990s. Hill provides information on several schools which made deep playoff runs over the years covered in this chapter.

We mentioned the 1990 Andress Eagles in Chapter 4, and the next 11-man school noted by Hill was the 2001 Del Valle Conquistadors. This school opened in 1987 and through the current school year, the student body is overwhelmingly Hispanic (over 97 percent). This team finished the 2001 season with a 10–2 mark and moved all the way to the regional playoffs, where they lost to De Soto, 56–28. The next school to make a deep run in the playoffs, the El Paso Riverside Rangers, has a similarly proportioned student body. In 2003 and 2004, the Rangers went three-deep, losing at the regional level to North Crowley, 35–8, and then to Wichita Falls Rider, 49–7. 2005 was a banner year for El Paso area high schools, as two teams, the Chapin High Huskies (a bit more diverse than the other schools noted so far, but still around 70 percent Latino) and the El Paso Franklin Cougars (around 80 percent Latino) both went three-deep. Chapin continued its impressive run in 2006 and 2009, again getting to the third round before bowing out. In 2012, the El Paso Burgess Mustangs (91 percent Latino) repeated the same feat, finally losing to Wichita Falls Rider, 64–35, at the regional level.

What has been referred to as probably the best team in the El Paso area in recent years was the Canutillo Eagles. In 2013, this team (the school is 96 percent Latino), like so many others before it, made it to the third round. However, unlike other representatives from this area, they managed to keep the regional contest close, losing to Wichita Falls, 19–10. As Charles Hill noted, "Canutillo led this game 10–7 at halftime. The second half was a disaster for the Eagles … [they] had plenty of chances to win this game but was [sic] unable to take advantage of them. There have been many chances and several El Paso teams have been close, and yet the coveted state championship title remains only a dream." The Texas High School Coaches Association ranked the Eagles the ninth-best team in the region spanning from El Paso to Dallas in 2013.

They improved on this feat in 2014, finishing 13–2 and losing to Ennis in the state semi-final match, 41–13. In 2016, El Paso teams had a respectable 6–10 record against out-of-town teams (such as squads from the Lubbock and the Odessa-Midland area). Even Bowie got into the act, finishing 9–1. Of all the teams to make it to the playoffs, however, only El Paso Americas (94 percent Latino) made it past the first round before being crushed in the second, 55–0, by Abilene. Overall, Hill summarizes the year as a "step backward" for the region's football.

Hill does express a qualification regarding the "lack" of state titles in football for the El Paso area. In 2016, El Paso Cathedral High did win a state crown in 11-man ball for TAPPS (Texas Association of Parochial and Private Schools), defeating Houston Village, 37–14. Hill then goes further afield, to Ft. Hancock, which is around 50 miles from the city and plays 6-man ball. This school, which in 2017 was 100 percent (126 students total) Latino, has been a consistent power in this sport since the late 1980s. Between 1986 and 1993, the Mustangs won five consecutive state titles and rang up a 70-game winning streak. The string and championship run ended in a title game against Panther Creek, 54–26.[19]

Another topic worth examining regarding El Paso football is whether some of these Latino players are making it to the next level. For this information, we turned to a wonderful website, www.epgridiron.com for information concerning the colleges and universities that are recruiting Latino athletes out of the area's institutions. This data dated back to 2005.[20] Several interesting trends are evident. First, the number of athletes signing letters of intent is increasing. In 2005, for example, there were seven players (of which two had Hispanic surnames) who committed to Division I schools. Four accepted offers from Division II through NAIA institutions (again, two were Latino). Compare that with the evidence from more than a decade later. In 2017, there were 15 players from area schools who signed with the larger schools (six were Spanish-surnamed). It is with the smaller schools, however, where the numbers have increased significantly. This class had 20 such players, and half were Latino. In certain years, the numbers committing to the smaller schools have exceeded the 2017 figure.

A second important trend noted is which Division I colleges were scooping up such players. Overwhelmingly, the most common school was the hometown UTEP Miners, certainly no major power, but they are providing an opportunity for Latinos to continue to play and develop. There are some notable exceptions, however. For example: Alex Torres from Franklin signed with Texas Tech in 2006, as did Orlando Garcia in 2013. JD Ybanez of Coronado signed with Army in 2010. Eddie Lopez, another Coronado graduate, signed with the University of Colorado Buffaloes in 2014. Steven Montez of Del Valle also went to Boulder in 2015. Isaac Garcia and Antonio Gomez of Eastwood signed with New Mexico State in 2017. Elijah Ruiz signed that same year with the Arizona Wildcats. Between 2005 and 2017, there were 17 area commits to the Miners. Although not a local product (he is from Las Vegas), Will Hernandez was a standout for the Miners through the 2017 season, and is now considered a potential first round draft pick for the 2018 NFL draft. The next in the line of Munoz and Montoya? Perhaps.[21]

Although not from the El Paso area, there is one other player we would like to discuss at this point: Jacob Gutierrez, who played running back for San Antonio's James Madison High. He was the named the Offensive Player of the Year in 2002 by the San Antonio Quarterback Club and was a three-year starter for the Mavericks. He rushed for more than 4,500 yards and scored 52 touchdowns. Such gaudy statistics, even though he stood 5'6" and weighed 186 pounds, and at the 6A level no less, got him noticed, and he signed with the University of Oklahoma. While he started only three games for the Sooners, one of these was against Baylor and it turned out to be a magical night.

David Flores of the *San Antonio Express-News* touted Gutierrez's performance against the Bears in an October 26, 2005, column. Backing up Adrian Peterson, Gutierrez would only touch the ball a few times per contest. Flores made certain that his readers knew that Gutierrez was not in the mold of Rudy Tuettiger, though there were some similarities. "Gutierrez is like Rudy in one important way, though. He refused to accept that he couldn't play with the big boys. 'You just have to keep believing in yourself.... You have to be ready when you get the opportunity.'" On this night, Jacob Gutierrez would answer the door. He rushed for 173 yards and scored twice, on runs of 7 and 28 yards. Gutierrez finished his career with 473 yards on 94 carries, for a 5.0 average.

While it was certainly exciting to note this great game by a local Latino, Flores contextualized the moment and Gutierrez's career as a model for other Spanish-surnamed athletes and coaches to emulate:

> Gutierrez' career stands as a testament to perseverance and the power of faith. It should also inspire young Hispanic football players to work harder in the classroom and on the field. As I've noted here time and again: *Si se puede* ... "I'm just glad to be able to be in a position to represent my people in a positive way." Art Gutierrez, Jacob's father, can relate to the challenges his son has faced. Although he was a bigger running back ... he bucked the odds when he started on Angelo State's 1978 NAIA Division I national championship team. "When I went up there, some people told me I wouldn't play because I was Hispanic," said the elder Gutierrez, an assistant football coach at Harlandale High School.

In addition to his success on the field, Gutierrez finished his degree in sociology, became an assistant coach in Oklahoma City for a few years, and now serves his community as a firefighter. The former Sooners runner summarized his athletic career and life by saying, "We're a proud people with a proud culture. My grandfather always told me to take pride in my last name and do things the right way. You try to have the same attitude in everything you do."²²

A bit further afield from El Paso, around 190 miles east, we find another school that is over 90 percent Latino and has recently made a name for itself on the football field. That team is the Balmorhea Bears. The institution had 152 students, pre–K through 12th grade in 2017. There were 48 students in the high school. The team has compiled a record of 38–4 since the 2015 season.

Jacob Gutierrez, 2005 (Mario Longoria, photographer, San Antonio, Texas).

In 2016, they played the Texas power (eight state titles) in 6-man football, the Richland Springs Coyotes. The game for the state championship took place on the glistening turf of AT&T Stadium, the home of the Dallas Cowboys. Although the Bears held on through halftime (trailing only 40–30), the Coyotes crushed them in the second half and mercy-ruled Balmorhea, 96–50. While a Cinderella ending would have been wonderful, the Mexican American kids on the team competed to the very end. One of the stars of the contest for BHS was Kyle Garcia, who noted after the loss, "We came out here and we fought. We never gave up. I wish it didn't end like this, but we're here, we came to Dallas. That was our goal. We didn't win it, but we'll be back next year." Garcia was right, the Bears did make it back to Dallas in 2017, though they lost again, this time to the Strawn Greyhounds, 78–42.²³

While Balmorhea made the news due to overcoming obstacles and got to the state title game, another Texas community, Harrold, which is about 30 miles northwest of Wichita Falls, gained the national spotlight for a totally different reason—for the kindness and unselfishness of a Mexican American young woman who stands 5'2" and weighs 135 pounds: Olivia Perez. The story, written by Elizabeth Merrill, documented the tale of the Hornets, and the unlikely friend and hero who saved their 2016 season.

The town of Harrold is just like many small Texas communities: football is life. The school has fielded a team every year since 1938, but in 2016, there was a real possibility that there would be no Friday night lights. The squad, you see, was down to five players, due to an athlete transferring out of district. One of the remaining players, a senior named Brady Blakely, desperately wanted to play this campaign in honor of his recently deceased father. "Outside of cloning someone … [the coach] was running out of options." Into this scenario stepped Olivia Perez, an all-district setter on the volleyball team who had also worked as water girl for the squad over the two previous years. She would play—after all, Olivia was good friends with Brady and wanted to help grant him this wish. It would not be easy. "'She was scared to death when she got out there,' [Coach] Templeton says." To protect Perez, the Hornets flanked her out as a receiver and tended to run plays away from her side of the line of scrimmage. Templeton also did the best he could to hide her on special teams and on defense, "as much as you can hide someone when you have only six players on the field."

Like many of the other athletes described in the previous pages, Olivia comes from a family that had struggles. Her mother, Maryann, suffered a stroke in her 30s. Her father, works at a factory in Altus, across the state line in Oklahoma. Between work and helping his spouse, there was little time for him to attend contests, so Maryann's sister, Malinda Vazquez, was present under the lights. Further, Olivia worked at the local United Supermarket. Now she would be an employee, a two-sport athlete, and a member of the National Honor Society.

At this point, it would be wonderful to inform readers that the Hornets, through miraculous play, went to the playoffs and were a version of the Balmorhea Bears. Of course, this is history, not a counterfactual. The Hornets were steamrolled consistently. Still, Olivia made it possible for her friend to play his senior year in honor of his late father. Certainly, that counted more than just the points on the scoreboard. "Despite all the losses, Brady had no regrets. He'll have a Harrold team photo, just like his dad…. They were like every other school in Texas: They played football." After the season and graduation, Brady fulfilled another dream by being accepted into the military police program in the Army. Olivia, like so many Latinos/as, hopes to go on to college; she would be the first in her family to do so. Her three other siblings all work in the food service industry. Perez hopes to move into the medical field, either as a nurse or a veterinarian. As other football players of Spanish-speaking descent have heard, Olivia's aunt reassures her niece that "You can be whatever you want to be. It's up to you." Sadly, there was no 2017 season for the Hornets as, with graduations, the team was down to three boys and Olivia. Coach Templeton had no choice but to cancel the season. "Right now, we're focusing on cross-country and getting ready for basketball."[24]

Before leaving the high school scene of the Lone Star State, it is worth noting the increased presence of the men who are following in the footsteps of the Lerma, Leal, and Villarreal clans on the sidelines. As of 2014, according to the *Texas Guide of High Schools and Colleges*, there were approximately 130 Spanish-surnamed head coaches prowling the sidelines of Texas.[25] Although that is a decent number, it is nowhere near representative of this population in the state (there are more than 3,700 high schools, both public and private, in the state). Additionally, most these coaches are in, not surprisingly, the Valley, Brownsville, El Paso, and Laredo.

A 2015 article in the *Dallas News* noted the small number of such coaches in the Metroplex. At that time, approximately 4 percent of the head coaches in the area (out of 202 schools) were Latino, this in a region where this group makes up more than 40 percent of the student population. Additionally, many of the coaches of this background who had jobs in the north Texas region were in "reclamation project" schools. The eight area programs that were headed by Spanish-surnamed field generals, in the three years before the article appeared, had a 36–173 record. These coaches wanted to continue in the tradition of the men noted earlier in this work, but the hyper-competitiveness for jobs in larger schools (6A) makes things even more difficult. Still, the process is opening up and some are being given opportunities. As one coach from this region noted, "It's a responsibility that I feel I certainly have, trying to perform and be successful, in order that you might be able to earn some opportunities for those who come after you."[26]

All this Latino talent on the playing fields of Texas generated a few players who, during the years covered in this chapter, have made it to the pinnacle of football, the NFL. We have already discussed the career and significance of Juan Castillo. There are a few others we would like to cover briefly (it is interesting that they are all offensive linemen): Roberto Garza, Louis Vasquez, and Manny Ramirez.

Roberto Garza hails from Rio Hondo and played his high school football for his hometown Bobcats; he lettered in track and field as well. As with many other Mexican Americans, he was encouraged to join the military after high school, and a Marine recruiter actually told him that his dream to play professional football was not going to happen, as "Mexicans do not play in the NFL." He refused to give up on his desire to play professionally and attended TAMUK as a walk-on starting in 1997. He was a two-time AP Little All-American and American Football Coaches Association First Team All-America selection. He also competed in track and field for the Javelinas, claiming the national title in DII shot put in 2000. While playing at a smaller school, as so many Latinos have done previously, he attracted the attention of the Atlanta Falcons, who made him their fourth-round pick in 2001. He remained with the team until 2004. He signed with the Chicago Bears and played in the Windy City until the end of his career in 2015. He was part of the

2006 NFC championship team which lost in Super Bowl XLI to the Indianapolis Colts. He played a total of 206 NFL games and started 176.

In addition to his success on the field, he also broke a couple of barriers for Latinos in the sport. First, he was on the cover of Madden 09 *En Espanol*, after the Chargers' Luis Castillo graced the first cover the previous year. He was also the Bears' nominee for the Walter Payton Man of the Year Award for 2006 due to his charitable work with the United Way and Big Brothers and Big Sisters in Chicago. In a selection that resonated with the folks in the Valley, Garza was selected as part of the 2012 "All Joe" Team chosen by *USA Today*. The goal of this squad is to honor "first-rate players who receive second-rate recognition." Finally, he was part of the Fox Sports broadcast of Super Bowl XLVIII and a commentator for ESPN Deportes' broadcast of Super Bowl L. Of his opportunities to be part of these telecasts, he noted, "There are not a lot of ex–NFL players who speak Spanish and [are] able to talk about the game, so I'm looking forward to that opportunity." As a tribute to Garza, his home town designated December 2 as "Roberto Garza Day."[27] Not a bad body of work for a "Mexican" who should have never played in the NFL.

The story of Louis Vasquez shares commonalities with that of Garza. When the future NFL All-Pro and Super Bowl winner lined up on the offensive line of the Corsicana Tigers in the early 2000s, he was reminded regularly of how unusual it was for a Mexican American to be on the gridiron. As he noted in a 2013 interview, one of the most oft-repeated comments he heard was "Man, there aren't many in the NFL or anything." This Latino did get attention, however, as he earned a place on the All-Area Team (in the Dallas region), as well as first team All-State Honors in Class 4A.

He persisted and came to the attention of the major programs in Texas: the Longhorns and the Aggies. He quickly ruled out A&M, and after a visit to Austin, "it just didn't feel right for me, for whatever reason." The next stop was Lubbock, and there he met Manny Ramirez (whom we will highlight below) in 2005. The impact of having a fellow *vato* from Texas sealed the deal, and the two wound up playing not only on the Red Raiders' offensive line, but also sharing time with the Denver Broncos during their Super Bowl run in 2013. Vasquez was an anchor on the line for a Tech offense that dominated collegiate passing statistics during the late 2000s. In 2007, he was named first team All-Conference and did not allow a sack, quite an accomplishment, considering that the running game is little more than an afterthought for the Red Raiders. He made second team All-Conference in 2008.

After the completion of that season, Vasquez was a third-round draft choice of San Diego and made the 2009 *Sporting News* All-Rookie Team. He remained with the Chargers through the 2012 season, starting in all 54 games in which he played, primarily working at right tackle. After that campaign, he became a free agent and signed with Denver for an estimated $23.5 million for four years. It was during his time in Colorado that he reunited with his colleague from Lubbock, who was now the team's center. During the Broncos' run toward Super Bowl XLVII, the two men got the opportunity to interact with Anthony Munoz. As the USC legend noted, the presence of these two players on a Super Bowl team was significant to the broader Spanish-surnamed community. "I love how happy those two guys are in each other's company. I've always been proud of my heritage, and it's great to see more and more Latino names on the back of the jerseys. And they aren't all kickers."

Vasquez remained with Denver through the team's next title game visit and earned a ring in Super Bowl L versus the Carolina Panthers. Shortly thereafter, he was released as part of a cost-cutting move. Additionally, Broncos management argued that Vasquez's style of blocking did not mesh with the zone-blocking scheme installed by Gary Kubiak. After his release, Vasquez visited other clubs, including the Tennessee Titans, but was not signed.

Louis Vasquez, 2009 (courtesy Texas Tech Athletics).

If this was the end of the road, the trip was certainly worthwhile. Just like Munoz and Montoya a generation earlier, the tandem of Vasquez and Ramirez did much to focus the NFL on the contributions of Latinos to the sport. Just before Super Bowl XLVII, this native Texan noted that the opportunities are there for the Spanish-surnamed who want to play football, even at the highest levels. "We take great pride in being Hispanic, showing the younger Hispanic generation that it is possible to play in the NFL. We're just showing them that the door is open, regardless of what the outside world says. We're living proof."[28]

Manny Ramirez officially retired from the NFL in June of 2016. He returned to Texas Tech to complete his degree (which he promised his young daughter he would do). He has since graduated and taken on the role of mentor to the current generation of Red Raiders football players. He and his family live in the Lamb County community of Earth, his wife's Iris' hometown, approximately 60 miles northwest of Lubbock.

The storyline for Ramirez is analogous to many of the others noted throughout this work. His parents, Rosalinda and Manuel, were both from Mexico and came to work in the Houston area at an early age. One interesting note about Manny's parents is that they met on a roofing job site; his father worked for the company owned by his future wife's grandparents. His parents were hard-working individuals who continued to work in roofing and janitorial posts. Manny "assumed I was going to do what my parents did." This is what he, his brother and sister saw while growing up. They lived in a poorer section of a Houston suburb called Missouri City. Ramirez always had substantial bulk, so much so that he was not able to play YFL because he was too large. He played football with his friends in the neighborhood, in large part to stay out of trouble. He eventually attended Willowridge High School, graduating in 2002. Even before he played football at this level, his size and background earned him the moniker of "Munoz" from one of his junior high coaches. At first, he did not know the story of this great athlete. With encouragement from his coach, and an assignment to do a report on the legend, he soon discovered that there were some Mexican American football players who had made it to the heights of the sport.

As with his offensive linemate, Manny Ramirez soon noticed that he was a rarity on the Eagles' gridiron roster. In his senior season, there were no more than eight to ten Mexican Americans on the squad. There were plenty of African Americans on the football team, but the Spanish-surnamed athletes were represented almost exclusively on the soccer pitch. As Ramirez's skills improved on the field, his parents were determined not to have him work during the school year. He would chip in during summers, but there was a sense in the Ramirez household that football might be the ticket to an education and better financial opportunities. Manny would eventually garner multiple scholarship offers, and initially committed to attend Kansas State. When he visited Lubbock, however, there was another Latino on the team who befriended him, so Ramirez decommitted from the Wildcats and became a Red Raider.

Things did not go smoothly at first, given the new-found freedom, particularly in the classroom. "I had the high school mindset of being 'OK' [as an athlete] no matter what." He soon met his future wife, an athletic trainer for the softball team, changed his study habits, and things began to improve. The couple married just before his senior year in 2006. Ramirez earned All-Big 12 Second Team honors in 2005 and Honorable Mention in 2006. He started all 36 regular season games after redshirting in 2003. The Detroit Lions selected him in the fourth round of the 2007 draft. One of the individuals who helped him in his pro-day for that upcoming draft was Juan Castillo, who recognized the significance of helping to bring along yet another Latino into the NFL.

After four years in the Motor City, Ramirez was cut by Detroit after 2010.

After his release, the Broncos got in touch and remained in contact until the 2011 season. Ramirez finally signed with Denver, though he played in only two games that year. In 2012, he played in 15 contests and started 11. The next season, he moved from right guard to center, and more importantly, helped convince his college teammate to sign to play in the Mile High City. By 2013, he was part of the offensive line that helped carry the Broncos to the Super Bowl. Unfortunately, that game did not go well for Ramirez or the team, as Seattle trounced Denver, 43–8. He started all 16 games in 2014. In April of 2015, the Broncos traded Ramirez back to the Lions, and he started seven games while playing in all 16. A final stop was with the Chicago Bears, with whom he signed for 2016. Here, he made another contact, Roberto Garza, with whom he is still in touch.

Before the start of the 2016 campaign, Manny Ramirez believed he could play for another three or four years, but back problems eventually led to his decision to retire. It was at this time, now back in Earth, where the nine-year-old voice of experience helped bring Ramirez back to the Lubbock campus. At his wife's and daughter's insistence, he completed his degree. He also contacted Kliff Kingsbury, the Red Raiders' head coach, about a possible volunteer position. This eventually lead to a full-time post with the team.

As with others noted in this work, Manny Ramirez recognizes the importance of what he has achieved, as well as giving back to his community and the Spanish-speaking populace. It is important to battle against preconceived notions of what a Latino can and cannot do. Football, given its popularity, is an important place to have mentors and role models. Ramirez had Castillo, Garza, and Munoz to lean upon, and now it is his turn. "Where I'm from, people aren't shy to tell you to your face, 'You're not going to make it. You're a Mexican, for one thing.'" It is moments such as this that help spur Ramirez on. "It's important to me for kids to look at me, maybe Mexican American kids who are growing up like I grew up, and see the NFL is out there for them if they work and believe."[29]

Manny Ramirez, 2007 (courtesy Texas Tech Athletics).

We turn again to the work of Dan Ford for information on New Mexico's Latino coaches and players. Dan Ford and Dusty Young of the New Mexico Athletic Association (NMAA) indicated to us that, regarding coaches who have impacted the sport over this time-period, it was imperative to start with Mario Martinez, who spent 38 years as a teacher, coach, and NMAA administrator. Other coaches who merit specific attention are San Juan Mendoza, Dickie Roybal, Mario Trujillo, Jose Porras, Robert Zamora, and Louie Baisa.

Mario Martinez, a native New Mexican, was an 1972 graduate of Springer High School and a University of New Mexico alum. He was inducted into the NMAA Hall of Fame in 2012, shortly before his passing. He endured a lifetime of jokes about his diminutive size. But his small stature was a direct contrast to the major impact he had on the state's sport history. At Springer High School, he lettered in football, basketball, and track for the Red Devils. From the beginning, he always had that "fire in his eyes," a phrase that became his trademark while coaching football at Fort Sumner High School. Current Fort Sumner girls basketball coach Ben Segura, a Foxes quarterback under Martinez, recalled a 1994 pre-game pep-talk by his mentor. "He said something that day that is still said before every Fort Sumner football game. 'Fire in your eyes!' That day he went from five-feet-four to seven-feet-four in our eyes."

Former Springer High player Joey Martinez (no relation) competed under coach Martinez in football, basketball, and track, and was a part of his first state basketball championship team. Of Coach Martinez, Joey Martinez said, "coach meant the world to me and we stayed in touch regularly after my graduation in 1991. He taught us to set goals but not to be comfortable just reaching the goal. Be satisfied but keep moving forward to be better and achieve more. Coach always brought out the best in us."

After earning a degree in education with an emphasis on special education and recreation from UNM, Mario Martinez embarked on a highly successful career in teaching and coaching. His calling first took him to Moriarty, where he worked under legendary coach Connie Hewitt, who became his mentor and best friend. It then took him to Tucumcari, Pojoaque, Springer, Carlsbad, and finally Fort Sumner. Coach Martinez's biggest successes came in his hometown of Springer and in Fort Sumner. His football, basketball, and track teams captured 11 NMAA state championships, making him one of the most successful coaches in state history. On the gridiron, his Fort Sumner Foxes won Class A titles in 1995, 1997, 1998 and 2001. They lost in the title game against Hagerman in 2000.

Mario Martinez preached multi-sport participation to his student-athletes. He was adamant that this was a formula for academic success while also creating a way for students to have a full high school experience and give back to their school and community. Former NMAA Executive Director Gary Tripp credited Mario Martinez with being "one of New Mexico's true lifetime coaching leaders."

Martinez credited his time in the special education classroom as a "Godsend" which provided him with the perspective of how fortunate most of us are.

> The love, enjoyment, and satisfaction that those special kids brought to my life was unbelievable. In fact, I convinced many special needs students to participate on my teams. I am proud to say that my coaching staff and I played a large role in enhancing their self-worth and making them believe that they could accomplish great things in life; including becoming state champions, which many of them did!

Martinez's career has also impacted many young coaches in the state. His message to young leaders was, "take the time to learn from coaches who have dedicated their lives to young people. I am not talking about x's and o's but life's challenges and experiences. Remember you are a teacher first and a coach second and your athletes are students first. It has to be that way if you want them to be successful for the long haul." NMAA Executive Director Sally Marquez echoed his focus by saying,

> Mario had an incredible passion for athletics and the impact they had on kids. He was not concerned about wins and losses. His concern was on the impact each practice and game would have on a student's future. Mario believed that athletics teaches kids life lessons; how to be successful, how to overcome adversity, and how to foster teamwork and collaboration. He made sure that all of his student-athletes had the tools necessary to become good and productive citizens.

Later, Mario Martinez joined the New Mexico Activities Association where he served as Associate Director. He had served on the group's board, commission, and various other committees throughout his coaching career. He was a strong advocate for all schools and sports, but especially the smaller institutions. His leadership within the association led to many significant changes, including the reformatting of the girls and boys state basketball tournament, the state's largest sporting event, into a same-week format. Concerning football, he helped usher in the creation of 8-man football for the Land of Enchantment. New Mexico began 6-man ball in 1988. As Dusty Young noted in an email:

> Although this option was available to small schools, there was still a group [of institutions] that didn't quite fit the 6-Man designation but struggled to compete and/or even field a team throughout the full [11-man] football season. Because of that, Mario worked hard to find a solution. 8 & 9 Man football are sanctioned by the National Federation of High School Associations, so Mario decided to start the process of creating the 8-Man classification for New Mexico. This came to fruition in 2006 and has been part of the NMAA ever since.

Among the schools that have benefited since the introduction of this version of the sport are Melrose (coached by Dickie Roybal) and Mountainair (coached by Robert Zamora), which we will discuss later in this chapter.

Former NMAA colleague Robert Zayas, who now works in a similar agency in New York State, said, "It was an incredible experience to work side-by-side with him. He was a big mentor of mine. I probably talked to him every week during my first months in New York. Mario always told me, 'just make a decision!' That was a simple but important piece of advice." Considering all his coaching accomplishments, Mario Martinez put things in perspective by crediting his greatest sporting moment by stating, "none have been more satisfying than taking part in my daughter Candida's and son Montana's state championship experiences in sports that they loved." He cited "being a good father, husband, and grandfather" as his most important life accomplishments. Mario Martinez, lifetime educator, coach, and family man, may have been diminutive in stature, but he was a giant. The fire in his eyes was extinguished when he passed away at age 58 in December of 2012 in the presence of his loving wife, Mary Ann, family members, and loved ones.[30]

San Juan Mendoza currently serves as the Assistant Principal and Dean of Students at St. Pius X Catholic High School in Albuquerque. He moved into that position after retiring from the sidelines just after the 2016 season. He went out in style, as his Sartans defeated Artesia for the 5A state title, 34–24, that December. This wrapped up a 12–1 campaign in Mendoza's 25th year on the sidelines with St. Pius X, 21 of them as head coach. At the time of his retirement from the sidelines, Mendoza was the second longest-tenured coach in the Albuquerque area. He also guided his squad to a 22–12 victory over Artesia for the state title in 1999. His overall mark was 160–82. It should be noted that Coach Mendoza's track record against the Artesia squad merits special attention. The Bulldogs have amassed 30 state titles in football, so a 2–1 mark in title games versus this opponent was certainly a significant accomplishment.

Coach Mendoza was born in Indio, California, in 1969. He played offensive line for his hometown Rajahs and walked on at the College of the Desert, where he lined up for the Roadrunners in 1988 and 1989. He followed this opportunity with two years with the Cavaliers of St. Mary's of the Plains in Dodge City, Kansas. The institution ceased operations in 1992, and Mendoza followed one of his coaches, Ken Peralta, to St. Pius X in Albuquerque, where he has been ever since.

Mendoza began his coaching career in 1992 as an assistant and took over as field general in 1996. There were many successes, including another tilt versus Artesia for the state title in 2001, a 28–20 loss. In recent years, the school had suffered declining enrollment, and St. Pius' football program bottomed out in 2013 at a 3–7 mark, with no in-district victories. After that nadir, a rebirth took place and the squad went 8–3 in 2014, 10–2 in 2015, and finally captured the brass ring in 2016. Shortly after being carried off the field by his charges, Mendoza reflected on his years at the school. "I've just been blessed to be able to coach there for 25 years and be able to work with these young men. I have so many memories." The tradition of winning will, hopefully, continue under Mendoza's replacement, Dave Montoya, who not surprisingly played for his mentor from 1991 to 1994 and then coached under him, starting in 1998. "Getting to coach where you played, being around the program for so long, it's incredibly humbling to be given a chance to be the head coach." The first team under Montoya's guidance finished 7–5 and lost in the first round of the state playoffs.

When asked to name one outstanding player for the era covered in this chapter, Coach Mendoza was hesitant to name just one individual. After more discussion, he noted that one of his final players, Drew Ortiz, who was a senior member of the Sartans' 2016 title team, merited some specific attention. Ortiz was named Player of the Year in the Albuquerque metropolitan area, and his statistics behind center were certainly eyepopping. He finished that season with 60 touchdowns, 38 via the air and 22 on the ground. For his career, he completed passes for over 7,100 yards and 103 scores. On the ground, he was just as impressive, totaling 3,555 yards and another 46 touchdowns.[31]

As happens all too often with Latino athletes, however, his stature of 5'10" and 190 lbs. was too much to overcome, even with the lofty numbers. He generated offers from smaller institutions, such as Eastern New Mexico, Western New Mexico, and New Mexico Highlands, and even signed with an NAIA school in Chicago, Olivet Nazarene. Still, Ortiz felt that he could play at the higher level. That is where the UTEP Miners came through with an offer as a "preferred walk-on." He redshirted in 2017 and as of 2018 was no longer listed on the Miners' roster.[32]

As noted in our discussion of Mario Martinez, many schools in New Mexico are too small for 11-man ball, but large enough to field an 8-man team. One such institution is Melrose High School in Curry County, south of Tucumcari and west of Clovis. The school played the "regular" version of the game through 1993 and did not have much success. Between the years when the state instituted the 6-man game (1988) and this school's last year in this version (1993), the Buffaloes were not a powerhouse. Their best season in that stretch was a 2–7 mark in 1988. Indeed, the institution canceled the remainder of the 1992 season after just two games, when they were outscored by a combined 96–12. Things began to turn around when Melrose moved to the reduced number of players in 1993, as they made the playoffs in their first year of competition, losing to Roy, 19–14, in the first round. Starting the following year, a long string of success began with Melrose claiming its first state title.

A second championship trophy came to the school in 1996. The school lost in the finals in 1995 to Ramah, 41–30.

While the Buffaloes became a force to be reckoned with in 6-man ball, the arrival of Dickie Roybal in 1998 took the program to a higher level in the 8-player category. The first title under this coach came in 1999, as Melrose defeated two-time defending champion Roy, 42–36, to avenge their only defeat that year. Between that season and the Buffaloes' final year in at the 6-man level, in 2005, the team made the playoffs every year, save 2002, and had three more appearances in the title tilt, losing in 2003 and 2005 and winning in 2004 by defeating Floyd, 74–60. The school then moved up to 8-man. Between 2007 and 2017, the Buffaloes made the playoffs nine times and won seven more titles.

At the helm of all these successes was Roybal, who retired after an undefeated season in 2017. In 2018, he earned the highest possible recognition: induction into the New Mexico Hall of Fame. He also won the Coach of the Year award for the 2017–2018 academic year. The induction came as surprise to Roybal, who jokingly claimed not to know that there was such a facility in the state. At the celebration, the coach's superintendent, Jaime Widner, reminisced about the challenges Roybal faced when taking over the program, and the impact it had on the young men in the community. "I think when he started it was difficult, but after that first year the boys bought in. And they do that with everything, and I'm not just talking about sports.... And I attribute that to Roybal and the environment he created." Overall, the total haul for the now–high school principal and athletic director is impressive indeed: 23 seasons as head coach, 19 playoff appearances, 14 visits to the state title game, and nine trophies, including the last four seasons he coached. As he heads into the newest phase of his career, Dickie Roybal has many great memories and the satisfaction of knowing the impact he has had on his players and community. "I'd say the biggest thing I'm going to miss is Friday night lights. I'm still associated with the kids in the hallway.... But there's nothing like walking out on the field."[33]

During Coach Roybal's tenure with the Buffaloes, there have been many athletes worthy of note; however, Jeremy Sena and Carlos Ruiz, both of whom helped the Buffaloes claim state titles, were particularly remarkable. An early 2000 article noted that Sena had already racked up over 700 yards on the ground on just 57 touches (12.3 yard per carry). His speed was legendary and helped to carry his team to the 1999 title. Sena accounted for 1,900 yards on the ground during that season. Impressive as his statistics were, the same question as noted with Drew Ortiz was asked about this athlete. He stood 5'10" and weighed 180 pounds. Coach Roybal claimed that he could play 11-man ball and at the collegiate level as well. "He runs hard, and some of the hits he takes.... He does things on the field that other kids can't do." Still, there was little attention paid to this star athlete outside of his home state.

Carlos Ruiz also led the Buffaloes to a state title, in 2004, and scored eight touchdowns in the title game against Floyd, as Melrose triumphed, 74–60. Ruiz even made several key defensive plays as Floyd mounted a late comeback. Even more impressive, Ruiz scored 13 touchdowns in the semifinal game, a 100–50 victory over Animas. In total, Ruiz racked up over 2,200 yards on the ground during the title run. Not surprisingly, other coaches in the district feared what was to come in 2005. Robert Zamora, no slouch in his own right, noted that going into this campaign, "Because they've got him, they'll probably be favored to win it again." Zamora was not far off regarding his prediction, as the Buffaloes made it all the way to the title game, but lost to Gateway Christian, 78–47. Ruiz did more than his part, as he earned the Offensive Player of the Year award for the state of New Mexico. He graduated in 2006. We were unable to uncover whether he continued to play on the gridiron after high school.[34]

Among the most successful coaches in New Mexico over the past few years is Mario Trujillo, who guided his Santa Rosa Lions to state titles in 2010, 2011, and 2012, as well as district titles in 2013 and 2017 at the AA level. This school is (as of 2015–2016) over 93 percent Latino. Another great success has been the performance of the Lake Arthur Panthers under the direction of Jose Porras. This small institution, with a total of 30 students (as of 2015–2016), is 83 percent Latino and is a juggernaut on the gridiron, with championships in 6-man in 2011, 2012, 2013, and a loss in the title game in 2016. In 2015, a Santa Fe paper noted that the Panthers had claimed five state titles since 2005. Finally, continuing the tradition started by Ernest Renteria (see Chapter 4), Robert Zamora has guided the Mountainair Mustangs to much success, with playoff appearances in 8-man ball in 2006, 2007, 2009, 2010, and 2016.[35]

A final sideline mentor worth mentioning specifically is Louie Baisa of Lordsburg High School. Coach Baisa was born and raised in the community and, save for his time in college (New Mexico State and Western New Mexico) plus one year in Douglas, Arizona, he has spent his entire career with the Mavericks. Born in 1951, Baisa attended the elementary school (Wilson) "on the wrong side of the tracks" in his hometown. He eventually moved on to the high school, where he played football and basketball and ran track. He did not play any sports at the collegiate level. He spent his first two years as an undergraduate at Las Cruces, then took some time off before returning to NMSU and finally finishing off his degree in physical education, with a minor in history, at Western New Mexico in Silver City.

After coaching for one year outside of the Land of Enchantment, Baisa returned and worked as a track and field coach in junior high, and assistant football coach at the high school. He finally had the opportunity to take over the reigns of the Mavericks in 1990, and that year produced one of the most significant victories in school history: a 9–8 triumph over Animas to snap the Panthers' 69-game winning streak. "That day was like several Fourth of Julys," Baisa noted. This was just the start of a successful run of over two decades under trying circumstances. As the community's population decreased, so has that of the school. Louie Baisa noted that by the time he coached his last game, wherein he claimed a second state title in 2016, there were only approximately 115 students in the entire student body.

Still, the Mavericks and Coach Baisa (now also athletic director for the district) refused to go down to 8-man or 6-man ball. Even with limited numbers of athletes and facilities, Baisa continued to mold his charges into successful squads year after year. Overall, he posted 187 victories with the Mavericks, the most wins by one coach at a single institution in New Mexico. He has been named New Mexico High School Football Coaches Association Coach of the Year twice, most recently in 2017. He has also been inducted into that organization's Hall of Honor (in 2017), as well as the state's Hall of Fame (in 2018). After the 2018 scholastic year, Coach Baisa finally became "fully" retired. He will still keep an eye on his Mavericks, however, as his house is located directly across the street from the newly opened high school facility in his beloved Lordsburg.[36]

Dan Ford informed us about two players from the historically significant community of Escalante, near Tierra Amarilla (home of the memorable Alianza movement during the late 1960s) in Rio Arriba County, with particularly noteworthy statistics. This area, which is considered one of the poorest in the nation, is approximately 70 percent Latino. Ford indicated that the Escalante High Lobos, a school with around 150 students, have certainly made a name for themselves in the A classification. The school was the result of the consolidation of the Chama and Tierra Amarilla high schools, combined since the late 1960s. Starting in the 2012 season, the Lobos have gone 62–9 and won titles in 2012, 2014, and 2015. Many great players have taken the field for coach Dusty Giles, but two stand out: Reynaldo Atencio, who scored 322 points for that first title team and 640 overall between 2010 and 2013. He totaled 4,940 yards on the ground in his career. Following on the heal of Atencio was Dominic Montano, who tallied 270 points in 2015 and finished his high school years with 608. One highlight in his senior year came against Ft. Sumner, when Montano rushed for 419 yards. That year, the Lobos defeated the Foxes twice, 42–25 during the regular season, and 28–20 for the state title. Even with all the trophies, Ford ranked a 2017 victory by Escalante as an even more impressive accomplishment. The Lobos took on a 6A school, Santa Fe High (with approximately 1,600 students), in a seeming mismatch. It was indeed: the final score was Lobos 39, Demons 6.[37]

We now move on to California. Not a great deal of research focuses on

5. Latinos on the Gridiron from Coast to Coast, 1991–2018 267

specific Latino high school players in the state. Therefore, this first section examines how the sport has impacted Spanish-speaking populations, both urban and rural. Here we note two recent ESPN documentaries, one on the farming community of Mendota and "The Lettermen," which is about Helen Bernstein High School in Hollywood. And also, an excellent movie produced by Billy McMillin, which updates the story of the East LA Classic. In addition, we interviewed two individuals, Coach Javier Cid and linebacker Jeremy Aguilar, concerning their participation and the significance of that contest to this community. In many ways, these films encapsulate many of the key issues/themes that we have highlighted, both positive and negative, throughout previous chapters.

In 2013, ESPN produced a documentary on the Mendota High School Aztecs that examined the circumstances confronted by the school's athletes and their families, as well as the importance of the sport (and a successful team) to a town that suffers from high unemployment and many other tribulations. The film focuses on the experiences of head coach Robert "Beto" Mejia and running back Edgar Segura. Mejia, a native of Mendota and a graduate of Fresno State, arrived at the institution in 2010 and quickly informed his players that things would be different under his guidance. "Negativity is a disease I want to kill," he stated at the very start of the documentary. While not able to overcome all obstacles, Mejia produced results on the field, leading the Aztecs to sectional championships in 2011 and 2012. Much of the success came via the athletic ability of Segura, who, like many of his teammates, came from a single-parent home and worked the nearby fields.

The film took viewers through the 2013 season, when the Aztecs again made the playoffs and went several rounds deep before succumbing. The run gave great satisfaction to the community and challenged the notions held by many that this squad (and town) was only comprised of, as one player put it, "stupid Mexicans without papers." The film made reference to how others (mostly majority) schools felt about the team in general and Segura specifically. In one scene, a rival coach, apparently upset by Mejia's ebullience, indicated that the coach and his team were "classless." Another such instance occurs later in the film when the Aztecs are going to play against an opponent that used "Segura es basura" ("Segura is trash") as a rallying cry. In both cases, Mendota came out on top, and Mejia reminded his charges that others did not determine their value as persons or as players.

While there was no doubt about Segura's abilities—he finished his gridiron career with over 8,000 yards on the ground, scored 137 touchdowns, and ran a 4.6 40-yard dash Division I schools shied away because of academics. Segura did not always do well in the classroom, earning five Ds in his last year of high school. He graduated in 2014. Segura wound up at Mt. San Antonio College, given an opportunity to play via the generosity of athletic agent Jerry

Argovitz, who paid his tuition. While we found Segura listed on the roster of the Mounties for 2016, he was not part of the squad for the 2017 season. No further information relating to his athletic career was found.

Simultaneously, Coach Mejia also faced troubles of his own, as he was accused of insurance fraud in September of 2014. He eventually pleaded no contest to a misdemeanor, received probation, and was required to complete 250 hours of community service. In addition, he paid a small fine and made restitution to the insurance company of around $2,000. He was suspended for the rest of the 2014 season but returned for 2015. Mejia once again led the Aztecs to the playoffs, losing in the sectional title game to Immanuel, 35–20. That team finished the year 9–5. His lawyer summarized the events surrounding the case by noting that "Mejia had a brief lapse of judgement and felt immediate remorse. Robert wanted to deal with what he did and move on. He recently received his master's degree. He's doing everything he can do to renew his teaching credential." In 2017, Mendota finished 5–5. As of the end of that academic year, Mejia continues to coach and is listed on the school's staff directory as a special education teacher.

The post-documentary trajectory of both Mejia and Segura provides a glimpse into the positives and negatives surrounding Latino participation in football at the current time. The coach and player did much to ignite the passion of local fans, provided a challenge to the assumptions of the majority regarding the abilities and capabilities of Mexican Americans, and provided role models for youths in the community. On the other hand, however, both fell short of living up to the standards they presented to the broader society. It is our hope that these two men, whose stars shined so brightly on the gridiron, will reassert themselves and help to continue to bring positive change to the town of Mendota, both on the field and off.[38]

Along the same lines is the story of John "Scrappy" Ramirez, a wide receiver for the Bernstein High School Dragons in Hollywood. This documentary focused on the importance of the gridiron in providing Latino athletes with male role models as well as a sense of family. The team's coach, Masaki Matsumoto, served as a father figure for many of the (mostly Latino) team's members. When "Coach Mat" took over, the Dragons had gone 4–36 over the previous four years. Ramirez, who had a troubled youth—including getting kicked out of school—enrolled at Bernstein in 2011 as part of a last-ditch effort to complete his education. He joined the varsity as a sophomore, the same year that Matsumoto arrived on campus. It was exactly what Ramirez needed to get some guidance in his life. His mentor noted in the documentary that "we use football as a tool to help boys become better future workers, husbands and fathers." Along with helping the Dragons' players get a sense of their potential as citizens, the staff hoped to help them get a sense of family.

In one particularly poignant scene, Coach Matsumoto talked to the players about what "love" means. Not necessarily what one would expect to hear in a locker room. However, the definition was exactly what these inner-city youths needed to hear: love means "You can depend on me." Football helped Matsumoto meet "amazing men and coaches" in his youth, and he came to understand that this was what his Dragons needed. If they learned to depend on each other, and on their families, they could achieve great things, on the field and off. One ingenious idea by this field general was to get parents to write letters to their sons/players about what they meant to them and their families. The campaign took place in the summer of 2013.

The response was dramatic and helped the team gain the confidence necessary to play well in the 2013 season. One player who benefited greatly, and responded as a team leader and better student, was John Ramirez. In 2014, Bernstein finished 9–2 and went on to the playoffs. "That's when they really started buying into [the program] and started playing for each other." In their first post-season contest, the Dragons battled back from a 20–7 halftime deficit and defeated Rancho Dominguez, 21–20. Ramirez scored the winning touchdown with less than one minute to go. They lost in the next round. Scrappy Ramirez, however, graduated in 2015 and played at Los Angeles Valley College. We were unable to determine whether he played his two years at LAVC and did not see his name in the "transfers" listing to four-year institutions after 2017. Still, as ESPN notes, this story is a wonderful example of "the power of sports" to change the lives of, in this case, mostly Latino young men. While Coach Matsumoto moved on (he is now coaching in the Seattle area), he certainly left an impact on the youths of southern California.[39]

In late January 2018, we interviewed Billy McMillin concerning his project, "The Classic," which is an updated consideration of this important contest. While the flavor of East Los Angeles and Boyle Heights is certainly still present in the film, McMillin noted that there have been changes in the composition of the teams. While generations of Mexican Americans continue to celebrate the contest, many players now are from other nations, such as El Salvador. Some are also undocumented or members of families with persons in that status. This fact, McMillin asserted, was one key reason why so many of these athletes do not go on. He noted one player who had a high GPA and was a good athlete, but "neither parent speaks English and there is no support for him to go to school." The lack of infrastructure, both within the family and in the broader community, holds back many such competitors. This is a timely film that sheds light on issues of poverty and immigration through the lens of football. While a contemporary story, much of what is seen in mid–2010s Los Angeles has been present in the lives of other Latino football players at other times and in other locales. Indeed, we most certainly agree with one reviewer who summarized the circumstances documented by this film as being about "what it means to be American" through the blood, sweat, and tears shed on the gridiron.[40]

Some of these players do go on to the collegiate game, but they wind up playing, at least initially, at institutions such as Cerritos College (the Falcons) and East Los Angeles College (the ELAC Huskies). McMillan did not know of many who had moved on to four-year institutions, though he did mention that Christian Campos, who was a Roughrider, earned a scholarship to Wayne State in Nebraska. He was on the team's roster during the 2016 fall term and made the Dean's List for the Spring 2016 semester.[41]

As a result of our interactions with Mr. McMillin, we were able to reach out to Javier Cid, who coached most recently at Roosevelt, but who has ties to both institutions involved in the Classic. He is a Roughrider alum, played varsity (linebacker and offensive line) through 1983, and graduated in 1984. Cid played for the Huskies at ELAC and graduated from Pacific in 1989. He got an opportunity to join the Garfield staff while serving as a probation officer and substitute teacher at a nearby middle school. After one year of this schedule, the principal at his alma mater asked him to move to Roosevelt. There he served as an assistant on the JV squad for four years before moving on to become varsity defensive coordinator in 1994. The head job came open in 1996, but he did not get the appointment. Disappointed, Cid briefly joined the college ranks, with Occidental College, as a defensive backs coach, but for only one season. He then gave up coaching for two years to focus on his family responsibilities.

In 1999, the principal at Garfield called him to help coach the Bulldogs. This season was difficult and earned him the moniker of the "Benedict Arnold of the Classic," as he continued to teach at Roosevelt. When the head post came open with the Roughriders again in 1998, he applied and was again rejected. He coached at Cathedral High through 2005. The Roosevelt post came open again in 2006, and Cid finally got an opportunity to lead his alma mater.

Javier Cid was now at a crossroads in his career. He understood the importance of the contest to the community and alumni, but also felt that it was more important for him to get his kids focused on graduating and going to college. In many ways, Cid's situation intersects with key elements of McMillin's story: is winning on the field the most important aspect of the Classic, or is it teaching these young men to compete and succeed both on the field and in the classroom?

Coach Cid was head coach of the Roughriders for a total of ten Classics (2006 to 2015); his record was an unimpressive 2–8. He stated, "The longer I coach, the less it becomes about the game and the more it is about them going to college." He continues to serve fellow Roughriders as Dean of Students. The notice in the *Los Angeles Times* announcing his resignation indicated that

5. *Latinos on the Gridiron from Coast to Coast, 1991–2018* 271

"his proudest achievement is six consecutive years of football players all graduating from high school." Going into the 2017 game, the Bulldogs had won seven consecutive Classics. The final score on the evening of October 27 was not unexpected: Garfield won yet again, 34–14.[42]

One of Coach Cid's athletes not only graduated from Roosevelt, but also got an opportunity to play at the collegiate level. In order to accomplish this, he had to leave California and travel to Kingsville, Texas, to play for the Javelinas. Jeremy Aguilar was born in 1990. His mom was a single parent, and he and his siblings grew up in the projects. Aguilar described his environment as "gang infested." One way to avoid trouble was to play football, and this he did, starting in fifth grade with the East LA Bobcats. He moved on to higher levels of competition. Unfortunately, his mother's job did not allow her to drop him off at practices, and he dropped out of the game and school for a while. Richard Zepeda, Coach Cid's defensive coordinator (and current head coach at Roosevelt), got Aguilar back to school after he hadn't played for almost two years. Aguilar did well and made All-City. His grades did not allow for an immediate jump to a four-year institution, so he played for two years at Pasadena City College, where he earned All-Conference and All-State honors in 2008 and 2009. Division I schools followed his career, but academic concerns mitigated interest.

Enter smaller schools into the picture. A friend of Aguilar introduced him to Kingsville and gave him a sense of the history and importance of that program. He visited south Texas and liked what he saw. We asked him to discuss the differences in lifestyle in this small Texas town as compared to Los Angeles. "I liked the school and knew that I had to isolate myself. I had a lot of pressure to stay straight." He majored in criminology and earned his bachelor's degree from TAMUK. On the gridiron, Aguilar made a name for himself as a two-time All-American. The Javelinas were very successful during his tenure and made the playoffs twice, losing to Northwest Missouri in 2010 and Abilene Christian in 2011. He did not get a chance to try out for any NFL team, though he did get a call from the Montreal Alouettes.

Aguilar feels that there is not as much of an urge to play the sport among the young people in East Los Angeles as in the past. For example, in 2016, only 29 players tried out for the Roughriders. He believes that the presence of gangs in the area has had a negative impact on the sport. He hopes to help his community by becoming either a corrections officer or a member of the county sheriff's office. He believes that football gave him a chance to achieve his academic and, hopefully, professional goals. Aguilar does not care to go to the Classic anymore because "Garfield always wins." When kids in the neighborhood approach him concerning success on the field and in the workplace, he likes to tell them, "Don't be like me, be better than me!"[43]

In late 2017, another Mexican American athlete from California made his mark in Texas, as well as on the national stage. Luis Perez, a native of San Diego, guided the Texas A&M Commerce Lions to the national title in Division II against the West Florida Argonauts. That season, Perez passed for over 5,000 yards, completed almost 71 percent of his throws, and threw 46 touchdown passes against only 11 interceptions. In addition to the national title, Perez also garnered the Harlon Hill Trophy, the equivalent of the Heisman Trophy for Division II. To say that he took a circuitous route to success on the gridiron is certainly an understatement.

Perez's father was a professional soccer player from Mexico. His parents moved to San Diego, and Perez was born there. Given his father's passion for the pitch, it was expected that Luis would follow in his footsteps. Though Luis wanted to play, "I was too chubby and did not like to run very much, so I only played goal." Thus began his interest in football, which he played at the JV level at Otay Ranch High. He also was a member of the basketball team. He never took a snap for the Mustangs, nor a down at the varsity level. He graduated in 2012.

Having grown up watching the Chargers and becoming an aficionado of Aaron Rodgers, Perez decided to walk on at Southwestern College in Chula Vista. Initially he ranked dead last in the depth chart of the Jaguars' quarterbacks. After transfers and injuries, Luis Perez played in 11 games for Southwestern in 2011 and racked up 18 touchdown passes with only three interceptions. This drew the attention of the Lions, and Perez transferred in 2015 (when he redshirted). In 2016 he passed for over 3,300 yards and was a Hill Trophy nominee. The Lions finished 11–2 and made it to the second round of the playoffs, losing to Grand Valley State, 55–32. The 2017 season was even more successful, and Perez capped off his career with 323 yards passing against the Argonauts. Though not selected in the 2018 NFL draft, he was impressive at A&M's pro-day, and was invited to rookie mini-camp by the Los Angeles Rams.[44]

Since a not unsubstantial number of Latino athletes wind up playing at the many community colleges in California, it would be instructive to discuss the experiences of such athletes at these schools. We visited with Coach Daniel Ruiz (offensive line and strength coordinator) of Mesa San Diego College and discussed his background, his experiences in football, and how this level of competition can be of benefit to Latino athletes.

Coach Ruiz was born and raised in the San Diego area. His father was an all-star athlete at Chula Vista High School in the late 1960s but did not participate in his upbringing until Daniel was around 18. By the time Daniel reached the fourth grade, he and his mother moved to the small northern Idaho town of Priest River. There, he became a star athlete, though many in the community were hesitant to embrace a Mexican American. Initially, locals thought he was of Native American background (and he is, on his mother's side). Always a large and powerful individual, the hesitancy to embrace him melted away as the youth demonstrated impressive skills on the baseball diamond and the basketball court. It was at this point in his life when he began to recognize the value of success in athletic endeavors as a way of breaking down barriers. Suddenly he went from being an "outsider" to having all of the parents in town ask, "Is Daniel going to be on our son's team?"

When he turned 11, Ruiz and his mother returned to southern California, and he looked forward to attending junior high and eventually Upland High School. He played a great deal of unorganized football, in part because he was simply too large and exceeded the weight limits of the YFL program. Here is where fate intervened. Ruiz's aunt had enrolled her kids in Catholic schools in the La Verne area, and they were set to attend all-girl or all-boy high schools. She convinced her sister to place Daniel at Damien High School, in part because of his affinity for football and the success of the Spartans' program. While not pleased with this decision at first, Daniel Ruiz came to love the institution and did well; his size and strength permitted him to start as a sophomore, and he still holds the school's record for most games played at the varsity level.

Like many other athletes discussed in this work, Daniel Ruiz turned to sport in part to seek out male role models, and he found one significant mentor in Coach Tom Carroll at Damien. Carroll not only taught Ruiz the intricacies of the sport, he also spent a great deal of time talking with him about his experiences in the game and life in general. Most of these conversations took place over the summers, as Ruiz did a great deal of custodial and maintenance work to help offset the cost of his education. Between 1982 and 1987, he earned numerous local and regional recognitions and attracted a great deal of attention from Division I programs.

As we have seen previously, the problem was that Daniel Ruiz "did not take care of business" in the classroom and did not excel on his SATs. By the time that he earned a sufficient score, he was down to one possibility: Idaho State University. In 1988, the Bengals had a typical season, that is, not particularly successful. The coach who recruited Ruiz got fired, and Ruiz eventually left Pocatello and returned to California. He attended Citrus College and played for the Fighting Owls. He and his wife, Harmony, married during their first year at Citrus. Shortly thereafter, he was offered an opportunity to continue his career at Southern Utah, but the couple stayed in California to have their first child. He eventually got a job as an offensive line coach at Chula Vista High School, in part due to his father's influence and reputation at the school.

After four successful years with the Spartans, the team went undefeated each season, Daniel Ruiz got involved in law enforcement until the early 2000s, when he was forced to retire due to an on-the-job injury. While in this field, he continued to play at the semi-pro level, including with a law enforcement squad. In addition, he became more and more immersed in coaching. After leaving the sheriff's office, Ruiz moved to Las Vegas, worked as a personal trainer, and played and coached for a minor league team, the Las Vegas Express. Eventually, the family returned to southern California, and he worked private security.

Then another gridiron opportunity presented itself. He became acquainted with the website http://europlayers.com/ and registered. He eventually got a job as a coach in Victoria, Espirito Santo state, in Brazil. His success there lead to another post, this time in Denmark. Given how the season runs for these non–U.S. teams, Ruiz had an opportunity to return to San Diego with approximately one month left in the collegiate season. He approached Mesa College and was given an opportunity as a volunteer. He returned to Denmark for one more season and was then hired full-time by the Mesa College Olympians for the 2017 season.

Another key aspect of Ruiz's job is to recruit athletes for the team. His area of responsibility is the South Bay, which is heavily Hispanic. As noted throughout this work, the impediments Ruiz encounters in increasing these numbers are threefold: (1) many of these kids are undersized and underdeveloped, which can be remedied to an extent; (2) many have to work to help support their families; and (3) academics. Ruiz understands how significant these obstacles can be. Still, he emphasizes to potential recruits how the sport of football can help them to change the trajectory of their own, and their families' futures. He indicated that, coming into spring football in 2018, there were about 60+ athletes on the roster; with only 10–12 Latinos. Hopefully, he and others like him at similar institutions in California and elsewhere, will be successful in attracting more and more such athletes. Obviously, the number of these players who will go on to the NFL is minuscule, but the number who earn degrees through their participation on the gridiron can continue to expand in the future.[45]

We now turn to a few athletes from California who have made it to the professional ranks during this period. While there were many to choose from, we selected Donnie Edwards and Mark Sanchez from the NFL. We will also discuss the careers of Anthony Calvillo in the CFL, and Aaron Garcia, the all-time leading passer in Arena League Football. Lengthier discussions at the end of this chapter will focus on David Diaz-Infante, Tony Romo, Ron Rivera, Jeff Garcia, and Tony Gonzalez.

Donnie Edwards had a long and successful career with the Kansas City Chiefs and San Diego Chargers. While he accomplished much on the field, the story of his life off the gridiron is even more impressive, both before and after his time in the NFL. Edwards, who is part Mexican American, Native American, and African American, had to struggle to get to where he is, and embraces wholeheartedly his role model status in athletics, academics, and philanthropy.

Edwards' family consists of eight brothers and sisters; he was the second-born. His father was not in the picture, and this led him to become highly self-directed and self-dependent. Of his missing parent, he stated in 1994, "He gave me life, and I thank him for that, but I have no respect for him." He grew up in National City, but his mother, Beverly, arranged it so that Donnie could attend Chula Vista High, "where opportunity lay." Once on campus, he quickly came to the attention of Coach George Obnesorgen. "He was a diamond in the rough, a kid from the wrong side of the tracks, when he came to us."

Even getting on to the field for the Spartans was an accomplishment, as Edwards had to take on a father's responsibility by around age 12, working first as a paper deliverer, then at a pizza shop. By age 15, he had saved enough to buy a car with his own funds. Obnesorgen noted that "He took a job to help the family ... but he wouldn't tell kids about himself. He would hide his grades, because ... it wasn't cool to be too smart.... He had to put on two or three different faces. I think it was only on the football field that he found a stable family life."

The way out of these difficulties lay on the field and in the classroom. His grades were not an issue, but for a 200-pound linebacker, not many large schools were beating a path to his door. Several institutions from the WAC came calling, such as San Diego State, but he chose to pursue his career with the only major power that showed interest: UCLA. Once at Westwood, he became a star for the Bruins, but there were "issues" on campus directly related to his upbringing. He was accused of taking money from an agent, though it turned out that he merely received a bag of groceries. Subsequently, Edwards raised a concern that is all too familiar today: whether student-athletes are "compensated" fairly for the billions in revenue they help generate. "Stop treating us like slaves ... [athletes need] more money so we can wash our clothes and take a girl to the movies like we should." Not surprisingly, such statements brought attention, both positive and negative.

While such sentiments have a genesis in his difficult upbringing, Edwards also took advantage of his academic opportunities. As he was set to finalize this career, he was present on the Honor Roll, and he eventually graduated with a degree in political science. The Chiefs selected Edwards with the third pick of the fourth round of the 1996 draft. He played his first six seasons in Arrowhead, and his finest year came in 2001, when he recorded 129 tackles/assists and intercepted four passes. This led to an opportunity to sign with his hometown Chargers, where he spent five seasons. His numbers there were even more impressive, capped by 122 solo stops in 2003. He made the Pro Bowl in 2002 and 2004. He returned to Kansas City for his final two seasons. The Chiefs released him in early 2009 and he retired. In his career, he recorded exactly 1,000 tackles, 23.5 sacks, and 28 interceptions.

Since finishing his career, Donnie Edwards has been highly active in a series of charities that are near and dear to his heart. First, he is a strong supporter of children in need. He started the Donnie Edwards Best Defense Foundation in 2002 to help support causes such as the Boy and Girl Scouts, the Child Abuse Prevention Foundation, and Read Across America. "Having grown up in San Diego's foster care system, I understand the importance of raising awareness, as well as funds, to help children in our community who are suffering from abuse and neglect."

Another area of interest is in serving military personnel. While Edwards might not have too much respect for his biological father, he is certainly proud of members of his family who have worn our nation's uniform. "My family has been in the military since grandpa, who is a Pearl Harbor survivor with the 25th infantry division. His service and sacrifice ... pushed me to support our military and so I'm a life-long supporter of our military." His other grandfather served in Korea. Edwards has made many trips to visit American troops all over the world. Finally, and most important to historians, "he is an avid student of military and war history." Given the above, Donnie Edwards is certainly an excellent role model for Latino and other youths, both on the field and off.[46]

One of the principal themes presented throughout this work has been the notion of the significance of Latino athletes and coaches beyond what they accomplish on the field and sidelines. We recognize that success on the gridiron is crucial, but what statement does a player's/coach's life and career make to the Latino population in general, as well as to the broader society? Here, the story of Mission Viejo and USC quarterback Mark Sanchez is particularly instructive. Yes, we certainly acknowledge that his time in the NFL has not lived up to the lofty expectations of Jets (and other) fans beginning in 2009. Additionally, we recognize that Sanchez will forever be the butt (sorry, could not resist) of jokes because of his fumble against the New England Patriots in November of 2012. We accept all of the above. Still, Mark Sanchez's career, particularly at USC and in his early days with the Jets, had broader significance than the totality of his NFL statistics. It is on that aspect that we will focus.

Sanchez, whose father played quarterback at ELAC and whose brothers played at Yale and Depauw, had an incredibly successful career with the Mission Viejo Diablos, finishing 27–1 as a starter and guiding his team to the state title in 2004. He was known around campus simply as "the Man." Not a common status for a Mexican American in Orange County. Even though he was beloved in his community, when Sanchez decided to attend "Quarterback U," he was forewarned that as the first Mexican American signal caller for the Trojans he should "'Get ready for the Hispanic community to go wild when you start playing.' It was a huge surprise. I just didn't know how big it would be." By the time he became a starter and looked forward to the NFL draft, TV Azteca was among the outlets eager to get media credentials to cover his story back in his ancestral homeland.

While on one hand perceived as a positive role model, on the other, Sanchez endured harsh criticism from some Trojans alumni and fans when he wore a "tri-color" mouthpiece in a game against the Notre Dame Fighting Irish in October of 2007. Although his teammates rallied around their triumphant quarterback (after all, he led USC to a 38–0 victory while using that mouthpiece), Sanchez decided not to use it a second time. "It taught me a lot about the position I am in—how many people you reach." As a result of such events, Sanchez took it upon himself to become active in the community and accepted his status as a role model. For example, he worked with Los Angeles mayor Antonio Villaraigosa in helping to mentor at-risk youths.

Mark Sanchez, 2012 (courtesy New York Jets).

After a stellar career, culminating with a superb performance at the 2009 Rose Bowl—28 of 35 for 413 yards passing in a 38–24 triumph over the Penn State Nittany Lions—Sanchez was selected by the New York Jets in the NFL draft. Things started well, as he helped guide the Jets to two consecutive AFC title games, though both resulted in defeats for New York. From then on, success on the field, with a plethora of teams, was spotty at best. Still, it is imperative to acknowledge what Sanchez's career has meant to other Latinos, particularly those of Mexican descent. What *ESPN the Magazine* reporter Jorge Arrangue, Jr., noted back in late 2008 it still relevant today:

> Sanchez realizes that he is playing not just for himself and his team. Whether he likes it or not, he's playing for people whose names sound like his; for those who work thankless jobs for little pay; for those who are reminded daily that they live in a country that does not know what to do with them. These are the fans who once cheered

for Valenzuela and Plunkett and now cheer for Garciaparra and De La Hoya. They are his fans, too. On this day, Sanchez has arrived in Los Angeles.

One final point that we would like to highlight regarding Mark Sanchez comes from an unlikely source: a fan and graduate of the Trojans' hated rivals, the UCLA Bruins. Right after Sanchez's triumph in the Rose Bowl, Gustavo Arellano penned a blog directed at the signal caller. He was blunt about his request: "Stay in school for Mexicans." While Arellano praised (grudgingly, of course) the talents of the Trojans signal caller and referred to him as "a brown boy slinging it like Sammy Baugh," Arellano felt it would be even more noteworthy for Sanchez to get his degree. Sanchez did just that, earning his bachelor's degree in May of 2009. Arellano, certainly seeking even more ostracizing from his fellow Westwood colleagues, summarized this player's significance thusly: "You've already taught thousands of Mexican kids who play football in high school, in schools and divisions always ignored by the media … that Mexis can and do succeed." We could not agree more strongly with this assessment, butt fumble or not.[47]

Another Californian who made his mark in the professional ranks is Anthony Calvillo, the all-time leading passer in CFL history. We previously discussed his childhood and time at Utah State University in Chapter 4, and now summarize his 20-year stint north of the border. For a man who was recently inducted into the CFL Hall of Fame (in 2017), Calvillo's career did not have a particularly auspicious start. His first go-round with the association came with one of the ill-fated, U.S.-based CFL franchises, the Las Vegas Posse. The team started off well, winning its first two contests, but things then quickly went south (as did the entire U.S.-based clubs experiment), and the Posse finished 5–13. Calvillo showed potential during that campaign, throwing for almost 2,600 yards, though he did have more interceptions (15) than scores (13). He was subsequently picked by Hamilton during the dispersal draft and spent three seasons with the Tiger-Cats, completing passes for almost 7,600 yards and 45 touchdowns. The club released him in March of 1998, and he subsequently signed with the Montreal Alouettes.

Like all young quarterbacks, particularly those who back up legends (in this case, another future CFL Hall of Famer, Tracy Ham—inducted in 2010), the former Aggie did not get much opportunity on the field at first. Calvillo served his apprenticeship in 1998 and 1999 until Ham's retirement. He became the starter in 2000 and started every game for Montreal over the next seven seasons. During that time, the Alouettes went to the Grey Cup five times (2000, 2002, 2003, 2005 and 2006), but came out on top only in 2002. After dealing with family and medical issues, Calvillo also guided the team to titles in 2009 and 2010. As we noted in our introduction, Anthony broke the record for most yards passing in October of 2011 and finished his career with almost 80,000 yards passing (and over 450 touchdown passes). He suffered a concussion in 2013 and retired at the end of the season.

The story of Anthony Calvillo is much more than just what he accomplished on the field. He has faced many obstacles in his lifetime (many discussed earlier), including helping his wife overcome cancer and being a survivor of that dreaded disease as well. Once he defeated his illness, he began to speak before civic and business groups. He summarized this new aspect of his life by saying, "the fact that I'm able to share this intimate story with them, it kind of brings me down to earth. I'm just another person like them." In addition to sharing his story, Calvillo, in 2014, completed another important task: getting his Utah State degree. As noted in a *Salt Lake Tribune* article from May of that year, Calvillo, did this in part for his daughters, Athena and Olivia. He brought his entire family to Logan to see him participate in the graduation ceremony. "I wanted them to have that visual, of me crossing the stage." One of the legendary quarterback's teammates with the Alouettes, Ben Cahoon (a BYU alum), noted the significance of this accomplishment. "He didn't need a degree. He's set up for life in Montreal, with endorsements and business opportunities.... It shows that he's a finisher." After retirement, Anthony Calvillo continued to serve the franchise as a coach (offensive coordinator), though he was not rehired after the team finished 3–15 and scored the fewest points and touchdowns in the league in 2017.

Interviewed in April of 2016, Calvillo looked beyond his time on the field and the sidelines, to reflect on the significance of his career. It all goes back to La Puente, he insisted. What he has accomplished in his life "gives students there some inspiration that they can do it." Like so many other athletes examined in this work, Calvillo embraced the opportunities provided by the game and now seeks to pay it forward, in Montreal, Logan, and most especially, among other Mexican Americans in southern Califor-

Anthony Calvillo, 1995 (courtesy Canadian Football League).

nia. As he was reminded in 2011 by a lifelong friend, his story is truly the American (or is it Canadian?) dream. "Dude, you're poor. Your grades stink. You're just another Mexican kid from La Puente, why would anyone think you could make it?" To which the humble, soon-to-be Hall of Famer replied, "I look back at my life ... it's really hard to believe."[48]

The career of another record-setting quarterback of Mexican American background occurred even further under the radar than Calvillo's in the CFL: Aaron Garcia, who made his mark in the Arena Football League (AFL). His father, Hank, the son of immigrants from Mexico, played three sports at Sacramento's Grant High School and earned a baseball scholarship to the University of New Mexico. Later, the elder Garcia coached Aaron at the same secondary school, where his son did the unthinkable: breaking all of John Elway's California passing records. Not surprisingly, such lofty statistics attracted attention from universities in major conferences. Eventually, thanks to the salesmanship of Dennis Erickson, Aaron Garcia chose to attend Washington State in 1989.

It seemed a match made in pigskin heaven, and it was, but for just one season. Garcia did his part, leading the Pac-10 in passing efficiency as a freshman, with a quarterback rating of 139.1. Then Erickson "took his talents" down to south Florida, taking over as head coach of the University of Miami Hurricanes. The next field general, Mike Price, recruited Drew Bledsoe, and that was pretty much the end of Garcia's opportunities with the Cougars. Still, Garcia did not hold a grudge against his former coach. Erickson thought that Garcia had NFL-caliber talent and encouraged his protégé to play in the CFL or AFL to better prepare for an opportunity at the highest level of the sport. When asked to comment about Erickson while playing in the AFL, Garcia noted, "Coach Erickson is someone that I always respected.... That's why I went to Washington State. But the other thing is, he's telling me something I've always known.... There are times when I'm watching an NFL quarterback struggling to get through the game, and I get bitter to some extent." Given his ties to Sacramento, Garcia decided to return home and played his final two years with Sacramento State University. In his time with the Hornets, Garcia was injured and had less than impressive statistics, so he was not drafted or given a tryout by NFL squads. Enter the AFL.

Garcia's travels throughout the indoor game demonstrated both his talent and the chaotic nature of the league. Over an 18-year career, he played for ten different teams, his longest stint being with the New York Dragons (2001–2008). None of the franchises for which he played were still in existence as of the 2018 season. While things were often tumultuous in the league and with individual clubs, Garcia shined on the field. He did get one chance with the NFL, in 2002, signing with the 49ers to compete to back up another Latino, Jeff Garcia. That opportunity did not work out, and he returned to the

Dragons. He last played with the ill-fated LA KISS in 2014. All told, Garcia passed for more than 62,000 yards and 1,336 touchdowns. He finished with a quarterback rating of 115.7 for his career. In a 2015 fan publication, Garcia was ranked as the greatest quarterback in league history. He retired as an active player and became head coach of the expansion Las Vegas Outlaws for the 2014 season. The team folded in 2015.[49]

Although Aaron Garcia and Anthony Calvillo did not make it to the "big show," their careers are indicative of the possibilities that do exist for Latino athletes outside of the NFL. As we have noted, there is a growing number of Spanish-surnamed athletes who are playing at smaller collegiate programs. While there is still a long way to go before the number of such competitors is more in line with this group's percentages in the overall population, it is possible to say that the trend is moving, albeit slowly, in a positive direction. Just as did other ethnic groups in the late 19th and early 20th centuries, it appears that Hispanics are beginning to claim a more substantial presence for themselves on the gridirons of the United States (and Canada).

A quick perusal of the "Miami-Dade's Best Football Players of All Time" list (the most recent one we encountered was from 2008), published by the *Miami Herald*, revealed but a handful of Spanish-surnamed players. The ones we have most focused on previously in this work are Ralph Ortega of Coral Gables High and Fuad Reveiz of Miami Sunset High. We were surprised that Carlos Alvarez did not make this list. As in places such as the Valley in Texas, many Latinos play the game in this region, but not very many are considered to be truly outstanding. Still, they are on the field, and some have made their mark as players, others as coaches. This section will briefly cover the careers and significance of the following: Orlando Iglesias, Mario Cristobal, Alex Mirabal, and Manny Diaz.

Anyone familiar with the history of high school football in south Florida knows that one school that seldom makes an appearance in discussions of "best of" is the Miami Coral Park Rams (of which Jorge Iber is an alumnus—class of 1980). While the school has had success in baseball—the Canseco brothers played there—the gridiron has been another matter altogether. For many years, the Rams have consistently been among the least successful teams of the talent-rich city's football programs.

Every so often, however, there comes along an athlete who provides at least a bit of delight to long-suffering aficionados. One such individual was Cuban American Orlando Iglesias, who in the late 1990s helped guide the Blue and Gold to the state playoffs for the first time in school history. In the first-round playoff game, he caught four scores, and a Miami–Dade County record 17 touchdown grabs during the regular season. He made first team all-county two consecutive years. He was pursued by Ohio State, Florida, and Iowa State, but ultimately chose to play for the University of Houston Cougars. Over his career he did well, with his best season coming in 1998, when he caught 63 passes for 772 yards. This ranked him sixth in Conference USA and 30th nationwide. He was injured in 2000 and came back for his senior season in 2001, when he averaged 11.3 yards per reception (on 63 catches) and had four games over 100 yards. Overall, he caught over 220 passes for more than 2,800 yards and 17 scores. While Iglesias did not get a chance to pursue a professional career, he did earn a degree in business management from Houston and is currently working in the financial services sector in Calgary, Alberta. The most important point about Iglesias' athletic career is how success on the gridiron helped him get the opportunity to pursue a higher education. Not all Latino football athletes will play professionally, of course, but if they can get a chance to attend college on an athletic scholarship, they certainly have the prospect to change the trajectory of their, and their families' lives.[50]

While the Coral Park Rams are one of the least successful programs in Miami-Dade County, just up the road, heading south on 87th Avenue from the CPHS campus, is one of the most triumphant, a Catholic institution, Columbus High. One of the most important Hispanic gridders to come out of that school in recent years is Mario Cristobal, in 2017 named the head coach of the Oregon Ducks. Cristobal played for the Explorers and earned a scholarship to play offensive tackle for the Hurricanes under the leadership of Jimmy Johnson and Dennis Erickson. While at "the U," he was part of two national championship teams and eventually graduated with a degree in business administration in 1993. Not through with the football bug quite yet, he signed with the Broncos as a free agent, but he never played for Denver. He played for the Amsterdam Admirals of the World League of American Football in 1995 and 1996. After finishing his playing career, he went back to Miami to serve as a graduate assistant. He also applied to the U.S. Secret Service and was accepted in 1998. At the last moment, he decided to forgo this career path and remained in coaching, beginning the long, grinding, and often relocating path of an assistant collegiate coach. He graduated with his MA in 2001, moved on to Rutgers to work with offensive linemen, and returned to Miami in a similar capacity.

In 2007, the collegiate football stepchild of the city of Miami, otherwise known as Florida International University, came calling, and Mario Cristobal took on what can only be described as a Bill Snyder–type (with Kansas State) undertaking with the Golden Panthers. Not only was the team new (started in 2002), they were not very good. Facilities were less than ideal. The disparity between the two South Florida institutions, at least on the gridiron, were evident, particularly when the Golden Panthers played the Miami Hurricanes. One of these contests resulted in an embarrassing brawl between the two teams. It was into this cauldron that Mario Cristobal stepped when he signed on to replace Don Strock at the helm of the FIU program. Cristobal's first season, with mostly underclassmen playing, finished with a 1–11 mark. However, Cristobal began to prove himself on the recruiting trail, and the Golden Panthers commenced a slow, but steady, climb. The culmination of his efforts came in 2010 and 2011, when FIU went to the first two bowl games in school history. A drop-back to a 3–9 mark in 2012 led to what many considered to be a hasty firing by athletic director Pete Garcia.

Cristobal was not out of work for long, as Nick Saban and the Alabama Crimson Tide came calling less than two months later. He was charged with running the offensive line and serving as recruiting coordinator. Cristobal earned another national championship ring in 2015. He then moved on to Oregon to become part of Willie Taggart's staff with the Ducks. After Taggart's departure to Florida State in December of 2017, Mario Cristobal was named head coach. Many in the Pacific Northwest expressed concern, given Cristobal's 27–47 mark at FIU. Little did they know and understand how remarkable an achievement this record was.

In a summary for Ducks fans posted on http://www.oregonlive.com, an anonymous author noted both Cristobal's first-generation Cuban American background as well as his aptitude on the recruiting trail. "Cristobal was named the nation's top recruiter by 247 Sports in 2015, and he ranked No. 2 in 2017. Cristobal's recruiting expertise will be especially key in the short term, give the flurry of Duck recruits who had decommitted following Willie Taggart's departure." No doubt that this is a Latino gridiron story worth following. It appears that for the next few years, this son of South Florida's vibrant Cuban culture will make his mark in a locale about as far removed as possible from his beginnings.[51]

Mario Cristobal did not have to look far to bring in an offensive line coach for the Ducks. Alex Mirabal is another Cuban American who had ties to the Columbus Explorers and FIU. Starting in 1993, Mirabal held a similar post at the Catholic institution and helped produce three district titles over a four-year span. He also served in other coaching capacities at the school until 2001. He then worked in the Miami-Dade system, coaching the offensive line at G. Holmes Braddock High until 2003 before returning to the Explorers. He served as Assistant Head Coach at FIU for the entirety of Cristobal's tenure with the Golden Panthers. After 2012, he moved on to Marshall University and had much success in West Virginia. During his tenure with the Thundering Herd, he coached several All-Conference USA linemen and helped make this team one of the highest-scoring offenses in the nation. In 2014, the Herd joined (coincidentally) the Ducks as the only two teams in the country to rank in the top 12 in scoring (third), rushing (sixth) and passing (twelfth). Hopefully, this pair of Cuban Americans will be important cogs in the leadership of one of the most important collegiate football programs in the nation for years to come.[52]

A final Floridian (and Cuban American) we would like to highlight briefly is Manny Diaz, who is currently serving as the defensive coordinator of the University of Miami, the team known for its "turnover chain," a symbolic piece of jewelry presented to players when they recover a forced fumble or make an interception. Diaz, the son of two-time Miami mayor Manuel Alberto Diaz, left South Florida to pursue his collegiate education in journalism at Florida State; serving as sports editor for the school newspaper. He completed that degree and hired on to ESPN, working in production of their NFL pregame show. It appeared that this would be his calling, and Diaz was even offered a promotion within the network. Instead of taking that job, he convinced his wife (who was pregnant at the time) that he would instead follow a career in coaching, hopefully starting with the Seminoles.

A meeting with defensive coordinator Chuck Amato led to a glamorous post stuffing envelopes and other menial, though critical for recruiting, tasks. When Amato got the head coaching position with the North Carolina State Wolfpack, Diaz followed him as a graduate assistant, working primarily with safeties. From there, he found defensive coordinator posts with Middle Tennessee, Mississippi State, and Texas. The job at Austin, seemingly about as significant a coordinator position as is possible, ended disastrously with Diaz being fired by Mack Brown after the Longhorns' defense surrendered 550 yards on the ground to BYU in September of 2013.

As with so many of our subjects, adversity brought out the best in Diaz, and he moved on to Louisiana Tech, then back to Mississippi State to reestablish his bona fides. He helped guide both defenses to substantial improvements over the 2014 and 2015 campaigns. This led to a return to South Florida in the same capacity with the University of Miami Hurricanes. In 2016, Diaz was nominated for the Broyles Award, which is presented to the nation's top assistant football coach. As a native Miamian, Diaz understands what the Hurricanes mean to the area. He carries his Cuban American background, and his ties to South Florida, with great aplomb. "The youth and high school football here is outstanding, arguably as good as anywhere in the country. I think people down here want to see the University of Miami represent that. They want to see us represent their community. Those are our young men out there playing against the rest of the world." It seems that for the time being, there will also be a local Latino helping to lead these charges.[53]

We briefly turn to two Latino athletes who played their football in other states. We have previously discussed the presence of such individuals in places such as Iowa, Kansas, Oklahoma, and Arkansas. The number of such tales will only grow the further we move into the 21st century. The two athletes profiled here are Alex Tejada (who was born in California but is part of the growing Salvadoran community in Arkansas) and Kiko Alonso (who is of Cuban and Colombian descent, born in Massachusetts and raised in Texas and California).

As discussed in Chapter 4, Spanish-surnamed individuals have been working in the Natural State since the early part of the 20th century. By the late 1980s, a growing number of Latino families began to migrate (many from places such as California, as with the Tejada clan), drawn by tough, but better-paying jobs in industries such as poultry processing. Alex's parents, Samuel and Milagro, brought their young son to Arkansas, and he was part of a cadre of Latino youths who began attending Springdale (and other local) schools in the 1990s. Alex learned English and became involved in the typical pursuits of youths in American schools. By the time he was in the ninth grade, not surprisingly, he was playing soccer. Then fate (in the way of a knee injury) intervened. During his recovery, friends suggested he try out for the Bulldogs' football team as a kicker. Not only did he take to the new sport (he connected on 174 of 184 extra points), he eventually earned a scholarship to play for his home-state University of Arkansas Razorbacks. "When I got the phone call, I was really excited. I never thought I would get a scholarship to play somewhere. It was an unbelievable feeling."

One important aspect of Tejada's press conference was that it was bilingual. When asked about this, he made a very powerful point by stating that "I just wanted to represent myself, and never forget where I come from and never forget my family or my roots." Tejada had a notable career with the Hogs, hitting on 136 of 141 extra points and connecting on 68.5 percent of his field goal attempts. More importantly, Tejada purposely chose to be a role model for the Latino youths in Northwest Arkansas. His success has helped motivate many to stay in school and give this "other" version of football a try. "Being a local, I think it has played a role in the number of Hispanic kids from Springdale … trying a new sport like football." A fellow Bulldogs gridder, Chris Melchior (whose parents are from Mexico), summarized Tejada's impact very succinctly when he stated, "I think he will [be a role model] because he stands out as a Hispanic, and not many Hispanics play American football … [but] with the success that he's had, that will encourage more kids to play."[54]

Kiko Alonso is the son of a Cuban father (who was raised in Puerto Rico) and a Colombian mother. He spent much time on a farm owned by his grandparents in his mother's homeland. He tallied 150 total tackles in his senior season at Los Gatos High School in California and was offered a scholarship to play at the University of Oregon. While in Eugene, he did well, highlighted by being named the Defensive Player of the Game in the 2012 Rose Bowl (a Ducks victory over the Wisconsin Badgers, 45–38). In that contest, he tallied five tackles, 1.5 sacks, and one interception. He also had some issues while in college, being suspended in 2010 for a DUI.

Alonso was a second-round draft choice of the Buffalo Bills in 2013 and quickly justified his selection when he was named NFL Defensive Rookie of the Month in September. He recorded 159 tackles (87 unassisted) and four interceptions that season. He was also recognized by the Professional Football Writers Association as Defensive Rookie of the Year. While he had an impressive first season, he tore his ACL during the off-season and was lost to Buffalo for all of 2014. The Bills traded Alonso to the Philadelphia Eagles in exchange for Sean McCoy before the 2015 season. A final, and appropriate, trade took place in March of 2016, as the Eagles shipped Kiko off to southern Florida to play with the Dolphins.

While proud of his heritage, the linebacker was not, as his father Carlos noted, well versed about many issues relating to Cuba. "He knows about what happened with Castro dying. But he's busy playing football." Alonso, however, was knowledgeable about Colin Kaepernick's stance on the late Cuban dictator. It just so happened, that in 2016 (week 11—November 27) the Miamians played the 49ers on their home turf. It also just so happened that Kaepernick deemed the days leading up to the game an appropriate time to mention his admiration for Castro and his regime. Armando Salguero, another Cuban American, noted the tension in the stadium before and during the game. The scribe gave voice to the sentiments that he and other locals (including the Alonso family) felt when Kaepernick praised the "universal health care in Cuba and [how Castro] invested in the educational system." Alonso noted, "I was waiting for Kaepernick to say he liked how Mussolini made the trains run on time." It was clear that Alonso took this as an affront to his family and culture. He had an excellent game (12 tackles and an interception), assisting in a stop of the 49ers' signal caller by Ndamukong Suh on the Miami two-yard line to preserve a 31–24 Dolphins victory. After the contest, Kiko Alonso remarked, "usually, I just try to play my game. But I did want to hit him." Shortly thereafter, an Instagram picture of the tackle, with the hashtag #cubalibre, appeared on Alonso's account. The point of this discussion is not to take sides, but to document an interesting example of a manifestation of Latino (in this case, Cubano) pride on a football field.[55] Alonso is now with the Saints.

We will now turn to more extensive overviews of the lives and careers of the following individuals: David Diaz-Infante, Tony Romo, Ron Rivera, Jeff Garcia, and Tony Gonzalez.

Gustavo David Miguel Diaz-Infante

Gustavo David Miguel Diaz-Infante was born on March 31, 1965, in San Jose, California. He is the son of a Mexican immigrant and *Zapatista*[56] named Marco Ignacio Diaz-Infante, who immigrated to the United States. His mother, whose name was not available, is of Finnish American background. The Diaz-Infante family made their home in San Jose, where David Miguel flourished in an academic and athletic environment. He attended the Bellarmine College Preparatory High School, where he attained the necessary credentials to pursue a college education. On the collegiate football field, he worked just as hard to master the sport to compete eventually at the professional level. Throughout a nine-year pro career, Diaz-Infante played for six teams in four leagues and enjoyed two Super Bowl victories with the Denver Broncos.

His gridiron journey began on the campus of San Jose State University, which he attended between 1983 and 1987, earning a degree in the Social Sciences. He also developed into a formidable football player who contributed greatly to the Spartans' success. Diaz-Infante was a four-year starter on the offensive line. The Spartans played in the Pacific Coast Athletic Association (PCAA) and experienced winning campaigns in 1984 and 1986. Their best year was the latter. The Spartans finished 10–2 and captured the PCAA Championship and the opportunity to play in the California Bowl. Their opponents were the Miami (Ohio) Red Hawks from the Mid-American Conference (MAC). The game was played at Bulldog Stadium, Fresno, where the Spartans were victorious, 37–7. Interestingly, Diaz-Infante's Latino teammate, quarterback Mike Perez, was named Most Valuable Player. Post-season honors for Diaz-Infante included honorable mention All-PCAA in 1985, Senior Team Co-Captain, First Team All-PCAA, UPI First Team, All-West Coast, and AP honorable mention All-America Team.[57]

After a successful collegiate career, Diaz-Infante looked forward to playing professional football but was not selected in the 1987 NFL draft. That season was notable because the NFL Players' Association negotiated with owners over contract matters that resulted in a player strike. During the strike, replacement players were hired to fill in and play a short schedule of games. Diaz-Infante signed as a free agent with the San Diego Chargers and played four games as a replacement.[58] After this first time in the NFL, Diaz-Infante attended tryouts in both 1988 and 1989 with the Rams. He was not signed and returned to his collegiate alma mater, where he secured a coaching position. In 1990, he was hired as an assistant and entrusted with scouting report responsibilities.[59] He remained with the SJSU football program until the following year, when the NFL organized another association to develop players.[60] The new league was named the World League of American Football (WLAF). In a 1991 article entitled "Mexican Gridders in World Adventure," the World League's opening day was recalled as anything but auspicious:

> The World League of American Football (WLAF) kicked off its premier season on March 23, 1991. It was an unspectacular beginning due to new league jitters and organizational problems. Some of the teams did not have front offices and for others, bus

transportation was late or never materialized. In Europe, the Americans were larger than the rooms they were supposed to occupy. In short, the league's season start was an adventure for its owners, coaches and players.[61]

In addition to the six U.S.-based clubs,[62] there were teams in Montreal, Frankfurt, Barcelona, and London.[63] In the league's initial lottery, Diaz-Infante was drafted in the third round (24th offensive lineman overall) by the Frankfurt Galaxy.[64] He became a ten-game starter on the Galaxy team for two seasons and was used primarily as a center and long snapper on special teams.[65] In two seasons, the Galaxy recorded 10 wins and 10 losses in league play before the WLAF suspended football operations in 1992 (and returned under a new structure in 1995).[66]

Less than a year later, Diaz-Infante continued his search for another opportunity in the NFL. In 1993, he attended the San Francisco 49ers' camp, hoping to sign as a free agent. He was released prior to the start of the regular season. Nonetheless, he continued his search and found an opportunity in Sacramento as the CFL sought to expand into the United States. The CFL chose Sacramento as their first south of the border franchise. They became the Sacramento Gold Miners, who inherited staff, stadium, and much of the roster from the Sacramento Surge of the defunct WLAF.[67] Once again, opportunity knocked on Diaz-Infante's door; he signed with the club in September of 1993 and became the starting left offensive guard.[68] In their initial season, the Gold Miners finished 6–12, a last-place finish in the Western Division. In 1994 they improved to 9–8–1 and a 5th-place finish, one win short of the playoffs. That season introduced three new U.S. teams: the Las Vegas Posse, Shreveport Pirates, and Baltimore Stallions. However, the Canadian football adventure did not last beyond 1995. The Sacramento Gold Miners moved to San Antonio to become the Texans, who played a single season before the CFL exited the United States market.[69]

At this point in his career, Diaz-Infante had already played in the NFL plus two seasons in the WLAF and two in the CFL. His experiences helped bring him to the attention of the Denver Broncos, who acquired his services as a backup offensive lineman. The timing of his acquisition could not have been more fortuitous, as the Broncos posted 13 wins in 1996, 12 in 1997, and 14 in 1998. This run included Super Bowl Championships in 1997 and 1998.[70] David Diaz-Infante's Denver Broncos career lasted three seasons (1996–1998), where he started nine games and played a total of 35 games.[71]

After being let go by Denver, there remained two other stops on this Latino's football journey. He received an offer from the Philadelphia Eagles in 1999 and signed on as a free agent, once again serving as a backup offensive lineman. He played in 15 games as the Eagles posted a 5–11 mark.[72] During his single season with the Eagles, *Philadelphia Daily News* sports writer Kevin Mulligan wrote an article entitled "Against All Odds: Eagles Guard Diaz-Infante Hopeful His Hard-earned Spot in the NFL Sets an Example for Youth in Latino Communities." The title of the article itself is a meaningful tribute to Diaz-Infante's determination to overcome the perceptions and obstacles he had to deal with as a Mexican American professional athlete.73

The final stop on Diaz-Infante's on-field timeline was with the eXtreme Football League (XFL).74 The league was comprised of eight teams: Birmingham Thunderbolts, Chicago Enforcers, New York/New Jersey Hitmen, Orlando Rage, Las Vegas Outlaws, Los Angeles Extreme, Memphis Maniax, and San Francisco Demons.75 The league presented a new style of football that only lasted a single, unimpressive season that attracted a small percentage of the national TV audience along with poor attendance at games. The season actually began on February 3, 2001 and concluded on April 21. The Outlaws acquired Diaz-Infante from the San Francisco Demons for offensive tackle Harvey Goins.76 He was the starting center for the Outlaws, who posted a 4–6 mark, last in the XFL's Western Division. After the league's demise, Diaz-Infante re-signed with the Denver Broncos as a backup guard and center. According to team records, he rejoined the team to bolster the Broncos' offensive line and played his last season in professional football. According to several Denver coaches, Diaz-Infante is remembered as one of the sport's most persistent and reliable performers.77

After a diverse football playing career, Diaz-Infante became a football analyst and assistant coach. He worked collegiate football games with FSN and ESPN and hosted a radio talk show in Denver.78 In 2013, he returned to the NFL as an offensive line coach with the Arizona Cardinals, and later the New York Jets. To date, Diaz-Infante and family reside in Parker, Colorado.79

David Diaz-Infante, 1987 (courtesy New York Jets).

Antonio Ramiro "Tony" Romo

San Antonio Express-News sportswriter David Flores wrote an insightful feature story on Dallas Cowboys quarterback Tony Romo's family, in particular about his grandparents, whose pride in their *nieto* (grandson) was fiercely emotional and unshakable. The reason for the pride was described as the *sueno* (dream) of his success and the family's gratitude for a successful outcome of their difficult times in Mexico and their struggles when they first arrived in the United States. Flores noted, "That a Mexican immigrant would someday have a grandson quarterbacking one of the most glamorous teams in pro sports, his grandparents, Ramiro Sr. and Felicita Romo, said, is a testament to the power of the American dream."[80] Additionally, the David Flores' story sketched three generations of Romo's family migration into the United States, their hopes and dreams, and the values of their cultural identity. The young Romo was taught to be careful with the temptations of prestige and money, and importantly, to be proud of being Hispanic.[81] Romo emerged as an exceptional multi-sport athlete, who learned and mastered the sport of football at each level.

The Antonio Ramiro "Tony" Romo story began with the journey of his grandparents from Musquiz, Coahuila, Mexico, and Robstown, Texas, as well as his parents' journeys within the United States. Ramiro Jr. and Judy met and married in Burlington, Wisconsin, but moved to San Diego, where he was stationed in the U.S. Navy. During this period in the military, their son, Antonio Ramiro Romo, was born in San Diego on April 21, 1980. He was the youngest of three children, with two sisters. The family remained in San Diego until Ramiro Jr. was discharged from the Navy in 1982 and returned home to Burlington.[82]

Back in Wisconsin, Tony attended the local high school, where he participated in sports and became a standout athlete in football, basketball, and golf.[83] According to internet sources, Tony Romo began his sophomore season (1996) with a slight injury that did not interfere with his quarterback duties. He quickly recovered and for the next two seasons guided the Cougars to a 16–3 mark, including the 1997 State Championship. He was twice named to the All-State Football Team.[84]

Tony Romo graduated in 1998 and investigated his opportunities for higher education and a chance to play collegiate football. Division I scouts overlooked his abilities, and he attended nearby Eastern Illinois University in Charleston, where he majored in communications. On the Panthers, he spent his first year (1999) learning the offense and earned playing time his sophomore year. EIU experienced a fine season and posted an 8–4 record (6–1 in Ohio Valley Conference play). In the 2000 NCAA I-AA playoffs Romo passed for 212 yards and two touchdowns in a losing effort (45–13) against the top-ranked Montana Grizzlies.⁸⁵ In the 2001 season, Romo quarterbacked the team to their first outright Ohio Valley Conference championship with a 9–2 season (6–0 in conference). However, victory in the NCAA I-AA playoffs eluded the Panthers once again, losing to Northern Iowa, 49–43.⁸⁶ Romo's senior year was productive, and his team once again made it to NCAA I-AA post-season play. Eastern lost to Western Illinois, 48–9.

Statistically, Romo concluded his collegiate career at Eastern Illinois in grand fashion with season and career records in passing attempts, yardage, and completions. His three-year totals included 7,816 passing yards and 82 touchdowns. He surpassed the 300-yard passing mark eight times in his Panthers career.⁸⁷ Romo was named Ohio Valley Conference Player of the Year three times (2000–2002), consensus All-American his senior year, and received the prestigious Walter Payton Award in 2002 (as most outstanding offensive player in NCAA I-AA).⁸⁸ His experiences at Eastern Illinois provided Romo with a hope that he would be able to move on to the NFL.

Tony Romo was overlooked and went undrafted, but it wasn't a long wait before he received a call from the Cowboys, who signed him as a rookie free agent in 2003.⁸⁹ When Romo signed on with Dallas in 2003, he joined an elite fraternity of Latino professional quarterbacks dating back to 1959. The first was Joe (Garcia) Kapp, who began that year with the Calgary Stampeders of the CFL⁹⁰; he was followed in 1960 by the Oakland Raiders' Tom Flores; in 1962 Chon Gallegos, also with the Silver and Black; in 1964, the San Francisco 49ers took George Mira; and in 1971, the New England Patriots took Jim Plunkett.⁹¹ Thus, Tony Romo began his career as a free-agent backup and holder for the Cowboys. Over the next few years, his place on the depth chart changed dramatically.

In 2003, Quincy Carter was the starting quarterback for "America's Team," while Tim Hasselbeck was his backup. The Cowboys enjoyed a successful season but lost in the NFC wildcard playoffs.⁹² In 2004, just prior to the start of the season, Dallas released Carter due to violations of the league's drug policies and signed veteran Vinny Testaverde to be their starter. Testaverde's backup was Drew Henson but the two struggled and the Cowboys posted a 6–10 record. The quarterback shuffle continued into the off-season, and Dallas signed former Buffalo Bills signal caller Drew Bledsoe. Bledsoe played the entire 2005 season with Drew Henson as the backup, while Romo stood on the sidelines holding the clipboard. The Cowboys finished 9–7 and did not make the playoffs.⁹³

In 2006, Bledsoe lasted six games and was replaced by Romo. The opportunity came after halftime in a game against the Giants. The hope was that the youngster would stabilize the Dallas offense. Romeo threw two touchdown passes in the fourth quarter and ran for a two-point conversion to make the final score a more respectable 36–22 victory for the New Yorkers.⁹⁴ In the next game against Carolina, Romo earned the first regular season start of his career. The Cowboys responded well and defeated the Panthers, 35–14. In that contest, Romo passed for 270 yards, a touchdown, and an interception. Romo started the rest of the year, and the Cowboys managed to return to the playoffs. They played the Seattle Seahawks in the NFC wildcard game but lost, 21–20.[95] After the 2006 season, Tony Romo was named to the Pro Bowl.

For the next ten years (2007–2016), Tony Romo led the team through good and not-so-good seasons. He produced four winning campaigns, three NFC East Division titles and four post-season appearances, played in four Pro Bowls, and sustained four major injuries—one being career-ending. In 2007, Romo and the Cowboys were magnificent, finishing with a 13–3 record; but they lost in the divisional round to the New York Giants.[96] That year, Romo earned a second trip to Honolulu. In 2008, he broke a finger early in the season but returned after a few games to lead an injured Dallas squad to a 9–7 record, but not a playoff appearance. In 2009, injuries continued to plague the Cowboys. Their practice facility collapsed during a workout and injured a dozen players and coaches. However, they rebounded from their misfortune to post an 11–5 record to clinch the NFC East crown. Regrettably, the Cowboys lost in the divisional round to the Minnesota Vikings, though Romo went to the Pro Bowl for a third time. The next four seasons (2010–2013) were a transitional time for the Cowboys. The start of the 2010 season began with the firing of Coach Wade Phillips, who was replaced by Jason Garrett. The team finished 6–10. On October 25, 2010, Romo fractured his left collarbone against the Giants, and he went on injured reserve in December.[97]

Tony Romo, 2006 (courtesy Dallas Cowboys/James D. Smith).

In each of those three seasons, the Cowboys posted identical 8–8 records and did not participate in the post-season. In 2011, Romo suffered a rib injury that sidelined him temporarily, and he was replaced by Jon Kitna. The 2012 season was more of the same although Romo started all 16 games, threw for a club-record 4,903 passing yards, and tied the touchdown mark with 28. In 2013, Romo started 15 games but missed the final contest with a back injury. In a game against the Green Bay Packers, Romo notched his 44th career 300+-yards passing game.⁹⁸ During that off-season, he underwent back surgery.

In 2014, Romo experienced a banner statistical year as he improved on existing club records and set new ones in: pass attempts, completion percentage, passing yards, and career starts. Of particular note was his performance of 218 passing yards against the Indianapolis Colts that gave him 32,971 career yards to top Troy Aikman as the club's all-time passing leader.⁹⁹ The Cowboys posted a 12-4 record and won the NFC East Division title. In the wildcard game, they beat Detroit, 24–20. However, in the divisional round, they stumbled and lost to the Green Bay Packers, 26–21. Romo earned his fourth Pro Bowl appearance and garnered AP second team All-Pro honors.¹⁰⁰

The 2015 season was Romo's 13th in the NFL. *Texas Monthly* writer Michael J. Mooney addressed the Cowboys' 2015–2016 seasons as a hope for Tony Romo and the Cowboys to become Super Bowl contenders:

> Consider the 2015 campaign: with him the Cowboys were 3–1 and looked like Super Bowl contenders; without him, the Cowboys were 1–11 and floundered toward the worst record in the league. The team has plenty of weapons, but everything starts and stops with Romo.¹⁰¹

Mooney's contention was the hope Romo symbolized to lead the Cowboys out of their troubled times and, ultimately, to the Super Bowl. Unfortunately, the 2015 season was riddled with injuries and poor performances that dashed those hopes. The season began with two victories but changed as Tony Romo was injured and replaced by his backup—Brandon Weeden, who started but was unsuccessful in three starts. In turn, Matt Cassel replaced Weeden but did not fare any better. After a few more contests, Romo returned briefly and posted a win, but re-injured the collarbone and was out for the season. Following Romo's departure, backup quarterback Kellen Moore took over. The Cowboys finished with a 4–12 mark, the team's worst since 1989.¹⁰²

Romo's final season (2016) offered some hope due to his recovery, and he was listed as the starting quarterback. The backups were rookie Dak Prescott and veteran Kellen Moore. In preseason action, Romo sustained another back injury. Initially, it was reported as not serious, but in actuality this ended his career. A *Sports Illustrated* internet article described the situation:

> Romo left the game clutching his back after being sacked by Seahawks defensive end Cliff Avril on his third play from scrimmage. Romo scrambled outside the pocket to his left and was chased down, landing awkwardly and hunching forward as he fell. He walked off under his own power and was examined at length by training staff. He would not return to the game as a precaution and coaches' decision.¹⁰³

He was done for the majority of the schedule, and rookie quarterback Dak Prescott replaced him to lead the Cowboys to a 13–3 record. However, Romo was not completely done, and the Cowboys honored him later in the season. He suited up for one last time for the Baltimore Ravens game as a backup to conclude his last season.

Romo's legacy as an undrafted Mexican American is exceptional although it did not include a Super Bowl triumph. He did, however, serve as the Cowboys' primary starting quarterback from 2006 to 2015. Recently, *Texas Monthly* writer Michael J. Mooney described part of Tony Romo's history with the Cowboys, by comparing him to the three most storied quarterbacks in Dallas' illustrious history:

> Don Meredith, Roger Staubach and Troy Aikman…. In the sixties, Meredith brought the young franchise to two consecutive NFL Championship games…. Staubach, the Navy veteran and Heisman Trophy winner, helped lead the team to five Super Bowl appearances—and two wins—in the seventies. And Aikman, of course, took the Cowboys to three Super Bowl wins in four years. Over time, that role—quarterback of the Dallas Cowboys—evolved into perhaps the most iconic position in all of sports.[104]

As the Cowboys' quarterback for many years, Romo left his imprint upon the team. He played competitively and made plays when the odds were against him. He was constantly driven to succeed and, barring injuries, was a clutch player. Romo produced an impressive set of numbers that are of historic caliber. For example, in the Cowboys' listings of "All-Time Passing Leaders," Romo is ranked ahead of Staubach, White, Aikman, and Meredith.[105] Other team marks include most touchdowns and passing yards. Romo also broke records in the following categories: games with at least 3 touchdowns passes—40, previously held by Danny White (20); games with at least 300 yards passing–46, previously held by Troy Aikman (13); lowest career interception percentage—2.6 percent, previously held by Troy Aikman (3.0 percent); and most fourth quarter comebacks/game-winning drives—28, previously held by Roger Staubach (23).[106] The above information is just a sample of the numbers Antonio Ramiro "Tony" Romo accumulated throughout his 14-year career.

Romo retired from the NFL on April 4, 2017, and put his EIU training to work by pursuing a broadcasting career with CBS Sports. Currently, he is the lead color analyst on the network's NFL telecasts. Here he is presenting yet another positive role model for Latinos/as, along the lines of what Jessica Mendoza is doing for MLB broadcasts at ESPN. Tony Romo married the former Candice Crawford and they have two sons, Hawkins and Rivers.

Ronald Eugene "Ron" Rivera

Coach Ronald Eugene "Ron" Rivera of the Carolina Panthers is the third Latino head coach in the history of the National Football League (NFL). The two previous coaches were Thomas Jesse Fears of the New Orleans Saints, 1967–1970, and the California Sun of the World Football League (WFL), 1974–1975, and Thomas Raymond Flores of the Oakland Raiders, 1979–1980, Los Angeles Raiders, 1981–1988, and Seattle Seahawks, 1992–1994.

All three Latino coaches were former NFL players who also served as assistant coaches prior to their head coaching responsibilities. Each of the Latinos experienced very successful playing careers that elevated them into the coaching ranks. Fears was a member of the Los Angeles Rams' 1951 NFL Championship team and a Pro Football Hall of Fame inductee as a player. Flores earned Super Bowl rings as a player and assistant coach and coached two Super Bowl Championship teams. The most recent member of this fraternity, Ron Rivera, was a Super Bowl XX Champion as a Bears player in 1985, participated in Super Bowl XLI as an assistant coach with Chicago in 2006, and coached the Carolina Panthers to Super Bowl L in 2015. The information is little known to many aficionados, but an important part of the Latino American sports history. Significantly, the focus of the story is Carolina Panthers head coach Ronald Eugene "Ron" Rivera and his journey from the fields of the Salinas Valley to his current responsibilities.

In 2017, Rivera was interviewed by CNN Money reporter Ahiza Garcia about his personal history and the issue of race.[107] Asked if he had experienced any racism in the NFL, he replied he had not and added he had not experienced any racism until the family returned to the United States (from his father's time stationed overseas). One incident occurred in the Salinas Valley of California as his family worked in the fields. He was in the eighth grade and was called "wetback" by an unnamed person. He recalled getting into a fight over the incident, and this instance impacted the rest of his life. The next time racist remarks were made about him occurred when Rivera was a student and football player at that bastion of tolerance, Berkeley. There the comments came from a white teammate. Rivera commented, "I was one of the best players on my team, and seriously bothered by the racist comments because I was treated that way and looked at that way."[108]

These were indeed hurtful comments that had no justification. However, the young Rivera endured and survived the experience for no other reason than family support and values he learned and accepted. The family values were articulated clearly when the interviewer asked, "As the only Hispanic coach in the league, a lot of people within the Hispanic community look up to you…. How do you feel about that?" He replied,

> I feel I have to succeed to the highest level I can…. I am at that level now. Once I realized this is what I wanted … to be the best…. I wanted to reach the pinnacle of what I do, and I have been … and, I take from this … and I hope people can take from this … you can be whatever you want … it's up to you…. You have to put in the work because at the end of the day … all you need is the opportunity.[109]

In other words, the race issue that pertained to labels and the contempt which confronted Rivera did not affect his drive to succeed, his personal/family values, his work ethic, and his commitment to take full advantage of opportunities.

His story begins in Fort Ord, California. Ronald Eugene "Ron" Rivera is one of four sons of Eugenio and Dolores Rivera. His father was a farmer in Puerto Rico who left the island to pursue a military career and attained the rank of a commissioned officer in the United States Army. While stationed at Fort Ord, Eugenio Rivera met Dolores. Her journey to the United States began in Mexico, continued into Colorado as a farmworker, and eventually reached the Salinas Valley. According to Ron, the couple met at a United Service Organization (USO) event and married shortly thereafter.[110] Their third son, Ronald was born on January 7, 1962, and raised, like his brothers, in a military environment. Due to his father's service, the family moved often, and the Rivera children were initially educated at military bases in Germany, Panama, Washington, D.C., and Maryland. When they returned to the Golden State, they settled in Seaside, where Rivera attended the local public school. His time with the Spartans provided him the opportunity to play and learn the sport of football.[111] His play on the gridiron earned Rivera a scholarship with the Golden Bears. According to the *1991 Pacific-10 Conference Media Guide*, Rivera was a consensus All American; PAC-10 Player of the Year on Defense; and First Team All-Conference Linebacker in 1983.[112] He finished his career at California as the school's all-time leader in sacks with 22 and tackles with 336. In his senior year, he established the team's single-season record for sacks with 13 and tackles for loss with 26.5.[113] Shortly after his collegiate career ended, Rivera was honored with induction into his alma mater's Hall of Fame in 1994; in 2003, he was inducted into the College Football Hall of Fame.[114]

With his collegiate career concluded, Rivera looked forward to hearing from the NFL. He was not disappointed and was selected in the second round in 1984 by the Chicago Bears. He was the 44th pick overall in the draft, and when the training camp opened, he wasted no time adjusting to the Bears' aggressive style of football. During his rookie season, Rivera played outside linebacker and saw regular action in the last 15 games.[115] It was a grand NFL start for Rivera, who constantly improved on the Bears' defense, playing alongside and learning from future Pro Football Hall of Famers such as Mike Singletary, Dan Hampton, and Richard Dent. In his remaining eight seasons with the Bears, Rivera appeared in 149 games with 62 starts and posted 392 tackles, 7.5 sacks, 5 forced fumbles, 4 fumble recoveries, 9 interceptions, and 15 passes defended. His career also included a Super Bowl XX Championship victory over the New England Patriots, 45–10, six NFC Central Division Championships,[116] and, for his community service, the Chicago Bears' 1989 Ed Block Courage Award and the team's Man of the Year in 1988.[117] With his

5. Latinos on the Gridiron from Coast to Coast, 1991–2018

Ron Rivera looming over a flattened opponent, 1984 (courtesy Cal Athletics).

playing days over, Rivera went into sports broadcasting, working with WGN and Sports Channel Chicago to cover both Bears and collegiate games between 1993 and 1996. According to various accounts, Rivera pursued the possibility of coaching during his years on the air. He found an opportunity with the Bears but required a little help from former teammate Walter Payton, who served as a member of the Bears' Board of Directors and supported Rivera's assignment to the Bears' staff in 1997.[118] He became the Bears' defensive quality control coach for two years, 1997–1998.

Thus began a 14-year assistant coaching career. After his time with the Bears, Rivera moved on to the following teams: Philadelphia Eagles (1999–2003), Chicago Bears (2004–2006), and San Diego Chargers (2007–2010). In Philadelphia, Rivera was initially the Eagles' linebackers coach and later became the defensive coordinator. In each of his responsibilities, the team's defenses flourished. During his time in Philadelphia, the Eagles advanced to play in the NFC Championship games in each of the three seasons in which their defense finished second in the league in scoring defense. During the 2001 season, the Eagles' defense also held all of their opponents to fewer than 21 points.[119]

After the 2003 season at Philadelphia, Rivera returned to the Chicago Bears as defensive coordinator. The Bears were in transition in 2004 but improved the next season. The 2005 Bears went 11–5 to make it to the playoffs. In the process, Rivera's defense produced nine more takeaways and 17 more sacks than the previous year, and tallied six defensive touchdowns. But the team was unsuccessful in the divisional playoff game against the Arizona Cardinals. In 2006, the Bears won 13 games and advanced to the playoffs to capture the NFC crown, but were unsuccessful in Super Bowl XLI, losing to the Payton Manning–led Indianapolis Colts, 29–17.[120]

Although Rivera looked forward to continuing his coaching tenure with the Bears, other teams were interested in his services. On February 19, 2007, the San Diego Chargers hired Rivera as their inside linebackers coach. He coached the linebackers his first season and part of the next season until October 2008, when the Chargers released Ted Cottrell and promoted Rivera to defensive coordinator.[121] In his new responsibility, he worked with the Chargers through 2010. Under his leadership, the defense improved markedly in the last eight games of 2008: the Chargers intercepted nine passes, yielded only 229.9 pass yards per game, and gave up only 11 touchdowns.[122] In the 2009–2010 campaigns, San Diego's defense continued their improvement and finished in the top five in 11 different defensive categories; the Chargers ranked 16th in total defense and 11th against the pass. In four seasons with the Chargers, Rivera's coaching impacted their defense and overall performance as they won two AFC West Division titles and made the playoffs on three occasions.[123]

During his successful tenure as an assistant coach, Rivera did not go unnoticed. The Arizona Cardinals, Pittsburgh Steelers, Dallas Cowboys, and the San Diego Chargers expressed interest in Rivera as a potential head coach.[124] However, it was the last-place Carolina Panthers who moved him up to the field general position. On January 11, 2011, the organization named Rivera the fourth head coach in team history.[125] At the time, football internet sources cited Rivera's military background as a positive aspect of his coaching style. His player and assistant coaching experience, as well as his post-season experience, were valuable attributes that included 19 playoff games, nine conference championships and three Super Bowls on his resume.[126] In 2011, Coach Rivera's Panthers managed a 6–10 record. Although his first-season record does not reflect a positive start, *The Football Outsiders*, an independent source, summarized the season as improved and credited the Panthers with the biggest year-to-year offensive enhancement in their history.[127]

For the next three seasons (2012–2014), Rivera and the Panthers experienced modest success. They finished the 2012 season with a record of 7–9. The defense had improved and showed their determination by winning five of their last six games. However, the Panthers' home office was not satisfied with Rivera's efforts and considered the possibility of firing him at the end of the season.[128] Although the idea to fire a coach after only two years seemed harsh and unwarranted, it later became apparent that the perceived threat was nothing more than a motivator for Coach Rivera to change his approach.

In 2013, Rivera displayed a more aggressive approached in his leadership role and play-calling. The Panthers posted a 12–4 record. They won the NFC South title and made it to the playoffs for the first time since 2008.[129] At season's end, Rivera was honored as the 2013 Associated Press (AP) NFL Coach of the Year.[130] Rivera's aggressive approach made a difference and impacted the team, but the immediate improvement and success did not continue into the next season.

The 2014 season was a letdown. The Panthers posted a 7–8–1 record. But there is no specific documentation that specifies the reason(s) for the letdown, or any mention of Ron Rivera's status. However, the fact that they won the final four regular season games to clinch the NFC South title indicates the team regained the necessary momentum that would benefit them the next season.[131] In 2015, Rivera and the Panthers continued their improvement from the precious season and posted a 15–1 record, the best season record in the history of the franchise. They won the NFC Conference Championship and played the Denver Broncos in Super Bowl L (50). It was a grand accomplishment for the Panthers that unfortunately ended with a loss to the Broncos, 24–10. However, the defeat did not exclude Coach Rivera from being honored once again as the 2015 Associated Press (AP) NFL Coach of the Year.[132] The 2016 and 2017 seasons produced a mixed bag as the Panthers went 16–16. They did not make the playoffs in 2016. In 2017, Carolina made the playoffs but lost to the New Orleans Saints; nonetheless, their run defense ranked as the third-best in the NFL.[133]

Coach Ron Rivera's wife, Stephanie, is of Filipino ancestry, a former basketball player at California and also former assistant coach with the Washington Mystics of the Women's National Basketball Association (WNBA). She also coached at Trinity International University (Deerfield, Illinois) and with the Chicago Condors of the American Basketball Association. The couple has two children, Christopher and Courtney.

Jeffrey Jason "Jeff" Garcia

The Jeffrey Jason "Jeff" Garcia football story began in the setting of a strong and closely-knit family that experienced many personal losses but survived because they loved and supported each other. From this experience, Jeff Garcia emerged a determined young man who, despite the obstacles encountered, persevered to succeed in both life and in football.

Jeff Garcia was born on February 24, 1970, in Gilroy, California, a town known as the garlic capital of the world. His father, Bob Garcia, is of Mexican ancestry, and his mother, Linda Elder, of Irish descent. He was the third of seven children who worked as farmworkers in the nearby farm fields. In 1999,

Los Angeles Times sportswriter Paul Gutierrez quoted Jeff Garcia about his family background:

> Settling in the Central California farming town of Gilroy, the Garcias quickly found work and established themselves. My dad grew up in the fields, picking cucumbers, strawberries ... and really my grandmother wanted my dad to be in the fields rather than going to school and trying to further his education. But he pressed on and fell in love with sports.... Obviously, my mom's side, the Irish side had a little more influence, as far as my looks go. But I'm definitely proud of my heritage, having the Latino side. It's definitely something I want to represent proudly.[134]

His father was also a former athletic director and football coach at Gavilan Community College, which Garcia attended after high school. Also in the family are his paternal grandparents, who hailed from San Juan de Los Lagos, Jalisco.[135] On the Irish side of the family there was his maternal grandfather, Maurice "Red" Elder, a well-known collegiate football player in the 1940s at Kansas State University.[136]

The Garcia family was very close and hard-working; however, several tragedies took a toll upon them. Twin sisters died before Jeff's birth. Later, his younger brother, Jason, drowned on a camping trip in 1977, and 14 months later, younger sister Kimberly died after falling out of a truck. The loss of a child is an incredible emotional strain, but losing several is almost unimaginable. Jeff Garcia's two surviving sisters, Jene and Melissa, were born after the deaths of their siblings.[137] Although the Garcia family was devastated by their losses, they stayed strong and unified. Many years later, Jeff Garcia was asked to comment about the tragedies. The reporter described Garcia's response, "spoken without tears but with hints of how unimaginable the loss has shaped his life and career."

> I think I'm very conscientious of how precious life is and how quickly life can be taken away from you, especially at times when it can be least expected.... To experience that personally with family tragedies, it's one of those things where I really value where I am today and everything I've been able to achieve.... And I think it's created so much gratification within my family and so much satisfaction within myself.[138]

Sportswriter Jere Longman recorded Gavilan College football coach John Lango's commentary about Garcia's character:

> Jeff has said that sport is really what kept the family together after all this tragedy.... I think that's what's driving him ... that and his fiery desire. People have said, the family will never overcome this, or he's not big enough to play Division I.... There has always been a negative thing that he has used as a positive thing.[139]

For Garcia, it was the very essence of family love and togetherness that helped them through the unexpected losses. Sports helped him to deal with his bereavement.[140] With the Gilroy High School Mustangs, he played football and basketball. He lettered in both sports, and in his senior year was selected to play in the Charlie Wedemeyer All-Star Football Game.[141] He played defensive back in high school before switching to quarterback in college.

Unfortunately, there were no college offers after graduation. He was unsigned by any major college but was not deterred and attended Gavilan Community College (1988–1989), where he began the quarterback phase of his career. His father, Bob, was a coach with the Rams. In 1989, his second year at Gavilan, Jeff Garcia became the starting quarterback. He experienced a very good statistical season that included 2,038 passing yards and 18 touchdowns, plus 584 rushing yards for another four touchdowns. It was a superlative junior college career that netted him a Junior College Honorable Mention All-America designation.[142] In 1990, he enrolled and walked on to the campus of San Jose State University, and he made the Spartans' football team. He was red-shirted his first year due to his inexperience. However, for the remainder of his career (1990–1993) at SJSU, Garcia played at a high level. According to both the *San Jose State University Sports Fact Sheet* and the *Philadelphia Eagles 2006 Media Guide*:

> Garcia was a three-year starter for the Spartans who was ranked 15th in the Nation in 1992 in total offense; and was a Big Western Conference Offensive Player of the Week several times in the season. Career-wise he completed 504 passes for 6,545 yards and 48 touchdowns. He was ranked first in San Jose State University history with 7,274 yards total offense, and earned UPI All-America honors as a junior.[143]

Garcia played in the 69th Annual East-West Shrine All-Star game, held on January 15, 1994. In the contest, he alternated at quarterback with Doug Nussmeir from the University of Idaho. The game was lopsided until the fourth quarter, when Garcia guided an incredible comeback. *The Deseret News* summed up the West's fourth-quarter, frantic drive to victory:

> San Jose State quarterback Jeff Garcia threw three fourth-quarter touchdown passes and ran for the decisive two-point conversion, rallying the West to a 29–28 victory Saturday in the East-West Shrine Game…. The East led 28–7 at the end of three quarters,

Jeff Garcia, 1999 (photographs by Ron Fried).

but the West narrowed the gap with the two fourth quarter touchdown passes by Garcia.... The West began its climactic march at its own 20 with 2:52 remaining and scored in seven plays. Garcia threw 8 yards to Jamal Anderson of Utah for a touchdown and then ran up the middle for the winning points. Garcia finished with 22 completions in 32 attempts for 266 yards.[144]

After a successful collegiate career, Jeff Garcia anticipated the opportunity to play in the NFL. Unfortunately, in 1994 he went undrafted. One individual stated, "he was too small for the NFL," while another scout exclaimed, "he wasn't supposed to be in the league at all."[145] Whatever the reasons for being overlooked, Garcia was happy because the Calgary Stampeders of the Canadian Football League contacted and signed him. Thus, Garcia spent the first five years of his professional football career as a back-up and then a starter in the CFL.[146] He began the 1994 season as Calgary's third-stringer behind Doug Flutie and Steve Taylor. He remained in that slot for almost two seasons until Flutie was sidelined with an elbow injury. In his first two games in the CFL, Garcia led the Stampeders to a victory over the Birmingham Barracudas 37–14, completing 26 of 34 passes for 445 yards and two touchdowns,[147] then established a team record with 546 passing yards and six touchdowns against Edmonton. These performances in his first two starts created controversy over who should continue as starter once Flutie returned.[148] The debate lasted the remainder of the 1995 season but intensified when Calgary lost the Grey Cup championship to the Baltimore Stallions, 37–20, with Flutie at the helm. Flutie asked for a release and signed with the Toronto Argonauts.[149]

The next three seasons (1996–1998) with the Stampeders, Garcia guided the team to records of 13-5, 10-8, and 12-6. In 1997, he was awarded the Jeff Nicklin Memorial Trophy as the outstanding player in the Western Division.[150] But the crowning achievement of his career, a CFL championship, came in 1998. On November 22, 1998, the 86th Annual Grey Cup Championship was played in Winnipeg. The weather produced icy conditions and the temperature was just ten degrees as Calgary and Hamilton met to determine the championship. The game was primarily a defensive affair that produced only four touchdowns (two per side), and a series of field goals eventually made the difference. Calgary's kicker, Mark McLoughlin, kicked three field goals in the fourth quarter to give the Stampeders the victory over the Tiger-Cats, 26–24. Key plays in the second half included a Garcia rushing touchdown in the third quarter and the 80-yard drive that set up the winning field goal. Garcia was named the Grey Cup's MVP on top of his selection to the CFL All-Star team for the fourth time.[151]

Although Garcia did not continue in the CFL, his tenure in the league was beneficial, as it provided the young Latino quarterback an opportunity to be noticed by the NFL. His efforts were rewarded when 49ers coach Steve Mariucci recruited Garcia and signed him in 1999 as a backup to Steve Young.

5. Latinos on the Gridiron from Coast to Coast, 1991–2018

Interestingly, Garcia's NFL bio page now notes that he was well-suited for the 49ers' offensive scheme as he was quick and elusive, with the ability to avoid the rush and throw on the run.[152]

The 1999 season began with both Jeff Garcia and Steve Stenstrom as backups to Young. However, early into the season against the Arizona Cardinals, the BYU legend suffered a concussion that sidelined him for the rest of the season. Garcia and Stenstrom alternated until Garcia claimed the starter's role.[153] In 2000, Garcia continued as the starting quarterback and set new San Francisco records with 4,278 passing yards and 31 touchdowns. Although the team's record was only 6–10, Garcia earned his first Pro Bowl selection.[154] In 2001, the team improved to a 12–4 mark, with Garcia netting 32 touchdowns. The 49ers made it to post-season play but lost to Green Bay, 25–15, in the first round.[155]

In his fourth year (2002) with the 49ers, Garcia experienced a statistical decline, but the team played well enough to get into the playoffs. They won the NFC West and played the New York Giants in the NFC Divisional game on January 5, 2003. The 49ers mounted an inspired comeback after the first three quarters of the game belonged to the Giants. In the fourth quarter, Garcia and the 49ers scored 25 unanswered points to beat the Giants, 39–38. Their season ended the next week in a 31–6 loss to the Tampa Bay Buccaneers.[156] The 2003 season was Garcia's final year in San Francisco. It was a disappointing campaign (7–9) due to many disruptive factors off the field that resulted, in part, from that loss to the Buccaneers, and numerous coaching and player moves. Among those changes was Garcia's release by the new coach, Dennis Erickson. Nonetheless, it was another valuable experience for Garcia, who set a few passing records and played in three Pro Bowls (2000–2002) The unfortunate and worst part of Garcia's 49ers experience was the unprofessional behavior and commentary by a fellow teammate and wide receiver who was commonly known for his disrespectful behavior and demeanor. Garcia responded to his unfounded outbursts intelligently and moved on with hopes to play elsewhere in the NFL.[157] For the next three seasons (2004–2006), Garcia signed and played a single season each with Cleveland, Detroit, and Philadelphia.

As the Browns' quarterback, Garcia struggled with injuries and was unable to turn Cleveland into a successful team. With Detroit, he broke his fibula in a pre-season game, and other injuries prevented him from any significant production. The Lions did not offer a new contract. Still confident he could regain his form, Garcia met with the Eagles, who signed him to a one-year contract as the primary backup to Donovan McNabb. McNabb was injured on November 19, 2006, and that made Garcia the starter. For the rest of the season, the re-energized signal caller led the Eagles to five consecutive victories and the NFC East crown. In the playoffs, the Eagles beat the New York Giants but lost to the New Orleans Saints.[158] As a tribute to Garcia's five-game winning streak, he made the front cover of *Sports Illustrated*, in which Paul Zimmerman summarized the coach's decision to use Garcia rather than A.J. Feeley, and his assessment of Garcia's two previous seasons. He wrote:

> Instead, they got Jeff Garcia. Poor guy; Cut by the San Francisco 49ers in 2004. His body practically shattered by two years of hard labor in the lead mines of the NFL, Cleveland and Detroit, Garcia was picked up this year by Philly because offensive coordinator Marty Mornhinweg remembered the good days they had shared in San Francisco.[159]

At season's end, Garcia was pleased with his performance, but the Eagles decided not to offer a new contract. Disappointed, he did not have to wait long for an offer and signed with the Tampa Bay Buccaneers as their starting quarterback on March 3, 2007. The Buccaneers had just experienced a 4–12 mark in 2006 and were hopeful Garcia would change their fate. Garcia started 13 games for a Buccaneers team that posted a 9–7 record and qualified for the playoffs by capturing the NFC South. Garcia passed for 2,440 yards, 13 touchdowns, and a rushing score. Tampa Bay played in the wild card game, where they lost to the eventual Super Bowl champion Giants, 24–14.[160] Garcia's performance as a Buccaneer also earned him a fourth Pro Bowl selection. The second season (2008) in the Sunshine State was radically different. Garcia injured his leg again and rotated starting duties with two other quarterbacks— Brian Griese and Luke McCown. Although Garcia did have some success, the uncertainty of the quarterback situation, and a reported tension between Garcia and head coach Jon Gruden over his injury, did not help matters. The Buccaneers posted another 9–7 record. Garcia passed for 2,712 yards and 12 scores. In the end, Tampa did not re-sign him.[161] Nonetheless, the Jeff Garcia football journey continued with four more stops: Oakland, Philadelphia, Omaha, and Houston.

The four-year sojourn began with the Oakland Raiders. He was signed to a single-year contract that lasted only five months. The expected backup role to quarterback JaMarcus Russell ended during the team's final cuts on September 5. Nine days later, Garcia heard from the Eagles, who offered a one-year contract to once again backup McNabb. That deal was good for only 16 days as former quarterback Michael Vick returned to Philadelphia from his suspension. Garcia was released on September 29, 2009.[162]

At this point in his career, Garcia had played for or was associated with one CFL and six NFL teams. The experience was invaluable in many respects, but he was not yet finished with his playing career. The next entry on his resume was the United Football League (UFL). In 2010, he signed with the Omaha Nighthawks as their quarterback and signature player. The UFL played a traditional fall schedule and, according to their brief history, the league occupied a second-tier status in pro football. The teams consisted primarily of former NFL players, but there was no official connection to the

NFL.¹⁶³ In his single season with the Nighthawks, Garcia starred in two games that earned him "Player of the Week" honors. The Nighthawks finished 3–5.¹⁶⁴ At season's end, Garcia left the UFL with no other football prospects evident until late in the 2011 NFL season, when the Houston Texans offered him the opportunity to serve as backup to T.J. Yates. He signed on December 6, 2011,¹⁶⁵ but did not play in any of the remaining games.

This was the end of his professional playing career. With his time on the field over, Garcia expressed a desire to coach with the San Francisco 49ers, but there was no interest. Instead, the Montreal Alouettes of the CFL hired him in August 2014 as an offensive consultant/quarterback coach. The job lasted one year, and Garcia's influence helped to improve Montreal's record to 9-9 and a tie for the East Division title. Next, the Los Angeles Rams¹⁶⁶ hired him in May 2015 as an offensive assistant. That tenure was also limited to a single year.

Thus, the Mexican/Irish quarterback Jeff Garcia, who was too small and wasn't supposed to be in pro football at all, played five years north of the border; was selected a CFL All-Star four times, quarterbacked a team to the Grey Cup Championship and was named the game's MVP. Additionally, he played almost ten years in the NFL, where he was a four-time Pro Bowl selection and quarterbacked three different teams into the playoffs, winning three division titles.¹⁶⁷ Jeff Garcia's resolve and determination carried him far in the sport of football. In retirement, Garcia is now a full-time family man who spends time with his wife, Carmella, two daughters, Presley and Faith, and two sons, Jason and Jax.

Anthony David "Tony" Gonzalez

Sacramento Bee sportswriter Paul Gutierrez wrote an October 24, 2007, feature titled "Not just kickers anymore—More Latino players—at more positions—are finding success." The title addressed the Latino professional football player stereotype of being small in stature. The story addressed their representation in the NFL and the stereotype that Latino athletes are "predestined" to play soccer, baseball, or boxing rather than take to the gridiron. Gutierrez interviewed several Latino professional football players including Joe Kapp, Tony Romo, and Jim Plunkett. One of the first Spanish-surnamed individuals he interviewed was the Kansas City Chiefs' Tony Gonzalez, who had just set an NFL record for the most career touchdowns by a tight end. He commented, "Now that football's become more popular, you're going to start seeing a lot more players of Latin descent. And it's great. I love it…. We're not just kickers anymore. It's across every position."¹⁶⁸

The other Latinos players each commented about the changing participation of Latinos in pro football, as well as their personal experiences in the NFL, both good and bad. The consensus of these subjects indicated that, despite the obstacles they faced, the numbers are on the increase. Toward the end of the article, Gonzalez commented on the idea of current Latino players as role models for the younger athletes of that background. He stated, "To me, you better take it as a responsibility because there are many kids looking up to you."[169] As a follow-up to Gonzalez's statement, Paul Gutierrez noted that this was especially true for Gonzalez because he was not only a role model for youths, he was also on track to become the fifth individual of this background in the Hall of Fame.[170]

The football story of Tony Gonzalez is a tale of extraordinary success and adaptability that began with his brother Chris' guidance in sports, followed by stops at Huntington Beach High, the University of California at Berkeley, the Kansas City Chiefs, and the Atlanta Falcons in the NFL. Each of these experiences became a period of learning and mastery of the sport and eventually culminated in great success.

Anthony David "Tony" Gonzalez was born on February 27, 1976, in Torrance, California. His mother, Judy, raised her sons, Chris and Tony, as a single parent. Concerning the family's ancestry, an internet article titled "Tony Gonzalez Biography" documented very diverse roots on both sides. Tony's father's family hailed from Jamaica and Scotland; his mother's lineage is a mixture of African American, Mexican American, and Native American. The resource also specified the name "Goncals" in his mother's background. When Americanized, this is pronounced "Gonzalez" and attests to a Portuguese lineage.[171] The Tony Gonzalez ancestry is rich, diverse, and proud.[172] The immediate clan lived in Huntington Beach, where Judy's sons grew up and attended the local high school.[173]

The young Tony Gonzalez was not initially interested in sports. Instead he preferred skateboarding, bicycle riding, and beach activities which consumed his early years. Older brother Chris sparked Tony's interest in organized athletics by encouraging him to take to the gridiron. The younger Gonzalez tried Pop Warner football but quit after a few games. Also during this time, Tony was bullied at school, though he eventually confronted his tormentor and overcame his fears. As a result, he gained a new sense of confidence, and this redirected him to sports.[174]

By 1990, Tony Gonzalez was a growing young man when he entered Huntington Beach High. In the process, he tried out for sports and adjusted exceptionally well to basketball and then football. He played hoops whenever he could and ultimately gained national attention as a junior (in 1992), averaging 17.1 points and 9.1 rebounds per game to receive All-USA Honorable Mention by *USA Today*.[175] In football, he soon matched his on-court skills and became a star his junior year on defense with 68 tackles and six sacks.

As a tight end, he caught 38 passes for 800 yards and 7 scores. His athletic successes drew the attention of Division 1 recruiters. In football, Gonzalez was named first team All-American at tight end and linebacker; in basketball he broke the Huntington Beach High School career scoring record, averaging 26 points per game and shooting 65 percent from the field. He was named Orange County's and Sunset Basketball League's Most Valuable Player.[176] An additional honor was being named "Orange County High School Athlete of the Year," an award he shared with Tiger Woods, who attended Western High in nearby Anaheim.[177]

The young Gonzalez was recruited by several colleges but attended the University of California at Berkeley. He arrived on campus in 1994 and spent three years working toward a degree in communications and developing his athletic skills. As a member of the 1994–1995 Bears football teams, he played tight end. Over those campaigns, he hauled in 45 pass receptions for 603 yards and three touchdowns. In his junior and final year in college football (1996), Gonzalez caught 44 passes for 699 yards and five touchdowns, helping the Bears to a 6–6 record and an invitation to play the Naval Academy in the Aloha Bowl on Christmas Day. A January *Sports Illustrated* story summed up Gonzalez's final football game and career at Berkeley, in which he also publicly announced his decision to forgo his senior year to participate in the NFL Draft:

> After finishing the regular football season on November 23, 1996 with 44 receptions for 699 yards—the most yardage in the nation for a tight end—Gonzalez joined the basketball team the next day in Maui for the start of its season. He had scored in the Bears' opening win over Iowa and four other games.... On December 9, the football team called him back to prepare for the December 25th match up with Navy in the Aloha Bowl. On Christmas he caught nine passes for 69 yards in California's loss to Navy. On December 26, Gonzalez arrived in Sunset Beach, California, for a delayed holiday with his family.... Several days later, he held a press conference announcing that he would forgo his final year of college football to make himself eligible for the NFL draft.[178]

After the 1996 football season, Tony Gonzalez turned his attention to basketball. Gonzalez played in 28 games and averaged 6.8 points and 5.4 rebounds per game.[179] The crowning glory of Gonzalez's time at Cal was making it to the "Sweet Sixteen" of the NCAA Basketball Tournament.[180] On April 19–20, 1997, the annual NFL draft took place at the Paramount Theatre in Madison Square Garden in New York. According to sources, Gonzalez was ranked as one of the top tight ends in the draft and was considered a first-round selection.[181] He was the 13th selection of the first round by the Kansas City Chiefs. In actuality, the Chiefs traded up five spots with the Houston Oilers (now the Tennessee Titans) to obtain the selection.[182]

The draft process was complex, but worthwhile for all parties involved.

The draft of Gonzalez was also historically significant to Latino professional football history as he became the first Latino tight end chosen in the first round. The first Latino drafted at this position—Joe Aguirre—was drafted out of St. Mary's College of California by the Washington Redskins in the ninth round in 1941. The second Latino tight end drafted was future Pro Football Hall of Famer Tom Jesse (Valdez) Fears, a tight end out of UCLA who was selected in the 11th round in 1945 by the Cleveland Rams. Tom Fears was the first Mexican-born Latino selected in the NFL draft.[183] The third Latino draftee at this position was Dan Garza, from the University of Oregon. He was selected in 1948, in the 15th round, by the New York Giants. The former Duck also played for the New York Yankees of the rival All-American Football Conference (AAFC).[184] There have been ten Latino tight ends in the NFL since the 1950s.[185]

Gonzalez's rookie season with the Kansas Chiefs was very successful. The team posted a 13–3 record to win the AFC West, but lost to the Denver Broncos in the playoffs. Gonzalez's contributions included 33 pass receptions for 368 yards and two touchdowns. He was named to the NFL All-Rookie Team for 1997.[186] Over the next five seasons (1998–2002), the Chiefs posted just one winning season, in 1999. That year, they finished 9–7, and Gonzalez caught 76 passes for 849 yards and 11 touchdowns. This led to his being named to the first of ten Pro Bowl appearances and the first of five First-Team All-Pro selections.[187] From 2000 to 2002, Gonzalez shined on offense for the struggling Chiefs, who respectively posted 7–9, 6–10, and 8–8 records. In 2003, the Chiefs finished 13–3, and Gonzalez continued to chalk up the receptions, yards, and touchdowns. He was now recognized as the most productive tight end in the NFL.[188] More Pro Bowl and All-Pro team selections followed. In 2004, the Chiefs stumbled to a 7–9 record, but Gonzalez forged on with probably his best statistical season. That year, he caught 102 passes for 1,258 yards and set an NFL record that stood for eight years, until surpassed by Dallas Cowboys tight end Jason Witten in 2012.[189] He played in the Pro Bowl after that season, and again in 2005.

In 2006, Kansas City finished 9–7, and Gonzalez closed in on numerous team records. He broke legendary receiver Otis Taylor's receiving yards and touchdowns marks, and surpassed running back Priest Holmes' figure for total yards from scrimmage.[190] In 2007, he grabbed 99 receptions for 1,172 yards, to break Shannon Sharpe's career touchdown reception record and, in the process, also passed Ozzie Newsome for second place in career receiving yards for a tight end. Gonzalez's record-breaking pace continued into December 23, 2007, as he notched his third 1,000+-yard season. Finally, a week later, he surpassed Shannon Sharpe's all-time receptions number.[191] In his final season with the Chiefs (2008), Gonzalez recorded additional receptions and yardage to become the NFL's all-time leader in receiving yards for a tight end. As in previous seasons, he was named to the Pro Bowl and honored as a First Team All-Pro selection.[192] He helped re-define the tight end position, proving it to be a highly effective weapon in a team's offensive arsenal, and was recognized for his style of play and results. However, at the end of that year, Gonzalez requested a trade, and he was shipped to the Atlanta Falcons.[193]

As a Falcon, Gonzalez played five more productive and record-breaking seasons (2009–2013). In three of these campaigns, the team recorded ten-plus wins and reached post-season play. In his first game with Atlanta, Gonzalez achieved another milestone in his receiving career. His first pass reception moved him onto the list of players in the history of the NFL to reach the 11,000 receiving yards milestone.[194] In 2010, he notched his 1,000th career reception as Atlanta won the NFC South. In 2011, the Falcons posted a third consecutive winning season. They finished 10–6 and lost in the wild card game. As usual, Gonzalez returned to the Pro Bowl.[195] The 2012 season set the stage for another Gonzalez career landmark; he achieved his 100th career touchdown reception and complemented that record with 93 receptions, 930 yards, and eight touchdowns. The Falcons enjoyed another great year that enabled them to the play for the NFC Conference Championship, where they fell short of going to the Super Bowl. Nonetheless, and this sounds like a broken record, Gonzalez gathered post-season honors that included another First Team All-Pro and Pro Bowl selection.[196]

The 2013 season was Gonzalez's final year on the professional gridiron. He finished in grand style with 83 receptions for 859 yards and eight touchdowns, in spite of the team's 4–12 season. On December 29, 2013, *New York Times* reporter Ray Glier wrote a salutatory and complimentary farewell to Gonzalez's success in perfecting the tight position as an offensive weapon, and his legacy of breaking records. He wrote:

> The 6-foot-5 Gonzalez was agile and quick, and relatively fast. He started in Kansas City and continued in Atlanta in 2009. He was split wide, allowed to stand up and motor into the secondary, catch passes out of the backfield, and worry a defense down the middle of the field.... Gonzalez finished his career with 1,325 receptions, the most ever by a tight end and second-most catches on the career list, behind Jerry Rice (1,549).... It is unlikely that no one will soon take the position to the heights Gonzalez took it. He caught passes for 15,127 yards in his career and had 111 touchdown receptions.... He missed only two games in 17 seasons.[197]

At the end of the article, Glier described Gonzalez's exit from the field after the final game:

> As he walked off the field for the last time, he appeared to wipe away tears and then gave a wave to family members in the stands and blew a kiss.... "My career, it's turned out to be something more than I ever thought, and more than I ever dreamed.... I'm still looking back and saying I can't believe this has happened to me. It's humbling."[198]

After retirement from football, Tony Gonzalez has worked as an analyst for several national sports news networks, including CBS Sports, Fox Sports, and others. He was also involved in a number of business ventures that included co-authoring a book on nutrition and helping to establish a sports nutrition company. He has appeared in several movies and television shows. All that remains as a culmination to Anthony David "Tony" Gonzalez's ties to the sport is his enshrinement in the Pro Football Hall of Fame. This event, as most knowledgeable aficionados of the game will attest, is all but assured.

Conclusion
The Historical Significance of Latinos on the Gridiron and Their Future in the Game

The preceding pages have provided an overview, extensive but by no means exhaustive, of the role/participation/contributions/impact of Spanish-surnamed athletes and coaches on the football fields of the United States and Canada. Given current demographic trends, as we noted in Chapter 5, it is safe to say that there will be even more such athletes and field generals in the future. There are many positive signs which indicate an expanded presence for Hispanics in the game, both on the field and off. There have been some recent articles (both academic and popular) that demonstrate this trend. While there are a plethora of stories to chose from, we will focus here on the following: the position of Mario Cristobal at the helm of one of the most important collegiate football programs in the country; the rise of a Honduran-American in the ranks of NFL assistant coaches; the ties between "America's Team," the Dallas Cowboys, and the overwhelmingly Latino (Mexican/Mexican American) population in the Valley of southern Texas; and the presence of Latino athletes in increasing numbers in "new" areas of concentration, such as Georgia.

We previously discussed the selection of Mario Cristobal as the new head coach of the Oregon Ducks and his hiring of his Cuban American compadre, Alex Mirabal, to work with his team's offensive linemen. An article entitled "10 Things to Know About the Oregon Ducks' New Head Football Coach" places emphasis on Cristobal's heritage as well as his affinity for Cuban coffee. This, in part, is a way to fuel his typical 16-hour workdays. Needless to say, it might not be practical to find a can of Cuban American mother's milk, also known as *Café Bustelo*, in the Eugene area, so Cristobal's mom is charged with making sure that he and Mirabal are well-lubricated with good doses of the potent substance. It will certainly serve as a reminder of how far these coaches have come from their days with the Golden Panthers and the Explorers. Beginning in the fall of 2018, it appears that the 3:05 p.m. *cafecito* break (so prevalent in Miami) might now help to fuel the fast-paced offense of this Pacific Northwest powerhouse. One last note regarding Oregon: yet another Latino member of Cristobal's staff is Marcus Arroyo, a native of Colfax, California, and a three-year letterman with the Spartans at San Jose State. He had served as an assistant at his alma mater, Wyoming, California, Southern Mississippi, and Oklahoma State. He also worked as interim offensive coordinator with the Tampa Bay Buccaneers in 2014. Arroyo has signed on to be co-offensive coordinator and quarterbacks coach with the Ducks.

As impressive and significant as it may be to have Latinos in positions of influence at an important collegiate program, it is even more noteworthy to have another working and learning from the legendary coach in New England, Bill Belichick. Brian Flores, a son of Honduran immigrants who grew up in the housing projects of Brownsville in Brooklyn, has, since 2004, climbed the assistant ranks in that organization. Soon after the departure of Matt Patricia to become head coach of the Detroit Lions, Belichick elevated Flores from coaching linebackers to calling the signals for the Patriots' entire defense. There is now talk about Flores being in line for a possible stint as a field general in the not-too-distant future. The path to Flores' current post was anything but smooth.

The Brownsville area is notorious for its violence and for its many housing projects. Brian and his four brothers, sons of Raul (a merchant marine) and Maria (a housewife), faced many difficulties to survive in this area. The hard streets, though full of danger and temptations, helped to shape this young man. "It made me tough. I learned how to deal with adversity and it motivated me to get out of there…. It's a tough environment, and there's violence and drugs. There are a lot of good people there too. I was fortunate to be around them." One of these good people, Brian's uncle Darrel Patterson (a firefighter), took the boys over to a park in Queens to visit the Lynvet youth football program. While there, a coach timed Brian in the 40-yard dash and immediately told him to go pick out equipment. "The young Flores put his first pair of shoulder pads on backwards, and the rest is football history in a basketball town."

Success in the Lynvet program attracted the attention of former NFL lineman Dino Mangiero, who was coaching at Brooklyn's Poly Prep Country Day School. Flores' talent on the field, in addition to his excellent grades, made it possible for him to attend the elite institution. The 90-minute ride to Poly, for Brian and his brothers, made the Floreses realize that "they were a long way from Brownsville in every literal and figurative way." Brian Flores became a star (as a safety and running back) with the Blue Devils, and his varsity team did not taste defeat during his time there, though they did tie one game against a school from New Jersey. He had many offers to play football but decided to attend Boston College "because of its academic standing and proximity to home." He was second on the Eagles in tackles in 2003 (as a linebacker). He seemed destined at least to get an opportunity to play in the NFL, but a torn quadricep ended that aspect of his gridiron dream. After graduating (with a degree in English, and later, an MA in Administrative Studies), Flores came to the attention of Scott Pioli, vice president of player personnel with the Patriots. He learned how to evaluate talent under Pioli's tutelage, then moved on to coaching starting in 2008. After Matt Patricia's departure to Michigan, Belichick assigned Flores the defensive coordinator duties, though not the specific title.

Flores, who is married and has two children of his own, has been able to move his family out of Brownsville and into better surroundings in Massachusetts. While they have moved out of the projects, the Flores clan does not forget where they came from. While his youngest brother, Christopher, did not go to college (he has autism), all the siblings earned degrees: Raul Jr. from Virginia Tech, Danny from Albany, and Luis from Bucknell. Thus, on the field, sidelines, or in the classroom, Brian Flores and his family are the embodiment of the American Dream. He certainly understands that he is a role model for other Latinos. As he noted in a recent interview after his promotion:

> I hope it's a powerful image. I hope they look at me and hear my story, and there's a hope and an understanding that they can do it too. That would be exactly what I would want them to feel. To see that regardless of what your circumstances are, or where your parents are from, of where you live … you can write your own story. I've written my own story.[1]

As a result of the success of the Patriots, and Brian Flores' fierce determination to triumph, it may not be too much longer before there is another Latino head coach in the NFL ranks. Flores was named the Dolphins' head coach before the start of the 2019 season.

Given the growth of the Latino population, it has become imperative for the NFL and college football to reach out to this market segment. Many articles have appeared in recent years concerning efforts to attract/solidify this fan base. Among the most successful teams in achieving this presence is, not surprisingly, the Dallas Cowboys. Not only are there rabid fans in Texas, but pretty much anywhere there is ample Mexican American representation, one will find a Cowboys display.[2] The team's history has played a substantial role in this development.

First, Tom Landry hailed from the Valley city of Mission, so he and Tex Schramm were cognizant of appealing to this population since the 1970s by broadcasting games in Spanish. Next, there have been several individuals of Mexican/Mexican American background (mentioned in previous chapters) who linked the team to this group. The league has also been broadcasting games into Mexico (and other parts of Latin America) since the 1990s, though what is now TV Azteca has been broadcasting the NFL (particularly, the Steelers and the Cowboys) since the 1970s. Finally, the Cowboys have been involved in community affairs targeting Spanish-speakers/Spanish-surnamed individuals (such as students) for many years as well, as noted by Victor Villalba, director of Spanish language broadcasting for the club.

A recent article by Cecilia Balli in *Texas Monthly* provided an "on the ground" examination of just how fanatical and socialized into the fabric of Valley existence is Cowboys mania. She describes various events and locales that teem with fans every time Dallas takes the field. From the more "traditional" surroundings, such as watching the contest at the local Buffalo Wild Wings, to the more Mexican-based *pitadas* (horn parades down Southmost Boulevard), the love for a franchise located 550 miles north of the border is palpable. The key issue to consider here is not only the zealousness of the connection, but also the duration of the bond to the sport and the team. As Balli noted, "the team is remembered directly in relation to treasured family stories and rituals, usually involving at least three generations. There are grandfathers who made the kids watch the games each week, the grandmothers who followed just as fervently." Later in the article, the author quoted Patricia Sanchez, an education professor at UT San Antonio, who well summarized many of the points that we have discussed throughout this work. "'When I was growing up in El Paso, the daughter of Mexican immigrants, we were acclimated right away that the two teams we rooted for were *los Cowboys y los Dodgers*.... We want to see ourselves and our people on America's biggest stage—sports arenas—because maybe then this country will accept us.'" A more academic, though with similar sentiments, discussion of this topic is presented in a recent article by Haylee Uecker Mercado and Matthew J. Bernthal which appeared in *Sports Marketing Quarterly* in 2016 concerning Cuban Americans.[3]

In the wake of the 2016 election season, and the increased dispersal of Latinos into "new" areas, such as the South, it is not surprising to see a tie between the sport of football and the debate concerning immigration. In August of 2016, the principal of Travelers Rest (known as the Devildogs) High School decreed that students would not be permitted to bring in American flags to a contest against the Berea High Bulldogs. The administrator believed that the standards would be utilized to taunt the numerous Latinos who played for Berea. A *Time* article noted that Devildogs fans had also shouted "go home" toward the Berea sidelines. We will not take sides on this matter. Some argued it was xenophobia, while others argued it was a matter of free speech, but suffice it to say that this issue will continue to play out on gridirons in the future. As Kristen Salyer summarized, "Regardless of whether the individual students planned to taunt their Hispanic football opponents or wave our country's flag in pride, the outrage on both sides is a reminder of the power of symbols and the importance of having serious conversations about what values we choose to hold most dear."[4]

A quick perusal of reports noting the expansion of the Latino population in the South augurs that this might not be the last time for such events. For example, a 2018 report about the expansion of this group in places such as Georgia indicated that there will be more and more Hispanics playing football in locales not considered to be "traditional" places of residence. The second-most heavily Latino locale in the Peach State offers a good illustration. The community of Dalton, in Whitfield County, was estimated to have a population of 33,653, and Spanish-surnamed individuals comprised 49.44 percent of that total. The roster of the hometown Catamounts (98 student athletes) for the upcoming 2018 campaign included 30 players with Spanish surnames. It would be of interest to see if the Catamounts face similar issues to those of the Berea Bulldogs (or the Grulla Gators) when they are the visiting team this season. On the one hand, it is positive to see the growth of the number of Latinos playing the South's favorite sport. On the other, it may take a while for some folks to accept the presence of athletes named Rodriguez and Perez in such locales.[5]

By 2018, the Latino presence in the game of football was of long standing, but there are two current issues that continue to plague the group in regard to opening up further opportunities: the relatively low number of Latinos who play beyond the high school level, and the small number of mentors, such as Cristobal and Mirabal, who coach at any collegiate level.

An interesting article by Juan Vidal appeared in *Rolling Stone* in September of 2016 concerning such matters. Vidal noted that this population "continues to grow in power and influence in areas ranging from politics to pop culture," but we still "don't see them reflected more in professional, televised sports." In American sports, there are endeavors which necessitate that an athlete go on to college before having a shot at the professional ranks. Football is, of course, just such a game. While we have documented that many Latinos play high school football throughout the nation, relatively few go on to play collegiately. A recent publication by The Institute for Diversity and Ethics in Sport (TIDES), which is headed by Richard Lapchick at the University of Central Florida, indicated that (as of 2017) Latinos comprised a scant 2.9 percent of all gridders at the Division I level. While the number had doubled since the first such study (1991–1992, 1.4), it has hovered around the upper 2 percent level since the early 2000s. Why is that? Vidal proffers the following argument:

> It's no secret that Latinos consistently dominate in sports like boxing and MMA, where college participation is not a requirement. Generally … and especially in

immigrant households ... sports are not viewed as something to seriously pursue....
Latinos may be some of the most bombastic, spirited fans, [but] the fact that we don't
see ourselves reflected ... on the football field ... can frustrate some from trying to
reach the next level.

In order to move to the professional game, it is necessary to pursue football at the collegiate level. Granted, we have discussed many such players, but the current numbers do not lie. Not only are Latinos not making it to the Division I schools, not many are playing at the lower ranks either. The report did not specify the Latino presence in smaller schools by sport but overall, Hispanics accounted for 4.8 percent of all (male) athletes at DI, with higher numbers at DII (7.0 percent) and DIII (5.6 percent). In total, individuals of this background accounted for 5.7 percent of all athletes. It is safe to assume that the increased number of Latinos is made up of athletes who are participating for colleges and universities on the soccer pitch as well as the baseball diamond.

In a 2009 dissertation by Rafael Romo, the researcher interviewed eight former collegiate football players of Mexican American descent concerning their experiences. Many of the responses by these men about the issues they confronted at various schools confirmed points we have made throughout this work. Many of their families needed financial assistance, and that complicated the possibilities to play the sport. Those who were from immigrant families often were discouraged from playing any sports. Others did not get much information about the college application process, or the methods required to put out their information (such as game film) to attract the attention of college recruiters. Some participants intimated that scouts simply did not visit places such as the Valley or Laredo.

These players are hungry for opportunities, and many of them can play at locales such as Incarnate Word, TAMUK, and elsewhere. The combination of financial, social, educational, and familial issues prevents many players who could move on from doing so. Of course, few of these youths will play professionally, but an opportunity to gain a college degree is certainly worth the effort. One of Romo's subjects summarized this plight by saying:

> I don't think we're well informed.... No one talks to us about what's out there. And what we are capable of doing. But you're right, there are a lot of small colleges and you know you're going to get an education and you're going to continue to play ball. Granted, it might not be the University of Texas, but it's college and you still get a college degree. You need to continue what you love to do, play football. If only I had known more ... known what to do.

One other detail presented by the TIDES report is of note to this discussion. Just as Latinos are severely underrepresented on the field, they are likewise not present in significant numbers on the sidelines. In 2017, there was one Hispanic head coach at the DI level: Tony Sanchez at UNLV (accounting for .4 percent of all field generals). Of course, he has now been joined by Cristobal. The numbers at all divisions was little better, .5 percent (three coaches). Concerning assistant coaches, there were 102 across all divisions (1.6 percent of the total). In order to increase these numbers, much work needs to be done. There are many athletes and coaches in the trenches who can move up, but it will take a broadening of the notion of who "belongs" on the gridiron and the sidelines to bring these figures more into line with the demographic reality of the United States at the end of the second decade of the 21st century. As Vidal noted at the end of his article:

> Sports are a connective tissue that bring people together from all backgrounds, and it's important to continue pushing budding Latino athletes to compete. The talent is there, in some cities overwhelmingly so. It's not just being showcased and encouraged on a broader scale.... [Current athletes and coaches serve] as much-needed inspiration and a reminder of what can be accomplished through hard work and the right support. But this doesn't mean there won't be opposition. Our current cultural and political moment makes that clear.[6]

From the time of Ignacio Saturnino Molinet to Tony Romo, and all others in between, the story of the participation of Latinos in football is one of perseverance and triumph extending over almost one century. This narrative will only continue to expand in significance as this population becomes a larger and larger percentage of the life, society, and totality of the United States. It is our hope that this historical accounting will aid in bringing the lesser-known of these many heroes to a broader audience, but also demonstrate that what is now the largest minority in the nation has, like African Americans, Native Americans, and others, used this sport to claim a space for themselves in the national sporting consciousness. The Spanish-surnamed football player has many great role models to look up to; it is now the turn of the young men on the rosters of 2018 high schools and colleges throughout the nation to write the next chapter in this history.

Chapter Notes

Introduction

1. Quoted in Gerald R. Gems, *Sport and the Making of Italian American Identity* (Syracuse: Syracuse University Press, 2014), 137.
2. Evan Andrews, "Why Do Americans Watch Football on Thanksgiving?" accessed September 1, 2016, http://www.history.com/ask-history/why-do-americans-watch-football-on-thanksgiving. See also: "Thanksgiving and the NFL," https://www.profootballhof.com/football-history/thanksgiving-and-the-nfl/.
3. The CFL began operations in its current format in 1958, though most of the teams now in the League well predate the establishment of the CFL.
4. https://en.wikipedia.org/wiki/Thanksgiving_Day_Classic#By_appearance.
5. "Alouettes' Calvillo Breaks Pro Football's Passing Record," *Postmedia News*, October 10, 2011, accessed August 4, 2016, http://news.nationalpost/sports/cfl/calvillo-breaks-pro-footballs-passing-record. For further information on Anthony Calvillo's life and career, please see "The Kid from La Puente," documentary, produced by Dugald Maudsley, Infield Fly Productions, 2014.
6. The amount of work on this topic is extensive and the following list is not meant to be exhaustive: Michael Oriard, *Reading Football: How the Popular Press Created an American Spectacle* (Chapel Hill: University of North Carolina Press, 1993); John Watterson, *College Football: History, Spectacle, Controversy* (Baltimore: Johns Hopkins University Press, 2002).
7. Ralph Hickok, *Bibliography of Books About American Football, 1891–2015* (Self-published, 2015), 41–88, 286–288.
8. Michael Oriard, *King Football: Sport and Spectacle in the Golden Age of Radio and Newsreels, Movies and Magazines, the Weekly & Daily Press* (Chapel Hill: University of North Carolina Press, 2001). The chapter of particular interest in this regard is Chapter 8, "Ethnicity."
9. *Ibid.*, 260.
10. *Ibid.*
11. Gerald R. Gems, *For Pride, Profit and Patriarchy: Football and the Incorporation of American Cultural Values* (Lanham, MD: Scarecrow Press, 2000); Gems, *Sport and the Shaping of Italian American Identity*.
12. Gems, *Sport and the Making of Italian American Identity*, 128.
13. *Ibid.*, 168.
14. *Ibid.*, 196.
15. Gems, *For Pride, Profit and Patriarchy*, 112.
16. *Ibid.*
17. Jorge Prieto, *The Quarterback Who Almost Wasn't* (Houston: Arte Publico Press, 1994).
18. *Ibid.*, 9.
19. *Ibid.*, 14.
20. *Ibid.*, 17.
21. *Ibid.*, 65, 66 and 119.
22. *Ibid.*, 143–144.
23. Gray Levy, *Big and Bright: Deep in the Heart of Texas High School Football* (Lanham, MD: Taylor Trade Publishing, 2015), 210.
24. Jorge Iber, "On-field Foes and Racial Misperceptions: The 1961 Donna Redskins and Their Drive to the Texas State Football Championship," in *Mexican Americans and Sports: A Reader on Athletics and Barrio Life*, eds. Jorge Iber and Samuel O. Regalado (College Station: Texas A&M University Press, 2007), 121–144. Quotations on pages 134 and 136.
25. *Ibid.*, 134.
26. Joel Huerta, "Friday Night Rights: South Texas High School Football and the

Struggle for Equality, 1930–1960s," *The International Journal of the History of Sport* 26 (June 2009): 981–1000.

27. *Ibid.*, 212.
28. *Ibid.*, 216 and 220.
29. *Ibid.*, 221.
30. Corbett Smith, "Why Are Latino High School Head Football Coaches so Scarce in the D-FW?" accessed September 1, 2016, https://sportsday.dallasnews.com/high-school/highschools/2015/10/17/d-fw-area-latino-head-coaches-high-school-football-scarce.
31. For example, while writing this introduction in August of 2016, a story on an incident at a football game at Traveler's Rest, South Carolina well exemplified such issues. The principal of TRHS refused to allow fans of his institution to enter the stadium where the game was held while carrying U.S. flags. The reasoning behind this was that the administrator believed that the flags were being used as a way to taunt the athletes and fans of that evening's opponent, Berega High School from Greenville, SC, which is an entity with a substantial Latino population. The principal, under heavy pressure, eventually reversed the ban on bringing in flags to his school's stadium. See: Colin Ward-Henninger, "South Carolina High School Bans American Flags from Football Game," August 29, 2016, accessed August 31, 2016, http://www.cbssports.com/general/news/south-carolina-high-school-bans-american-flags-from-football-game/. See also: Todd Starnes, "High School Reverses American Flag Ban at Football Stadium," August 29, 2016, accessed August 31, 2016, http://www.foxnews.com/opinion/2016/08/29/high-school-bans-american-flag-at-football-stadium.html.
32. Jorge Iber, Samuel O. Regalado, Jose M. Alamillo, and Arnoldo De Leon, *Latinos in U.S. Sport: A History of Isolation, Cultural Identity, and Acceptance* (Champaign, IL: Human Kinetics, 2011), 228–229. For info on Springdale, AR, please see pages 1–5.
33. Mario Longoria, *Athletes Remembered: Mexicano/Latino Professional Football Players, 1929-1970* (Tempe, AZ: Bilingual Press/Editorial Bilingue, 1997), ix.
34. Frederick Luis Aldama and Christopher Gonzalez, *Latinos in the End Zone: Conversations on the Brown Color Line in the NFL* (New York: Palgrave McMillan, 2014), 108.
35. Iber, et al., *Latinos in U.S. Sport*, 6–7.
36. *Ibid.*
37. Jorge Moraga, "Remembering Super Bowl 50 Through a Meztiz@ Sports Consciousness." Accessed July 26, 2016, https://ussporthistory.com/2016/02/22/remembering-super-bowl-50-through-a-mestiz-sport-consciousness/.

Chapter 1

1. Mark C. Anderson, "'What's To Be Done with 'Em?': Images of Mexican Cultural Backwardness, Racial Limitations, and Moral Decrepitude in the United States Press, 1913–1915," *Mexican Studies/Estudios Mexicanos* 14, no. 1 (Winter, 1998): 23–70. Quoted in Iber, et al., *Latinos in U.S. Sport*, 72.
2. Carlos Kevin Blanton, "'They Cannot Master Abstractions, but They Can Often Be Made Efficient Workers': Race and Class in the Intelligence Testing of Mexican Americans and African Americans in Texas during the 1920s," *Social Science Quarterly* 81, no. 4 (December 2000): 1014–1026. Quotes are from pages 1017 and 1018.
3. Miroslava Chavez-Garcia, "Intelligence Testing at Whittier School, 1890–1920," *Pacific Historical Review* 76, no. 2 (May 2007): 193–228. Quotes from 217 and 227.
4. Rodolfo Acuna, *Occupied America: A History of Chicanos, 6th Edition* (New York: Pearson/Longman, 2007), 146.
5. Lillian Emrick, "A Survey of the Recreational Interests of High School Pupils in Nogales, Arizona" (Master's thesis, University of Southern California, 1944), 59.
6. Charles Dinnijes Withers, "Problems of Mexican Boys" (Master's thesis, University of Southern California, 1942), 48 and 49.
7. Quoted in Iber, et al., *Latinos in U.S. Sport*, 72.
8. *Ibid.*, 75.
9. For an excellent overview of the life, times and influence of Walter Camp, please see Julie Des Jardins, *Walter Camp: Football and the Modern Man* (New York: Oxford University Press, 2015).
10. Quoted in Iber, et al., *Latinos in U.S. Sport*, 90. See also David Barron, "The Birth of Texas Schoolboy Football," in *King Football: Greatest Moments in Texas High School Football History*, ed. Mike Bynum (Birmingham, AL: Epic Sports Classics, 2003), 26–39.
11. Iber, et al., *Latinos in U.S. Sport*, 74.
12. Emrick, "A Survey of the Recreational Interests of High School Pupils in Nogales, Arizona," 61.
13. Greg Selber, *Border Ball: The History of High School Football in the Rio Grande Valley* (Deer Park, NY: Linus Publications, 2009), 9.
14. Iber, et al., *Latinos in U.S. Sport*, 90. For more information on the career of Amador Rodriguez, please see his web page at the Rio

Grande Valley Sports Hall of Fame: https://https://www.rgvshof.net.

15. Selber, *Border Ball*, 5.

16. Joel Huerta, "Friday Night Rights: South Texas High-school Football and the Struggle for Equality," *The International Journal of the History of Sport* 26 (June 2009): 981–1000.

17. Iber, et al., *Latinos in U.S. Sport*, 127.

18. Quoted *ibid.*, 129. See also: Victor M. Aguilar, "Mexican Americans in Sports: A Survey of Ex-Bowie High School Football Players, 1932–1954," Unpublished paper, copy in possession of Jorge Iber.

19. Fred M. Morales, *History of Bowie High School, 1922–1973* (El Paso, TX: Self-published, 2015), 1, 4 and 6.

20. *Ibid.*, 8, 10, 12, 13, 21 and 23.

21. *Ibid.*, 40.

22. Dan Ford, *The History of New Mexico High School Football* (CreateSpace, 2010), locations 199, 261, 878, 1107, 1139 and 1668, Kindle.

23. Ricardo Dow Anaya, "An Historical Prospective of Influence Sport Had on Sport Legends of New Mexico, 1925–1975" (PhD diss., University of New Mexico, 1997), 53.

24. *Ibid.*, 152.

25. Walter Hines, "Aggie Sports: The Early Years," last modified March 25, 2006, accessed April 13, 2017, http://bleedcrimson.net/aggiesports_theearlyyears. See also: Longoria, *Athletes Remembered*, 141–142.

26. Joel Franks, "California and the Rise of Spectator Sports, 1850–1900," *Southern California Quarterly* 71, no. 4 (Winter 1989): 287–310. Quotes from pages 304–306.

27. Iber, et al., *Latinos in U.S. Sport*, 58–59.

28. Deana Anderson Lamont, "Sport and Leisure in the Building of an Urban Community: The Case of Oakland, California 1850–1906" (PhD diss., University of California at Berkeley, 1996), 299–300 and 323–330. Quote is from page 330.

29. Marshall Stimson, "History of Los Angeles High School," *The Quarterly: Historical Society of Southern California* 24, no. 3 (September 1942): 98–109.

30. Jose Alamillo, "Playing Across Borders: Transnational Sports and Identities in Southern California and Mexico, 1930–1945," *Pacific Historical Review* 79, no. 3 (August 2010): 360–392.

31. Mark Wild, "'So Many Children at Once and so Many Kinds': Schools and Ethno-Racial Boundaries in Early Twentieth-Century Los Angeles," *Western Historical Quarterly* 33, no. 4 (Winter 2002): 453–476. Quote is from page 457.

32. "Symbol of Heart: The Official Documentary of the East L.A. Classic," Carmona Productions, 2003.

33. Gary Ross Mormino and George E. Pozzeta, *The Immigrant World of Ybor City: Italians and Their Latin Neighbors in Tampa, 1885–1985* (Gainesville: University of Florida Press, 1998), 252.

34. Santiago Eagles, 2013, accessed October 24, 2016, http://santiagoeaglesfootball.blogspot.com/2009/12/xalapaveracruzen-1896-raul-dehesa-y.html; "Impulsor del Football Americano en la UNAM: Arthur Constantine," 2013, accessed October 24, 2016, https://www.youtube.com/watch?v=XpXqt5XruGk.

35. ESPN Deportes, "Campeones de la Liga Mayor," 2001, accessed October 24, 2016, https://www.youtube.com/watch?v=XpXqt5XruGk.

36. "Cronologia del football Americano en Mexico," 2007, accessed October 24, 2016, http://www.tackleo.com/index.php?option=com_content&view=article&id=22&Itemid=98.

37. Eduardo Reig-Romero, *Memorias de deporte universitario: sus inicios* (La Habana: Editorial Unicornio, 2009), 44–48.

38. Michael T. Wood, "American Football in Cuba: A Brief Introduction," 2015, accessed October 24, 2016, https://ussporthistory.com/2015/07/30/american-football-in-cuba-a-brief-introduction/; "American Football in Cuba: L.S.U. vs. University of Havana, 1907," 2015, accessed October 24, 2016. https://ussporthistory.com/2015/12/31/american-football-in-cuba-l-s-u-vs-university-of-havana-1907/.

39. "American Football in Cuba: L.S.U. vs. University of Havana, 1907," 2015.

40. Michael T. Wood, "Bacardi Bowl: American Football in Cuba," 2016, accessed May 10, 2016, http://bacardibowl.blogspot.com/.

41. Iber, et al., *Latinos in U.S. Sport*, 93.

42. "Football in Cuba," 2014, accessed May 10, 2016, http://profootballdaly.com/football-in-cuba/.

43. "LU Facilities," 2014, accessed October 24, 2016. http://lulions.com/sports/2014/7/2/GEN_0702141729.aspx.

44. Jason Aiken (Collections Coordinator, Pro Football Hall of Fame) telephone call with author, June 26 2000.

45. Teresa Van de Carr telephone call with author, July 3, 2000.

46. "Ignacio Saturnino Molinet '27," Cornell Athletic Communications Office, June 27, 2000.

47. *Ibid.*
48. *The 1927 Cornellian*, 111.
49. "Ignacio Saturnino Molinet '27," Cornell Athletic Communications Office, June 27, 2000.
50. Robert B. Haines letter to I.S. Molinet, July 21, 1927.
51. *Ibid.*
52. *Ibid.*
53. Frankford Athletic Association telegram to Ignacio Molinet, August 19, 1927.
54. Ignacio S. Molinet letter to Robert S. Haines, August 20, 1927.
55. *Ibid.*
56. Frankford Athletic Association telegram to Ignacio Molinet, August 28 1927.
57. Ignacio S. Molinet letter to Robert S. Haines, August 29, 1927.
58. *Ibid.*
59. Ignacio S. Molinet letter to the American Consul, Havana, Cuba, August 29, 1927.
60. *Ibid.*
61. "Moran Trips Legions, Fanning 14 Players: Yellow Jackets Win Close Game Though Only Making Four Hits, The Same as Garnered of Volte," *Philadelphia Record*, September 18, 1927, 3.
62. *Ibid.*
63. *Frankford Yellow Jackets Game Program*, October 22, 1927, 7.
64. "Yellow Jackets Win Fray from New Britain: Forward Pass Attack Aids Frankford Eleven in National Football League Contest," *Philadelphia Record*, October 1, 1927, 1 and 3.
65. Jesse Rodriguez letter to Mario Longoria, December 27, 1982.
66. *Ibid.*
67. T. Edward Davis letter to Mario Longoria, December 8, 1982. Mr. T. Edward Davis was the Director of Athletics at Salem College during the time Jesse Rodriguez was a student.
68. Art Goldchien letter to Mario Longoria, January 18, 1985.
69. Longoria, *Athletes Remembered*, 3.
70. Bruce Harton, "Jesse Rodriguez, Clarksburg's Own Star at Salem College, Will Have Greatest Year of His Life in 1927," *Clarksburg Exponent*, September 23, 1927.
71. "Here Today, Rodriguezes, Kelly and Jesse, Two Brothers Pitted One Against the Other, Score Both Touchdowns of Game," *Clarksburg Exponent*, October 8, 1927.
72. Longoria, *Athletes Remembered*, 4.
73. "Rodrieguez and Kistler Lead Salem's Attack Throughout," *Clarksburg Exponent*, October 31, 1928.
74. Longoria, *Athletes Remembered*, 4.
75. Jim Durfee refereed both collegiate and pro football games. Because the NFL was not as organized as it is today with their own scouts, they relied on reporters, game officials, and others to spot pro football talent and share information with them. Durfee was not officially tied to the Bison Club, but it appears his opinion of Jesse's pro capability was their motive for contracting him.
76. Jesse Rodriguez letter to Mario Longoria, December 27, 1982.
77. *Ibid.*
78. "Bison Pros Open Season Today with Chicago Cards: Chief Elkins with Rivals," *Buffalo Courier Express*, September 29, 1929.
79. "Sports-O-Rama. The Remembered Art of Punting," *Clarksburg Exponent*, August 12, 1964.
80. *Ibid.*
81. Longoria, *Athletes Remembered*, 5.
82. "Buffalo Pros Hold Hornets to Three Points," *Buffalo Courier Express*, October 6, 1929.
83. "Galloping Ghost Aids Mate in Scoring 2 Touchdowns: Locals Threaten to at Close," *Buffalo Courier Express*, October 14, 1929.
84. "Ties Steam Rollers, 7-7 Buffalo Comes from Behind to Knot Count in Pro Football," *The New York Times*, October 12, 1929.
85. "Bears Misplays Present Bisons with 19-7 Win, Fumbles and Intercepted Passes," *Chicago Daily Tribune*, November 25, 1929.
86. Jesser Rodriguez letter to Mario Longoria, December 27, 1982.
87. Art Goldchien letter to Mario Longoria, January 18, 1985.
88. Kelly Rodriguez letter to Mario Longoria, August 12, 1984.
89. Palmira Rodriguez letter Mario Longoria, August 3, 1984.
90. Kelly Rodriguez letter to Mario Longoria, September 29, 1984.
91. *1935 Boston Redskins Press Guide.*
92. Longoria, *Athletes Remembered*, 7.
93. *Ibid.*, 8.
94. Kent Kessler, *Hail West Virginians!* (Parkersburg, WV: Park Press, 1959), 145–146.
95. John J. Carroll letter to Kelly Rodriguez, January 6, 1975.
96. "Navy Swamps Bobcat Eleven," *Clarksburg Telegram*, November 13, 1928.
97. Longoria, *Athletes Remembered*, 8.
98. *Ibid.*
99. Robert B. Haines letter to Kelly Rodriguez, April 26, 1930.
100. David S. Neft, Richard M. Cohen and Rich Korch, *The Football Encyclopedia: The*

Complete Year-by-Year History of Professional Football From 1892 to the Present (New York: Martin's Press, 1994), 86.
101. Kelly Rodriguez letter to Mario Longoria, September 29, 1984.
102. Longoria, *Athletes Remembered*, 11.
103. Kelly Rodriquez letter to Mario Longoria, November 20, 1984.
104. L.E. Mansean letter to Kelly Rodriguez, June 8, 1935.
105. Longoria, *Athletes Remembered*, 10.
106. W.E. Don Carlos letter to Mario Longoria, June 27, 1996.
107. *Ibid.*
108. *Ibid.*
109. *1930 QUAX Drake University Yearbook.*
110. *1931 QUAX Drake University Yearbook.*
111. Paul Morrison, "Memorandum of Information on Waldo Don Carlos," Drake University, Department of Intercollegiate Athletics, July 16, 1996.
112. W.E. Don Carlos letter to Mario Longoria, June 27, 1996.
113. *Ibid.*
114. Longoria, *Athletes Remembered*, 12.
115. Neft, et al., *The Football Encyclopedia*, 89.
116. W.E. Don Carlos letter to Mario Longoria, June 27, 1996.
117. Longoria, *Athletes Remembered*, 12–13.
118. *1928 Naval Academy Annual—The Lucky Bag*, 90.
119. *Ibid.*
120. "Boand System National Championship Selections," *College Football Data Warehouse*, May 5, 2010.
121. "Deke Houlgate Dead at 54," *Pasadena Independent*, August 1, 1959, 9.
122. Herschel Nissenson, *Tales From College Football's Sidelines* (New York: Sports Publishing, 2001), 93.
123. "Helms Athletic Foundation," https://en.wikipedia.org/wiki/Helms_Athletic_Foundation.
124. "Jeff Sagarin," https://en.wikipedia.org/wiki/Jeff_Sagarin.
125. *1928 Naval Academy Annual—The Lucky Bag*, 294.
126. "Obituary—James Bushanon Schuber '28," *Shipmate Magazine*, September 1, 1982, 116–117.
127. *Ibid.*, 117.
128. E. Leroy Hatch, "Mormon Colonies: Beacon Light in Mexico," *Ensign*, September 1972.
129. *Ibid.*
130. "Al Richins," accessed April 17, 2016, https://www.profootballarchives.com/playerr/rich10200.html.
131. "Aldo Richins and Hank Davies Win Athletic Award," *Utah Daily Chronicle*, May 24, 1934.
132. *Ibid.*
133. "Aldo Richins," accessed May 1, 2017, en.wikipedia.org/wiki/Aldo_Richins.
134. Mel "Buck" Bashore, "The Salt Lake Seagulls," *The Coffin Corner* 14, no. 02 (1992).
135. *Ibid.*
136. Jorge Prieto, *The Quarterback Who Almost Wasn't*, 65.
137. *Ibid.*, 66.
138. "Jose Martinez-Zorrilla—Class '32," Cornell University, Sports Publicity Office, May 31, 1979.
139. *Ibid.*
140. *Ibid.*
141. *Ibid.*
142. Cornellbigred/com/hof.aspx
143. Although Jorge Prieto did not play professional football, there are a total of 47 Latino athletes from various countries who did beginning in 1927. Out of these 47, 21 pro football athletes were from Mexico.
144. Jorge Prieto, *The Quarterback Who Almost Wasn't*, 59.
145. *Ibid.*, 9.
146. *Ibid.*, 11, 25.
147. *Ibid.*, 12.
148. *Ibid.*, 11.
149. *Ibid.*, 15.
150. *Ibid.*, 10.
151. *Ibid.*
152. Prieto, *The Quarterback Who Almost Wasn't*, 13. See also Richard Delgado, "Words That Wound: A Tort Action for Racial Insults, Epithets, and Name-calling," in *Critical Race Theory: The Cutting Edge* (Philadelphia: Temple University Press, 1995), 160.
153. Prieto, *The Quarterback Who Almost Wasn't*, 30.
154. *Ibid.*, 31. "Pocho" is a derogatory term given to Mexicans living in the United States whose English speaking lessens their Spanish language competency.
155. *Ibid.*, 32.
156. *Ibid.*, 49.
157. *Ibid.*, 50.
158. *Ibid.*, 51.
159. *Ibid.*, 47.
160. *Ibid.*, 50.
161. *Ibid.*, 71.
162. *Ibid.*, 115.
163. Janet G. Messenger, "Chicago Names Public School for Evanston Physician, Dr.

Jorge Prieto," *EVANSTON RoundTable*, October 13, 2009.
164. *Ibid.*

Chapter 2

1. Zaragosa Vargas, *Crucible of Struggle: A History of Mexican Americans from Colonial Times to the Present Era* (New York: Oxford University Press, 2011), 245.
2. *Ibid.*, 243 and 245.
3. For more information on this topic please see Maggie Rivas-Rodriguez, *Mexican Americans and World War II* (Austin: University of Texas Press, 2005).
4. Vargas, *Crucible of Struggle*, 259. See also: Jorge Iber, *Mike Torrez: A Baseball Biography* (Jefferson, NC: McFarland, 2016), 25.
5. Patrick J, Carroll, *Felix Longoria's Wake: Bereavement, Racism, and the Rise of Mexican American Activism* (Austin: University of Texas Press, 2003).
6. Vargas, *Crucible of Struggle*, 267. See also: Richard Griswold del Castillo, ed., *World War II and Mexican American Civil Rights* (Austin: University of Texas Press, 2008).
7. Vargas, *Crucible of Struggle*, 247.
8. Estela Godinez-Ballon, *The Mexican American Experience: Mexican Americans and Education: El Saber es Poder* (Tucson: University of Arizona Press, 2015), 20 and 21.
9. *Ibid.*, 26.
10. *Ibid.*, 26–27.
11. *Ibid.*, 27.
12. See the following: Genevieve King, "The Psychology of a Mexican Community in San Antonio, Texas" (MA thesis, University of Texas, 1936), 60; Albert Folsom Cobb, "Comparative Study of the Athletic Ability of Latin American and Anglo American Boys on a Junior High School Level" (MA thesis, University of Texas, 1952), 2; Clyde Ira Kramme, "A Comparison of Anglo Culture with Spanish Culture Elementary Students in Physical Development as Determined by Height, Weight, and Vital Capacity Measurements" (MA thesis, Texas A&I University, 1939); Andrew Lee Habermacher, "Physical Development of Anglo and Spanish Culture Boys and Girls, Ages 13–18, Inclusive" (MA thesis, Texas A&I University, 1940); Bruce Walsh Shaw, "Sociometric Status and Athletic Ability of Anglo American and Latin American Boys in a San Antonio Junior High School" (MA thesis, University of Texas, 1951), 18–19; and Merrell E. Thompson and Claude C. Dove, "A Comparison of Physical Achievement of Anglo and Spanish American Boys in Junior High School," *Research Quarterly* 13 (October 1942): 341–346.
13. Gary R. Mormino and George E. Pozzetta, *The Immigrant World of Ybor City: Italians and their Latin Neighbors in Tampa, 1885–1985* (Gainesville: University of Florida Press, 1998), 252 and 287–291. See also: Iber, et al., *Latinos in U.S. Sport*, 160–161.
14. Selber, *Border Ball*, 58.
15. Huerta, "Friday Night Rights," 981–1000. Quote is from page 990.
16. Jorge Iber, "Mexican Americans of South Texas Football: The Athletic and Coaching Careers of E.C. Lerma and Bobby Cavazos, 1932–1965," *Southwestern Historical Quarterly* 55, no. 4 (April 2002): 616–633.
17. *Ibid.*, 628.
18. Quoted in Iber, et al., *Latinos in U.S. Sport*, 130.
19. See the following: Jorge Iber, "The Pigskin Pulpito: A Brief Overview of the Experiences of Mexican American High School Football Coaches in Texas," in *Sports and the Racial Divide: African American and Latino Experience in an Era of Change*, ed. Michael E. Lomax (Jackson: University Press of Mississippi, 2008), 178–195; and Ignacio M. Garcia, "William Carson 'Nemo' Herrera: Constructing a Mexican American Powerhouse While Remaining Colorblind," *Journal of the West* 54, no. 4 (Fall 2015): 40–46. Information on Coach Martinez is from an email to Jorge Iber by Greg Selber on March 24, 2017.
20. See the Rio Grande Valley Sports Hall of Fame for individual pages, https://www.rgvshof.net.
21. Morales, *History of Bowie High School*, 49 and 53.
22. *Ibid.*, 100.
23. "Bowie Plays Lanier at 8 Tonight," *El Paso Times*, September 26, 1941, 14.
24. Grenville Mott, "Bowie Gains Scoreless Tie in El Paso," *El Paso Times*, September 27, 1941, 8.
25. Morales, *History of Bowie High School*, 60–61.
26. *Ibid.*, 64 and 65.
27. *Ibid.*, 108, 112–115, and 136–139.
28. Quoted in Iber, et al., *Latinos in U.S. Sport*, 128–129.
29. Dan Ford, *The History of New Mexico High School Football—Vol. I The First 100 Years* (CreateSpace, 2011), 42 and 68.
30. http://www.menaulschool.org/student-life/athletics/football-2/.
31. Ford, *The History of New Mexico High School Football—Vol. I The First 100 Years*, 72. For more information on Sam Etcheverry, see also http://www.cfhof.ca/members/

sam-etcheverry/; https://www.legacy.com/obituaries/currentargus/obituary.aspx?n=-sam-etcheverry-the-rifle&pid=132618103. Both accessed April 12, 2017.

32. According to Dan Ford and the NMAA, the state championship prior to 1953 was "mythical," given that champions were not crowned on the field, but rather through a polling process. This information comes from two sources: Dan Ford, "Las Cruces Suspension," December 14, 2015, accessed April 11, 2017, https://nmsportsblog.com/2015/12/14/las-cruces-suspension-by-dan-ford/; and "New Mexico State Football Champions," https://www.nmact.org/file/Football_Past_Champs.pdf.

33. Ibid. See the following for information specifically on Coach Camunez: "LCPS Board May Consider Field of Dreams Name Changes," *Las Cruces Sun News*, accessed April 11, 2017, http://www.lcsun-news.com/story/news/2016/03/02/lcps-board-may-consider-field-dreams-name-changes/81245576/; accessed April 11, 2017, https://www.findagrave.com/cgi-bin/fg.cgi?page=gr&GRid=86552938; "Walking Tour: Mesquite Historic District," accessed April 11, 2017, http://lascrucesmagazine.com/walking-tour-mesquite-historic-district/.

34. Anaya, "An Historical Perspective of Influence Sport Had on Sports Legends," 176–195. See also: Obituary for Gilbert S. "Gillie" Lopez, accessed April 10, 2017, http://www.genlookups.com/nm/webbbs_config.pl/noframes/read/269.

35. Anaya, "An Historical Perspective of Influence Sport Had on Sports Legends," 196–220.

36. Longoria, *Athletes Remembered*.

37. Ibid., 27–29. See also: http://www.nfl.com/player/johnsanchez/2524844/careerstats.

38. Longoria, *Athletes Remembered*, 30–32. See also: http://www.profootballarchives.com/playerm/mora00400.html and http://www.sfgate.com/sports/article/WHERE-ARE-THEY-NOW-Gonzalo-Morales-Early-man-2840478.php.

39. Longoria, *Athletes Remembered*, 47–50. See also: "The Road to the Hall: 1950 Loyola Foootball," January 18, 2011, http://www.lmulions.com/genrel/011811aaa.html; "Gene Brito," https://en.wikipedia.org/wiki/Gene_Brito; and "Remembering Gene Brito," http://www.profootballresearchers.org/archives/Website_Files/Coffin_Corner/21-03-803.pdf. All accessed April 24, 2017.

40. George J. Sanchez, *Becoming Mexican American: Ethnicity, Culture and Identity in Chicano Los Angeles, 1900–1945* (New York: Oxford University Press, 1993), 257.

41. Iber, et al., *Latinos in U.S. Sport*, 175. See also: http://www.tbo.com/sports/former-jefferson-high-nfl-star-rick-casares-dies-at-82-20130914/; and Longoria, *Athletes Remembered*, 53.

42. Juan Garcia, *Mexicans in the Midwest, 1900–1932* (Tucson: University of Arizona Press, 2004); Zaragosa Vargas, *Proletarians of the North: A History of Mexican Industrial Workers in Detroit and the Midwest, 1917–1933* (Berkeley: University of California Press, 1993); and Iber, *Mike Torrez*.

43. Longoria, *Athletes Remembered*, 21–22.

44. Ibid., 39–41. See also: "Ray Romero of the Philadelphia Eagles (1951)," accessed May 1, 2017, http://notesfromaztlan.tumblr.com/post/81328528614/ray-romero-of-the-philadelphia-eagles-1951.

45. Longoria, *Athletes Remembered*, 42–43. See also Page 71, accessed May 1, 2017, https://s3.amazonaws.com/sidearm.sites/nebomaha.sidearmsports.com/documents/2017/6/22/Football_History.pdf

46. *1947 Los Angeles Dons Player Profiles*, 16.

47. Longoria, *Athletes Remembered*, 17.

48. Brother L. Dennis (archivist, St. Mary's College of California—Office of the Librarian, Programs and Press Handbook Information), letter to Mario Longoria, January 21, 1983.

49. Longoria, *Athletes Remembered*, 17.

50. Beau Riffenburgh, *The Official NFL Encyclopedia* (New York: New American Library, 1986), 461.

51. Kingsley Childs, "Redskins Beat Brooklyn, 3 to 0, on Aguirre's Third-Period Boost," *The New York Times*, October 5, 1941, 23.

52. *1947 Los Angeles Dons Player Profiles*, 16.

53. Longoria, *Athletes Remembered*, 17.

54. Ibid.

55. "Aguirre, Redskins Beats Cards, 24–21," *The New York Times*, November 5, 1945.

56. *1982 Washington Redskins Fan Guide*, 122.

57. Longoria, *Athletes Remembered*, 18.

58. Ibid.

59. Neft, et al., *The Football Encyclopedia*, 171.

60. Riffenburgh, *Official NFL Encyclopedia*, 83.

61. Ibid.

62. Fritz Pollard was the first black coach/co-coach in pro football. He coached for the following teams/years: Akron Pros, 1920–1921; Milwaukee Badgers, 1922; Hammond

Pros, 1923–1925, and Akron Pros, 1925. See Riffenburgh, *Official NFL Encyclopedia*, 441.
63. Riffenburgh, *Official NFL Encyclopedia*, 83.
64. Longoria, *Athletes Remembered*, 2, 7, 11, 17, 21, 23, 27, 30, 33.
65. "Dons Crush Bisons with Record 62–14," *The New York Times*, December 2, 1946, 35.
66. "Dons, Bisons Even at Buffalo, 21–21," *The New York Times*, September 30, 1946, 30.
67. "Aguirre's Field Goal for Dons in Last 20 Seconds Tops Browns," *The New York Times*, November 4, 1946.
68. *1947 Los Angeles Dons Player Profiles*, 16.
69. Neft, et al., *The Football Encyclopedia*, 187, 213, 223.
70. *1994 Winnipeg Blue Bombers Media Guide*, 69.
71. *1988 Edmonton Eskimos Media Guide*, 63.
72. *1953 Saskatchewan Roughriders Game Program*, 163.
73. *1982 Canadian Football League Official Record Manual*, 33.
74. Mario Longoria and Carlos Guerra, "Recuerdos…Moments of Glory," *PRO MEX SPORTS Publication* II, issue I (February 1991): 11–13.
75. Edward D. Saenz letter to Mario Longoria, January 24, 1985.
76. Longoria, *Athletes Remembered*, 23.
77. "San Francisco (UP)," *The New York Times*, October 12, 1942, 22.
78. *1944 University of Southern California Yearbook*.
79. *1944 Official National Collegiate Athletic Association Football Guide and Official Rules*, cover.
80. "Sailors Play Ft. Sheridan in Grid Opener Saturday," *Great Lakes Bulletin*, September 15, 1944, 6.
81. *Ibid*.
82. "Bluejackets Play Wisconsin at Madison Saturday," *Great Lakes Bulletin*, October 27, 1944, 5.
83. "Great Lakes Routs Wisconsin by 40–12," *The New York Times*, October 29, 1944, 1.
84. Irving Vaughan, "40–12 Defeat on Badgers," *Chicago Tribune*, October 29, 1944, 1, 5.
85. "Dozen Bluejacket Gridders Detached," *Great Lakes Bulletin*, January 12, 1945, 7.
86. *Ibid*.
87. Riffenburgh, *Official NFL Encyclopedia*, 463.
88. Paul Zimmerman, "Washington Redskins Sign Eddie Saenz," *The Los Angeles Times*, June 4, 1946.
89. "87-Point Total Sets a New Mark as Eagles Top Redskins, 45–42," *The New York Times*, September 29, 1947.
90. Joseph M. Sheehan, "Baugh and Saenz Pace 28-20 Victory," *The New York Times*, October 13, 1947, 33.
91. Frank Finch, "Halfback Saenz Joins Redskins," *The Los Angeles Times*, August 3, 1948.
92. *Ibid*.
93. Longoria, *Athletes Remembered*, 28.
94. *Ibid*.
95. Jim Gallagher, "Informational Letter," Philadelphia Eagles Football Club, December 19, 1984.
96. "Steve Van Buren," accessed August 7, 2017, https://en.wikipedia.org/wiki/Steve_Van_Buren.
97. *Ibid*.
98. *Ibid*.
99. *Ibid*.
100. *Ibid*.
101. *Ibid*.
102. Mario Longoria telephone interview with Steve Van Buren, May 16, 1996.
103. *Ibid*.
104. Steve Van Buren, television interview, *La NFL en Telemundo Sports Show*, November, 1993.
105. Morio Longoria telephone interview with Steve Van Buren, May 16, 1996.
106. "Van Buren, Steve," profile information, LSU Sports Information Office, April 22, 1996.
107. "L.S.U. Vanquishes Texas Aggies, 19–14," *New York Times*, January 2, 1944, L1.
108. *Ibid.*, 2.
109. *Ibid*.
110. Riffenburgh, *Official NFL Encyclopedia*, 463.
111. Louis Effrat, "New Order Fails as Tigers Bow to Eagles in Rough Game," *The New York Times*, November 6, 1944, 23.
112. William D. Richardson, "Versatile Eagles Rout Giants, 38–17," *The New York Times*, November 12, 1944, 24.
113. "Eagles Set Back Steelers by 30-6: Van Buren Scores twice for Philadelphia—His Fumble Leads to Loser's Tally," *The New York Times*, November 19, 1945, 14.
114. Louis Effrat, "Van Buren Sets Touchdown Mark as Eagles Turn Back Yanks, 35–7," *The New York Times*, December 19, 1945, 25.
115. *1983 Philadelphia Eagles Media Guide*, 101.
116. "Steve Van Buren," accessed August

7, 2017, https://en.wikipedia.org/wiki/Steve_Van_Buren.
117. "87-Point Total Sets a New Mark as Eagles Top Redskins, 45–42," *The New York Times*, September 29, 1947.
118. *Ibid.*
119. Longoria, *Athletes Remembered*, 25.
120. Louis Effrat, "Eagles Win National Football League Title in Snow Storm: Philadelphia Tops Cardinals by 7 to 0," *The New York Times*, December 20, 1948.
121. *Ibid.*
122. *Philadelphia Eagles 1983 Media Guide*, 101, 137.
123. "Eagles Win Second Straight National Football League Championship—Philadelphia Tops Los Angeles, 14–0," *The New York Times*, December 19, 1949.
124. "2 New Ground-Gaining Records Set by Van Buren, Eagles' Star," *The New York Times*, December 19, 1949.
125. "Eagles Win Second Straight National Football League Championship- Philadelphia Tops Los Angeles, 14–0," *The New York Times*, December 19, 1949.
126. Riffenburgh, *Official NFL Encyclopedia*, 291. The Latino historical significance of the championship game is, of course, the play of Honduran-born Steve Van Buren as well as Los Angeles Rams' receiver Tom Fears. Fears led the NFL in pass receptions in 1949 with 77 receptions for 1,013 yards. He only managed two receptions, however, in the championship game. Tom Fears was born in Guadalajara, Mexico.
127. "Steve Van Buren: A Rarified Eagle," *The Victoria Advocate*, October 16, 1981, 3F.
128. "Steve Van Buren." accessed August 7, 2017, https://en.wikipedia.org/wiki/Steve_Van_Buren.
129. *Ibid.*
130. Mario Longoria telephone call with Louella Fears, January 19, 2000.
131. Earl Gustkey, "What's Left for Fears: Round Pegs in Round Holes," *The Los Angeles Times*, August 1975.
132. *Ibid.*
133. *Ibid.*
134. *Ibid.*
135. *Ibid.*
136. *Ibid.*
137. College Football Data Warehouse 2000–2017.
138. wwii-pows.mooseroots.com/1/77682/Charles-w-Fears.
139. "Tom Fears of the Rams—League Leading Receiver," Hall of Fame Profile, *Pro!* 1972.
140. Riffenburgh, *Official NFL Encyclopedia*, 464.
141. Gustkey, "What's Left for Fears."
142. *1992 UCLA Football Media Guide*, 188.
143. *Ibid.*
144. *Ibid.*, 154.
145. *1946 Los Angeles Rams Press Book*.
146. *1982 Los Angeles Rams Media Guide*, 90.
147. *Ibid.*
148. "Browns Rule Smashed—Rams Capture Pro Grid Crown, 24–17," *San Antonio Express*, December 24, 1951, 2A.
149. *1986 Los Angeles Rams Media Guide*, 112.
150. *Ibid.*, 174.
151. *1956 Los Angeles Rams Press Book*, 3.
152. George A. Frazier, "Two for the Show," Untitled source, missing year and date, 5D.
153. Gustkey, "What's Left for Fears."
154. *1967 New Orleans Saints Press Book*
155. *Ibid.*
156. *1982 Saints Official Media Guide*, 102.
157. *Ibid.*, 103.
158. Riffenburgh, *Official NFL Encyclopedia*, 87–88.
159. *Ibid.*
160. *1967 New Orleans Saints Press Book*.

Chapter 3

1. Vargas, *Crucible of Struggle*, 274.
2. *Ibid.*
3. *Ibid.*, 276.
4. *Ibid.*, 292.
5. Guadalupe San Miguel, Jr., *"Let Them All Take Heed": Mexican Americans and the Campaign for Educational Equality in Texas, 1910–1981* (Austin: University of Texas Press, 1987); Thomas H. Kreneck, *Mexican American Odyssey: Felix Tijerina, Entrepreneur and Civic Leader, 1905–1965* (College Station: Texas A&M University Press, 2001).
6. San Miguel, Jr., *"Let Them All Take Heed,"* 158–159.
7. Ruben Donato, *The Other Struggles for Equal Schools: Mexican Americans During the Civil Rights Era* (Albany: State University of New York Press, 1997), 61.
8. Vargas, *Crucible of Struggle*, 288–289.
9. There are a plethora of research material that documents this history. Here is but a brief listing of some key works (not exhaustive by any stretch of the imagination): F. Arturo Rosales, *Chicano! The History of the Mexican American Civil Rights Movement* (Houston, TX: Arte Publico Press, 1997); Mario T.

Garcia, *The Chicano Movement: Perspectives from the Twenty-First Century* (New York: Routledge, 2014); and Mario T. Garcia, *The Chicano Generation* (Berkeley: University of California Press, 2015).

10. Vargas, *Crucible of Struggle*, 286–287.
11. *Ibid.*, 290.
12. *Ibid.*, 292; Mario T. Garcia, *The Making of a Mexican American Mayor: Raymond L. Telles of El Paso* (El Paso: Texas Western Press, 1999).
13. Vargas, *Crucible of Struggle*, 292.
14. *Ibid.*, 293.
15. See Ignacio M. Garcia, *Viva Kennedy: Mexican Americans in Search of Camelot* (College Station: Texas A&M University Press, 2000).
16. Vargas, *Crucible of Struggle*, 294.
17. *Ibid.*, 295.
18. See Jose Angel Gutierrez, *We Won't Back Down: Severita Lara's Rise from Student Leader to Mayor* (Houston: Pinata Books, 2006).
19. Vargas, *Crucible of Struggle*, Chapter 10, "Mexican Americans in the Protest Era" for specific information, 306–343. For more information on the Chicano Movement in the West please also see Jorge Iber and Arnoldo De Leon, *Hispanics in the American West* (Santa Clara, CA: ABC-Clio, 2005), Chapter 6, "The Great Depression Through 1965," Chapter 7, "The Era of the Chicano Movement, 1965-1980," and 211–316. For information on the blowout in Kansas City, please see Leonard David Ortiz, "La Voz de la Gente: Chicano Activist Publications in the Kansas City Area, 1968–1969," *Kansas History* 22, no. 3 (Autumn, 1999): 228–244.
20. Vargas, *Crucible of Struggle*, 308.
21. Dave Meggyesy, *Out of Their League* (Lincoln, NE: Bison Books, 2005).
22. Jorge Iber, "Mexican Americans of South Texas Football," 616–633. Quote is from page 627.
23. Ty Cashion, *The Pigskin Pulpit: A Social History of Texas High School Football Coaches* (Austin: Texas State Historical Association, 1998). See also Jorge Iber, "The Pigskin Pulpito: A Brief Overview of the Experiences of Mexican American High School Football Coaches in Texas," in *Sports and the Racial Divide: African American and Latino Experience in an Era of Change*, ed. Michael E. Lomax (Jackson: University Press of Mississippi, 2008), 178–195.
24. Quoted in Iber, et al., *Latinos in U.S. Sport*, 171.
25. Corbett Smith, "Why Are Latino High School Head Football Coaches so Scarce in the D-FW," October 1, 2015, accessed September 1, 2016, https://sportsday.dallasnews.com/high-school/high-schools/2015/10/17/d-fw-area-latino-head-coaches-high-school-football-scarce.
26. Selber, *Border Ball*, 79. See also "Rene Manuel Hinojosa," accessed June 9, 2017, http://rgvsportshalloffame.org/?inductee=-rene-manuel-hinojosa.
27. Selber, *Border Ball*, 77 and 87–92. See the following websites: http://siempre.tamu.edu/index.php?pg=21&nav=3; http://siempre.tamu.edu/index.php?pg=60&nav=7; and http://rgvsportshalloffame.org/?inductee=-carlos-esquivel.
28. Selber, *Border Ball*, 149, 157, 160–163. See also: http://www.srlobos.com/news/2015/9/1/FB_0901152107.aspx?path=football and http://rgvsportshalloffame.org/?inductee=-alfredo-avila.
29. Quoted in Iber, et al., *Latinos in U.S. Sport*, 172.
30. *Ibid.* See also Jorge Iber, "On Field Foes and Racial Misconceptions: The 1961 Donna Redskins and Their Drive to the Texas State Football Championship," in *Mexican Americans and Sports: A Reader on Athletics and Barrio Life*, eds. Jorge Iber and Samuel O. Regalado (College Station: Texas A&M University Press, 2007); 121–144; and Selber, *Border Ball*, 164–168.
31. Selber, *Border Ball*, 201–208.
32. *Ibid.*, 169–171. See also: http://diversity.tamu.edu/VPDiversity/media/library/inclusion/docs/Diversity-Timeline-FINAL-11-1-2013.pdf.
33. Selber, *Border Ball*, 221–238. See also: accessed June 21, 2017, http://www.themonitor.com/sports/high_school/article_2db3c90c-7bb0-516f-99c8-e6f06b621b58.html.
34. Accessed June 21, 2017, http://www.pressboxservices.com/teams/18828.
35. See: Iber, "Mexican Americans of South Texas Football," 617–633; and accessed June 21, 2017, http://www.themonitor.com/sports/high_school/article_2db3c90c-7bb0-516f-99c8-e6f06b621b58.html.
36. See also: Jorge Iber, "Bobby Cavazos: A Vaquero in the Backfield," *College Football Historical Society* 14, no. 4 (August 2001): 1–5; Jorge Iber, "Becoming Raiders Rojos: Using Sport to Claim Hispanic 'Space' at Texas Tech University," *West Texas Historical Association Yearbook* 77 (2001): 139–151.
37. See the following: https://www.youtube.com/watch?v=VGlj1zA6YhM; http://nbclatino.com/2013/11/01/mexican-american-college-football-legend-honored-at-ut-hall-of-honor/; https://news.utexas.

edu/1997/06/18/nr-ball. All accessed June 21, 2017.

38. Gutierrez, *We Wont Back Down!*, 54 and xiii. See also: Armando Trujillo, *Chicano Empowerment and Bilingual Education: Movimiento Politics in Crystal City, Texas* (New York: Garland Publishers, 1998), 50 and Quoted in Iber, et al., *Latinos in U.S. Sport*, 201.

39. A rough approximation of nifu-nifa is "nothing" or "not of interest." De La Cruz, for example, when giving out a score will say something like "Cardinals 7, Yellowjackets "nifu-nifa," to relay a 7-0 score.

40. Joel Huerta, "Friday Night Rights: South Texas High School Football and the Struggle for Equality," *International Journal of the History of Sport* 26, no. 27 (June 2009). See also: "High School Football Music to Rio Grande Valley," accessed June 21, 2017, http://www.espn.com/sports/news/story?id=2210540.

41. www.rgvshof.net, accessed June 8, 2017.

42. Quoted in Iber, et al., *Latinos in U.S. Sport*, 202.

43. R. Gaines Baty, *Champion of the Barrio: The Legacy of Coach Buryl Baty* (College Station: Texas A&M University Press, 2015), 93–103.

44. *Ibid.*, 104–193. See also: Fred Morales, *History of Bowie High School, 1922–1973* (El Paso: self-published, 2015), 164.

45. Morales, *History of Bowie High School, 1922–1973*, 167, 169, 171, 177, 183, 186, 192, 198, 202, 218, and 222.

46. See: Dan Ford, *The History of New Mexico High School Football, Vol. VIII* (San Bernardino, CA: self-published, 2017), 154. All of the state title games information comes from http://www.nmact.org/file/Football_Past_Champs.pdf. Accessed May 23, 2017.

47. See: Ford, *The History of New Mexico High School Football, Vol. VIII*, 244 and 309. See also: http://www.legacy.com/obituaries/santafenewmexican/obituary.aspx?pid=178103124; and Ford, *The History of New Mexico High School Football, Vol. I—The First 100 Years*, 99–100.

48. Ricardo Dow Anaya, "An Historical Perspective of Influence Sport Had on Sports Legends of New Mexico, 1925–1975" (PhD diss., University of New Mexico, 1997), 239–251.

49. See the following: Ford, *The History of New Mexico High School Football, Vol. VIII*, 108, 151 and 166; http://www.nmstatesports.com/news/2009/2/12/3628641.aspx; Dan Ford email to Jorge Iber, June 26, 2017; and Iber, et al., *Latinos in U.S. Sport*, 173.

50. Ford, *The History of New Mexico High School Football, Vol. VIII*, 108, 114 and 135.

51. Longoria, *Athletes Remembered*, 68–72. See also: http://www.latimes.com/local/obituaries/la-me-danny-villanueva-20150621-story.html; https://www.nytimes.com/2015/06/23/business/daniel-villanueva-creator-of-univision-dies-at-77.html. Both accessed June 27, 2017.

52. Longoria, *Athletes Remembered*, 112–114. See also: https://www.si.com/vault/1992/08/31/127063/worst-team-the-end-of-the-line-for-the-past-20-years-losing-football-games-has-been-the-woeful-tradition-at-new-mexico-state#; http://amarillo.com/stories/070197/fires.html#.WVKVy-lOljU.

53. Mario T. Garcia and Sal Castro, *Blowout! Sal Castro and the Chicano Struggle for Educational Justice* (Chapel Hill: University of North Carolina Press, 2011).

54. *Ibid.*, 51, 86, and 93.

55. *Ibid.*, 95–97 and 119.

56. *Ibid.*, 110–111.

57. *Ibid.*, 261.

58. *Ibid.*, 262.

59. Longoria, *Athletes Remembered*, 63–67. See also: http://bcrfahalloffame.com/past-inductees/.

60. Longoria, *Athletes Remembered*, 82–86. See also: Tom Flores and Frank Cooney, *Fire in the Iceman: Autobiography of Tom Flores* (Chicago: Bonus Books, 1992), 3, 15–17, 19, 22, 29–31, 35, 47, 52–54, and 57; and Aldama and Gonzalez, *Latinos in the End Zone*, 96.

61. Frederick Luis Aldama, "Shaper of Sports History: An Interview with Latino Football Pioneer Hank Olguin," *Journal of the West* 54, no. 4 (Fall 2015): 66–70; Hank Olguin, "Who Let the Mexicans Play in the Rose Bowl?" last modified December 31, 2014, accessed June 30, 2017, http://www.thecalifornian.com/story/news/2014/12/31/let-mexicans-play-rose-bowl/21126805/.

62. Aldama, "Shaper of Sports History," 101–105. See also: http://www.sports-reference.com/cfb/players/jim-plunkett-1.html; http://www.sports-reference.com/cfb/schools/stanford/1970-schedule.html; and http://www.davidpietrusza.com/Plunkett.html. All accessed July 3, 2017.

63. Iber, et al., *Latinos in U.S. Sport*, 202. See also: "Symbol of Heart: The Official Documentary of the East Los Angeles Classic (Ground Zero Latino and Carmona Productions, 2003), and "The East Los Angeles Classic," accessed July 3, 2017, http://laeastside.com/2008/11/the-east-los-angeles-classic/.

64. Nancy Klingener, "When Key West

Was Cuban," January 7, 2015, accessed July 3, 2017, http://wlrn.org/post/when-key-west-was-cuban.
  65. Jose A. Cobas and Jorge Duany, *Cubans in Puerto Rico: Ethnic Economy and Cultural Identity* (Gainesville: University Press of Florida, 1997), 26. See also "Cubans in Miami: An Historic Perspective," accessed July 3, 2017, http://cuban-exile.com/doc_001-025/doc0016.html.
  66. Longoria, *Athletes Remembered*, 103–107. See the following: http://archive.tcpalm.com/sports/100-years-of-florida-high-school-football-the-100-greatest-players-ep-404810200-349234841.html; http://www.sports-reference.com/cfb/players/george-mira-1.html; http://www.mccookgazette.com/story/2045545.html; https://news.google.com/newspapers?id=8Xc0AAAAIBAJ&sjid=Ep0EAAAAIBAJ&pg=5617%2C1722120; http://www.fiusports.com/roster.aspx?rp_id=4612; http://thegroveguy.blogspot.com/2010/10/george-mira-native-conch.html. All accessed July 3, 2017.
  67. Iber, et al., *Latinos in U.S. Sport*, 204. See also: http://www.gatorsports.com/article/20110517/ARTICLES/110519590/1136?template=printpicart. Accessed July 3, 2017. Jorge Iber conducted three interviews with Carlos Alvarez during October and November of 2016. Mr. Alvarez is currently working on a biographical manuscript (so far, unpublished), to which Jorge Iber has access.
  68. "Genaro G. Brito," Standard Certificate of Birth, County of Los Angeles—Registrar—Recorder/County Clerk, August 23, 1995.
  69. "Genaro Herman Brito," Certificate of Death, County of Los Angeles—Registrar—Recorder/County Clerk, September 5, 1995.
  70. *1960 Los Angeles Rams Media Guide*, 14.
  71. *The Lair: 1951 Loyola University of Los Angeles Yearbook*, 163.
  72. *1958 Washington Redskins Media Guide*, 36.
  73. Longoria, *Athletes Remembered*, 48.
  74. Riffenburgh, *Official NFL Encyclopedia*, 176.
  75. Ibid.
  76. Tim Hansen, Public Relations, Calgary Stampeders Football Club. Letter to Mario Longoria, Dec. 20, 1982.
  77. "Brito Named Pro Player of the Year," *The Los Angeles Times*, December 13, 1955.
  78. Ibid.
  79. Riffenburgh, *Official NFL Encyclopedia*, 176.
  80. Longoria, *Athletes Remembered*, 48.
  81. Cal Whorton, "McElhenny, Brito Get Grid Awards," *The Los Angeles Times*, January 9, 1959, 3.
  82. "Nixon Praises Brito in Last Skins Game," *The Los Angeles Times*, December 15, 1958.
  83. *1960 Los Angeles Rams Media Guide*, 13.
  84. Mal Florence, "Brito Shuns '59 Ankle Injury to Steal Raves in Ram Camp," *The Los Angeles Times*, August 1, 1960.
  85. Mal Florence, "Illness Forces Brito to Quit Pro Football," *The Los Angeles Times*, August 30, 1961.
  86. Ibid.
  87. Mal Florence, "Ex-Pro Grid Star Gene Brito Dies: Former Loyola, Redskins, Rams' Player Succumbs After Four Year Paralysis," *The Los Angeles Times*, June 9, 1965.
  88. Ibid.
  89. Longoria, *Athletes Remembered*, 49.
  90. "Gene Brito's Four-Year Fight Ends," *Burbank California Review*, June 9, 1965.
  91. Longoria, *Athletes Remembered*, 50.
  92. "Gene Brito Award Information," The Touchdown Club of Washington, D.C., November 22, 1991.
  93. "Washington Hall of Stars Elects 5 D.C. Sports Greats," *StarPlex Press Release*, Washington, D.C., September 9, 1982.
  94. Mario Longoria, letter to David Alonzo (National Italian American Sports Hall of Fame), September 10, 1995.
  95. Frank del Olmo, "The Ice Man," *NUESTRO*, October 1979, 18.
  96. Flores and Cooney, *Fire in the Iceman*, 30.
  97. Frank del Olmo, "The Ice Man," 18.
  98. Flores and Cooney, *Fire in the Iceman*, 26.
  99. Ibid., 28.
  100. Ibid., 33–34.
  101. Mario Longoria, letter and questionnaire to Tom Flores, June 30, 1982.
  102. Ibid.
  103. Longoria, *Athletes Remembered*, 83.
  104. Scotty Stirling, "…But What a Finish! Raiders Nip Oilers, 52–49," *The Oakland Tribune*, December 23, 1963, 25–26.
  105. Flores and Cooney, *Fire in the Iceman*, 95.
  106. Ibid.
  107. *1981 The Oakland Raiders Media Guide*, 92; *1986 The Los Angeles Raiders Media Guide*, 100.
  108. Mario Longoria, letter and questionnaire to Tom Flores, June 30, 1982.
  109. *Official 1981 National Football League Record Manual*, 137.

110. Flores and Cooney, *Fire in the Iceman*, 118.
111. Longoria, *Athletes Remembered*, 88.
112. Bob Oates, "Flores Hit Perfect Pitch for Raiders—His Calm Approach Before and During Game Rubbed Off," *The Los Angeles Times*, January 27, 1981, 1, 8.
113. Dwight Chapin, "Dos de la Misma Clase," *PRO! The Magazine of the National Football League*, Premier Issue, August 1981, 49.
114. Flores and Cooney, *Fire in the Iceman*, 172.
115. *Ibid.*, 185.
116. *Ibid.*, 187–188.
117. *Ibid.*, 189.
118. "50th League Win For Raider Coach," *Gameday Program*, Raiders vs. Chargers, September 24, 1984, 178.
119. Neft, et al., *The Football Encyclopedia*, 835.
120. "Tom Flores Retires from Football Coaching," *Raiders Release*, January 20, 1988.
121. Flores and Cooney, *Fire in the Iceman*, 240.
122. *Ibid.*, 247.
123. Neft, et al., *The Football Encyclopedia*, 945.
124. *Ibid.*, 967.
125. *Ibid.*, 989.
126. Richard Keeton, "A Minority of None—Why are there no black coaches in the National Football League?" *The Main Event: Monthly Sports Journal for Physicians*, December 1988, 45–46, 48, 50–52.
127. *Ibid.*, 50.
128. *Ibid.*, 50–51.
129. Marlin Briscoe with Bob Schaller, *The First Black Quarterback: Marlin Briscoe's Journey to Break the Color Barrier and Start in the NFL* (Grand Island, NE: Cross Training Publishing, 2002), 197–200.
130. *Ibid.*, 198.
131. "Latin American International Sports Hall of Fame Program," January 21, 2006, 4. Ceremony was held at the Laredo Civic Center, 7:00 PM, in Laredo, Texas.
132. "Tucumcari, New Mexico—Legend Surrounding the Area," accessed March 2018, https://en.wikipedia.org/wiki/Tucumcari,_New_Mexico#Legend_surrounding_the_area.
133. Margalit Fox, "Daniel Villanueva, a Creator of Univision, Dies at 77," *The New York Times*, June 22, 2015, http:///www.nytimes.com/2015/06/23/business/daniel_villanueva_creator_of_univision_dies_at_77.html.
134. *Ibid.*

135. *1961 Los Angeles Rams Media Guide*, 30.
136. Fox, "Daniel Villanueva."
137. Gary Libman, "He Gets His Kicks Serving Latino Community," *The Los Angeles Times*, September 29, 1985, Part VI, 6.
138. Jeane Hoffman, "Classes Ended When Rams Blew Horn for Teacher Villanueva," *The Los Angeles Times*, September 12, 1961.
139. Fox, "Daniel Villanueva."
140. *1961 Los Angeles Rams Media Guide*, 30.
141. *Ibid.*
142. *1992 Los Angeles Rams Media Guide*, 197.
143. *Ibid.*, 145, 197.
144. *Ibid.*, 197.
145. *Ibid.*, 221.
146. *1982 Los Angeles Rams Media Guide*, 91.
147. Al Wolf, "Danny Boy's Now a Cowboy," *The Los Angeles Times*, July 31, 1965.
148. *Ibid.*
149. *1988 Dallas Cowboys Media Guide*, 123
150. *The Official National Football League 1991 Record & Fact Book* (New York; Workmand Publishing, 1991), 311.
151. Carlton Stowers, *Journey to Triumph: 110 Dallas Cowboys Tell Their Stories* (Dallas: Taylor Publishing, 1982), 124; "Cowboys Defeat Redskins, 31–30, Kick by Villanueva with 15 Seconds to Play Wins," *The New York Times*, November 14, 1966.
152. Carlton Stowers, *Journey to Triumph*, 124.
153. *1988 Dallas Cowboys Media Guide*, 159, 161, 167.
154. Longoria, *Athletes Remembered*, 71.
155. Mike Shropshire, *The ICE BOWL: The Green Bay Packers and Dallas Cowboys Season of 1967* (New York: Donald T. Fine Books, 1997), 184.
156. *Ibid.*, 194.
157. Libman, "He Gets His Kicks," part VI, 1, 6–7.
158. Fox, "Daniel Villanueva."
159. The surname "Casares" originates in Castile as well as in north central Spain, the regions of Galicia, the Basque, and Andalucia. According to Heraldry historical documentation, Casares settlers to the New Spain date back to 1599; Richard Jose "Rick" Casares (1931–2013), American college and NFL fullback who played from 1955 through 1966, is listed as a contemporary notable of the name "Casares" (post 1700). His mother's name is listed as Eleanor Casares.
160. Paul Guzzo, "Tampa's NFL Hero: Rick

Casares," *Cigar City History Magazine* 6, issue 32 (January/February 2011): 23.
161. *Ibid.*
162. *Ibid.*
163. *Ibid.*
164. *Ibid.*, 26.
165. *1951 Florida Football Facts & Figures*, 18.
166. Longoria, *Athletes Remembered*, 54.
167. *1951 Florida Football Facts & Figures*. 18.
168. *1952 Florida Football Facts & Figures—The Fighting Gators*, 9–10.
169. *1981 University of Florida Media Guide*, 73.
170. *Ibid.*, 73; Longoria, *Athletes Remembered*, 54.
171. "Florida Nips Tulsa in Gator Bowl on Conversion by Casares, 14–13," *The New York Times*, January 2, 1953, 20L.
172. Riffenburgh, *Official NFL Encyclopedia*, 474; Longoria, *Athletes Remembered*, 54.
173. Guzzo, "Tampa's NFL Hero: Rick Casares," 26.
174. *Ibid.*
175. "Flashback of a Fullback," unknown Tampa newspaper, 1977. Article provided to Mario Longoria by Rick Casares, July 20, 1995; Longoria, *Athletes Remembered*, 54.
176. Longoria, *Athletes Remembered*, 54.
177. Louis Effrat, "Bears Win Western Title by Beating Lions: Fisticuffs Mark 38 to 21 Contest," *The New York Times*, December 17, 1965.
178. Richard M. Cohen, Jordan A. Deutsch, Roland T. Johnson and David S. Neft, *The Scrapbook History of Pro Football* (New York: The Bobbs-Merrill Company, 1976), 147.
179. *Ibid.*, 146.
180. *Ibid.*, 147.
181. *1986 Chicago Bears Media Guide*, 131, 134, 144, 160.
182. "The Fabulous Fifties," television program, narrated by Harry Kalas, about NFL teams and players during the 1950s; The program was produced by NFL Films; Date and year of production are unknown.
183. Irv Goodman, "New Monsters of the Midway," *SPORT: The Magazine For the Sports-Minded* 24, no 6 (December 1957): 53.
184. *Ibid.*, 61.
185. *1986 Chicago Bears Media Guide*, 153.
186. Charles Callahan (Public Relations Director, Miami Dolphins) "Rick Casares—Press Release," June 19, 1966.
187. *Ibid.*
188. *1976 Miami Dolphins Media Guide*, 104.
189. "Flashback of a Fullback," unknown Tampa newspaper, 1977. Article provided to Mario Longoria by Rick Casares, July 20, 1995.
190. Jan Smith, "The Team That Came from Nowhere," *San Antonio Magazine*, October 1976, 72.
191. Mario Longoria, "1962 Texas Schoolboy Class AAAA Football Champions: The Brackenridge Eagles—A Mexican-American, African-American Team of Destiny, Diversity, and Courage" (unpublished compilation of excerpts, September–December 1962, from the San Antonio Light and San Antonio Express, microfilm archives, San Antonio Public Library).
192. "Brackenridge's 1962 Title a Legendary Victory," January 7, 2013, https://www.mysanantoni.com/default/article.Barckenridge-s-1962-title-a-legendary.
193. Johnny Williams, "Eagles Win, 21–3: Highlands Ousted in Playoff Scrap," *San Antonio Express and News*, December 1, 1962.
194. Johnny Williams, "Brack Downs Brownsville, 38–13," *San Antonio Express and News*, December 8, 1962.
195. "Versatility Big Factor in Spring Branch Success," *San Antonio Express and News*, December 13, 1962.
196. Johnny Williams, "Eagles Upset Spring Branch," *San Antonio Express and News*, December 16, 1962.
197. "Eagles, Borger Play in Abilene: Brackenridge Underdog Again for Big Battle with Borger," *San Antonio Express and News*, December 17, 1962.
198. Mike Wester, "Speedy Eagles Prep For Borger," *San Antonio Express and News*, December 18, 1962.
199. Johnny Williams, "Eagles Relaxed, Gay as Borger Test Nears," *San Antonio Express and News*, December 21, 1962.
200. "Brack Wins State Championship in Thriller," *San Antonio Express and News*, December 23, 1962.
201. Johnny Williams, "Eagles Drill on Defensive Plans," *San Antonio Express and News*, December 19, 1962.
202. "Jefferson's Gaiser on AAAA All-State," *San Antonio Express and News*, December 27, 1962.
203. David Flores, "Brack's '62 Champs Remain Close After All These Years," March 17, 2011, http://www.kens5.com/sports/DAVID-FLORES-Brack-62-champs-have-remained-close.

Chapter 4

1. Aldama and Gonzalez, *Latinos in the End Zone*, 6.
2. Zaragosa Vargas, *Crucible of Struggle: A History of Mexican Americans from Colonial Times to the Present Era* (New York: Oxford University Press, 2011), 345–359.
3. Neil Foley, *Mexicans in the Making of America* (Cambridge: The Belknap Press of Harvard University Press, 2014), 182.
4. *Ibid.*, 182–188.
5. *Ibid.*, 189.
6. *Ibid.*, 191.
7. *Ibid.*, 192–196.
8. *Ibid.*, 198.
9. Zaragosa Vargas, *Crucible of Struggle: A History of Mexican Americans from Colonial Times to the Present Era* (New York: Oxford University Press, 2011).345–359.
10. *Ibid.*, 370.
11. Mark Overmeyer-Velazquez, *Latino America: A State-by-State Encyclopedia* (Westport, CN: Greenwood Press, 2008).
12. Steve Striffler and Julie M. Weise, "Arkansas," in *Latino America: A State-by-State Encyclopedia*, 63–75.
13. Jerry Garcia, "Iowa," in *Latino America: A State-by-State Encyclopedia*, 289–310.
14. Iber, "Mexican Americans of South Texas Football," 628.
15. Selber, *Border Ball*, 286–287. See also: http://rgvsportshalloffame.org/?inductee=john-lerma; http://rgvsportshalloffame.org/?inductee=john-lerma.
16. Selber, *Border Ball*, 289–292. See also: Kenn Rodriguez, "Lerma Out as Football Coach at Belen," December 17, 2015, http://www.news-bulletin.com/sports/lerma-out-as-football-coach-at-belen/article_b88d8da8-a439-11e5-8c66-3f5976bb7a55.html.
17. Armando Garza, "Leal Steps Down as Raymondville Football Coach," *Valley Morning Star*, December 18, 2010, http://newsok.com/article/feed/228583. See also: http://rgvsportshalloffame.org/?inductee=alex-leal.
18. Selber, *Border Ball*, 293–305.
19. *Ibid.*, 321–328. See also: Dennis Silva, "Joe Solis Out as Edcouch-Elsa Coach," December 8, 2012. See http://www.valleymorningstar.com/sports/football/uil-sec-suspends-solis-orders-e-e-forfeit-non-district/article_ed95737c-236c-11e2-99ac-0019bb30f31a.html; Dennis Silva, "E-E Football Fallout: I'm Getting Blamed for It," *Valley Morning Star*, September 28, 2012, http://www.valleymorningstar.com/news/local_news/e-e-football-fallout-i-m-getting-blamed-for-it/article_cf24c922-0929-11e2-aeb1-001a4bcf6878.html.
20. Roy Hess, "Zavaletta, 82, Leaves Behind a Rich Coaching Legacy," *Brownsville Herald*, October 6, 2011, http://www.brownsvilleherald.com/sports/zavaletta-leaves-behind-rich-coaching-legacy/article_a8289b85-ca47-5729-852d-086ae4c59bfb.html. See also: http://rgvsportshalloffame.org/?inductee=gus-zavaletta.
21. Charlie Robinson, "Unique Brother Combination," *Texas Coach*, April 1973, 34 and 35.
22. Mario Aguirre, "Valdez, Valley's All-Time Receiver Leader, to Be Inducted into Hall of Fame," June 23, 2015, http://www.themonitor.com/premium/article_ebb1e0d0-1a28-11e5-9896-e301aef43a3c.html. See also: "Texas Sports Hall of Fame: Valdez, Nati," http://tshof.org/about/thsfhof/details/index.html?staff_id=701.
23. David Flores, "From UTEP Star to Scouting the Cowboys' Next Rising Star," July 29, 2010, http://www.mysanantonio.com/sacultura/conexion/article/From-UTEP-star-to-scouting-Cowboys-next-rising-779176.php. See also: http://rgvsportshalloffame.org/?inductee=sammy-garza.
24. Kelsey Conway, "Where It All Began for Juan Castillo," July 16, 2015, http://www.baltimoreravens.com/news/article-1/Where-It-All-Began-For-Juan-Castillo-/1e2b8ce7-8ed9-4159-88dc-ea8b5642cffc. See also: Iber, et al., *Latinos in U.S. Sport*, 245.
25. "Two Ex-Area Gridders Now Playeing for U.T. Longhorns," *Alice Echo News*, October 15, 1972, https://newspaperarchive.com/alice-echo-news-oct-15-1972-p-19/.
26. Scott Sinclair, "Senor Sack…the Steeler that Never Was," April 24, 2013, https://stillcurtain.com/2013/04/24/senor-sack-the-steeler-that-never-was/. See also: Joe Starkey, "Gabe Rivera Finds Peace," May 20, 2012, http://triblive.com/sports/columnists/1821676-74/rivera-says-starkey-watts-lucky-accident-alive-antonio-car-finds; Texas Tech Athletic Department, "Rivera to Be Enshrined Into Ring of Honor," http://www.texastech.com/news/2014/7/2/Rivera_To_Be_Enshrined_Into_Ring_of_Honor.aspx.
27. Victor Anthony Castillo, "Pathfinders: A Life History Study of 10 Academically Successful Latinos From San Antonio," (PhD diss., University of Texas at San Antonio, 2012), 209 and 210.
28. Morales, *History of Bowie High School, 1922–1973*, 221, 222, 233 and 242.
29. http://www.lonestarfootball.net/team.asp?T=978 and http://www.kvia.com/sports/chapter-1-football/56141161.
30. Evan Berkowitz, "Where Are They

Now: Texas DL Julian 'Kiki' De Ayala," *The Daily Texan*, September 11, 2014, http://www.dailytexanonline.com/2014/09/10/where-are-they-now-texas-dl-julian-kiki-deayala; Jim Lassiter, "Family History Influences Texan's Thoughts on 'War,'" *The Oklahoman*, October 6, 1982, http://newsok.com/article/1998100. See also the following: http://www.houstongamblers.com/id52.html and https://www.statscrew.com/football/stats/p-deayakik001.

31. See the following: "Army Salinas Coach of the Year," *Santa Fe New Mexican*, November 23, 1971, 10; "Hagerman's Salinas UPI Coach of the Year," *Albuquerque Journal*, December 15, 1971, 40; *Clovis News-Journal*, May 22, 1973, 10; Norval Pollard, "Salinas Resigns as LHS Coach," *Lubbock Evening Journal*, October 20, 1983, D1; "Seminole Indians Preview," *Odessa American*, August 31, 1997, 27; "Resurgent Seminole Looking Straight Ahead," *Odessa American*, August 22, 1999, 52; John Erfort, "Seminole Believes Time Is Right to Get Back to Playoff Competition," *Odessa American*, August 25, 2002, 12; and Adam Zuvanich, "New Seminole Coach Should Have Help," *Lubbock Avalanche Journal*, August 22, 2004.

32. See the following: "Socorro Advances in AAA Playoff," *Silver City Daily Press*, November 27, 1976, 7; Walter K. Lopez, "Sports Eyeview," *Santa Fe New Mexican*, December 1, 1977, 1; "Previews," *Albuquerque Journal*, August 24, 1988; Bob Larkin, "Socorro Dilemma Offers a Lesson for High Schools," *Albuquerque Journal*, September 15, 1989; Darryl Seibel, "Resurgent Socorro Is Weathering Hard Times," *Albuquerque Journal*, October 11, 1989, 21; and, Bob Larkin, "For N.M. Preps, It's an Upbeat Week of Sports," *Albuquerque Journal*, September 28, 1990.

33. Dan Ford, email to Jorge Iber, January 18, 2018. See also: Ford, *The History of New Mexico High School Football, Volume VIII*, 368–369; James Yodice, "Tatum Sizes Up Heavyweight Loving in Quest for Fourth Straight Title," *Albuquerque Journal*, November 9, 1989; Richard Rickerd, "Menaul Should Be Formidable Again," *Albuquerque Joural*, August 28, 1992; Bill Lebzelter, "Stangs Put Sting on NMSD," *Santa Fe New Mexican*, October 1, 1993; Jean VanAman, "Momentum on Mustangs' Side," *Albuquerque Journal*, August 10, 2000; and Eric Butler, "Mountainair Looks for Summit," *Albuquerque Journal*, August 25, 2000.

34. Ford, *The History of New Mexico High School Football, Volume 1—The First 100 Years*, 138, 139, 147, 180, 184, and 189.

35. *Ibid.*, 143 and 156.

36. *Ibid.*, 152. See also: Dan Ford, email to Jorge Iber, January 18, 2018; "Little Big Man in N.M. Scoring," *Hobbs Daily News-Sun*, September 26, 1977; and Jim McElroy, "AA Team Has Scoring Punch," *Las Vegas Optic*, December 7, 1977.

37. Ford, *The History of New Mexico High School Football, Volume 1—The First 100 Years*, 146.

38. Dan Ford, email to Jorge Iber, January 17, 2018.

39. https://www.youtube.com/watch?v=-Pr5zDpzwt-E and https://www.youtube.com/watch?v=1JUFzFUaSnM.

40. Julian Wick, "Rival High Schools to Face Off Friday at Legendary East L.A. Classic," https://laist.com/2017/10/28/east_la_classic.php.

41. Aldama and Gonzalez, *Latinos in the Endzone*, 92–93.

42. Robert W. Cohen, *The 50 Greatest Players in New England Patriots Football History* (Lanham, MD: Down East Books, 2015), 220. See also: Bernd Buchmasser, "Pats' Past: The Patriots Trade QB Jim Plunkett to the San Francisco 49ers," November 17, 2016, https://www.patspulpit.com/2016/11/17/13609884/pats-past-new-england-patriots-trade-jim-plunkett-san-francisco-49ers-1976-brock-fox-clayborn-ivory.

43. "49ers Year-by-Year: 1976," February 20, 2009, https://www.ninersnation.com/2009/2/20/766547/49ers-year-by-year-1976; "49ers Year-by-Year: 1977, February 27, 2009, https://www.ninersnation.com/2009/2/27/773882/49ers-year-by-year-1977. See also: https://www.pro-football-reference.com/players/P/PlunJi00.htm.

44. Flores and Cooney, *Fire in the Iceman*, 110.

45. *Ibid.*, 111–117.

46. *Ibid.*, 177–126.

47. *Ibid.*, 133 and 147. See also: https://www.pro-football-reference.com/boxscores/198010050rai.htm.

48. See: https://www.pro-football-reference.com/teams/rai/1980.htm#all_passing. See also: Dwight Chapin, "Dos de la Misma Clase," *Pro: The Magazine of the National Football League* 1, no. 1 (August 1981): 45–51.

49. Chapin, "Dos de la Misma Clase." See also: https://www.pro-football-reference.com/boxscores/198101250phi.htm; Flores and Cooney, *Fire in the Iceman*, 166.

50. See: Brandon Gurney, "Top 10 Games in BYU-USU History," September 30, 2011, https://www.deseretnews.com/top/246/10/1993-Utah-State-58-BYU-

56-Top-10-games-in-BYU-USU-history. html; http://sltrib.cougarstats.com/games. php?show=details&game_id=234.
51. See: http://www.mtsacathletics.com/hof; Les Carpenter, "Football Thursday: Anthony Calvillo, Greatest QB You Have Never Seen, Didn't Need Steelers to Validate Career," https://sports.yahoo.com/news/football-thursday—anthony-calvillo—greatest-qb-you-have-never-seen—didn-t-need-steelers-to-validate-career-041617509.html; Bill Plaschke, "Pass Master," *Los Angeles Times*, October 11, 2011, 7; "La Puente vs. Covina," *Los Angeles Times*, November 2, 1989; "La Puente 75, Bosco Tech 73," *Los Angeles Times*, February 14, 1990; "El Camino vs. Mt. San Antonio," *Los Angeles Times*, November 8, 1991.
52. Michael Liedtke, "Fernandez Disqualified, Arrested," *Spartan Daily*, February 1, 1982, 6.
53. See: "Fernandez, Star Wide Receiver in Canada, Signs with Raiders," March 5, 1987, http://articles.latimes.co/1987-03-05/sports/sp-7726_1_cfl-contract; Marh Heisler, "Fernandez Taking Crash Course: Ex-Canadian Leaguer Hopes to Catch on to Raider Way," March 17, 1987, http://articles.latimes.com/1987-03-17/sports/sp-12385_1_canadian-football; Mark Heisler, "Breaking the Ice: Fernandez Comes from Frozen North and Fits in Just Nicely with Raiders," September 3, 1987, http://articles.latimes.com/1987-09-03/sports/sp-5659_1_frozen-north; Chris Dufresne, "Whatever Comes to Pass Is Fine with Fernandez," September 19, 1991, http://articles.latimes.com/1991-09-19/sports/sp-3716_1_canadian-football-league; "Jurisprudence," January 15, 1992, http://articles.latimes.com/1992-01-15/sports/sp-182_1_mervyn-fernandez; "49ers Get Fernandez from Raiders for Draft Choice," *Santa Cruz Sentinel*, May 9, 1993; "Fernandez Retires After 11 Seasons," *Ukiah Daily Journal*, August 8, 1993; https://www.pro-football-reference.com/players/F/FernMe00.htm; and http://www.cflapedia.com/Players/f/fernandez_mervyn.htm.
54. Mark Powell, *Legends of the Jungle: Introducing the Initial Candidates for a Possible Cincinnati Bengals Hall of Fame* (Bloomington, IN: iUniverse, 2017).
55. Ibid., 119–123. See also: "Raiders Sign Bengal Max Montoya," February 27, 1990, http://articles.latimes.com/1990-02-27/sports/sp-1632_1_bengal-max-montoya; Geoff Hobson, "Full Circle," February 11, 2012, http://www.bengals.com/news/article-1/Full-circle/f8ad7508-c67e-4125-83cc-38f237bec463; "Memories to the Max," April 22, 2017, http://www.bengals.com/news/article-1/Memories-to-the-Max/a291aa11-198a-4390-9a9d-9486f0b3c9b5; Eric Sondheimer, "La Puente to Welcome Max Montoya in Super Bowl Honor," October 8, 2015, http://www.latimes.com/sports/highschool/varsity-times/la-sp-vi-football-la-puente-to-welcome-max-montoya-in-super-bowl-honor-20151008-story.html; and http://mtsacathletics.com/hof.
56. Powell, *Legends of the* Jungle, 180.
57. Tim Layden, "Chips Off the Old Block: Michael and Michelle Munoz Are Following in the Enormous Footsteps of Their Pro Football Hall of Fame Father," *Sports Illustrated*, May 29, 2000, https://www.si.com/vault/2000/05/29/281472/chips-off-the-old-block-michael-and-michelle-munoz-are-following-in-the-enormous-footsteps-of-their-pro-football-hall-of-fame-father; Jorge Iber, "Anthony Munoz," in *Latino and African American Athletes Today: A Biographical Dictionary* (Westport, CT: Greenwood Press, 2004), 270–271; Mark Powell, *Legends of the Jungle*, 175–180; Anthony Munoz Foundation, http://www.munozfoundation.org/default.asp; and NFL Hall of Fame, "Destined for Canton," October 1, 2005, http://www.profootballhof.com/news/destined-for-canton/.
58. Longoria, *Athletes Remembered*, 19.
59. Jose Miguel Romero, "Catching Up with Efren Herrera: Ex-Kicker Fields Range of Goals," *Seattle Times*, December 6, 2003, http://old.seattletimes.com/html/sports/2001808904_oldhawk06.html; "Herrera Not Kicking After Outlaws Replace Him with Rookie Zendejas," *Spokesman Review*, January 26, 1985, 20. See also: https://www.pro-football-reference.com/players/H/herreefr01.htm.
60. Rick Gonsalves, *Placekicking in the NFL: A History and Analysis* (Jefferson, NC: McFarland, 2014), 197; David Zink, "Inland Super Bowl: Frank Corral, the Wild Card Kicker," *The Press Enterprise*, February 6, 2016, https://www.pe.com/2016/02/06/inland-super-bowl-frank-corral-the-wild-card-kicker/. See also: https://www.riversidesporthalloffame.com/frank-corral/.
61. See: "The Zendejas Boys Find Life Is a Relative Kick," September 17, 1984, http://people.com/archive/the-zendejas-boys-find-life-is-a-relative-kick-vol-22-no-12/; "Zendejas Not Guilty of Raping Woman," March 10, 2009, http://www.espn.com/nfl/news/story?id=3968620; http://www.nfl.com/player/tonyzendejas/2503856/profile; Bob Eger, *Maroon and Gold: A History of Sun*

Devil Athletics (Champaign, IL: Sports Publishing, 2001), 202 and 205; https://www.pro-football-reference.com/players/Z/zendelui01.htm?redir; https://www.sports-reference.com/cfb/players/luis-zendejas-1.html; https://www.sports-reference.com/cfb/leaders/fgm-player-career.html; and http://www.nfl.com/player/maxzendejas/2529643/profile.

62. Scott Bordow, "Luis Sharpe Looks Forward to Release and a New Life," *The Arizona Republic*, http://archive.azcentral.com/sports/cardinals/articles/2011/07/02/20110702arizona-cardinals-luis-sharpe.html; See also: http://bleacherreport.com/articles/231585-the-all-time-ucla-bruins-football-team; http://bleacherreport.com/articles/231585-the-all-time-ucla-bruins-football-team; http://bruingold.com/BGpedia/index.php?title=Sharpe,_Luis; http://www.12news.com/article/sports/nfl/cardinals/arizona-cardinals-great-luis-sharpe-shares-new-message-since-prison-release/491580303; http://www.espn.com/espn/wire/_/section/nfl/id/3342461; http://goleathernecks.com/roster.aspx?rp_id=14154&path=; and https://www.youtube.com/watch?v=TRntqP5I4gI.

63. Walter Villa, "The 'Cuban Comet' to Soar Again at Chamber Sports Hall of Champions Ceremony," *Miami Herald*, October 24, 2017, http://www.miamiherald.com/sports/college/football/article180577021.html.

64. See: http://miamiherald.typepad.com/hssports/2008/06/miami-dades-bes.html and http://miamisouthpaw.blogspot.com/2007/08/dade-countys-100-greatest-high-school.html.

65. "Steelers Pic, Stars, Ready," *Tampa Tribune*, August 1, 1975.

66. See: https://www.facebook.com/ghostsoftheorangebowl/posts/1545735048793998:0

67. "Ortega One of the 'Smart Boys,'" *Palm Beach Post*, November 3, 1974.

68. Jack Hairston, "Two More Sophs on Gator First Team," *Pensacola News Journal*, February 11, 1972; Tom Kelly, "UF Challenge: Get Great Quick," *St. Petersburg Times*, August 12, 1972.

69. Tom Cornelison, "Ralph Ortega Is Difference for U-F," *The Miami News*, November 27, 1972.

70. Steve Rajtar and Gayle Prince Rajtar, *Gone Pro: Florida Gator Athletes Who Became Pros* (Covington, KY: Clerisy Press, 2014), 137–138.

71. Steve Hummer, "Remember 40 Years Ago, When Falcons Grits Blitz Dominated on D," August 10, 2017, http://www.myajc.com/sports/remember-years-ago-when-falcons-grits-blitz-dominated/SEtrerBUsPDgrBIPJCzqUP/.

72. https://www.pro-football-reference.com/players/O/OrteRa20.htm.

73. http://www.nfl.com/player/buckortega/2506637/profile; http://hurricanesports.cstv.com/sports/m-footbl/mtt/ortega_buck00.html.

74. http://www.nfl.com/player/carloshuerta/2501261/profile; http://www.umsportshalloffame.com/carlos-huerta.html; and http://www.arenafan.com/players/Carlos_Huerta-761/.

75. "Dolphins' Reveiz Is Working Hard," *Ocala Star Banner*, October 3, 1985, https://news.google.com/newspapers?id=-X5RAAAAIBAJ&sjid=UAYEAAAAIBAJ&pg=6835,2516323&dq=fuad-reveiz+miami+sunset&hl=en; "Vikings' Reveiz Retires Because of Painful Foot," *Los Angeles Times*, August 10, 1996, http://articles.latimes.com/1996-08-10/sports/sp-32916_1_minnesota-vikings. See also: http://www.floridapreprecords.com/field-goal-kicking-records; http://diglib.lib.utk.edu/fbpro/main.php?bid=193&pg=57&catid=44&s=reveiz; http://diglib.lib.utk.edu/fbpro/main.php?bid=738&pg=106.

76. Berry Trammel, "Casillas: An Epic Sooner," *NewsOK*, September 11, 2008, http://newsok.com/article/3296394. See also: https://www.oklahomasportshalloffame.org/tony-casillas.html.

77. John Rhode, "Casillas Shares Memories—'Oklahoma Will Always be Special,'" *NewsOK*, September 11, 2008, http://newsok.com/casillas-shares-memories-oklahoma-will-always-be-special/article/3296432; Bob Hersom, "Improving Casillas '10 Times Better,'" *NewsOK*, August 30, 1984, http://newsok.com/improving-casillas-10-times-better/article/2079819.

78. Gene Wojcieshowski, "Calm Storm: Successful Therapy Lets Falcons' Tony Casillas Cause Stress for Foes," *Los Angeles Times*, October 7, 1989, http://articles.latimes.com/1989-10-07/sports/sp-588_1_tony-casillas,.

79. See: http://articles.latimes.com/print/1991-07-23/sports/sp-72_1_tony-casillas; https://www.pro-football-reference.com/players/C/CasiTo20.htm.

80. Gerald Eskenazi, "Pro Football: Jets' Casillas Seems to Be in Right Frame of Mind," *New York Times*, October 21, 1994, http://www.nytimes.com/1994/10/21/sports/pro-football-jets-casillas-seems-to-be-in-right-frame-of-mind.html?wanted=print,; "Jets Sign Casillas, Plus His Baggage," *New York Times*, September 20, 1994, http://www.nytimes.com/1994/09/20/sports/pro-

football-jets-sign-casillas-plus-his-baggage.html? wanted=print. See also: "Casillas Due for Back Surgery: Jets Tackle to Be Sidelined for 8 Weeks," *NewsOK*, July 30, 1995, http://newsok.com/casillas-due-for-back-surgery-jets-tackle-to-be-sidelined-for-8-weeks/article/2509799.

81. University of Oklahoma Athletics Communications, "Tony Casillas Inducted into College Hall of Fame," August 14, 2005, http://www.soonersports.com/ViewArticle.dbml?DB_OEM_ID=31000&ATCLID=208387846.

82. See the following: Dan Verdun, *Southern Illinois Salukis Football* (Carbondale, IL: Southern Illinois University Press, 2017), 54–57; https://www.sports-reference.com/cfb/players/andre-herrera-1.html; Neil Amour, "Herrera: no. 2 in Yardage After Trying Harder," *New York Times*, December 26, 1976, http://www.nytimes.com/1976/12/26/archives/herrera-no-2-in-yardage-after-trying-harder.html; 76; John Sonderegger, "SIU's 'Miracle Man' Seeks Encore," *St. Louis Post-Dispatch*, August 14, 1977; Tom Barnidge, "Herrera Still Waiting for His Chance," *St. Louis Post-Dispatch*, August 15, 1978; and "Chiefs Are Pleased with NFL Draft Picks," *Chillicothe Constitution-Tribune*, May 5, 1977.

83. Ron Fimrite, "Surprise Marriage of the Year: Joe Kapp and Cal," *Sports Illustrated—The First College and Pro Football Spectacular*, September 1, 1982, 106.

84. Joe Kapp and Jack Olsen, "We Were Just a Bunch of Party Poopers," *Sports Illustrated*, August 3, 1970, 24.

85. Joe Kapp and Jack Olsen, "A Man of Machismo," *Sports Illustrated*, July 20, 1970, 28.

86. Sports Information Office, University of California Berkeley, "Kapp Comes Home!" *CAL Athletic News—Special Edition*, 1982, 1, 4.

87. Longoria, *Athletes Remembered*, 75.

88. Fimrite, "Surprise Marriage of the Year: Joe Kapp and Cal," 110.

89. *1991 Pacific-10 Conference Football Media Guide*, 161.

90. "Kapp Comes Home!" *CAL Athletic News—Special Edition*, August 1982, 4.

91. Kapp and Olsen, "A Man of Machismo," 28.

92. *Ibid.*; Lour Goodwin, ed., *Fall Madness: A History of Senior and Professional Football in Calgary, Alberta* (Calgary, Alberta: Calgary Stampeder Football Club, 1979), 51.

93. Kapp and Olsen, "A Man of Machismo," 29.

94. Goodwin, *Fall Madness*, 51.

95. *1987 Calgary Stampeders Fact Book*, 80.

96. Goodwin, *Fall Madness*, 54.

97. *Ibid.*, 94.

98. Gorde Hunter, "4 for 1 Trade," *Touchdown: The All-Canadian Sports Magazine*, August 31, 1961, 5.

99. *Ibid.*, 17.

100. Longoria, *Athletes Remembered*, 76.

101. *1982 Canadian Football League Official Record Manual*, 52; *1987 B.C. Lions Fact Book*, 110.

102. *B.C. Lions Fact Book*, 99.

103. Kapp and Olsen, "A Man of Machismo," 29.

104. Jack Sullivan, *The Grey Cup Story: The Dramatic History of Football's Most Coveted Award* (Toronto: Pagurian Press Limited, 1970), 159.

105. *Ibid.*, 160–161.

106. *1983 Minnesota Vikings Fact Book*, 67.

107. *Ibid.*, 75–77.

108. *Ibid.*, 67.

109. "Kapp Passes for 7 Touchdowns as Vikings Crush Colts, 52 to 14: Quarterback Equals League Mark for Scoring Tosses," *The New York Times*, September 29, 1969; *Official 1981 National Football League Record Manual*, 231.

110. *1983 Minnesota Vikings Fact Book*, 68.

111. Riffenburgh, *Official NFL Encyclopedia*, 267.

112. Kapp and Olsen, "We Were Just a Bunch of Party Poopers," 23.

113. *Ibid.*, 25.

114. Carlos Guerra, "What's in a Name? Chicanos May Be Too Confused to Know," *San Antonio Express-News*, June 4, 1993.

115. Jack Olsen, "He Goes Where the Trouble Is," *Sports Illustrated*, October 19, 1970, 22.

116. Larry Fox, "Welcome to the DMZ," in *The New England Patriots: Triumph & Tragedy* (New York: Atheneum, 1979), 104.

117. Jack Olsen, "He Goes Where the Trouble Is," 23.

118. Fox, "Welcome to the DMZ," 104.

119. Longoria, *Athletes Remembered*, 77.

120. Fox, "Welcome to the DMZ," 103.

121. *Ibid.*, 108.

122. "Mexican Joe Thrown for Million-Dollar Loss," unnamed newspaper, April 3, 1976, article provided by the Canadian Football League. This and other un-signed newspaper articles were mailed to Mario Longoria by Susan Loney, Secretary to Larry Robertson—Information Officer, Canadian Football League, on October 21, 1982.

123. "Where are they now?" Joe Kapp tele-

vision interview, *Inside the NFL* (HBO sports program), November 1993.
124. Fimrite, "Surprise Marriage of the Year: Joe Kapp and Cal," 104.
125. Longoria, *Athletes Remembered*, 78.
126. Chris Baker, "Cal Beats Stanford and Its Band on Last Play," *The Los Angeles Times*, November 21, 1982, Part III, 1, 4.
127. "B.C. Lions in Football Hall of Fame," *1987 B.C. Lions Fact Book*, 106.
128. *1991 Pacific-10 Conference Football Media Guide*, 144.
129. *Ibid.*
130. Longoria, *Athletes Remembered*, 78.
131. "Joe Kapp," https://en.wikipedia.org/wiki/Joe_Kapp.
132. Longoria, *Athletes Remembered*, 81.
133. Laredo Latin-American International Sports Hall of Fame—Salon de Fama. *Induction Banquet Program*, February 3, 2001, 2.
134. Jim Plunkett and Dave Newhouse, *The Jim Plunkett Story: The Saga of a Man Who Came Back* (New York: Arbor House, 1981), 19–20.
135. Herb Michelson and Dave Newhouse, *Rose Bowl Football Since 1902* (New York: Stein and Day, 1977), 199.
136. Plunkett and Newhouse, *The Jim Plunkett Story*, 20.
137. Chapin, "Dos de la Misma Clase," 45.
138. Plunkett and Newhouse, *The Jim Plunkett Story*, 13.
139. *Ibid.*, 43, 44.
140. *Ibid.*, 47.
141. *Ibid.*, 38–39.
142. *Ibid.*, 50.
143. *1991 Pacific-10 Conference Football Media Guide*, 141.
144. *1969 Stanford Football Facts For Press-Radio-TV*, 34, 76.
145. Plunkett and Newhouse, *The Jim Plunkett Story*, 65.
146. Rick Telander, "In the Eye of the Storm," *Sports Illustrated*, September 7, 1981, 102. Plunkett's senior season, called by many sportswriters "The Year of the Quarterback," included Archie Manning, Dan Pastorini, Rex Kern, Joe Theismann, Scott Hunter, Ken Anderson, Chuck Hixson and Lynn Dickey. All were enjoying fine seasons. Competition for the Heisman Trophy was unusually fierce, with certain schools running pushy, almost garish campaigns. At Stanford, however, the hype was subdued.
147. *1991 Pacific-10 Conference Football Media Guide*, 141.
148. Frank del Olmo, "The Born Again Quarterback," *NUESTRO Magazine*, March 1981, 18.

149. Michelson and Newhouse, *Rose Bowl Football Since 1902*, 202–204.
150. *Ibid.*, 204.
151. del Olmo, "The Born Again Quarterback," 18.
152. Plunkett and Newhouse, *The Jim Plunkett Story*, 90.
153. "Patriots Shock Raiders, 20–6, in Plunkett's Debut," in *The Scrapbook History of Pro Football*, Richard Cohen et al. (New York: Bobbs-Merrill, 1976), 274.
154. Telander, "In the Eye of the Storm," 104.
155. del Olmo, "The Born Again Quarterback," 18; Plunkett and Newhouse, *The Jim Plunkett Story*, 112.
156. Plunkett and Newhouse, *The Jim Plunkett Story*, 121–122.
157. San Francisco gave up two number 1 draft picks in 1976, a number 1 and number 2 in 1977, and reserve quarterback Tom Owen.
158. del Olmo, "The Born Again Quarterback," 21.
159. *1983 San Francisco 49ers Media Guide*, 174.
160. Murray Olderman, "Cinderella After the Bowl," *SPORT Magazine*, August 1981, 30.
161. *Ibid.*, 30–31.
162. Plunkett and Newhouse, *The Jim Plunkett Story*, 185.
163. *Ibid.*, 198.
164. Danny Peary, ed., "Super Bowl XV—Jim Plunkett," in *Super Bowl: The Game of Their Lives* (New York: Simon & Schuster, 1997), 209–214.
165. del Olmo, "The Born Again Quarterback," 22.
166. *The Los Angeles Raiders 1986 Media Guide*, 148; *Decades of Destiny: 1960–1984—The Historic First 25 Years* (Los Angeles: CWC Sport Publications, 1985), 30.
167. *Decades of Destiny*, 35.
168. *Ibid.*, 37.
169. Neft, et al., *The Football Encyclopedia*, 814.
170. Plunkett and Newhouse, *The Jim Plunkett Story*, 256.
171. Robert Markus, "Along the Sports Trail," *Chicago Tribune*, July 27, 1971.
172. Bill Braucher, "Looms the Stork," *SPORT Magazine*, 1972, 63–64.
173. Linda Robertson, "Hendricks Enshrinee Has Trouble Adjusting," *Knight Ridder Newspapers—Packer Report*, August 11, 1990, 4.
174. Paul Zimmerman, "Who Is This Mad Hatter," *Sports Illustrated*, October 17, 1983.
175. Ray Crawford, "The Mad Stork—

Miami For No. 1 Player," *The Sporting News*, November 9, 1968.
176. "Miami Hails Ted Hendricks as Greatest All-Time Gridder," *The Football News*, October 26, 1968.
177. *Ibid.*
178. "Hendricks Game: Book and Tackle," *The Philadelphia Inquirer*, November 8, 1968.
179. *The Oakland Raiders 1981 Media Guide*, 38.
180. "Memories—Colts' Ted Hendricks," *Game Day: Saints Edition*, August 31, 1990, 46.
181. *Baltimore Colts 1983 Media Guide*, 142.
182. *Ibid.*
183. *Baltimore Colts 1983 Media Guide*, 96; *Green Bay Packers 1983 Media Guide*, 104; *The Los Angeles Raiders 1986 Media Guide*, 112, 121.
184. John Crittenden, "Hendricks to Stay with Colts—Thomas," *The Miami News*, February 14, 1973.
185. Charlie Nobles, "Stork Wants Miami," *The Boston Globe*, January 27, 1973.
186. In 1971, in addition to Hendricks, there were Norm Bulaich, Bill Curry, Mike Curtis, Jerry Logan, Bubba Smith, Bob Vogel, and Rick Volk. In 1972, Bill Curry and Bruce Laird. In 1973 Ted Hendricks was the only Colts player in the Pro Bowl. *Baltimore Colts 1983 Media Guide*, 97.
187. Charlie Nobles, "Hendricks Can't Tell Without a Program," *The Miami News*, February 18, 1974.
188. Jim Selman, "Changed Colts Swap Hendricks to Pack," *The Tampa Tribune*, August 14, 1974.
189. Dale Hoffman, "Hendricks Could Be Free Agent Again," *Milwaukee Sentinel*, October 9, 1974.
190. *1983 Green Bay Packers Media Guide*, 105.
191. "Ted Hendricks: Oakland/ Los Angeles Raiders," accessed May 25, 2018, https://en.wikipedia.org/wiki/Ted_Hendricks#Oakland_/_Los_Angeles_Raiders.
192. Warren Wells, "NFL History: Ted Hendricks Used His Head, Heart and Hands as an Oakland Raider," May 6, 2011, https://raidersonline.org/?.
193. *The Oakland Raiders 1981 Media Guide*, 87.
194. *Ibid.*, 73.
195. "Ted Hendricks," *Red, White & Green Magazine* 8, no. 11 (December 1988/January 1989).
196. *The Los Angeles Raiders 1986 Media Guide*, 139; *Decades of Destiny*, 56.
197. *Decades of Destiny*, 56–57.
198. *The Los Angeles Raiders 1986 Media Guide*, 112, 121.
199. *Ibid.*, 30.
200. *Ibid.*, 139.
201. *Decades of Destiny*, 37.
202. "Hendricks Receives Hall of Fame Ring During Pregame Ceremony," *Gameday—Raiders/Packers*, November 11, 1990.
203. Longoria, *Athletes Remembered*, 115.
204. Jorge Iber, interview with Manny Fernandez, April 2016.
205. *Ibid.*
206. *Ibid.*; Longoria, *Athletes Remembered*, 115.
207. Jorge Iber, interview with Manny Fernandez, April 2016.
208. *1992 Utah Football—100 Years Media Guide*, 82.
209. *Ibid.*
210. Jorge Iber, interview with Manny Fernandez, April 2016.
211. *1976 Miami Dolphins Media Guide*, 37.
212. *Ibid.*
213. Dave Anderson, "Larry Little and Manny Fernandez—The Dolphins' Irresistible Force & Immovable Object," *SPORT*, January 1974, 43.
214. Jorge Iber, interview with Manny Fernandez, April 2016.
215. *1976 Miami Dolphins Media Guide*, 119.
216. Jorge Iber, interview with Manny Fernandez, April 2016.
217. *1976 Miami Dolphins Media Guide*, 105.
218. *Ibid.*, 80.
219. *Ibid.*, 36.
220. Riffenburgh, *Official NFL Encyclopedia*, 270.
221. "Pressure on Kilmer Called Key Factor," *The Los Angeles Times*, January 15, 1973.
222. "Manny Fernandez," https://en.wikipedia.org/wiki/Manny_Fernandez.
223. Edwin Pope, "A Super Bowl Hero Re-Enters Reality," *Miami Herald*, January 6, 1978.
224. Longoria, *Athletes Remembered*, 116.
225. Riffenburgh, *Official NFL Encyclopedia*, 271.
226. *Ibid.*
227. William N. Wallace, "Dolphins Go After Unsigned," *The New York Times*, April 2, 1974.
228. *Ibid.*

229. *1976 Miami Dolphins Media Guide*, 105.
230. Gary Long, "Fernandez Taking His Lumps in Dolphin Comeback Attempt," *Miami Herald*, July 7, 1977.
231. Dave Anderson, "NFL's Best of the Best: The All-Time Super Team," *The New York Times*, January 1981.
232. Jorge Iber, interview with Manny Fernandez, April 2016.
233. "Obituary—Peter Paul Rodriguez," November 30, 2014, accessed April 6, 2018, https://www.dignitymemorial.com/obituaries/oceanside-ca/peter-rodriguez-6220721.
234. Bart Hubbuch, "A Special Coach: Rodriguez Brings Unique Style to Jaguars' Special Teams," *The Florida Times-Union*, September 26, 2004.
235. Don Pierson, "From Railroad Boxcar to NFL Sideline—Seattle Coach Special," *Chicago Tribune*, September 17, 1999.
236. *Ibid.*
237. *Ibid.*
238. "Obituary—Peter Paul Rodriguez."
239. "Leaving a Legacy—A Feature Story on Western's Former Head Coach Kay Dalton," accessed April 9, 2018, https://rmacsports.org/news/2017/6/20/general-leaving-a-legacy-a-feature-story-on-westerns-former-head-football-coach-kay-dalton.aspx?path=baseball.
240. "Mountaineer Legend Pete Rodriguez Passes Away," accessed April 7, 2018, http://www.gomountaineers.com/news/2014/12/4/HOF_1204142452.aspx?print=true.
241. "Former Football Head Coach Pete Rodriguez Passed Away," WIU Athletic Communications Football, December 4, 2014.
242. "Florida State Football—1974 Year in Review," accessed April 9, 2018, http://www.nolefan.org/summary/f1974.html.
243. "1976 Iowa State Cyclones Football Team," accessed April 9, 2018, https://en.wikipedia.org/wiki/1976_Iowa_State_Cyclones.
244. "Former Football Head Coach Pete Rodriguez Passed Away."
245. "Pete Rodriguez," accessed September 22, 2015, https://en.wikipedia.org/wiki/Pete_Rodriguez_(American.
246. Neft, et al., *The Football Encyclopedia*, 774.
247. "Michigan Panthers—USFL," accessed April 7, 2018, http://www.usflsite.com/panthers.php.
248. "Pete Rodriguez—Special Teams," *1993 Phoenix Arizona Cardinals Media Guide*.
249. *The Sporting News Official USFL Guide and Register* (St. Louis: The Sporting News Publishing, 1985), 108, 113.
250. "A Brief History of the USFL," http://www.usflsite.com/panthers.php.
251. *Denver Gold 1985 Media Guide*, 23.
252. *1987 Ottawa Rough Riders Guide Media*, 8.
253. Rick Reilly, "Staying Away in Flocks," *Sports Illustrated*, November 9, 1987.
254. Pete Rodriguez' NFL career included the Los Angeles Raiders 1988–1989; Phoenix Cardinals 1990–1993; Washington Redskins 1996–1997; Seattle Seahawks 1998–2003; and Jacksonville Jaguars 2004–2006.
255. Bart Hubbuch, "A Special Coach: Rodriguez Brings Unique Style to Jaguars' Special Teams," *The Florida Times-Union*, September 26, 2004.
256. *Ibid.*, 18.
257. *Ibid.*
258. *Washington Redskins 1994 Press Guide*, https://fc.net/ndlojacon/skins/rodrig.html.
259. Rich Camarillo was born in Whittier, California. He played collegiate football at University of Washington and professionally with the New England Patriots 1981–1987; Los Angeles Rams 1989; and Phoenix Cardinals 1989–1993. He was selected 1st Team All Pro in 1992 and is a 5-time Pro Bowl player in 1983, 1989, 1991, 1992 and 1993.
260. *Washington Redskins 1994 Press Guide*; *1993 Phoenix Cardinals Media Guide*, 24.
261. Brent Schrotenboer, "Special Delivery: Seattle's Pete Rodriguez Consistently Delivers Great Special Teams," *American Football Monthly* 7 (September 2001): 18.
262. *Seattle Seahawks 2004 Media Guide*, 265.
263. Hubbuch, "A Special Coach."
264. *Ibid.*
265. *Seattle Seahawks 2004 Media Guide*, 388.
266. Hubbuch, "A Special Coach."
267. *2006 Jacksonville Jaguars Media Guide*, 26.
268. *Ibid.*
269. Hubbuch, "A Special Coach."
270. Mark Long, "Del Rio Fires 5 Jaguars Assistants," *The Associate Press*, January, 2, 2007, accessed April 17, 2018, http://www.washingtonpost.com/wp-dyn/content/article/2007/01/02/AR2007010200901_p.
271. "Best NFL Coordinators of the Past 25 Years," accessed September 21, 2017, http://www.espn.com/nfl/story/_/id/20746026/nfl-best-offensive-defensive-specialteams-coordinators-25-years.

272. "2009 New York Sentinels Season," accessed April 7, 2018, http://en.wikipedia.org/wiki/2009_New_York_sent.
273. "Obituary–Peter Paul Rodriguez," www.dignitymemorial.com.
274. *Ibid.*

Chapter 5

1. Wayne Drehs, "Cultures Are Teammates at Iowa High School," October 11, 2006, accessed March 20, 2018, http://www.espn.com/espn/hispanichistory/news/story?id=2618295.
2. For a discussion on this topic, please see: Iber, et al., *Latinos in U.S. Sport*, 225–230. See also: A.G. Sulzberger, "Hispanics Reviving Faded Towns on the Plains," *The New York Times*, November 13, 2011, accessed March 20, 2018, http://www.nytimes.com/2011/11/14/us/as-small-towns-wither-on-plains-hispanics-come-to-the-rescue.html.
3. Rogelio Saenz and Maria Cristina Morales, *Latinos in the United States: Diversity and Change* (Malden, MA: Polity Press, 2015).
4. *Ibid.*, 45, 56 and 59.
5. *Ibid.*, 51–54.
6. *Ibid.*, 55, 56 and 229.
7. *Ibid.*, 66.
8. *Ibid.*, 93–95.
9. William Kandel and John Cromartie, "New Patterns of Hispanic Settlement in Rural America," United States Department of Agriculture, Economic Research Service, Rural Development Research Reports Number 99, May 2004, 32 and 33. Quoted in Iber et al., *Latinos in U.S. Sport*, 233–234.
10. Felipe Fernandez-Armesto, *Our America: A Hispanic History of the United States* (New York: W.W. Norton, 2014).
11. Vargas, *Crucible of Struggle*, 344–370.
12. Fernandez-Armesto, *Our America*, 308–309.
13. *Ibid.*, 310 and 322.
14. Ena Capucion, "McAllen-Edinburg-Mission now 5th Largest MSA in Texas," *Rio Grande Guardian*, August 2, 2016, http://riograndeguardian.com/mcallen-edinburg-mission-now-5th-largest-msa-in-texas/.
15. Selber, *Border Ball*, 329–337. See also: "Pete Vela," http://rgvsportshalloffame.org/inductees.
16. Selber, *Border Ball*, 339–351. "Villarreals Talk Life, Football Ahead of RGV Hall of Fame Ceremony," *Brownsville Herald*, June 24, 2017, http://www.brownsvilleherald.com/premium/the-herald-s-gridiron-greats-villarreals-talk-life-football-ahead/article_bc3c4b08-5949-11e7-8380-4bd7b57c6917.html. See also Greg Luca, "Villarreal Reassigned at Weslaco High," *The Monitor*, January 30, 2017, http://www.themonitor.com/mvtc/sports/article_c1f7c836-e73b-11e6-bead-7f018c1fadd3.html.
17. Selber, *Border Ball*, 371–381. See also: http://heraldcast.blogspot.com/2012/01/grulla-coach-abel-gonzalez-iii-named.html and Brian Sandalow, "Unsportsmanlike Conduct," *Brownsville Herald*, November 19, 2007, http://www.brownsvilleherald.com/news/local/unsportsmanlike-conduct/article_7929ace5-9bb3-5c9e-be0c-463e2e8eb7d8.html.
18. Selber, *Border Ball*, 421–435. See also: E.J. Holland, "Legends of the Ball," April 6, 2011, https://www.texasfootball.com/legends-of-the-ball/.
19. See the following links: http://www.kvia.com/sports/chapter-1-football/56141161; http://www.lonestarfootball.net/tcam.asp?action=schedule&T=979&S=2001&GUID=7936964631; https://nces.ed.gov/ccd/schoolsearch/school_detail.asp?Search=1&DistrictID=4846680&ID=484668006496; https://nces.ed.gov/ccd/schoolsearch/school_detail.asp?Search=1&DistrictID=4846680&School Num=4&ID=484668005337; https://nces.ed.gov/ccd/schoolsearch/school_detail.asp?Search=1&DistrictID=4818300&School Num=2&ID=481830008776; https://nces.ed.gov/ccd/schoolsearch/school_detail.asp?Search=1&Zip=79932&Miles=20&DistricType=1&DistrictType=2&DistrictType=3&DistrictType=4&DistrictType=5&DistricType=6&DistrictType=7&NumOfStudentsRange=more&NumOfSchoolsRange=more&ID=481830003786; https://nces.ed.gov/ccd/schoolsearch/school_detail.asp?Search=1&DistrictID=4818300&ID=481830001669; https://nces.ed.gov/ccd/schoolsearch/school_detail.asp?Search=1&DistrictID=4818300&ID=481830001669; http://www.canutillo-isd.org/news/archived_news/c_h_s_eagle_football_among_best_in_texas/; http://www.lonestarfootball.net/team.asp?action=schedule&T=1337&S=2014&GUID=4593976736; https://www.elpasotimes.com/story/sports/high-school/football/2016/11/07/cathedral-excited-title-win/93437006/; and https://nces.ed.gov/ccd/schoolsearch/school_detail.asp?Search=1&Zip=79839&Miles=20&DistrictType=1&DistrictType=2&DistrictType=3&DistrictType=4&DistrictType=5&DistricType=6&DistrictType=7&NumOfStudentsRange=more&NumOfSchoolsRange=more&ID=482013010849.

20. http://nextlevel.epgridiron.com/

21. Alex Kirshner, "Will Hernandez Played an Anonymous Position for an Anonymous College Team. He's Now a 2nd-Round Guard for the Giants," March 2, 2018, https://www.sbnation.com/nfl/2018/3/2/17067794/will-hernandez-utep-guard-draft-2018.

22. David Flores, "Gutierrez's Diligence Reaping Big Rewards," *San Antonio Express News*, October 26, 2005, 1C and 10C. See also: http://www.soonersports.com/ViewArticle.dbml?DB_OEM_ID=31000&ATCLID=208799313 and "Ex-OU Player Becomes Firefighter," June 6, 2012, https://www.mysanantonio.com/sacultura/conexion/article/Ex-OU-player-Gutierrez-becomes-a-firefighter-3613709.php.

23. Ryan Cox, "Strawn Ends Historic Season with 6-Man State Title," *Fort Worth Star-Telegram*, December 20, 2017; https://nces.ed.gov/ccd/schoolsearch/school_detail.asp?Search=1&DistrictID=4809330&ID=480933000392; and Justin Lee, "Balmorhea Falls Short of Championship With Loss to Richland Springs," December 14, 2016. http://www.oaoa.com/oavarsity/article_0872a060-c27f-11e6-9e49-cb920f29644b.html. Also see: http://www.lonestarfootball.net/team.asp?action=schedule&T=94&S=2016&GUID=3608522415; https://nces.ed.gov/ccd/schoolsearch/school_detail.asp?Search=1&DistrictID=4809330&ID=480933000392.

24. Elizabeth Merrill, "Six Man Forever," August 4, 2017, http://www.espn.com/espn/feature/story/_/id/20229005/high-school-girl-saves-football-season-fading-texas-town. See also: Zach Duncan, "Texas Six-Man Team Featured on ESPN Unable to Play Football in 2017," August 9, 2017, https://www.reporternews.com/story/sports/high-school/football/2017/08/09/texas-six-man-team-featured-espn-unable-play-football-2017/554409001/.

25. Texas Guide of High Schools and Colleges (published by T.S.G., El Paso, Texas, 2017).

26. Corbett Smith, "Why Are Latino High School Head Coaches So Scarce in D-FW?" October 17, 2015, https://sportsday.dallasnews.com/high-school/highschools/2015/10/17/d-fw-area-latino-head-coaches-high-school-football-scarce.

27. http://www.lonestarconference.org/hof.aspx?hof=42; http://www.nfl.com/player/robertogarza/2504538/careerstats.

28. See the following: Bill Vourvoulias, "Los Dos Amigos: Louis Vasquez and Manny Ramirez Key to Denver Broncos' Gallop to the Super Bowl," January 31, 2014, http://www.foxnews.com/sports/2014/01/30/los-dos-amigos-louis-vasquez-and-manny-ramirez-enjoy-broncos-ride-to-super-bowl.html; "2008 All-Big 12 Football Awards Announced," December 2, 2008, http://www.big12sports.com/ViewArticle.dbml?ATCLID=3626465; "Louis Vasquez," https://web.archive.org/web/20140219104650/; http://www.denverbroncos.com/assets/docs/UpdatedBios/2013/VasquezLouis.pdf; and Andrew Mason, "Broncos Release Louis Vasquez, Owen Daniels and Aaron Brewer," March 8, 2016, http://www.denverbroncos.com/news-and-blogs/article-1/Broncos-release-Louis-Vasquez-Owen-Daniels-and-Aaron-Brewer/070ed5d9-69c5-430a-a8b3-4750ea56554c.

29. Jorge Iber, interview Manny Ramirez, January 13, 2017. See also: Vourvoulias, "Los Dos Amigos."; "Manuel Ramirez," https://texastech.com/roster.aspx?rp_id=1052; Larry Mayer, "Ramirez Retires After Eight Seasons," June 8, 2016, http://www.chicagobears.com/news/article-1/Ramirez-retires-after-eight-seasons/fd466f21-37ee-4231-9ee4-d229cf4c84db; Jeff Legwold, "Denver Linemen Are Happy to Inspire," September 22, 2013, http://www.espn.com/espn/hispanicheritage2013/story/_/onenationbroncos130923/hispanic-heritage-month-denver-broncos-linemen-manny-ramirez-louis-vasquez-happy-inspire; and Gabe Salgado, "Manny Ramirez's Sudden Retirement from the NFL Raises Questions About Why," June 15, 2016, http://www.foxnews.com/sports/2016/06/15/manny-ramirezs-sudden-retirement-from-nfl-raises-questions-about-why.html.

30. Dusty Young, email to Jorge Iber, February 26, 2018, about Mario Martinez's induction ceremony into the NMAA, 2012. See also: New Mexico State Football Champions, https://www.nmact.org/file/Football_Past_Champs.pdf.

31. Coach San Juan Mendoza email to Jorge Iber, May 5, 2018.

32. James Yodice, "Sartans Coach Mendoza Is Retiring with State Crown," *Albuquerque Journal*, December 4, 2016; "Sartans Choose Montoya as New FB Coach," *Albuquerque Journal*, January 17, 2017; and "Sports Week in Review," *Albuquerque Journal*, January 21, 2017; Jorge Iber, interview with San Juan Mendoza on April 27, 2018; Van Tate, "Drew Ortiz Hopes He Can Shire with the UTEP Miners," http://www.krqe.com/news/drew-ortiz-hopes-he-can-shine-with-the-utep-miners_20180104030017553/900337223.

33. Peter Stein, "Roybal Named Foot-

ball Coach of the Year," *Eastern New Mexico News*, April 19, 2018, http://www.easternnewmexiconews.com/story/2018/04/19/sports/roybal-named-football-coach-of-the-year/157268.html; Rick Wright, "NM Sports HOF Inductees Include Moyas," *Albuquerque Journal*, February 25, 2018.

34. Mike Hall, "Melrose Back Sena Is the Real Deal," *Albuquerque Journal*, September 28, 2000; Greg Rosales, "Runnin' Ruiz," *Albuquerque Journal*, August 21, 2005; Eric Butler, "Melrose Captures Six-Man Crown," *Albuquerque Journal*, November 18, 2004; and "Football: Six Man All State," *Albuquerque Journal*, December 16, 2005.

35. "Six Man Championship," *Albuquerque Journal*, November 11, 2007; James Barron, "Cardinals Set Sights on Class 4A Crown," *The Santa Fe New Mexican*, December 5, 2015; https://nces.ed.gov/ccd/schoolsearch/school_detail.asp?Search=1&DistrictID=3501950&ID=350195000473; https://nces.ed.gov/ccd/schoolsearch/school_detail.asp?ID=350147000375.

36. Jorge Iber, interview with Coach Louie Baisa, May 7, 2018.

37. Dan Ford, email to Jorge Iber, April 29, 2018.

38. See the following: https://mhs.musdaztecs.com/apps/staff/; http://mtsacathletics.com/sports/fball/2017-18/roster; Andrew L. John, "Act of Kindness Helps Young Athletes Fulfill Dreams," *The Desert Sun*, May 9 2015, https://www.desertsun.com/story/sports/football/2015/05/09/act-kindness-helps-young-athletes-fulfill-dreams/27060267/; Scott Harves, "Drive, Determination at Mendota High," February 16, 2014, http://www.espn.com/espn/story/_/id/10450321/from-farm-fields-football-fields-there-drive-determination-mendota-high; Daniel Casarez, "ESPN Documentary, Coach's Arrest: Adversity Powers Mendota High's Aztecs," *Vida En El Valle*, November 26, 2014, http://www.espn.com/espn/story/_/id/10450321/from-farm-fields-football-fields-there-drive-determination-mendota-high; and Bryant-Jon Anteola, "Mendota High Football Coach Beto Mejia Pleads No Contest to Insurance Fraud," *Fresno Bee*, January 6, 2016, http://www.fresnobee.com/sports/high-school/prep-football/article53453955.html. For the documentary, please see here: https://video.search.yahoo.com/yhs/search;_ylt=AwrEwNKkz_FafKcAKPgPxQt.;_ylu=X3oDMTByMjB0aG5BGNvbG8DYmYxBHBvcwMxBHZ0aWQDBHNlYwNzYw--?p=mendota+football+documentary&fr=yhs-pty-pty_maps&hspart=pty&hsimp=yhs-pty_map s#id=1&vid=17124529cb98a61482fa3148881 57500&action=view.

39. See the following: https://www.lavc.edu/athletics/football/Monarchs-on-the-Move.aspx; http://www.maxpreps.com/athlete/john-ramirez/dhKK6hAeEeOZ5AAmVebBJg/default.htm; and http://www.espn.com/video/clip?id=14368870.

40. Eric A. Gordon, "'The Classic': High School Football and What It Means to Be American," June 30, 2017, http://www.peoplesworld.org/article/the-classic-high-school-football-and-what-it-means-to-be-american/.

41. Jorge Iber, interview with Billy McMillin, January 31, 2018. See also: https://www.wsc.edu/news/article/218/spring_2016_deans_list and http://www.wscwildcats.com/roster.aspx?rp_id=3083; http://athletics.elac.edu/sports/fball/2017-18/roster.

42. Jorge Iber, interview with Javier Cid, February 2, 2018. See also: Julian Wick, "Rival High Schools to Face Off at Legendary East L.A. Classic," October 27, 2017, http://laist.com/2017/10/27/east_la_classic.php; Eric Sondheimer, "Garfield Takes Seven-Game Win Streak into East L.A. Classic," *Los Angeles Times*, October 23, 2017, http://www.latimes.com/la-sp-high-school-sports-updates-garfield-takes-seven-game-win-streak-1508768958-htmlstory.html; and "Football: Roosevelt Coach Javier Cid Has Resigned," *Los Angeles Times*, December 12, 2015, http://www.latimes.com/sports/highschool/varsity-times/la-sp-vi-football-roosevelt-coach-javier-cid-has-resigned-20151212-story.html.

43. Jorge Iber, interview with Jeremy Aguilar, March 2, 2018.

44. John Maffei, "Perseverance Paying Off for Former Southwestern QB," *San Diego Union Tribune*, December 6, 2016; http://www.latimes.com/sports/highschool/varsity-times/la-sp-vi-football-roosevelt-coach-javier-cid-has-resigned-20151212-story.html; Arivel Velazquez, "Luis Perez Apunta A La NFL." December 16, 2016, http://www.universodeportivo.mx/article/2016/12/16/luis-perez-le-apunta-la-nfl; http://lionathletics.com/roster.aspx?rp_id=2578; and http://lionathletics.com/news/2018/3/22/football-perez-player-of-the-year-honor-leads-six-lions-on-don-hansen-all-american-teams.aspx.

45. Jorge Iber, interview with Daniel Ruiz, April 12, 2018. See also: http://www.gosdmesa.com/sports/fball/coaches/Ruiz_Dan?view=bio.

46. See the following: http://www.nfl.com/player/donnieedwards/2500516/profile;

Jim Hodges, "Edwards Finds a Niche Among UCLA Defenders," *Los Angeles Times*, September 7, 1994, http://articles.latimes.com/1994-09-07/sports/sp-35551_1_donnie-edwards; http://www.chargers.com/news/2017/11/14/chargers-nominate-donnie-edwards-salute-service-award; https://cvhsfoundation.com/donnie-edwards/; and http://www.eagsportsmanagement.com/donnie_edwards.html.

47. For information on Mark Sanchez, please see the following: Jorge Iber, "'Introduction: The Perils and Possibilities of 'Quarterbacking While Mexican': A Brief Introduction to the Participation of Latino/a Athletes in U.S. Sports History," in *More Than Just Peloteros: Sport and U.S. Latino Communities*, ed. Jorge Iber (Lubbock: Texas Tech University Press, 2014): 3–14; Gustavo Arellano, "A UCLA Bruin Plea for USC's Mark Sanchez to Stay in School," *OC Weekly*, January 2, 2009, http://blogs.ocweekly.com/navelgazing/2009/01/a_ucla_bruin_plea_for_uscs_mar.php; Jennifer Allen, "Sanchez's Impact Can Go Beyond Field with Mexican American Roots," March 31, 2009, http://www.nfl.com/draft/story/09000d5d80f85db6/article/sanchezs-impact-can-go-beyond-field-with-mexicanamerican-roots; and Gustavo Arellano, "A Mouthpiece Says it All," *Los Angeles Times*, October 26, 2007, http://articles.latimes.com/2007/oct/26/opinion/oe-arellano26.

48. Jorge Iber, interview with Anthony Calvillo, April 2016. See also: "Anthony Calvillo," http://www.cflapedia.com/Players/c/calvillo_anthony.htm; Les Carpenter, "Football Thursday: Anthony Calvillo, Greatest QB You Have Never Seen, Didn't Need Steelers to Validate Career," October 24, 2013, https://sports.yahoo.com/news/football-thursday—anthony-calvillo—greatest-qb-you-have-never-seen—didn-t-need-steelers-to-validate-career-041617509.html; Kurt Kragtorpe, "USU Degree a Big Completion for Anthony Calvillo," *Salt Lake Tribune*, May 7, 2014, http://www.sltrib.com/sltrib/sports/57913283-77/calvillo-usu-cfl-football.html.csp; Herb Zurkowsky, "Alouettes Name New Assistants, but Anthony Calvillo Won't Be on Staff," *Montreal Gazette*, January 8, 2018, http://montrealgazette.com/sports/football/cfl/montreal-alouettes/alouettes-name-new-assistants-but-anthony-calvillo-wont-be-on-staff; Bill Plaschke, "Pass Master: Anthony Calvillo's Journey from La Puente to Football Fame Has Come in Virtual Anonymity," *Los Angeles Times*, October 11, 2011, http://articles.latimes.com/2011/oct/11/sports/la-sp-1011-plaschke-anthony-calvillo-20111011.

49. George J. Tanber, "Aaron Garcia Sees Himself in the Right Place, at the Right Time," October 1, 2008, http://www.espn.com/espn/hispanicheritage2008/news/story?id=3618363; Tim Ball, "Interview with Aaron Garcia and His Agent," May 2, 2002, http://www.arenafan.com/news/?=origcol&article=841; Daniel Gallen, "KISS Quarterback Garcia, 43, Reaches Crossroads," *Orange County Register*, July 14, 2014, https://www.ocregister.com/2014/07/14/kiss-quarterback-garcia-43-reaches-crossroads/; and Ben Heck, "Top 10 Quarterbacks in Arena Football League History," *All Out Blitz*, March 7, 2015, http://bensalloutblitz.com/top-10-quarterbacks-in-arena-football-league-history/#sthash.qxIo9qdH.dpbs.

50. See: "Orlando Iglesias," https://www.sports-reference.com/cfb/players/orlando-iglesias-1.html; "18-Orlando Iglesias," http://www.uhcougars.com/sports/m-footbl/mtt/iglesias_orlando00.html; "Orlando Iglesias, Wholesaler," https://ca.linkedin.com/in/orlando-iglesias-76913844.

51. Greg Cote, "FIU's Decision to Fire Mario Cristobal Was Inpatient and Unfair," *Miami Herald*, December 6, 2012, http://www.miamiherald.com/sports/article1945180.html; Tim Rohan, "When Best Still Isn't Good Enough," *New York Times*, December 5, 2012, https://www.nytimes.com/2012/12/06/sports/ncaafootball/florida-international-fires-football-coach-mario-cristobal.html; "Mario Cristobal: 10 Things to Know About the Oregon Ducks' New Head Football Coach," December 8, 2017, https://www.oregonlive.com/ducks/index.ssf/2017/12/mario_cristobal_new_oregon_duc.html.

52. "Alex Mirabal," http://www.herdzone.com/sports/m-footbl/mtt/alex_mirabal_838638.html; and "Ducks Hire Mirabal to Coach Centers and Guards," February 28, 2018, http://goducks.com/news/2018/2/28/football-ducks-hire-mirabal-to-coach-centers-and-guards.aspx.

53. Matt Porter, "Miami DC Manny Diaz Named a Broyles Award Nominee," *Palm Beach Post*, November 23, 2016, http://caneswatch.blog.palmbeachpost.com/2016/11/23/miami-dc-manny-diaz-named-a-broyles-award-nominee/; "Manny Diaz Ignores Coaching Carousel, Thankful to be a Miami Hurricane," November 29, 2017, http://caneswatch.blog.palmbeachpost.com/2017/11/29/manny-diaz-ignores-coaching-carousel-thankful-to-be-a-miami-hurricane/; "Miami Native Diaz Named Hurricanes' Defensive Coordinator,"

January 2, 2016, https://hurricanesports.com/news/2016/1/2/210611698.aspx; and Doug Samuels, "Manny Diaz's Coaching Journey Involves Initial Journalism Aspirations, a Job at ESPN, and Convincing His Pregnant Wife to 'roll the dice,'" November 30, 2017, http://footballscoop.com/news/manny-diazs-coaching-journey-involves-initial-journalism-aspirations-job-espn-convincing-pregnant-wife-roll-dice/.

54. Iber, et al., *Latinos in U.S. Sport*, 2–4; "Alex Tejada," https://www.sports-reference.com/cfb/players/alex-tejada-1.html; and Andres Focil, "Tejada: Choosing Football Over Futbol," http://www.arkansasrazorbacks.com/tejada_choosing_football_over_futbol_204832757/.

55. Almando Salguero, "Kiko Alonso Turns 'Bad Blood' for Colin Kaepernick into Great Preformance," *Miami Herald*, November 27, 2016, http://www.miamiherald.com/sports/spt-columns-blogs/armando-salguero/article117426693.html; Omar Kelly, "Embracing His Hispanic Heritage Has Helped Kiko Alonso Blossom," *Sun Sentinel*, November 4, 2016, http://www.sun-sentinel.com/sports/miami-dolphins/fl-dolphins-1105-20161104-story.html; and Andrea Canales, "Kiko Alonso Has It Made in the Shade in Miami," April 19, 2017, http://www.espn.com/blog/onenacion/post/_/id/7354/kiko-alonso-has-it-made-in-the-shade-of-miamis-sunshine.

56. The term "Zapatista" in Mexican History refers to General Emiliano Zapata and his campesinos—defined as the people of the fields, ordinary farmers, farm workers, and field hands—who revolted in 1910–1920 against the Mexican Federalist Government's control of the land and resources. They fought and eventually achieved Agrarian Land Reform that today is still being challenged by the Mexican Government. See: John Womack, Jr., *Zapata and the Mexican Revolution* (New York: Vintage Books, 1968), x, 329–330, 335.

57. *San Jose State University 1990 Football*, 16

58. *Sacramento Gold Miners 1994 Media Guide*, 29.

59. *San Jose State University 1990 Football*, 16.

60. Bob Rose, "Beginnings—Founding of the World League." *GAMETIME: The Official Magazine of the World League of American Football* 1, no. 2 (1991): 19.

61. Mario Longoria, "Mexican Gridders in World Adventure," *PRO MEX SPORTS Publication* II, issue III (April 1991): 10.

62. The U.S. WLAF clubs are: New York/New Jersey Knights, Sacramento Surge, Raleigh-Durham Skyhawks, Orlando Thunder, Birmingham Fire, and San Antonio Riders.

63. Longoria, "Mexican Gridders," 10.

64. Kent Olinger, "Galaxy Frankfurt," *GAMETIME: The Official Magazine of the World League of American Football* 1, no. 2 (1991): 28.

65. *Sacramento Gold Miners 1994 Media Guide*, 29.

66. "Sacramento Gold Miners," accessed June 6, 2018, https://en.wikipedia.org/wiki/Sacramento_Gold_Miners

67. Ibid.

68. *Sacramento Gold Miners 1994 Media Guide*, 29.

69. "Sacramento Gold Miners," https://en.wikipedia.org/wiki/Sacramento_Gold_Miners

70. "1997 Denver Broncos Season," accessed June 6, 2018, https://en.wikipedia.org/wiki/1997_Denver_Broncos_season; "1998 Denver Broncos Season," accessed June 6, 2018, https://en.wikipedia.org/wiki/1998_Denver_Broncos_season.

71. "1997 Denver Broncos Season," accessed June 6, 2018, https://en.wikipedia.org/wiki/1997_Denver_Broncos_season; "1998 Denver Broncos Season," accessed June 6, 2018, https://en.wikipedia.org/wiki/1998_Denver_Broncos_season.

72. https://www.footballdb.com/teams/nfl/philadelphia-eagles/roster/1999.

73. Kevin Mulligan, "Against All Odds: Eagles Guard Diaz-Infante Hopeful His Hard-earned Spot in NFL Sets an Example for Youth in Latino Communities," *Philadelphia Daily News*, October 13, 1999.

74. "XFL," accessed June 7, 2018, https://en.wikipedia.org/wiki/XFL.

75. Ibid.

76. "David Diaz-Infante," accessed June 7, 2018, https://www.all-xfl.com/lasvegasoutlaws/team/roster/daviddiazinfante.htm.

77. Ibid.

78. Dan Leberfeld, "Bio on Jets New Assistant Offensive Line Coach," accessed June 7, 2018, https://www.jetsconfidential.com/news/bio-on-jets-new-assistant-offensive-line-coach-david-diaz-infante.

79. "David Diaz-Infante," accessed June 7, 2018, https://www.all-xfl.com/lasvegasoutlaws/team/roster/daviddiazinfante.htm.

80. David Flores, "From Their Dreams, a Star Is Born," *San Antonio Express-News*, November 3, 2006, 1D, 3D.

81. Ibid., 1D.

82. Ibid., 3D.

83. Tom Osborn, "America's Cowboy:

Quarterback's Merchandise Atop Many Christmas Wish Lists as Romo Mania Grips the Country," *San Antonio Express-News*, December 10, 2006, 23A.
84. Dave Delozier, "Tony Romo's Football Legacy Started at Wis. High School," last modified January 7, 2015, https://www.channel3000.com/news/local-news/tony-romos-football-legacy-started-at-wis-high-school/156546659.
85. *The 2006 Eastern Illinois Panther Media Guide*, 61.
86. *Ibid.*, 62.
87. *Ibid.*, 47, 48, 49, 55.
88. *Ibid.*, 48.
89. Osborn, "America's Cowboy," 23A.
90. Longoria, *Athletes Remembered*, 75–81. Joe Kapp started his career in the CFL and began his NFL career with the Minnesota Vikings in 1967.
91. Mario Longoria, unpublished research paper, "Master Mexican American/Latino/Spanish Surname/Birthright Pro Football Roster by League, 1927–2014," May 9, 2019. The other Latino quarterbacks include: 1982 Montreal Concordes—Steve AlaTorre; 1982 Montreal Alouettes—Tom Porras; 1987 Kansas City Chiefs—Alex Espinoza; 1987 St. Louis Cardinals—Sammy Garza; 1988 New York Giants—Mike Perez; 1994 Edmonton Eskimos—Chris Vargas; 1994 Las Vegas Posse—Anthony Calvillo; 1995 Ottawa Rough Riders—Jay Macias; 1996 Oakland Raiders'—David Montez; 1998 Miami Dolphins—Dan Gonzalez; 1998 Pittsburgh Steelers—Pete Gonzalez; 1998 Chicago Bears—Moses Moreno; 1999 San Francisco 49ers—Jeff Garcia; 2001 San Diego Chargers—Zeke Moreno; 2002 San Francisco 49ers—Aaron Garcia.
92. "2003 Dallas Cowboys Season," accessed July 18, 2018, https://en.wikipedia.org/wiki/2003_dallas_cowboys_season.
93. "2004 Dallas Cowboys Season," accessed July 18, 2018, https://en.wikipedia.org/wiki/2004_dallas_cowboys_season.
94. *Dallas Cowboys 2015 Media Guide*, 147.
95. *Ibid.*, 309.
96. *Ibid.*, 369.
97. *Ibid.*, 144.
98. *Ibid.*, 142–143.
99. *Ibid.*, 423.
100. *Ibid.*, 141.
101. Michael J. Mooney, "The Last Best Hope of Tony Romo," *Texas Monthly* 44, issue 9 (September 2016): 90.
102. "2015 Dallas Cowboys Season," accessed July 12, 2018, https://en/wikipedia.org/wiki/dallas_cowboys_season.
103. "Tony Romo Leaves Cowboys' Preseason Game with Back Injury," *Sports Illustrated*, August 25, 2016, accessed July 22, 2018, https://www.si.com/nfl/2016/08/25/tony-romo-dallas-cowboys-preseason-injury-update.
104. Mooney, "The Last Best Hope of Tony Romo," 150.
105. *Dallas Cowboys 2015 Media Guide*, 268.
106. "Tony Romo," accessed July 16, 2018, https://en.wikipedia.org/wiki/tony_romo; "Tony Romo," accessed July 16, 2018, https://www.pro-football-reference.com/players/R/Romoto00.htm.
107. "Ron Rivera on Immigration, Trump and Race in the NFL," interview by Ahiza Garcia, February 28, 2017, accessed June 10, 2018, https://money.cnn.com/video/news/2017/02/27/ron-riveracarolina-panthers-nfl-immigration.cnn/index.html.
108. *Ibid.*
109. *Ibid.*
110. Pat Yasinskas, "Rivera Embraces Role as Pioneer," accessed June 10, 2018, https://www.espan.com/espn/print?id=8483164.1/20/2017.
111. "Ron Rivera Early Years," https://en.wikipedia.org/wiki/Ron_Rivera.
112. *1991 Pacific-10 Conference Football Media Guide*, 168, 172, 180.
113. "Carolina Panthers: Ron Rivera," http://www.panthers.com/team/coaches/ron-rivera/848931a2-11cf-4e45-84db-f5745b09e275.
114. "Coaching Staff—Ron Rivera," accessed December 10, 2001, https://www.philadelphiaeagles.com/store/players_personnel/coachesContent.asp?id=14.
115. "Ron Rivera," *PROMEX SPORTS Publication* I, issue IV (August 1990): 13.
116. "Carolina Panthers: Ron Rivera."
117. "Coaching Staff—Ron Rivera."
118. *Ibid.*
119. *Ibid.*
120. "NFL History—Super Bowl Winners," accessed June 12, 2018, https://www.espn.com/nfl/superbowl/history/winners.
121. "Carolina Panthers: Ron Rivera."
122. *Ibid.*
123. "Ron Rivera, Assistant coach," https://www.pro-football-reference.com/teams/sdg/2007.htm; https://www.pro-football-reference.com/teams/sdg/2008.htm; https://www.pro-football-reference.com/teams/sdg/2009.htm; https://www.pro-football-reference.com/teams/sdg/2010.htm.
124. "Ron Rivera," https://en.wikipedia.org/wiki/Ron_Rivera.
125. *Ibid.*

126. "Carolina Panthers: Ron Rivera."
127. https://en.wikipedia.org/wiki/2011_Carolina_Panthers_season 6/18/2018.
128. *Ibid.*
129. "Ron Rivera," https://en.wikipedia.org/wiki/Ron_Rivera.
130. *Ibid.*
131. *Ibid.*
132. "2011 Carolina Panthers Season," accessed June 18, 2018, https://en.wikipedia.org/wiki/2011_Carolina_Panthers_season.
133. *Ibid.*
134. Paul Gutierrez, "Heritage Haul 49ers' Garcia One of a Slowly Increasing Number of Latinos in NFL," *Los Angeles Times*, November 24, 1999, D-12.
135. "Jeff Garcia," accessed June 22, 2018, https://ethnicelebs.com/jeff-gracia.
136. "Jeff Garcia," accessed June 22, 2018, https://en.wikipedia.org/wiki/jeff_garcia.
137. *Ibid.*
138. Jere Longman, "Shaped by Tragedies, Garcia Has Built Career with Resolve," *The New York Times*, January 5, 2007.
139. *Ibid.*
140. *Ibid.*
141. "Jeff Garcia," accessed June 22, 2018, https://en.wikipedia.org/wiki/jeff_garcia.
142. *Ibid.*
143. *San Jose State University Sports Fact Sheet*, 4, 11; and Philadelphia *Eagles 2006 Media Guide*, 103.
144. "San Jose State's Garcia Rallies West to Shrine Win," accessed June 24, 2018, https://www.deseretnews.com/article/331532/San-Jose-Status-Garcia-Rallies-West-To_Shrine-Win.html.
145. Patrick Holloway, "Jeff Garcia: A Man Too Small to Be in the NFL, Won Division Titles with 3 Different Teams," accessed June 22, 2018, https://www.ninernation.com/2017/6/24/15860244/jeff-garcia-nfl-career-49ers-steve-young-replacement.
146. The Grey Cup Championship in Canada is the equivalent to the Super Bowl in the NFL. The history of the game begins in 1909 when Earl Grey, the Governor of Canada, donated a trophy for the Rugby Football Championship of Canada. The trophy, which subsequently became known as the Grey Cup, was originally only for teams which were registered with the Canadian Rugby Union. Since 1954, only the nine teams of the CFL have challenged for the Grey Cup. Source: "The Grey Cup," *Canadian Football League Facts Figures & Records* (Toronto: The Canadian Football League, 1985), 2.
147. *Calgary Stampeders 1997 Media Guide*, 29.
148. "Jeff Garcia," accessed June 22, 2018, https://en.wikipedia.org/wiki/jeff_garcia.
149. *Ibid.*
150. The Jeff Nicklin Award is given annually to a player in the Western Division considered to be the most valuable to his team. The trophy was donated in 1946 by the First Canadian Paratrooper Battalion in memory of its commanding officer, Lt. Colonel Jeff Nicklin, killed in action on March 24, 1945. He had been an outstanding end with the Winnipeg Blue Bombers. Since 1973 the award has gone to the most outstanding player in the Western Division. Source: "Jeff Nicklin Memorial Award," *Canadian Football League Facts, Figures & Records* (Toronto: The Canadian Football League, 1985): 3.
151. "86th Grey Cup," accessed July 2, 2018, https://en.wikipedia.org/wiki/86th_Grey_cup. The other CFL Latino quarterback that was named Grey Cup MVP is Anthony Calvillo who quarterbacked the Montreal Concordes in 2002.
152. "Jeff Garcia," accessed December 10, 2001, http://www.nfl.com/players/146325_bios.htm.
153. "Jeff Garcia," accessed June 22, 2018, https://en.wikipedia.org/wiki/jeff_garcia.
154. *Ibid.*
155. *Ibid.*
156. *Ibid.*
157. *Ibid.*
158. "Pro Football Reference," https://www.pro-football-referenc.com/teams/cle/2004.htm; https://www.pro-football-reference.com/teams/det/2005.htm; https://www.pro-football-reference.com/phi/2006.htm.
159. Paul Zimmerman, "Armed and Dangerous," *Sports Illustrated*, January 8, 2007, 38.
160. "Jeff Garcia," accessed June 22, 2018, https://en.wikipedia.org/wiki/jeff_garcia; "Pro Football Reference," https://pro-football-reference.com/teams/tam/2007.htm.
161. "2008 Tampa Bay Buccaneers Season," https://en.wikipedia.org/wiki/2008_Tampa_Bay_Buccaneers-seaon; "Pro-Football-Reference," https://www.pro-football-reference.com/teams/tam/2008.htm.
162. "Jeff Garcia," accessed June 22, 2018, https://en.wikipedia.org/wiki/jeff_garcia.
163. "United Football League (2009–2012)," https://en.wikipedia.org/wiki/United_Football_League_(2009%E2%80%9312.
164. "2010 Omaha Nighthawks Season," https://en.wikipedia.org/wiki/2010_Omaha_Nighthawks_season.
165. "Jeff Garcia," accessed June 22, 2018, https://en.wikipedia.org/wiki/jeff_garcia.

166. Holloway, "Jeff Garcia."
167. Ibid.
168. Paul Gutierrez, "Not Just Kickers Anymore—More Latino Players—at More Positions—Are Finding Success," *The Sacramento Bee*, October 24, 2007. C-1.
169. Ibid., C-3.
170. Ibid., C-3. Note: The first Latino Pro Football Hall of Famers are Steve Van Buren, Class of 1965; Tom Fears, Class of 1970; Ted Hendricks, Class of 1990; and Anthony Munoz, Class of 1998.
171. The Latino name "Goncals" is pronounced as follows; "Goan-cal-es"
172. Gutierrez, "Not Just Kickers Anymore," C-3.
173. "Tony Gonzalez Biography," accessed July 6, 2018, https://www.jockbio.com/Bios/Gonzalez/Gonzalez_bio.html.
174. Ibid.
175. Ibid.
176. "Tony Gonzalez," accessed July 6, 2018, https://en.wikipedia.org/wiki/Tony_Gonzalez.
177. Ibid.
178. "A Swingman, of Sorts," *Sports Illustrated*, January 13, 1997, 85.
179. Tony Gonzalez," accessed July 6, 2018, https://en.wikipedia.org/wiki/Tony_Gonzalez.
180. Jack Carey, "Cal's Two-Sport Gonzalez Realizes How Sweet It Is," *USA Today*, March 19, 1997, 6C.
181. "1997 NFL Draft," accessed July 10, 2018, https://en.wikipedia.org/wiki/1997_NFL_Draft.
182. Wesley Roesch, "Throwback Thursday: Chiefs Traded Up to Select Tony Gonzalez in 1997 Draft," https://chiefswire.usatoday.com/2017/4/13/throwback-thursday-chiefs-traed-up-to-select-tony-gonzalez-in-1997-draft/.
183. Riffenburgh, *Official NFL Encyclopedia*, 464.
184. Longoria, *Athletes Remembered*, 34–35.
185. There are a total of 10 Latino tight ends: Joe Aguirre, Washington Redskins-1941; Tom Fears, Los Angeles Rams-1945; Dan Garza, New York Giants-1948; Robert Coronado, Pittsburgh Steelers-1961; Emilio Vallez, Chicago Bears-1968; Ray Rowe, Washington Redskins-1992; Tony Gonzalez, Kansas City Chiefs-1997; Aaron Hernandez, New England Patriots-2010; Jace Amaro, New York Jets-2014; and Gavin Escobar, Dallas Cowboys-2014.
186. "Tony Gonzalez 1998 Game Log," acceseed on July 10, 2018, https://www.pro-football-reference.com/players/G/GonzTo00/gamelog/1998/.
187. "Tony Gonzalez 1999 Game Log," accessed July 10, 2018, https://www.pro-football-reference.com/players/G/GonzTo00/gamelog/1999/.
188. Ibid.
189. *2007 Kansas City Chiefs Media Guide*, 478.
190. Ibid., 508–507.
191. Steve Weiberg, "Gonzalez Grabs TD Record as Chiefs Get Back to .500," *USA Today*, October 14, 2007, https://usatoday30.usatoday.com/sports/football/nfl/2007-10-14-bengals-chiefs_N.htm.
192. "Gonzalez Breaks Tight Ends Record for Most Catches," December 30, 2007, https://www.espn.com/nfl/news/story?id=3174064.
193. In 2010, the Chiefs drafted Mississippi Running back/Wide receiver Dexter McCluster. Source: "Chiefs Trade Gonzalez for 2010 Draft Pick," April 24, 2009, https://www.espn.com/nfl/news/story?id=4092471.
194. "Tony Gonzalez," accessed July 6, 2018, https://en.wikipedia.org/wiki/Tony_Gonzalez.
195. Ibid.
196. Ibid.
197. Ray Glier, "1325 Catches Later, Gonzalez Wraps Up His Career," *The New York Times*, December 29, 2013, https:///www.nytimes.com/2013/12/30/sports/football/1325-catches-later-gonzalez-wraps-up-his-career.html.
198. Ibid.

Conclusion

1. Ian O'Connor, "The Patriots' New Coaching Star? His Odds Were Incredibly Long," March 7, 2018, http://www.espn.com/nfl/story/_/id/22262842/brian-flores-new-england-patriots-next-coaching-star-emerge-bill-belichick-tree.
2. Of course, the Cowboys may be the most popular team among Mexican Americans, but the Raiders, 49ers, and the newly returned Rams also claim substantial followings. Among Cuban Americans, the Dolphins, and to a lesser extent, the Buccaneers also have followings. Please see: Jorge Iber, "Sports and Consumerism" and "Football" in Oxford Bibliographies: Latino Studies, http://www.oxfordbibliographies.com/obo/page/latino-studies.
3. For a discussion of the marketing of football to Latinos, please see the following (in addition to the Oxford Latino Studies

bibliography noted above): Haylee Uecker Mercado and Matthew J. Bernthal, "Hispanic Subcultural Sport Socialization: An Initial Investigation," *Sports Marketing Quarterly* (2016): 25, 103–114; "Spenders in the Grass: The Reach of College Football Is Formidable and Its Viewers Have Buying Power," December 29, 2016, http://www.nielsen.com/us/en/insights/news/2016/spenders-in-the-grass-the-reach-of-college-football-is-formidable.html; Cecilia Balli, "How 'America's Team' Became South Texas's Team," *Texas Monthly*, January 15, 2017; Eric Diaz, "Hispanic Football Marketing with 'America's Team,' the Dallas Cowboys," *The Nativa*, October 2, 2011, http://thenativa.com/blog/hispanic-football-marketing-dallas-cowboys/; Silvana Pagliuca, "Jerry Jones Has Been a Pioneer in Marketing Cowboys, NFL to the Latino Fan Base in U.S. and Beyond," *Dallas News*, July 21, 2017, https://sportsday.dallasnews.com/dallas-cowboys/cowboys/2017/07/21/jerry-jones-pioneer-marketing-cowboys-nfl-latino-fan-base; Alicia Jessop, "How The NFL Built a 25 Million Person Hispanic Fan Base," *Forbes*, September 26, 2013, https://www.forbes.com/sites/aliciajessop/2013/09/26/how-the-nfl-built-a-25-million-person-hispanic-fan-base/#54ca18df121d; Martin Rogers, "Dallas Cowboys Aren't Just America's Team. They're Mexico's, Too," *USA Today*, November 17, 2016, https://www.usatoday.com/story/sports/nfl/2016/11/17/dallas-cowboys-americas-team-mexico-nfl/93985644/; and Steve Wulf, "Fandom Without Borders," ESPN, November 16, 2016, http://www.espn.com/espn/feature/story/_/id/18055465/when-visiting-mexico-city-signs-nfl-popularity-everywhere.

4. Kirsten Salyer, "The American Flag was Banned at a South Carolina High School," *Time*, August 30, 2016, http://time.com/4472433/american-flag-ban-south-carolina/.

5. Chris Kolmar, "These Are the 10 Georgia Cities with the Largest Hispanic Population for 2018," *HomeSnacks*, January 6, 2018, https://www.homesnacks.net/most-hispanic-cities-in-georgia-1210756/; and "Dalton Football Preseason Roster," http://www.maxpreps.com/high-schools/dalton-catamounts-(dalton,ga)/football/roster.htm. Although a bit dated by this point, a good place to start any examination of the burgeoning Latino presence in the South is here: http://www.pewhispanic.org/2005/07/26/the-new-latino-south/.

6. See the following: Juan Vidal, "Why Does American Sports Have a Latino Problem?" *Rolling Stone*, September 16, 2016; Richard Lapchick, "2017 College Sport Racial and Gender Report Card," University of Central Florida Institute for Diversity and Ethics in Sport, February 28, 2018, 5, 6, 17, 19, 49, 50, 52, 53, and 65; and Rafael E. Romo, "A Phenomenological Study of the Perceptions and Experiences of Mexican Americans Participating in Collegiate Football," (PhD diss., Capella University, 2009), 51.

Bibliography

Books

Acuna, Rodolfo. *Occupied America: A History of Chicanos, 6th Edition.* New York: Pearson/Longman, 2007.

Aldama, Frederick Luis, and Christopher Gonzalez. *Latinos in the Endzone: Conversations on the Brown Color Line in the NFL.* New York: Palgrave McMillan, 2014.

Balzer, Howard, ed. *The Sporting News Football Register, 1981.* St. Louis: The Sporting News Publishing Company, 1981.

Baty, R. Gaines. *Champion of the Barrio: The Legacy of Coach Buryl Baty.* College Station: Texas A&M University Press, 2015.

Berger, Phil. *Great Moments in Pro Football.* New York: Julian Messer Publishing, 1969.

Briscoe, Marlin, and Bob Schaller. *The First Black Quarterback: Marlin Briscoe's Journey to Break the Color Barrier and Start in the NFL.* Grand Island, NE: Cross Training Publishing, 2002.

Bynum, Mike, ed. *King Football: Greatest Moments in Texas High School Football History.* Birmingham, AL: Epic Sports Classics, 2003.

Carroll, Patrick J. *Felix Longoria's Wake: Bereavement, Racism, and the Rise of Mexican American Activism.* Austin: University of Texas Press, 2003.

Cashion, Ty. *The Pigskin Pulpit: A Social History of Texas High School Football Coaches.* Austin: Texas State Historical Society, 1998.

Clary, Jack. *Pro Football's Great Moments.* New York: Bonanza Books, 1983.

Cobas, Jose A., and Jorge Duany. *Cubans in Puerto Rico: Ethnic Economy and Cultural Identity.* Gainesville: University Press of Florida, 1997.

Cohen, Richard, et al. *The Scrapbook History of Pro Football.* New York: Bobbs-Merrill, 1976.

Cowen, Robert W. *The 50 Greatest Players in New England Patriots Football History.* Lanham, MD: Down East Books, 2015.

Des Jardins, Julie. *Walter Camp: Football and the Modern Man.* New York: Oxford University Press, 2015.

Donato, Ruben. *The Other Struggle for Equal Schools: Mexican Americans during the Civil Rights Era.* Albany: State University of New York Press, 1997.

Fernandez-Armesto, Felipe. *Our America: A Hispanic History of the United States.* New York: W.W. Norton, 2014.

Flores, Tom, and Frank Cooney. *Fire in the Iceman: Autobiography of Tom Flores.* Chicago: Bonus Books, 1992.

Foley, Neil. *Mexicans in the Making of America.* Cambridge: The Belknap Press of Harvard University Press, 2014.

Ford, Dan. *The History of New Mexico High School Football.* CreateSpace, 2010. Kindle.

_____. *The History of New Mexico High School Football, Vol. 1-The First 100 Years.* CreateSpace, 2011.

_____. *The History of New Mexico High School Football, Vol. VIII.* San Bernadino, CA: CreateSpace, 2017.

Garcia, Ignacio M. *Viva Kennedy: Mexican Americans in Search of Camelot*. College Station: Texas A&M University Press, 2000.
Garcia, Juan. *Mexicans in the Midwest, 1900–1932*. Tucson: University of Arizona Press, 2004.
Garcia, Mario T. *The Making of a Mexican American Mayor: Raymond L. Telles of El Paso*. El Paso: Texas Western Press, 1999.
Garcia, Mario T., and Sal Castro. *Blowout! Sal Castro and the Chicano Struggle for Educational Justice*. Chapel Hill: University of North Carolina Press, 2011.
Gems, Gerald R. *For Pride, Profit and Patriarchy: Football and the Incorporation of American Cultural Values*. Lanham, MD: Scarecrow Press, 2000.
_____. *Sport and the Making of Italian American Identity*. Syracuse: Syracuse University Press, 2014.
Godinez-Ballon, Estela. *The Mexican American Experience: Mexican Americans and Education: El Saber es Poder*. Tucson: University of Arizona Press, 2015.
Gonsalves, Rick. *Placekicking in the NFL: A History and Analysis*. Jefferson, NC: McFarland, 2014.
Goodwin, Lou, ed. *Fall Madness: A History of Senior and Professional Football in Calgary, Alberta, 1908–1978*. Calgary, Alberta: Calgary Stampeders Football Club, 1979.
Gutierrez, Jose Angel. *We Won't Back Down: Severita Lara's Rise from Student Leader to Mayor*. Houston: Piñata Books, 2006.
Hickok, Ralph. *Bibliography of Books about American Football, 1891–2015*. New Bedford, MA: CreateSpace, 2015.
Iber, Jorge. *Mike Torrez: A Baseball Biography*. Jefferson, NC: McFarland, 2016.
_____. *More than Just Peloteros: Sport and U.S. Latino Communities*. Lubbock: Texas Tech University Press, 2014.
Iber, Jorge, and Arnoldo De Leon. *Hispanics in the American West*. Santa Barbara, CA: ABC-Clio, 2006.
Iber, Jorge, and Samuel O. Regalado, eds. *Mexican Americans and Sport: A Reader on Athletics and Barrio Life*. College Station: Texas A&M University Press, 2007.
Iber, Jorge, Samuel O. Regalado, Jose M. Alamillo, and Arnoldo De Leon. *Latinos in U.S. Sport: A History of Isolation, Cultural Identity, and Acceptance*. Champaign, IL: Human Kinetics, 2011.
Kessler, Kent. *Hail West Virginians!* Parkersburg, WV: Park Press, 1959.
Kreneck, Thomas H. *Mexican American Odyssey: Felix Tijerina, Entrepreneur and Civic Leader, 1905–1965*. College Station: Texas A&M University Press, 2001.
Levy, Gray. *Big and Bright: Deep in the Heart of Texas High School Football*. Lanham, MD: Taylor Trade Publishing, 2015.
Longoria, Mario. *Athletes Remembered: Mexicano/Latino Professional Football Players, 1929–1970*. Tempe, AZ: Bilingual Press/Editorial Bilingue, 1997.
Meggysey, Dave. *Out of Their League*. Lincoln, NE: Bison Books, 2005.
Mendell, Ronald L., and Timothy B. Phares. *Who's Who in Pro Football*. New Rochelle, NY: Arlington House, 1974.
Michelson, Herb, and Dave Newhouse. *Rose Bowl Football Since 1902*. New York: Stein and Day, 1977.
Morales, Fred. *History of Bowie High School, 1922–1973*. El Paso, TX: self-published, 2015.
Mormino, Gary Ross, and George E. Pozzeta. *The Immigrant World of Ybor City: Italians and Their Latin Neighbors in Tampa, 1885–1985*. Gainesville: University of Florida Press, 1998.
Neft, David S., Richard M. Cohen, and Rich Korch. *The Football Encyclopedia: The Complete Year-by-Year History of Professional Football From 1892 to the Present*. New York: Martin's Press, 1994.
Newlon, Clarke. *Famous Mexican Americans*. New York: Dodd, Mead and Company, 1972.
Nissenson, Herschel. *Tales From College Football's Sidelines*. New York: Sports Publishing, 2001.
Oriard, Michael. *King Football: Sport and Spectacle in the Golden Age of Radio and Newsreels, Movies and Magazines, the Weekly & Daily Press*. Chapel Hill: University of North Carolina Press, 2001.
_____. *Reading Football: How the Popular Press Created an American Spectacle*. Chapel Hill: University of North Carolina Press, 1993.
Overmeyer-Velazquez, Mark. *Latino America: A State-by-State Encyclopedia*. Westport, CT: Greenwood Press, 2008.
Peary, Danny, ed. *Super Bowl: The Game of their Lives*. New York: MacMillan, 1997.

Plunkett, Jim, and Dave Newhouse. *The Jim Plunkett Story: The Saga of a Man Who Came Back.* New York: Arbor House, 1981.
Powell, Mark. *Legends of the Jungle: Introducing Initial Candidates for a Possible Cincinnati Bengals Hall of Fame.* Bloomington, IN: iUniverse, 2017.
Prieto, Jorge. *The Quarterback Who Almost Wasn't.* Houston: Arte Publico Press, 1994.
Rajtar, Steve, and Gayle Prince Rajtar. *Gone Pro: Florida Gators Who Became Pros.* Covington, KY: Clerisy Press, 2014.
Reig-Romero, Eduardo. *Memorias de deporte universitario: sus inicios.* Havana, Cuba: Editorial Unicornio, 2009.
Rescinti, Angelo C. *Super Bowl Victories.* Worthington, Ohio: Willowisp Press, 1985.
Riffenburgh, Beau. *The Official NFL Encyclopedia.* New York: New American Library, 1986.
Rivas-Rodriguez, Maggie. *Mexican Americans and World War II.* Austin: University of Texas Press, 2005.
Saenz, Rogelio, and Maria Cristina Morales. *Latinos in the United States: Diversity and Change.* Malden, MA: Polity Press, 2015.
San Miguel, Guadalupe. *"Let Them All Take Heed": Mexican Americans and the Campaign for Educational Equality in Texas, 1910–1981.* Austin: University of Texas, 1987.
Sanchez, George J. *Becoming Mexican American: Ethnicity, Culture and Identity in Chicano Los Angeles, 1900–1945.* New York: Oxford University Press, 1993.
Selber, Greg. *Border Ball: The History of High School Football in the Rio Grande Valley.* Deer Park, NY: Linus Publications, 2009.
Shropshire, Mike. *The Ice Bowl: The Green Bay Packers and Dallas Cowboys Season of 1967.* New York: Donald T. Fine Books, 1997.
Stowers, Carlton. *Journey to Triumph: 110 Dallas Cowboys Tell Their Stories.* Dallas: Taylor Publishing Company, 1982.
Sullivan, Jack. *The Grey Cup Story: The Dramatic History of Football's Most Coveted Award.* Toronto: Pagerian Press, 1970.
Trujillo, Armando. *Chicano Empowerment and Bilingual Education: Movimiento Politics in Crystal City, Texas.* New York: Garland Publishers, Inc., 1998.
Vargas, Zaragoza. *Crucible of Struggle: A History of Mexican Americans from Colonial Times to the Present Era.* New York: Oxford University Press, 2011.
_____. *Proletarians of the North: A History of Mexican Industrial Workers in Detroit and the Midwest, 1917–1933.* Berkeley: University of California Press, 1993.
Verdun, Dan. *Southern Illinois Salukis Football.* Carbondale: Southern Illinois University Press, 2017.
Waterson, John. *College Football: History, Spectacle, Controversy.* Baltimore: Johns Hopkins University Press, 2002.
Whittingham, Richard. *The Dallas Cowboys: An Illustrated History.* New York: Harper and Row, 1981.

Journal Articles, Website Articles and Essays

Alamillo, Jose M., "Playing Across Borders: Transnational Sports and Identities in Southern California and Mexico, 1930–1945." *Pacific Historical Review* 79, no. 3 (August 2010): 360–392.
Aldama, Frederick Luis. "Shaper of Sports History: An Interview with Latino Football Pioneer Hank Olguin." *Journal of the West* 54, no. 4 (Fall 2015): 66–70.
Anderson, Marc C. "'What Is to Be Done with 'Em?': Images of Mexican Cultural Backwardness, Racial Limitations, and Moral Decrepitude in the United States Press, 1913–1915." *Mexican Studies/Estudios Mexicanos* 14, no. 1 (Winter 1998): 23–70.
Blanton, Carlos Kevin. "'They Cannot Master Abstractions, but They Can Be Made Efficient Workers': Race and Class in Intelligence Testing of Mexican Americans and African Americans in Texas during the 1920s." *Social Science Quarterly* 81, no. 4 (December 2000): 1014–1026.
Chavez-Garcia, Miroslava. "Intelligence Testing at Whittier School, 1890–1920." *Pacific Historical Review* 76, no. 2 (May 2007): 193–228.
Franks, Joel. "California and the Rise of Spectator Sports, 1850–1900." *Southern California Quarterly* 71, no. 4 (Winter 1989): 287–310.

Garcia, Ignacio M. "William Carson 'Nemo' Herrera: Constructing a Mexican American Powerhouse While Remaining Colorblind." *Journal of the West* 54, no. 4 (Fall 2015): 40–46.
Huerta, Joel. "Friday Night Rights: South Texas High-school Football and the Struggle for Equality." *The International Journal of the History of Sport* 26 (June 2009): 981–1000.
Iber, Jorge. "Becoming Raiders Rojos: Using Sport to Claim Hispanic 'Space' at Texas Tech University." *West Texas Historical Association Yearbook* 77 (2001): 139–151.
———. "Mexican Americans of South Texas Football: The Athletic and Coaching Careers of E.C. Lerma and Bobby Cavazos, 1932–1965." *Southwestern Historical Quarterly* 55, no. 4 (April 2002): 616–633.
———. "On Field Foes and Racial Misperceptions: The 1961 Donna Redskins and Their Drive to the Texas State Football Championship." In *Mexican Americans and Sport: A Reader on Athletics and Barrio Life*, edited by Jorge Iber and Samuel O. Regalado, 121–144. College Station: Texas A&M University Press, 2007.
———. "The Pigskin Pulpito: A Brief Overview of the Experiences of Mexican American High School Football Coaches in Texas." In *Sports and the Racial Divide: African American and Latino Experiences in an Era of Change*, edited by Michael E. Lomax, 178–195. Jackson: University Press of Mississippi, 2008.
———. "Quarterbacking While Mexican: A Brief Introduction to the Participation of Latino/a Athletes in US Sports History." In *More Than Just Peloteros: Sport and US Latino Communities*, edited by Jorge Iber, 3–14. Lubbock: Texas Tech University Press, 2014.
———. "A Vaquero in the Backfield." *College Football Historical Society* 14, no. 4 (August 2001): 1–5.
Ortiz, Leonard David. "La Voz de la Gente: Chicano Activist Publications in the Kansas City Area, 1968–1969." *Kansas History* 22, no. 3 (Autumn 1999): 228–244.
Stimson, Marshall. "History of Los Angeles High School." *The Quarterly: Historical Society of Southern California* 24, no. 3 (September 1942): 98–109.
Thompson, Merrell E., and Claude C. Dove. "A Comparison of Physical Achievement of Anglo and Spanish American Boys in Junior High School." *Research Quarterly* 13 (October 1942): 341–346.
Uecker-Mercado, Haylee, and Matthew J. Bernthal. "Hispanic Subcultural Sport Socialization: An Initial Investigation." *Sports Marketing Quarterly* 25 (2016): 103–114.
Wild, Mark. "'So Many Children at Once and so Many Kinds': Schools and Ethno-Racial Boundaries in Early Twentieth-Century Los Angeles." *Western Historical Quarterly* 33, no. 4 (Winter 2002): 453–476.
Wood, Michael T. "American Football in Cuba: A Brief Introduction." Accessed July 30, 2015. https://ussporthistory.com/2015/07/30/american-football-in-cuba-a-brief-introduction/.
———. "American Football in Cuba: L.S.U. vs. University of Havana, 1907." Accessed December 31, 2015. https://ussporthistory.com/2015/12/31/american-football-in-cuba-l-s-u-vs-university-of-havana-1907/.
———. "Bacardi Bowl: American Football and Cuba." Accessed March 1, 2013. https://bacardibowl.blogspot.com/search/label/Bacardi%20Bowl.

Dissertations, Master's Theses and Government Reports

Anderson-Lamont, Deanna. "Sport and Leisure in the Building of an Urban Community: The Case of Oakland, California, 1850–1906." PhD diss., University of California at Berkeley, 1996.
Castillo, Victor Anthony. "Pathfinders: A Life History Study of 10 Academically Successful Latinos From San Antonio." PhD diss., University of Texas at San Antonio, 2012.
Dinnijes-Withers, Charles. "Problems of Mexican Boys." Master's thesis, University of Southern California, 1942.
Dow-Anaya, Ricardo. "An Historical Perspective of the Influence Sport Had on Sport Legends of New Mexico, 1925–1975." PhD diss., University of New Mexico, 1997.
Emrick, Lillian. "A Survey of the Recreational Interests of High School Pupils in Nogales, Arizona." Master's thesis, University of Southern California, 1944.
Folsom-Cobb, Albert. "Comparative Study of the Athletic Ability of Latin American and

Anglo American Boys on a Junior High School Level." Master's thesis, University of Texas, 1952.
Habermacher, Andrew Lee. "Physical Development of Anglo and Spanish Culture Boys and Girls, Ages 13–18, Inclusive." Master's thesis, Texas A&I University, 1940.
Kandel, William, and John Cromartie. "New Patterns in Hispanic Settlement in Rural America." United States Department of Agriculture, Economic Research Service, Rural Development, Research Report Number 99, May 2004.
King, Genevieve. "The Psychology of a Mexican Community in San Antonio, Texas." Master's thesis, University of Texas, 1936.
Kramme, Clyde Ira. "A Comparison of Anglo Culture with Spanish Culture Elementary Students in Physical Development as Determined by Height, Weight, and Vital Capacity Measurements." Master's thesis, Texas A&I University, 1939.
Romo, Rafael. "A Phenomenological Study of the Perceptions and Experiences of Mexican Americans Participating in Collegiate Football." PhD diss., Capella University, 2009.
Walsh-Shaw, Bruce. "Sociometric Status and Athletic Ability of Anglo American and Latin American Boys in a San Antonio Junior High School." Master's thesis, University of Texas, 1951.

Newspaper and Magazine Articles

"Aguirre, Redskins, Best Cards, 24–21." *The New York Times*, November 5, 1945.
"Aguirre's Field Goal for Dons in Last 20 Seconds Tops Browns." *The New York Times*, November 4, 1946.
"Aldo Richins and Hank Davies Win Athletic Award." *Utah Daily Chronicle*, May 24, 1934.
Anderson, Dave. "Miami's Immovable Object Meets Miami's Irresistible Force." *SPORT Magazine*, January 1974.
———. "NFL Best of the Best: The All-Time Super Team." *The New York Times*, January 1981.
Balli, Cecilia. "How 'America's Team' Became South Texas's Team." *Texas Monthly*, January 15, 2017. https://www.texasmonthly.com/the-culture/americas-team-became-south-texass-team/.
Barker, Chris. "Cal Beats Stanford and Its Band on Last Play." *Los Angeles Times*, November 21, 1982.
Bashore, Mel "Buck." "The Salt Lake Seagulls." *The Coffin Corner* 14, no. 02 (1992).
"Battles and Spanish Lad Are Scorers." *Clarksburg Telegram*, November 10, 1928.
"Bears Misplays Present Bisons with 19–7 Win, Fumbles and Intercepted Passes." *Chicago Daily Tribune*, November 25, 1929.
"Bison Pros Open Season Today with Chicago Cards: Chief Elkins with Rivals." *Buffalo Courier Express*, September 29, 1929.
"Bobcats in Decisive Win by 34–0 Tally: Thirty Seconds after Game Opens Rodriguez Runs 76 Yards to Score." *Clarksburg Telegram*, October 27, 1928.
Boyd, Denny. "It Was the Biggest Deal Since Sam and Hall. A Pair of Touchdown Experts Give Their Opinions on That." *Touchdown: The All-Canadian Sports Magazine*, August 31, 1961.
Braucher, Bill. "Looms The Stork." *SPORT Magazine*, 1972.
"Brito Named Pro Player of the Year." *Los Angeles Times*, December 13, 1955.
"Browns Rule Smashed—Rams Capture Pro Grid Crown, 24–17." *San Antonio Express*, December 24, 1951.
"Buffalo Pros Hold Hornets Three Points." *Buffalo Courier Express*, October 6, 1929.
Burton, Lewis. "NYU Defeats Wesleyan, 26–7." *New York Herald Tribune*, October 7, 1928.
Carey, Jack. "Cal's two-sport Gonzalez realizes how sweet it is." *USA Today*, March 19, 1997.
Chapin, Dwight. "Dos de misma clase." *Pro! The Magazine of the National Football League*, August 1981, 45–51.
Childs, Kingsley. "Redskins Beat Brooklyn, 3 to 0, on Aguirre's Third Period Boot." *New York Times*, October 6, 1941.
"Cowboys Defeat Redskins, 31–30; Kick by Villanueva with 15 Seconds to Play Wins." *The New York Times*, November 14, 1966.
Crawford, Ray. "The Mad Stork—Miami For No. 1 Player." *The Sporting News*, November 9, 1968.
Crittenden, John. "Hendricks to Stay with Colts—Thomas." *The Miami News*, February 14, 1973.

"Davis and Elkins Twice Cross Wesleyan Goal." *Clarksburg Telegram*, November 17, 1928.
del Olmo, Frank. "The Born Again Quarterback." *NUESTRO Magazine*, March 1981.
_____. "The Ice Man." *NUESTRO Magazine*, October 1979.
Dickey, Glenn. "Cal Program Has Reached a Plateau." *San Francisco Chronicle*, September 25, 1984.
"Dons, Bisons Even at Buffalo, 21–21, Aguirre Takes O'Rourke Pass Four Minutes from End to Tie for Los Angeles." *The New York Times*, September 30, 1946.
"Dons Crush Bisons with Record 62–14." *The New York Times*, December 2, 1946.
"Drake Air Game Beats Iowa State." *The New York Times*, November 23, 1930.
Drehs, Wayne. "Cultures are Teammates at Iowa High School." October 11, 2006. http://www.espn.com/espn/hispanichistory/news/story?id=2618295.
"Eagles Set Back Steelers By 30–6: Van Buren Scores Twice for Philadelphia—His fumble leads to Loser's Tally." *The New York Times*, November 19, 1945.
"Eagles Win Second Straight National Football League Championship—Philadelphia Tops Los Angeles, 14–0." *The New York Times*, December 19, 1949.
"Eddie Saenz, Ex-Trojan Dies." *Los Angeles Times*, April 29, 1971.
Effrat, Louis. "Bears win Western Title by Beating Lions: Fisticuffs Mark 38 to 21 Contest." *The New York Times*, December 17, 1965.
_____. "Eagles Win National Football League Title in Snow Storm: Philadelphia Tops Cardinals by 7 to 0." *The New York Times*, December 20, 1948.
_____. "New Order Fails as Tigers Bow to Eagles in Rough Game." *The New York Times*, November 6, 1944.
_____. "Van Buren Sets Touchdown Mark as Eagles Turn Back Yanks, 35–7." *The New York Times*, December 19, 1945.
"87-Point Total Sets a New Mark as Eagles Top Redskins, 45–42." *The New York Times*, September 29, 1947.
Eskenazi, Gerald. "Bengals' Blocking Technique Forward." *The New York Times*, January 18, 1989.
"Field Goal Saved Season for Danny." *Los Angeles Times*, November 18, 1966.
Fimrite, Ron. "Surprise Marriage of the Year: Joe Kapp and Cal." *Sports Illustrated*, September 1, 1982.
"Flashback of a Fullback." Unknown Tampa newspaper, 1977—article provided by Rick Casares, July 20, 1995.
Florence, Mal. "Ex-Pro Grid Star Gene Brito Dies: Former Loyola, Redskins, Rams Player Succumbs after Four Year Paralysis." *Los Angeles Times*, June 9, 1965.
_____. "Illness Forces Gene Brito to Quit Pro Football." *Los Angeles Times*, August 30, 1961.
Flores, David. "From their dreams, a star is born." *San Antonio Express-News*, November 3, 2006.
_____. "Kapp Taking High Hispanic Dropout Rate to Task." *San Antonio Express-News*, February 4, 2005.
_____. "Kapp's Toughness Made Him Unique." *Deportes Conexion—San Antonio Express-News*, February 3, 2005.
_____. "Munoz Carving a Trail to the Hall of Fame." *PROMEX SPORTS Publication*, March 1990.
Flores, John. "Uno, dos, tres…Hike! Latinos in the National Football League." *HISPANIC Magazine*, January/February 1998.
"Florida Nips Tulsa in Gator Bowl on Conversion by Casares, 14–13." *The New York Times*, January 2, 1953.
"Ft. Sheridan First Opponent for Great Lakes." *Great Lakes Bulletin*, August 25, 1944.
Goodman, Irv. "New Monsters of the Midway." *SPORT Magazine*, December 1957.
"Great Lakes Clashes with Ohio State at Columbus." *Great Lakes Bulletin*, October 20, 1944.
"Great Lakes, Marquette Tangle at Milwaukee." *Great Lakes Bulletin*, November 3, 1944.
"Great Lakes Routs Wisconsin by 40–12." *The New York Times*, October 29, 1944.
Greenberg, Jay. "The King of the Block." *Sports Illustrated*, September 10, 1990.
Gustkey, Earl, "What's Left for Fears: Round Pegs in Round Holes." *The Los Angeles Times*, August 1975.
Gutierrez, Paul. "Heritage Haul 49ers' Garcia One of a Slowly Increasing Number of Latinos in NFL." *Los Angeles Times*, November 24, 1999.

_____. "Not Just Kickers Anymore." *The Sacramento Bee*, October 24, 2007.
Guzzo, Paul. "Tampa's NFL Hero: Rick Casares." *Cigar City History Magazine*, January/February 2011.
"Hagsberg the Buffalo Star in Tough Game." *Buffalo Courier Express*, October 21, 1929.
"Happy Kapp Is Looking for 2 More." *San Antonio Express-News*, December 28, 1969.
Hardman, A.L. "Rodriguez Will Help, Herman Hoskins Feels." *Charleston Gazette*, November 13, 1970.
Hardman, Steve. "Tom Flores: L.A. Raiders." *Los Angeles Sports Profiles*, Spring Issue 1987.
Harton, Bruce. "Jesse Rodriguez, Clarksburg's Own Star at Salem College, Will Have Greatest Year of His Life in 1927." *Clarksburg Exponent*, September 23, 1927.
Hatch, E. Leroy. "Mormon Colonies: Beacon Light in Mexico." *Ensign*, September 1972.
"Hendricks Game: Book and Tackle." *The Philadelphia Inquirer*, November 8, 1968.
"Hendricks Receives Hall of Fame Ring During Pregame Ceremony." *GAMEDAY—Raiders/Packers*, November 11, 1990.
"Here, Today, Rodriguez' Kelly and Jess, Two Brothers, Pitted One Against the Other, Score Both Touchdowns of Game." *Clarksburg Telegram*, October 8, 1927.
Hoffman, Dale. "Hendricks Could Be Free Agent Again." *Milwaukee Sentinel*, October 9, 1974.
Hoffman, Jeane. "Classes Ended When Rams Blew Horn for Teacher Villanueva." *Los Angeles Times*, September 12, 1961.
Hooper, Al. "Think Big." *Touchdown: The All-Canadian Sports Magazine*, November 15, 1963.
Hubbuch, Bart. "A Special Coach: Rodriguez Brings Unique Style to Jaguars' Special Teams." *The Florida Times-Union*, September 26, 2004.
"Jesse Rodriguez on Football—Then and Now." *Clarksburg Exponent*, August 14, 1964.
"Jesse Rodriguez Star of Salem College Backfield." *Clarksburg Exponent*, October 31, 1928.
Jessop, Alicia. "How the NFL Built a 25-Million Person Hispanic Fan Base." *Forbes*, September 26, 2013. https://www.forbes.com/sites/aliciajessop/2013/09/26/how-the-nfl-built-a-25-million-person-hispanic-fan-base/#c1815e7121db.
"Kapp Comes Home." *Cal Athletic News: Special Edition*, University of California—Berkeley, August 1982.
Kapp, Joe and Jack Olsen. "A Man of Machismo." *Sports Illustrated*, July 20, 1970.
_____. "A Misfit Who Lives to Win." *Sports Illustrated*, July 27, 1970.
_____. "We Were Just a Bunch of Party Poopers." *Sports Illustrated*, August 3, 1970.
"Kapp Passes for 7 Touchdowns as Vikings Crush Colts, 52–14." *The New York Times*, September 29, 1969.
Kaufman, Michelle. "The Few, The Proud: For various reasons, the NFL hasn't been a hotbed for Hispanics. But times are changing." *Miami Herald*, January 25, 1999.
Keeton, Richard. "A Minority of None—Why are there no black coaches in the National Football League?" *The Main Event: Monthly Sports Journal for Physicians*, December 1988.
Keisser, Bob. "The Fabled Life of Joe Kapp." *Los Angeles Herald-Examiner*, October 22, 1982.
"Kelly Dashes 50 Yards for Lone Scores: Rodriguez's Punting Only Feature of the Wesleyan Play Against Georgetown." *Clarksburg Telegram*, October 20, 1928.
"Kelly Rodriguez Signs: Will Be Upon the Same Team as 'Gyp' Battles." *Clarksburg Telegram*, May 1935.
Laing, Jack. "Galloping Ghost Aids Mate in Scoring 2 Touchdowns: Locals Threaten at Close." *Buffalo Courier Express*, October 14, 1929.
_____. "Hornets Show Resourceful Varied Attack, Punish Line and Pass Over Bison Heads." *Buffalo Courier Express*, October 7, 1929.
_____. "McDonnell's Great Sprint Breaks 3–3 Tie at Stadium: Weimer Boots Bison Points." *Buffalo Courier Express*, September 30, 1929.
Libman, Gary. "He Gets His Kicks Serving Latino Community." *Los Angeles Times*, September 29, 1985.
Long, Gary. "Fernandez Taking His Lumps in Dolphin Comeback Attempt." *Miami Herald*, July 14, 1977.
Longman, Jere. "Shaped by Tragedies, Garcia Has Built Career with Resolve." *The New York Times*, January 5, 2007.
Longoria, Mario. "Jess Rodriguez: First Latino in Pro Football." *NUESTRO*, Jan/Feb. 1984.
_____. "Mexican Gridders in World Adventure." *PROMEX SPORTS Publication*, April 1991.

_____. "Ron Rivera." *PROMEX SPORTS Publication*, August 1990.
"L.S.U. Vanquishes Texas Aggies, 19–14." *The New York Times*, January 2, 1944.
Markus, Robert. "Along the Sports Trail." *Chicago Tribune*, July 27, 1971.
Merrill, Elizabeth. "Six Man Forever." August 4, 2017. http://www.espn.com/espn/feature/story/_/id/20229005/high-school-girl-saves-football-season-fading-texas-town.
Messenger, Janet G. "Chicago Names Public School for Evanston Physician Dr. Jorge Prieto." *Evanston Round Table*, October 13, 2009.
"Miami Hails Ted Hendricks As Greatest All-Time Gridder." *The Football News*, October 26, 1968.
Mooney, Michael J. "The Last Best Hope of Tony Romo." *Texas Monthly*, September 2016.
"Moran Trips Legions, Fanning 14 Players: Yellow Jackets Win Close Game Though Only Making Four Hits, the Same as Garnered of Volte." *Philadelphia Record*, September 18, 1927.
Mulligan, Kevin. "Against All Odds: Eagles Guard Diaz-Infante Hopeful His Hard Earned Spot in NFL Set an Example For Youth in Latino Communities." *Philadelphia Daily News*, October 13, 1999.
Newhall, Bob. "Rodriguez, Bullington Stars of Bobcat Win." *Clarksburg Telegram*, September 1928.
"Nixon Nominates Gene Brito for Football Hall of Fame." *Highland Park News Herald and Journal*, October 3, 1971.
"Nixon Praises Brito in Last Skins Game." *Los Angeles Times*, December 15, 1958.
Nobles, Charlie. "Hendricks Can't Tell Without a Program." *The Miami News*, February 18, 1974.
_____. "Stork Wants Miami." *The Boston Globe*, January 27, 1973.
"Notre Dame Rally Downs Drake, 19–7." *The New York Times*, November 10, 1929.
"Notre Dame Repels Drake by 28 to 7." *The New York Times*, November 16, 1930.
Oates, Bob. "Reaping the Harvest: Once a Fruit Picker, Tom Flores Worked His Way to Coach of Oakland Raiders." *Los Angeles Times*, September 1, 1979.
"Obituary—James Buchanon Schuber '28." *Shipmate Magazine*, September 1, 1982.
O'Connor, Ian. "The Patriots' Next Coaching Star?: His Odds Were Incredibly Long." *ESPN*, March 7, 2018. http://www.espn.com/nfl/story/_/id/22262842/brian-flores-new-england-patriots-next-coaching-star-emerge-bill-belichick-tree.
Olderman, Murray. "Cinderella After the Bowl." *SPORT Magazine*, August 1981.
_____. "The Hungriest Bear." *San Francisco Sunday Examiner & Chronicle*, July 24, 1983.
Olinger, Kent. "Galaxy Frankfurt." *GAMETIME: The Official Magazine of the World League of American Football* 1, no. 2 (1991).
Olsen, Jack. "He Goes Where the Trouble Is." *Sports Illustrated*, October 19, 1970.
Osborn, Tom. "America's Cowboy: Quarterback's merchandise atop many Christmas wish lists as Romo Mania grips the country." *San Antonio Express-News*, December 10, 2006.
_____. "Jones: Big contract calls for Romo to work harder." *San Antonio Express-News*, April 28, 2013.
"Packers Are Upset by Cardinals, 21–13." *The New York Times*, November 16, 1931.
"Packers Whip Frankford; Regain Lead." *Green Bay Press-Gazette*, November 28, 1930.
Pierson, Don. "From Railroad Boxcar to NFL Sideline—Seattle Coach Special." *Chicago Tribune*, September 17, 1999.
Pope, Edwin. "A Super Bowl Hero Re-Enters Reality." *Miami Herald*, January 6, 1978.
"Pressure on Kilmer Called Key Factor." *Los Angeles Times*, January 15, 1973.
"Rams Defeat Colts on Field Goal, 17–16." *The New York Times*, November 25, 1963.
"Rams Field Goal Top Packers, 33–31." *The New York Times*, November 21, 1960.
"Rams Upset Vikings on Late Kick, 27–24." *The New York Times*, October 21, 1963.
Reilly, Rick. "Staying Away In Flocks." *Sports Illustrated*, November 9, 1987.
Richardson, William D. "Versatile Eagles Rout Giants, 38–17." *The New York Times*, November 12, 1944.
Robertson, Linda. "Hendricks Enshrinee Has Trouble Adjusting." *Knight Ridder Newspapers –Packer Report*, August 11, 1990.
"Rodriguez and Kistler Lead Salem's Attack Throughout." *Clarksburg Exponent*, October 13, 1928.
"Rodriguez Scores Two Touchdowns on Philippi Baptist." *Clarksburg Exponent*, November 18, 1927.
"Rodriguez's Pro Team Loses to Portsmouth by the Score of 42–0." *Clarksburg Telegram*, December 7, 1930.

Rose, Bob. "Beginnings—Founding of the World League." *GAMETIME: The Official Magazine of the World League of American Football* 1, no. 2 (1991).
"Saenz Splurges against Badgers." *Great Lakes Bulletin*, November 4, 1944.
"Sailors Meet Ft. Warren in Final Home game." *Great Lakes Bulletin*, November 24, 1944.
"St. Mary's Triumphs 20 to 13, Withstanding Texas to Tech Rally." *The New York Times*, January 3, 1939.
"Salem Is Winner at Marietta College, 12–0." *Clarksburg Exponent*, October 13, 1928.
Schrotenboer, Brent. "Special Delivery: Seattle's Pete Rodriguez consistently delivers great special teams." *American Football Monthly*, September 2001.
Selman, Jim. "Changed Colts Swap Hendricks to Pack." *The Tampa Tribune*, August 14, 1974.
Sheehan, Joseph M. "Baugh and Saenz Pace 28–20 Victory." *New York Times*, October 13, 1947.
"Sports-O-Rama, The 'Remembered' Art of Punting." *Clarksburg Exponent*, August 12, 1964.
"Steelers Late Rush Surprises Redskins for a Tie at 14–14." *The New York Times*, September 30, 1946.
"Steve Van Buren: A Rarified Eagle." *The Victoria Advocate*, October 16, 1981.
Stirling, Scotty. "Raiders Nip Oilers, 52–49." *Oakland Tribune*, December 23, 1963.
Sulzberger, A.G. "Hispanics Reviving Faded Towns on the Plains." *The New York Times*, November 13, 2011. https://www.nytimes.com/2011/11/14/us/as-small-towns-wither-on-plains-hispanics-come-to-the-rescue.html.
"Swingman of Sorts." *Sports Illustrated*, January 13, 1997.
Tamez, Ana. "Latino Cowboys: Hispanics Are A Force To Be Dealt With in the NFL." *CONEXION—The weekly voice of la cultura—San Antonio Express-News*, September 22–28, 2005.
"Ted Hendricks." *Red, White & Green Magazine*, December 1988/January 1989.
Telander, Rick. "In the Eye of the Storm." *Sports Illustrated*, September 7, 1981.
"Three West Virginia Boys Among Ten Leading Eastern Grid Scorers." *Clarksburg Telegram*, November 30, 1928.
"Ties Steam Rollers, 7–7 Buffalo Comes from Behind to Knot Count in Pro Football." *The New York Times*, October 12, 1929.
"Tom Flores, Longtime Raider Is Named Coach." *Los Angeles Times*, February 9, 1979.
Vaughan, Irving. "Great Lakes Triumphs 40–12 Over Wisconsin." *Chicago Tribune*, October 29, 1944.
"Vikings Rally to Edge Rams, 23–20." *San Antonio Express-News*, December 28, 1969.
Vidal, Juan. "Why Does American Sports Have a Latino Problem?" *Rolling Stone*, September 16, 2016. https://www.rollingstone.com/culture/culture-sports/why-does-american-sports-have-a-latino-problem-122838/.
"Villanueva Rates Soccer Style Place Kicking as Best Method." *Los Angeles Times*, December 3, 1966.
Wallace, William M. "Dolphins Go After Unsigned." *The New York Times*, April 2, 1974.
"Wesleyan Has Easy Time in First battle." *Clarksburg Telegram*, September 21, 1928.
"Wesleyan Wins Over Concord, Rodriguez Plows Through for Two Scores, Final Count, 18–0." *Clarksburg Telegram*, October 13, 1928.
White, Gordon S. "Bears Rate Slight Favorites Over Steelers in Game at Pittsburgh Today: Chicago to Play Without Casares." *The New York Times*, November 1963.
Whorton, Cal. "McElenny, Brito Get Grid Awards." *Los Angeles Times*, January 9, 1959.
———. "33-Year-Old Veteran to Put Off Retirement." *Los Angeles Times*, March 5, 1959.
Wolf, Al. "Brito May End Grid Career in Pro Bowl." *Los Angeles Times*, January 7, 1958.
———. "Danny Boy's Now a Cowboy." *Los Angeles Times*, July 31, 1965.
"Yellow Jackets Win Fray from New Britain: Forward Pass Attacks Aids Frankford Eleven in National Football League Contest." *Philadelphia Record*, October 1, 1927.
Zimmerman, Paul. "Armed and Dangerous." *Sports Illustrated*, January 8, 2007.
———. "Villanueva Has Itchy Toe, Views Big Season." *Los Angeles Times*, June 17, 1964.
———. "Who Is This Mad Hatter?" *Sports Illustrated*, October 17, 1983.

Documentaries

"Impulsador del Football Americano en la UNAM: Arthur Constantine." https://www.youtube.com/watch?v=XpXqt5XruGk.

"Santiago Eagles." http://santiagoeaglesfootball.blogspot.com/.
"Symbol of Heart: The Official Documentary of the East L.A. Classic." Carmona Productions, 2003.

Interviews: All Interviews with Jorge Iber

Aguilar, Jeremy. March 2018.
Alvarez, Carlos. October & November 2016.
Baisa, Louie. May 2018.
Calvillo, Anthony. April 2016.
Cid, Javier. February 2018.
Fernandez, Manny. April 2016.
McMillin, Billy. January 2018.
Mendoza, San Juan. May 2018.
Ramirez, Manny. January 2017.
Ruiz, Daniel. April 2018.

Letters

Boatright, Brenda. Brenda Boatright to Mario Longoria, March 12, 1982, on Tom Flores.
Bonnell, Lori. Lori Bonnell to Mario Longoria, December 17, 1982, on Joe Kapp.
Clower, Clem. Clem Clower to Mario Longoria, October 8, 1982, on Jesse Rodriguez.
Cornell University, Sports Publicity Office to Mario Longoria, May 31, 1979, Jose Martinez-Zorrilla.
Davis, Edward T. Edward Davis to Mario Longoria, December 8, 1982, Jesse and Kelly Rodriguez.
Davis, Edward T. Edward Davis to Mario Longoria, November 9, 1982, Jesse Rodriguez.
Davis, Edward T. Edward Davis to Mario Longoria, January 4, 1985, Jesse Rodriguez.
Dennis, Brother L. Brother Dennis to Mario Longoria, January 21, 1983, Joe Aguirre.
Dennis, Brother L. Brother Dennis to Mario Longoria, February 23, 1989, Joe Aguirre.
Don Carlos, Waldo E. Waldo Don Carlos to Mario Longoria, June 27, 1996.
Flores, Tom. Tom Flores to Mario Longoria, June 30, 1982.
Gallagher, Jim. Jim Gallagher to Mario Longoria, December 19, 1984, Steve Van Buren.
Gates, Victoria. Victoria Gates to Mario Longoria, January 28, 1983, Gene Brito.
Goldchien, Art. Art Goldchien to Mario Longoria, January 18, 1985, Jesse Rodriguez.
Haines, Robert B. Robert Haines to Kelly Rodriguez, April 26, 1930.
Haines, Robert S. Robert Haines to Ignacio S. Molinet, July 21, 1927.
Haines, Robert S. Robert Haines to Ignacio S. Molinet, August 19, 1927. (Telegram)
Haines, Robert S. Robert Haines to Ignacio S. Molinet, August 28, 1927. (Telegram)
Hansen, Tim. Tim Hansen to Mario Longoria, December 20, 1982, Gene Brito and Joe Kapp.
Kordiala, Ray E. Ray Kordiala to Mario Longoria, April 27, 1983, Joe Aguirre.
Loney, Francine. Francine Loney to Mario Longoria, December 26, 1984, Joe Kapp.
LSU Sports Information Office. LSU Sports Information Office to Mario Longoria, April 22, 1996, Steve Van Buren.
Mansean, L.E. L.E. Mansean to Kelly Rodriguez, June 6, 1936.
Molinet, Ignacio S. Ignacio Molinet to American Consul, Havana, Cuba, August 29, 1927.
Molinet, Ignacio S. Ignacio Molinet to Robert S. Haines, August 20, 1927.
Molinet, Ignacio S. Ignacio Molinet to Robert S. Haines, August 29, 1927.
Morrison, Paul. Paul Morrison to Waldo Don Carlos, July 16, 1996.
Rodriguez, Jesse. Jesse Rodriquez to Mario Longoria, December 27, 1982.
Rodriguez, Jesse. Jesse Rodriguez to Mario Longoria, January 18, 1983.
Rodriguez, Jesse. Jesse Rodriguez to Mario Longoria, February 19, 1983.
Rodriguez, Jesse. Jesse Rodriguez to Mario Longoria, August 12, 1984.
Rodriguez, Jesse. Jesse Rodriguez to Mario Longoria, September 29, 1984.
Rodriguez, Jesse. Jesse Rodriguez to Mario Longoria, November 20, 1984.
Rodriguez, Jesse. Jesse Rodriguez to Mario Longoria, April 5, 1985.
Rodriguez, Palmira. Palmira Rodriguez to Mario Longoria, August 3, 1984, Kelly Rodriguez.

Saenz, Edward D. Edward Saenz to Mario Longoria, October 31, 1984, Eddie Saenz.
Saenz, Edward D. Edward Saenz to Mario Longoria, January 24, 1985, Eddie Saenz.

Media Guides

Baltimore Colts Media Guide: 1983.
Boston Redskins 1935 Media Guide.
Chicago Bears Media Guide: 1956.
Chicago Cardinals Press, Radio and Television Guide: 1954.
Dallas Cowboys Media Guide: 1967, 2015.
Denver Gold Media Guide: 1985.
Green Bay Packers Media Guide: 1983.
Jacksonville Jaguars Media Guide: 2006.
Kansas City Chiefs Media Guide: 1970, 1971, 2007.
Los Angeles Dons Players Profiles, 1947.
The Los Angeles Raiders Media Guide: 1986.
Los Angeles Rams Media Guide: 1960, 1961, 1964, 1982, 1986.
Los Angeles Rams Press Book: 1946, 1956,
Miami Dolphins Media Guide: 1966, 1976, 1977.
New England Patriots 1983 Facts Book.
New Orleans Saints Official Media Guide: 1982.
New Orleans Saints Press Book: 1967.
The Oakland Raiders Media Guide: 1981.
Official Chicago Bears Media Guide: 1982.
Philadelphia Eagles Media Guide: 1983, 2006.
Phoenix Cardinals Media Guide: 1992.
Sacramento Gold Miners Media Guide: 1994.
San Francisco 49ers Media Guide: 1983.
Seattle Seahawks Media Guide: 1992, 2004.
Southern California SUN Media Guide: 1974.
Washington Redskins Media Guide: 1946, 1951, 1958, 1959, 1994.

Canadian Football League

British Columbia Lions Fact Book: 1987.
Calgary Stampeders Media Guide: 1997.
Edmonton Eskimos Grey Cup Champions Media Guide: 1982.
Montreal Concordes Media Guide: 1985.
Ottawa Rough Riders Media Guide: 1987.
Saskatchewan Roughriders Fact Book: 1987.
Toronto Argonauts Media Guide: 1985.
Winnipeg Football Fact Book: 1982.

College/Universities

California Football Centennial Media Guide: 1982.
California Football Media Guide: 1986.
The Eastern Illinois University Panther Media Guide: 2006.
The Official National Collegiate Athletic Association Football Guide: 1944.
Pacific-10 Conference Football Media Guide: 1991.
San Jose State University Football Media Guide: 1990.
Stanford Football Facts For Press-Radio-TV: 1969.
UCLA Football Media Guide: 1992.
University of Florida Football Facts & Figures: 1951, 1952.

University of Florida Media Guide: 1981.
University of Miami Hurricanes Media Guide: 1976.
Utah Football-100 Years Media Guide: 1992.

Game Programs

"Frankford Yellow Jackets Game Program," October 22, 1927. Provided by Joe Horrigan, Curator, Pro Football Hall of Fame, Canton, Ohio. On Kelly Rodriguez.
"Frankford Yellow Jackets Game Programs," September 9, 1930. Provided by Joe Horrigan, Curator, Pro Football Hall of Fame, Canton, Ohio. On Kelly Rodriguez.
"Frankford Yellow Jackets Game Programs," November 15, 1930. Provided by Joe Horrigan, Curator, Pro Football Hall of Fame, Canton, Ohio. On Kelly Rodriguez.
"Frankford Yellow Jackets Game Program," October 12, 1930. Provided by Joe Horrigan, Curator, Pro Football Hall of Fame, Canton, Ohio. On Kelly Rodriguez.
"Tom Flores: 50 Victories," Raiders vs Chargers Gameday Program. September 24, 1984.

Press Information/Releases

Charles Callahan—Public Relations Director, Miami Dolphins, LTD. *Press Release*, Sunday, June 19, 1966. On Rick Casares.
"Washington Hall of Stars Elects 5 D.C. Sport Greats," *Press Release* on Gene Brito, Washington, D.C. September 9, 1982.
"Tom Flores Retires from Football Coaching." *Raiders Release*, January 20, 1988.

Public Records

Standard certificate of birth for Genaro G. Brito. California State Board of Health, Bureau of Vital Statistics. County of Los Angeles, Registrar/Recorder, County Clerk, local registration no. 937/6943, filed 10/28, 1925, and no. 10, 1925, obtained August 25, 1995. 19-005186.
Certificate of death for Genaro Herman Brito. State of California, Department of Public Health. County of Los Angeles, Registrar/Recorder, County Clerk, local registration district and certificate number 7026/23123, filed July 2, 1965, obtained August 25, 1995. 19-006014.

Index

A&M-Kingsville Javelinas 176, 249, 271
Abreu, Ernie 125
Abreu, James "Jim" 125-126
Acuna, Rodolfo 16, 98
addiction 198-199
Addie, Bob 143
AFC Championship (1982) 193
agricultural work 9, 116-117, 169-170, 300
Aguilar, Jeremy 267, 271
Aguilar, Victor M. 20, 68-69
Aguirre, Joe 80-85, 195-196, 308
Aikens, Jason 29-30
Akers, Fred 116, 180
Alabama Crimson Tide 283
Alamillo, Jose 25
Albuquerque High School 22, 126
Alcorta, Ruben 174
Aldama, Frederick Luis 10
All-America Football Conference (AAFC) 83-84
All-Time Super Bowl Team 234
Allen, Chatter 19
Allen, Damon 2
Allen, George 102
Allen, Marcus 148
Alonso, Carlos 286
Alonso, Kiko 284-286
Alvarez, Arturo 138
Alvarez, Carlos 109, 136, 138-139, 199
Alvarez v. Lemon Grove School District (1931) 61-62
Amato, Chuck 284
Amaya, Rene 177
Americanization 9-10, 244-245
Anderson, Mark C. 16
Andress Golden Eagles 179, 250
Andrew Jackson Industrial Arts High School 17
Andrew P. Hill High Falcons 190
Andrews, Mickey 121
Animas Panthers 182-183, 266
Anthony Gadsden High 184

Apodaca, Anastacio "Hookey" 22-23
Apodaca, Lauro 22-23
Arellano, Gustavo 278
Arenas, Guadalupe (Lupe) Joe 79
Arkansas, notable athletes from 169, 284-285
Armijo, Barbara 184
Army Air Corps Super Bombers 100
Arrangue, Jorge 277-278
Arroyo, Marcus 312
Artesia High School Bulldogs 72, 262
Asherton Trojans 121-122
assimilation 9-10, 244-245
Atencio, Reynaldo 266
Athletes Remembered: Mexicano/Latino Professional Football Players, 1929-1970 (Longoria) 10, 98-99
Atlanta Falcons 102-103, 200-201, 203-204, 309-310
Avila, Alfredo 113
Avila, Celestino 121
Avila, Oscar 7, 114-115

Baisa, Louie 183, 265-266
Balli, Cecilia 314
Balmorhea Bears 253
Baltimore Colts 226-227
barefoot kicking 38-39
Barni, Roy 142
Barzun, Jacques 241
Bashore, Mel "Buck" 52-53
Battles, Cliff 41, 43, 45
Baty, Buryl 122-124
Baugh, Sammy 82, 83, 141
Bautista, Pete 164
Bednarik, Chuck 96
Behring, Ken 149
Belen Eagles 171-172
Belichick, Bill 312
Belmont High Sentinels 129-130
Benavides High School (BHS) Eagles 64-65
Benedict, Chuck 152

363

Index

Berea High Bulldogs 314–315, 320n31
Bernstein High School Dragons 268–269
Bernthal, Matthew J. 314
Bethany College 38
Bibliography of Books About American Football, 1891–2015 (Hickok) 3
Birmingham Americans 137
black coaches, in NFL 150–151
black quarterbacks 151
Blakely, Brady 254
Blanda, George 145–146
Blanton, Carlos Kevin 16
Blowout: Sal Castro and the Chicano Struggle for Educational Justice (Garcia) 129
Borger Bulldogs 164–165
Boston College Eagles 313
Boston Patriots 135, 186, 212–213
Boston Redskins 41, 45
Boston Yanks 95
Bowie High School Bears 20–21, 66–68, 122–124, 179
Boyd, Denny 209
Boys Club of North Miami 138
Brackenridge Eagles 139–140, 162–165
Brigham Young University Cougars 174, 189
Briscoe, Marlin 151
British Columbia Lions 132, 191, 209–211, 216
Brito, Genaro Herman "Mean" Gene 74–75, 140–144
Broaddus College 37
Brooklyn Dodgers 51, 81
Brown, Doug 207–208
Brown, Ed 159
Brown, Paul E. 87
Brownsville High School 173, 246
Bryant, Paul "Bear" 111
Buffalo Bills 146–147, 176, 187, 286
Buffalo Bisons 38–40, 84
Bullos, Jesus "Jessie" 68
Buoniconti, Nick 232–233

Cahoon, Ben 279
Caldwell, Heidi 29–30, 35
Calexico High 127
Calgary Stampeders 133, 145, 207–209, 302
California: challenges facing Latino players in 129–131; football's arrival in 23–26; football's impact on Spanish-speaking populations in 267; Latino population in 104, 168; notable athletes from 73–76, 131–135, 140–151, 184–199, 217–224, 230–234, 266–281, 286–289, 294–310; segregation and educational impediments in 106
California Foot Ball League (CFBL) 24–25
California Professional Football League 45
call in-scoreboard shows 120
Calvillo, Anthony 2, 189–190, 278–280
Calvillo, David 189–190
Camarillo, Rich 340n259

Camp, Walter 5, 18
Campos, Christian 270
Camunez, Guillermo Rudolfo "Rudy" 69–71, 124
Canadian Football League (CFL) 1–2
Candelaria, Martin 183
Canutillo Eagles 250–251
Capello, Juan Jose 121
Cardozo, Silvio 199
Carillo, Joe 110
Carolina Panthers 298–299
Carrizozo Grizzlies 125, 181, 182
Carroll, John J. 42
Carroll, Tom 273
Carter, Quincy 291
Casares, origination of surname 331n159
Casares, Ricardo Jose "Rick" 63, 76–77, 156–162
Cashion, Ty 110
Casillas, Tony 202–204
Castaneda, Eddie 181–182
Castillo, Fernando 7
Castillo, Juan 175–177
Castillo, Victor 163, 164, 178–179
Castro, Fidel 286
Castro, Sal 129–131
Castro Revolution 109
Cavazos, Bobby 117–119
Cavazos, Dick 117
Cavazos, Lauro 117
Cementina, Al 135, 218
Chapin, Dwight 147–148, 189, 218–219
Chapin High Huskies 250
Chavez, Cesar 108
Chavez, Dennis 60–61, 107
Chavez, Theresa (Trecia Cheavez) 140
Chavez-Garcia, Miroslava 16
Cheavez, Trecia (Theresa Chavez) 140
Chicago Bears 39–40, 77–78, 79, 153, 158–161, 255–256, 296–298
Chicago Cardinals 39, 47, 95, 96
"Chicano" 212
Chicano Movement 106–109, 119–120, 135–136, 166, 167
Chula Vista High Spartans 275
El Cid 210; *see also* Kapp, Joseph Robert (Garcia) "Joe"
Cid, Javier 185, 267, 270–271
cigar industry 136
Cincinnati Bengals 180, 192, 193–195
Cisneros, Henry 167
civil rights movement 59; *see also* Chicano Movement
Clasico-Poli-Universidad (*Poli-University Classic*) 27
"The Classic" 267, 269–271
Cleveland Browns 84, 101–102, 155–156
Cleveland Rams 82–83, 100; *see also* Los Angeles Rams

Index

Cobas, Jose 136
Cobb, Albert Folson 62
Cohen, Richard M. 159
Coleman, Edward 164
College of the Pacific 145
Colonia Diaz, Mexico 51–52
Columbus High Explorers 201, 282
Confederacion Deportiva Mexicana (Mexican Sports Confederation, CDM) 25
Constantine, Arthur 26–27
Coral Gables High Cavaliers 200
Cornell University 53–54
Coronado, Robert 245
Coronado Thunderbirds 179
Corpus Christi Miller Bucs 171
Corral, Frank 197
Corsicana Tigers 256
Cortez, Robert 115, 116
Costello, Al 83
Cristobal, Mario 282–283, 311
Cromartie, John 243
Crow, John David 111–112
Crystal City High School 119–120
Crystal City revolt 108
Cuba, football's arrival in 27–29
Cubans: discrimination against 63; flee Castro Revolution 109; and football in Florida 136–139, 199–201, 281–284, 286; high school graduation rate of 243
Cuero High School Gobblers 247

Dallas Cowboys 153–156, 204, 291–294, 313–314
Damien High School 273
Davidson, Cotton 146
Davidson, Guy 21
Davis, Al 148, 187, 193, 222, 227–228
De Anza College Dons 190–191
De Ayala, Kiki 179–180
De Ayala, Ralph 180
Dehesa, Raul 26
De La Cruz, Hugo 120
De Leon, Arnoldo 24
Delgado v. Bastrop Independent School District (1948) 61, 62
delinquency, preventing 16–17
del Olmo, Frank 220
Del Valle Conquistadors 250
Democratic Party 107–108
Denver Broncos 259, 288
Denver Gold 237
deportation of Mexican Americans 107
Detroit Lions 52, 159–160, 258, 303
Diaz, Manny 284
Diaz-Infante, Gustavo David Miguel 286–289
Dickey, Doug 200
Dieciséis de Septiembre celebration 170
Dinnijes-Withers, Charles 17

discrimination: at Bowie High School 21; and Chicano Movement 106–107, 119–120; experienced by Abel Gonzalez 248; experienced by Carlos Alvarez 138; experienced by Danny Villanueva 128, 153; experienced by Eddie Saenz 89–90; experienced by Everardo Carlos Lerma 19–20; experienced by Jimmy Juarez 72; experienced by Joe Kapp 206; experienced by Ray Romero 78, 79; experienced by Ron Rivera 295; faced by war-era Latinos 60–64; in Texas 107–108, 115, 123; *see also* segregation
Dismar, Bill 80–81
Ditka, Mike 160
Division I level, Latinos at 315–317
Domingo, "Big Joe" 26
Don Carlos, Waldo Emerson 45–49
Donna Redskins 7, 111, 112, 113–115, 121, 171, 246
Dove, Claude C. 63
Dow Anaya, Ricardo 22, 71–72
Dowler, Boyd 103
Drake University Bulldogs 46–47, 51
Drehs, Wayne 241
Duany, Jorge 136
Dunn, Red 47
Durfee, Jim 38, 322n75
Durham, Aulton "Bull" 70

Earp, Jug 47, 48
East L.A. Classic 25–26, 135–136, 184–185, 267, 269–271
Eastern Illinois University Panthers 290–291
Eastern New Mexico Greyhounds 181
Edcouch-Elsa Yellowjackets 117, 120
Edmonton Eskimos 85
education: and legal status of immigrants 168; and segregation 61–63, 104–106, 115; and social reform 108–109, 119–120; and U.S. Latino demographic changes 242–243
Edwards, Donnie 273–275
Edwards, Fred 114
Effrat, Louis 159
El Paso Burgess Mustangs 250
El Paso Cathedral High 251
El Paso Franklin Cougars 250
El Paso High Tigers 67
El Paso Riverside Rangers 250
Eliot, Ray 77
Elkins, Chief 39
Elway, Jack 191
employment 9, 104, 116–117, 169–170, 300
Emrick, Lillian 16–17, 19
epgridiron.com 251
Escalante High Lobos 266
Esquivel, Carlos 111–112, 116, 117
Etcheverry Sam 69, 185
eXtreme Football League 289

Fears, Charles William, Jr. 99
Fears, Charles William, Sr. 99, 100
Fears, Louella 99
Fears, Tom Jesse (Valdes) 97, 98–103, 295, 308, 327n126
Featherstone, John 190
Fernandez, Manuel Jose "Manny" 200–201, 230–234
Fernandez, Manuel (Manny's father) 230
Fernandez, Mervyn 190–192
Fernandez-Armesto, Felipe 244–245
Fimrite, Ron 207
Finks, Jim 209, 211
Fleming, Willie 207
Flores, Bob 145
Flores, Brian 312–313
Flores, Cruz 126
Flores, David 165, 252, 290
Flores, Nellie 144–145
Flores, R.C. "Frito" 66
Flores, Thomas Raymond "Tom" 132–133, 144–151, 187–189, 191, 222, 228, 295
Flores, Tom Cervantes 144–145
Florida: Cuban immigration to 136; football's arrival in 26; notable athletes from 76–77, 136–139, 156–162, 199–202, 281–284
Florida International University Golden Panthers 282–283
Florida State Seminoles 236
Flutie, Doug 216
Foley, Neil 166, 167, 168
food processing and packaging 169, 170
football: arrival of, in California 23–26; arrival of, in Florida 26; arrival of, in New Mexico 21–23; arrival of, in Texas 18–21; discrimination in 19–20, 21; future of Latinos in 311–317; lack of Latino participation in 18–20; and negative perceptions of Latinos 15–18; origins of 18–19; scholarship on Latinos in 5–10, 15–16; scholarship on varied racial, ethnic, and religious groups in 3–5; spread of 18, 26–29
"Football Scoreboard" 120
For Pride, Profit and Patriarchy: Football and the Incorporation of American Cultural Values (Gem) 4, 5
Ford, Dan 21–22, 69, 70, 126, 180–181, 184, 260, 266, 325n32
Forren, Weldon 162–163, 164, 165
Ft. Hancock Mustangs 251
Fort Sumner High School 260
Fox, Larry 213
Frankford Athletic Association 31–34, 43
Frankford Yellow Jackets 30, 31–35, 39, 41, 43–45
Frankfurt Galaxy 288
Franks, Joel 23–24
"Freezer Bowl" 193

Fresno City College 132, 145
"Friday Night Lights" (Huerta) 8, 19

Gadsden High School Panthers 126
Gallagher, Jim 90–92
Gallegos, Willie 182
Gamon, Manny 241
Garcia, Aaron 280–281
Garcia, Bob 299–300
Garcia, Gonzalo 66
Garcia, Hank 280
Garcia, Jeffrey Jason "Jeff" 299–305
Garcia, Juan 77
Garcia, Kyle 253
Garcia, Linda Elder 299–300
Garcia, Mario T. 129
Garcia, Orlando 251
Garfield High School Bulldogs 25–26, 75–76, 135–136, 184–185, 270–271
Garza, Dan 84, 308
Garza, Leonel 121
Garza, Roberto 255–256
Garza, Sammy 175
Gastineau, Mark 216
Gavilan Community College Rams 300, 301
Gems, Gerald 4–5
Gene Brito Achievement Award 75, 143–144
Giddings, Mike 230, 231
Giles, Dusty 266
Gilroy High School Mustangs 300–301
Glier, Ray 309–310
Goddard Rockets 183
Godinez Ballon, Estela 61, 62
Goldchien, Art 37, 40
Gomez, Antonio 252
Gonzalez, Abel 248–249
Gonzalez, Al 127, 128–129
Gonzalez, Anthony David "Tony" 305–310
Gonzalez, Bob 133
Gonzalez, Chris (brother of Tony) 306
Gonzalez, Christopher (author) 10
Gonzalez, Henry B. 105, 107
Gonzalez, Juan 11
Gonzalez, Memo 124
Gonzalez, Rodolfo "Corky" 108
Gonzalez, Sal 126
Gonzalez, Vincent 79–80
Gonzalez, Zane 198
Goodbread, Royce 44
Goodman, Irv 160
Gossett, Bruce 153
Grange, Red 39
Great Depression 60–61
Great Lakes Naval Training Center 87–88
Green, Joe 245–246
Green Bay Packers 45, 47–48, 153, 155, 227
Gregg, Forrest 193
Grey Cup Championship 347n146; (1964) 209–210; (1998) 302

Grogan, Steve 186
Grove, Roger 47
Gruden, Jon 176
Grulla High School 249
Guerra, Ramiro 64
Gustkey, Earl 99, 100
Gutierrez, Jacob 252–253
Gutierrez, Jose Angel 108, 119–120
Gutierrez, Paul 300, 305
Gutierrez, Sally 183–184
Guzzo, Paul 157

Hagerman High School Bobcats 181, 182
Haines, Robert B. 31–32, 33–34, 43–44
Halas, George 158
Ham, Tracy 278
Hamilton Tiger-Cats 210, 278, 302
Hanson, Chris 239, 240
Harlingen High School Cardinals 115, 175
Harlingen South Hawks 172
Harrold, Texas 253–254
Hart-Cellar Act (1965) 166–167
Hart High School 206
Harton, Bruce 37
Havana University 28–29
Helen Bernstein High School 267
Hendricks, Angela Bonatti 224
Hendricks, Maurice "Sonny" 224
Hendricks, Theodore Paul "Ted" 224–230
Hendy, John 224
Henson, Drew 291
Hernandez, Louis 22, 69
Hernandez, Walter 22
Hernandez, Will 252
Hernandez v. the State of Texas (1954) 107
Herrera, Andre 204–205
Herrera, Efren 196
Herrera, Nemo 66, 68, 123, 124
Hickok, Ralph 3, 10
high school graduation rate 242–243
Highland Owls 163
Hill, Charles 250–251
Hines, Walter 23
Hinkle, Clarke 97
Hinojosa, Rene Manuel 66, 111
Hirsch, Elroy "Crazy Legs" 143
Hispanic: genesis of term 166; versus Latino 10–11
Hispanic Leadership Conference 79
"An Historical Prospective of Influence Sport Had on Sport Legends of New Mexico, 1925-1975" (Dow Anaya) 22
The History of New Mexico High School Football: Volume I: The First 100 Years, 1892-1992 (Ford) 21–22
Holmgren, Mike 238–239
Houston Gamblers 180
Houston Oilers 145–146, 210
Hubbard, Cal 47

Huerta, Carlos 201
Huerta, Dolores 108
Huerta, Joel 8, 19, 65, 120
Hunter, Gorde 209
Huntington Beach High 306–307

Iber, Jorge 9, 77, 110, 118
Iglesias, Orlando 199, 281–282
immigration: connection between football and 314–315, 320n31; of Cubans to Florida 136; increase in 166–167, 168; pan–Hispanism concerning U.S. 244
Immigration and Nationality Act (1965) 166–167
Immigration Control and Reform Act (IRCA, 1982) 168
Independent School District v. Salvatierra (1930) 61
Instituto Politecnico Nacional (National Technical Institute, NTI) 27
intermural football 183–184
Iowa, notable athletes from 169–170
Iowa State University Cyclones 236

Jackson, Robert C. 20–21
Jacksonville Jaguars 239–240
Jacksonville Sharks 227
James Lick High School 135, 218–219
James Madison High Mavericks 252
Janowicz, Vic 141, 142
Japanese-Americans 99–100
Jefferson High School Dragons 76–77, 157
Johnston, James 177
Jolly, Al 39
Juarez, Jimmy 72–73
juries 107

Kaepernick, Colin 286
Kandel, William 243
Kansas City Chiefs 146, 148–149, 187, 188, 204, 205, 211–212, 275–276, 307–309
Kansas State University (KSU) Wildcats 78
Kapp, Joseph Robert (Garcia) "Joe" 130–131, 133, 134, 185–186, 193, 206–217, 220
Keeton, Richard 150–151
Kessler, Kent 42
King, Genevieve 62
King Football: Sport and Spectacle in the Golden Age of Radio and Newsreels, Movies and Magazines, the Weekly & the Daily Press (Oriard) 3–4
Klosterman, Don 188
Knox, Chuck 149
Kramer, Ron 103
Kreneck, Thomas H. 105

La Joya High School Coyotes 171
La Puente High School Warriors 190, 196
Laing, Jack 39

Lake Arthur Panthers 265
Lambeau, Earl "Curley" 141
Lamont, Deana Anderson 24
Lango, John 300
Lara, Severita 120
Las Cruces High School (LCHS) Bulldawgs 69–71, 124
Las Vegas Outlaws 289
Las Vegas Posse 201, 278
Latin America, spread of football in 26–29
Latino(s): acclimation of, to United States 244; assimilation of 9–10, 244–245; changing participation in pro football 305–306; as coaches 8–9; Dallas Cowboys and 313–314; defining 49; demographic changes in U.S. 241–243; discrimination against 19–20, 21, 60–64, 78, 79, 89–90, 106–108, 115, 119–120, 123, 153, 206, 295; dispersal of 314–315; at Division I level 315–317; future of, in football 311–317; increase in, in United States 166–167, 243; increased presence of, in football 241, 243, 281; lack of participation in football 18–20, 205; negative perceptions of 15–18, 61–62, 68–69, 105, 134, 206, 259; non–U.S. born 49–58, 224–230; recent trends among 244; scholarship on, in football 5–10, 15–16; versus "Hispanic" 10–11
Latinos in the End Zone: Conversations on the Brown Color Line in the NFL (Aldama and Gonzalez) 10
Latinos in the United States: Diversity and Change (Saenz and Morales) 241–242
Latinos in U.S. Sport: A History of Isolation, Cultural Identity, and Acceptance (Iber et al.) 9
Leal, Alex 172
LeBaron, Eddie 141
Leonard, Lynn 174
Lerma, Everardo Carlos (E.C.) 8, 19–20, 64–65, 109–110, 170, 171
Lerma, John 110, 170–172
"The Lettermen" 267–269
Levy, Marv 176
Liedtke, Michael 191
Lincoln High School 130, 140
Little Schools of the 400 105, 106
Lombardi, Vince 4–5
Longman, Jere 300
Longoria, Felix 60
Longoria, Mario 10, 23, 98–99
Lopez, Eddie 251–252
Lopez, Gilbert S. "Gillie" 71–72, 125
Lopez, Mike 126
Lopez, Ruth 21
Lopez Tijerina, Reies 108
Lordsburg High Mavericks 183, 265–266
Los Angeles Chargers 256–257
Los Angeles Dons 84

Los Angeles Raiders 148–149, 151, 189, 191–192, 193, 229, 237–238
Los Angeles Rams 96–97, 101–102, 127, 128, 142, 152–154, 197, 305; *see also* Cleveland Rams
Los Angeles Wings 216
Los Gatos High School 285
Louisiana State University Tigers 28, 80, 92, 93–94
Loyola University Lions 75, 86, 140–141
Lugo, Alfredo 121
Luevano, Ernie 182

Madden, John 147, 188, 227–228
Maggard, Dave 215
Majors, Johnny 201–202
Mangiero, Dino 312
Manuel, Dolores 230
Manuel, H.T. 106
Markus, Robert 224
Marquez, Sally 261
Marshall College 43
Marshall University Thundering Herd 283
Marti, Jose 136
Martinez, Joe 65–66
Martinez, Joey 260
Martinez, Jose 125
Martinez, Mario 260–262
Martinez-Zorilla, Cristobal 54
Martinez-Zorilla, Jose C. 6, 53–55
Matsumoto, Masaki 268–269
McAllen-Edinburg-Mission metropolitan statistical area 245
McAllen Memorial High School 113, 171, 172, 246, 247
McLaughlin, Elvira 21
McMillin, Billy 267, 269–270
McNally, Johnny "Blood" 47
McVea, Warren 163, 164
McWilliams, David 119
Mejia, Robert "Beto" 267, 268
Melchior, Chris 285
Mello, Jim 88
Melrose High School Buffaloes 263–265
Menaul High School 69
Mendez v. Westminster (1947) 61, 62
Mendota High School Aztecs 267, 268
Mendoza, San Juan 262–263
Mercado, Haylee Uecker 314
Mercedes Tigers 246
Merlino, Sam 182
Merrill, Elizabeth 253–254
Messenger, Janet G. 58
Mexican American Movement (MAM) 76
Mexican Athletic Association of Southern California (MAASC) 25
Mexico City Y.M.C.A. 66–67
Mexico, football's arrival in 26–27
Miami Coral Park Rams 281

Index

Miami Dolphins 161, 200–201, 202, 227, 230, 231–234, 286
Miami (Ohio) Red Hawks 287
Miami Sunset High 201–202
Michalske, Mike 47
Michelson, Herb 220
Michigan Panthers 236–237
Midwest, notable athletes from 77–79, 169–170, 234–240
Millner, Wayne 83
Minneapolis Red Jackets 41, 44
Minnesota Vikings 185, 202, 210–212, 233
Mira, George Ignacio, Jr. 138
Mira, George Ignacio, Sr. 109, 137–138
Mira, Nick 138
Mirabal, Alex 283, 311
Mission Eagles 174
Mission Viejo Diablos 276
Mitchell, Elmer 17
Molenda, Bo 47
Molina, Gloria 167
Molinet, Conchita 30
Molinet, Ernesto 30, 54
Molinet, Igancio Saturnino 29–35, 53–54
Molinet, Joaquin Ernesto 31
Molinet, Joaquin, Jr. 30, 54
Molinet, Joaquin, Sr. 30, 32
Montano, Dominic 266
Monterrey Tech 173
Montez, Steven 252
Montoya, Dave 263
Montoya, Max 192–194
Montreal Alouettes 2, 69, 137, 278–279, 305
Mooney, Michael J. 293, 294
Moore, Dick 183–184
Morales, Fred 20, 66–67, 124, 179
Morales, Gonzalo 74
Morales, Maria Cristina 241–242
Moran de Constantine, Amanda 26–27
Mormino, Gary 26, 63
Mott, Grenville 67
Mt. San Antonio College 190, 192
Mountainair Bears 182
Mountainair Mustangs 265
Movimiento Estudiantil Chicano de Aztlan (Chicano Student Movement for Aztlan, MEChA) 108
Moynihan, Tim 47
Mudra, Darrell 235, 236
Mulligan, Kevin 289
Munoz, Anthony 192, 193, 194–195, 257
Munoz, DeDe 195
Munoz, Eneas 29
Munoz, Michael 195
Munoz, Michelle 195

names: misspelling of 140; pronunciation of 134, 203
Nash, Tom 47

National Association of Latino Elected and Appointed Officials (NALEO) 167
National Chicano Moratorium Committee (NCMC) 108
National Council for La Raza (NCLR) 167
National Football League (NFL): first Latino athlete in 30, 31–35; first Latino coaches in 294–295; Kapp's antitrust suit against 213–215; lack of black coaches and quarterbacks in 150–151; segregation of 128
Nava, Julian 185
Naval Academy 50–51
Neft, David 47, 51, 236
Nevers, Ernie 47
New England Patriots 220–221, 312, 313
New Mexico: football's arrival in 21–23; intermural football in 183–184; key events in 124–129; notable athletes from 69–73, 151–156, 180–182, 260–266; Spanish surnamed coaches in 124–125, 128–129
New Mexico State University Aggies 23, 127, 128–129, 152
New Orleans Saints 103
New York Giants 89, 95, 160, 161
New York Jets 277
New York, notable athletes from 204–205
New York Sentinels 240
Newhouse, Dave 218
Nieblas, Reuben 182–183
Nixon, Richard M. 142, 143, 167
Noriega, Alejandro 27
Noriega, Leopoldo 27
North Iowa University 237
Nosotros 134
Note, Kelly 74
Notre Dame Fighting Irish 46, 47, 56, 58

Oakland Raiders 133, 145–146, 147, 187–189, 220–224, 227–229, 304; *see also* Los Angeles Raiders
Oates, Bob 147
Obnesorgen, George 275
Ohio State Buckeyes 220
Oklahoma, notable athletes from 202–204
Oklahoma Outlaws 196
Oklahoma University Sooners 202–203
Olguin, Hank 133–134
Omaha Nighthawks 304–305
O'Malley, Peter 130
Operation Terror 107
Operation Wetback 107
Oregon Ducks 282, 283, 311
Oriard, Michael 3–4
Ortega, Buck 201
Ortega, Ralph 199, 200–201
Ortega, Tony 133
Ortiz, Drew 263
Ottawa Rough Riders 237
Our America: A Hispanic History of the

Index

United States (Fernandez-Armesto) 244–245
Overmeyer-Velazquez, Mark 169

Padilla, Al 185
Padilla, Evasalio 125
Pais, Abbie 22
Parseghian, Ara 87
Pastorini, Dan 147, 187, 188, 222
"Pathfinders: A Life History of 10 Academically Successful Latinos from San Antonio" (Castillo) 178–179
Patterson, Ruth 172
Pedraza, Luz 112, 113–115
Pena, Federico 167
Pendergrass, Cassey 184
Pennsylvania 48–49
Perez, Luis 272
Perez, Olivia 253–254
Perez, Paul 78
Perez, Pedro 78
Perez, Peter 77–78
Pharr-San Juan-Alamo High School Bears 112
Philadelphia Eagles: Castillo coaches for 176–177; defeated in Super Bowl XV 147, 188–189, 222–223, 228–229; Diaz-Infante plays for 288–289; Fears plays for 103; Garcia plays for 303–304; Morales plays for 74; Rivera coaches for 297; Saenz plays for 89; Van Buren plays for 90, 93, 94–97
Phillips, Red 103
Phoenix Cardinals 238
Pigskin Pulpit: A Social History of Texas High School Football Coaches (Cashion) 110
Pittsburgh Steelers 74, 177
Plunkett, Carmen Blea 217–218
Plunkett, James William "Jim" 134–135, 147–148, 151, 186–189, 203, 217–224
Plunkett, William Gutierrez 217–218
Plyer v. Doe (1982) 168
politics 166–168
Porras, Jose 265
Port Isabel Tarpons 171, 172, 175, 247
Portales Rams 181
Powell, Mark 192, 193, 194
Pozzetta, George 26, 63
Prado, Mike 133
Prieto, Jorge 5–7, 53, 55–58, 323n143
PRO! The Magazine of the National Football League 147–148, 189

Quanah Indians 114–115
Quemado, New Mexico 183–184

racism *see* discrimination; segregation
radio call-in/scoreboard shows 120
Ramirez, John "Scrappy" 268–269
Ramirez, Manny 256, 257–259
Ramirez, Manuel 258
Ramirez, Michael 9
Ramirez, Rene 117, 119
Ramirez, Rosalinda 258
Ramos, Manuel "Mel" 179
Raymondville Bearkats 172
Reagan, Ronald 168
Reeves, Daniel F. 143
Reid, Andy 177
Reiderer, Don 179
Renteria, Ernest 182
repatriation efforts 106–107
Reveiz, Fuad 199, 201–202, 281
Rhodes, Ray 176
Richardson, James Perkins 18
Richardson, Nolan 124
Richert, Pete 155
Richins, Aldo Osborn 49, 51–53
Richland Springs Coyotes 253
Richter, Les 143
Riffenburgh, Beau 83, 141, 233
Rio Grande City Rattlers 248–249
Rio Grande Valley Dorados 249
Rios, Jose 199
Rivas, Mishak 249–250
Rivera, Dolores 296
Rivera, Eugenio 296
Rivera, Gabe 177–178
Rivera, Ronald Eugene "Ron" 294–299
Rivera, Stephanie 299
Rivero, Manuel 29
Robert Vela High School SaberCats 117
Robinson, Charlie 174
Robinson, John 194
Robustelli, Lou 124
Rodriguez, B.R. "Poppy" 112–113
Rodriguez, Francisco 234–235
Rodriguez, Jesse 30, 35–40, 42, 43, 45
Rodriguez, Kelly 35, 37–38, 40–45
Rodriguez, Peter Paul "Pete" 234–240, 340n254
Rogers, Charley 35
Romero, Eli 79
Romero, Melvin 125
Romero, Ray 78–79
Romo, Antonio Ramiro "Tony" 290–294
Romo, Felicita 290
Romo, Judy 290
Romo, Rafael 316
Romo, Ramiro, Jr. 290
Romo, Ramiro, Sr. 290
Roosevelt High School Roughriders 25–26, 75–76, 130, 135–136, 184–185, 270–271
Root, Reginald 27
Rosas, Fred 123–124
Rose Bowl (1958) 207
Royal, Darrell 116, 119
Roybal, Dickie 264–265
Roybal, Edward 107

Index

Rozelle, Pete 213–214
"Rozelle Rule" 213–214
Ruiz, Carlos 264, 265
Ruiz, Daniel 272–274
Ruiz, Elijah 252
Rush, Clive 212
Rusk, Rod 135

Sacramento Gold Miners 288
Saenz, Daniel 86
Saenz, Eddie 74, 85–90, 95–96
Saenz, Edward D. 85–86, 89
Saenz, Edwin Matthew, 86
Saenz, Gabriel 86
Saenz, Jesus 85, 86
Saenz, Rogelio 241–242
St. Joseph Academy 173
St. Louis Cardinals 198–199
St. Mary's College of California 80, 86–87
St. Michael's Horsemen 182
St. Pius X Catholic High School Spartans 262–263
Salem College Tigers 36–38, 42, 43
Salguero, Armando 286
Salinas, Army 181
Salt Lake Seagulls 52–53
Salyer, Kristen 314–315
Sam Houston State Bearkats 121
Samano, Rodolfo 19
San Antonio Lanier Volks 67
San Antonio Toros 115
San Benito Greyhounds 116
San Diego Chargers 298
San Francisco 49ers 186–187, 221–222, 286, 302–303
San Jose State University Spartans 130, 190–191, 287, 301–302
San Lorenzo High School 230
San Miguel, Guadalupe, Jr. 105–106
Sanchez, George J. 76, 106
Sanchez, Joe R., Jr. 66
Sanchez, John C. 73–74, 84
Sanchez, Larry 183
Sanchez, Mark 276–278
Sanchez, Patricia 314
Sandalow, Brian 248
Sanger Union High School 132
Santa Clara University 100
Santa Rosa Lions 265
Santiago, Bobby 126
Saskatchewan Roughriders 85, 128, 208
Schaller, Bob 151
scholarships 130–131
Schuber, James Buchanan 49, 50–51
Scobee, Josh 239, 240
Sealy, John 18
Seattle Seahawks 149–150, 238–239
segregation 61–63, 104–106, 115, 123, 128, 162; *see also* discrimination

Segura, Ben 260
Segura, Edgar 267–268
Selber, Greg 18–19, 64, 111, 245, 246, 249
Sena, Jeremy 264–265
Shanahan, Mike 237–238
Sharpe, Luis 198–199
Sharyland High School Rattlers 110, 111
Shaw, Bruce Walsh 63
Sheehan, Joseph 89
Shofner, Del 103
Shropshire, Mike 155
Shula, Don 232
Simmang, Jerry 122, 123–124
Simpson College 46
Simpson-Mazzolli Bill (1982) 168
Smith, Corbett 9
Socorro Warriors 181–182
Solis, Joe 172–173
Somerall, Robert 155
South: expansion of Latino population in 314–315; Latino players in 79–80
Southern California Sun 103
Southern Illinois University Salukis 205
Southernmost Brownsville Eagles 163
Southwestern College Jaguars 272
Spoonemore, Carl 172
"Sport and Leisure in the Building of an Urban Community: The Case of Oakland, California, 1850–1906" (Lamont) 24
Sport and the Shaping of Italian American Identity (Gem) 4
Spring Branch Bears 163–164
Springer High School Red Devils 260
Stabler, Ken 222
Stallings, Gene 116
Stanford Indians 135, 215, 219–220
Stenstrom, Steve 303
Stephen F. Austin High 123
Stetson University 29
Stirling, Scotty 146
Stowers, Carlton 121–122, 154–155
Striffler, Steve 169
Sul Ross State Lobos 113–114
Sullivan, Jack 210
Super Bowl IV (1970) 211–212
Super Bowl VII (1973) 232–233
Super Bowl VIII (1974) 233
Super Bowl XI (1977) 228
Super Bowl XV (1981) 147, 188–189, 222–223, 228–229
Super Bowl XVIII (1984) 148
Svare, Harlan 143
Sweeny Bulldogs 114
Sweigert, William T. 214
Switzer, Barry 202–203
"Symbol of Heart" 25

Tackwell, Cookie 44
"Taco Bowl" *see* East L.A. Classic

Taggart, Willie 283
Talavera, Chano 183
Tampa Bay Buccaneers 304
Tarleton Junior College Plowboys 118
Tedesco, Fred 53
Tejada, Alex 284
Tejada, Milagro 285
Tejada, Samuel 285
Telles, Raymond 107
Terman, Lewis 16
Testaverde, Vinny 291
Texas: Chicano Movement in 119–120; discrimination against Latinos in 107–108, 115, 119–120, 123; football's arrival in 18–21; Latino population in 104; Mexican American coaches in 109–117; notable athletes from 64–69, 121, 162–165, 170–180, 245–259; segregation and educational impediments in 105–106, 123, 162; significance of football to Latino Americans in 178–180; underdogs in 121–124
Texas A&M Aggies 94, 116
Texas A&M Commerce Lions 272
Texas Schoolboy Class AAAA State Football Championship (1962) 162–165
Texas Tech University Red Raiders 117, 118, 177, 256, 258–259
Thanksgiving Day Classic 1–2
Theder, Roger 215
Thomas, Joe 227
Thompson, Alexis 96
Thompson, Merrell E. 63
Tijerina, Felix 105–106
Tomlinson, Dave 69
Toronto Argonauts 2, 137, 205, 302
Torres, Alex 251
Touchdown Club of Washington D.C. 143–144
Travelers Rest High School Devildogs 314–315, 320n31
Tripp, Gary 261
Trujillo, Dennis, Jr. 125
Trujillo, Mario 265
Tularosa Wildcats 182
Tuloso-Midway High School Warriors 245–246

UCLA Bruins 100, 131–132, 192, 198, 275
UNAM 25, 26–27
Underwood, John 137
United Farmworkers of America 108
United Football League (UFL) 238, 240
University of Arizona Wildcats 235–236
University of Arkansas Razorbacks 285
University of California Berkeley Golden Bears 133–134, 186, 206–207, 215–216, 296, 307
University of Denver Pioneers 69
University of Florida Gators 138–139, 157–158, 200

University of Havana 28–29
University of Houston Cougars 281–282
University of Illinois 77–78, 100
University of Iowa Hawkeyes 207
University of Miami Hurricanes 136–138, 201, 225–226, 282, 284
University of Omaha-Mavericks 79
University of Oregon 285
University of San Francisco Dons 73, 87
University of Southern California (USC) Trojans 86–87, 194, 276–277
University of Tennessee Volunteers 201–202
University of Texas at El Paso Miners 251–252, 263
University of Texas Longhorns 117, 119, 177, 180
University of Utah Redskins 52
University of Utah Utes 230
University of Wisconsin Badgers 87–88
Upland High School 273
USFL 197, 236–237
Utah State University Aggies 189, 190, 279
Uvalde Coyotes 174

Valdes, Carmen 99
Valdez, Nati 174
Valdez, Tony J. 22
Van Brocklin, Norman 101–102
Van Buren, Ebert 93, 97
Van Buren, Steve 89, 90–98, 327n126
Van De Carr, Teresa 30
Vargas, Zaragoza 59, 60, 77, 104, 106–109, 166, 168–169, 244
Vasquez, Louis 256–257
Vaughan, Irving 87–88
Vedado Tennis Club (VTC) 28
Vela, Efraim 66
Vela, Ernesto 121
Vela, Pete 245–246
Vela, Robert 115, 116–117, 246
Veterans of Foreign Wars (VFW) 60
Victory High School 42
Vidal, Juan 315–316, 317
Vigil, Danny 183
Villanueva, Daniel Dario "Danny" 127–128, 151–156, 195–196
Villanueva, Jimmy 155
Villanueva, Pilar 152, 156
Villanueva, Primitivo 152, 156
Villanueva, Primo 127, 131–132, 152
Villarreal, Tony, Jr. 246
Villarreal, Tony, III 246–248
Villarreal, Tony, IV 247–248
Voss, Walter "Tillie" 39

Wade, Robert 163, 164
wartime production 59, 60
Washington Redskins 73–74, 80–83, 88–90, 95–96, 141–142, 154–155, 161, 232–233, 238

Waterfield, Bob 101, 142–143, 152, 153
Watkins, Bobby 159
We Won't Back Down!: Severita Lara's Rise from Student Leader to Mayor (Gutierrez) 119–120
Weise, Julie M. 77, 169
Weslaco Panthers 249–250
West Las Vegas High School (WLVHS) Dons 125–126
West Virginia Wesleyan College 37–38, 42–43
Western Illinois University Leathernecks 236
Western State Colorado University 235
Whitney, Caspar 5
Wick, Julia 185
Widner, Jaime 264
Wiley, Ralph 215
Williams, Charlie 247
Willow Ridge High School Eagles 258
Wilson, George 161
Wilson, Marc 223
Winnipeg Blue Bombers 84–85, 175
Wolf, Al 153–154
Wood, Michael T. 28
Woodson, Warren 126

World Football League (WFL) 103, 227, 233
World League of American Football (WLAF) 287–288
www.epgridiron.com 251
Wyche, Sam 193

Xavier College of Cincinnati, Ohio 42

Yale University 18
Ybanez, JD 251
Young, Dusty 260, 261
Young, Steve 302–303

Zamora, Lupe "Chipper" 115, 173
Zamora, Robert 265
Zavaletta, Gus 121, 173–174
Zayas, Robert 262
Zendejas, Genaro 197
Zendejas, Joaquin, Sr. 197
Zendejas, Luis 197–198
Zendejas, Max 197, 198
Zendejas, Tony 197
Zepeda, Richard 271
Zimmerman, Paul 225, 304
Zorn, Jim 190